CONTENTS

D0551591

Preface *xvi*

About the Authors xxii

Chapter 1 MINORITIES, DIVERSITY, MULTICULTURALISM, GLOBALIZATION, AND THE CRIMINAL JUSTICE SYSTEM 1

Learning Objectives 1

Key Terms 1

Introduction 2

Defining the Term "Minority" 4

Defining Cultural Diversity 5

Multiculturalism and Globalization 7

    Immigration and the Influx of Differing Cultures 8

    Immigration Issues (Mexico) 8

    Immigration Issues (Asian Immigrants) 11

    The Combined Impact of Latino and Asian Immigration 13

The Challenge to Law Enforcement 13

    The Impact of the Global Community on American Jurisprudence 14

    Implications for the American Criminal Justice System 16

Homegrown Challenges, Historical Trauma, and Minority Groups 17

    Historical Trauma and Native Americans 18

    Historical Trauma and African Americans 20

Conclusion 23

    Chapter 1 Learning Check 24 • Essay Discussion Questions 25 • References 25

Chapter 2 ASSIMILATION, ACCULTURATION, STEREOTYPING, AND CLASSISM IN A DEMOCRATIC SOCIETY 26

Learning Objectives 26

Key Terms 26

Introduction 27

What Is Cultural Competence? 27

A Brief Discussion of Race and Ethnicity 28

Acculturation, Assimilation, Social Integration, and Multiculturalism 29

Personal Attributes and Assimilation 30

iii

Melting Pot or Myth—Is There an American Way of Life? 33

Social Dominance and Disparities 34

Stereotyping Behavior 35

Institutional Racism and Racial Bias in American History 36

Skin Color and Bias 37

Criminal Justice Disparities 37

Law Enforcement and Arrests 38

Minorities and Racial Profiling 39

Sentencing Disparities 41

Disparities of Incarceration 42

Lack of Reentry Services 44

Conclusion 44

Chapter 2 Learning Check 45 • Essay Discussion
Questions 45 • References 46

Chapter 3 MINORITIES BASED ON AGE AND DISABILITY 47

Learning Objectives 47

Key Terms 47

Introduction 48

The Elderly and Impaired as Minority Groups 49

Age Discrimination 50

Disability Discrimination 50

Disabilities Common to the Criminal Justice System 52

Mental Impairments 53

    Mental Retardation 54

    Psychosis and Psychotic Disorders 55

    Mood Disorders—Major Depression 57

    Dementia—Alzheimer's Disease 57

    Mentally Ill Offenders 57

Access to Care: The Four Standards of Mental Health Care 58

Physical Disabilities 59

    Hearing and Visual Impairments 60

The Elderly as Criminal Justice Employees 61

The Disabled as Criminal Justice Employees 62

    Traumatic Stress and Police Agencies 62

Exemptions for Criminal Justice Agencies, Litigation, and Client Remedies 64

The Disabled as Victims of Crimes 64

The Elderly as Victims of Crimes   66

Elder Financial and Property Crimes   69

Elder Suicide   70

Elderly Offenders   70

Elderly Inmates   72

Special Consideration for Elders   72

Conclusion   73

> *Chapter 3 Learning Check   73   •   Essay Discussion
> Questions   74   •   References   74*

**Chapter 4 MINORITIES BASED ON GENDER AND SEXUAL
PREFERENCE   75**

Learning Objectives   75

Key Terms   75

Introduction   76

Women in the Criminal Justice Field   76

Women in Law Enforcement   76

Women in Corrections   78

Women in the Judicial System   80

Women in the Juvenile Justice System   81

The Glass Ceiling   82

Women as Supervisors in the Criminal Justice System   83

Violence against Women   83

Crime Victim's Movement   84

Violence Against Women Act   84

Domestic Violence   84

Demographics of the Female Offender   85

Other Issues Associated with the Female Offender   86

Physical and/or Sexual Abuse   86

Sex Industry Activity   86

Sexually Transmitted Diseases   86

Drug Abuse   87

Mental Health Issues among Female Offenders   87

The Female Offender as Single Mother   88

Separation between Mother and Child   89

Negative Effect on Children   91

*Gay and Lesbian Employees of the Criminal
Justice System   91*

Lifestyle   91

Professionalism in Agencies   93

Coping for Gay/Lesbian Employees
in Paramilitary Agencies 93

An Organizational Culture of Tolerance 94

Discrimination in the Professional Setting 96

Hate Crimes against the Gay and Lesbian Population **96**

Violent Actions 96

Sexual Harassment 97

Other Forms of Victimization **98**

Primary and Secondary Victimization 98

Victim Characteristics 99

Victimization of LGBT Offenders in Prisons 100

Responses to Anti-Gay Crime 102

Conclusion **103**

Chapter 4 Learning Check 104 • Essay Discussion
Questions 105 • References 105

**Chapter 5 CULTURAL COMPETENCE AND INTERCULTURAL
COMMUNICATION 107**

Learning Objectives **107**

Key Terms **107**

Introduction **108**

*The Spectrum of Competency: The Cultural Competence
Continuum* **109**

An Overview of the Six States of the Cultural Competence
Continuum 110

*Cultural Competence: Common Issues Facing Diverse
Minority Groups* **111**

Generational Status in the United States 111

Degree of Acculturation and Assimilation 112

Comfort with and Competence in English 113

Religious Beliefs and Cultural Value Orientation 113

Intercultural Communication **115**

Intercultural Communication: Early Studies and
Prospective Research 116

The Impact of Schemas on Intercultural
Communication 117

Intercultural Communication and Linguistic
Competence 119

Availability of Trained Bilingual and Bicultural Staff 120

Dissemination of Crime-Fighting Information 120

Language and Sign-Language Interpretation 122

Cross-Racial Issues 122

Multi-Linguistic Issues in Interviewing and
Interrogations 124

Intercultural Communication with Citizen Relations and
Agency Operations 126

Conclusion 127

Chapter 5 Learning Check 128 • Essay Discussion
Questions 129 • References 129

**Chapter 6 LAW ENFORCEMENT AND MINORITIES: SPECIFIC
DEMOGRAPHIC GROUPS, VICTIMS, AND
OFFENDERS 131**

Learning Objectives 131

Key Terms 131

Introduction 132

African Americans 132

Slavery in the Colonies and Later United States 133

The End of Slavery in the United States 134

The Modern-Day African American Community 134

Structural Racism 135

Marginalization of African Americans 135

Historical Victimization 136

Impact of Structural Racism, Crime, Violence,
and Criminal Justice 136

African Americans and Law Enforcement 137

Racial Profiling, Policing, and the African American
Community 139

Latino Americans 140

Mexican Americans 141

Immigration Concerns 143

Puerto Ricans 143

Cuban Americans 146

Other Groups 147

Native Americans 147

Native American Values 148

Native American Victimization 149

Unique Legal Status 149

Asian Americans 151

Difficulties and Challenges in Establishing a Rapport 152

Generational Status in the United States 152

Asian American Crime Victimization 152

Domestic Violence in Asian American Families   153
Asian American Criminal Activity   153
Middle Eastern Americans   154
Iranians and Turks   154
Arab Americans   155
Victimization of Middle Eastern Americans   156
Minority Victims of Crime   157
Minority Offenders and the Police   158
Conclusion   159
Chapter 6 Learning Check   160   •   Essay Discussion
Questions   160   •   References   160

**Chapter 7 LAW ENFORCEMENT AND MINORITIES: COMMUNITY
RELATIONS, HIRING, AND TRAINING   162**
Learning Objectives   162
Key Terms   162
Introduction   163
Trust-Building and Community Involvement   163
Challenges Specific to Immigrant Communities   165
Language Barriers   167
Reluctance to Report Crime   167
Fear of Police   168
Federal Immigration Enforcement Can Affect
Local Trust-Building Efforts   168
Individual Officers Can Damage a Department's
Efforts   168
Lack of Awareness of Cultural Differences   170
A Model Police Response to Immigrant Communities   172
Recruitment and Hiring of Minorities in Policing   174
Benefits of Diversity   174
Commitment to Hiring   175
Legal Considerations   176
Planning and Techniques   179
Community Involvement   180
Broadening the Recruiting Age Pool—Hiring the Young
and Old   181
Minority Retention in Policing   182
Diversity Training in Police Agencies   184
Immigrant-Specific Diversity Training   187
Multiculturalism and Volunteerism in Policing   189
Bilingual Volunteer Assistance   190

   Cultural Liaisons   190

   Immigrant Communities and Ethnic-Specific Responses   191

  Conclusion   192

   Chapter 7 Learning Check   193   •   Essay Discussion
   Questions   193   •   References   194

Chapter 8 THE COURTS AND MINORITIES   195

  Learning Objectives   195

  Key Terms   195

  Introduction   196

  The Myth of Colorblindness   197

  Implicit Bias within the Courtroom   198

  Overview of the American Court System   200

  Methods for Selecting Judges   201

  Tribal Courts   203

  An Overview of Sentencing Circles   205

  Goals   206

  Implementation   206

  Special Courts That Affect Minorities   207

   Juvenile Courts   207

   Family Courts   207

   Elder Courts   208

   Drug Courts   208

   Mental Health Courts   208

  Diversity and the Courts   209

  Judicial Professionals and Cultural
  Competence   209

   Minority Legal Representation: Minority Public
   Defenders   211

  Notable Historic Minority Judiciary Figures   211

   William Henry Hastie, Jr.   212

   Thurgood Marshall   212

   Frank Howell Seay and Michael Burrage   213

   Florence Ellinwood Allen   213

   Sonia Sotomayor   213

   Sandra Day O'Conner   214

   Lance Ito   215

   Reynaldo Guerra Garza   215

   Herbert Young Choy   215

   Constance Baker Motley   216

Eric Hampton Holder   216
Johnnie L. Cochran, Jr.   217
Diversity and the Bench: Some Additional Comments   217
Conclusion   219
Chapter 8 Learning Check   219   •   Essay
Questions   220   •   References   220

Chapter 9   MINORITIES IN THE COURT SYSTEM   221
Learning Objectives   221
Key Terms   221
Introduction   222
Minority Defendants and Legal Representation   222
Historical Precedence: Scottsboro Case   222
Historical Case: *Gideon v. Wainwright*   223
The Current Indigent Defender System   223
Racial Minorities and Bail-Making Decisions   225
Bail Discriminations   227
Prosecutorial Discretion   228
Initial Screenings   230
Dismissal   230
Charge Reduction   230
Plea Bargaining   231
Jury Selection and Minorities   231
Voir Dire   232
Jury Nullification   233
Disparity and Discrimination in Sentencing Procedures   235
Discrimination Continuum   236
Crime as an Intra-Racial Phenomenon   237
Minority Sentencing Issues   238
Death Penalty Convictions   239
Race of Offender and Victim in Death Penalty Cases   239
Conclusion   242
Chapter 9 Learning Check   242   •   Essay
Discussions   243   •   References   243

Chapter 10   CORRECTIONS, CLASSISM, POVERTY, AND MINORITY GROUPS   244
Learning Objectives   244
Key Terms   244
Introduction   245
Institutions of Confinement   247

The Rationale Behind the Use of Jails   248

   Debtor's Gaols   249

   Workhouses, Poorhouses, and Houses of Correction   250

   Transportation   250

The Prison   251

Hospitals and Asylums   252

   Modern Asylums   252

Slavery   253

   Race-Based Slavery: The Myth of Inferiority   254

   Modern Minorities within the Prison System   256

Behavioral Illnesses as a Minority Status   256

Persons with Addictions   256

   The Substance Addiction–Crime Connection   257

Persons with Mental Illnesses   258

Immigrants   259

   Detainment on Arrival   259

   Post-Arrival Arrest/Imprisonment   260

   The Newest Immigrants: Hispanic Americans   261

   Middle Eastern Muslims   261

   Asian Americans   262

   African Americans   262

The Poor/Undereducated   264

Religion in Corrections: General Rights to Minority Religious Beliefs   266

   Legality of "Non-traditional" Religions   267

   Religious Diets and Holy Days   268

Conclusion   268

   Chapter 10 Learning Check   269   •   Essay Discussion Questions   270   •   References   270

Chapter 11 CORRECTIONS AND MINORITIES: MINORITIES, GANG AFFILIATION, GENDER, AND STAFF ISSUES   272

Learning Objectives   272

Key Terms   272

Introduction   273

The War on Drugs and the Era of Drug Criminalization   274

Minorities and Incarceration   276

Women and Incarceration   279

Institutional Racism and Corrections   280

A History of Minority Treatment in Imprisonment 281
   The Convict Lease System (1865–1910) 282
   The Trusty System (1910–1975) 282
   Chain Gangs 284
   Old School Corrections, Prison Reform, and LSP Angola during the Trusty System 284
Types of Modern Prison Facilities and Affirmative Action 285
Correctional Workers 287
   The Racial Composition of Correctional Officers 288
   The Gender Composition of Correctional Officers 288
   The Need of Bilingual Workers 289
   Diversity Training Programs in Corrections 289
Race and Prison 289
   Racial Segregation Case Law 289
Prison Gangs: Structured along Racial Lines of Allegiance 290
Religion and Prison 294
Staff and Inmate Dynamics: Prison Culture and Prisonization 295
   The Prison Subculture and Women in Corrections: Both Inmate and Staff Subculture 296
Sexual Orientation and Corrections 297
   Male Prison Hierarchies and Sexual Victimization 298
   Prison Rape Elimination Act of 2003 298
   Implementing Organizational Change to Counteract the Prison Subculture 299
Cross-Racial Inmate and Staff Supervision Issues 299
   Education and Training of Staff 300
Conclusion 301
    Chapter 11 Learning Check 301 • Essay Discussion Questions 302 • References 302

Chapter 12 JUVENILE MINORITY WELLNESS AND HEALTH DISPARITIES, GENDER, SEXUAL IDENTITY, YOUTH CULTURE, AND SOCIAL CLASS 304
Learning Objectives 304
Key Terms 304
Introduction 304
Health and Wellness among Juveniles 305
   Family 306

Education 308

Violence in Schools as Wellness Indicator 309

Sexual Activity and the Juvenile Population 310

Gender as a Minority Status among Juveniles 311

Teenage Mothers and Unwanted Pregnancies 312

Impact of Racial Discrimination on Health and Wellness of Juvenile Minorities 315

Sexual Minority Youth 319

Sexual Minority Youth Who Carry a Gun to School 320

Sexual Minority Youth and Reports of Physical Fights at School 321

Sexual Minority Youth and Sexual Assault 321

Sexual Minority Youth and Attempted Suicide 322

Peer Groups, Subculture, Minority Issues, and Socialization 325

Culturally Relevant Considerations 325

Social Class, Poverty, and the Underclass 326

Conclusion 328

Chapter 12 Learning Check 330 • *Essay Discussion Questions* 331 • *References* 331

Chapter 13 TYPES OF JUVENILE OFFENDING, GANG AFFILIATION BY RACE AND GENDER, AND DISPROPORTIONATE MINORITY CONTACT IN THE JUVENILE SYSTEM 333

Learning Objectives 333

Key Terms 333

Introduction 333

Rates and Types of Offending by Age and Gender 334

DMC in the Juvenile Justice System 337

DMC at All Stages of Justice System 338

Social Contexts Associated with Juvenile Minorities 340

Youth Composition of Gangs and Reasons for Joining 341

Minority Youth, Gang Involvement, and Reasons for Joining 343

Gangs and Racial Affiliation 345

Gangs and Juvenile Females 348

Youth, Gangs, and Corrections 350

Female Juveniles in Custody 350

Disparity in Juvenile Detention and Incarceration 352

Factors That Contribute to Disparate Minority Confinement   353

A Model Program to Respond to Minority Juveniles in Secure Environments   355

Prevention and Intervention Efforts Needed in the Future   356

Conclusion   358

Chapter 13 Learning Check   359   •   Essay Discussion Questions   359   •   References   360

Chapter 14 CULTURAL COMPETENCE TRAINING, ASSESSMENT, AND EVALUATION OF CULTURAL COMPETENCE, AND EVIDENCE-BASED PRACTICES IN CULTURALLY COMPETENT AGENCIES   362

Learning Objectives   362

Key Terms   362

Introduction   363

Assessing Agency Cultural Competence   363

Implementation of Agency Cultural Competence   366

Cultural Competence Training in Large and Small Agencies   368

Training beyond the Classroom and Using Ill-Structured Problems in Developing Cultural Competence   371

Beyond the Training: Individual Staff Recognition for Utilizing Culturally Competent Practices   374

Evaluation Research and Cultural Competence in the Agency   377

Implementation Evaluation   377

Process Evaluation   378

Outcome Evaluation   378

Program Quality and Staffing Quality   378

Feedback Loops and Continual Improvement   379

Community Harm with Ineffective Programs, Separating Politics from Science in the Evaluative Process   380

Evidence-Based Practices   381

EBP #1: Assess the Needs of Organizational Participants   381

EBP #2: Enhance Motivation of Participants   381

EBP #3: Target Operational Changes   382

EBP #4: Provide Skill Training for Staff and Monitor Their Delivery of Services   382

EBP #5: Increase Positive Reinforcement   382

EBP #6: Engage Ongoing Support   382

EBP #7: Measure Relevant Processes/Practices 382

EBP #8: Provide Measurement Feedback 382

Individual Case-Level Implementation of EBP 383

Agency-Level Implementation of EBPs 383

System-Level Implementation of EBPs 383

Research Evaluation for Effectiveness of EBPs 383

Conclusion 384

Chapter 14 Learning Check 386 • Essay Discussion Questions 387 • References 387

Chapter 15 FUTURE MULTICULTURAL TRENDS IN CRIMINAL JUSTICE 388

Learning Objectives 388

Key Terms 388

Introduction 388

Continued Globalization 389

An Emphasis on Cultural Competence Will Continue to Be Important 389

There Will Be a Continued Reliance on Community Involvement and Community Justice 390

Police Will Need Increased Knowledge about Immigrant Populations and Younger Populations 391

There Will be a Movement away from Prisons toward Community Supervision 392

Disable/Elderly Offender Populations Will Continue to Increase and Be Shifted to Community Supervision 393

Sentencing May Become More Indeterminate in Nature 393

Early Prevention of Criminal Behavior/Addictions Will Continue to Be Promoted 395

Drug Enforcement Strategy Will Be Adjusted to Represent Demand-Side Strategies 396

Treatment Strategy Will Become of Greater Importance as Enforcement Strategy Changes 397

There Will Continue to Be a Strong Emphasis on Reentry 400

A Continued Development of Varied Supervision/Community Techniques 402

Conclusion 403

Chapter 15 Learning Check 403 • Essay Discussion Questions 404 • References 404

Index 405

PREFACE

INTRODUCTION

This text was written at a time when multiculturalism is a primary issue in society, in general, and criminal justice, in particular. Since the dawn of the current millennium, both multicultural issues and trends toward globalization have impacted the United States in a manner that may likely be unprecedented. For instance, the tragedy of 9/11 resulted in an international War on Terror that generated a number of racially based incidents within the United States and also required thousands of U.S. service men and women personnel to serve in the Middle East, where they would be exposed to cultural groups with whom they were not familiar.

This demonstrates how an international incident on American soil can impact the behaviors of citizens at home and, at the same time, require others to go abroad and return home with new knowledge and views that make peoples of the Middle East more familiar. This also shows how multiculturalism and globalization are often inter-related, as well. What happens on American soil does not necessarily affect only the United States and, conversely, what happens abroad does not stay abroad. Rather, there is an intersection of the two concepts.

We wanted to begin our introduction with this point because this is, perhaps, a defining aspect of this text. The United States does not exist in a worldwide vacuum but instead is a complicit partner with the rest of the global community. Going further, what happens in the world impacts the United States internally and especially with regard to how cultural groups intermingle within the borders of the United States. We no longer have any true separation; rather, our borders and our cultures are all semipermeable.

The semipermeable nature of the world's cultural and lifestyle boundaries has impacted the field of criminal justice. Furthermore, this impact affects all segments of the criminal justice system and does so regardless of whether one examines these issues from the role of a practitioner or from the perspective of an offender who is processed through the system. In either case, the impact of a more diversified society has a continual influence upon the United States. It is from this perspective that we present *Multiculturalism and the Criminal Justice System*.

INTENDED AUDIENCE AND INTENDED USE

This book is written primarily for the undergraduate criminal justice student. While it is plausible that this text could be used at the graduate level, its focus on systemic issues in criminal justice might be a bit basic for many graduate students. Regardless, this text is ideal for courses that address minorities or diversity in the criminal justice system. This text could also be used in some social justice courses, but it is not, of itself, written with a purely or even predominantly social justice orientation. Rather, this text attempts to provide a detailed view of various facets of multiculturalism that are encountered in the realm of criminal justice.

In addition, it should be noted that each chapter is written so that it can either be used as a standalone chapter to provide a framework for a specific lecture on a specific minority group or, in another vein, be used to focus on a specific segment of the criminal justice system with which different minority groups come into contact. One could approach the use of this text from either perspective. No matter what is desired, the text is comprehensive and is very contemporary when considering issues related to diversity in the criminal justice system as well as society as a whole.

ORGANIZATION OF THIS BOOK

Generally speaking, this text is organized in a manner that addresses multiculturalism, cultural competency, and diversity issues, while also following these issues throughout each segment of the criminal justice system. The first five chapters of this text provide the reader with a basic understanding of multiculturalism and the need for cultural competence. Of equal importance, those five chapters lay the groundwork for understanding specific diverse populations. The remaining chapters address the primary areas of the criminal justice system in a progressive manner, going from law enforcement to the courts, then to corrections, along with a couple of chapters addressing the juvenile justice system. We believe this approach portrays comprehensively the multicultural issues in the criminal justice system. More specifically, the content of the chapters is as follows:

Chapter 1, "Minorities, Diversity, Multiculturalism, and Globalization and the Criminal Justice System," begins by presenting the case that in the United States the demographics of the population, views on religion, sexuality, and cultural mores have resulted in a very fluid social system. This social system is greatly impacted by influences within and beyond the nation's borders. Moreover, economic and political developments have resulted in a large degree of interdependence between the United States and other nations. In addition, we show that a trend has emerged among lawmakers and the judiciary to adopt, or at least consider, social views from the global community. Altogether, these developments have required that the U.S. criminal justice system be dynamic and adaptable. The criminal justice system of the United States will find itself in contradictory roles, with demands for maintaining positive community relations among diverse groups being countered with the need to provide tougher protections against criminal activity that is imported into the United States.

Chapter 2, "Racial Minorities, Assimilation, Acculturation, and Classism in a Democratic Society," discusses issues associated with the assimilation and acculturation of minorities into mainstream society; stereotyping and prejudice have also been presented to serve as a groundwork for future chapters that will be more specific to topics related to the criminal justice system and the interface of minority groups in that system. When addressing multiculturalism in the criminal justice system, there is always the likelihood that these issues will be relevant at one point or another. In this chapter, we address these foundational terms and concepts and note that they apply to the remainder of the text.

In Chapter 3, "Minorities Based on Age and Disability," we discuss how the elderly and disabled are two minority groups that frequently overlap. Both are known as cultural minorities because of disadvantages that they possess due to preferences that have been established in our social system. These two minority groups are participants in courts, and correctional and law enforcement systems as employees, victims, and offenders.

As our population ages the elderly and disabled will themselves be tasked to identify each population subset and to determine how the disabled need special considerations.

In Chapter 4, "Minorities Based on Gender and Sexual Preference," we cover two specific populations that have struggled to gain acceptance and respect within the criminal justice system, particularly in policing and correctional agencies. Both women and the LGBT population have been marginalized in society and also suffer from sexualized violence, victimization, and harassment. It is in this manner—through the gendered experiences of these two groups—that they share similarities in experiences though, of course, the challenges each have faced are not identical. Throughout the remainder of the text, it will be noticeable that we make an active effort to integrate boxes and sections within each chapter that include these two minority groups.

Chapter 5, "Cultural Competence and Cross-Cultural Communication in Agencies," explains the concept of cultural competence and provides an overview of the different levels of competency along a continuum of possibilities. In this chapter, we also discuss the means by which cultural competence can be implemented and maintained within criminal justice agencies. Amidst this discussion, we believe that religious diversity must also be considered if we are to be competent with many of the cultural groups that we will encounter in the criminal justice field. Intercultural communication is another key aspect of this chapter. We likewise provide an overview of the use of interpreters as well as bilingual individuals. Additional considerations regarding cross-racial communication are provided, as well as information related to intercultural interviews and interrogations.

In Chapter 6, "Law Enforcement and Minorities: Specific Demographic Groups, Victims, and Offenders," we cover issues related to police–community relations with respect to African Americans, Latino Americans, Native Americans, Asian Americans, and Middle Eastern Americans. For each group, we provide demographic and/or historical background. It is our intent to avoid rehashing the same material that has been covered on each group in previous chapters. Yet, at the same time, it is necessary to provide history in some circumstances if it relates to how police relations with a given group have developed over time and/or demonstrates how that group has been impacted in the past. Past experiences in previous generations will be part of the social teaching that younger generations acquire today, so the historical context of policing with respect to these groups can be very important.

Chapter 7, "Law Enforcement and Minorities: Community Relations, Hiring, and Training," largely focuses on police–community relations with respect to various racial and/or ethnic groups that we discussed earlier in Chapter 6, as well as other diverse groups discussed in Chapters 3 and 4. The key point of this chapter is to demonstrate how police agencies can benefit from positive relationships with the surrounding community that they serve. In this chapter, we again point out how globalization has impacted diversity in the United States and discuss likely trends in policing as a result of this.

In Chapter 8, "The Courts and Minorities," we show how minorities are underrepresented within the judicial realm of the criminal justice system. Indeed, as we show, there is a serious underrepresentation of minorities among judgeships as well as other positions (such as district attorneys). Issues related to bias in the court system, based on race, are also discussed. The key message in this chapter is that the judicial system of the United States must become more diverse; otherwise bias and skewed outcomes in meting out justice will be the continued final product.

Chapter 9, "Minorities in the Court System," first confronts readers with the grim circumstances for minorities who need legal assistance. We begin with a historical overview of the tainted forms of representation that existed in times past, citing historical precedence, and continue with a presentation of the indigent defender system. The public defender system, bail-setting, and prosecutorial discretion are also further discussed. Disparity and discrimination in sentencing are discussed, along with jury nullification. We likewise present a section that highlights disparity in the application of the death penalty and provide a detailed analysis of this issue.

In Chapter 10, "Corrections, Classism, Poverty, and Minority Groups," we provide an extensive discussion on how poverty correlates strongly with those who get prison sentences. The impact of slavery on corrections during the pre–Civil War era is also examined. To some extent, this helped set the stage for the demographics we currently observe in the United States. In this chapter, we also discuss the addicted population, the mentally ill in prison, and immigrant offenders as people in need of specialized services. We then discuss Hispanics, Middle Easterners, Asian Americans, and African Americans, explaining how these groups contend with negative services. Lastly, in this chapter, we also discuss religion inside prison facilities and explain how this is an important aspect of multicultural correctional operations.

In Chapter 11, "Corrections and Minorities: Minorities, Gang Affiliation, Gender, and Staff Issues," we provide an overview of some of the historical antecedents that have shaped prison dynamics today. For instance, the War on Drugs has had a significant impact on the prison population, in terms of both numbers incarcerated and racial group. This chapter also addresses the prison subculture and explains how this impacts and reflects both the coalescing and conflicting nature of these norms and mores, which are inverted from the outside society. In addition, we discuss the professionalization of corrections. We demonstrate that the means by which employees have been trained in correctional agencies greatly impact the organizational culture within prison systems. Furthermore, the informal subculture within prisons has typically been paramilitary and male-dominated. More frequent integration of female staff and the intentional diversification of staff have ameliorated some of the negative aspects of this strict and often oppressive internal culture. All of these changes in prison operations have been rapid and difficult to transition, sometimes requiring statewide monitoring by the federal government.

We turn to juvenile issues next, in Chapter 12, "Juvenile Minority Wellness and Health Disparities, Gender, Sexual Identity, Youth Culture, and Social Class," and explain that youth are a distinct class and category of individuals in society who share a common characteristic (age) and also have specific challenges that are unique to their group. Furthermore, we note a number of issues associated with youth related to their likelihood of being processed through the juvenile system. In addition, many of the variables that lead to a youth being in contact with the juvenile system have to do with aspects of their development, such as family life, educational access and achievement, sexual activity and pregnancy, as well as health and wellness indicators. In addition, we pay specific attention to the effects of discrimination on the development of youth, including potential health effects as well as the psychological impact of discrimination. Likewise, this chapter provides specific attention to sexual minority youth, or youth who have same-sex preferences. This population has grown among the younger generation and we consider our coverage of this aspect of diversity in the juvenile population to be quite progressive. Lastly, we discuss the impact of social class and poverty on youth, particularly minority youth, because minority youth are disproportionately represented among the lower-income strata of the population.

In Chapter 13, "Types of Juvenile Offending, Gang Affiliation by Race and Gender, Disproportionate Minority Contact in Juvenile System," we focus on minority youth based on racial and/or ethnic group and we provide an overview of disproportionate contact at multiple points in the justice system, which ultimately result in the disparities in confinement that we see today. We further discuss disproportionate minority contact (DMC) in the juvenile system and make this a large part of our discussion on multiculturalism and juvenile justice. We also further address issues related to female youth in the justice system. We have identified women and, just as correctly, young girls, as a minority group worthy of exploration when addressing diversity and the need for gender-appropriate knowledge and response in the justice system.

In Chapter 14, "Cultural Competence Training, Assessment and Evaluation of Cultural Competence, and Evidence-Based Practices in Culturally Competent Agencies," we provide students with information on how agencies can assess and implement culturally competent practices. We begin with a discussion of how one might assess the cultural competence of an agency and provide understanding of how agencies can develop policies that encourage, establish, and sustain cultural competence throughout. Beyond this, the agency must then be evaluated, over time, to determine whether these initiatives have been effective and to determine where improvements can be made.

Lastly, in Chapter 15, "Future Multicultural Trends in Criminal Justice," we provide an analysis of what we have covered thus far, in this text, and speculate as to the likely trends that we will see in the future.

THE BOOK'S ORIENTATION AND THEME

The text addresses a wide range of diverse groups in society as they relate to the criminal justice system. It examines perspectives from the vantage point of the practitioner, offender, and victim. In addition, this text uniquely integrates globalization issues, with multiculturalism, in the United States, and demonstrates how the two aspects work in tandem to impact the criminal justice system. This text makes a point to address diversity and multicultural issues in the policing, judicial, correctional, and juvenile justice segments of the criminal justice system. Most textbooks on this topic do not provide similar breadth and depth in discussing multicultural issues in the criminal justice system. Our theme of presenting these topics amidst the reality of globalization is unique to our text; to date, we can find no other that truly acknowledges the impact of globalization and immigration on our understanding of diversity and multiculturalism within the U.S. borders.

INSTRUCTOR SUPPLEMENTS

MyTest and *TestBank* represent new standards in testing material. Whether you use a basic test bank document or generate questions electronically through MyTest, every question is linked to the text's learning objective, page number, and level of difficulty. This allows for quick reference in the text and an easy way to check the difficulty level and variety of your questions. MyTest can be accessed at www.PearsonMyTest.com.

PowerPoint Presentations Our presentations offer clear, straightforward outlines and notes to use for class lectures or study materials. Photos, illustrations, charts, and tables from the book are included in the presentations when applicable.

Other supplements are:

- Instructor's Manual with Test Bank
- Test Item File for ingestion into an LMS, including Blackboard and WebCT.

To access supplementary materials online, instructors need to request an instructor access code. Go to **www.pearsonhighered.com/irc,** where you can register for an instructor access code. Within 48 hours after registering, you will receive a confirming email, including an instructor access code. Once you have received your code, go to the site and log on for full instructions on downloading the materials you wish to use.

ALTERNATE VERSIONS

eBooks This text is also available in multiple eBook formats including Adobe Reader and CourseSmart. *CourseSmart* is an exciting new choice for students looking to save money. As an alternative to purchasing the printed textbook, students can purchase an electronic version of the same content. With a *CourseSmart* eTextbook, students can search the text, make notes online, print out reading assignments that incorporate lecture notes, and bookmark important passages for later review. For more information, or to purchase access to the *CourseSmart* eTextbook, visit **www.coursesmart.com**.

ACKNOWLEDGMENTS

Robert Hanser would like to thank his wife Gina. She has been patient and understanding while he spent hours typing away on one project or another. Lastly, he would like to extend special gratitude to all of the practitioners who carry out the daily tasks of our criminal justice system, whether it be in law enforcement, the courts, corrections, or juvenile justice. These individuals deserve the highest praise as they work in a field that is demanding and undervalued—we thank you all for the contributions that you make to our society.

Mike Gomila would like to thank his wife Sunny. Through good times and bad, she has always been his greatest advocate and best friend.

Both authors are grateful to the many reviewers who spent time reading the document, making a considerable number of recommendations that helped shape the final product. Every effort was made to incorporate those ideas. We fully believe these suggestions and insights only helped improve the final product.

ABOUT THE AUTHORS

Dr. Robert Hanser is the Coordinator of the Department of Criminal Justice Program, and the Director of the Institute of Law Enforcement at the University of Louisiana at Monroe. He is also a past administrator of North Delta Regional Training Academy, a regional police and corrections academy in Northeast Louisiana. In addition to teaching undergraduate and graduate courses in criminal justice, Dr. Hanser conducts pre-service and in-service training for police officers, jailers, and mental health workers and is an active Crisis Intervention Team (CIT) trainer for Northeast Louisiana. He is a Licensed Professional Counselor (LPC) in the states of Texas and Louisiana and conducts group work with substance abuse and domestic batterer offenders in prison and on community supervision. His research and teaching interests focus on mental health, multicultural, and multinational issues in criminal justice. Dr. Hanser has authored and coauthored numerous textbooks and peer-reviewed articles; he is also an active researcher, both nationally and internationally.

Michael Gomila, Ph.D., is an adjunct faculty member at the University of Louisiana Monroe's Criminal Justice Department. He holds a Ph.D. from the University of North Carolina–Greensboro in counseling and has worked almost exclusively in the behavioral health treatment field since the earning of his degree. Dr. Gomila has been instrumental in developing and supervising various offender treatment programs that include drug courts prison-based and outpatient programs. He has also been involved in policymaking decisions on a state level, advocating for treatment reforms that would ultimately have a substantial impact on minority offenders. He currently resides in Louisiana with his wife and three children.

Minorities, Diversity, Multiculturalism, Globalization, and the Criminal Justice System

LEARNING OBJECTIVES

After reading this chapter, students should be able to do the following:

1. Identify and discuss the terms "minority," "cultural diversity," and "racial diversity."
2. Explain how the impact of globalization has created new demands for the U.S. criminal justice system, both inside and outside the nation's borders.
3. Discuss multiculturalism and explain how current immigration processes are increasing the need for this approach in our criminal justice system.
4. Discuss how historical trauma has been inflicted on, and how it has impacted, specific groups within the United States.
5. Assess the likely future of the criminal justice system due to challenges within and without the nation's borders.

KEY TERMS

Atkins v. Virginia

Cultural diversity

Department of Homeland Security

Globalization

Grutter v. Bollinger

Historical trauma

Immigration

Immigration and Customs Enforcement (ICE)

Comprehensive Immigration Reform Act of 2007

Jim Crow laws

McCreary County v. ACLU of Kentucky

Minority

Multiculturalism

North American Free Trade Alliance (NAFTA)

Racial diversity

Secure Fence Act of 2006

Strive Act

Minority status

Intergenerational trauma

INTRODUCTION

When writing about multicultural issues in the criminal justice system, it quickly becomes clear that the topic is broad and multifaceted. The precise reason for this is that this topic, when handled correctly, is one that splinters into a multitude of groupings and issues that, from a layperson perspective, are not readily apparent at the mere mention of the words "minority" and "diversity," whether from a criminal justice perspective or otherwise. However, the aim of this text is to demonstrate that the term "diversity" itself has diverse meanings. This is actually not just a matter of semantics; rather one should consider that numerous experts in the field have crafted numerous definitions and perspectives that are all valid yet unique in many respects.

In this chapter, we will seek to develop definitions for the terms "minority" and "diversity." The notion of multiculturalism will be explored from what we believe is a contemporary perspective; we will discuss both domestic issues internal to the United States and its multicultural fabric and international issues external to the United States that are the result of globalization. Indeed, it is important for students to understand that the diversity within the United States comes from both within and outside the borders of the nation. This is important because the pushes and pulls that are inherent to various competing groups come from within and without any country. Indeed, many of the strains and stresses experienced within the "melting pot" of the United States are also experienced in countries such as France, Germany, England, Australia, China, and Russia, to name a few. This is, we believe, an important observation that is not often showcased in other texts.

Many authors and criminal justice experts attempt to separate diversity studies within a country from the study of cross-border international issues. We believe that this separation results in an artificial distinction that is not truly pragmatic for the practitioner who is confronted with issues that are both local and global in nature, particularly in densely populated urban areas with complicated demographic features. This text will rectify this aspect of studying multiculturalism within the criminal justice process and will also examine numerous vantage points that are not always sufficiently addressed in other texts. For instance, the issue of hate crimes is often discussed, but many criminal justice texts that address diversity tend to overlook the fact that, in most cases, gang offenders (both on the streets and in prison systems) tend to group themselves along racial lines. While doing so, they tend to be pitted against one another along racial lines and, in the process, may hold members of other racial groups as the enemy of their own affiliation, regardless of whether that person is a member of a rival gang or not. These types of intricate distinctions in racially motivated crimes are often not brought to bear by many authors.

We believe that such additional microcosms within these areas of study are important to the day-to-day criminal justice practitioner, regardless of whether their involvement is in policing, courtroom sentencing, the operation of prisons, or work in the juvenile system, and regardless of whether the practitioner falls within the ranks of security or treatment-oriented professions. Simply put, there are a multiplicity of perspectives from which one can approach the notion of diversity and from which one can classify a minority, and although this text is focused on the criminal justice system's interface with a multicultural society, this emphasis on crime and criminal justice actually makes the study of these issues more complicated while also providing with a sense of focus—contradictory concepts that work hand in hand with one another at the same time. Perhaps a good example might be something akin to a combination of peanut butter and jelly sandwich: The flavors are both salty and sweet, but when combined they both contrast and complement each other at the same time. So, too, do many of the approaches that we will use to investigate what the terms "minority," "diversity," and "multiculturalism" mean.

In this chapter, we will highlight certain aspects of the criminal justice system and its operations. The intention is to demonstrate how multiculturalism impacts and, is impacted by, the criminal justice system. For instance, consider the use of community policing within a diverse neighborhood. Given that, in many cases, the rapport between police agencies and minority communities is not always optimal, it makes sense to use approaches that attempt to involve community members as a means of developing rapport. Likewise, it is perhaps useful to hire persons who are representative of the surrounding community, thereby further enhancing the sense of continuity between the agency and its service community. However, making such hiring practices a priority is sometimes thought to lead to reverse discrimination. Likewise, the integration of community citizens into citizen review panels, neighborhood watches, and police patrol ride-along programs requires that the agency be transparent to these citizens—even in cases where this may lead to discomfort to some agency personnel and/or misunderstanding among persons outside the agency.

In a different context, consider issues related to domestic violence victims. Diversity entails, among other things, awareness and understanding of gender issues just as much as it does of racial or ethnic issues. For instance, women who are victims of domestic violence may not feel comfortable talking with male police officers, or, when in treatment, they may be less likely to divulge details to male therapists. Further still, consider crimes of elder abuse; in such cases, knowledge of geriatrics and/or issues related to the elderly and indicators for victimization can be particularly useful. Thus, age, as well as gender and race, falls within the realm of diversity studies.

Other issues related to diversity may not often be considered by most people. For instance, persons with disabilities are considered a minority class. Numerous laws exist to provide protection for these individuals. Indeed, even prison inmates must be given a degree of consideration to ensure their safety and security while in custody. This is also true for elderly inmates. Living arrangements that do not exacerbate a disability and safely housing disabled and elderly inmates in areas where they will not be victimized are expectations that have been set by the U.S. Supreme Court.

Lastly, consider the impact of immigration and its relationship to globalization. During the past decade, increasing attention had been given to issues related to immigration in the United States. Immigration issues have impacted law enforcement quite substantially in the past decade and have recently resulted in controversial legislation in some states. Further, immigration, whether legal or illegal, has impacted the cultural landscape of the United States. This has had an impact on our court and correctional systems, in terms of both the offender population who are processed and the composition of the practitioner population who do the processing. In other words, as immigration into the United States continues to increase, the demographics of offenders and practitioners have reflected this influx of cultural and racial groups that has occurred.

Thus, it can be seen that there are a number of considerations, from a variety of perspectives, to explore when discussing multicultural issues in the criminal justice system. In the examples provided, we can see that ethnic and racial considerations must be made when dealing with the offender population (e.g., racial motivations and racial allegiances of gang members, the need for culturally competent interventions) and with victims (e.g., the need for gender-specific interventions). Such issues related to diversity may involve communication between criminal justice agencies and the broader community, and diversity concerns may center on the need for agencies to be more reflective of the broader population that they serve. All of these (and more) are important aspects of any examination of multiculturalism within the criminal justice system and its processes of response.

We will now turn our discussion to the concept of minorities and diversity as well as the interplay of multiculturalism within the United States and the impact of globalization beyond the nation's borders. Throughout this text, we will address various aspects of diversity and multiculturalism that have existed throughout the history of the United States but, in particular and distinct from many other similarly grounded texts, we will also infuse discussions related to the more recent globalized social landscape in the United States, demonstrating the consistencies in the melting pot philosophy and the distinctions between modern-day influxes of persons into the United States and those in past generations.

DEFINING THE TERM "MINORITY"

For the purpose of this text, we would like to take a moment to provide our own definition of the term "**minority**." Our use of the term *refers to any group of people who are substantially different from the broader society in political, economic, religious, or racial terms. It also includes persons who have diminished access to resources or ability to compete in a market economy*. While this may not be an all-inclusive use of the term, we believe that it captures the essence of the term for this text without being overly cumbersome. While this definition of "minority" is primarily for this text, we also wish to explore the term from some other perspectives, to ensure a thorough discussion of this subject.

First, in the strictest interpretations, a minority group might be defined most readily by its numerical relationship to the larger society of which it is a part. In other words, groups that consist of smaller number of people may be defined as minority; figures are based solely on the head count of that group compared to other groups. While, from a mathematical perspective, this may make sense, it is basically a one-dimensional interpretation. It does not indicate why sensitivity to the plight of minorities might be an issue of concern; just because a group is numerically small does not mean it warrants additional concern or assistance. Indeed, the greatly affluent are a minority group in the United States. However, few would agree that this group merits additional concern. Rather, this group typically has sufficient political and economic clout to ensure adequate representation.

Similarly, the term "minority" can be used to describe those who have minimal political and/or economic power. However, this approach can also be deceptive and one-dimensional. For instance, consider Asian Americans in the United States; they are often labeled the "model minority" due to their higher-than-average education and wealth as estimated in census reports. However, this fact cannot ignore some of the factors associated with this group that, upon closer examination, reveal a history of discrimination upon their immigration to the United States, racial hatred against them, and distrust of many other racial and ethnic groups throughout the nation. Thus, there is perhaps more to consider than just political and economic indicators, though these are, of course, part of what may be used to identify a minority group.

Likewise, the term "**minority status**" may be used to identify those who have been or are susceptible to unfair treatment by the dominant culture. Since some groups (i.e., African American and Native American people, or women as a whole, for that matter) that constitute a numerical majority in certain areas of the United States also enjoy minority status, this alone cannot be the sole means of identifying a minority group. While there are some groups that may have received unfair treatment by the majority culture, this may not, in and of itself, be the key factor that makes them a minority. For example, consider the Jewish population in America. Though their history is one that has been riddled with historical trauma, they have largely been free of most violent forms of mistreatment in the United States. Further, many people equate the Jewish community with affluence, yet they are still very much a minority due to their unique history and their religious precepts. Because of the persecution that they have endured, they are still a minority in most countries where they reside, largely due to social and historical circumstances.

Thus, the term "minority" encompasses a number of aspects that work together to establish such a status. The fact is that, over time, the United States will ultimately consist of a splintered group of minorities across the nation. In other words, the United States will continue to become more and more diverse over time. In fact, it may well be that the dominant culture will cease to exist within another 50 years or so. This trend has been noted by demographers and can also be readily observed from the social changes occurring throughout the nation. Just a few years ago, most people would not have thought that an African American president would have been a reality in the United States. However, this reality stands as a stark testament to the changing nature of the social and cultural landscape of the United States.

DEFINING CULTURAL DIVERSITY

The term "diversity" is itself subject to diverse forms of meaning. Indeed, many people think of diversity in terms of physical characteristics, but this is a simplified understanding of diversity. We use the term "**cultural diversity**" to refer to a concept whereby the history, beliefs, behavior, language, traditions, and values of racial and/or ethnic groups are what make them distinct. Thus, cultural diversity includes a variety of features specific to a given group of people. The sum total of these differences is what specifically identifies individuals who belong to a specific group.

Diversity characteristics also include religious beliefs and political viewpoints. In some cases, these can be mixed, such as in Muslim nations where governments are theocratic (run by religious authority). Immigrants to the United States who come from Middle Eastern countries may have a difficult time understanding concepts such as the separation of church and state; in their countries of origin, this concept may not exist. These differences in viewpoints and in defining what is "normal" according to a specific group are where challenges and friction emerge.

However, it is important that students and practitioners understand that cultural diversity is something that is here to stay and will only become more pronounced in the future. Indeed, even the United Nations has acknowledged that cultural diversity is a prime concern, even though it would seem that a worldwide culture of homogeneous standards on human rights has evolved. A report drafted by UNESCO, entitled

"Investing in Cultural Diversity and Intercultural Dialogue," speaks to this very issue. The key premise of this report is that even though the world community is developing a sense of common knowledge due to improvements in technology, transportation, and educational exchange, the identities of various groups is still an important feature in developing effective human relations around the world. In fact, the report advocates the preservation of the unique aspects of different cultures. If the United Nations has had to come to terms with the issue of diversity and its impact on all spheres of government operation, then it is only natural that the United States will have to do the same.

Lastly, it should be clear from our discussion of diversity that we are referring to ethnic and cultural differences, not necessarily racial differences, among people. (For a list of racial definitions, students should refer to Table 1-1 for examples provided from the federal government.) Racial diversity is another important concept when considering a multicultural society such as the United States. However, it is not identical to cultural diversity. **Racial diversity** is a term that describes the existence of numerous racial groups within a given society. Naturally, the United States has a racially diverse composition. In addition, numerous atrocities, based on racial categories, have occurred in the United States. Perhaps the most memorable would be the history of slavery, during which the United States maintained a slave population of African descent.

TABLE 1-1   Definitions of Race According to the U.S. Bureau of the Census.
Categories of Race Established by the U.S. Bureau of the Census
White. A person having origins in any of the original peoples of Europe, the Middle East, or North Africa. It includes people who indicate their race as "White" or report entries such as Irish, German, Italian, Lebanese, Arab, Moroccan, or Caucasian.
Black or African American. A person having origins in any of the Black racial groups of Africa. It includes people who indicate their race as "Black, African Am., or Negro" or report entries such as African American, Kenyan, Nigerian, or Haitian.
American Indian and Alaska Native. A person having origins in any of the original peoples of North and South America (including Central America) and who maintains tribal affiliation or community attachment. This category includes people who indicate their race as "American Indian or Alaska Native" or report entries such as Navajo, Blackfeet, Inupiat, Yup'ik, or Central American Indian groups or South American Indian groups.
Asian. A person having origins in any of the original peoples of the Far East, Southeast Asia, or the Indian subcontinent including, for example, Cambodia, China, India, Japan, Korea, Malaysia, Pakistan, the Philippine Islands, Thailand, and Vietnam. It includes people who indicate their race as "Asian Indian," "Chinese," "Filipino," "Korean," "Japanese," "Vietnamese," and "Other Asian" or provide other detailed Asian responses. A person having origins in any of the original peoples of Hawaii, Guam, Samoa, or other Pacific Islands. It includes people who indicate their race as "Native Hawaiian," "Guamanian or Chamorro," "Samoan," and "Other Pacific Islander" or provide other detailed Pacific Islander responses.
Some other race. Includes all other responses not included in the "White," "Black or African American," "American Indian or Alaska Native," "Asian," and "Native Hawaiian or Other Pacific Islander" race categories described above. Respondents reporting entries such as multiracial, mixed, interracial, or a Hispanic, Latino, or Spanish group (for example, Mexican, Puerto Rican, Cuban, or Spanish) in response to the race question are included in this category.
Two or more races. People may have chosen to provide two or more races either by checking two or more race response check boxes, by providing multiple responses, or by some combination of check boxes and other responses.

Source: U.S. Bureau of the Census. (2010). *Race definitions.* Washington, DC: U.S. Bureau of the Census.

MULTICULTURALISM AND GLOBALIZATION

It has been well established that the demographic composition of the United States will be considerably different in the future. In short, the United States is becoming more diverse than ever, and the Caucasian American group will become the minority by the year 2050, at the latest. This raises a number of interesting possibilities for the country as a whole and its criminal justice system in particular. The United States has often been referred to as *the melting pot* because since its early history, it has been open to immigrants and cultural groups from many different countries. However, we contend that current trends in diversity and immigration are distinct from much of the past history of the United States. In particular, the influx of cultural groups is much more disparate, consisting of groups from a variety of world regions, rather than being dominated by one or two primary groups of immigrants. One key factor that has led to this distinction is globalization. **Globalization** is the process by which societies, cultures, and economies around the world have become integrated due to advances in communication and transportation technology, as well as the passage of laws and treaties that facilitate this integration. This results in a transnational sharing of ideas, cultures, and mores that become interlaced. The impact of globalization has, in turn, led to an increased interest in multiculturalism. **Multiculturalism** *refers to the policy-setting agenda to adopt equitable forms of consideration for distinct ethnic, religious, and racial groups without promoting any particular group as being dominant or central in identification.* This term can also include official belief systems and lifestyle choices, with none being held as preferable or superior to others.

The state of change within the cultural fabric of the United States continues in a fast pace. Cultural norms are, to some degree, in a state of flux, with resulting friction between groups who find themselves losing status and privilege within this new fabric and other groups who find that they have more social clout and capital than they did in the past. This has led to a morphing of the United States where traditional aspects of American culture are challenged more than ever. For instance, issues related to religion have been questioned, in terms of both continued courthouse practices integrating Judeo-Christian overtones (see *McCreary County v. ACLU of Kentucky*) as well as the validation and acceptance of the Muslim religion in the United States, despite the events that transpired with the World Trade Center tragedy on September 11, 2001. Issues related to race have broadened, even in the criminal justice literature. Consider as an example the racial profiling concerns shifted in the early 2000s from being centered on possible African and Latino American suspects to those of Middle Eastern origin.

Given the current state of affairs, the modern criminal justice practitioner is only likely to face further cultural complexities. Whether good, bad, or indifferent, it is not at all likely that these issues will become easier to address; rather, they will certainly become more complicated in the future. This creates unique and ever-changing demands on criminal justice practitioners, whether they are employed within the law enforcement, judicial, or correctional arena. The criminal justice system does not operate in a social vacuum; rather, it is directly impacted by this sense of rapid and continual cultural change. It is because of this that law enforcement, court personnel, and correctional personnel will find themselves continually challenged beyond the scope of their standard recruit training and it is because of this that continued attention will need to be provided to this area within the criminal justice system.

Immigration and the Influx of Differing Cultures

Immigration issues have come to the forefront of public debate and immigration itself is a very important topic for modern-day criminal justice practitioners. When we talk of **immigration**, we are referring to those persons who choose to live in the United States and willingly move within the borders of the United States even though their area of origin is outside of the United States. This includes both legal and illegal movement into the United States. The **Department of Homeland Security** is a federal agency that tracks the movement of persons who enter and exit the borders of the United States. The Department of Homeland Security reports that there were one million immigrants (permanent residents with green cards) in the United States during fiscal year 2005 and 1.3 million immigrants during fiscal year 2006. However, even these numbers are not accurate as Gelatt and Coffey (2007) point out, indicating that most likely there are 1.8 million immigrants in the United States during any given fiscal year. This is largely attributed to the nature of certain types of temporary immigration as well as out-of-date immigration papers. When restricting the discussion to those immigrants who have been legally accounted for, the Department of Homeland Security statistics count immigrants as those who obtain lawful resident status in the United States (Gelatt & Coffey, 2007).

It is estimated that of these immigrants, roughly 60 percent are not new or temporary immigrants but are instead in the process of obtaining some type of permanent status (Gelatt & Coffey, 2007). These immigrants, seeking adjustment of their immigration status, are drawn from temporary workers, students who came to the United States for study, refugees and/or asylum seekers, or persons seeking nonimmigrant visas. It is estimated that this accounts for approximately 632,000 immigrants seeking status adjustment each year. This is important because these immigrants, for all practical purposes, become permanent members of the community. However, the immigration data just discussed does not include the large numbers of illegal aliens within the nation.

When considering these individuals, the numbers amount to millions of persons within the U.S. border. In fact, it has been estimated from 2000 Census Bureau data that the probable number of residual foreign-born persons was likely to be around 8.7 million (Costanzo, Davis, Irazi, Goodkind, & Ramirez, 2001). These estimates also conclude that of the 8.7 million, 5.4 million were Latino and 3.9 million (44.5 percent) Mexican (Costanzo et al., 2001). This then means that Mexican immigrants, whether legal or illegal, account for the largest influx of persons in the United States. The next largest group of immigrants consists of a variety of Asian nationalities, with percentages being quite varied among several nationalities. Because Latino and Asian groups constitute the majority of immigrants into the United States, discussions related to immigration will stay focused on these populations. Lastly, it is important to note that the influx of immigrants into the United States is unprecedented in relation to the proportion that accounts for the overall national population.

Immigration Issues (Mexico)

Immigration tensions have mounted between the United States and Mexico. In states such as California, Arizona, New Mexico, and Texas, there has been a substantial backlash from citizens of the United States toward persons migrating to the United States, whether legally or illegally. To a large extent, this is simply the result of the growing pains of a nation that continues to maintain its multicultural origins. However, the difference in this case is because of a mass exodus of immigrants from nearby, rather than overseas, and these same immigrants send much of their hard-earned money and income to their family directly across the U.S. border.

The result, according to some, is a displacement of available jobs in certain areas of the United States as well as an economic vacuum that develops as money is channeled into another country's economy. On the other hand, the jobs that many Mexican American immigrants are taking are those that other persons in the United States will not fill, for whatever reason. Further, the drain on the U.S. economy may, in actuality, not be that great but instead may be producing a blurring of economies between the United States and Mexico. Some evidence of this could be seen when the **North American Free Trade Alliance (NAFTA)** came into vogue during the early to mid-1990s. This agreement made much more lenient immigration for Mexican citizens wishing to work in the United States. While there were advantages and disadvantages associated with this agreement, it is noteworthy that this treaty, when taken together with the third national partner, Canada, constituted the largest trade bloc in the world in terms of combined GDP purchasing power parity.

The sheer economic impact of NAFTA on the landscape of the United States has actually been unparalleled. In examining the impact of NAFTA, consider that the trading relationship between the United States and Canada is the largest in the world in terms of bilateral exchange of money, goods, and services (Davy & Meyers, 2006). Indeed, the two-way trade in commodities between these countries equaled over $428 billion in 2004, and since the 1994 implementation of NAFTA, trade has nearly doubled (Davy & Meyers, 2006). Further, Mexico is the United States' second largest trading partner following Canada, with trade between Mexico and the United States reaching $268 billion in 2004 (Davy & Meyers, 2006). These figures demonstrate the enormous economic interconnections that exist between the United States and its immediate neighbors. It is then no wonder that immigration has become so widespread. This is especially true when an affluent country such as the United States borders a less affluent one such as Mexico.

The pull and incentives for Mexican citizens to enter the United States is (understandably) very strong. In fact, immigration (both legal and illegal) of Mexican citizens, as well as other Central American and South American citizens, has had such an impact throughout the United States that it is now common for signage along roads and throughout cities to be written in both Spanish and English. This is unique in many respects because the United States, while being classified as the world's "melting pot," has had the advantage of maintaining one official language: English. But this is no longer the case, and it is becoming increasingly necessary that traditional outlooks on language be challenged; many citizens find themselves now no longer at home knowing only English. For Europe and other countries around the world, the need to know more than one language has not been so problematic. For the United States, this issue has vexed many citizens and continues to build resistance among groups of people in southwestern states.

During the year 2000, Mexico pushed for the free flow of people across the U.S.–Mexican border as a second phase of the NAFTA agreement. However, the events that followed the World Trade Center tragedy on September 11, 2001, raised border security concerns throughout the nation. Naturally, this impacted immigration policies and eventually resulted in national debate among citizens and the U.S. Congress in 2006. The emergence of the **Secure Fence Act of 2006**, which implemented 700 miles of high-security fencing along the Mexican–U.S. border, demonstrated the desire of the nation to curtail illegal border crossings.

American politics being as they are, there was likewise a call for a countermeasure to assuage those who disagreed with what appeared to be heavy-handed tactics to discourage border crossings. The **Comprehensive Immigration Reform Act of 2007** was proposed in Congress, and it would have granted illegal immigrants who were already in the country a means to stay and obtain citizenship status. However, this bill failed in the Senate due to serious public complaints and the negative media attention that was generated. During the later part of 2007, various House Representatives introduced the **Strive Act**, which was designed to strengthen border security, eliminate the excessive number of family immigration applications, and limit the provision for legalization to those immigrants who first entered the United States and agreed to pay fees, fines, and back taxes as a condition for legal status.

In 2007, politicians in Washington, DC, had informally considered a similar proposal around the same time. Its notable differences from the Strive Act are as follows: (1) eliminating preferences for family immigration and (2) instituting a points system that would have given priority to education, skills, work experience in the United States, and English proficiency for employment-based immigration. This proposed bill was intended to significantly boost enforcement of immigration laws (both at the borders and through mandatory verification by employers of the legal status of their employees), created a new temporary worker program, eliminated family immigration backlogs, instituted a points system, and allowed most of the country's millions of unauthorized immigrants to earn legal status. The Senate bill represented a "grand compromise" among widely differing points of view and political interests. President Bush even made a rare visit to Capitol Hill to speak with Republican leaders.

Although it was the strongest enforcement bill yet to be considered by the Senate, the public perceived it primarily as an amnesty measure. Public opposition to the idea of amnesty undermined the work of this group and, as a result, the House abandoned further consideration of the Strive Act. Further still, subsequent attempts to pass specific pieces of the immigration reform bill also failed. This means that federal agencies are left with few options other than strict enforcement of existing laws. Currently, **Immigration and Customs Enforcement (ICE)**, the agency charged with enforcing immigration laws, continues to be active in the vigorous enforcement of various border issues.

CURRENT EVENTS IN MULTICULTURAL CRIMINAL JUSTICE
Immigration Controversies and Criminal Justice

In the recent past, there have been numerous lawsuits and other actions taken against local law enforcement agencies that embrace the enforcement immigration law. Among them is the well known Sheriff Joe Arpaio, of Maricopa County, in Arizona (Wian & Martinez, 2012). The sheriff's department of Maricopa County was sued through a class-action filed by the ACLU and other attorneys who represented Latino Americans in the area. The accusations allege violations of civil rights and Constitutional violations. At issue is that the 14th Amendment's requirement for equal protection under the law has been violated, as well as other Constitutional violations (Wian & Martinez, 2012). The plaintiffs, in this case, allege a policy of racial discrimination and mistreatment of Latino Americans (Wian & Martinez, 2012). Regardless of whether an agency is found to be guilty of Civil Rights violations, there is no arguing that the process of defending against such allegations is costly in terms of legal expense. When and where possible, it is prudent, both from a fiscal and from a public relations standpoint, to avoid such controversial allegations. The exception being, of course, for sheriffs and politicians who seek to use such notoriety as a mechanism for political ascension.

There is additional past precedence of local police agencies that have faced civil litigation and liability for their involvement in immigration enforcement. For example, the Katy, Texas Police Department participated in an immigration raid with federal agents in 1994. A total of 80 individuals who were detained by the police were later determined to be either citizens or legal immigrants with permission to be in the country. The Katy police department faced suits from these individuals and eventually settled their claims out of court. Consider also that in San Francisco, the Lawyers Committee in that city reported that it has settled at least eight cases during the last decade that have cost the city over $640,000 (Morawetz & Das, 2010; Ward, 2008). Because local agencies currently lack clear authority to enforce immigration laws, are limited in their ability to arrest without a warrant, are prohibited from racial profiling and lack the training and experience to enforce complex federal immigration laws, it is more likely that local police agencies will face the risk of civil liability and litigation if they chose to enforce federal immigration laws.

Further, in many cases, there are a number of illegal immigrants who live in the community amidst friends and relatives who have legally immigrated. Morawetz and Das (2010) call households where both illegal and legal immigrants reside "mixed families" denoting the mix in immigration statuses that may exist among various members of the home (p. 73). In fact, they estimate that up to 85% of all immigrant homes have family members of mixed immigration statuses. They also note that, in relation to liability issues, mixed-status families can present local police with two problems. First, they may inadvertently detain citizens or lawful residents while seeking a person who is illegally in the country. If they do so, they can be held accountable for infringing the individual's right to liberty. Second, it can occur that minors may be left unsupervised and/or in the supervision of unauthorized persons when they detain their parents and

thereby violate their general responsibility for the care and well-being of the children residing in the community. These types of circumstances have happened in some jurisdictions that has resulted in litigation (Morawetz & Das, 2010).

Further, for these and other reasons, immigrant families are often hesitant to call police, even when they know of crimes that have been committed against them or others whom they know. Lysakowski, Pearsall, Pope (2009) found that participants reported that when immigrants call police they may be taking a risk if they disclose their immigration status, or the status of their family members or neighbors, to authorities. Indeed, participants from a Latino community in this study found that these persons often knew who committed many of the crimes in their area, but they were not willing to come forward out of fear that their immigration status would be questioned. As one can imagine, there are a number of means by which the immigrant is victimized and that this victimization is made worse by their failure to report these crimes. Thus, many of these individuals feel trapped in a world where their own needs for safety are perpetually compromised, creating a bleak future picture for them and their families.

References: Wian, C. & Martinez, M. (2012, July 20). Arizona sheriff faces civil trial in alleged targeting of Latinos. CNN Justice, retrieved from http://www.cnn.com/2012/07/19/justice/arizona-arpaio-trial/index.html

Lysakowski, M., Pearsall, A. A., & Pope, J. (2009). *Policing in immigrant communities.* Washington, DC: Office of Community Oriented Police Services, United States Department of Justice.

Morawetz, N. & Das, A. (2010). Legal issues in local police enforcement of federal immigration law. In Anita Khashu (Ed.). *The Role of Local Police: Striking a Balance Between Immigration Enforcement and Civil Liberties.* Washington, DC: Police Foundation. Retrieved from www.policefoundation.org.

Ward, S. (2008). *Illegal Aliens on I.C.E: Tougher Immigration Enforcement Tactics Spur Challenges,* ABA JOURNAL (June 2008), available at http://www.abajournal.com/magazine/illegal_aliens_on_ice/

Immigration Issues (Asian Immigrants)

It is estimated that the Asian American community, currently consisting of approximately 4.5 percent of the U.S. population (United States Census Bureau, 2008), will grow to account for 9.3 percent of the overall U.S. population by the year 2050 (Centers for Disease Control, 2005). Between 2000 and 2008, the increase in the Asian American population (26.8 percent) was more than three times the increase in the total U.S. population (7.8 percent) (United States Census Bureau, 2008). Simply put, this growth is unprecedented and reflects even more how immigration continues to impact the overall composition of the U.S. racial and cultural landscape.

The Asian American population tends to be predominantly located in California, New York, Illinois (mainly Chicago), and various regions around the nation's capital. Among those who immigrated to the United States in 2007, 4.4 percent came from the Philippines, 4.1 percent came from the People's Republic of China, 4.1 percent came from India, 3 percent came from Vietnam, and 2.7 percent came from Korea. Although collectively these countries account for only about one-fifth to a quarter of all foreign-born persons in the United States, their numbers and the rate of immigration are growing faster than average.

In addition to this growth, there is an increasing tendency among Asian Americans to intermarry and have children with partners of other racial categories. Figure 1-1 shows the average population of two categories of the Asian American population, the "Asian Alone" and the "Asian Alone or in Combination with Another Race." This second category of Asian Americans demonstrates how the immigration of Asians into the United States has contributed to the notion of the melting pot in the United States. This also demonstrates how Asian culture impacts mainstream culture and at the same time how U.S. mainstream culture affects Asian families, traditional lineages, and ultimately traditional cultural views that are passed down from one generation to the next.

The fact that the Asian American population is growing at such a rapid rate underscores this population's emerging importance throughout the nation and points toward the need for further accommodation in the United States. Thus, law enforcement officers in the United States will increasingly need to have an understanding of Asian groups in their area. This also demonstrates the need for training and attentiveness to community-relations issues and also makes it clear that that there is a need for culturally competent law enforcement (specific to the Asian American groups in a given jurisdiction) in the United States. Further, these groups tend to be quite varied from one another. This presents numerous challenges since there are more languages and cultural systems with which law enforcement personnel must become familiar. In addition, a substantial portion of the Asian population in the United States does not know English. This is particularly true among the Southeast Asian groups. Indeed, nearly 38 percent of all Vietnamese Americans do not speak English (Shusta, Levine, Wong, Olson, & Harris, 2011). In addition, it has been determined that an approximate 23 percent of Chinese Americans also do not speak English (Shusta et al., 2011). Naturally, this leads to further difficulties for police agencies attempting to establish rapport with these communities.

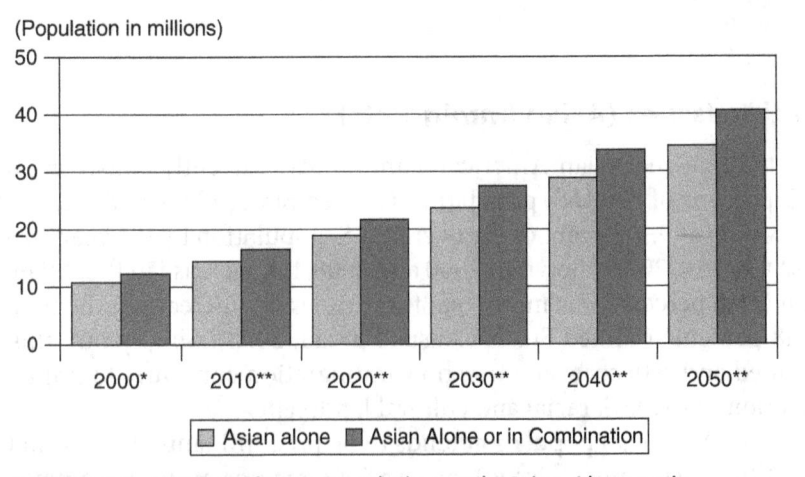

FIGURE 1-1   "Asian Alone" Population and "Asian Alone or in Combination with Another Race Population, 2000–2008.
Source: United States Census Bureau. (2008). *National population estimate and national population projections.* Washington, DC: United States Census Bureau.

*Means population as of 01 July, 2000.
**Means population projection after 01 July of that year from 2010 onward.

The Combined Impact of Latino and Asian Immigration

As noted earlier in this chapter, the current state of immigration is touted to be unique and different from previous periods in U.S. history. Importantly, the predominance of immigration from Mexico and Asian countries in the early part of this century contrasts with immigration from mostly European countries in times past. This is even true when compared with groups that immigrated during the later 1900s, such as the influx of Italian immigrants that occurred during the 1960s. At that time, Italian immigrants made up nearly 13 percent of all foreign-born Americans, followed by those born in Germany and Canada, with both accounting for approximately 10 percent of the foreign-born population in the United States. No single country accounted for more than 15 percent of the total immigrant population in 1960, unlike in 2008 (Gelatt, 2013; Coffey, 2011).

Now, in this decade, we are seeing that the United States is contending with cultural groups that have a diverse array of subgroups (i.e., Latino populations consisting of numerous national identities such as Mexican, El Salvadoran, and Cuban; Asian populations consisting of Chinese, Korean, Indian, and Vietnamese). These groups are also contributing to substantial social change. Asian groups bring with them languages that are new for many agencies, adding linguistic barriers. Religious and cultural orientations are quite different from those originating from Europe, adding additional complexity. Latino groups, particularly those from Mexico, may not be new to the United States, but their sheer numbers have led to the need for the United States to make accommodations for this group that go well beyond those that have been made for other groups in the past.

THE CHALLENGE TO LAW ENFORCEMENT

Building trust with diverse communities has not always been easy for police agencies. This is exacerbated by the fact that the United States has had a shift in the amount and type of immigration that has occurred. Researchers continue to point toward the rapid change that has occurred due to immigration into the United States, and Khashu, Bush, and Latiff (2005) go so far as to state that such an impact from immigration has not been witnessed since the early twentieth century. Further, they indicate that never has the immigrant population been so diverse and geographically dispersed (Thomas, 2011). This new demography, combined with the era of terrorism being a national priority, has law enforcement agencies throughout the country exploring the means by which they can build relationships with immigrant communities who are distanced from agency personnel. The need for trust building has been identified as essential. Some suggestions provided by Khashu et al. (2005) of the Vera Institute as well as the Community Oriented Policing Services of the Department of Justice include the following:

- Agencies must develop regular channels of communication between immigrant community representatives and police, which will help build trust and create a climate where tensions can be resolved before they escalate (Khashu et al., 2005). Police personnel must reach out to a variety of community representatives since racial, cultural, and/or political divisions within immigrant communities may otherwise impede progress in rapport building (Khashu et al., 2005).
- Engaging a diverse group of immigrants should involve the inclusion of community representatives. With this in mind, it is also important for police to remain neutral in intragroup rivalries and hostilities (Khashu et al., 2005).

- If high-level police officials and policy makers do not participate, or if community participants do not see immediate changes in police policy and procedures, the community representatives may perceive an initiative as little more than public relations (Khashu et al., 2005). This is especially true if high-level policy makers are absent from the process since police representatives must communicate the specific ways they intend to use community feedback (Khashu et al., 2005).

Though these may seem like simplistic suggestions, they have proven to be challenging to implement. However, as we will see in the subsequent section, the justice system does not operate in a social vacuum. As police are addressing the day-to-day concerns associated with diverse communities who have international origins, the judicial system is increasingly adopting standards and concepts from multinational sources. This proves that the U.S. system is one that is in flux, with the nation's process of administering justice increasingly resembling the notions and philosophies of the global community.

The Impact of the Global Community on American Jurisprudence

As an example of how the international community is impacting the landscape of the United States and its justice system, consider the fact that many attorneys are now integrating precedents from other national jurisdictions within their own legal arguments. In fact, this is being done with the approval (or at least toleration) from lower courts. The Supreme Court itself has accepted such arguments in some circumstances as valid and applicable to a number of legal issues. This is perhaps one of the strongest evidence that the U.S. judicial and criminal justice systems will be further impacted by the global community.

Indeed, immigration lawyers in the United States have cited decisions of the International Court of Justice as well as the International Covenant on Civil and Political Rights. This has been particularly true in the states of Illinois, Michigan, California, and Texas (Leavitt, 2003). There are even cases in the state of Michigan where criminal defense lawyers have cited decisions of the Constitutional Court of South Africa and the Inter-American Commission on Human Rights (Leavitt, 2003). In addition, there have been cases where U.S. companies are being held accountable by foreign courts due to Internet defamation, such as that involving Dow Jones, the publisher of *The Wall Street Journal* and *Barron's* magazine, which agreed to pay the plaintiff, an Australian by the name of Joe Gutnick, a combined total of $443,500 for damages and legal fees in Australian courts. Since this case was settled in November 2004, Canadian, UK, and U.S. attorneys have cited this precedent when applicable (The Associated Press, 2004).

The tendency to cite foreign courts and to consent to their rulings has even extended to the U.S. Supreme Court. This has been directly observed in three important cases where the majority and/or concurring opinions (not just the dissenting opinions) have specifically noted foreign legal jurisprudence. The first case is **Atkins v. Virginia**, which resulted in a ruling that prohibited the execution of the mentally retarded. In *Atkins*, the Court specifically noted that "within the world community, the imposition of the death penalty for crimes committed by mentally retarded offenders is overwhelmingly disapproved" (p. 221), specifically citing the Brief for The European Union as an amicus curiae in *McCarver v. North Carolina*. In *Atkins*, the Court further noted that though the use of international factors was by no means dispositive, their consistency with the legislative evidence lent further support that there is a consensus among those who have addressed the issue of the death penalty. The Court likewise

INTERNATIONAL FOCUS

Medellin v. Texas (2008), the United States and the International Court

Further demonstration of the impact of international courts on U.S. judicial decision making would include the case of Jose Medellin, a Mexican citizen who was on death row in the United States for murder in Texas. In this case, the nation of Mexico sued the United States because the Mexican national consulate had not been notified about Medellin's case, a requirement of the Vienna Convention on Consular Relations. The state of Texas rejected this notion and continued to pursue the death penalty for Medellin. What is most interesting about this case is that the Bush administration sought to influence the Supreme Court, entering the case on behalf of Medellin in an attempt to get the U.S. Supreme Court to overturn the Texas court's ruling.

The concern of the Bush administration was that the Texas ruling and the completion of the death sentence would place the United States in breach of its obligation to comply with the World Court and its oversight (Stanford University, 2005). Further, this situation was noted to have a negative impact on the foreign policy interests of the United States, adding friction to the already difficult relations regarding crime and justice between the two countries. Thus, the Bush administration hoped to overrule Texas' own death penalty as a means of staying in compliance with World Court standards.

Despite the persistence of federal government officials, Texas maintained its stance on the death penalty and its own authority to implement judicial decisions within its jurisdiction. Ultimately, this led to an unexpected decision by the Bush administration where the U.S. government withdrew from the Vienna Convention's optional protocol that gave the International Court of Justice jurisdiction over disputes related to the treaty between the United States and Mexico. Even with this in mind, in July 2008 the International Court of Justice asked for a stay of execution for Medellin on the grounds of unfair trial practices. The state of Texas did not heed this request and executed Medellin in August 2008.

noted *Thompson v. Oklahoma* (1988), considering the views of professional organizations respected by other nations that share our Anglo-American heritage, as well as the leading members of the Western European community.

A second important case where the Supreme Court considered international precedent was ***Grutter v. Bollinger* (2003).** This case involved the University of Michigan Law School's policy of permitting the consideration of race in affirmative action claims (Leavitt, 2003). The concurring opinion given by Justices Ginsburg and Breyer starts with the statement that "the Court's observation that race-conscious programs 'must have a logical end point', accords with the international understanding of the office of affirmative action" (*Grutter v. Bollinger*, 2003, p. 311). These two Justices pointed to United Nations documents, citing the International Convention on the Elimination of All Forms of Racial Discrimination, as ratified by the United States in 1994. This document endorsed "special and concrete measures to ensure the adequate development and protection of certain racial groups or individuals belonging to them, for the purpose of guaranteeing them the full and equal enjoyment of human rights and fundamental freedoms" (p. 312). These justices then implied that U.S. laws in agreement with their international equivalents would be more likely to be upheld by the Court than those that disagree. There are also other instances where there was an allusion to similar programs (similar to affirmative action) in other areas of the world and the idea that there was an international and quasi-collective understanding of affirmative action.

Implications for the American Criminal Justice System

The implications of cases like *Medellin* for the American judicial and criminal justice systems should be fairly clear to the average reader. This case demonstrates that American criminal justice and criminal law is directly impacted by international treaties, concerns, and mores. While in this case, the state of Texas maintained its stance, it did so in contradiction of the desires of the president's initial requests. Certainly, the United States will find itself contemplating international implications in future judicial rulings as well. Further, the astute reader will recall that economic benefits of trade due to NAFTA and other agreements are quite important to both the United States and Mexico. These types of considerations add to the layers of complication that can arise in incidents such as the *Medellin* case.

It is important to consider that such cases can have implications in other areas of the world for the United States. For instance, consider what overtones this will have with respect to other countries in Central and South America. After all, the United States has grown accustomed to entering some of those countries to fight its War on Drugs and it also has continued economic interests in those nations. It is not likely that these other countries will be content with lopsided compliance with international agreements for an indefinite period.

While it is still too early to say what the ultimate results could be, it is clear that the global legal community is having an impact on judicial decisions in the United States. Further, police agencies find themselves needing more detailed training on other cultures, languages, and customs than ever before. The commonality of this challenge is becoming increasingly clear in areas of the United States (such as the Midwest and the Southeast—excluding Florida) that did not have to contend with such issues nearly as often. Now, cultural diversity consists of a much greater mix of groups and identities in communities whose police agencies may not be prepared to deal with such an influx of variety.

Likewise, correctional systems are increasingly having to contend with populations who are diverse. This has proven quite costly for the Federal Bureau of Prisons. Indeed, the Government Accountability Office noted that in federal prisons "the number of criminal aliens incarcerated increased from about 42,000 at the end of calendar year 2001 to about 49,000 at the end of calendar year 2004—a 15 percent increase. The percentage of all federal prisoners who are criminal aliens has remained the same over the last 3 years—about 27 percent" (2005, p. 2).

Likewise, this same report indicates that the federal cost of incarcerating criminal aliens from 2001 through 2004 was approximately $5.8 billion. This demonstrates that the processing of persons from other countries has an impact on all areas of the U.S. criminal justice system. In response to the influx of criminal aliens within U.S. borders, Immigration and Customs Enforcement has implemented the Secure Communities: A Comprehensive Plan to Identify and Remove Criminal Aliens agenda as a means of transforming the way the federal government cooperates with state and local law enforcement agencies to identify, detain, and remove all criminal aliens held in custody (U.S. Immigration and Customs Enforcement, 2008). In addition, the overrepresentation of African American and Latino American inmates in state prisons has been widely written about throughout the research literature. The racial diversity and high representation of minorities among inmates provide challenges to correctional workers, agencies, and administrators. Further, the diversity of religious affiliations (including Muslim inmates) has generated a need for added training. All in all, correctional officials, like law enforcement officials, will find themselves challenged by the continual influx of a diverse population. From this, it is clear that all three branches of the criminal justice system (law enforcement, the courts, and corrections) will continue to be impacted by a broader social structure that will continually change.

HOMEGROWN CHALLENGES, HISTORICAL TRAUMA, AND MINORITY GROUPS

Although issues related to immigration are undoubtedly an important challenge for the American criminal justice system, there are other long-standing challenges that have existed within the United States for multiple generations. In particular, the United States has struggled to make peace with two minority groups who have suffered a great deal of historical trauma: Native Americans and African Americans. **Historical trauma** or **intergenerational trauma** is the cumulative psychological damage that specific groups of people suffer throughout multiple generations. It becomes a shared group experience that, at least in part, defines that group's role in society. Because these two groups are interlaced within the history of the United States from the very early period of the nation's inception, we refer to the social challenges in meeting the needs of these two racial groups as having been "homegrown" within the United States. This simply implies that the United States, and specifically its criminal justice system, bred and developed this problem on its own accord and, as a result, has an ethical obligation to be accountable for the atrocities that it has committed against these groups, to include a criminal justice system that is adept at understanding and addressing the issues that have led to the state of affairs that now exist.

In this chapter, we will focus on both Native Americans and African Americans in discussing diversity challenges related to race. We do this for several reasons. First, juxtaposed against the new concerns related to the immigration of Latino and Asian populations is the even longer and more traditional history associated with racial disparities among populations that were either here prior to the arrival of European Americans or have been in the United States through most of that country's history. Second, these two groups have a much different history from other minority groups in that they were either nearly eradicated or placed into outright slavery and bondage, making them a particularly disadvantaged group. Third, though these two groups will be covered in detail in future chapters, an introductory chapter regarding racial and cultural diversity would be remiss without the specific coverage of these two groups.

Lastly, we do, of course, understand that the Latino population has lived within the United States for a substantial period of time. Indeed, in most southwestern states they were part of the original citizenry, even prior to the state's founding. Indeed, in 1847 at the close of the Mexican–American war, Mexico was forced to sign the Treaty of Guadalupe Hidalgo. This treaty resulted in a shift in citizenship of over 80,000 Mexicans. Likewise, Puerto Ricans were made citizens upon the U.S. victory in the Spanish–American war. Despite the fact that each of these groups of people (both are classified as Latino) preceded European Americans, they were treated as substandard citizens, with most of them losing their property and status. Over time, these regions were classified as the modern-day states of California, Arizona, New Mexico, Texas, Nevada, Utah, and Colorado. In addition, tax laws and property laws were passed that essentially stripped most Mexican Americans of their wealth and set them back economically to an impoverished state of existence.

Certainly, we do not condone these historical occurrences nor do we wish to make light of them. However, from a historical and legal perspective, we believe that there are some genuine differences in the traumatic effects upon Latino Americans as compared with the Native American and African American people. The Latino American population, by the time of the United States' existence, had already acquired independence from Spain. At the hands of Spain, native Latinos had suffered slavery, mass death and destruction, and pillage. But by the time of the Mexican–American war, these were issues for which Spain was accountable and, perhaps (to a lesser extent), the Mexican government.

When the United States obtained these vast regions of territory, this was done through an officially declared and legally recognized war between the two nations. While this might seem like hairsplitting, it is not. Although the war might not have been fought on fair grounds militarily, such arguments go well beyond the scope or purpose of this text. Rather, we intend to focus on the simple legal and historical reality that occurred. Thus, in essence, these acquisitions were the spoils of war. Further, there is no history of mass executions, murder, rape, and pillage of citizens in this area. This is true even according to Mexican accounts of the war. To be sure, injustices did occur (as they do in all types of warfare) but the extent to which these occurred cannot be classified as a systemic process deliberately instituted by the U.S. military and/or government. In addition, Mexican Americans were, at the very least, granted citizenship and were voting members who could (and often did) own property and/or have the ability to engage in politics. They were not relocated to other areas of the United States as a group and did not suffer mass extermination to the point of near extinction (as was true for Native Americans), and their families were not separated from one another so that they could be bred for labor as is done with common livestock (as was true for African Americans).

Thus, overall, we believe that the dynamics and issues related to Latino populations and Asian populations are substantially different from those related to Native American and African American groups who suffered mass extermination and/or mass enslavement. Again, we do not intend to minimize the sense of victimization, economic disadvantage, and unfair treatment that has been endured. However, we do believe that the means by which this type of disadvantage occurred, as well as the depth to which the damage was inflicted (i.e., the loss of property as opposed to mass death at the hands of the U.S. government), present different circumstances. Further still, in today's contemporary setting, large numbers of Latinos and Asians are vigorously trying to immigrate to the United States of their own accord. The same cannot be said of Native Americans in other countries and Africans overseas; at least not to the same extent as is true for Latinos and Asians. It is because of these reasons that we have chosen to address these two groups with a separate yet concise overview.

Historical Trauma and Native Americans

For Native Americans, history in the Americas is thought to have begun about 40,000 years ago, when humans migrated from Asia, across the Aleutian chain (islands between Alaska and Kamchatka, Russia), and eventually settled throughout North and South America. This means that they were the first true Americans. The term "Indian" is simply one that was given by Europeans (namely Christopher Columbus) who arrived in 1492 and thought that they had landed ashore in the nation of India. Further, it should be pointed out that when we say that Columbus discovered America, we ignore the fact that Native Americans were already present; we thus fail to acknowledge them as people who were the first true founders of the Americas.

Throughout American history, Americans of European descent "settled" the continent and, through force, relocated Native Americans to less desirable areas of the United States. Through a process of genocide (mass extermination), the population of Native Americans was decimated across the continent. Entire tribes were eradicated. This type of mass death, abuse, and mistreatment is precisely what has caused the historical trauma that exists among Native American groups. Indeed, military campaigns, massacres, the deliberate spread of foreign disease epidemics, and forced relocations completely undermined the ability of the Native American population to resist their near extinction. To gain an understanding of how profound these measures were, consider that from the late 1700s to the early 1900s, the total Native American population dropped from around 12,000,000 people to around 250,000 people (Toth, Crews, & Burton, 2008, p. 8). In other words, they decreased in numbers by around 97 percent, if not more.

Today, the Native American population remains very small, but has stabilized and, in fact, has grown in the past few years. This growth, however, still pales in comparison to that in the height of Native American culture before Europeans arrived on the shores of North America. The U.S. Census Bureau, and the federal government as a whole, uses the official term "American Indian and Alaska Native Population." While we consider this terminology to be outdated, truth in reporting requires that we at least acknowledge this term, as used by the federal government, when presenting data on the Native American population from the Census Bureau. Figure 1-2 shows the average population of two categories of the Native American population, *the American Indian/ Alaska Native (AIAN) Alone* and the *Native American population, the American Indian/ Alaska Native (AIAN) Alone or in Combination (AOIC) with Another Race.* This second category of Native Americans demonstrates that even though Native Americans may be a bit reclusive when living in tribal or reservation grounds, many do intermix with

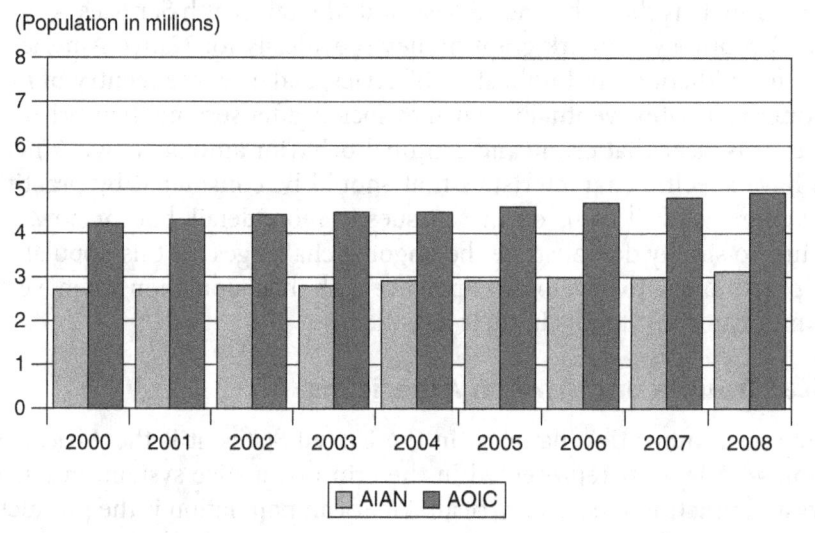

FIGURE 1-2 Native American Population, the American Indian/Alaska Native Alone (AIAN) or in Combination with Another Race (AOIC), 2000–2008. *Source:* United States Census Bureau. (2008). *National population estimate and national population projections.* Washington, DC: United States Census Bureau.

other racial groups. Naturally, this has impacted the traditional culture of many Native American groups.

Native Americans who did survive the systematic process of brutalization were forced to live in reservations constructed on lands that had little value and/or use. Boarding schools were constructed and Native American children were abducted, en masse, and forced to attend. These youth were punished physically for using their own original language, attempting to make contact with their families, or for refusing to learn the values and rules of the dominant European culture (Toth et al., 2008, p. 8). The U.S. government, through the use of Bureau of Indian Affairs agents, continued to regulate the lives of Native Americans. Indeed, "Indian Agents had the right to determine who married, who could work, who got farming tools and medicines, and were not above using starvation and violence" to gain obedience (Nielson, 2000, p. 49). Today, those Native Americans who remain may or may not live on reservations and may or may not retain remnants of their heritage. However, the intergenerational trauma and the psychological devastation that began generations ago, magnified by poverty, mistreatment by the United States, and the sense of distrust, have led to increased problems for this group of people, regardless of their tribal lineage (see Figure 1-3). Rates of drug abuse, family violence, suicide, and other types of mental health problems among them tend to be higher than the national average.

Consider that most crimes in America tend to be intraracial (meaning that perpetrators of a certain racial group tend to victimize others from their own racial group); thus, this means that Native Americans are also at an increased risk of criminal victimization. This is particularly true for Native American women. This means that the criminal justice system in areas where Native Americans tend to be present will see heightened rates of domestic violence, mutual assaults, and other crimes among intimates. Likewise, as with much of the rest of the nation, crimes often occur where substance abuse exists. This is particularly true with the Native American population, who have pronounced problems with alcohol and other drug use. This is so true that federal agencies such as the Substance Abuse and Mental Health Services Administration (SAMHSA) routinely earmark grant money specifically for Native Americans to gain treatment for addictions and unhealthy lifestyles, and even the reentry of incarcerated Native Americans who eventually return to society after serving their prison sentence.

Thus, it is clear that crime and criminal behavior among Native American populations have specific characteristics that should be considered by practitioners. In future chapters, we will focus on these issues in more detail, but for now, we provide these points to simply demonstrate the ongoing challenges for this population and the need for practitioners to develop competence with this population whenever they have Native American constituents in their jurisdiction.

Historical Trauma and African Americans

Of all the racial minorities that exist in the United States, it is the African American population who is most represented in the criminal justice system, in terms of both offenders and practitioners. The African American population is the product of one of the greatest forms of mass victimization that has occurred in the history of the United States. Literally kidnapped from their homes overseas in Africa, Africans were brought to the United States en masse and placed into bondage. For generations, African Americans were bought and sold by wealthy plantation owners, raised as property, and given no rights to self-governance whatsoever.

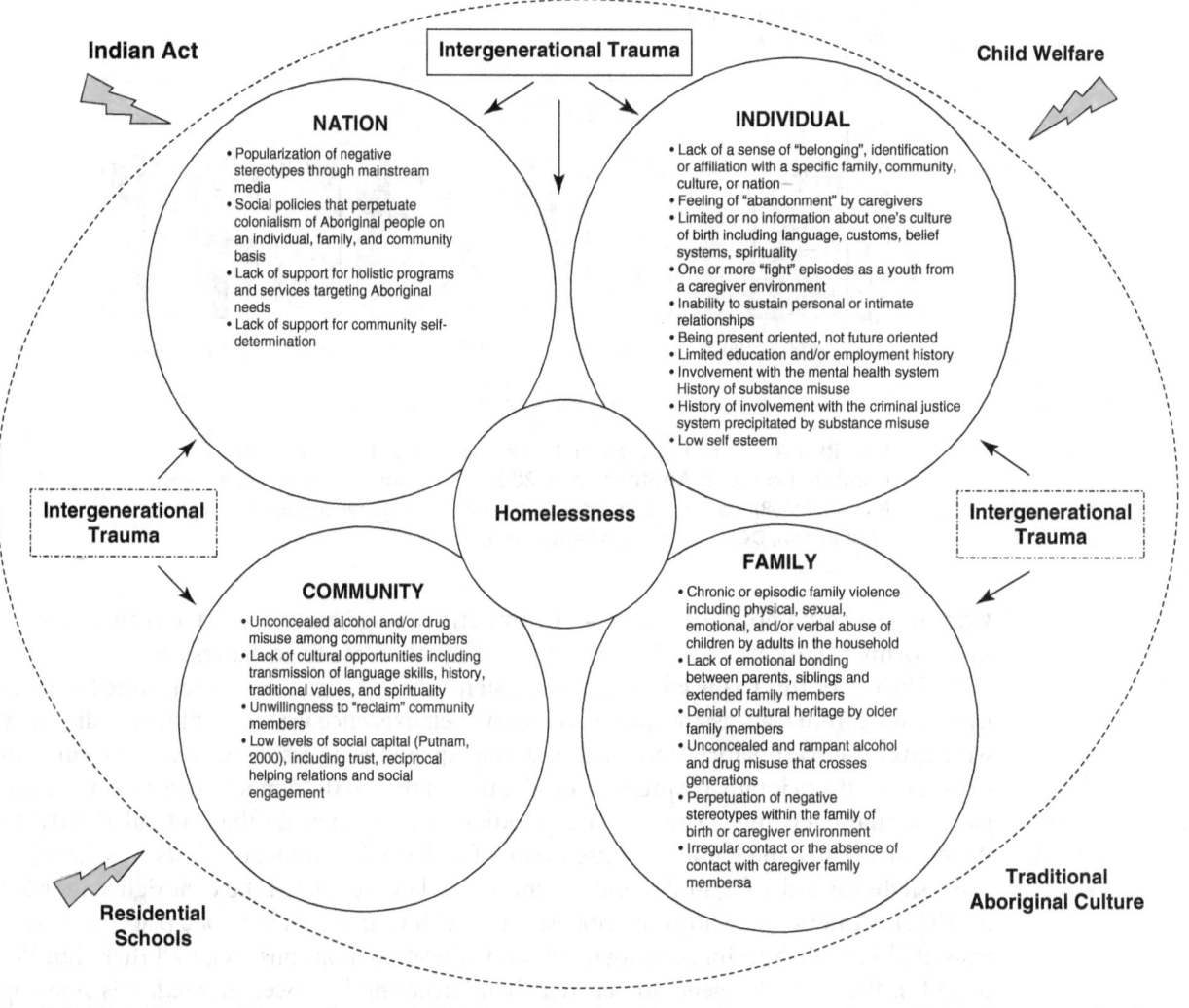

FIGURE 1-3 Intergenerational Trauma Model for Native Americans. *Source:* Menzies, P. (2010). Intergenerational trauma from a mental health perspective. *Native Social Work Journal, 7,* 63–85.

Nowadays, the population of blacks alone or blacks in combination with another race remains stable and is growing, but the disparity in income and access to resources continue to put them at a disadvantage. Figure 1-4 shows the average population of two categories of the African American population—the Black Alone and the Black Alone or in Combination with Another Race. This second category of African Americans demonstrates how the melting pot concept has literally infused the African American population with other racial groups within U.S. society, providing a blurring in distinctions and further pointing toward the multicultural society in which we live.

While all of this is generally known by the majority of the population in the United States, how debilitating this can be to a group of people is not genuinely appreciated by much of the public. Simply put, one cannot enslave an entire group of people and then, overnight, proclaim them to be free of generations of bondage without expecting social disadvantages to emerge. This is particularly true when considering that, even though freed, these people were not given the right to vote, did not own any property

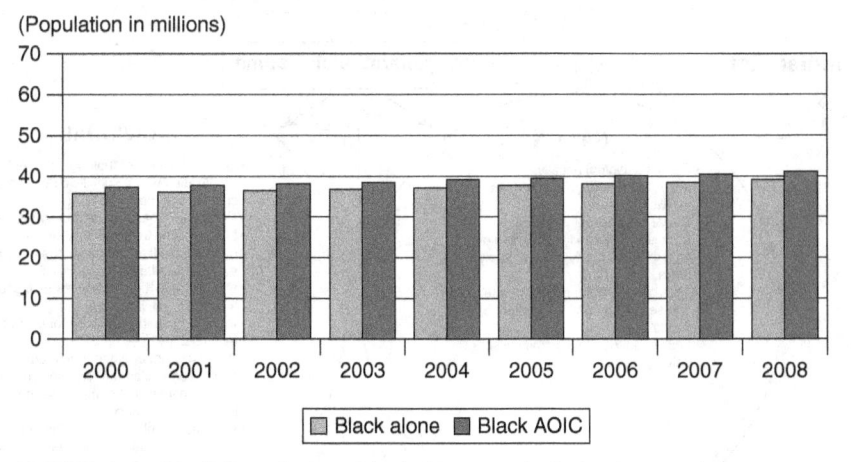

(Population in millions)

FIGURE 1-4   Black Population, Black Alone and Black Alone or in Combination with Another Race, 2000–2008. *Source:* United States Census Bureau. (2008). *National population estimate and national population projections.* Washington, DC: United States Census Bureau.

whatsoever, could not earn a decent or competitive wage, were restricted from access to most forms of education, and were not given equal access to social resources.

The use of **Jim Crow laws** created a system where African Americans were forced to live separate from Caucasians, where in theory their existence was equal but, in reality, they were given discriminatory treatment and inadequate resources. However, the term "Jim Crow" is itself a pejorative expression originating in the 1800s to mock African Americans, using a character, Jim Crow, from a popular sarcastic parody that ridiculed African Americans. Thus, the commonly used name for these discriminatory laws was, itself, an overt slight toward African Americans. Jim Crow laws restricted the civil rights afforded to African Americans, who could not associate with Caucasians in public places and were restricted in their housing, employment, and educational options. With all these hurdles placed in their way, for generations after their "freedom" had been granted, it is amazing that this racial group has been able to preserve any semblance of cohesion whatsoever.

The fact that African Americans suffered intergenerational trauma from living at such disadvantage and that laws were continually passed to keep them at a disadvantage for years after their freedom simply ensured that social ills, mental health challenges, and criminal behavior would be pronounced problems among this group. See Figure 1-5 for an illustration of the multisystemic effect that this intergenerational trauma can have in various spheres of social functioning. Further, the victimization (and consequent trauma) of this group at the hands of a racially discriminatory system explains why a sense of distrust developed between the African American community and government officials, whether at the local, state, or federal level persons.

Because this group will be discussed in greater detail in future chapters, we will not go into greater depth in this subsection. However, we believe that it is important to illustrate that this group, just like Native Americans, has been impacted by a long history of trauma that, while not identical, has been just as damaging (Menzies, 2010). Indeed, Africans were removed from their homes to an entirely new continent, and in the present day, few could claim to know their actual historical or tribal roots in Africa; this is not as true for Native Americans. African Americans, when brought to the Americas, were prevented from speaking their tribal tongues and/or dialects, had most of their

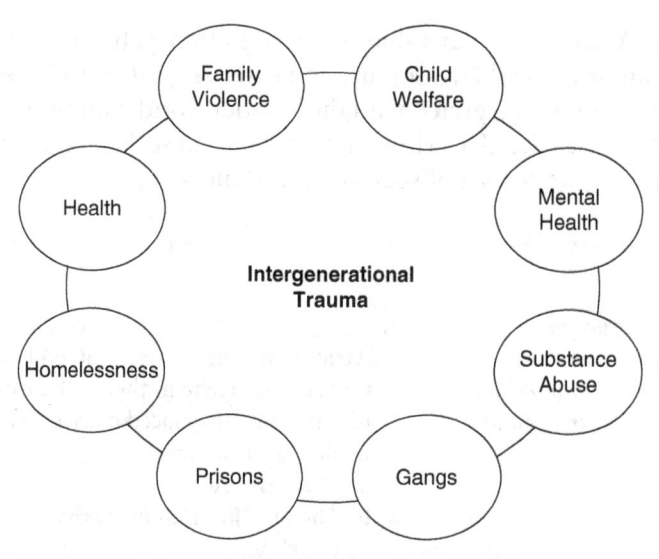

FIGURE 1-5   Impact of Intergenerational Trauma on Various Spheres of Social Functioning for Affected Racial/ Cultural Group. *Source:* Menzies, P. (2010). Intergenerational trauma from a mental health perspective. *Native Social Work Journal, 7,* 63–85.

family kin separated from one another, and were essentially fragmented and splintered apart as a people. Native Americans were decimated in their numbers but, at the same time, were able to retain some of their family cohesion and tribal groupings (Menzies, 2010). Though this is no comfort for the pain they endured and though there is no way to gauge the difference in the levels of the victimization between these two groups, we think that it is worth observing that African Americans have had their entire sense of original ancestral identity stolen from them. Because of this, we believe that this warrants acknowledgment as another aspect of the historical trauma that they have endured.

CONCLUSION

The U.S. cultural scheme is currently in a state of flux. The ever-changing demographics of the population, views on religion, sexuality, and cultural mores have resulted in a very fluid social system. This social system is greatly influenced by factors within and beyond the nation's borders. Further, economic and political developments have resulted in a large degree of interdependence between the United States and other nations. Further, there has emerged a trend among lawmakers and the judiciary to adopt, or at least consider, social views from the global community. Altogether, these developments have required that the U.S. criminal justice system be dynamic and adaptable. The criminal justice system of the United States will find itself in contradictory roles, where demands for maintaining community relations among diverse groups are countered with the need to provide tougher protections against criminal activity that is imported into the United States.

Whether fair or unfair, the modern criminal justice system will need to traverse the difficult and sometimes competing demands of a society that is increasingly becoming diverse. Homegrown diversity among groups who have traditionally been a central social feature in the United States and the increased representation of Latino

Americans and Asian Americans due to immigration patterns reflect the internal pushes from domestic social stresses and the external pulls on U.S. society, which is required to become more integrated with the broader world community. Only time will tell the final outcome as the U.S. criminal justice system seeks to meet the expectations of an ever more complicated set of social circumstances.

Chapter 1 Learning Check

1. _____ to any group of people who are substantially different from the broader society in political, economic, religious, or racial terms. It also includes persons who have diminished access to resources or ability to compete in a market economy.
   a. Minority
   b. Special Interest Group
   c. Victimized culture
   d. Multicultural system

2. _____ is the cumulative psychological damage that specific groups of people suffer throughout multiple generations. It becomes a shared group experience that, at least in part, defines that group's role in society.
   a. Victim culture
   b. Past transgressions
   c. Intergenerational trauma
   d. All of the above
   e. None of the above

3. Which group is the fastest growing minority group in the United States?
   a. Native Americans
   b. African Americans
   c. Latino Americans
   d. Asian Americans
   e. None of the above

4. The historical trauma of Native Americans and African Americans is more profound than that experienced by Latino Americans and Asian Americans.
   a. True
   b. False

5. _____ is the process by which societies, cultures, and economies around the world have become integrated due to advances in communication and transportation technology, as well as the passage of laws and treaties that facilitate this integration.
   a. Racial diversity
   b. Globalization
   c. Multiculturalism
   d. International influx
   e. Immigration

6. _____ created a system where African Americans were forced to live separate from Caucasians, where in theory their existence was equal but in reality they faced discriminatory treatment and inadequate resources.
   a. The Strive Act
   b. The J.D. "Jim Dandy" Barham Separate but Equal Act
   c. Jim Crow laws
   d. None of the above

7. The Strive Act and the Secure Fence Act are examples of how immigration has encouraged lawmakers to tighten and secure the porous borders of the United States.
   a. True
   b. False

8. _____ refers to the policy-setting agenda to adopt equitable forms of consideration for distinct ethnic, religious, and racial groups without promoting any particular group as being dominant or central in identification.
   a. Racial diversity
   b. Globalization
   c. Multiculturalism
   d. International influx
   e. Immigration

9. In the case of _____, issues related to courthouse practices integrating Judeo-Christian overtones have been questioned and scrutinized.
   a. *Atkins v. Virginia*
   b. *Grutter v. Bollinger*
   c. *Batson v. Kentucky*
   d. *McCreary County v. ACLU of Kentucky*
   e. None of the above

10. _____ is a term that describes the existence of numerous racial groups within a given society.
   a. Racial diversity
   b. Globalization
   c. Multiculturalism
   d. International influx
   e. Immigration

Essay Discussion Questions

1. Discuss historical/generational trauma. How does this type of trauma relate to Native Americans and African Americans?
2. Identify and discuss the ways in which globalization has impacted diversity within the United States. Be sure to discuss how macro-level acts and legislation have added to this social change, such as with the North American Free Trade Agreement (NAFTA), the development of Immigration and Customs Enforcement, and various court cases.
3. Discuss the various challenges faced by the criminal justice system due to the rapid social changes in the United States.

References

Atkins v. Virginia, 536 U.S. 304 (2002).

Centers for Disease Control. (2005). *Asian American Populations*. Retrieved from: http://www.cdc.gov/omh/Populations/AsianAm/AsianAm.htm.

Coffey, D. (2011). *Limits to experimental evaluation and student attendance in rural indian schools: A field experiment*. Presented at the Population Association of America Annual Meeting. Washington, DC.

Costanzo, J., Davis, C., Irazi, C., Goodkind, D., & Ramirez, R. (2001). *Evaluating components of international migration: The residual foreign born*. Washington, DC: U. S. Bureau of the Census.

Davy, M., & Meyers, D. (2006). *United States-Canada-Mexico fact sheet on trade and migration*. Washington, DC: Migration Policy Institute.

Gelatt, J. (2013). Looking down or looking up: Status and subjective well-being among asian and latino immigrants in the United States. *International Migration Review, 47*(1), 39–75.

Gelatt, J., & Coffey, C. (2007). *Annual immigration to the United States: The real numbers*. Washington, DC: Migration Policy Institute.

Grutter v. Bollinger, 539 U.S. 306 (2003).

Khashu, A., Busch, R., & Latif, Z. (2005). *Building strong policeimmigrant community relations: Lessons from a New York City project*. New York, NY: Vera Institute of Justice.

Lawrence et al. v. Texas, 539 U.S. 558 (2003).

Leavitt, N. (2003). *Legal Globalization: Why U.S. Courts should be able to consider the Decisions of Foreign Courts and International law*. Petrolia, CA: Counterpunch. Retrieved from: http://www.counterpunch.org/leavitt10252003.html.

McCreary County v. ACLU of Kentucky, 545 U.S. 844 (2005).

Nielson, M. O. (2000). Stolen lands, stolen lives: Native Americans and criminal justice. In Criminal Justice

Collective of Northern Arizona University (Ed.), *Investigating difference: Human and cultural relations in criminal justice* (pp. 47–57). Boston: Allyn & Bacon.

Shusta, M., Levine, D. R., Wong, H. Z., Olson, A.T., & Harris, P. R., (2011). *Multicultural law en-forcement: Strategies for peacekeeping in a diverse society* (5th ed.). Upper Saddle River, NJ: Prentice Hall.

Stanford University. (2005). *Foreign Judges gather on campus to weigh the impact of International Courts*. Stanford, CA: Stanford Report. Retrieved from: http://news-service.stanford.edu/news/2005/march30/justs-033005.html.

The Associated Press. (2004). *Internet Libel case with global implications ends in settlement*. Retrieved from: http://www. Firstamendmentcenter.org/news.aspx?id=14379.

Thomas, D. J. (2011). *Professionalism in policing: An introduction*. Clifton Park, NY: Cengage Learning.

Thompson v. Oklahoma, 487 U. S. 815, 830, 831, n. 31 (1988).

Toth, R. C., Crews, G. A., & Burton, C. E. (2008). *In the margins: Special populations and American justice*. Upper Saddle River, NJ: Pearson/Prentice Hall.

United States Government Accountability Office. (2005). *Information on criminal aliens incarcerated in Federal and State prisons and local jails*. Washington, DC: United States Government Accountability Office. Retrieved from: http://www.gao.gov/new.items/d05337r.pdf.

United States Immigration and Customs Enforcement. (2008). *Secure communities: A comprehensive plan to identify and remove criminal aliens*. Washington, DC: U.S. Immigration and Customs Enforcement. Retrieved from: http://www.ice.gov/pi/news/factsheets/secure_communities.htm.

Assimilation, Acculturation, Stereotyping, and Classism in a Democratic Society

LEARNING OBJECTIVES

After reading this chapter, students should be able to do the following:

1. Discuss cultural competence and why it is important for criminal justice practitioners.
2. Identify the terms "discrimination" and "disparity" and discuss their differences within the criminal justice system.
3. Discuss disparities in arrest, sentencing, incarceration, and the death penalty for different racial groups.
4. Discuss the "melting pot" concept, social dominance theory, and skin tone/pigmentation theory.
5. Explain how issues of race and racism have impacted society, in general, and the criminal justice system, in particular.

KEY TERMS

Acculturation

American exceptionalism

Assimilation

Colorism

Discrimination

Disparate recidivism rates

Disparity

Ethnic group

Ethnicity

Evil other

External locus of control

Integration

Internal control

Internal locus of control

Internal responsibility

Jim Crow laws

Locus of control

Locus of responsibility

Minority group

Multiculturalism

One-drop rule

One-eighth rule

Person-blame

Person-centered

Phrenology

Pigmentocracy

Prejudices

Racial profiling

Racism

Social dominance theory

Stigmatization

... Give me your tired, your poor,
Your huddled masses yearning to breathe free,
The wretched refuse of your teeming shore.
Send these, the homeless, tempest-tost to me,
I lift my lamp beside the golden door!

—EMMA LAZARUS, "THE NEW COLOSSUS"

INTRODUCTION

Inscribed on the Statue of Liberty are these words that have greeted multiple generations into the democratic society that is unique to the United States. No country has
ever welcomed such a diverse group of peoples from virtually every nation on earth
as has the United States. Its freedoms, opportunities, and acceptance of diversity have
drawn those in search of better lives to its shores. At its core, it is a society made of
many cultures, religions, ethnic groups, races, and sexual orientations living together in
a heterogeneous society.

Owing to the nature of our unique society, law enforcement officers, courts,
and corrections personnel are forced to contend with people from all backgrounds.
Invariably, when mixtures of people with different languages, values, customs, and
beliefs come to live together, differences obviously arise, thereby straining relationships and making the jobs of criminal justice personnel even more difficult. Because
of the services that criminal justice fields provide, cultural competence is required
to minimize cultural strain and improve community relationships. This competence can be obtained through awareness of cultural differences and exposure to
different cultural groups. Over time, competence can be fostered in order to build
rapport with various groups, thereby enhancing the work performed by the criminal
justice personnel.

Justice, fairness, and equality are all mandates of the criminal justice system; yet
these mandates have not been equitably applied cross-culturally. It is reasonable to
assume that until law enforcement, courts, and corrections become more culturally
competent, disparities in arrests, punishment, and incarceration will continue. For one
to say that they are fair and treat persons of other cultures equally diminishes the value
of the other's culture as well as forces the ideas, values, and beliefs of criminal justice
personnel on those that they serve and protect. True fairness, equality, and justice cannot be obtained independent of cultural competence.

WHAT IS CULTURAL COMPETENCE?

Cultural competence describes the process of effectively attending to the needs of
individuals by integrating the salient aspects of the culture to which they identify
themselves. One definition that is congruent with our assertion that cultural competence is a theoretical construct is provided by the Department of Health and Human
Services (DHHS, 2003) in its report titled *Developing Cultural Competence in Disaster
Mental Health Programs*: "Cultural competence is a set of values, behaviors, attitudes,

and practices within a system, organization, program, or among individuals that enables people to work effectively across cultures. It refers to the ability to honor and respect the beliefs, language, interpersonal styles, and behaviors of individuals and families receiving services, as well as staff who are providing such services. Cultural competence is a dynamic, ongoing, developmental process that requires a long-term commitment and is achieved over time" (DHHS, 2003, p. 12). This definition was chosen because its essence implies a philosophy that is meant to incorporate all necessary components of providing fair and equitable criminal justice treatment to all individuals, including minorities. We will discuss the notion of cultural competence and its application to criminal justice operations in greater detail in Chapter 5 of this text.

A BRIEF DISCUSSION OF RACE AND ETHNICITY

The term "race," as applied in scientific investigation, refers to the categorization of populations or ancestral groups based on certain heritable characteristics as measured by phenotypic and genotypic traits. These physical characteristics commonly include visual traits such as eye color, skin color, facial or cranial structures, and hair texture. Interestingly, at a genetic level, differences that can be attributed to different world origins (say between a blond-haired, blue-eyed Scandinavian and a dark-skinned, dark-eyed African) account for less than 10 percent of the genetic variation, indicating that humans are more similar than dissimilar (Shriver et al., 2003).

Our social conceptions of what constitutes race have little grounding in genetic facts. For example, of those who classify themselves as "white" in the United States, 30 percent or more have at least one distant relative of African descent (Shriver et al., 2003). African Americans, on average, have 17–19 percent of their heritage made up of European descent (Shriver et al., 2003). Scientifically speaking, there is no such thing as "black" or "white" per se, just those that are more or less genetically akin to those from sub-Saharan Africa or Northern Europe.

In sociological categorizations of race, such as information used in compiling the U.S. Census or other categorizations where race is studied, the term "race" refers to a socially constructed concept that is distinct to the culture in which it exists. This socially constructed concept is ever changing to keep up with the sociopolitical changes of the day. Our common conception of what it means to be "white" or "non-white" in America is based on the historical past as well as on present commonly held ideas of what those terms mean. To some extent, this trait is even personally ascribed to oneself as evidenced by the U.S. Census Bureau (2007) form's question that asks, "To what race or races does this person considers himself/herself to be?" For example, our current conception of what constitutes being "white" has not always been a widely held view of the nation's citizenry. At different points in American history, Irish, Germans, Ashkenazi Jews, Italians, Portuguese, Slavs, and Welsh were all considered "non-white." It is important to acknowledge this distinction between "white" and "non-white" races because "white" as a group has become the hegemonic majority group, and because "non-white" groups have traditionally received poor treatment and have had difficulty integrating into the culture, they are known as **minority groups**.

A further social categorization of people is that of ethnicity. An **ethnic group** is a group of people that identify with each other based on a heritage that is real or assumed. Until about 1900, ethnicity was believed to be determined by racial features. It was in this time period that **phrenology**—the study of cranial structures—dominated the determination of cultural and behavioral traits. In this line of thought, by examining pronounced features of the skull, differences that existed between races and subsequent cultural patterns could be explained. One example of this is the cultural superiorities that Belgium and subsequent German occupiers assumed between the Tutsis and the Hutus of Rwanda. Tutsis, as determined by phrenology, were assumed superior to and different from the Hutus. Because of this, Tutsis were allowed to socially integrate into the colonial governments having opportunities to be educated as well participate in the government. In the post-colonial period, Hutus were once again allowed a voice in Rwanda and thus seized power. This ethnic division, dictated largely by physical appearances, has precipitated recent genocidal conflicts, resulting in over 500,000 Tutsi deaths. Ironically, although the Tutsi and Hutus are ethnically and culturally diverse, genetically they are very similar.

Ethnicity, in modern terms, means belonging to a group with a shared history, common ancestry, kinship, religion, shared language, shared nationality, or shared appearance. In the United States, because of the nature of the socially constructed concepts, one can belong to a number of racial and ethnic categories at the same time. The U.S. Census Bureau (2007) identifies the following racial categories: White, Black or African American, American Indian or Alaska Native, Asian, Indian, Chinese, Filipino, Japanese, Korean, Vietnamese, other Asia, Native Hawaiian, Guamanian or Chamorro, Samoan, other Pacific Islander, and Other. The following are the ethnic categories included on the U.S. Census (2007): ethnicities of Hispanic origin subdivided into Mexican, Mexican American, Chicano, Puerto Rican, Cuban, and other Spanish/ Hispanic/Latino. It is important to understand that because both ethnicity and race are socially constructed concepts, they are frequently used interchangeably.

ACCULTURATION, ASSIMILATION, SOCIAL INTEGRATION, AND MULTICULTURALISM

Virtually every U.S. citizen, with the exception of Native Americans, is a direct descendent of a non-native immigrant lineage. These immigrant forbearers, drawn to the country by myriad reasons, were subjugated to adjusting to the new life abroad. Many sociological terms are used to describe the immigrants' adjustments to life, work, and culture. **Acculturation** refers to the sharing of cultural values that occurs when two cultures come into contact. Child (1943) and Lewin (1948) conceived that, more specifically, acculturation referred to the minority groups' strategic reaction to constant contact with the dominant group. They posited that immigrant minority groups, when adjusting to a new culture, had a number of possible outcomes as to how they acculturated, which include (1) assimilating with the majority culture, (2) a defensive assertion of the minority culture, (3) a bicultural blending of the two cultures, (4) a bicultural alternation between cultures, or (5) diminishment of each culture. **Integration** is a term that refers to a minority population's movement into the mainstream, thus being afforded the same opportunities, rights, and services that are possessed by the dominant culture. **Cultural assimilation** is a political response that encourages the minority demographic to adopt the customs, values, and language of the dominant culture in order to receive the benefits of social integration. **Multiculturalism** is an opposing political viewpoint that encourages the minority demographic to retain their cultural, linguistic, ethnic, and religious values, while also receiving the benefits of integration.

Some people would argue that the United States, albeit multiethnic, has promoted policies of **assimilation** that favor the adoption of predominate Anglo-Saxon values. In this viewpoint, through the propagation of myth and public policy, American society has encouraged immigrants to shed their native cultures, languages, and values to become more like white-Anglos. In this system, by becoming indistinguishable from Anglo-America, the immigrant then gains access to the rights and benefits of the culture. These rights and benefits may include the building of wealth, prominence, and social standing as well as political involvement. Multiculturalism, as a social philosophy, acknowledges the disparities that have existed in American history and works to celebrate and promote multiple ethnic viewpoints. The objective of the philosophy of multiculturalism is that diverse people can retain their individuality while at the same time inheriting societal rights and privileges.

PERSONAL ATTRIBUTES AND ASSIMILATION

To some degree, a group's ability to assimilate is dictated by self-perceptions that the group has about itself in relation to the world. **"Locus of control"** is a term that describes a person's orientation to the world and his/her ability to effectively make changes or take action. The locus of control rests either with the individual or with some external force. Lefcourt (1966) and Rotter (1975) have summarized research findings that correlate high internal control with (a) greater attempts at mastering the environment, (b) superior coping strategies, (c) better cognitive processing of information, (d) lower predisposition to anxiety, (e) high achievement motivation, (f) greater social action involvement, and (g) placing greater value on skill-based rewards. In essence, because an internal locus of control is so fundamental to the historical values of the United States, individuals possessing these qualities naturally assimilate better.

Many minorities, individuals of lower socioeconomic status, and women score significantly higher on the external end of the "locus of control" continuum. Hence, these groups have traditionally had more difficulty assimilating into the U.S. culture. In addition, how this externalization is often viewed by the mainstream is that these groups are inherently apathetic, procrastinating, lazy, depressed, and anxious about trying to achieve (Sue and Sue, 2012). Naturally, this can skew perceptions that law enforcement or other criminal justice practitioners may have of cultural groups who operate more from an **external locus of control**. This observation has been made even by well-known criminologists cited in criminological literature. Consider, for example, the work of Walter B. Miller who wrote the classic article "Lower Class Culture as a Generating Milieu of Gang Delinquency" in 1958. According to Miller, those in the lower socioeconomic groups have several focal beliefs, among them being the notion that life's outcome is due to fate and that a person's outcomes are preordained. Miller (1958) states that:

> Many lower class individuals feel that their lives are subject to a set of forces over which they have relatively little control. These are not directly equated with the supernatural forces of formally organized religion, but relate more to a concept of "destiny," or man as a pawn of magical powers. Not infrequently this often implicit world view is associated with a conception of the ultimate futility of directed effort towards a goal: if the cards are right, or the dice good to you, or if your lucky number comes up, things will go your way; if luck is against you, it's not worth trying (p. 11).

Miller further adds that people from lower socioeconomic backgrounds also tend to believe in the idea that:

> once things start going your way, relatively independent of your own effort, all good things will come to you. Achieving great material rewards (big cars, big houses, a roll of cash to flash in a fancy night club), valued in lower class as well as in other parts of American culture, is a recurrent theme in lower class fantasy and folk lore (p. 12).

It should be noted that although Miller's work is certainly dated, it nonetheless is consistent with observations by clinicians, law enforcement personnel, and social workers. Many people from disadvantaged backgrounds tend to have similar thoughts as those presented by Miller (1958). Furthermore, since African Americans and Latino Americans are disproportionately represented within disadvantaged communities, it is not uncommon to observe these beliefs among those racial groups who dwell in the inner-city ghettos and barrios of America.

However, this same orientation can also be seen among groups in a quite adaptable manner, even in a capitalist society like the United States. Consider that, in part, immigrant views of internal versus external locus of control are built on one's culture. For example, Chinese and Native American cultures place a high value on "the group" over "the individual," social roles and expectations, and harmony with the universe—thus an external orientation is highly valued in these cultures. Dissonance between one's own cultural expectations and the assimilating expectations of the host country can produce negative stereotypes of the minority group (such as with Native Americans). On the other hand, as with Chinese immigrants and/or perhaps Vietnamese immigrants, this group cohesion can be a strength that allows these groups to work themselves into economically superior positions, over time. This is, in part, why Asians are referred to as the "model minority" in the media.

Another important dimension in world outlooks is the locus of responsibility. **Locus of control/responsibility** measures the degree of responsibility or blame placed on an individual or a system. The degree of emphasis placed on an individual as opposed to the system in affecting a person's behavior is important in the formation of life orientations. The terms "**person-centered**" and "**person-blame**" indicate the focus of the individual. Individuals believing in the person-centered orientation (a) emphasize the understanding of the person's motivations, values, feelings, and goals, (b) believe that success or failure is attributable to the individual's skills or personal inadequacies, and (c) believe that there is a strong relationship among ability, effort, and success in society. In essence, these people strongly adhere to the Protestant ethic and idealize "rugged individualism."

Conversely, "situation-centered" or "system-blame" individuals believe that the environment is more potent than the individual is. Social, economic, and political powers are powerful; failure usually depends on the socioeconomic system and not necessarily on personal attributes (Sue and Sue, 2012). Assimilation is difficult for system-blame-oriented individuals, because in the United States there are social myths regarding a person's ability to control his or her own fate. Those that fit into these social myths are often rewarded. Many minority groups, owing to adverse experiences they have had trying to socially integrate, view the majority culture as being opposed to their attempts and thus adopt the "system blame" stance. This stance has been portrayed by many minorities as "angry and defiant"

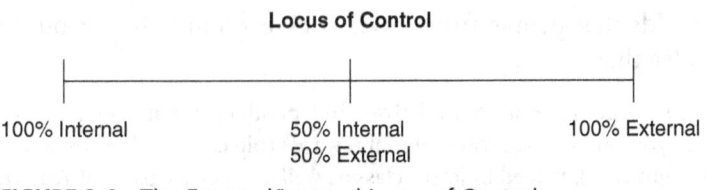

FIGURE 2-1 The External/Internal Locus of Control Spectrum. *Source:* Foy, A. (2011). The left's psychological assault on independence. *American Thinker*. Retrieved from: http://www.americanthinker.com/2010/07/the_lefts_psychological_assaul.html

and "learned helplessness." These characterizations further propel racial biases, which work against minority groups and reinforce views that the system works against them.

As shown in Figure 2-1, most portrayals of the Locus of Control/Responsibility Spectrum include extremes at two polar ends, with a middle point being identified as a point of balance. Interestingly, this diagram was obtained from an article that demonstrates that the United States, in its more inclusive posture, has undermined the rugged sense of independence that has been a traditionally showcased quality of American culture (Foy, 2008). To separate the two ends of the spectrum and to portray one as being superior to the other are probably not effective uses of this construct because each polar end, when taken to the extreme, is maladaptive and has consequences. Both have their respective benefits and drawbacks; hence, understanding the parameters of each and, perhaps, knowing when and where each is beneficial can optimize a person's social performance.

However, we present the following four possible descriptive quadrants in which we describe the various types: (1) an internal locus of control combined with a locus of internal responsibility, (2) a locus of internal control combined with a locus of external responsibility, (3) a locus of external control combined with an internal locus of responsibility, and (4) an external locus of control with an external locus of responsibility. Of these four responsibility/control loci, **internal control/internal responsibility** best fits the majority culture in the United States. Under this worldview, individuals are rewarded for their individualism, uniqueness, and self-reliance. A high value is placed on problem-solving abilities, noting that individuals in this system are supposed to be self-reliant, pragmatic, individualist, and are expected to achieve by placing strong controls over their environment. American ideals, such as those reflected by the phrases "equal access to opportunity," "liberty and justice for all," "God helps those that help themselves," and "fulfilling one's own personal destiny," are common expressions of this worldview. This view tends to be held by most white middle-class males living in the United States.

Because of cultural views, individuals residing in the West are prone to making assumptions about other ethnic groups. According to Sue and Sue (2012), Western values emphasize the following: (1) a high desirability for active engagement, (2) transitory and friendly social relations, (3) a high degree of competition, (4) a degree of separateness from the world, and (5) a high degree of emphasis on the individual instead of on the group. There should be a clear understanding on how these concepts can impact an immigrant or minority group's ability to integrate into mainstream society in the United States. The influx of immigrants (discussed extensively in Chapter 1) has resulted in shifts on this emphasis, thus stressing agencies that must navigate between individuals who have different "tempos" from which they operate and who may have different motivators to their behavior.

MELTING POT OR MYTH—IS THERE AN AMERICAN WAY OF LIFE?

Many Americans have been exposed to the popular belief of the "American way of life." At the foundation of this folklore is the idea of American exceptionalism. **American exceptionalism** suggests that the United States holds a special position among nations because of its unique status as the first modern democracy. This ideology holds that, because the United States was formed based on Judeo-Christian values, God ordained the formation of the United States. The purpose of this new "Godly Nation" was to provide a moral beacon to the world. Because the overwhelming majority of U.S. citizens are Protestants and because the idea of American exceptionalism has been politically reinforced, this thought has persisted through multiple generations. Examples of this reinforcement include Ronald Regan's famous "Shining City Upon a Hill" speech where he proclaimed, "I have always believed that there was some divine plan that placed this great continent between two oceans to be sought out by those who were possessed of an abiding love of freedom and a special kind of courage," and similar comments fashioned by George W. Bush: "our nation is chosen by God and commissioned by history to be a model to the world."

One of the tenets of **American exceptionalism** is the idea that America is a vast melting pot where immigrants from many nations have come to form a new alloy called "the American." Alloys, in a metallurgical sense, are stronger than the base metals that are combined. The "melting pot" metaphor holds that what is formed from the "smelting process" is a greater culture than the immigrant (or the rest of the world) has ever known; hence, the pride and national ethos of the American people reside in its unique assimilated cultural alloy. Once more, the "Great Smelter" is God himself.

The use of the term "melting pot" did not come into regular usage until 1908 after the premier of the play *The Melting Pot* by Israel Zangwill. In this play, the protagonist, a Russian-Jewish immigrant, proclaimed:

> America is God's Crucible, the great Melting Pot where all races of Europe are melting and reforming… Germans and Frenchmen, Irishmen and Englishmen, Jews and Russians—into the Crucible with you all! God is making the American.

The message of the play was that if men and women of various cultures were willing to leave behind their old cultures and assimilate to the "American Way," then all of the benefits of this great society would be made readily available. This play, as well as other cultural metaphors, gave rise to the belief that America was founded on the principle of assimilation. Subsequent reinforcements such as James Truslow Adams's coinage of "The American Dream" perpetuated the idea that all immigrant groups are inheritors of egalitarian rights of prosperity and social prominence. The idea of the "melting pot" is a romanticized story that purports the virtues of becoming more like the dominant Anglo-culture of the United States, but the question remains, "Has this smelting process actually forged a homogeneous culture like is suggested?"

History provides a very different view of the ease of immigrant assimilation and integration into American culture. Numerous examples exist of the problems of immigrants integrating into culture, and thus receiving the societal wealth that the culture has to offer. Native Americans, the earliest immigrants to North America, were decimated by warfare, disease, and enslavement and were ultimately moved to reservations; African Americans were captured and smuggled from their homelands to work as slaves in the colonial plantation system; Irish Catholics were denied equal employment opportunities; Asian Americans were denied immigrant status, and so on.

Examples like these demonstrate that historically there have been barriers to social progression within the United States, and that these barriers have largely been constructed based on race, ethnicity, and religion.

SOCIAL DOMINANCE AND DISPARITIES

One popular sociological theory, **social dominance theory (SDT)**, postulates that cultures are organized on layers of hierarchical social groups (Sidanius & Pratto, 1999). The key principles of SDT are that cultures are stratified based on age, sex, and groups (groups include divisions based on race, ethnicity, religion, etc.) and that hegemonic groups hold positions of power and social consequence. According to SDT, the dominant group (majority group) exerts social pressure on subordinate minority groups in order to maintain a position of dominance. The dominant group maintains power through a number of sociological forces whose ultimate aim is not to allow the nondominant group access to positions of power and authority. These sociological forces include (1) individual discrimination, (2) institutional discrimination (discrimination by government or business), and (3) behavioral symmetry of the subordinate group (attitudes, values, and beliefs that the minority group holds that reinforces subordination) (Sidanius & Pratto, 1999).

There are a number of ways that the dominant group maintains power through common sociological processes. These processes include **prejudices**, **racism**, **discrimination, and stigmatization**. **Prejudice** refers to a person's belief that some possessed characteristic makes him/her superior to someone who does not hold it. One can be prejudiced toward people of different sexes, sexual orientations, races, ethnicities, religions, social classes, etc. **Racism**, a form of prejudice, is the term used to describe a person's view that he/she is superior to another because of racial differences. **Discrimination** refers to the behaviors that one takes against someone toward which they hold a prejudice. **Stigma** refers to social disapproval based on personal characteristics or behaviors that deviate from what has been determined as normal society. The following are the three groups of social stigma: (1) external deformities (e.g., leprosy, cleft lip, or clubfoot), (2) known deviations in personal traits (e.g., mental illness, sexual orientation), and (3) tribal stigma, which are associations with races, ethnicities, and religions that are unpopular. **Disparities** are inequalities that exist between people of different races, sexes, ethnicities, and religions. **Disparities** between groups do not have to be a result of discriminatory practices, but often are caused by a plethora of interacting influences.

In American culture, the hegemonic culture (the dominant group) has long been Protestants of English heritage. E. Digby Batzell (1964), in his famous sociological work *The Protestant Establishment: Aristocracy and Caste in America*, coined the term WASP (White Anglo-Saxon Protestant) to describe what he viewed as an aristocratic group that controlled America's democracy. Batzell noted that despite the fact that America was a modern democracy, a privileged group of elites was continually promoted into positions of prominence. He once more argued that persons of different racial and ethnic backgrounds, by virtue of their culture, were hemmed into non-elite castes. Once segregated into these social castes (that were largely associated with race/ethnicity), members of these classes had difficulty obtaining social status. The history of social prominence of WASPs can be traced back to the founding of the country. WASPs were responsible for forming much of the societal framework of the country, including many of the political, business, educational, and financial institutions. Consequently, because people of English heritage were responsible for founding these institutions, this group maintained positions of authority and influence within these institutions. One need only look at a history of U.S. presidents to begin to understand the elite status of white Protestant males. Of the 44 elected presidents, only 4 were not from Protestant backgrounds, one was non-white, and none have been female.

STEREOTYPING BEHAVIOR

Although it is not something that most people are comfortable admitting, it is true that everyone stereotypes from time to time. Our tendency to stereotype begins early in life in infancy, as we attempt to make sense of our environment and categorize phenomenon so that they are recognizable to us. In making sense of the world, we group together experiences and store them for future reference. During this process, our brains receive a variety of external stimuli from our senses and these stimuli are organized into *diagnostic packages*, according to cognitive psychologists (Perez, 2011; Schneider, 2005). Once a diagnostic package has been created, our brain uses it as a type of perceptual shorthand where we see something and reference it to preexisting categorizations, then recognize what it is, and act in accordance with what we identify. This is how all humans store all information and knowledge they accumulate in life (Perez, 2011; Schneider, 2005).

The main point to understand here is the way we store all information that we accumulate in the world. Because of this, stereotyping occurs all of the time and we all do it (Perez, 2011). Indeed, "to have knowledge—to be able to recognize any thing, event, person, or concept—and to act effectively upon this knowledge recognition is to stereotype" (Perez, 2011, p. 24). Thus, stereotyping is a common and typical human behavior that eases our identification of circumstances and phenomenon and makes everything more readily understandable. Indeed, stereotyping is something that, in reality, we all must do; otherwise, we would all go about our daily existence in a state of confusion. Unfortunately, we have to label anything we encounter or we will not have any way to identify it in the future.

However, people do use their stereotyping skills for more than simply identifying people, events, and concepts. This is precisely when stereotyping becomes problematic and negative in its outcome. People stereotype others in many ways, not merely aimed at keeping them straight in their minds, but also for nefarious reasons. People stereotype to make themselves feel comfortable and superior to others. We stereotype human characteristics and create perceptions that we then attribute or place upon other social groups (Perez, 2011).

Box 2.1 Reasons Why People Stereotype

To simplify life—to make things easier.
To categorize knowledge into understandable elements.

To feel comfortable about their lives and themselves.
To feel superior to others.

Source: Perez, D. W. (2011). *Paradoxes of police work* (2nd ed.). Clifton Park, NY: Cengage Learning.

Stereotyping other groups of people can make us feel comfortable as being a member of the "us" as opposed to being a member of the "them" group (Perez, 2001). More simply put, using group stereotypes—such as our group and the "other" group—helps create a sense of solidarity in our own group. In fact, if we are not able to truly define what our own group *is*, we can then use the stereotype of the other group to determine what we *are not*. This also creates an individual level of comfort, which allows us to be part of something greater than just ourselves. This is so much of our daily dynamics in behavior that researchers have studied the propensity to create in foreign groups of people the fearful concept of the **evil other**. This is also seen in many criminal justice agencies that develop subcultures that think in terms of "us against them" when viewing the outside society. Naturally, this can lead to poor agency–community relationships, especially when such views are maintained with marginalized communities.

Thus, it is important to remember that although stereotyping is, unto itself, not always a bad thing, when it serves to divide groups, it can have very negative implications, particularly when it results in the attribution of negative characteristics to an entire group. Ultimately, this type of separation into "us" and "them" becomes an issue of being "good" or "bad," making it seem acceptable to confront the evil others in the world with contempt, disdain, hatred, and violence (Perez, 2011). These are precisely the types of thought that are seen among hate groups and extremists throughout the world, and this type of thinking tends to be found in the doctrine and teachings of these groups.

Thus, stereotyping can at the same time be a necessary, important, logical part of everyday life; moreover, it can develop into counterproductive, hostile, and evil ways of thinking and behaving. This is a paradox of life, not just criminal justice work. Stereotyping can be good and utilitarian, but it also can be bad and counterproductive (Perez, 2011). Understanding how stereotypes affect us all can aid us when we consider the frame-of-reference for others who are faced with the challenge of assimilation and/or acculturation. Such introspective awareness, coupled with a sense of empathy, can allow us to avoid many mistakes that are often showcased in the media, both personally and professionally.

INSTITUTIONAL RACISM AND RACIAL BIAS IN AMERICAN HISTORY

The socially constructed racial divide between "white" and "non-white" people can be traced back to the founding of the country itself. In the colonial period, indentured servitude and Indian enslavement were common practices of colonists of the New World. The majority of immigrants in the colonial period found their way to the colonies in the form of servitude. Many of the immigrants either could not afford passage to the New World or were considered the scourge of English society, and thus coerced into servitude in exchange for passage and eventual freedom. Black and white immigrants alike were initially treated as indentured servants. It was not until a 1640 court case, *Re Negro John Punch,* that distinctions were drawn between white and non-whites with regard to servitude. In this case, two white men and one black man all ran away from a plantation to which they were bonded. The two white men were given 30 lashes and an additional four years of servitude; the black man was permanently enslaved. In 1661, Virginia enacted laws that introduced race-based slavery. It is widely held that the institution of slavery created a permanent race-based class system that persists even today. The official recognition between "whites" and "non-whites" probably did not occur until the 1790 Naturalization Act was enacted. In this Act, "white" became a label that separated African Americans and Asians from all other immigrant populations. This act limited naturalization to "free white persons" of "good moral character."

Other historical conceptions of race included the *one-drop rule* and the *one-eighth rule* that once politically dictated racial divisions. The **one-drop rule** is a historical colloquial term used to classify people of African ancestry as belonging either to the white or to the non-white races. This colloquialism was brought about through the Virginia Racial Integrity Act of 1924 (and similar laws in several other states) that stated that all those with any amount of African blood were considered black for legal purposes. The Virginia Racial Act of 1924 was one of the many "**Jim Crow Laws**" that became enacted in the years following the Civil War in the South. These laws were designed to segregate "white" from "black," which often resulted in non-whites being disenfranchised. The **one-eighth rule**, much like the one-drop rule, was another legal way of differentiating "whites" from "non-whites." Other variations of this classification system included the one-fourth, one-sixteenth, and one-thirty-second rules.

SKIN COLOR AND BIAS

Because the most salient feature of race is skin color, skin color itself is a source of bias. This is relevant because, to some degree, the more one's skin color diverges from the dominant class in the United States, the greater the difficulty an individual has integrating into the culture. Dark skin discrimination occurs within as well as across races (Turner, 1995). Among African Americans, darker-skinned blacks have been shown to have more difficulty integrating into the culture and/or more often have been the targets of within-race discrimination. Lighter-skinned African Americans, in contrast, have advantages in earning potential, social advancement, and educational attainment (e.g., Hill, 2000; Hughes & Hertel, 1990). The term used to describe discrimination based on skin color is called "**colorism.**" A social system that discriminates based on skin pigment is called **pigmentocracy**. Although this term has most frequently been associated with social structures in Latin American countries, there is evidence that the United States also functions in a similar capacity.

Colorism and its impact on criminal justice issues remain a largely unexplored area. It is conceivable that due to inherent biases, darker-skinned individuals may be targeted for criminal activity more frequently. These shared biases may presume that darker-skinned individuals are more menacing and dangerous. Arguably, criminal justice disparities may exist between lighter-skinned and darker-skinned racial groups (both among and within) because of cultural biases. Investigations are required to determine the effect of colorism on arrests, adjudication, and sentencing.

CRIMINAL JUSTICE DISPARITIES

Racial disparities in criminal justice are inequalities that exist "when the proportion of a racial or ethnic group in the control of the system is greater than the proportion of such groups in the general population" (The Sentencing Project, 2008, p. 1). It has been suggested that the reasons for disparities between racial and ethnic groups are multifaceted and can include factors such as the level of crime in a particular area, policing's emphasis on certain communities, and the decision-making process at all levels of the criminal justice system (The Sentencing Project, 2008).

African Americans and Hispanic Americans have notoriously been overrepresented within the criminal justice system. It has been estimated that approximately one in three African American males ages 22–29 are under correctional control. In contrast to their white male counterparts, African American men are five times more likely to spend time in prison. Although African Americans constitute approximately 13 percent of the U.S. population, they represent 38 percent of the prison and jail populations. Similarly, African Americans represent 17 percent of the juvenile population, but account for 46 percent of the juvenile arrests. Similarly, Hispanic Americans also face disparities in the U.S. criminal justice system. For instance, Hispanics in the United States constitute 19 percent of the prison population but only 15 percent of the general population.

Minorities suffer disparities at each step of the criminal justice system. These include inequalities in law enforcement arrests, pre-adjudicatory decisions, sentencing, probation, and alternatives to incarceration, incarceration, and prison reentry. The following sections will discuss disparities encountered by African Americans in the aforementioned areas.

LAW ENFORCEMENT AND ARRESTS

The entry stage into the criminal justice system begins with the law enforcement officers and arrests. Law enforcement officers are the most visible members of the criminal justice system. They are responsible for responding to calls of citizens, monitoring behaviors, intervening with warnings, making arrests, and assembling evidence to be used in prosecution of cases that result in arrests. Law enforcement officers, responding to the charge of their occupation, spend a disproportionate amount of time in high-crime areas (Thomas, 2011). Often times, these high-crime areas are populated with minority populations, making their encounters with minorities and subsequent arrests more likely. In addition, law enforcement officers use broad discretion in arrests, thereby increasing the potential for expressed racial bias. A further compounding problem is an overall lack of cultural competency training that exists for many law enforcement personnel (Shusta, Levine, Wong, Olson, & Harris, 2011). The failure to understand language, norms, and behaviors has often created confusion between citizen and officer and has created barriers of trust for minority populations (Shusta et al., 2011; Thomas, 2011).

There are a number of reasons why arrests of minorities are higher than their counterpart white Americans. One obvious reason why arrests are more pronounced is that persons in these areas commit crimes at an increased frequency. To simply state that minorities commit crimes at higher rates fails to address the psycho-social-demographic reasons why minority youths are at greater risk for criminal activity and also fails to accurately portray actual crime as compared to arrests. The reasons why minorities are at greater risk involves a myriad of factors that blend toward antisocial behaviors that ultimately result in crimes (Shusta et al., 2011; Thomas, 2011). For example, many impoverished minority communities, due to a lack economic opportunity, opt for alternative sources of income. Often times, these alternate income sources include illegal activities such as drug sales, prostitution, gambling rings, etc. A number of factors, such as poverty, inability to legally obtain social standing, poor education, lack of adequate supervision, substance abuse, and the provocative experiences of trauma and street life, blend to push minority youth toward lives of crime. Once more, because criminal activity becomes a way of life for many communities, the idea of being a criminal becomes reinforced because ultimately, many in the community have a vested interested in keeping that activity going (Shusta et al., 2011; Thomas, 2011).

Despite increased risk for criminal activity experienced by many minorities, the totality of the disparity of arrest records cannot completely be explained by criminal activity. More insidious social forces come into play when discussing the reasons why minorities are disparately arrested. The prevalence of police officers in high crime areas and the frequent contact with minorities, to some degree, influences who is arrested. However, minorities experience greater arrest rates even when not in high-crime areas. Stops, searches, and arrests occur at higher rates for minorities than for whites despite the fact that there are often no distinguishing differences in behaviors of whites and minorities that would warrant these stops. To some degree, disparities might be explained through overt racists attitudes of some police officers, but often times, a more subtle form of racial bias occurs that many officers themselves are left unaware of. Because many minorities have become associated with crime and criminal activity, **racial profiling** can occur, where race and ethnicity become the primary means by which law enforcement decides who gets stopped, searched, and arrested (Thomas, 2011).

MINORITIES AND RACIAL PROFILING

One of the cited reasons for the disparities that exist for minorities is because of racial profiling. Euphemistically, the phrase "driving while black" is applied to traffic stops of African Americans because of racial profiling. As a play on words, the phrase was meant to draw attention to the fact that many African American drivers were being stopped for nothing more than being black. Evidence supports this notion of racial profiling for African Americans. Numerous studies have indicated that African Americans are more likely to be stopped and searched at higher rates than whites despite there being no evidence of increased incidences of violations or contraband (Leinfelt, 2006). The most famous of these studies is the New Jersey Turnpike Study performed by Dr. John Lambert of Temple University. The study was conducted in a response to a state court case, *State v. Pedro Soto*. In the court case, Mr. Soto alleged that he had been stopped because of his ethnicity. A total of 42,000 cars were examined to measure the percentage of African American males stopped and ticketed versus their makeup of total drivers. The results of this study found that despite the fact that blacks and whites violated traffic laws at comparable rates, blacks represented 35 percent of all those stopped while only representing 13.5 percent of the people on the road.

A second study, the Maryland Study, examined a stretch of highway between Baltimore and Delaware. Again, this study was prompted by a court case: the plaintiff being Robert Wilkins, a Harvard Law School graduate, against the Maryland police. In his complaint, Mr. Wilkins alleged that he had been stopped and searched because of his race. During the case, a State Police memo was brought into evidence that instructed police officers to be aware of drug couriers who were described as "predominately black males and black females." In the settlement phase, the police agreed to give the court data on every stop followed by a search, with data on the racial makeup of the occupant for the three years following the case. Over the course of the three years, 6,000 cars were examined that had been stopped and searched. Of those cars, it was concluded that blacks and whites violated traffic laws at about the same rate. Despite this fact, black men were stopped and searched at a rate four times greater than the number of black drivers represented on the road. A third case, the Ohio Study, was conducted in response to the Ohio legislators' request for police officers to begin to collect information on race in traffic stops. Before the legislators would agree to draft such a law, they first wanted to study if there actually was a problem. To do this, data was collected from municipal court records. From this data, the racial makeup of those ticketed was examined. This study revealed, through conservative estimates, that blacks are twice as likely to be stopped and ticketed as non-whites.

Racial profiling creates an image of police officers as racist, punitive, and enforcers rather than as community protectors. This negative image of officers has impeded the way that many officers interact with minorities, ultimately hindering the police efforts to reduce crime. Racial profiling affects issues that go beyond racial division and mistrust. As Professor David Harris explained when discussing the problem of racial profiling:

> Because police will look for drug crime among black drivers, they will find it disproportionately among black drivers. More blacks will be arrested, prosecuted, convicted, and jailed, thereby reinforcing the idea that blacks constitute the majority of drug offenders. This will provide a continuing motive and justification for stopping more black drivers as a rational way of using resources to catch the most criminals.

This phenomenon of the "self-fulfilling prophesy" can be observed when studying African Americans charged and arrested for drug-related crimes. Despite the fact that African Americans constitute approximately 13 percent of the population and likewise represent 13 percent of drug use, they disproportionately represent 59 percent of those convicted for drug offenses (Shusta et al., 2011). This has created an image for many law enforcement officers that in order to deter crime, they must focus their attention on African Americans. More on this will be discussed in Chapter 6 on policing.

CURRENT EVENTS IN MULTICULTURAL CRIMINAL JUSTICE
Assimilation, Acculturation, Religion, and Criminal Proceedings

It is perhaps inevitable that, as the demographics of individuals processed through the justice system become more and more multicultural and international, cultural practices will clash.

Recently, Major Nidal Hasan has resisted institutional regulations that he shave his head before appearing in court. Hasan, in 2009, was a U. S. Army psychiatrist who served at Fort Hood in Texas. On November 5th, 2009, he opened fire using army automatic rifles and killed 13 people while injuring several others.

While his military trial was pending, he was to be required, by military regulations, to shave his head prior to his appearance. Hasan refused and the military considered forcing him to comply. At issue, in particular, was Hasan's beard, which was in violation of U. S. Army custom but was part of Hasan's traditional and cultural practice according to his Muslim faith.

Hasan contended that, as a Muslim male, Allah required that he wear his beard, particularly in public circumstances. In support of his claim, Hasan's attorney filed an appeal to thwart the order to shave. The appeal pointed toward the Religious Freedom Restoration Act - intended to safeguard individuals from governmental burdens that can prevent or obstruct their ability to practice their religion - as the legal and moral basis for Hasan's right to keep his beard as a practice of his faith (Nussbaum, 2008; Shaughnessy, 2012). According to his legal defense, Hasan's beard is a display of his faith and the sincerity of his desire to be publicly associated with Allah. Further, because Hasan claimed that his act of mass murder was tied to his own personal Jihad, in the name of Allah, the beard was considered important in showcasing the intent and defense that he would provide in relation to his crime (Shaughnessy, 2012).

However, federal prosecutors noted that, by allowing him to keep the beard, it was providing a sense of moral support and triumph for fanatical Islamic warriors around the world who were, through international news media, tracking Hasan's case. These warriors, known as the Mujahedeen, came from a long tradition of Muslim soldiers who had fought together in Afghanistan against the prior Soviet Union and whom had fought in other areas of the world, on behalf of Islam and in the name of Allah. By wearing the beard, according to federal prosecutors, Hasan was associating himself with the Mujahedeen, even though he was not, in actuality, a member of this group (Shaughnessy, 2012). Though speculative, such public allegiances could have a variety of national security implications.

Ultimately, Hasan's beard was shaved off, against his will and through force, after the appeal delayed his court martial trial for several months (Goldman, 2013). Though there was some debate regarding orders to shave the beard, by one official and acquiesce to allow Hasan to keep the beard, by another, Hasan's attorney has vowed to appeal, though the actual benefit to such an appeal is questionable. The possibility of damages, in violation of Hasan's First Amendment protections to freedom of religion may be an issue, but the merit of such a claim is yet to be seen, as the appeal is still pending.

This is not the first time that issues related to Muslim religious practices have led to clashes with U. S. legal requirements. In another case (see *Freeman v. Florida*, 2002), Sultana Freeman, a Muslim woman in Florida, sued the state because of a requirement that she remove her veil from her face before taking a photo for her driver's license identification photo (Cosgrove, 2003). Ultimately, in this case, as well, governmental powers prevailed over the religious freedoms exercised by the individual, with public safety reasons being provided for grounds of enforcing this requirement.

References: Cosgrove, p. (2003). Muslim woman cannot wear veil in driver's license photo. Associated Press, retrieved from: HYPERLINK "http://usatoday30.usatoday.com/news/nation/2003-06-06-license-%09veil_x.htm"http://usatoday30.usatoday.com/news/nation/2003-06-06-license-veil_x.htm

Goldman, R. (2013, September 04). Nidal Hasan's lawyer to sue after army forcibly shaves Ft. Hood shooter. ABC News, retrieved from: http://abcnews.go.com/US/nidal-hasans-lawyer-sue-army-forcibly-shaves-ft/story?id=20154963

Nussbaum, M. (2008). *Liberty of Conscience: in defense of America's tradition of religious equality.* New York: Basic Books.

Shaughnessy, L. (2012, September 06). Judge orders accused Fort Hood shooter to have his beard shaved. CNN Justice, retrieved from:HYPERLINK "http://www.cnn.com/2012/09/06/justice/fort-%09hood-trial/index.html?iref=obnetwork"http://www.cnn.com/2012/09/06/justice/fort-hood-trial/index.html?iref=obnetwork

SENTENCING DISPARITIES

The disparities experienced by minorities begin with arrest procedures and continue throughout the arraignment and sentencing phases of prosecution. During the arraignment phase, multiple players coalesce to make a determination about the arrest. Often times, misdemeanor charges are quickly disposed of and given non-incarcerated sentences at arraignment. These sentences are often reflected in bail amounts being set to reflect the seriousness of the crime that was committed. For minority populations, resources to make bail and pay fines can be limited, thus promoting detention that might have otherwise been avoided. Detention, in turn, increases the likelihood that a subsequent conviction will be rendered, followed by further incarceration.

Because of limited resources, minorities are also disadvantaged in preparing for the adjudication process. It has been suggested that minorities involved in adjudication processes have less-skilled defense teams that are overburdened by court caseloads. It is a widely held view among minorities that public defenders, because of limited investment in the case, produce disparate outcomes for their clients. This creates an image that "wealth" purchases "justice." This image is supported by research evidence that indicates the type of counsel (i.e., private, public, none) determines the outcome in sentencing.

In juvenile cases, African Americans seem to suffer from racial biases from probation officers who formulate presentencing reports. Probation officers often characterize juvenile African American's delinquent behaviors as stemming from attitudinal and personality traits, whereas white juveniles were portrayed as being involved in poor peer groups. This information translates into the perception that juvenile African Americans are more dangerous and thus deserve harsher sentences. One example of the disparities that exist between juvenile youth is the disproportionate rates of sentencing of youth to *life without parole*. Black youth are sentenced to *life without parole* 10 times the rate of white youth. More on this will be discussed in Chapter 9, which discusses the courts and sentencing issues.

DISPARITIES OF INCARCERATION

African Americans and Hispanics comprise a dramatically disproportionate share of those incarcerated in jails and prisons. *African Americans represent approximately 13 percent of the population; however, they represent nearly 38 percent of the prison and jail population. This number compares to that for white Americans, who comprise 76 percent of the population, but only 37 percent of the prison and jail population* (Sabol, West, & Cooper, 2009). Although Hispanics have a lower overall rate of incarceration per capita compared to African American males, they are incarcerated at nearly 2.5 times that of whites. The reasons for this increased incarceration rate is not only due to environmental factors that may expose minorities to an increased potential for criminal involvement, but also for an exponentially increasing bias that occurs at each stage of the criminal justice process.

When discussing the potential for criminal involvement, it is important to first understand why the majority of offenders are locked up. Overwhelmingly, addictions and psychiatric concerns play convincing roles in criminal involvement. It has been estimated that in excess of 50 percent (as compared to 15 percent of the general population) of all those incarcerated have a diagnosable substance abuse disorder. Moreover, untreated psychiatric conditions such as schizophrenia and bipolar disorder can potentiate crime. When making an honest appraisal of the reasons as to why individuals are incarcerated, a picture begins to emerge that suggests that what is being incarcerated is not necessarily a moral-criminal issue per se, but rather an untreated healthcare issue. More on this will be discussed in Chapters 10 and 11, which discuss issues related to corrections.

Disparities for minorities are by no means limited to the criminal justice system; healthcare disparities are perhaps even more pronounced. Minorities living in low-income communities are less likely to seek and receive services, especially for the critical adolescent age ranges where addictions are assumed to develop. In addition, minorities who do receive psychiatric diagnoses often times receive more severe diagnoses than their white counterparts do. This fact has caused many in the public to believe that minorities suffering from mental illness have tendencies toward violence whereas whites do not.

As is common for many minority low-income communities, education levels are also disparate. With limited opportunities, low education, and prevalent crime, it is little wonder why minorities are drawn to criminal activity. Once incarcerated, few opportunities are afforded in the way of education, substance abuse and mental health treatment, and vocational training. Given that the majority of incarcerated individuals eventually return to community settings, education, the ability to engage in meaningful legal employment, and recovery skills are crucial to ensuring that the offender does not recidivate.

INTERNATIONAL FOCUS

Increase in Radicalized Muslim Prison Inmates Vexes France

About a year ago, President Nicolas Sarkozy funded a study that examined the growing threat of violence that has originated from the nation's prisons. This recent interest was generated by an act of mass murder in the town of Toulouse, France, where a man, Mohamed Merah, went on a shooting spree, killing seven people.

Mohamed Merah had been in prison, prior to this, for a year and a half for the crime of theft and had no prior history of violence. Merah, it was reported, had read the Quran alone and, through his own interpretation, turned to radicalized Muslim beliefs. Merah, had made trips to Afghanistan and Pakistan after he served his prison sentence in France, and returned with an even more radical Islamic orientation (Ganley, 2012).

Merah is one of several radicalized Islamic offenders who French officials have dubbed 'lone wolf radicals' because, while they claim to commit their acts of violence in the name of Islam, they act alone, rather than in tandem with official or organized Islamic groups (Ganley, 2012; Sage, 2013).

French prison officials have implemented numerous improvements in training and in intelligence gathering processes, but there are still numerous challenges. Further, officials are hesitant to scrutinize the Muslim prison population even more closely as they are already closely watched and are given heightened security, particularly those who have been identified as associates of known terrorists.

In French prisons, Muslims are a growing population, with self-proclaimed imams leading the faith and recruiting individuals in organized practice. In addition to these numbers who are part of these organized Islamic activities, many seek the Muslim faith as a form of individual identity, something to hold to and to which they can identify, while serving time in a world where one's sense of personal identity is made anonymous. According to Sage (2013), this is not completely unusual in France as well as other countries like the United States and England, where a young male is confined in an overcrowded and/or violent facility after conviction of a minor offense, and comes out both a converted and a hardened individual committed to a radical faith bent on Jihad.

While the French have implemented training and better security practices, both in and out of the prison, there are problems with adequate services being provided for Muslim inmates. Consider, for instance, that while it is estimated that the French prison system's inmate population is at least half Muslim, with some noting that as much as 60 to 70 percent of the prison system's population is Muslim (Ganley, 2012; Moore, 2008; Sage, 2013), there is an underrepresentation of Muslim chaplains, particularly when compared to those of the Christian faith. This alone, has caused numerous problems. In some cases, Muslims on the outside volunteer their time to those who are locked up, including El Alaoui Talibi, an Islamic holy woman who ministers to female Muslim inmates at the women's cellblock of the Lille-Sequedin Detention Center in far northern France (Moore, 2008).

There are some who contend that the disparity in Muslim representation in French prisons reflects a failure of the nation to integrate that population into its broader society, pointing out that while 60 to 70 percent of the prison population may be Muslim, only 12 percent are Muslim in broader French society. The 12 percent Muslim population, however, lives mostly in poverty and represents a disproportionate amount of the jobless population in france, as well. Incidentally, it is these regions from which most extremist groups tend to recruit, as there are numerous disillusioned, desperate, and angry individuals in these areas who are easy to recruit. When young men (and even women) from these areas are incarcerated, they may identify with radicalized beliefs quite easily and take solace in a belief system that blames the infidel government for the problems that they have encountered. Whether right or wrong, it is a security problem that plagues France and several other nations in Europe.

Source: Ganley, E. (2012, April 10). France takes new look at radicalization in prisons. *Associated Press*, retrieved from: http://www.thejakartapost.com/news/2012/04/10/france-takes-new-look-radicalization-prisons.html

Moore, M. (2008, April 29). In France, prisons filled with Muslims. *The Washington Post*.

Sage, A . (2013, May, 07). France struggles to fight radical Islam in its jails. *Reuters*, retrieved from: http://www.reuters.com/article/2013/05/07/us-france-radicalisation-insight-idUSBRE9460OQ20130507

LACK OF REENTRY SERVICES

At least 90 percent of the 650,000 prisoners incarcerated every year will eventually reenter the society (Prisoner Reentry, 2007). Two-thirds of those returning to their communities are racial minorities compared to one-third in the general population (Petersilia, 2005). Many of those returning are from communities in which residents are of lower socioeconomic standing, have a lower educational status, and are either unemployed or underemployed. Moreover, these underprivileged communities are plagued by illegal activities such as drug use, drug sales, prostitution, etc. Those underprivileged offenders returning to these low-income communities, because of their inability to find employment and sustain an independent lifestyle, place an even larger stressor on an already heavily burdened community. This repetitive cycle of minorities facing barriers and returning to socially impoverished communities has produced **disparate recidivism rates** that are higher for minority offenders (BJS, 2002). With this in mind, African Americans are more likely than whites and other minorities to be rearrested, reconvicted, and ultimately return to prison (BJS, 2002).

In order for minorities to appropriately reenter the community, effective programming, including education, skills training, substance abuse treatment, and work programs, should be presented to offenders well before the intended release. This means that for the American criminal justice system there will be an increased need to be "all things" related to service delivery. If the criminal justice system cannot meet this demand, then it will be necessary that we ask the community itself to aid in integrating these people into our society. That community that would receive such a request and the society into which offenders will return are becoming increasingly diverse with each passing day. Thus, it is clear, the American criminal justice system will be greatly impaired if it does not embrace the diversity that exists within its society. Indeed, a failure to do so can likely be equated to a risk in our public safety.

CONCLUSION

This chapter, like Chapter 1, has covered a wide array of topics and introduced numerous new concepts and ideas regarding minorities, diversity, and the changing nature of society in the United States. Issues associated with the assimilation and acculturation of minorities into mainstream society, stereotyping, and prejudice have also been presented to serve as a groundwork for future chapters that will be more specific to topics related to the criminal justice system and the interface of minority groups in that system. When addressing multiculturalism in the criminal justice system, there is always the likelihood that these issues will be relevant at one point or another.

As with Chapter 1, we have also presented some general discussion on criminal justice issues related to the topics presented in this chapter. These introductory segments also provide the groundwork for future chapters, which will discuss in much greater detail each of these specific topics. The goal of this chapter, as with Chapter 1, is to provide you with a framework of concepts related to race, culture, minority identities, and diversity that can be applied to chapters that will follow. It is very important that students become very familiar with the terms and concepts introduced in this chapter since they will be a point of reference when we delve further into the means by which multiculturalism impacts the U.S. criminal justice system.

Chapter 2 Learning Check

1. _____ describe(s) a repetitive cycle where minority offenders face systematic barriers beyond that of the typical offender, returning to socially impoverished communities that served, in part, as the genesis of their criminal lifestyle.
   a. Disparate recidivism rates
   b. Offender minority reentry
   c. Disparate reentry
   d. None of the above

2. The term _____ refers to the idea that the United States holds a special position among nations because of its unique status as the first modern democracy.
   a. American Ingenuity
   b. American Exceptionalism
   c. American Pride
   d. All of the above
   e. None of the above

3. _____ refers to the behaviors that one takes against someone toward which they hold a prejudice.
   a. Disparity
   b. Discrimination
   c. Stigma
   d. All of the above
   e. None of the above

4. Disparities are inequalities that exist between people of different races, sexes, ethnicities, and religions.
   a. True
   b. False

5. _____ refers to social disapproval based on personal characteristics or behaviors that deviate from what has been determined as normal society.
   a. Disparity
   b. Discrimination
   c. Stigma
   d. All of the above
   e. None of the above

6. _____ means belonging to a group with a shared history, common ancestry, kinship, religion, shared language, shared nationality, or shared appearance.
   a. Race
   b. Ethnicity
   c. Multiculturalism
   d. None of the above.

7. Stigma refers to social disapproval based on personal characteristics or behaviors that deviate from what has been determined as normal society.
   a. True
   b. False

8. The internal-control/internal responsibility best fits the majority culture in the United States.
   a. True
   b. False

9. Cultural competence describes the process of effectively attending to the needs of individuals by integrating the salient aspects of the culture to which they identify themselves.
   a. True
   b. False

10. _____ is a term that describes when race and ethnicity become the primary means by which law enforcement officials decide who gets stopped, searched, and arrested.
    a. Racial profiling
    b. Racial discrimination
    c. Ethnic stereotyping
    d. None of the above

Essay Discussion Questions

1. Fully discuss and describe the differences and similarities between the terms "race" and "ethnicity." Be sure to distinguish the two terms and comment on why they are frequently used as if they are interchangeable.

2. Compare and contrast the terms "discrimination" and "disparity." Explain why this is important to know if one is to become culturally competent.

3. Identify and discuss the "melting pot" concept, social dominance theory, and skin tone/pigmentation theory.

References

Batzell, E. D. (1964). *The Protestant establishment: Aristocracy and caste in America.* New Haven: Yale University Press.

Child, I. L. (1943). *Italian or American? The second generation in conflict.* New York: Russell & Russell.

Hill, M. (2000) Color differences in the socioeconomic status of African American men: Results of a longitudinal study. *Social Forces, 78*(4): 1437–1460.

Hughes, M., & Hertel, B. (1990). The significance of color remains: A study of life chances, mate selection, and ethnic consciousness among black Americans. *Social Forces, 68*(4), 1105–1120.

Lefcourt, H. M. (1966). Internal versus external control of reinforcement: A review. *Psychological Bulletin, 65,* 206–220.

Leinfelt, F. H. (2006). Racial influences on the likelihood of police searches and search hits: A longitudinal analysis from an American Midwestern City. *Police Journal, 79*(3), 238–257.

Lewin, K. (1948). *Resolving social conflicts.* New York: Harper & Row.

Miller, Walter B. (1958). Lower class culture as a generating milieu of gang delinquency. *Journal of Social Issues, 14*(3), 5–19.

Perez, D. W. (2011). *Paradoxes of police work* (2nd ed.). Clifton Park, NY: Cengage Learning.

Rotter, J. B. (1975). Some problems and misconceptions related to the construct of internal versus external control of reinforcement. *Journal of Consulting and Clinical Psychology, 43,* 56–67.

Sabol, W. J., West, H. C., & Cooper, M. (2009). *Prisoners in 2008.* Washington, DC: Bureau of Justice Statistics.

Schneider, D. J. (2005). *The psychology of stereotyping.* New York: Guilford Press.

Shriver, M. D., Parra, E. J., Dios, S., *et al.* (April 2003). Skin pigmentation, bio-geographical ancestry and admixture mapping. *Human Genetics 112*(4), 387–99.

Shusta, M., Levine, D. R., Wong, H. Z., Olson, A. T., & Harris, P. R., (2011). *Multicultural law en-forcement: Strategies for peacekeeping in a diverse society* (5th ed.). Upper Saddle River, New Jersey: Prentice Hall.

Sidanius, J., & Pratto, F. (2001). *Social dominance: An intergroup theory of social hierarchy and oppression.* Cambridge: Cambridge University Press.

Sue, D. W., & Sue, D. (2012). *Counseling the culturally different: theory and practice* (6th ed.). New York: Wiley.

The Sentencing Project. (2008). Reducing racial disparity in the criminal justice system: A manual for practitioners and policymakers. Retrieved from http://www.sentencingproject.org/doc/publications/rd_reducingracialdisparity.pdf.

Thomas, D. J. (2011). *Professionalism in policing: An introduction.* Clifton Park, NY: Cengage Learning.

U.S. Department of Health and Human Services. (2003). *Developing cultural competence in disaster mental health programs: Guiding principles and recommendations.* DHHS Pub. No. SMA 3828. Rockville, MD: Center for mental health services, substance abuse and mental health services administration.

United States Census Bureau (2007). 2006 American Community Survey. Available online at: http://www.census. Gov/acs/www/index.html.

Minorities Based on Age and Disability

LEARNING OBJECTIVES

After reading this chapter, students should be able to do the following:

1. Discuss how the demographics regarding the elderly have changed throughout the past few years.
2. Identify types of impairments and abuse commonly experienced by the elderly population.
3. Identify and discuss different types of age discrimination.
4. Identify and discuss different types of disability discrimination.
5. Identify and discuss mental health disabilities and physical disabilities encountered in the criminal justice system.
6. Identify and discuss various disabilities and stresses that affect criminal justice practitioners.
7. Identify types of victimization suffered by the elderly and the disabled.

KEY TERMS

Active neglect

Activities of daily living

ADA Amendments Act of 2008

Administration on Aging

Adultism

Advocacy groups

Age discrimination

Age Discrimination in Employment
    Act of 1967

Ageism

Age of majority

Alzheimer's disease

Americans with Disabilities
    Act of 1990 (ADA)

Assistive aids

Baby boomers generation

Burnout

Civil Rights Act of 1964

Community stakeholders

Critical-incident occupations

Cultural Adultism

Culturalism

Deafness

Delusions

*Diagnostic and Statistical Manual IV—Text
    Revision (DSM-IV—TR)*

Disability

Discrimination

Elder Abuse

Eldercide

Elderly discrimination

Failure to thrive

Four standards of mental healthcare

Gerontocracy

Hallucinations

Health concerns

Health insurance fraud

Hearing impairments

Impairment

International and Statistical Classification of Diseases and Related Health Problems 10th Revision

Inverse age–crime relationship

Investment schemes

Mental health providers

Minors

Passive neglect

Posttraumatic stress disorder (PTSD)

Reverse mortgages

Ruiz v. Estelle

Social exchange theory

Social Security Administration

Social Security Disability Insurance

Status offenses

Substantial gainful activities

Suicide by cop

Suicide prevention

Supplemental Security Income

Telemarketing fraud

Thought disorder

Visual impairments

INTRODUCTION

Owing to life-prolonging medical advances and a declining fertility rate, the population of the United States is getting older. In the early 1900s, the number of elderly (over 65 years) living in the United States was approximately 1 in 25. Today, the elderly account for one in every 8 U.S. citizens. It is expected by the year 2050, the number of elderly living in the United States will double the current levels, noting that 1 in 5 citizens will be elderly (AoA, 2011). Of the elderly, the "oldest old" is the most rapidly growing elderly group. In the next 20 years, survivors of the **baby boomers generation** are expected to contribute substantially to those over the age of 85. In less than 40 years, 24 percent of the elderly will be over the age of 85 (AoA, 2011).

The implications of this aging of America are far reaching—particularly as it relates to the "oldest old." Those that live to the oldest ages will be forced to contend with a number of chronic illnesses including arthritis, diabetes, osteoporosis, and dementia. Because of illnesses common to geriatrics, increasing numbers of individuals will be forced to rely on others to maintain activities of daily living. It is estimated that 1 in 4 elderly over the age of 85 will live in nursing homes, and of those living independently, 50 percent will need assistance performing routine activities such as bathing, getting around in the home, and preparing meals.

Likewise, in an overlapping fashion, a substantial number of Americans suffer from disabilities. It is estimated that 1 in 5 Americans suffer from disabilities (17 percent). Of the disabled living in the United States, one-third are elderly citizens. Fifteen percent of those who are disabled are related to congenital illness (illnesses that are present at birth), whereas the bulk of disabilities occur over the course of the lifespan. According to the Centers for Disease Control (2009), the three most common forms of disabilities are the age-related illnesses of: (1) arthritis and rheumatism, (2) back and spine problems, and (3) heart problems. It is expected the amount of disability will continue to increase as the population ages, advancing the need for more public health and medical care.

THE ELDERLY AND IMPAIRED AS MINORITY GROUPS

In any culture, the dominant group is the group that has greater wealth, power, prestige, and resources to affect the environment in which they live. Minority groups, in contrast, have disadvantages related to the ability to have a voice and affect changes in a personal and communal fashion. The elderly and impaired, because of the attributed social roles common to life in the United States, both lack the social standing to command their environments. All too often, these groups are overlooked and discriminated against because of this lack of social regard.

It is noteworthy that not all cultures discriminate against their elderly and impaired populations. In fact, many cultures exist in the form of a **gerontocracy**, which favors those of advanced ages. A **gerontocracy** is a social-political system in which one's political authority is derived from years of service to that system. Communist countries as well as many theocratic states use this as a governing principle. In these cultures, the elderly are held in higher esteem and therefore are looked to as leaders. Likewise, not all cultures view those who are impaired as being disabled. **Impairment** refers to the loss of regular human functioning. Impairments come in various forms ranging from limitations of cognitive, emotional, and physical attributes. This might include a lack of physical functioning (e.g., loss of limbs, paralysis, blindness), mental impairment (e.g., autism, Alzheimer's, mental retardation, cognitive deficits), and emotional impairments (e.g., depression, schizophrenia, etc.). A **disability**, in contrast, is a socially constructed concept that captures the relationship between the person with the impairment and the society in which he/she lives. Impairments become disabilities when those who have the impairments cannot meet the demands of the society. For instance, someone with sight impairment might not be able to function as aptly in a traditional work environment as someone who does not suffer from the same impairment. The reason for the lesser functioning is that the system is constructed around the needs of sighted individuals. Because of this favoring of sighted individuals, the impaired person is disadvantaged and thus disabled by the system. In order for the sight-impaired person to function on a level comparable to the sighted colleague, environmental changes are needed to account for sight deficiencies. Examples of these environmental changes include the provision of Braille materials or other assistive aids.

Although the differences in the terms **impairment** and **disability** are subtle, knowing the difference illustrates why those with disabilities are considered minority status. Those who are disabled, by definition, are unable to perform at the desired social level. These persons do not have the capabilities for work and civic participation that is expected by the culture, so therefore they are relegated to a lesser social role.

The elderly and impaired often overlap as a group, noting that the elderly contribute to the majority of impaired persons living in the United States. Understandably so, with age, the chances of someone becoming disabled increases too. This is because of the aging process itself and the many injuries and disease that are presented over the course of a lifespan. Nearly 50 percent of all elderly men and 60 percent of all elderly women are considered disabled.

AGE DISCRIMINATION

Age discrimination, also known as **ageism**, is the stereotyping of and discrimination against individuals or groups because of their age. It is a set of beliefs, attitudes, norms, and values used to justify age-based prejudice and discrimination. Ageism exists in two forms: (1) the discrimination of those based upon youthfulness, sometimes known as **cultural adultism**, and (2) discrimination against the elderly.

Cultural adultism, although not typically thought of when referring to age discrimination, refers to the culturally different responses given to adolescents and children that may be different from when dealing with adults. Most cultures discriminate against youth through a formulation of different expectations of behavior of youth than what is expected of the adult population. The reason for this discrimination is the belief that young people are unable to reason and perform responsibly as adults. These culturally expected differences in behavior may include rules that are used to deliver punishment (e.g., corporal punishments), legal mandates such as **status offenses** (refers to legal offenses that adults can engage in without penalty, e.g., drinking, truancy, running away from home), and rules that govern work. **Minors**, those persons viewed by the culture as not being equal to adults, are considered individuals who have not reached the age of majority. The **age of majority** refers to reaching the age in which someone is considered an adult. Other age thresholds that may or may not be the same as the age of majority include the age of criminal responsibility, the legal working age, the age of sexual consent, the age of eligibility to marry, vote, and obtain a driver's license, the age required for compulsory education, and the age for the ability to purchase certain items (e.g. tobacco, alcohol, pornography). It is because of the lack of the ability for youth to completely direct their own lives that they are viewed collectively as a minority group.

Elderly discrimination more commonly comes to mind when the topic of ageism is broached. **Elderly discrimination** refers to the unwarranted bias and stereotyping of the elderly solely based on advanced age without considering the merits of that person. Most commonly, the topic of elderly discrimination is associated with workplace discriminations. It can, however, refer to a lack of services being afforded to the elderly based on the differences of needs they experience. The elderly are more likely to suffer from physical and mental impairments than most other people. Hence, they are also more likely to not be accommodated for their impairments. Seniors may not have appropriate transportation, medical attention, and educational opportunities (e.g., bridging the technological gap) that would otherwise improve the quality of their lives.

Attention to workplace discrimination involving the elderly gained attention through the **Age Discrimination in Employment Act of 1967 (ADEA)**. This act forbids the discrimination of anyone over the age of 40. Specifically, the ADEA forbids the: (1) discrimination in hiring, wage increases, promotions, wages, termination of employment, and layoffs, (2) specification in job notices of age preferences, (3) denial of benefits to older employees, and (4) requirement of mandatory retirement.

DISABILITY DISCRIMINATION

Inherent to the idea that persons are "disabled" is the notion that discrimination is common to the system in which the impaired person lives. **Discrimination** is the way in which a system caters to some members while excluding others. Incumbent to our social system is a catering to persons with "normal" capabilities. For instance, social provisions ranging from transportation, housing, work, entertainment, education, etc. are designed to meet the average person's needs. Those with special needs are often an afterthought of this design process. To protect individuals with special needs and impairments, legislation has been adopted that prevents the most overt discriminatory practices. These laws model similar legislations that were passed to protect the rights of other minority groups. Probably the most recognizable piece of law, and the one that has done more to advance the needs of minority groups, is the **Civil Rights Act of 1964**.

The **Civil Rights Act of 1964** ushered in a new era of workplace and civil protections that prevented discrimination based on race, religion, sex, national origin, and other characteristics. As an extension of the protections of the Civil Rights Act, the **Americans with Disabilities Act of 1990 (ADA)** was passed to afford similar protections to those with physical and mental impairments. The ADA, coupled with the **ADA amendments Act of 2008 (ADAAA)**, offers a wide range of protections over a variety of settings that include employment, public entities (e.g., public transportation), public accommodations, telecommunications, and other miscellaneous provisions. Under the provisions of ADA, discriminations against those with impairments became illegal, stating that employers could not unfairly target those with impairments, using those impairments as a basis for not hiring, not promoting, or else terminating an employee. In addition to workplace protections, ADA established a number of public protections that afforded access to public programs and services besides creating building standards in order that those with impairments would be able to physically access those public entities. As a final provision of ADA, communication companies are required to make reasonable accommodations for functionally equivalent services for those with speech and hearing impairments.

Under ADA, the term **"disability"** is defined as being a physical or mental impairment that substantially limits one or more major life activities. A number of impairments that are considered "disabilities" are covered as a part of ADA. Among the most common are mobility, vision, hearing, or speech impairments, learning disabilities, chronic health conditions, emotional illnesses, AIDS, HIV positive, and a history of alcoholism or prior substance abuse. It is important to know that although ADA recognizes many disabilities, not all are covered under the enactment's protections. Among the categories specifically excluded from protections are those that are related to sexual behaviors (e.g., voyeurism, pedophilia, etc.), those that are related to compulsive behaviors (e.g., kleptomania, pyromania, gambling), and substance dependency issues (e.g., alcohol dependence, cocaine dependence abuse).

Persons are considered to be disabled if they can produce a record of having such a mental or physical impairment and/or are regarded as having impairments. Commonly, a person proves that he/she has a disability by providing documentation from a physician or psychiatrist naming the specific condition as well as how that condition substantially limits major life activities. The level of proof required is dictated by the individual policy of the program or agency for which the impaired person is claiming a disability. For instance, the Department of Motor Vehicles may request that a form be completed by a physician that requires proof of disability. Provided the person meets the agencies' standards, they are entitled to receive the accommodation offered. Because there is no one unified body that pronounces a person as "disabled," one must continue to prove disabilities to each agency where special provisions are being requested.

The pronouncement body most referred to when discussing the issue of disability is the **Social Security Administration (SSA)**. This is because of a twofold reason: the SSA is often seen as the highest arbitrator of disability claims and it is the federal agency responsible for paying monetary benefits related to being "disabled." Once the SSA determines someone to be disabled, this alone is often proof enough to meet the standards of other programs.

The SSA provides monetary benefits that are often referred to in common vernacular as "being on disability." These two benefits are known as **Supplemental Security Income (SSI)** and **Social Security Disability Insurance (SSDI)**. SSI is a benefit for persons who are disabled, aged (over 65), or blind persons and have little or no income. Disability is determined based on a person's ability to participate in **substantial gainful activities (SGA)**. **SGA** is defined as any activity that can be done for profit for a specified period of time. Often, SGA is determined by a dollar amount that a person is able to produce as a result of work. SSI is used for the basic provisions of food, clothing, and shelter. SSI extends to both adults and children and the only requirement for the disabled person is that they are below a certain income level. SSDI is the federally sponsored insurance program funded by payroll taxes. SSDI is a work disability program for those who become disabled to such an extent that it prevents them from engaging in SGA. In order to receive SSDI one has to have a condition that is expected to last at least 12 months or result in death. In addition, the person must be under the age of 65 and have worked 5 out of the last 10 years as of the determined date of onset of the disability.

DISABILITIES COMMON TO THE CRIMINAL JUSTICE SYSTEM

Persons with disabilities impact every area of the criminal justice system. Disabled persons represent employees and potential employees of criminal justice agencies, victims, and offenders. All of the aforementioned are protected under ADA; thus, certain accommodations are legally required. Moreover, disabled persons affect how criminal justice personnel perform their jobs. Increasingly, criminal justice personnel are becoming involved in special trainings in order to better protect persons with disabilities.

Disabled persons have unique obstacles that must be considered when they are interacting within the criminal justice system. First, isolation is a common problem for disabled persons because society has traditionally segregated those that suffer from disabilities. One such example is how individuals with mental impairments have been institutionalized or else placed in special homes. Another example would be that of the disabled elderly who are placed in nursing homes, sometimes to be forgotten. Because of the isolation that occurs with persons with disabilities, the person with the disability may not be aware of available services and resources or they might not be routinely informed of their rights under the law. This often promotes a situation where the disabled can be victims of negligence and they do not know that they have the right to different treatment. Second, physical accessibility remains problematic for disabled persons who become involved with the criminal justice system. Disabled persons often need special accommodations from the criminal justice system in order to participate in the process like other citizens. Continued vigilance has to be made toward creating spaces for those with disabilities that are accommodating to their special needs. Finally, attitudes toward those with disabilities have negatively influenced the quality of treatment that these persons receive in the criminal justice system. Because of a lack

Most Prevalent Reasons for Disabilities Among Adults Living in the United States

1. Arthritis or rheumatism
2. Back or spine problems
3. Heart trouble
4. Lung and respiratory problems
5. Mental and emotional problems
6. Diabetes
7. Deafness or hearing problem

8. Stiffness or deformity of limbs/ extremities
9. Blindness
10. Stroke

Source: CDC. (2009). Prevalence and most common disability among adults. Retrieved from: *http://www.cdc.gov/mmwr/preview/mmwrhtml/mm5816a2.htm*

of understanding on the part of those that are not impaired, unrealistic expectations and attitudes toward the disabled often impact the care that these persons receive. For example, improperly trained law enforcement officers may respond to a person with mental illness in a similar fashion as they might respond to someone who is being defiant and aggressive. In the former case, the individual may have no control over their behavior because of the disability, but may still be subjected to interventions that could cause physical harm. Improved competency in caring for the disabled becomes an ongoing responsibility of criminal justice agencies.

MENTAL IMPAIRMENTS

Mental impairments are one of the most prevalent causes of disability in society, and therefore they are also commonly found within criminal justice agencies. The term mental impairment is a broad term to represent any kind of noticeable performance deficits of the brain. These deficits come in numerous forms representing various brain injuries, learning deficits, intellectual functioning problems, as well as mental illnesses.

Owing to the numerous changes or deficits that can occur in the brain over the course of a lifespan, systems have been developed to categorize changes and deficits. The two most commonly used diagnostic systems are the **Diagnostic and Statistical Manual IV—Text Revision (DSM-IV—TR)** and the **International Statistical Classification of Diseases and Related Health Problems 10th Revision (ICD 10 Chapter V)**. The DSM-IV—TR, the manual most commonly used in the United States, has 16 different sub-classifications that are further broken down into 297 different diagnoses. The DSM VI—TR uses a multiaxial system that further breaks each of the diagnoses into different aspects of the disorder or disability:

Axis I: Clinical disorders, including major mental disorders, and learning disorders

Axis II: Personality disorders and mental retardation

Axis III: Medical problems

Axis VI: Acute medical conditions and physical disorders

Axis V: Global Assessment of Functioning (GAF) or Children's Global Assessment Scale (CGAS) for children and teens under the age of 18

Although there are numerous mental impairments, not all mental impairments are considered to cause disability. For them to rise to the point of disability, one must substantiate the claim that the impairment substantially limits the person's life. There are numerous mental impairments that are not thought to substantially limit one's life; therefore, one will usually not be declared disabled related to the disorder. An example might be that of anti-social personality disorder (ASPD). ASPD is probably the most common mental impairment encountered by law enforcement officials. However, because ASPD is not considered to severely limit major activities, it is therefore not considered a disability. The following section will detail common mental impairments that often result in disability.

Mental Retardation

Mental Retardation is a disorder that appears before adulthood in which a person experiences impaired intellectual functioning or has deficits in two or more adaptive skill areas. Intellectual functioning level is defined by standardized tests that measure the ability to reason in terms of mental age (also known as Intelligence Quotient–IQ). Mental retardation is defined as an IQ score below 70–75. "Adaptive skills" is a term that refers to skills that a person needs for the average life. These skills include language skills, home life skills, health, leisure, use of community resources, self-care, social skills, self-direction, functional academic skills, and job-related skills.

The common causes for mental retardation are genetic disorders (e.g., Down's syndrome, Klinefelter's syndrome) and fetal alcohol syndrome, which account for anywhere from one-third to one-half of all cases. Other common causes of mental retardation are problems experienced in pregnancy, problems encountered at birth, exposures to diseases and toxins, iodine deficiencies, and malnutrition. It is estimated that 2 percent to 3 percent of the population suffers from mental retardation—75–95 of which are in the mild range.

According to the *DSM-IV-TR* (American Psychiatric Association, 2000), mental retardation is divided into four categories, reflecting the severity of the retardation. The ranges of mental retardation, as noted by the American Psychiatric Association (2000), are listed below:

Severity	IQ	Percentage of MR Population
Mild	51–69	89.0
Moderate	36–50	6.0
Severe	21–35	3.5
Profound	Under 20	1.5

Generally speaking, it is estimated that mental retardation has a prevalence of 3 percent in society, with roughly 89 percent having mild retardation. Similar percentages have been found to exist in the correctional population as well. As expected, these individuals are not likely to be employees within criminal justice agencies. Rather, the contact between the criminal justice system and the mentally retarded is likely, instead, to be when such individuals are processed within the system.

When considering those individuals who are processed through the criminal justice system, it is often difficult to identify mildly retarded offenders since their handicap is not especially pronounced so as to be easily identified. This is further compounded among the offender population when one considers that the offender population tends to have intellectual scores (IQs) that are slightly lower than the majority of the non-offending population (much of this is due to lower socioeconomics and lack of education among the majority of the lower-income offending population within the correctional system).

Moderately retarded offenders are more easily identifiable. Their deficits usually manifest in early childhood periods and exhibit some delayed muscular-motor development. These persons can usually learn to take care of themselves and can do simple tasks. However, they often have difficulty with more complex tasks. They can usually progress to the third or fourth grades of academic ability. These offenders do require fairly extensive training for community living and often need some form of structured employment setting.

On the other hand, offenders with severe or profound retardation are often either unlikely to commit crime or they are diverted in the early stages of processing through the criminal justice system. Offenders with severe retardation often show marked delays in motor development early in life and are extremely hindered from functioning independently. These offenders need constant supervision to just function and communicate. These individuals often need constant nursing care and often have other existing physical and/or mental impairments beyond their mental retardation. These individuals need extensive training for the simplest of basic skills. Because of this, they are seldom kept in the institutional or community correctional systems. Offenders with this level of impairment are extremely rare.

It is important to provide a clear distinction between mental retardation and mental illness. In technical terms, mental illness is a disease, whether temporary, periodic, or chronic. Mental retardation, on the other hand, is a developmental disability and therefore not considered a disease. A person suffering from mental illness may recover; however, the state of mental retardation is a permanent characteristic that will limit the individual's ability to learn indefinitely.

Psychosis and Psychotic Disorders

Psychosis (sometimes confused with psychopathic) is a state in which someone has a partial or complete break from reality. There are three symptoms psychotic individuals demonstrate: **hallucinations**, **delusions**, and **thought disorder**. **Hallucinations** refer to someone experiencing sensory perceptions in the absence of external stimuli. These sensory perceptions are most commonly experienced as auditory or visual

Box 3.1 The Mentally Retarded and Capital Punishment

In June of 2002, the Supreme Court of the United States abolished the execution of mentally retarded offenders in the landmark case of *Atkins v. Virginia* (536 U.S. 304). The Court passed its ruling with a 6 to 3 vote and used the fact that 18 out of 38 death penalty states specifically banned the practice of executing the mentally retarded offender. Such punishment was held to be "cruel and unusual," in violation of the 8th Amendment. Justice Stevens wrote in a majority opinion that "because of their disabilities in areas of reasoning, judgment and control of their impulses... they so not act with the level of moral culpability that characterizes the most serious adult criminal conduct." From this ruling it has since been determined that punishment objectives grounded in deterrence and obtaining retribution are not legally valid when the offender is of an intelligence level that is so far below average as to be considered mentally retarded. Generally speaking, this is typically an offender that has an Intelligence Quotient of 70 or less (*DSM-IV-TR*).

Source: Atkins v. Virginia (536 U.S. 304).

hallucinations, but also can be experienced through the gustatory (taste), tactile (touch), and olfactory (smell) senses. **Delusions** are pathological false beliefs. Examples of delusions are a person believing that he/she is a religious figure, has special powers, or is being persecuted by unknown forces. **Thought disorder** is a term that refers to incomprehensible speech, language, or writing. Example of a thought disorder is when someone is difficult to understand due to a flight of ideas that does not allow them to complete sentences or else incoherent babbling, sometimes known as "word salad."

Psychosis can be caused by brain damage, general medical conditions, schizophrenia, severe depression, bipolar disorder, poisonings, drug abuse, and drug withdrawals. Psychotic individuals may or may not be oriented and able to control behaviors. Those who suffer from psychotic disorders represent approximately 1 percent of the population.

As was mentioned in the subsection on physical disabilities, law enforcement officials are, in modern times, more well trained in their response to persons with mental health challenges. Various training initiatives have been implemented in law enforcement agencies throughout the United States. An example of this can be found in law enforcement agencies' increasingly specialized role in working with mentally ill citizens through crisis intervention teams (CIT). It is perhaps worth noting that

Box 3.2 Crisis Intervention Teams, "The Memphis Model"

The Crisis Intervention Team (CIT) is a police-directed, first responder model that pairs police officers with community agencies to improve crisis interventions for the local community. Police officers who are part of CIT have specialized training in mental illness and are taught techniques for dealing with persons that may have mental impairments. This specialized training and response style has been shown to improve crisis intervention outcomes for police officers, consumers, family members, and citizens in the community.

CIT is sometimes referred to as the "Memphis Model" because it was first applied in Memphis, TN. It has since grown to be a nationally recognized program that is used in most parts of the United States. The CIT model's goal is to reduce stigma and prevent further involvement of mentally ill persons in the criminal justice system. It achieves this goal by facilitating problem solving with the mental healthcare system that creates a context for sustained change (Dupont, Cochran, & Pillsbury, 2007).

The Core Elements of CIT involve collaborations between law enforcement agencies, advocacy groups, mental health providers, and community stakeholders. Law enforcement agencies, in this system, are trained to interact with crisis situations through the use of de-escalation techniques in order to improve the safety of the officer, consumers, and family members. Officers are also trained to provide care and help consumers by taking them to the appropriate facility that can meet their mental health needs. **Advocacy groups** are involved throughout the entire process of CIT formation in order to provide strong support from "passionate and dedicated individuals" whose goal is to improve the quality of life for those suffering from mental illness. Through the advocacy partnership, a feedback loop is formed that provides ongoing information about the concerns of consumers and their families. **Mental health providers**, which includes professional mental health clinicians (e.g., psychologists, counselors, social workers), behavioral health agencies, and hospitals, all collaborate to provide training for officers and interventions for consumers. This combined effort on the part of multiple community mental health partners improves existing mental health networks by clarifying how each agency and professional responds during a crisis. A final group involved in the CIT team formation is that of **community stakeholders**. **Community stakeholders** are involved in all aspects of the formation and implementation of the CIT program in order to produce a team that is owned and accepted by the local community. This involvement establishes a level of trust between the law enforcement agency and the community, which is required to assure the success of crisis interventions.

Source: Author.

one of the authors of this text administrates a police and corrections academy and is a CIT instructor for his region in the state of Louisiana. From personal experience, this author can attest to the efficacy of this training for those in both law enforcement and corrections.

Mood Disorders—Major Depression

Mood disorders, the most common of which is major depression, consist of a number of mental illnesses where mood is thought to be the underlying cause of the illness. Approximately, 22 percent of the population will, at one point, suffer from a mood disorder, with the highest rates being experienced by women and those between the ages of 30 and 60 years. Those suffering from depression may have symptoms of helplessness, hopelessness, anhedonia (the inability to experience pleasure), suicidal thoughts and behaviors, and psychosis in some rare cases. Mood disorders are also closely tied to death by suicide.

Suicide prevention is an area in which criminal justice employees are often called to intervene. It is estimated that 90 percent of those who complete suicide have a mental health or substance abuse diagnosis, the most common of which is Major Depressive Disorder. Women *attempt* suicide at higher rates than men do, where men *complete* suicide at higher rates. The reason for the higher rates of death for men is largely due to the method used to harm oneself (Joiner, 2007). Men frequently use more violent means (most commonly handguns), whereas women commonly use poisonings (i.e., overdoses).

One fairly recent form of suicide that places law enforcement officers at great risk is known as **suicide by cop**. Suicide by cop is where an individual pulls and/or fires a weapon at the law enforcement officer in order to provoke lethal force. The intent is not necessarily to injure the officer as much as it is to commit suicide with the aid of the officer. It has been estimated that approximately 11 percent of all law enforcement shootings are related to **suicide by cop**. Males are more likely to commit suicide by this method because of their more common use of firearms.

Dementia—Alzheimer's Disease

Dementia refers to a loss of cognitive functioning related to aging that is greater than normal expected memory loss. **Alzheimer's disease**, the most common form of dementia, is an incurable, degenerative, and terminal disease that most often affects the elderly. The most common and earliest symptom of dementia is the inability to form new memories. As the disease progresses, confusion, irritability, mood swings, language breakdown, loss of long-term memory, and withdrawal become present. The disease leads to a gradual loss of bodily functioning over time, culminating in death. The average life span for a person diagnosed with **Alzheimer's disease** is seven years from the onset of symptoms.

Mentally Ill Offenders

In 2005, nearly 776,000 prison inmates had been identified as possessing some type of mental health problem, according to the Bureau of Justice Statistics (2006). This number included over 705,000 in state prison systems as well as another 70,000+ inmates in the federal Bureau of Prisons. When added with another 479,900 inmates in local jails who were also found to have an identified mental health problem, the total count of

Box 3.3 Diagnostic Criteria for Dementia of the Alzheimer's Type as found in the *DSM-IV-TR*

A. The development of multiple cognitive deficits manifested by both
   1. Memory impairment (impaired ability to learn new information or to recall previously learned information)
   2. One (or more) of the following cognitive disturbances:
      a. aphasia (language disturbance)
      b. apraxia (impaired ability to carry out motor activities despite intact motor function).
      c. Anosia (failure to recognize or identify objects despite intact sensory function)
      d. Disturbance in executive functioning (i.e. planning, organizing, sequencing, abstracting)
B. The cognitive deficits in Criteria A1 and A2 each cause significant impairment in social or occupational functioning and represent a significant decline from a previous level of functioning.
C. The course is characterized by gradual onset and continuing cognitive decline.
D. The cognitive deficits in Criteria A1 and A2 are not due to any of the following:
   1. Other central nervous system conditions that cause progressive deficits in memory and cognition.
   2. Systemic conditions that are known to cause dementia.
   3. Substance-induced conditions.
E. The deficits do not occur exclusively during the course of delirium.
F. The disturbance is not better accounted for by another Axis I disorder.

incarcerated persons with a mental health issue in 2005 was over 1,255,000 offenders throughout the nation. The estimates mean that, during the prior year, approximately 56 percent of state inmates and 45 percent of federal inmates have some type of mental health issue, along with another 64 percent of all jail inmates.

Students should look to Table 3-1 for an illustration of the data just discussed). With the current trend toward increased sentence length, it is clear that this number will continue to rise. In fact, the proportion of inmates needing mental health assistance will most assuredly continue to rise from the current statistics as the correctional population continues to age behind bars. Problems with dementia and other cognitive disorders are steadily increasing as a natural consequence of mandatory sentencing, habitual offender, and 3-strike laws that are in place.

ACCESS TO CARE: THE FOUR STANDARDS OF MENTAL HEALTH CARE

Correctional facility administrators are legally required to implement an adequate healthcare delivery system that can ensure inmate's access to healthcare and healthcare providers (Hanser, 2006). This legal requirement for adequate healthcare also extends to mental healthcare (Hanser, 2006). An adequate care delivery system for mental health services in a correctional facility must address a range of specialized needs. In the Supreme Court case of ***Ruiz v. Estelle***, the Court focused on several issues required to meet minimally adequate standards for mental healthcare in a correctional environment. The following requirements articulated by the *Ruiz* Court are pertinent to this chapter:

1. Correctional administrators must provide an adequate system to ensure mental health screening for inmates,

TABLE 3-1   Recent Symptoms and History of Mental Health Problems among Prison and Jail Inmates

Mental health problem	Percent of inmates in —		
	State prison	Federal prison	Local jail
Any mental health problem	56.2%	44.8%	64.2%
Recent history of mental health problem[a]	24.3%	13.8%	20.6%
Told had disorder by mental health professional	9.4	5.4	10.9
Had overnight hospital stay	5.4	2.1	4.9
Used prescribed medications	18.0	10.3	14.4
Had professional mental health therapy	15.1	8.3	10.3
Symptoms of mental health disorders[b]	49.2%	39.8%	60.5%
Major depressive disorder	23.5	16.0	29.7
Mania disorder	43.2	35.1	54.5
Psychotic disorder	15.4	10.2	23.9

Note: Includes inmates who reported an impairment due to a mental problem. Data are based on the Survey of Inmates in State and Federal Correctional Facilities, 2004, and the Survey of Inmates in Local Jails, 2002. See *Methodology* for details on survey sample. See *References* for sources on measuring symptoms of mental disorder based on a Structured Clinical Interview for the Diagnostic and Statistical Manual of Mental Disorders, fourth edition (DSM-IV).

[a]In year before arrest or since admission.

[b]In the 12 months prior to the interview.

Source: James, D. J., & Glaze, L. E. (2006). *Mental health problems of prison and jail inmates.* Washington, DC: Bureau of Justice Statistics.

2. Correctional facilities must provide access to mental health treatment while inmates are in segregation or special housing units,
3. Correctional facilities must adequately monitor the appropriate use of psychotropic medication.
4. A suicide prevention program must be implemented.

These **Four Standards of Mental Healthcare** are common to all jail and prison systems in the United States. The case of *Ruiz v. Estelle* was instrumental in laying much of the groundwork for correctional responsibilities to provide adequate mental healthcare. Other cases would soon follow that would clarify various fine points of law regarding liability issues, involuntary confinement, and so forth, but the **Four Standards of Mental Health Care** for prison systems are generally considered to have evolved from the decisions in the case of *Ruiz v. Estelle*.

PHYSICAL DISABILITIES

Physical disabilities represent a broad range of disabilities including orthopedic, neuromuscular, cardiovascular, and pulmonary disorders. Often, persons with these disabilities require **assistive aids** such as canes, crutches, walkers, wheel chairs, and scooters. There are many different causes of physical disabilities including congenital disorders, injuries, muscular dystrophy, multiple sclerosis, cerebral palsy, amputation, heart disease, and pulmonary disease. It is important to consider that many persons have disabilities that are not outwardly visible such as heart disease and epilepsy.

Box 3.4 The Case of *Ruiz v. Estelle* and *Mental Illness* in Prison Environments

In 1972, David Ruiz sued the director of the Texas Department of Corrections (William J. Estelle) over dangerous and inhumane working and living conditions. This was a long-battled suit that ended in 1982 with a final consent decree that the Texas prison system was resolved to obey. In this class action suit, it was held that the Texas prison system constituted "cruel and unusual punishment," which is prohibited by the 8th Amendment to the U.S. Constitution. Some of the specific problems noted from this case are as follows:

1. Overcrowding—the prison system had been placing two or three inmates within a single cell designed for only one inmate.
2. Inadequate Security—the prison system utilized a system of security that incorporated selected inmates as guards. This practice led to numerous injustices and civil rights violations.
3. Inadequate healthcare—the prison system did not have an adequate number of medial personnel and also used the services of non-professional personnel (including inmate "surgeons" and orderlies) to deliver medical care. Likewise, the therapy for psychiatric patients was deficient.

4. Unsafe working conditions—unsafe conditions and procedures were the norm for inmate laborers.

Ultimately, all of these complaints were rectified within the Texas prison system. However, this case held even more stipulations that would affect the future of all mentally ill and mentally challenged inmates in Texas and throughout the entire nation. In this case, it was further ruled that it was also cruel and unusual punishment to confine mentally ill inmates in solitary confinement. In response to this ruling, the prison administration in Texas developed the Administrative Segregation Maintenance Psychiatric Program to provide intensive counseling to inmates with serious mental illness in need of high-security housing as well as a program to transition these inmates back to the general prison population. Correction officials also increased mental health training for security staff and established oversight through regular onsite audits by various outside review bodies.

Source: Ruiz v. Estelle, 503 F. Supp. 1265 (SD Tex. 1980), in Out of State Models. Retrieved from: *http://www.correctionalassoci-ation.org/PVP/publications/Out%20of%20State%20Models.pdf*

Persons with physical disabilities may face a number of barriers when interacting in society. For example, buildings (other than public buildings) are often not built to accommodate individuals with mobility disabilities. Certain employment or activities that require physical exertion may be too strenuous for a person with physical disability. Physically disabled persons, particularly in rural areas, may lack transportation in order to receive medical attention or else perform routine tasks (e.g., grocery shopping, bank deposits). In severe cases of physical disability, individuals are unable to care for basic needs.

Hearing and Visual Impairments

Hearing impairments, also known as **deafness**, is when a person has lost partial or complete ability to detect certain frequencies of sound. These impairments are classified into the following two forms: 1) pre-lingual deafness and post-lingual deafness. In the case of the latter, language was acquired prior to the hearing impairment; therefore, the person may have some use of language or else use the assistance of hearing aids or other devices. In the case pre-lingual deficits, no verbal language was acquired and therefore communication techniques are limited to sign language. Of all age groups, the elderly represent 43 percent of all those who are hearing impaired.

Visual impairments is where an individual has significant sight loss such as to qualify for extra visual supports. Vision and visual impairments are represented by a range of visual capabilities including: (1) normal vision, (2) moderate visual impairment, (3) severe visual impairment, and (4) blindness. Visual impairments are most widely found in the elderly age group, which constitute 82 percent of all visual impairments.

THE ELDERLY AS CRIMINAL JUSTICE EMPLOYEES

Many criminal justice professions have physical demands that are a routine part of the occupation. Although the **ADEA** protects the rights of criminal justice employees against discriminations based on age, it does not protect inabilities to perform basic job functions. Over the course of the ADEA enactment, some municipalities and states have required mandatory retirement ages of police officers and firefighters under the assumption that older police officers and firefighters could not perform on the same physical level as their younger counterparts. The ADEA, as amended, has found that these practices are allowable and therefore have been adopted by many police and fire-fighting agencies.

The most recent challenge of this provision for the ADEA came from a group of Chicago police officers who challenged the use of mandatory retirement through a case filed in the 7th circuit court of appeal entitled *Minch v. The City of Chicago*. In this case, the city filed a motion to have the case dismissed noting that the U.S. Supreme Court case *Public Employees Retirement System of Ohio v. Betts* and *United Airlines Inc. V. McMann* had both offered rulings that made clear that mandatory retirement ages were allowable. In both cases, the Court had ruled that mandatory retirement ages did not necessarily "subterfuge" the ADA provided that the "early retirement provision ... has some economic or business purpose other than arbitrary age discrimination." *Minch v. The City of Chicago* was dismissed reaffirming that mandatory retirement ages are acceptable under the ADEA. Chicago, as with many other police agencies, requires retirement at age 63.

Despite the fact that many states and municipalities have mandatory retirement ages, this has not resulted in the complete absence of elderly from criminal justice agencies. Administrative jobs within the criminal justice system often do not have mandatory restrictions, and therefore elderly involvement is more common. Elderly volunteers are also common to criminal justice agencies.

Elderly volunteers are becoming increasingly present within criminal justice agencies. This, in part, is due to increases in the number of senior citizens living within communities as well as the criminal justice systems' increased awareness of the effectiveness of using elderly volunteers. Agencies that manage to recruit elderly volunteers often use these volunteers to perform clerical work, issue parking tickets, and surveillance. One such example is that of "Granny Patrol." The "Granny Patrol" is a Delray Beach, Florida program that has enlisted the help of 70 senior citizens to issue parking violations. It has been estimated that this group writes over 10,000 tickets per year.

Agencies, for the most part, that enlist elderly volunteers have found their presence to be very rewarding for both the agency and the volunteer. Elderly volunteers often have good work ethics and are pleasant to be around. It is said that their presence has a calming influence on the agencies in which they volunteer and that they relate well to community issues. Once more, their added labor helps offset expenses that criminal justice agencies incur.

Although elderly volunteers are mostly beneficial to criminal justice agencies, their presence can create some disadvantages. Among these are difficulties in training elderly volunteers and safety concerns that may exist. The elderly, as a general rule, are less well versed in many modern computer application and technological advances. Training these individuals may result in an inordinate amount of time being spent on teaching basic technological skills (e.g., word processing, using databases, basic computer functions). Trainers and employees may feel that these volunteers are in the way and creating "double work." Safety of volunteers is also of concern. Using elderly in surveillance and ticketing efforts can expose them to risks of violence or other health concerns.

THE DISABLED AS CRIMINAL JUSTICE EMPLOYEES

Title I of the ADA deals with employment issues. Under this section, it is illegal to deny employment to qualified individuals with disabilities based on the disability (Rubin, 1994). Equal employment opportunities covered under Title I include the application and hiring process as well as how employees are treated with respect to transfers, promotions, and benefits (Rubin, 1994). In order to be qualified for jobs in the criminal justice system, an applicant must first be qualified and able to perform the essential functions of the job without accommodations (Rubin, 1994). Essential functions are defined as those parts of the job that are fundamental to the performance of the job (Rubin, 1994). If the applicant cannot perform the essential functions of the job, then the criminal justice agency must determine whether a reasonable accommodation can be made in order that the person could perform the essential function of the job (Rubin, 1994). Reasonable accommodations are those improvements or purchases that do not produce undue expense or burden on the criminal justice agency (Rubin, 1994).

Disabled persons are also provided equal access to employment opportunities. This means that applicants are allowed to participate in the application process in a meaningful way. An example of this might be that sight-impaired applicants are read questions for a written exam or learning-impaired individuals are given more time to answer questions.

Fitness standards, both physical and psychological, can be part of the essential functions of a job. When these standards are applied, they must be consistently applied to all candidates. If disabled applicants are screened out because of an inability to meet the physical or psychological standard, the agency must show that the disabled individual could not meet the standard even when reasonable accommodations were made.

Persons working in police and corrections agencies, because of the stressful nature of the work, are prone to stress-related concerns such as mood and anxiety disorders and other physical ailments. The stressful nature of police work is evidenced in the high rate of suicide that is common to the profession, which is two to three times that of the general population. Concomitant physical reactions such as cardiovascular disease and high blood pressure are also linked to stressful work environments.

Because of the physical and mental demands that are common to criminal justice setting, ongoing fitness evaluations are required. Inmates or detainees who are injured as a result of an officer's lack of fitness for duty places the agency at great risk for litigation. When these diagnoses are made, reasonable accommodations should be made related to the condition. These reasonable accommodations could be light-duty assignments until the displayed symptoms subside.

Traumatic Stress and Police Agencies

Law enforcement has been classified as a critical-incident occupation. **Critical-incident occupations** are the occupations where workers are subjected to traumatic stressors as a normal part of their job responsibilities. Persons in these professions experience work-related trauma in various forms including threats to personal safety (e.g., being shot at, entering a burning building), witnessing individual death (e.g., failed resuscitation attempts, car fatalities), viewing dead bodies and violent deaths (e.g., burn and gunshot victims), personal injury, etc. Stressors may also include secondary exposures that result from helping someone who has been traumatized. Secondary exposures are common to helping professionals such as psychologists, police support personnel, social workers, and counselors (Stamm, 1999).

There are a number of stress and traumatic stress-related symptoms that are common to critical stress occupations. The most common of these reactions is **burnout**. **Burnout** has been defined as a deterioration in job satisfaction and job performance that leads to "higher turnover rates, decreased job performance, lack of social support to other staff, low morale, negative attitudes and loss of concern for clientele" (Brownstone, Shatoff, & Duckro, 1983, p.36). Moreover, burnout has been linked to low job satisfaction, increased incidence of employee illness and turnover, alcohol and drug misuse, psychosomatic complaints, and interpersonal staff conflict (Maslach & Jackson, 1981). A second reaction is that of increased incidences of **health concerns**. Police officers, in general, suffer from elevated incidences of burnout, disability, and premature death compared to other professional groups. Police officers have been found to have higher rates of coronary artery disease, cancer, and hypertension (Violanti, Vena, & Marshall, 1986) than other professions. In addition, they have been found to have higher rates of alcoholism, suicide, depression, and other forms of mental illness when compared to the general population. A final well-documented reaction is that of **Posttraumatic stress disorder (PTSD)** (Martin, McKean, & Veltkamp, 1986). **PTSD** is a severe anxiety disorder in which a person who has been exposed to a severe stressor continues to display symptoms well after the stressful event occurs. It has been estimated that 7 percent of police officers suffer from PTSD and another 35 percent have symptoms bordering on a diagnosis (Carlier, Fouwels, Lamberts, & Gersons, 1997).

Because of the risk of morbidity and mortality related to stress disorders, careful evaluation and treatment are required to ensure the long-term well being of police officers. Unfortunately, as often is the case in critical stress occupations, stress reactions are often blamed on the organizational structure of agencies or else denied all together. Officers often do not consider the activities that they participate in to be stressful, but rather blame bureaucracies and leadership for symptoms of burnout and discontentedness. Once more, officers and agencies alike insulate themselves from the stress of the occupation by unspoken codes of silence where neither discusses the painfulness of events. When an officer does succumb to the stressfulness of the occupation, he/she is inadvertently shunned from the "normal group" of officers. This isolation can further exacerbate the stress reaction.

Consider the case of a career police officer who was injured in the line of duty. This officer was a veteran of the force who had been trained in elite schools and was very confident in his ability to protect himself and the community. One night, while on a routine patrol, the officer was directed to the house of a person suspected of knowing the whereabouts of a wanted criminal who lived in the area. This person invited the officer in his home, welcomed him to sit down, and proceeded to answer the officer's questions in a respectful and courteous way. The officer recalled the event,

> I noticed that the informánt had his arms tucked closely to his sides, but I thought nothing of it. In an instant, he pulled a box cutter from his pocket and proceeded to cut me from one side

> of my face circling my head to the base of my neck right above my back. In one second, that guy had jumped on me cutting me so badly that I was forced to hold up my face in order to see! With one hand I held up my face and with the other I pulled my weapon. I chased the man to the parking lot where he jumped into a car and came careening towards me. I shot him five times through the front windshield.

Months passed and the officer's emotional state continued to deteriorate.

> I had crying spells and became overwhelmed by fear. I couldn't stand the thought of going out on patrol. I replayed the thoughts over and over in my head. I stopped talking to my wife. She finally told me I had to go get some help.

The officer went to see the police psychologist.

> When I went to see the shrink things went from bad to worse. They put me on light duty and took away my gun. Everyone stopped talking to me. It was like I had a disease that was catching. I thought of taking my own life.

This story illustrates several points as it relates to critical-incident occupations. First, all persons, regardless of training or other personal attributes, are susceptible to stress reactions, given the significant exposures to stressful events. The officer in the above example believed in his own "immunity" thinking that he had been prepared to cope with almost anything. Second, the agency and fellow officers isolated the distressed officer. This was probably the case because most officers have experienced stressful events that are difficult to talk about and because few people know just what to say to their injured colleague. This isolation probably compounded the event. Finally, training and preparation for the encounter of traumatic stress are often lacking.

EXEMPTIONS FOR CRIMINAL JUSTICE AGENCIES, LITIGATION, AND CLIENT REMEDIES

After the enactment of the ADA, the International Association for the Chiefs of Police (IACP) sought exemption standards for state and local police as well as sheriff departments. Their request was denied. The only exemptions that were given were in cases involving the Federal government. Because of this, the Federal Bureau of Investigation (FBI) and Drug Enforcement Administration (DEA) are not required to comply with the ADA while state and local agencies are.

Agencies that fail to comply with the ADA can result in litigation on behalf of those who were harmed. Plaintiff's who were targets of discrimination have access to a number of remedies that include injunctive relief, reinstatement, back pay, and attorney fees and costs (Alpert and Smith, 1993). In addition, compensatory damages of varying amounts can be awarded as well as punitive damages (Alpert & Smith, 1993).

THE DISABLED AS VICTIMS OF CRIMES

Persons with disabilities overall are at a heighted risk for victimization. It has been estimated that persons with disabilities are estimated to become the victim of crime at a rate 4–10 times higher than persons without disabilities. Likewise, children with disabilities are twice as likely as non-disabled children to become victims of sexual and physical abuses.

The reasons for this advanced victimization are manifold. First, disabled victims are more likely to become victims related to their perceived inability to fight or flee. Disabled victims are less likely to be able to defend themselves and thus are easy targets. Second, disabled victims are less likely to notify others or else testify to the victimization. This is particularly true when the disability is related to a mental impairment such as mental retardation where the victim has difficulty communicating victimization. Third, many disabled persons require assistance to perform daily activities. Caregivers often take advantage of the disabled person's relative helplessness. Finally, persons with disability, because of preexisting social stigmas, are more likely to intensify emotions of self-blame or guilt that occur as a result of victimization. In doing so, they are less likely to tell others of the victimization out of fear of further abuse or else because they feel that the abuse was justified.

CURRENT EVENTS IN MULTICULTURAL CRIMINAL JUSTICE
Elderly, Crime, Neglect, and Caring Law Enforcement

In Florida, officer Zach Hudson, of the Lake Mary Police Department, implemented the Seniors Intervention Group after responding to a call for service that involved two women, a mother (aged 90) and a daughter (aged 70) who were living together and, due to their state of poverty, had decided to alternate on a monthly basis between buying food and buying medicine. Officer Hudson had witnessed many of these types of circumstances among senior citizens, and this is precisely what prompted him to begin the Seniors Intervention Group. As of 2009, his group has aided over 1,000 seniors in the Seminole County, Florida region (Berger, 2012).

The group partners with faith-based organizations, local businesses and other nonprofits assistance of all types is provided, including food, monetary provisions, transportation, as well as household maintenance. This group will, on a monthly basis, select a neighborhood or region and will provide yard work, home repairs, and other major tasks to assist the area's senior citizens with tasks and issues that they may not be able to do on their own without risking potential injury (Berger, 2012).

In addition, the elderly are often at-risk of criminal victimization. The National Crime Prevention Council has numerous suggestions to aid in preventing criminal victimization of the elderly. The elderly are prone to be victimized by burglars, purse snatchers, and con artists. The Crime Prevention Council has provided a strategy for reducing crime against the elderly as well as reducing the fear of crime that many elderly may have. This strategy entails the following:

1. A communication network to keep the elderly alert to potential crime in their area.
2. Information and training on how to report crime.
3. Services to support the elderly who are victims of crime.
4. Access to products to prevent crime.

The above recommendations are basics to any elderly victimization reduction program. It is important that programs not sensationalize the likelihood of crime as many elderly are often fearful. Rather, the point is to educate them, get them involved, and have them become informed members of their community.

One innovative program, implemented by the Fairfield, Connecticut police department, is the Alzheimer's registration program, where citizens who have family members with Altzheimer's disease can register the individual through an identification process. The purpose being to allow police or other individuals to more readily identify the family member and help to ensure that they are brought back to their family or household quickly and safely, should they wander off or become lost. The use of photos, a national registry program, and internal agency processes help to optimize the likelihood of providing aid to elders who may end up missing.

Throughout the nation, many police agencies have what are referred to as TRIAD programs and SALT committees. TRIAD programs represent a membership of three community aspects – law enforcement, the senior citizen community, and local community groups. The purpose of a TRIAD is to promote senior citizen safety and to reduce the unwarranted fear of crime that some seniors may experience. When a community develops and official TRIAD, the next step is to develop SALT committees. SALT stands for **S**eniors **A**nd **L**aw enforcement working **T**ogether. Usually, a TRIAD will be a county-level governing body with multiple SALTs being developed in various areas of that county. The SALT committees often consist of approximately 10 to 20 volunteers who will be active in aiding senior citizens with various social issues and engaging in various crime prevention programs, as well.

The National Association of Triads is a far-reaching and active organization that provides training and a good deal of resources to the elderly and those who work with this population.

References: Berger, D. (2012, July 06). Fed up officer says "enough," starts senior outreach. CNN Heroes, retrieved from http://www.cnn.com/2012/07/05/us/cnnheroes-hudson-seniors/index.html

Fairfield Police Department (2012). *Community policing programs: Alzheimer's registration program.* Fairfield, CT: Fairfield Police Department.

National Association of Triads (2013). *About NATI:* Who we are, what we stand for, and the services we provide your community. Retrieved from: http://www.nationaltriad.org/About_NATI.htm

National Crime Prevention Council (2013). *Strategy: crime prevention services for the elderly.* Arlington, VA: National Crime Prevention Council.

THE ELDERLY AS VICTIMS OF CRIMES

The common perception of the elderly is that they are the victims of crimes more often than the other groups. The truth of the matter is that overall, the elderly, as compared to other age groups, experience lower victimization rates. It is perhaps their physical vulnerabilities and living alone that have perpetuated this myth of victimization.

Although the elderly have low levels of victimization, it might be fair to say that the average elderly persons fear being victimized more than other age groups. In part, this fear might be related to the female makeup of the elderly age group. Women constitute approximately 60 percent of the elderly population. Women, in general, express high levels of fear related to victimization. Once more, elderly women are more likely to live alone then elderly men, which may compound these fears. Perhaps another reason why the elderly fear being victimized more often is that the perceived consequences of that victimization may be greater as related to their age. When these seniors were younger, they probably felt more able to defend themselves or else steer clear of harm's way. Now that they are older, they feel both physically and economically vulnerable to victimizations. Because of physical and economic frailties, the elderly person may feel that, if victimized, recovery may not be possible.

Despite these heightened fears, the elderly are not at heightened risk for victimization. As a general rule, age is negatively correlated to a person's likelihood of being a victim of a crime. Older individuals are significantly less likely to become the victims of violence of younger age groups. In almost every category of crime, those over the age of 65 are less likely to be victims than those under 65. The two exceptions to this trend are personal thefts and pick pocketing. In these two categories, the elderly are just as likely to be victims as other age groups.

Elderscide—**Eldercide** refers to someone over the age of 65 who is the victim of a homicide. Of the total number of homicides committed in the United States, eldercides represent only 5 percent. Of those who were the victims of eldercide, males were found to be slightly more common victims. Eldercides has been on a sharp downward trend since 1975, having leveled off to approximately 350 annually for both males and females.

Elder Abuse—According to the **Administration on Aging**, elder abuse is a term that refers to "any knowing, intentional, or negligent act by a caregiver or other person that causes harm or serious risk of harm to a vulnerable adult." This abuse may consist of:

- *Physical abuse*—the inflicting of pain or injury on a senior (e.g., slapping, bruising, or restraining by physical or chemical means).
- *Sexual Abuse*—non-consensual contact of any kind.

- *Neglect*—the failure of those responsible to provide food, shelter, healthcare, or protection for the vulnerable elder.
- *Exploitation*—the illegal taking, misuse, or concealment of funds, property, or assets of a senior for someone else's benefit.
- *Emotional Abuse*—inflicting mental pain, anguish, or distress on an elder person through verbal and non-verbal acts (e.g., humiliating, intimidating, or threatening).
- *Abandonment*—desertion of a vulnerable elder by anyone who has assumed the responsibility for care or custody of that person.
- *Self-neglect*—characterized as the failure of a person to perform essential, self-care tasks and that such failure threatens his/her own health or safety.

The precise annual number of elderly who are the victims of abuse in the United States is unknown; this is due to several reasons. First, definitions as to what constitutes abuse vary. Because of this, it is difficult to pinpoint what constitutes abuse and what does not—therefore the abuse remains hidden. Second, there is no uniform reporting system. This lack of uniformity has resulted in varied estimates of abuse from a number of different studies. Because of the lack of uniformity, comparing the results of these studies is practical. Third, underreporting of abuse cases is also likely. It is estimated that only 1 in 14 incidents of abuse is reported. Finally, there is no national reporting system that collects and confirms data on elderly abuse.

Despite the lack of precise information on the number of elderly who suffer abuses, estimates have been created indicating the number of likely cases. According to the National Center on Elder Abuse (2011), approximately 1–2 million Americans aged 65 or older "have been injured, exploited, or otherwise mistreated by someone whom they depended on for their care." It is estimated that anywhere from 2 percent to 10 percent of all elderly will be victims of abuse. Those mostly to be the victims of elderly abuse are the "oldest of the old," indicating that those over age 80 suffer abuse rates at two to three times that of all other elderly. The most common type of abuse experienced by seniors is neglect (58.5 percent), followed by physical abuse (15.7 percent), and financial exploitations (12.3 percent).

Neglect occurs when basic **activities of daily living (ADLs)** go unmet. ADLs is a medical term that refers to self-care activities that occur in one's own residence or somewhere else. Healthcare professionals refer to performance of ADLs as being a measure of the ability or inability of an elderly person to function independently. ADLs are two types—basic ADLs and instrumental ADLs. Basic ADLs include basic functions of self-care such as personal hygiene, the ability to feed oneself, dressing and undressing, functional transfers (i.e., mobility), the ability to voluntarily control urinary and fecal discharge, as well as the ability to walk. Instrumental ADLs refer to those more complex needs such as the ability to provide groceries and pay bills, the ability to perform routine housework, the ability to take care of one's own financial situation, as well as the ability to prepare one's own meals. When one becomes incapable of caring for his/her own ADLs, it is said that that person has a **failure to thrive** and therefore assistance is needed. Neglect occurs when the assistance provided does not meet the ADL needs.

Neglect comes in two types—**passive neglect** and **active neglect**. Passive neglect occurs when the caregiver is unable to provide adequate care. This is a common form of abuse when caregivers take in the elderly person with the best of intentions of providing for their loved one. Despite these intentions, life circumstances or else the caregivers' inability or inadequacy to provide care create a situation of abuse. It is not all that uncommon that one of the partners of an elderly marriage will opt to take care of the infirmed spouse. Owing to the caregivers' own impairments, proper care may not be provided to the infirmed person. In these cases, basic ADLs are not maintained and the infirmed person experiences neglect. Living conditions can become unhealthy, that is basic sanitation, cleanliness, and safety are not practiced.

Neglectful conditions that lead to fires are a great risk for the elderly. The elderly die in fires more than any other age group. The reasons for this heightened risk of injury and death are manifold. The elderly may live in homes built of older materials and/or that are in states of neglect or disrepair, due to their inability to afford maintenance or complete the maintenance themselves. Their cognitive abilities may be diminished, enhancing the possibility of fire hazards (e.g., leaving irons on). They also may not have the capacity to recognize signs of a fire and exit the structure quickly. **Passive neglect** leaves the elderly person in very unsafe conditions, which can lead to fires and deaths.

Active neglect is a much more sinister form of neglect. Active neglect occurs when someone purposely withholds necessities in order to gain something in return. For instance, a son may withhold life-saving medications from a father in order to expedite his death so as to collect an insurance benefit. Another example might be someone withholding food from an elderly person in order to gain their compliance on some issue.

Approximately, 20,000 elderly are the victims of physical abuse annually. The exact number of victims is difficult to determine due to concealment that often occurs by both the victim and the victimizer. In part, the reasons for the concealment are largely due to the present family social setting. Elderly who are the victims of physical abuse by their own children often inflicted physical abuse on those same children. Retribution for previous assaults by the adult child caregiver is a common reason for abuse. Elderly victims often conceal their injuries in order to prevent further victimizations, prevent from being placed in a nursing home, or because of conflicting emotions over being victimized. It is not uncommon for victims to feel as if they have caused the attack, deserved to be injured, or else to feel helpless over not being able to prevent the injury.

Baumhover and Beall (1996) presented five theories to explain elder abuse and neglect. First, the mental health of the caregiver affects the quality of care for the infirmed. Emotional outbursts such as bouts of aggression and hostility may result in the taking out of frustrations on the elderly person. Cognitive deficits (e.g., dementia, mental retardation, schizophrenia) may prevent adequate care from being provided. Second, transgenerational violence is often to blame for patterns of abuse. Violent families, as a general rule, remain violent through the willing of violence to the younger generation. Children who were once abused become the victimizers of their infirmed parents. The third cause is demonstrated through the **social exchange theory**. The **social exchange theory** states that persons respond to a number of punishments and rewards. In a caregiver-dependent relationship, the caregiver may feel justified in abusing the dependent person's feeling as if the relationship did not provide the deserved rewards. Abusiveness in these relationships continues as long as the caregiver feels that he/she is capitalizing off of it. Fourth, the vulnerability and impairment of the person may prompt the abuse. Defenseless persons lack the ability to fight back and injure their assailants. Assailants typically will not continuously injure someone if they know the risk of personal injury is significant. It is of little consequence that physical assaults as well as corporal punishments cease when young persons are old enough to defend themselves. Finally, stressors common to delivering care to a dependent person may increase tension, thereby transforming the caregiver's response.

Other social risk patterns for abuse include social isolation as well as parent–adult child-dependency relationships. Social isolation in which the caregiver and elderly person live alone without contact with the outside community encourages abuse. This is because abuse is unlikely to be discovered and the victimizer may become emboldened thinking the abusive behavior will go unnoticed. Living situations where an adult child still relies on the elderly parent also present a pattern of risk. In the adult child-dependency relationships, the child often feels that their role of dependency is socially unacceptable and therefore they try to gain power over the elderly person.

ELDER FINANCIAL AND PROPERTY CRIMES

According to FBI (2011), seniors are a prized target for scam artists. In fact, they are so vulnerable to victimizations that street lingo has been developed to represent the fleecing of the elderly. "Crib job" is a term that describes the ease to which con artists can "get over" on their elderly targets.

The reasons why they are targets of scams are numerous. First, the elderly often have a "nest egg" in the form of home equity or other savings accounts. Assets combined with good credit make them appealing to the con artist. Second, people who grew up before World War II were likely to have been groomed to be polite and trusting. Because of these traits, they often have difficulty saying "no" or hanging up a telephone. Third, elderly victims are less likely to report scams. The reasons for their failure to report include a lack of awareness of whom to report the crime to, embarrassment over being taken advantage of, and/or because they lack the mental faculties to know they are being taken for a ride. Compounding the problem of reporting, when the elderly do report, they frequently make poor witnesses. This is because they may have difficulty reporting detailed information that investigators need. Finally, the elderly are particularly susceptible to advertisements of products that promise rejuvenation and vitality. These miracle products have become increasing possible, or so the elderly person thinks, because of their experience with medical advances that have occurred through their lifetimes.

Common frauds include reverse mortgage schemes, investment schemes, telemarketing fraud, fraudulent "anti-aging products," funeral and cemetery fraud, counterfeit prescription drugs, and health insurance fraud. **Reverse mortgages**, also known as home equity conversion mortgages (HECM), are often used fraudulently to cheat elderly victims out of their investments. In this scheme, victims are promised free homes, investment opportunities, and foreclosure and/or refinance assistance. Home flippers will then use the elderly victim as a "straw buyer" in a house-flipping scheme. **Investment schemes** occur by fraudulently convincing an elderly person to invest in a fake investment. These schemes come in many forms such as pyramid schemes, advanced fee schemes, prime bank note schemes, and Nigerian letter fraud schemes. **Telemarketing fraud** involves the selling of false products over the telephone. Women living alone are particularly susceptible to this type of fraud, which may involve the offering of discount vitamins, prizes, or other healthcare products. **Health insurance fraud** involves the improper billing of insurance claims or else the fraudulent sale of unnecessary healthcare products. Common health insurance schemes involve "rolling lab" schemes where improper or fake tests are conducted for members of churches, retirement homes, and other locations where the elderly congregate.

ELDER SUICIDE

Despite popular belief that teens and young people are at the greatest risk for suicide, the opposite is true. As a general rule, as age increases, so does the occurrence of suicide. Elderly people, particularly the oldest of the old, are at heightened risk for self-harm. Those over the age of 75 commit suicide at a rate three times that of other age groups. The elderly who do take their own lives commonly are divorced or widowed and/or suffering from a disease.

According to Thomas Joiner's Universal Theory of suicide (2005), suicide deaths have many common features. One such feature is that those who eventually succeed in killing themselves became desensitized to painful experiences. According to the theory, pain is the natural warning mechanism that prevents us from harming ourselves. Suicide victims, through their experiences of pain, have become desensitized over time. The elderly in particular, through the aging process and painful experiences that have occurred along the way, no longer fear death and therefore are at the highest risk for suicide. Other groups that experience provocative painful experiences are also at risk. Examples of these include police officers who witness death and violence as a part of their work, adolescents who have suffered through mental and physical abuses, as well as others who have experienced acts of overwhelming violence.

ELDERLY OFFENDERS

The public's view of the elderly is not one that is often attached to images of that of the criminal offender. This is because, generally, as age increases criminal involvement decreases. This phenomenon is known as the "**inverse age–crime relationship**." Criminal involvement reaches its peak at adolescence and slowly decreases thereafter.

The fact that elders have the least involvement in crime is true for all crime categories. Despite the images of elder shoplifters and elder pedophiles, there is no truth to their heightened involvement as a group. Elder involvement in crime is negligible in every crime category, and therefore the attention to elder crime as a source of concern or inquiry is not warranted.

Even though elderly account for the least amount of crime committed by all age groups, they represent a unique group within the criminal justice system on two counts. First, when the elderly do commit crimes, they often need special care and consideration related to disabilities, frailties, and age. Second, the area in which elderly come into contact the most with the criminal justice system is in the prison system. Many of these offenders committed crimes with lengthy sentences while younger, and have since "grown old" behind bars. Compounding the problems of aging in prison is the fact that inmates age faster than the general public. It has been estimated that by adding 11.5 years to an inmate's actual age establishes the chronological age. For this reason, inmates over 50 are considered to be elderly. This fact creates many unique problems, as related to access, healthcare, and housing, which will only magnify as America's prison population continues to age.

INTERNATIONAL FOCUS

The Elderly in Prison – An International Problem

In the United States, the geriatric population behind bars is a phenomenon that has generated substantial attention. This same issue has been witnessed in other industrialized nations, as well. Like many countries, England faces challenges of dealing with an aging prison population. England defines geriatric offenders as those who are 50 to 55 years of age or older (Wahidin & Aday, 2006). The reason for this is because the incarcerated tend to have health problems due to a series of poor decisions throughout the life-course as well as the vagaries of prison life, which lead to a physiological aging that tends to be 10 years (or more) senior to their chronological age.

The issue with the elderly prison population applies to both the male and female population. For instance, between 1995 and 2003, the number of women incarcerated who were over 50 rose by a full 87 percent, while the number of men incarcerated over the age of 50 rose by an even more staggering 113 percent; this is in only an 8 year period (Wahidin & Aday, 2006).

As can be guessed, elderly inmates require medical services and also have social care needs that can and do burden the English prison system due to the enormous expense involved. This has challenged the British, who must contend with a greying of their offender population. At this time, there is no comprehensive national policy or strategy to address this segment of the population. Further, when considering those inmates with chronic illnesses, the English system is extremely ill-equipped, having only one 16-bed facility at Norwich Prison, available for such inmates (The Economist, 2013).

In Canada, circumstances are not as bad as in England, but they are not at all ideal. In that country, during the past decade, the elderly population has grown by over 50% and they comprise nearly 20% of the prison population in Canada (Crawford, 2012). In that country, there is a pervasive disregard for policies and programming created in 2001 due to budgetary restrictions, leaving this population vulnerable, particularly those who are 60 years old and over; Canada documents at least 1,000 of these inmates who tend to require a host of needs that go beyond those of most elderly offenders (Crawford, 2012).

In Japan, during the past decade, the number of inmates who are aged 60 and above have doubled. This is a faster rate-of-growth than the 30 percent increase that has occurred among all other age groups of the inmate population in Japan. As of 2010, elderly inmates consisted of 16 percent of the nation's population (Yamaguchi, 2010). In Onomichi Prison, facilities for the elderly are state-of-the art but that country has still found it necessary to invest another $100 million into additional facilities for the greying offender population (Yamaguchi, 2010). Interestingly, many offenders in the Japanese system are there because they commit their crime... on purpose. The economy being bad and their having a lack of individual or family resources, the Spartan conditions of prison life are better than what they may experience on the outside; many, therefore, commit property crimes that are just serious enough to ensure that they are locked up, allowing them sufficient meals, a safe environment, and other basic commodities that they may lack, on the outside (Yamaguchi, 2010).

In all of these countries, the issues are the same – an ever-growing offender population who, because of a greying of the general national population, tight financial resources, and (in some cases) longer prison sentences. These dynamics, coupled with the burgeoning costs of medical care associated with the elderly and the provisions to the physical structures of facilities that house the elderly inmate population, create challenges that are difficult to navigate for correctional practitioners around the world.

Sources: Crawford, a. (2012, March 19). Canada urged to segregate elderly prisoners. CBC News, retrieved from: http://www.cbc.ca/news/world/canada-urged-to-segregate-elderly-prisoners-1.1296158

The Economist (2013, March 02). In it for life: Old prisoners are suffering from poor care—and putting a strain on jails, too. Retrieved from: http://www.economist.com/news/international/21572752-old-prisoners-are-suffering-poor-careand-putting-strain-jails-too-it-life

Wahidin, A. & Aday R. (2006). *The needs of older men and women in the criminal justice system: An international perspective.* London: Her Majesty's Prison Service.

Yamaguchi, M. (2010, December, 12). Japan's prison population getting old, fast. Associated Press, retrieved from: http://www.sfgate.com/news/article/Japan-s-prison-population-getting-old-fast-2524440.php

ELDERLY INMATES

A fivefold increase in the incarceration rate over the last 30 years has caused the United States to rank as a world leader in the number of offenders behind bars. Concomitant to the increased level of incarceration is a rapidly expanding population of elderly offenders. The number of elderly offenders (aged 55 and older) doubled between the years 1995 and 2003 and continues to be on the rise. This increase is largely due to lengthy more punitive sentencing guidelines that have been adopted since the mid-1970s. Because of the expansion in elderly offenders, unique problems have arisen for the prison system.

Problems experienced include an increased incidence of health concerns, the specialized needs of the population, and subsequent associated costs. Elderly inmates have health needs that exceed the needs of the elderly living freely in society. These needs may include an advanced reliance on special medications, special diets, improved accessibility, and additional healthcare. These advanced needs of elderly inmates are related to the fact that this group suffers from increased rates of disability and health concerns as compared to the same-age cohorts living in the general population. The reason for these increased health concerns is due to the quality of life that the prisoner maintained both before and after incarceration. Many inmates lived in unhealthy living environments or else maintained unhealthy lifestyles while a part of society. These unhealthy lifestyles and life situations included long-term histories of drug and alcohol use, long-term poverty, unprotected sex, and homelessness. Once incarcerated, confinement, a lack of social health, unnatural sexual practices, communicable diseases, ongoing drug use, and violence all work toward rapid aging and amplified disease processes.

In addition to the costly healthcare needs are specialized housing needs of the elderly population. Elderly inmates are more vulnerable to self-harm, suicide, and/or victimization than their younger counterparts. Because of this, special measures have to be taken to segregate elderly inmates who are at risk for victimization and protect inmates who are at risk for self-harm or suicide. It has been estimated that costs associated with elderly offenders is three time higher than the cost of housing a younger offender.

SPECIAL CONSIDERATION FOR ELDERS

There has been some discussion in recent years about special procedures being used with the elderly by law enforcement and with the courts. Most law enforcement agencies have policies that are used universally for all offenders that come into contact with the agency. One such example is the use of handcuffing and shackling offenders who are being transported. Elders, because of their physical vulnerabilities, are more susceptible to injury than the average person. Moreover, elderly criminals are less likely to fight back or flee, nullifying the main purpose for this kind of restraint. This questions the practical idea of using maximum restraint on an elderly person. A second example is the use of standard sentencing practices for all offenders regardless of age. A young person at age 24 given a prison sentence of 10 years may allow this person to reenter society and become a productive citizen. It is somewhat implied in sentencing guidelines that sentences that are less than the maximum sentence of "life" are meant to give the person committing the crime hope to reenter society. However, giving a 10-year sentence to a 65-year old is likely to be a death sentence. Should sentencing guideline be adjusted based on age?

The answer to age-based policy is not without precedence. In fact, both law enforcement and courts have already developed a separate system for dealing with adolescence because of their unique needs and vulnerabilities. Arguably, elders have similar concerns to adolescents in that they physically are not equal to the average offender and because of their age, they may experience more harmful incidents related to arrests, criminal proceedings, and incarceration than does the average offender.

CONCLUSION

The elderly and disabled are two minority groups that frequently overlap. They are known as cultural minorities because of disadvantages that they possess due to preferences that have been established in our social system. As it relates to criminal justice issues, these minority groups are prevalent participants in courts, correctional, and law enforcement systems. They engage in the criminal justice system as employees, victims, and offenders.

Special consideration has to be made for the elderly and disabled because of difficulties they may have in fully participating in the criminal justice system. Once more, as the aging of our culture progresses, the aged and disabled will be increasingly prevalent in the system. Criminal justice professionals will be tasked with identifying those who are aged and disabled and understanding how those who are disabled need special considerations. These same professionals will also need to be aware of their own risks of becoming disabled and the issues facing those of advanced age within their own ranks.

Chapter 3 Learning Check

1. As age increases, criminal involvement decreases. This phenomenon is known as the inverse age–crime relationship.
   a. True
   b. False

2. _____ leaves the elderly person in very unsafe conditions that can lead to fires and deaths, whereas _____ occurs when someone purposely withhold necessities in order to gain something in return.
   a. Passive neglect; Non-passive neglect
   b. Accidental neglect; Deliberate neglect
   c. Passive neglect; Active neglect
   d. Minimal neglect; Serious neglect
   e. None of the above

3. Which court case was instrumental in setting standards for mental healthcare in prisons?
   a. *Atkins v. Virginia*
   b. *Ruiz v. Estelle*
   c. *Grutter v. Bollinger*
   d. *Miller-El v. Cockrell*
   e. None of the above

4. Elder abuse is a term that refers to any knowing, intentional, or negligent act by a caregiver or other person that causes harm or serious risk of harm to a vulnerable adult.
   a. True
   b. False

5. The _____ is a police-directed, first responder model that pairs police officers with community agencies to improve crisis interventions for the local community.
   a. Crisis Intervention Team
   b. Critical Incident Team
   c. Emergency Community Response Team
   d. None of the above

6. The Four Standards of Mental Health Care include which of the following?
   a. Correctional administrators must provide an adequate system to ensure mental health screening for inmates.
   b. Correctional facilities must provide access to mental health treatment while inmates are in segregation or special housing units.
   c. Correctional facilities must adequately monitor the appropriate use of psychotropic medication.
   d. A suicide prevention program must be implemented.
   e. All of the above.

7. An Impairment refers to the loss of regular human functioning. Impairments come in a variety of forms ranging from limitations of cognitive, emotional, and physical attributes.
   a. True
   b. False

8. The term disability is defined as being a physical or mental impairment that substantially limits one or more major life activities.
   a. True
   b. False
9. The Age Discrimination in Employment Act of 1967 (ADEA) act forbids the discrimination of anyone over the age of 35.
   a. True
   b. False

10. _____ ushered in a new era of workplace and civil protections that prevented discrimination based on race, religion, sex, national origin, and other characteristics.
    a. The Civil Rights Act of 1964
    b. Americans with Disabilities Act of 1990 (ADA)
    c. The Four Standards of Mental Health Care
    d. None of the above

Essay Discussion Questions

1. Discuss some of the specialized responses that have been developed for the mentally ill in law enforcement and corrections.
2. Identify key legislation that has impacted the rights and services provided for the physically and mentally disabled.
3. Identify and discuss types of victimization experienced by the elderly.

References

Administration on Aging. (2011). Aging statistics. Retrieved from: http://www.aoa.gov/AoARoot/Aging_Statistics/index.aspx

Alpert, G., & Smith, M. (1993). The police and the americans with disabilities act—who is being discriminated against? *Criminal Law Bulletin, 29*, 516–528.

American Psychiatric Association. (2000). *Diagnostic and statistical manual of mental disorders* (4th ed., text rev.). Washington, DC: Author.

Baumhover, L. A., & Beall, S. C. (Eds.). (1996). *Abuse, neglect, and exploitation of older persons: Strategies for assessment and intervention.* Baltimore, MD: Health Professions Press.

Brownstone, J. E., Shatoff, D. K., & Duckro, P. N. (1983). Reducing stress factors in EMS: Report of a national survey. *Emergency Health Services Review 2*(1), 35–53.

Bureau of Justice Statistics. (2006). *Mental health problems of prison and jail inmates.* Washington, DC: Bureau of Justice Statistics.

Carlier, I. V. E., Fouwels, A. J., Lamberts, R. D., & Gersons, B. P. R. (1996). Post-traumatic stress disorder and dissociation in traumatized police officers. *The American Journal of Psychiatry, 153*, 1325–1328.

Centers for Disease Control and Prevention. (2009). Prevalence and most common disability among adults. *Morbidity and Mortality Weekly Report, 58*(16), 421–426. Retrieved from: http://www.cdc.gov/mmwr/preview/mmwrhtml/mm5816a2.htm

DuPont, R., Cochran, S., & Pillsbury, S. (2007). *Crisis intervention team core elements.* Memphis, TN: University of Memphis.

Federal Bureau of Investigations. (2011). Common fraud schemes. Retrieved from: http://www.census.gov/acs/www/

Hanser, R. D. (2006). Special needs offenders. Upper Saddle River, NJ: Prentice Hall.

Joiner, T. (2007). *Why people die by suicide.* Cambridge, MA: Harvard University Press.

Martin, C. A., McKean, H. E., & Veltkamp, L. J. (1986). Post-traumatic stress disorder in police and working with victims: A pilot study. *Journal of Police Science and Administration, 14*, 98–101.

Maslach, C., & Jackson, S. E. (1981). The measurement of experienced burnout. *Journal of Occupational Behavior, 2*, 199–215.

Nagin, D. S., & Farrington, D. P. (1992). The onset and persistence of offending. *Criminology, 30*, 501–528.

National Center for Elder Abuse. (2011). Statistics at a glance. Retrieved from: http://www.ncea.aoa.gov/Main_Site/Library/Statistics_Research/Abuse_Statistics/Statistics_At_Glance.aspx

Rubin, P. N. (1994). The Americans with Disabilities Act and criminal justice: Hiring new employees. Washington, DC: National Institute of Justice.

Stamm, B. H. (Ed.) (1999). *Secondary traumatic stress: Self-care issues for clinicians, researchers, and educators* (2nd ed.). Lutherville, MD: Sidran Press.

Violanti, J., Vena, J., & Marshall, J. (1986). Disease risk and mortality among police officers: New evidence and contributing factors. *Journal of Police Science and Administration, 14*, 17–23.

Minorities Based on Gender and Sexual Preference

LEARNING OBJECTIVES

After reading this chapter, students should be able to do the following:

1. Identify and discuss the history and role of women in police, judicial, correctional, and juvenile agencies.

2. Explain some of the means by which women have experienced discrimination in the criminal justice system.

3. Discuss some of the challenges that female offenders face.

4. Discuss some of the changes that agencies have had to make to be more inclusive of the gay, lesbian, bisexual, and transgender (LGBT) population.

5. Assess likely future changes that will occur in the criminal justice system when addressing issues relevant to the LGBT population.

KEY TERMS

Borderline personality disorder

Bowers v. Hardwick

Bradwell v. Illinois

Child Saver Movement

Collateral damage

Crime Victim's Movement

Equal Employment Opportunity (EEO) Act

Farmer v. Brennan

Glass ceiling

Homophobia

International Association of Women Police

Lawrence v. Texas

LGBT

Multiple personality disorder

Office on Violence Against Women

Post-traumatic stress disorder

Primary victimization

Secondary victimization

Sexual harassment

Shelter movement

Victims of Crime Act

Vilification

Violence Against Women Act (VAWA)

INTRODUCTION

Throughout history, the role that women have played in the criminal justice system has been significantly different from that of men. Throughout most of history, societal expectations of women have shaped the views of the public regarding what is appropriate for women. This is true whether the women was employed within a correctional capacity, one that was law enforcement oriented, or if the woman was an offender. We will discuss this in more detail throughout this chapter, but it is safe to say that women have often had restrictions placed upon them by expectations of what is gender-appropriate. These expectations, for the most part, were generated by a system that was usually led and governed by men.

WOMEN IN THE CRIMINAL JUSTICE FIELD

Throughout history, professions within the criminal justice field have tended to be male-dominated. In early U.S. history, women who worked in law enforcement usually did so in positions that dealt with social service functions, clerical work, juvenile work, or vice investigations (Martin & Jurik, 1996). In the field of corrections, women usually held the role of matron over women who had been incarcerated (Rafter, 1985).

The role of women in the criminal justice field saw more change during the 1970s than in any other period. In part, this was due to the passage of the **Equal Employment Opportunity (EEO) Act in 1972**. This act prohibited discrimination in hiring on the basis of race, color, religion, sex, or national origin. This meant that selection procedures, criteria, and standards were modified so that they had to be related to the job itself in order to be considered. This law was instrumental to opening up the field of law enforcement to women. The use of affirmative action processes as well as court injunctions helped ensure that women were included. It is from this point that we will proceed, discussing the role of women as employees in various facets of the criminal justice system.

Women in Law Enforcement

The first woman in law enforcement was Alice Stebbin Wells, born in 1873. Alice Wells began with the Los Angeles Police Department, but her eventual acceptance as a police officer with full powers of arrest did not come easy. Ms. Wells was, initially, a religious minister in Kansas and eventually desired a change of careers. In order to be considered for police work, she had to petition the Mayor, the Police Commissioner, and the City Council of Los Angeles. Alice Wells joined the Los Angeles police department on September 12, 1910. She eventually became the first president of the International Association of Police Women (now known as the **International Association of Women Police**), a major lobbying group for female officers.

Prior to 1890, police agencies had employed women only for the care of female prisoners. After Wells successfully petitioned for a place on the LAPD, she was equipped with a telephone call box, a police rule book and first aid book, and the "Policewoman's Badge Number One"; however, this was not always believed by the public. Wells was assigned to work with the LAPD's first juvenile officer, and was also assigned to crimes that involved female suspects, where it was her job, exclusively, to question female suspects of crime, whether juvenile or adult. Wells began her career supervising skating rinks and dance halls, as well as interacting with female members of the public. Two years after Wells joined the force, two other female officers were sworn in, with all female officers now under the control of the Civil Service. Sixteen other cities had hired female police officers as a direct result of Well's activities.

During the early years of women working in the police profession, there was a need for the police to work with juveniles and this led to women being assigned these positions. Indeed, the first women in policing were frequently assigned to the juvenile division. This was due to stereotypes that held women as maternal and therefore better able to deal with juveniles than male police officer might have been (Comeau & Klofas, 2010). These women were usually referred to as police matrons and were given different duties from male police officers. Often, these women would perform clerical duties, enforce minor city ordinance rules (such as parking tickets), or other similar tasks if they did not work with youth.

During World War I (1911–1915), women came into policing to fill the shoes of male officers as they would in a near mirroring of events that would occur a mere 20 years later (Price & Gavin, 1981). These new officers operated as auxiliary police and were tasked with war-related duties, such as ensuring prostitutes were not in or around military camps. They also served as general supervision within army camps (Price & Gavin, 1981). By the decade end, women were employed as officers in over 200 cities in the United States (Price & Gavin, 1981).

During the 1940s, both prior to and during World War II, women were again actively recruited and employed in tasks traditionally held by men—including policing. For the duration of the War women acted as auxiliary officers (Price & Gavin, 1981). After World War II, many women went back to home life, and this was often against their own desires (Price & Gavin, 1981). Women still engaged in policing or those who wished to pursue a career in the field were often required to be college graduates. Rather perplexingly, they would be considered for the position as long as they were not overly feminine or masculine (Garcia, 2003). The 1940s saw the rise of women in traffic control and parking enforcement among Southern police departments. This was in part due to personnel shortages caused by low wages; female traffic enforcers proved so successful that they began to be hired in this capacity throughout the United States (Grennan, 2000).

During the baby boom of the 1950s there was an influx of women into the world of work, including policing. In this decade over 2,500 women were employed as officers. For their appointment, these women were required to be attractive, empathetic, selfless, well-adjusted, dignified, tactful, and sensible (Garcia, 2003). As in prior decades, these women were officers in name, but performed as specialized social workers. Their sex was inextricably seen as tied to their ability to perform as officers; many departments believed that a woman could only successfully perform her work if she behaved in a stereotypically feminine manner (Garcia, 2003). Despite having higher qualifications than their male counterparts, female officers were made well aware of the fact that they were in no way replacing men, but rather aiding and assisting them to the best of their womanly capacity (Garcia, 2003).

At the start of the 1960s there were more than 5,000 female officers serving across the country (Garcia, 2003). However, they were largely placed in Womens' Bureaus, performing duties similar to what they had done for the previous half-century: protecting women and youths from society's ills, and handling juvenile cases and runaways (Grennan, 2000). The most notable change to occur in their duties for the previous

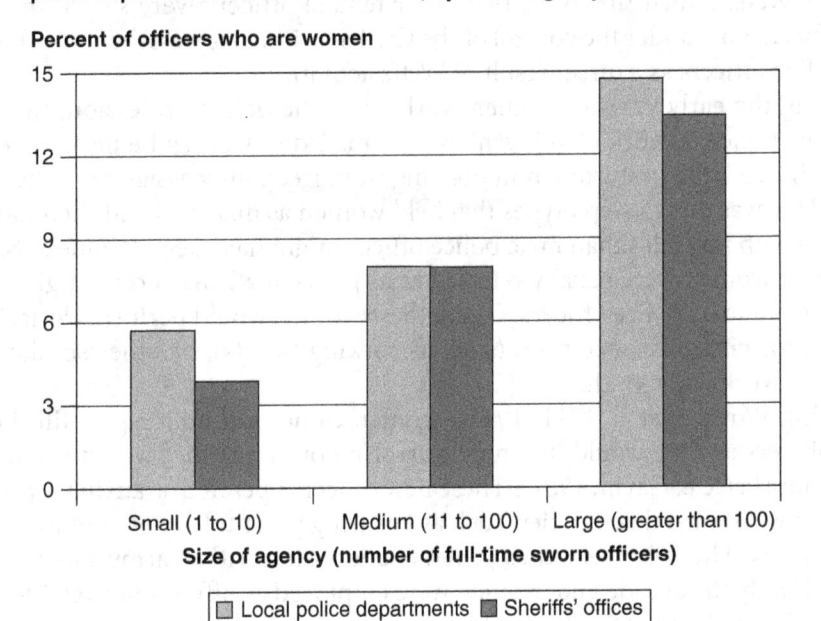

Percent of full-time sworn law enforcement officers who are women among local police departments and sheriffs' offices, by size of agency, 2007

FIGURE 4-1   Percent of Full-Time Female Law Enforcement in Police and Sheriff Agencies by Size of Agency. *Source:* Bureau of Justice Statistics. (2010). *Women in law enforcement, 1987–2008*. Washington, DC: Bureau of Justice Statistics.

50 years was the placement of women on traffic-control and enforcement in the 1940s (Garcia, 2003).

Nowadays, as a result of the 1960s' and the 1970s' push for changes for women in the workforce, female police officers engage in the full range of police activities that their male counterparts are involved in. Even though this is true, in 2007 women still accounted for only 12.7 percent of all sworn police officers in large agencies throughout the United States. Thus, while the majority of police officers do tend to be males, in most jurisdictions, social pressures that restrict them from taking policing as a profession seem to be much less in existence in modern society. Note that Figures 4-1 and 4-2 provide data that illustrate the representation of women in different types of police agencies.

Women in Corrections

With the professionalization of corrections has come the understanding that diversity in the workforce necessitates transparency and ethical behavior behind the walls. In other words, when correctional staff consist of various persons from various groups and backgrounds, there is less likelihood that biases in operations can continue undetected. This is particularly true in cases where the prison subculture, steeped in a staunch male-oriented view, is concerned. The inmate subculture tends to be quite sexist in orientation, with feminine characteristics being considered weak and inferior. Having women in the workforce can counter these biases among inmates and having female supervisors can be even more effective in developing acceptance of women in the field of corrections. The key issue is whether agencies make an effort to facilitate the

Percent of full-time sworn law enforcement officers who are women among state and local law enforcement agencies, 1987–2007

Percent of officers who are women

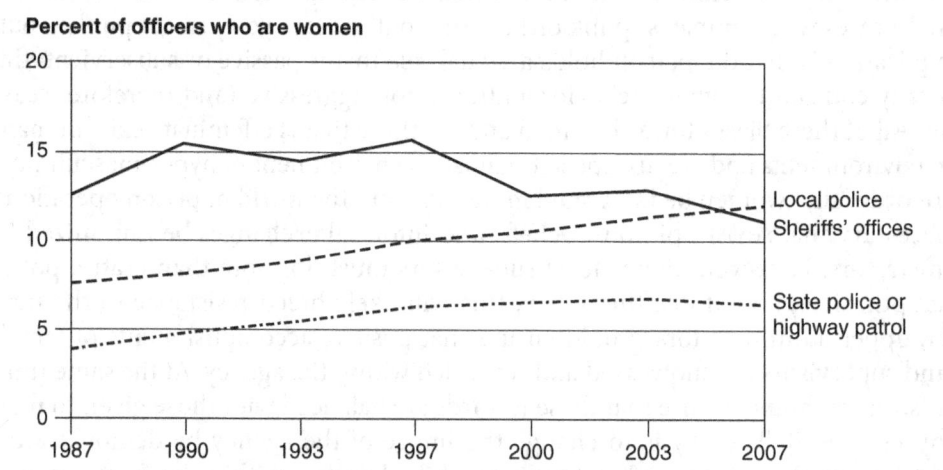

Note: Data on state police and highway patrol agencies were obtained from the Federal Bureau of Investigation's Uniform Crime Reports. Data on local police departments and sheriffs' offices were obtained from the BJS Law Enforcement Management and Administrative Statistics (LEMAS) series.

FIGURE 4-2 Percent of Full-Time Female Law Enforcement in State and Local Agencies. *Source:* Bureau of Justice Statistics. (2010). *Women in law enforcement, 1987–2008.* Washington, DC: Bureau of Justice Statistics.

careers of female security staff; it is very important that they do so in order for subcultural influences to be countered.

Carlson and Garrett (2013) noted that some women who work in male prisons may conduct themselves differently than their male coworkers as they perform the responsibilities of a correctional officer and/or correctional supervisor. Research on this subject has found that many women tend to adopt a service-oriented approach that is less confrontational than that used by their male counterparts. This is actually a very valuable asset to agencies because this minimizes the number of grievances, potential lawsuits, personal injury claims, and other legal pitfalls associated with conflicts in prison. Likewise, the overall climate on cellblocks and dorms that are handled in a less-aggressive manner tends to be calmer; this can add to institutional safety.

Though this approach has its benefits, there have been mixed results. In jail settings, research has found that women officers are perceived by male officers to be less effective in breaking up fighting inmates or controlling large and/or aggressive inmates. On the other hand, male officers do tend to view women as being skilled at calming inmates and working with those who are mentally or emotionally disturbed (Carlson & Garrett, 2013). Female supervisors tend to have these same skills and abilities and, even in cases where male inmates are aggressive, women who hold rank seem to be just as adept as men at maintaining control of the cellblock or dormitory.

However, the problem of sexual harassment affects the prison worksite, just as is the case in outside society, but it is much more pronounced and pervasive in prisons. Harassment can include behaviors such as cussing, intimidation, or inappropriate humor. In the prison or jail setting, male staff as well as inmates may present challenges to women through an atmosphere that is demeaning to women. For instance, a male staff member may say to a group of male inmates working in the field, "Okay, c'mon ladies, let's get back to work," which implies that women are less accepted and respected than are men. The fact that the guard is referring to the male inmates as "ladies" is meant to be demeaning and reinforces the notion that women have lesser stature within the prison. In cases where inmates "punk one another out" or say "you just got punked out" the implication is that the person holds a sexual role that is passive or subservient; this is typically equated to female behavior and/or a non-aggressive (and therefore weak) person. All of these biases toward women and anything that is effeminate exist in many prison environments and are juxtaposed against an environment of hyper-masculinity.

In order that women be integrated more fully into the world of prison operations, it is necessary that sexist opinions, beliefs, and informal exchanges be minimized by administrators. However, higher-level supervisors must do more than craft a policy and act punitively to enforce the policy; this will likely breed resistance to the idea. Rather, upper-administrators should ensure that positive accomplishments of female staff and supervisors are showcased and rewarded within the agency. At the same time, administrators should ensure that these rewards are balanced with those given to male employees as well. The key is to change the image of the agency by demonstrating support for female officers and supervisors while doing so within the framework of acknowledging, showcasing, and rewarding *all* officers within the agency. This will be particularly effective if women who perform difficult duties that are in close-contact with inmates are specifically noted within the agency. Such showcasing will counter stereotypes among inmates and other staff and will empower other women who might also wish to work among the direct security ranks rather than separated areas (i.e., count room, camera stations, or call centers), support services (i.e., food, laundry, or recreational programs), or auxiliary functions (such as security in protective custody, visitation, or religious services).

Furthermore, it is important that female supervisors be present and represented in male facilities, not just female facilities. Although this can lead to some complications in certain situations, agencies must be committed to working around and through legal issues related to cross-gender searches, privacy issues for male inmates in shower areas and/or locations where strip searches may occur, and so forth. Ultimately, this acknowledgment of women in corrections is healthy for the sexist subculture that tends to exist among inmates and some correctional officers. Providing training on sexual equality, sexual harassment, and other similar topics is also important and should not be made optional but should be mandatory.

Women in the Judicial System

As with other segments of the criminal justice system, it would appear that even the judicial component has fewer women than men represented therein. This is largely due to the fact that, historically speaking, there was a general impression that women were not fit to practice law. Indeed, in 1875, the Wisconsin Supreme Court denied admission to the state bar of Ms. Lavinia Goodell on the grounds that women were not suited for legal battles and judicial conflict. Prior to this, in 1872, the United States Supreme Court had also upheld a ruling from the Supreme Court in Illinois that denied another woman, Myra Bradwell, from admission into the state bar. The Court, in this case (**Bradwell v. Illinois**, 83 U.S. 110, 141–142, 1872), the rationale was that a married women could not engage in the practice of law without the consent of her husband because such a woman, according to state law, could not enter into contracts without the signature of their husband. The need for contracting was mandatory to represent clients and married women (most women would be married during this time) could not legally engage in such agreements on their own.

This ruling demonstrates the social views that were held of women, even in the court system. Women were, at this time, property of their husbands and were treated as children. Over time, exceptions did emerge throughout the United States, such as in California, where in 1878 Clara Foltz lobbied the state legislature for the removal of gender-biased restrictions from the statutes that precluded women from practicing law. Even then, she was denied admission to one law school due to the concern that a woman in the midst of male students would be too distracting to the male students. Ultimately, she argued her case in the California Supreme Court and was admitted into law school.

It should be clear from this brief historical synopsis that discrimination against women has existed in the judicial arena for over a hundred years. The struggle of women to attend law school, become attorneys, and to practice law would continue throughout the 1900s. Indeed, it really was not until the 1980s that women truly did experience substantial increases in their access to the courts as employees of the courthouse, practicing attorneys, prosecutors, and judges. This era led to more attention being given to women in the legal professions, with the National Association of Women Judges and the National Organization for Women Legal Defense and Education Fund working to encourage state and federal systems to address bias and discrimination against the activity of women in the court system. Throughout the 1980s, significant developments would take place, which eventually aided women to be active players within the judicial system.

Nowadays, it is of course not uncommon for women to practice law and there is even a higher proportion who make it to the position of judge within their jurisdiction. Indeed, it is perhaps the role of judge that is the most prestigious position within the courthouse. When considering this it is clear that women are represented in the judiciaries of all 50 states but their representation is less than a 50/50 split that one might expect between men and women. Indeed, according to the National Association of Women Judges (2010), there were 4,521 female judges out of a total of 17,108 total judges (male and female) around the nation. Essentially, this means that women accounted for only 26 percent of all the state-level judgeships around the nation. When examining the specific types of judgeships, it would appear that the representation is only slightly higher in appellate courts (about 31 percent) and is a bit lower in general jurisdiction courts (24 percent) throughout the nation (National Association of Women Judges, 2010).

Women in the Juvenile Justice System

Women as professionals in the juvenile justice system has been a longstanding accepted practice. Historically speaking, women have been involved in juvenile reform, including movements such as the Child Savers with whom one of the leading advocates was a woman by the name of Jane Addams, who was the first American woman to be awarded the Nobel Peace Prize. The **Child Saver Movement** emphasized redemption and prevention through early identification of deviance and intervention in the form of education and training (Platt, 1969).

As seen in the field of policing, it was common decades ago to view women as working in a gender-appropriate field when children and youth issues were involved. This was even more true if the youth were female. The matriarchal and nurturing image proscribed to women made juvenile work an area that was much easier for women to break into. In today's environment, women tend to be well represented among juvenile workers, whether this be as juvenile probation officers, security staff at facilities to reform youth, or working in an array of social services that provide assistance to youth.

We have deliberately not expounded much on this subsection simply because women have traditionally been well represented in this area of criminal justice employment for generations. In fact, one could conclude that women have shaped many of the youth services and juvenile systemic responses since 1899 when the first juvenile court was established in Cook County, Illinois. Because of this, we simply note that women have long been involved in this area of response and, as a result, are perhaps not a minority within this field of work.

The Glass Ceiling

There is some debate as to whether the glass ceiling still exists for women employed within the criminal justice system. The **glass ceiling** is a term for official or unofficial barriers to promotion that exist for women within the workforce. For all practical purposes, it should be considered that some sort of barrier does indeed exist because, if for no other reason, there are substantially fewer female supervisors than there are male supervisors within correctional facilities. Furthermore, throughout history, women who worked in corrections tended to do so in facilities for women and, since the female offender population was proportionally smaller than the male population, the need for women to work in corrections was much less than that for men.

In addition, there are social constraints in society that tend to frown upon women working within the prison environment. Historically, this type of employment was not considered "ladylike" and therefore instilled a social aversion toward this type of employment. Coupled with the intensely masculine nature of the prison subculture, the hard-nosed population of male guards who already worked in prisons, and the dangerousness of the job, it is not surprising that during the past 100 years women were not commonly employed in this field. However, the modern era of corrections is seeing a change and women are more commonly seen within this area of employment.

However, an employee's expectations and internal belief systems often determine success in the world of work. People placed in situations in which they are powerless and with limited promotional potential tend to lower their goals and develop approaches to work that are defensive and not postured for upward mobility. In many cases, women may not utilize the same set of aggressive social skills that their male counterparts employ and may therefore be at a socialized disadvantage. These skills may need to be learned on the job and, for women in particular, there may be a need to learn about the prison environment's social cues. This means that women may have to adjust their body language and facial expressions to assert an authoritative image rather than a pleasant one. In all cases, the stereotyped "subservient" image of women must be avoided. Likewise, attempts to make themselves attractive are also problematic within a prison setting. This means that the prison environment is often counter-intuitive to the socialization that many women may receive.

However, many women in corrections report that even when they have the skills and desire to work in corrections, they are often still at a disadvantage. This is due to the glass ceiling effect, which prevents them from being included in informal social circles, gaining appropriate mentoring and on-the-job training from their senior male counterparts, or having access to positions that are more dangerous but more prestigious within the informal guard subculture. Indeed, paternalistic desires to protect female officers may prevent them from working on some job assignments and this places female officers at a disadvantage in terms of training and experience, resulting in impaired promotional ability.

Women as Supervisors in the Criminal Justice System

It is important to have female supervisors in policing agencies from both an intra-agency perspective and a community relations perspective. It is advisable that police chiefs, particularly in larger jurisdictions, ensure that female officers receive opportunities for assignments and training that prepare them for promotion. A failure to do so can lead to underprepared candidates in their ranks and can be grounds for failure to train lawsuits. In addition, administrators can, quite naturally, leave themselves open to suits based on discrimination if they neglect their female officers in favor of male officers. Regardless, police chiefs should, in actuality, seek to prepare their female officers for promotion simply because it is ethical to do so and because, as leaders, it is their responsibility to ensure that all officers in their fold are treated with respect and professionalism.

Furthermore, chiefs, sheriffs, and other administrators should pay attention to whether women are applying for promotions in their agency. In short, this should be encouraged. If there is a disproportionately low number who apply, it is the leader's responsibility to determine the reasons for this. Leaders in police agencies will need to ensure that promotion processes are not overly subjective and will need to also ensure that the process is free from bias, whether intended or accidental.

In relation to the field of corrections, it is advisable that correctional agencies continue to recruit and promote more female representation within the management circles. The role of the supervisor requires effective communication skills and the ability to share the agency's mission and values. If the agency is truly sincere about professionalism, ethical behavior, and a desire to develop a safe institution, then having optimal female representation can add to all of these objectives. This is especially true since the inclusion of women with supervisory power will tend to counter the negative aspects of the prison subculture and since this will create an organizational culture that does not promote the sexist views that male inmates tend to hold within the institution.

Lastly, women as supervisors within the judicial system and the juvenile system have not been as controversial as it has been in policing and corrections (primarily institutional corrections). Indeed, many court workers, clerks, and other staff in courthouses around the nation are women. In addition, supervisors tend to be drawn from these ranks and are also often women. Likewise, as we have seen in this section, women have traditionally been well represented within the juvenile justice field. The same is true of women as supervisors in the juvenile justice system and its corollary services, such as with child protection and family services.

VIOLENCE AGAINST WOMEN

This subsection was included because much of the violence against women, particularly domestic abuse and sexual assault, are gender-based and disproportionate. This is not to imply that men are not frequently the victims of crime, including violent crime. Rather, it is the nature of the types of crime that are disproportionately experienced by women (rather than men) that make this subsection necessary. In many cases, the types of crime that will be especially considered are those that are often committed, at least in part, with gender being a motivator to their commission.

Crime Victim's Movement

The Crime Victim's Movement is one that is not, in and of itself, limited to women. However, the **Crime Victim's Movement** was originated mostly by women advocates and had its origins in campaigning against domestic violence crimes and sexual assaults committed against women. To some extent, this was a proclamation among women during an era of social consciousness (the 1960s and the 1970s) that women were not to blame for the victimization that might be committed against them. During this era of the Civil Rights Movement, advocates for women's rights were outspoken and feminism was widely touted. This was also the era in which the **shelter movement** started, which provided options for women who were victims of various forms of domestic violence. In later years, female victims of crime began to refer to themselves as survivors, rather than victims (Bass & Davis, 2008).

In 1984, the Victims of Crime Act was passed and this resulted in the creation of the Office for Victims of Crime by the United States Department of Justice (USDOJ). Later, with the passage of the **Victims of Crime Act** (commonly referred to as VOCA) and later the Violence Against Women Act (commonly referred to as VAWA), which was passed in the mid 1990s, the rights of crime victims were given more weight in the American criminal justice system. For women, these two pieces of legislation paved the way for a whole series of achievements related to crime and the victimization of women. For instance, the **Office on Violence Against Women** (OVW), created in 1995, was established to provide federal leadership in developing the nation's capacity to reduce violence against women and administer justice for and strengthen services to victims of domestic violence, dating violence, sexual assault, and stalking. The Office on Violence Against Women administers financial and technical assistance to communities across the country that are developing programs, policies, and practices aimed at ending domestic violence, dating violence, sexual assault, and stalking. In fact, the lead author of this text is also the director of a grant-funded project through OVW, to prevent dating violence, sexual assault, and stalking on his home campus in Louisiana.

Violence Against Women Act

In 1994 Congress passed the **Violence Against Women Act (VAWA)** in recognition of the severity of crimes associated with domestic violence, sexual assault, and stalking. This Act emerged from the efforts of a broad, grassroots coalition of advocates and survivors who informed the work of Congress. In the two decades prior to VAWA, a movement had grown within the United States to respond appropriately to violent crimes against women. Rape crisis centers and women's shelters were established in localities, and state and local laws had changed. However, the progress had been uneven around the country. VAWA was borne out of the need for a national solution. This Act enhances the investigation and prosecution of violent crimes against women.

Domestic Violence

The research on the prevalence of domestic violence and its impact on women in the United States is so abundant and obvious that it goes beyond the scope of this chapter to discuss. However, when limiting the discussion to female offenders and their experiences with domestic violence, it appears that they are at greater risk for physical abuse than those in the general population. One survey of female offenders shows that incarcerated women are very likely to have histories of physical abuse (American Correctional Association, 1990). This study indicated that 53 percent of adult women and nearly 62 percent of juvenile girls had been victims of physical abuse. Nearly half of both these groups (49 percent of adults and 47 percent of juveniles) reported experiencing multiple episodes of physical abuse. Furthermore, this study found that this violence is most likely to have been perpetrated by a boyfriend or husband in the case of adult women offenders (50 percent) or by a parent in the case of juvenile girls (43 percent).

For juvenile girls, most of the cases of domestic violence occur between the ages of 10 and 14 years (Bloom, Owen, & Covington, 2003). Adult incarcerated women report being subjected to the most violence at ages 15–24 (Bloom et al., 2003). This means that this abuse tends to follow the female offender throughout their lifespan, indicating that these offenders return to a lifestyle that is self-damaging. Because the women on probation and parole are likely to be somewhat socially isolated from common social circles, her peer network is likely to be limited (Bloom et al., 2003). At best, it will include other women in a similar situation, or perhaps persons from employment (keeping in mind the educational level, unemployment rate, and vocational skills of these women). More likely, these women are likely to continue to associate within the subculture of origin, meaning that many of the friends and family that they return to are likely to be, or have been, criminal offenders themselves. This may be much more common since many women who offend often tend to do so as secondary accomplices with a male primary offender. Thus, these women are not likely to have many resources to rely on and may find themselves quite dependent on a man, including an abusive man.

DEMOGRAPHICS OF THE FEMALE OFFENDER

When discussing female offenders, it becomes clear that the majority of female offenders are minority members. Furthermore, it likewise is the case that these women typically have few options and few economic resources. Thus, many of these offenders are marginalized in multiple ways from the access to success and stability commonly attributed to broader society. As of 2003, roughly 176,300 women were incarcerated in a state prison, federal prison, or local jail. Of these female inmates, about 76,100 or 44 percent were Caucasian American, 66,800 or 38 percent were African American, and 28,300 or 16 percent were Latino American (Harrison & Beck, 2003). Of those women who are incarcerated, approximately 44 percent have no high school diploma or GED and 61 percent were unemployed at the point of incarceration (Bloom et al., 2003). In addition, roughly 47 percent were single prior to incarceration while an approximate 65–70 percent of these women were the primary caretakers of minor children at the point that they were incarcerated (Bloom et al., 2003). Lastly, over one-third of those incarcerated can be found within the jurisdictions of the federal prison system, or the state prison systems of Texas and California (Harrison & Karberg, 2004).

With respect to community supervision, roughly 844,697 female offenders are on probation, with another 87,063 on parole (Bloom et al., 2003). Of those women on community supervision (both probation and parole combined), about 62 percent are Caucasian American, 27 percent are African American, and roughly 10 percent are Latino American (Bloom et al., 2003). Of those women on community supervision, roughly 40 percent have no high school diploma or GED, 42 percent are single while under supervision, and 72 percent are the primary caretakers of children under 18 years of age (Bloom et al., 2003).

Considering the above-mentioned demographic characteristics, we will now discuss several issues that have been found to be commonalities among the female offending population. The remainder of this introduction will consider each subcategory in an attempt to demonstrate the multitude of difficult problems that confound effective intervention for many female offenders.

OTHER ISSUES ASSOCIATED WITH THE FEMALE OFFENDER

Physical and/or Sexual Abuse

A study on the self-reported prior abuse conducted by the Bureau of Justice Statistics in 1999 found that female offenders are abused more frequently than male offenders. State prison inmates reported both physical and sexual abuse experiences prior to their being sentenced. The results found that 57.2 percent of females had experienced abusive treatment compared to 16.1 percent of males. Of this same group, 36.7 percent of the female offenders and 14.4 percent of the male offenders reported that the abuse occurred during their childhood or teenage years. Other findings from this study were:

1. Males tend to be mistreated as children, but females are mistreated as both children and adults.
2. Both genders reported much more abuse if they had lived in a foster home or other structured institution.
3. Higher levels of abuse were reported among offenders who had a family member who was incarcerated.
4. Offenders reporting prior abuse had higher levels of drug and alcohol abuse than those who did not report abuse. Furthermore, female offenders who were abused drugs or alcohol more frequently than did male offenders.

Sex Industry Activity

A large body of research shows that female criminals often have some sort of history of prostitution although the causal factor(s) and the order of causal factors are not very clear. A debate, indeed a schism, exists among researchers as to whether this is the case due to economic necessities or whether prior sexual victimization is at the root of this common form of female offense. Many researchers contend that prior victimization (especially sexual) is at the root, pointing toward the high rate of incidence of sexual abuse among female criminals and the high rate of female criminal's involvement in prostitution.

Sexually Transmitted Diseases

Simply put, sexually transmitted diseases (STDs) are those that are transmitted from one person to another through sexual contact. Because female offenders tend to be highly represented in the illicit sex industry, they are particularly at risk of contracting a STD. According to the Centers for Disease control, roughly 15 million cases of STDs are reported each year. Those within the age range of 15–24 are most at risk, with at least 3 million cases a year being reported from within this demographic group (Epigee, 2004). It is interesting to note that this is also the age range that is most likely to be engaged in criminal activity in general. This once again shows how populations engaging in risky behaviors are also more likely to engage in behaviors that are correspondingly criminal; a point that seems to be intuitively obvious but clearly demonstrates that criminal offending may have a multiplicity of issues surrounding the simple act of offending. Most STDs are treatable. However, even the once easily cured gonorrhea has become resistant to many of the older traditional antibiotics. Other STDs, such as herpes, AIDS, and genital warts, all of which are caused by viruses, have no cure. Some of these infections are very uncomfortable, whereas others can be deadly. Syphilis, AIDS, genital warts, herpes, hepatitis, and even gonorrhea have all been known to cause death (Epigee, 2004).

The Epigee Foundation (2004) notes that "it is important to recognize that sexual contact includes more than just intercourse. Sexual contact includes kissing, oral-genital contact, and the use of sexual 'toys,' such as vibrators. There really is no such thing as 'safe' sex." This is important to note because many offenders simply may not know this or they may not believe that they should have cause for concern. These individuals often believe that they are protecting themselves or are not armed with the information necessary to make prudent sexual choices. This is why offender education on these topics is a necessity.

Lastly, the rate of HIV infection is higher for female offenders than for male offenders. According to the Bureau of Justice Statistics (Snell, 1994), among state prisoners tested for HIV, women were more likely to test positive. An estimated 3.3 percent of the women reported being HIV positive, compared to 2.1 percent of the men. Among prisoners who had shared needles to inject drugs, more women than men were likely to be HIV positive (10 percent vs. 6.7 percent).

Drug Abuse

Drug use is a major contributor to female criminality. Female offenders use drugs more often than male offenders, although differences are not extreme and research focuses mostly on arrested and incarcerated subjects. Consider this: between 1985 and 1994, women's drug arrests increased 100 percent whereas men's drug arrests increased only by about 50 percent. Regardless, the point is that when dealing with female offenders, addressing drug use is critical to prevent recidivism. Furthermore, female offenders engage in riskier drug habits than male offenders as they report higher levels of needle usage and needle sharing (Snell, 1994). This social problem is further compounded because a high number of female offenders who are intravenous drug users likewise engage in prostitution and work in the sex industry to support their habit.

Mental Health Issues among Female Offenders

Mental health issues for female offenders are often tied to stages in their lifecycle and development, such as with puberty, adolescence, and phases of reproductive development (Seiden, 1989). However, because a disturbing number of women are sexually and physically abused as girls and as adult women, attention has been focused on the anxiety, depression, and other psychological illnesses resulting from these events (Seiden, 1989). The trauma of early sexual and physical abuse may be manifested in **borderline personality disorder** and **multiple personality disorder** as well as the more common **post-traumatic stress disorders** and alcoholism (Seiden 1989). As with most forms of mental illness, these disorders develop largely in response to stressors that push an already over-taxed psyche. Indeed, because of their higher rates of abuse and victimization, coupled with their drug offending, female offenders may have numerous "predispositions" that make them prone to mental illness when the stressor of incarceration is presented as a life experience.

Depression is a very common mental illness among the incarcerated and is even more pronounced among the female offending population because this is a disorder that tends to have higher prevalence rates among females in the general society. Furthermore, depression is a common symptom and dual diagnosis among drug abusers; hence, when the numerous problem variables are taken together, female offenders are found to be very susceptible to bouts of depression and to the full array of mood disorders.

Male offenders tend to mask their depression with anger and aggressive reactions, which serve as defensive "fronts" or displays of force that mask their underlying depression. Much of this is due to socialization, but for women, their socialization tends to ensure that their symptoms of depression are recognized for what they are. Thus, men who are incarcerated may simply be diagnostically labeled as aggressive and, when in a prison environment, this can go one step further into a classification of being assaultive. Though from the view of institutional security this is accurate, it nonetheless fails to detect the sense of depression that the male inmate may be experiencing. On the other hand, for female inmates, socialization provides a ready tolerance for acts of depression and the expression of emotional sorrow; thus, prevalence rates among female and male inmates in prison may be compounded by social expectations and norms that prison staff are accustomed to. Furthermore, as would be expected, prior abuse plays a role in addiction and depression, further cementing these two variables together as correlates among female offenders.

THE FEMALE OFFENDER AS SINGLE MOTHER

In 2007, female offenders in the criminal justice system were mothers to approximately 1.3 million children. Many female offenders under criminal justice supervision face losing custody of their children. Some female offenders do have relatives or friends who will care for their children while they are incarcerated but many do not. For those who are able to arrange placement with relatives, the likelihood of permanent separation between mother and child is significantly reduced. It has been observed that maternal grandmothers most often care for the children of female prison inmates (Bloom, Brown, & Chesney-Lind, 1996). If a mother is unable to place her children with relatives or friends, the local child welfare agency will most likely place the child in foster care. When children of imprisoned mothers are placed in foster care, caseworkers are expected to make concerted efforts to sustain family ties and to encourage family reunification (Bloom et al., 1996). Most incarcerated mothers, particularly those who are mentally ill, do not have access to the resources they need to meet other reunification requirements imposed by the court, such as parent education, counseling, drug treatment, and job training. Upon release form custody to community corrections, mothers face numerous obstacles in reunifying with their children. They must navigate through a number of complex governmental and social service agencies in order to regain custody of their children. Although differences may exist across jurisdictions, in many cases, it is considered to be beyond the purview of probation and parole agencies to intervene in child custody cases.

Box 4.1 Female Offenders as Mothers—"Thinking Out of the Box"

In an attempt to alleviate some of the pains of imprisonment for female offenders who are mothers and for children who have mothers in prison, the use of child nurseries has been developed in some prison systems. Child nurseries are an excellent concept for both the female offender and the child. These programs help female offenders "learn to become effective mothers" with a focus on meeting the mental health needs of both the mother and the child.

The Healthcare for pregnant inmates and Women and Infants at-Risk Program is a residential rehabilitation program in Detroit. It facilitates the natural relationship between mother and child. Inmates enter the program prenatally after 28 weeks and stay in the program up to 6 months post-partum.

Motheread Programs, such as those in North Carolina, simultaneously improves the literacy of female inmates and creates stronger bonds between mother and child. Mothers read to their children and write the stories to improve their own literacy.

Girl Scouts Beyond Bars with National Institute of Justice. Girls from 5 to 13 years join their mothers two Saturdays a month for a Girl Scout troop meeting in prison or jail. These are two-hour sessions where troop projects are carried out.

When fathers are incarcerated, there is usually a mother left at home to care for the children. However, when mothers are incarcerated, there is not usually a father in the home. This situation is further exacerbated by the fact that there are fewer women's prisons and because of the rarity of female prison units they tend to be at great distances from one another and from the likely location from which the female offender lived prior to incarceration. Because of this, there is a greater risk that female offenders will be incarcerated at a greater distance from their children than males (Bloom et al., 1996). Indeed, an average female inmate is more than 160 miles farther from her family than a male inmate and at least half the children of imprisoned mothers have either not seen or not visited their mothers since they were incarcerated (Bloom et al., 1996). This low rate of contact between mother and child tends to weaken family bonds, which then causes psychological and emotional damage both to the child and to the incarcerated mother. This low rate of contact also has a negative effect on the female offenders themselves, as recidivism rates tend to increase when inmate mothers have diminished contact with their children (Bloom et al., 1996).

Separation between Mother and Child

The separation between mother and child causes what has been called "**collateral damage**" to children and society by the current incarceration trends of female offenders who typically commit property and/or drug crimes (Crawford, 2002). Although female offenders separated from their children are at an increased risk of later recidivism, the damage done to the children is probably more serious than to the adult when a parent is incarcerated (Bloom et al., 1996; Crawford, 2002). A number of children display symptoms of posttraumatic stress disorder, namely depression, feelings of anger and guilt, flashbacks about their mother's crimes or arrests, and the experience of hearing their mother's voice.

The practice of incarcerating women who are mothers of minor children is extremely damaging and costly for the society (Crawford, 2002). It harms both the children during their developmental stages and their parent. The children are more likely to enter into the criminal justice system than their peers who do not have incarcerated parents, and the mother who is separated from her child is more likely to recidivate herself. This form of intervention is likely to cost society untold billions within the next generation, again resulting in ever more collateral damage (Crawford, 2002).

CURRENT EVENTS IN MULTICULTURAL CRIMINAL JUSTICE
Female Offenders as Mothers in Prison

As we have noted in this chapter, many female offenders who are in prison are often mothers (and were primary caretakers) of children. This issue, as a current event, is still one that has not been adequately addressed by most state correctional systems. In a report by the Rebecca Project and by the National Women's Law Center (2010), it was found the 38 states did not provide adequate prenatal care to incarcerated pregnant women. In addition, 36 states continued to shackle women during pregnancies without making allowances for their medical circumstances or for those of the expected newborn. This study also found that 17 states had no family-based treatment programs. Likewise, 38 states had no prison nursery for women giving birth so that mother-child bonding could occur.

The personal conditions for these women often have substance abuse as the central problem. For instance, consider the efforts of Kellie Phelan, who in 2007 was an expecting mother while serving a 90-day jail sentence related to an ongoing crack addiction – she ended up having her child while in jail (Berger, 2012). For Phelan, this proved to be a life-changing event after she found help with Hour Children, a non-profit organization that aids convicted mothers in the state of New York (Berger, 2012). In her case, unlike in many states, services were available for her.

With these conditions in mind, individuals who can identify with these circumstances sometimes volunteer their time to aid women in this plight. Sister Teresa Fitzgerald, the founder of Hour Children, has devoted substantial time and effort to aid these women (Berger, 2012), seemingly in response to the dearth of services that have been noted by the study conducted by the Rebecca Project and the National Women's Law Center (2010).

Programs like Hour Children are often staffed by volunteers, many of whom were themselves in similar circumstances as the consumers of their services, at one time. This is the case of Phelan, who now works with the program leading support groups and mentoring women who face pregnancy and other parenting issues while in the justice system (Berger, 2012).

Most recently, this issue has caught the attention of Hollywood, with celebrities on television such as Piper Kerman, playing on the series, *Orange is the New Black*. This series that has been viewed by millions highlights the challenges faced by women who are incarcerated.

Since filming this series, Kerman has advocated for mothers behind bars, noting the detrimental effect that incarceration has on the children of these mothers. She has also showcased the challenges involved when women are incarcerated in remote geographical regions, far from family with whom the child may be staying, making it difficult for families to participate in visitation programs. Further, many of these women and their families are economically challenged and the expense of the travel may limit prospects for visitation all the more.

This connection is important for the child and is also important for women doing time. Staying connected with the outside aids their ability to cope with incarceration and also aids their reintegration back into the community. Kerman has written about these challenges in a The New York Times op-ed column, increasing awareness on how the lack of more effective programming does not provide any additional benefit to crime prevention or public safety initiatives and, in actuality, just adds future costs to taxpayers and also adds suffering and trauma to those who do not deserve it.

It is important for students to understand that this issue impacts minority women and, by extension minority communities, disproportionately. As we have seen in previous chapters, economic deprivation is more common among minority groups in any society. These various factors coalesce into a scenario where minority women are disproportionately incarcerated (as are minority men), leading to a disproportionate number of minority children having one or both parents behind bars. All of these factors serve to exacerbate, one with the other, the circumstances for entire communities, not just the individual mothers and their child.

References: Rebecca Project for Human Rights & National Women's Law Center (2010). Mothers behind bars: a state-by-state report card and analysis of federal policies on conditions of confinement for pregnant and parenting women and the effect on their children. Washington, DC: National Women's Law Center.

Berger, D. (2012, August 10). Nun helps moms in prison move past their mistakes. CNN Heroes, retrieved from http://www.cnn.com/2012/08/09/us/cnnheroes-fitzgerald-hour-children/index.html

Huffington Post (2013, August 15). *'Orange Is The New Black' Author Piper Kerman Advocates For Community-Based Sentences For Women*. Retrieved from: http://www.huffingtonpost.com/news/mothers-in-prison

Negative Effect on Children

Children of incarcerated mothers display other negative effects such as school-related difficulties, depression, low self-esteem, aggressive behavior, and general emotional dysfunction (Bloom et al., 1996). These effects can be very pronounced and show how an "intergenerational transmission" of criminality can occur if interventions are not provided. For instance, some studies on children of incarcerated mothers have found that 40 percent of the boys aged 12–17 were delinquent, whereas the rate of teenage pregnancy among female children of incarcerated mothers was 60 percent (Bloom et. al., 1996). Frequently, the children are left with a caregiving arrangement that is inadequate, unreliable, or irregular, and this causes further long-term damage to the development of the child. Because of these deprivations and traumas, children of incarcerated parents may be six times more likely than their counterparts to become incarcerated themselves (Bloom et. al., 1996).

Problems with fetal alcohol syndrome and other forms of fetus damage from mothers who are substance abusers have majority of offenders in prison with women pushing perhaps 8 percent of the entire U.S. prison population (Clear, Cole, & Reisig, 2009). To ensure that the numbers are kept in perspective, consider that at the end of 2003, U.S. prisons held 1,368,866 men, which equates to a 2 percent compared to 2002. This means that in 2003, 1 in every 109 men was in prison. For women the figure was 1 in every 1,613. It should be noted that because of the War on Drugs, and because of the extended sentences associated with that era, many women were incarcerated for lengthier sentences and this has helped fuel the growth in the female inmate population. Given the rates of drug use among female offenders, the growth in their numbers behind bars is not surprising.

GAY AND LESBIAN EMPLOYEES OF THE CRIMINAL JUSTICE SYSTEM

This section largely focuses on the gay/lesbian population as criminal justice practitioners and also as victims within society. Unlike other groups of minorities, the gay and lesbian population is not covered under the Civil Rights Act, the Americans with Disabilities Act, or the Equal Rights Amendment. These lack of protections have enabled a culture in many criminal justice agencies that is anti-gay in nature or, at the very least, not tolerant of same-sex partner preference. Given the paramilitary nature of most criminal justice organizations and the fact that law enforcement and corrections tend to be conservative by nature, it is not surprising that gay and lesbian practitioners experience difficulties in these agencies.

Lifestyle

There are many challenges to providing effective police services in the gay community in most areas of the United States. Indeed, in order to do so, it would be expected that the agency would need to have at least some gay police officers within its ranks as a reflection of the population that it serves. However, it is difficult to hire gay police officers because of the stigma that still surrounds openly gay persons in organizational cultures such as with police agencies. As a result, the problem is self-perpetuating. In recent years, there have been cases where officers have filed suit in Los Angeles and New York due to harassment and discrimination from other officers on the force. This reflects the changing times, increased level of acceptance, and better recognized rights that gay and lesbian persons have in law enforcement.

Prior to this decade, there was open discrimination and a hostile environment toward gay and lesbian persons in policing. For instance, it was until 1991 that the psychological exam administered to LAPD applicants contained questions inquiring into the applicant's attraction to members of the same sex. Other agencies also allowed discrimination against gay and lesbian members throughout the 1980s and the 1990s as well. For instance, in New Jersey, police officers could be fired for being identified as homosexual until 1989 and the Dallas Police Department refused to hire gay candidates due to state laws that prohibited such behavior. In fact, the FBI terminated investigators who were found to be homosexual (Barlow & Barlow, 2000).

Today, most openly gay and lesbian police officers are employed in large urban police departments where they are more likely to be accepted and tolerated than in the smaller police agencies that are typically rural in nature. Even in these jurisdictions, gay and lesbian officers often find it necessary to lead double-lives, hiding their true sexual orientation from their fellow officers. This can cause very serious strain and psychological pressure on these individuals who must remain "in the closet," so to speak. This strain has been correlated with higher rates of suicide, alcoholism, and stress-related health problems (Arnott, 1994).

Furthermore, gay officers who do speak of their experiences often report a fear of being exposed and the potential for becoming victims of harassment. In addition, in their own spare time, these officers often must exercise care to not be seen in areas frequented by the gay community for fear of being identified by other officers. Moreover, gay officers may be hesitant to inform other members of the gay community that they are police officers due to bias within the community against the police (Barlow & Barlow, 2000).

Lastly, within the field of corrections, there is very little research on practitioners who are gay or lesbian. This is true for both the institutional- and community-based components of the profession. Although there are persons who are gay or lesbian who work in these areas of the criminal justice system, their roles are less public in nature and usually are not as prominently observable, because of this. While some members of their agency may be aware of their sexual preference or may at least suspect, the culture within community supervision agencies tends not to be as pronounced and, even in institutional corrections, gay or lesbian staff are able to mask their identity better.

Although this should not be necessary, there are some complications in institutional corrections that are not present in community correctional agencies or police agencies. First, within many prison subcultures, there is at least a topical reference to men who are "punked out" or made to play a subservient role among inmates. The inmate culture tends to have a negative view of the same-sex population, holding them to be lowest on the pecking order among inmates, being second only to pedophile sex offenders. If staff hold this identity, they are likely to have a difficult time gaining respect and maintaining control of inmates under their supervision. Likewise, there is concern (whether founded or unfounded) that such staff will be more prone to engage in inappropriate sexual contact with inmates under their supervision. This also means that, within prison and jail facilities, gay or lesbian personnel may be held under much more scrutiny by inmates and by fellow officers and, as such, will experience a lack of acceptance as well as a constant sense of skepticism and intimidation within these types of institutions.

Professionalism in Agencies

With regard to behavior on the job, there is often an unwritten perception among persons in criminal justice agencies that the same-sex population should conform themselves to heterosexual standards (Arnott, 1994; Toth, Crews, & Burton, 2008). Much of the resentment toward gay and lesbian officers is fed not only by the fear that these officers may carry HIV, but also the belief that such behavior is immoral and/or reprehensible. These biases can produce circumstances that are dangerous for the gay or lesbian officer who may not get support from his or her coworkers during calls for backup, whether as police or as correctional officers within a prison facility. Naturally, this is extremely unprofessional behavior amongst other members of the agency as the provision of support for one's fellow officers is the top-order priority in both fields of work.

Coping for Gay/Lesbian Employees in Paramilitary Agencies

Many police and corrections experts have indicated that, because of the "macho" image and requirements maintained by police and corrections agencies, a double standard exists with respect to the manner in which gay and lesbian colleagues are viewed. The traditional male dominance of the profession has made it difficult for many male officers to accept that women or gay males are equally capable of performing the same tasks. Many male police officers view their work as being reserved for the strongest and toughest. In fact, a male officer's self-esteem can be threatened by the ability of women and gay men to do this type of work successfully, because this contradicts many of the messages that are transmitted within the cultures of many paramilitary organizations.

Nevertheless, there are changes that are occurring, particularly in policing. Examples abound, such with the Baltimore, Maryland Police Department. This agency has made strides to provide for police liaisons between the agency and the gay community. Much of this stems from high-profile incidents where members of the gay community have been victimized, including the slaying of a married lesbian couple in Northeast Baltimore, a fatal shooting outside a lesbian club, and a series of attacks in Mount Vernon, a hub to the city's gay community (Fenton, 2009). A similar liaison unit has been established in the District of Columbia's Metropolitan Police Department. Although change has been slow, the fact that these police departments recognize the need for such units is indicative of the trends that are occurring in policing.

On the other hand, even in states that have been recognized to accept gay and lesbian relationships officially, even by marriage, problems still emerge. In 2007, a high-profile suit against the New York Police Department (Hartocollis, 2007) emerged due to claims of constant harassment against Officer Michael Harrington. These claims occurred prior to New York's passage of legislation recognizing gay marriage, but are reflective of underlying biases that are held by police members, regardless of the legal status that gay men or lesbian women may have within a given jurisdiction.

A study by Myers, Forest, and Miller (2004) demonstrates that, despite attempts to expand social diversity, policing is still dominated by a white, masculine, heterosexual ethos. Consequently, they content that employment of lesbians and gay men as police officers may be especially threatening to members of this occupation. Their study found that within the context of potential hostility and homophobia, nontraditional officers must negotiate their contradictory presence on the police force. Myers et al. (2004) investigated the process of negotiating these roles and coping with traditional police culture. They used the Bem Sex Role Inventory as well as open survey data from samples of open gay and lesbian officers as well as those who kept their same-sex preferences secret to determine how both groups managed their images as "good cops" in the face of gender norm violations associated with their sexual orientation (p. 17).

The findings by Myers et al. (2004) indicated that masculinity and femininity did not hold together in a cohesive, dichotomous manner for officers in their study. Instead, these officers relied on other characteristics that enhanced policing to support their sense of occupational competence. These officers saw themselves as good cops, in the process. The gendered/sexualized character of their self-perceptions mattered less than the context of the job when compared with a sample of heterosexual police officers. As a result, Myers et al. (2004) concluded that though gay and lesbian officers saw their sexuality as an occupational asset, they were also likely to work harder to prove themselves as effective police officers.

Myers et al. (2004) concluded that being a good cop was the major driving motivation behind the actions of gay and lesbian officers. The definition of being a "good cop" remained, for these officers, within the parameters of the traditional police subculture (p. 35). Thus, even though these individuals would struggle to navigate between competing internal messages regarding their own views on sex and sexism and those externally conveyed in the organization, they ultimately tended to go along with the culture of the organization due to fear of negative consequences. It is perhaps ironic, then, that fears that gay or lesbian officers may be more lenient on crime fighting were contrary to what was found to typically be the truth. Rather, the gay and lesbian officers were instead found to be more vigorously staying within the constrained definitions of the police role. Such findings demonstrate the challenges that these officers tend to experience in coping with the oppressive and intolerant nature that may exist within many agencies.

An Organizational Culture of Tolerance

As the issue of sexual orientation has become a more mainstream topic in public, gay and lesbian individuals have become more assertive and willing to confront discrimination. Recent events, such as the legal marriage of same-sex partners in states such as New York, as well as television portrayal of gay persons in criminal justice agencies have provided some impetus for this stance among the same-sex population. Fearful of litigation and negative publicity, most police and community supervision agencies have removed discriminatory language from their hiring criteria. Nevertheless, strong bias against this population continues to exist within many criminal justice agencies, but this bias is often covert rather than overt in nature.

The past decade has seen the removal of the explicit ban against the hiring of gay men and lesbians by most law enforcement and correctional agencies. Even though this has been the official trend, reality remains that the majority of police and correctional agencies seem to utilize means to surreptitiously avoid hiring members of the gay community. In some states, sodomy laws have been used to disqualify applicants, with the notion being that gay males will have a propensity to violate this law. In 2003, this practice was made void due to the Supreme Court ruling in **Lawrence v. Texas**, where the Texas anti-sodomy law had been struck down. This ruling invalidated similar laws in a total of 13 states. Thus, ultimately, agencies could not use sodomy laws as a rationale for not hiring gay applicants.

Despite the law, rejection of the gay community in some police and correctional agencies continues. As times change and public views on sexuality become more open, the tendency for agencies to continue with this discrimination does seem to be decreasing. Indeed, studies have shown that the presence of openly lesbian, gay, and bisexual personnel have not negatively impacted morale or unit cohesion in integrated police departments (Belkin & McNichol, 2002) as well as in the military (Belkin &

INTERNATIONAL FOCUS

Legal Precedents for the Gay/Lesbian Population in the International Community

There is also a precedent for using international legal developments regarding laws related to the gay/lesbian population in the United States. One important case was *Lawrence vs. Texas* (2003), which struck down state anti-sodomy laws that had been upheld by the Supreme Court in a prior case known as **Bowers v. Hardwick** (1986). In his sweeping majority opinion, Justice Kennedy referred to a similar case decided by the European Court of Human Rights. In particular, Justice Kennedy leveled his comments toward opinions enunciated by Chief Justice Burger, who alluded to the history of Western civilization and to Judeo-Christian moral and ethical standards as appropriate rationale for the decision in *Bowers*. In contradiction, Justice Kennedy noted that Chief Justice Burger did not take account European authorities who held opposing positions on the issue of homosexuality. Further illustrating his point, Justice Kennedy wrote that:

A committee advising the British Parliament recommended in 1957 repeal of laws punishing homosexual conduct. The Wolfenden Report: Report of the Committee on Homosexual Offenses and Prostitution (1963). Parliament enacted the substance of those recommendations 10 years later. Sexual Offences Act 1967, §1. Of even more importance, almost five years before *Bowers* was decided the European Court of Human Rights considered a case with parallels to *Bowers* and to today's case. An adult male resident in Northern Ireland alleged he was a practicing homosexual who desired to engage in consensual homosexual conduct. The laws of Northern Ireland forbade him that right. He alleged that he had been questioned, his home had been searched, and he feared criminal prosecution. The court held that the laws proscribing the conduct were invalid under the European Convention on Human Rights. *Dudgeon v. United Kingdom*, 45 Eur. Ct. H. R. (1981); 52. Authoritative in all countries that are members of the Council of Europe (21 nations then, 45 nations now), the decision is at odds with the premise in *Bowers* that the claim put forward was insubstantial in our Western civilization (p. 564).

As can be seen from the quote above, Justice Kennedy points out that the European Court's ruling holds authority throughout all countries who are members of the Council of Europe, and he even indicates that the United State's lack of agreement on this fundamental issue indicated that the Court should rethink its analysis of the issue.

Although some Justices, namely Justice Scalia, have been very resistant to the use of foreign jurisprudence as a means of formulating legal decisions in the United States, it is clear that the majority of the Court does not agree. Leavitt (2003) notes that while critics may assert that *Atkins*, *Grutter*, and *Lawrence* are aberrations rather than a sign of a larger shift in legal analysis on the part of the Supreme Court, it still stands that lawyers continue to file an increasing number of amicus briefs addressing international law. It is safe to say that, just as in the prior case law, the High Court will continue to consider the content of those briefs, just as it has done in the past (Leavitt, 2003).

McNichol, 2002). The fact that President Barak Obama initiated reform for gay men and women who serve in the military, allowing this population to serve while openly admitting to being gay, demonstrates how times have changed and continue to change toward more inclusive attitudes regarding sexual preference.

Discrimination in the Professional Setting

Status issues such as gender or race impact quality of life for the gay population employed within criminal justice agencies. In most cases, lesbians are subjected to less hostility than are gay men. This is likely due to the belief that lesbians are hyper-masculine and thus conform to the image of criminal justice employee, whereas gay men are usually thought of as being effeminate. Another reason may be that, simply put, men in an agency (and most agencies tend to be male dominated) are not questioned of their own sexuality among lesbians; identification with gay males may put into question their own sense of sexuality. Indeed, there is the perception among some men that two women being intimate with one another is erotic, but this is not generally the case for men when considering gay male sexual relations (Burke, 1994).

Much of the resentment toward gay and lesbian officers is fed not only by the fear that such officers may have HIV, but also by the belief that this type of behavior is morally reprehensible. Such resentment can sometimes be life threatening when other officers refuse to respond to calls for backup and other needed assistance. Many criminal justice agencies are largely populated by men, and this can lead to issues concerning their perceptions of their own masculinity, making the presence of a gay male officer seemingly a threat to the heterosexual officer's masculine identity (Barlow & Barlow, 2000). Because of this, lesbian officers are seemingly more accepted within the law enforcement community, at least among male officers (Barlow & Barlow, 2000).

Ultimately, the chief executive officer of an agency must establish departmental policies and regulations with regard to gay and lesbian employees. These policies should clearly note that discrimination, harassment, or a failure to assist fellow gay or lesbian members is unacceptable and such behaviors should carry serious penalties. All employees must be held accountable by these rules and those who refuse to support such nondiscrimination policies should be restricted from promotion or from desirable assignments. Evaluations of employees should reflect support from the agency for gay and lesbian officers. Lastly, agency executives should also remain aware that gay and lesbian officers may not report victimization by other employees and should, therefore, remain vigilant for any covert discriminatory behavior within their agency.

HATE CRIMES AGAINST THE GAY AND LESBIAN POPULATION

Violent Actions

Every year in the United States, thousands of gay, lesbian, and transgender persons are harassed, beaten, or murdered solely because of their sexual orientation or gender identity. According to the National Gay and Lesbian Task Force, hate violence against **LGBT** people has increased dramatically over the past decade, even when violent crime in the United States declined (National Gay & Lesbian Task Force News, 2000).

The FBI's Hate Crime Statistics in 2009 indicated that 17.8 percent of all hate crime victims were targeted because of a bias against a particular sexual orientation.

During this year, the FBI reported that 1,482 persons were victims of hate crimes due to sexual orientation within the following categories:

- 55.1 percent were victims because of an offender's anti-male homosexual bias.
- 26.4 percent were victims because of an anti-homosexual bias.
- 15.3 percent were victims because of an anti-female homosexual bias.
- 1.8 percent were victims because of an anti-bisexual bias.

Clearly, from the percentages above, it can be seen that the strongest bias seems to exist against the gay male population. This is, of course, consistent with other sources regarding bias against the same-sex population.

Going beyond the category of incidents, anti-LGBT murders are often distinguished from other murders by the level of brutality involved. LGBT murder victims are often dismembered, stabbed multiple times, or severely beaten. According to the National Coalition of Anti Violence Programs (NCAVP), the following statistics occurred in 2008:

- Of the total injuries reported in 2008, 216 (46 percent) were classified as—serious, meaning that the injury required medical attention.
- 2008, with 29 total murders, has the highest number of deaths since 1999, and an increase of 28 percent from 2007.
- Weapons use during the commission of a hate crime increased significantly; at least 382 out of the total 1,677 incidents (23 percent) involved weapons use in 2008.

The data presented above demonstrates that not only are the numbers of incidents increasing, but their level of violence is also increasing.

Sexual Harassment

A common form of discrimination that gay, lesbian, bisexual, and transgendered persons face in the criminal justice system is sexual harassment. This is encountered among employees and offenders processed through the system, alike. For clarity, we define **sexual harassment** as unwelcome sexual behavior directed at an individual, which makes them feel offended, humiliated, or intimidated, and in the circumstances, it is reasonable to conclude that this behavior would make a person feel this way. Both men and women can sexually harass and be harassed. Lastly, sexual harassment has nothing to do with mutual attraction and friendship between people. Consider the following example:

Box 4.2 Example of Sexual Harassment

Tim works at a steel works. One of his co-workers often asked personal question about his sexual preference and sex life. In the lunch room he suggested that Tim frequented gay bars, 'often had sex with little boys' and implied that he is a paedophile. Tim is being subjected to sexual harassment.

Source: Anti-Discrimination Commission Queensland (2009). Tracking your rights, lesbian, gay, transgender, and intersex people. Brisbane, AU.

Another common form of harassment that can occur, though not necessarily on the worksite, is vilification. **Vilification** is publicly inciting others to hate, have serious contempt for, or severely ridicule people because of their race, religion, sexuality, or gender identity. Vilification, like sexual harassment, is unlawful and often goes hand-in-hand with the commission of hate crimes against members of the LGBT population. Indeed, if this incitement involves threats of physical harm to people or their property, it is an assault and should be considered a hate crime. Consider this example for clarification:

Box 4.3 Example of Gender Identity Vilification

Gender identity vilification:

Bobbi is a 'sister girl'. One day she was sitting in the mall, having a break while shopping and was approached by one member of a group. The person verbally abused and taunted her because of her transgender status. When she didn't respond he encouraged his friends to join in the ridicule and harassment, and threatened to beat her up.

Source: Anti-Discrimination Commission Queensland. (2009). *Tracking your rights, lesbian, gay, transgender, and intersex people.* Brisbane, AU.

OTHER FORMS OF VICTIMIZATION

Of all concerns for the gay and lesbian community, becoming a crime victim is perhaps one of the greatest fears that impact this population. Anti-gay violence often is the result of homophobia among perpetrators of this type of crime. In defining **homophobia**, we will use a definition from Berrill (1994), in which the term refers to "the longstanding persistent, and baseless notion that gay and lesbian people are sick, evil, predatory people who hate and fear the opposite sex and who molest children" (p. 114). Homophobic individuals tend to view gay and lesbian persons as being one-dimensional, as if their sexual identity is the only aspect of their sense-of-self. Furthermore, homophobes—as the term is called for persons who are homophobic—tend to blame the gay population for three issues in society: HIV/AIDS, pedophilia, and the undermining of religious institutions (Perry, 2001; Toth, Crews, & Burton, 2008).

Lastly, there seems to be a connection between anti-gay violence and extreme rightwing religious views. In such cases, negative views of gay/lesbian community tend to be Biblical rhetoric that justifies the actions of those who discriminate and/or victimize this group. Perpetrators of anti-gay violence often consider the victims to be an abomination, using scripture from the Bible to substantiate their claim (Perry, 2001; Toth, Crews, & Burton, 2008). In a similar vein, many religious extremists in various Christian churches held the HIV/AIDS virus to be a punishment from God targeted at the gay population during the early 1980s, largely due to the fact that, at that time, it was thought that the virus was only transmitted by anal and oral sexual activity, such sexual activity being the primary means of sexual intimacy among the gay population.

Primary and Secondary Victimization

It has been suggested that the gay/lesbian population may experience victimization at two different levels (Berrill & Herek, 1992). The first is when they are directly victimized by the perpetrator and the second is when they are essentially double-victimized by society, particularly when they seek assistance for the initial victimization that they have endured. This initial victimization is referred to as **primary victimization**, and simply refers to the point at which a person becomes a direct victim of crime. **Secondary victimization**, on the other hand, is the negative response that the victim receives from the community, from the criminal justice, and or social services system, and from family, friends, coworkers, and other people whom they know (Berrill & Herek, 1992; Toth, Crews, & Burton, 2008). The issue of secondary victimization is important because this reflects the level at which a community has accepted its gay or lesbian population and, even more importantly, this can add to the trauma that these persons experience from their initial victimization. The lack of support and sense of alienation prevent these individuals from getting the care and assistance needed and can add to both the physical and emotional trauma that is experienced by these victims.

Victim Characteristics

According to the National Coalition of Anti-Violence Programs (2009), for the LGBT population, gay men and lesbians tend to consist of the majority of those reporting incidents to participating programs. This group represents 79 percent of all victims for whom sexual orientation was known. Bisexual-identified victims represented about 6 percent of reports whereas those who questioned their sexual orientation represented 2 percent (National Coalition of Anti-Violence Programs, 2009). Two percent of victims provided a self-identifying label such as queer. Figure 4-3 provides an overview of these statistics in a pie chart format.

Those identifying as heterosexual constitute 9 percent of victims, up slightly from the 6 percent who identified as such in 2007. Only a portion of these reports are from people of transgender experience who identify as heterosexual (see Figure 4-3). According to the National Coalition of Anti-Violence Programs (2009), perpetrators seldom differentiate between sexual orientation and gender identity in the bias-motivation for their attacks.

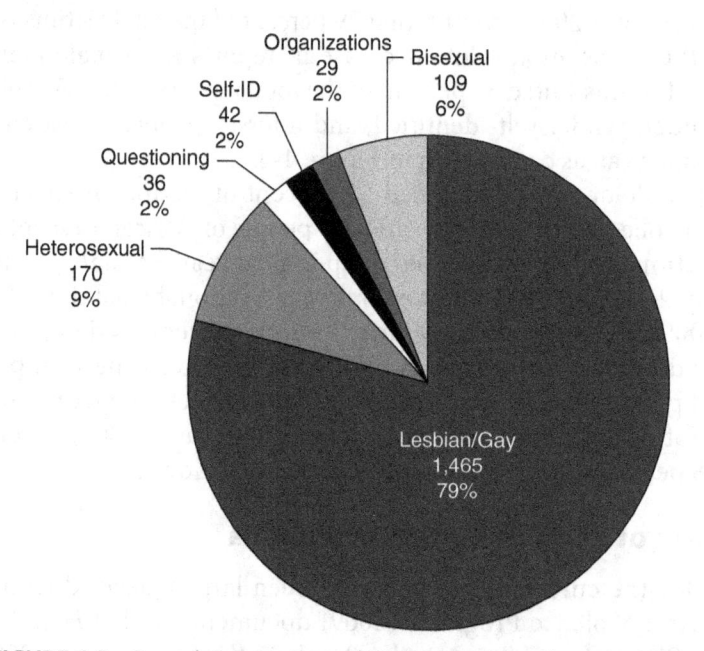

FIGURE 4-3 Sexual Orientation of Victims and Survivors in 2008.
Source: National Coalition of Anti-Violence Programs (2009).

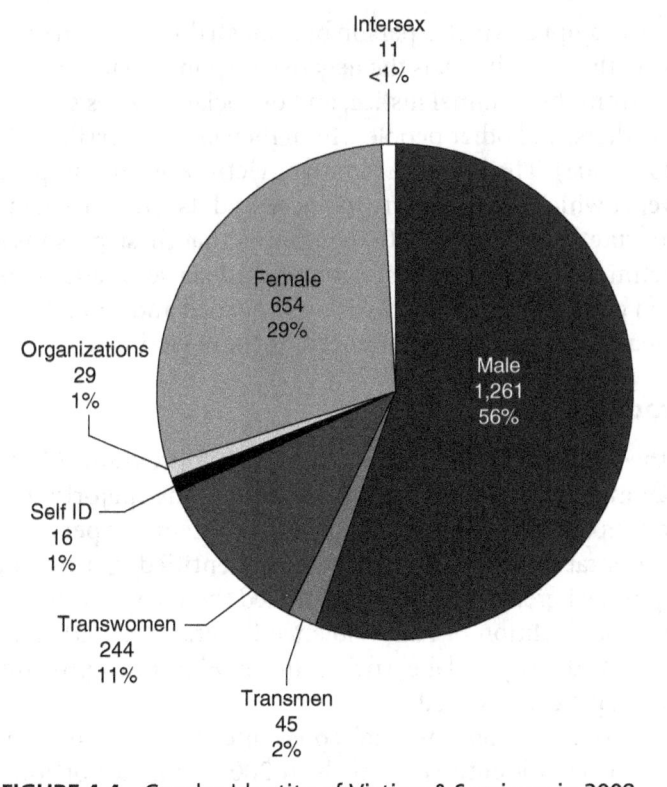

FIGURE 4-4   Gender Identity of Victims & Survivors in 2008.
Source: National Coalition of Anti-Violence Programs (2009).

Furthermore, it was found that there was an absolute increase of female-identified victims (6 percent over 2007), constituting 29 percent of the total victims (see Figure 4-4). In addition, there was an absolute decrease in reports from male identified victims (–3 percent), who constituted 56 percent of the total reports to NCAVP in 2008. Reports from transgender, gender self-identified, and intersex people increased by 12 percent during this same year, as can be seen in Figure 4-4.

Lastly, people of color comprised 52 percent of victims or survivors for whom data had been collected in 2008. Specifically, people of African descent constituted 20 percent of victims, up 3 percent over the previous year. Latina/o victims comprised 23 percent, up 2 percent from the previous year (National Coalition of Anti-Violence Programs, 2009). People of Arab/Middle Eastern descent made up about 3 percent of victims, as did those identifying as multi-racial. Native American people made up 2 percent and people of Asian descent comprised 1 percent of victims, down 2 percent from 2007 (National Coalition of Anti-Violence Programs, 2009). Caucasian persons comprised 48 percent of the total for whom race was known.

Victimization of LGBT Offenders in Prisons

The content for the current subsection has been largely derived from the National Coalition of Anti-Violence Programs (2009) document entitled *Hate Violence against Lesbian, Gay, Bisexual, and Transgender People in the United States, 2008*. This document provides an accurate, modern, and clear account of the plight of gay, lesbian, bisexual, and transgendered individuals who are kept behind bars. With this in mind, it is fairly common knowledge that LGBT inmates are at heightened risk of sexual abuse and sexual assault in prison facilities. Supreme Court rulings, such as ***Farmer v. Brennan***, have spoken to this issue and the parameters involved when liability can be attached to prison administrations.

As expected, LGBT inmates are often targeted for abuse because of their sexual orientation and/or gender identity. As with their status in broader society, these individuals are marginalized by the prison subculture, including both inmates and many correctional staff who have biases toward the LGBT population and/or who believe that such abuse is simply part of the cost of doing crime. In male prison facilities, the power hierarchy is shaped firmly by concepts that put a premium on strength and masculinity—and that places gay, bisexual, and transgender inmates firmly at the bottom of the social structure. Similarly, in facilities for female inmates, studies have shown that lesbian, bisexual, and gender non-conforming inmates in women's prisons are targeted by other inmates as well as by staff. Nevertheless, butch or gender non-conforming women and transgender men are frequently viewed as potential predators and automatically placed in punitive segregation—not for their own protection, but for the protection of other inmates.

Gay, bisexual, and transgender inmates entering male prisons and jails are often seen as fair game for attacks upon arrival, and marked as targets for further abuse that frequently continues for the duration of their time in detention. Survivors in men's prisons tend to be labeled as punks, queens, or described as having been turned out. Those who sexually abuse LGBT inmates use a range of tactics, from violent attacks to more subtle coercion. For example, powerful inmates often offer protection to vulnerable inmates in exchange for sexual and other favors—a phenomenon known as protective pairing or hooking up. Entering into such a relationship can give vulnerable inmates a sense of control and can sometimes prevent more brutal attacks. In some protective pairing scenarios, the survivor may develop feelings of gratitude and affection for, or positive identification with, the more powerful partner. These feelings can make the arrangement appear to be consensual to observers. However, the more powerful inmate always sets the terms of the relationship and the survivor is not able freely to choose to end the relationship, mirroring the dynamics of domestic violence in the community. In especially egregious cases, the vulnerable inmate's body becomes a commodity that is offered to friends, exchanged for contraband or commissary items, and used to pay off debts.

Corrections officials tend to confuse protective pairings with consensual relationships and will often discipline both the perpetrator and the victim, citing policies that prohibit any sexual contact between inmates. As a result, many survivors endure these abusive relationships in silence, not only fearing the wrath of the more powerful inmate, but also of being punished by corrections officials. Not surprisingly, most inmate rape survivors choose not to come forward and report abuse that occurs as part of protective pairing arrangements. To illustrate the circumstances that these LGBT inmates experience, consider the following two sexual assault survivor stories, taken from Just Detention International:

Jason, Texas

Jason is a 30-year-old gay male who is currently incarcerated by the Texas Department of Criminal Justice (TDCJ). In the past four years he has been transferred to six different facilities within the TDCJ and has faced harassment and discrimination at each facility. While in prison, he was assaulted and extorted relentlessly by members of the Aryan Brotherhood, a powerful prison gang. During each of the assaults he was physically beaten by at least three members of the gang until he agreed to perform oral sex. He was eventually transferred to another facility, but was never placed in the TDCJ's *Safekeeping* program—a special classification for vulnerable inmates who can not be safely housed in general population.

Shakria, Colorado

Shakria is a 36-year-old black transgender prisoner of the Colorado Department of Corrections. In 2007, she was raped by her cellmate, while a third prisoner acted as a lookout. After the first assault, she repeatedly requested protection but was denied each time. Months later, she was again raped by an inmate who didn't know how to take no for an answer. Shakria described her experience in a letter written days after being transferred from the facility where the assaults took place:

I was raped twice at the Limon Correctional Facility. When I was assaulted the first time, I was afraid to "snitch" because I was in fear that my life would end. I complained and wrote two letters to [two different officials] and requested to be transferred to a safer facility, that I no longer felt safe there. The two letters were given to them in November 2007 and still they kept me there. In January 2008, I was sexually assaulted again and they caught one of the inmates who did it the next day. I was sent to medical where I had to wait 3 hours to speak with a street investigator and out of fear, once more I refused to press any charges so they refused to give me medical treatment or do a rape kit on me. I was placed in segregation for 14 days and when I requested grievances, I was refused. Finally I was transferred to another facility.

Responses to Anti-Gay Crime

Anti-gay violence has resulted in the establishment of hundreds of gay and lesbian advocacy groups and other projects that provide services for victims. The presence of these groups and their active advocacy is, in large part, responsible for these types of crimes being classified as hate crimes. These types of groups were formed as a recognition of the problem and to reflect the changing social climate toward further inclusion within the United States. While law enforcement agencies have made efforts to address discrimination against gay members, there is room for improvement when addressing victimization within the gay community. Thus, it is recommended that police and correctional agencies increase training for LGBT-specific violence and victimization.

Specifically, agencies should establish—if they have not already done so—anti-bias units or hate crimes task forces in every major metropolitan and state police force. This should include training and resources that specifically address anti-LGBT violence at the cadet training academy and during in-service trainings over the law enforcement career and agencies should include effective follow-up and evaluation training programs to ensure that such training is effective in changing the police culture and attitudes toward the LGBT population. In addition, these agencies should ensure that policy and local legislation include guidance for the rigorous investigation and prosecution for harassment, intimidation, and abuse committed by employees against members of the LGBT population. Training on these policies for agency personnel should emphasize this enhanced response to communicate the seriousness of this issue.

Likewise, agencies should support cooperative projects between existing community anti-violence programs and civil courts and they should aid research on and initiate programs for cooperative work between these systems. The coordination of civil law responses in tandem with criminal law responses can optimize social change within the community. This is particularly true with youthful offenders and juvenile court systems. Because a large proportion of the hate-based offender population is young, this is one potentially effective area of response that is often under-utilized within communities and among agencies.

Lastly, agencies should encourage the participation of LGBT members on community boards and oversight committees. Furthermore, a strong community policing model should be implemented that is designed to build a rapport between the agency and the LGBT community. This is no different than would be utilized with other minority groups, particularly ethnic minority communities. Encouraging the LGBT community to actively participate in agency visits, participation in neighborhood watch programs, and other types of police-community crime prevention initiatives can bridge a rapport between the agency and LGBT individuals and also send a strong public message that the agency is earnest and sincere in its efforts to protect and serve all members of its community, including LGBT members.

CONCLUSION

This chapter has covered two specific populations that have struggled to gain acceptance and respect within the criminal justice system, particularly in policing and correctional agencies. Both women and the LGBT population have been marginalized in society and also suffer from sexualized violence, victimization, and harassment. It is in this manner—through the gendered experiences of these two groups—that they share similarities in experiences, though, of course, the challenges each have faced are not identical.

The history of women in law enforcement and corrections is one that has been difficult and has reflected social biases toward women who chose to do what might have been considered a "man's job," demonstrating the discrimination that was inherent to the allocation of jobs in society. Furthermore, even in modern criminal justice agencies (policing, in particular), women tend to be underrepresented. Likewise, there are barriers that exist for women within these agencies as many find it difficult to promote due to various forms of discrimination that occur in the decision-making process when shaping careers in agencies.

For female offenders, it is clear that services for female offenders are inadequate, both within institutional and community intervention programs. There is a need to address specific social ills that are fairly unique to female offenders since this population is likely to continue to grow in numbers. Among these social ills are domestic violence, sexual abuse, drug use, prostitution, sexually transmitted diseases, and child-custody issues. Many of the problems associated with female offenders have hidden costs that affect the rest of society in a multi-faceted manner. This is specifically the case given the "collateral damage" that emanates from the impairment of children whose mother (and likely sole caretaker) is incarcerated. When thinking long-term, it becomes both socially and economically sound practice to work to improve services and ensure that accommodations are made for the special needs of the female offender.

Lastly, the LGBT population has suffered discrimination, harassment, and violent victimization throughout history in the United States. They are particularly unwelcome in many criminal justice agencies that have a strong paramilitary culture. Both police and correctional agencies have made strides in correcting this type of discrimination but much more work must be done. Currently, gay males seem to bear the most direct and severe forms of discrimination. Hate crimes committed against the LGBT population are not uncommon and, in some cases, it would appear that many communities provide tacit approval of these types of crimes.

In addition, LGBT offenders suffer from sexual assault as well as other forms of abuse while in jails and prisons. This group is particularly vulnerable due to either their appearance/mannerisms or their sex preference. Prison subcultures tend to have hyper-masculine ideals, norms, and mores, which justify the victimization of weak or effeminate individuals. Furthermore, staff within these facilities may not take this issue seriously, believing that this type of victimization is simply part of an inmate's experience when doing time, or they may view such acts as consensual when LGBT victims choose to partner with a single protector in the inmate population as a means of avoiding repetitive victimization by multiple assailants. This is a tactic that is not always successful and, in many cases, this group of inmates tends to experience repeat incidents of harm.

Chapter 4 Learning Check

1. The "glass ceiling" is a term for official or unofficial barriers to promotion that exist for women within the workforce.
   a. True
   b. False
2. Many police and corrections agencies operate along a paramilitary structure.
   a. True
   b. False
3. Which Supreme Court case invalidated anti-sodomy laws in numerous states?
   a. *Atkins v. Virginia*
   b. *Ruiz v. Estelle*
   c. *Lawrence v. Texas*
   d. *Bowers v. Hardwick*
   e. None of the above
4. The acronym LGBT refers to Lesbian, Gay, Bi-Sexual, and Transgendered persons.
   a. True
   b. False
5. Women as professionals in the juvenile justice system have been a longstanding accepted practice. Historically speaking, women have been involved in juvenile reform, including movements such as the

   _____.
   a. Child Saver Movement
   b. Juvenile Justice Reform Movement
   c. Reformatory Era
   d. None of the above
6. The first woman in law enforcement was _____

   _____.
   a. Mary Kay Williams
   b. Lisa Louise McAdams

c. Cathy Kay Thomas
d. Alice Stebbin Wells

7. According to the text, sexual discrimination is an unwelcome sexual behavior directed at an individual, which makes them feel offended, humiliated, or intimidated, and in the circumstances, it is reasonable to conclude that this behavior would make a person feel this way.
   a. True
   b. False
8. According to the text, in order that women can be integrated more fully into the world of prison operations, it is necessary that sexist opinions, beliefs, and informal exchanges be minimized by administrators.
   a. True
   b. False
9. According to the text, there is often an unwritten perception among persons in criminal justice agencies that the same-sex population should conform themselves to heterosexual standards.
   a. True
   b. False
10. Which act prohibited discrimination in hiring on the basis of race, color, religion, sex, or national origin.
    a. Thehe Civil Rights Act of 1964
    b. Americans with Disabilities Act of 1990 (ADA)
    c. Equal Employment Opportunity (EEO) Act of 1972
    d. None of the above

Essay Discussion Questions

1. Fully discuss some of the changes that agencies have had to make to be more inclusive of the gay, lesbian, bisexual, and transgender (LGBT) population.
2. Discuss the history and role of women in: a. policing, b. the judiciary, c. corrections, or d. juvenile justice (pick option a, b, c, or d for this question).

3. Identify and discuss some of the challenges that female offenders face.

References

American Correctional Association. (1990). *The female offender: What does the future hold?* Washington, DC: St. Mary's Press.

Anti-Discrimination Commission. (2009). *Tracking your rights: Lesbian, bay, bi-sexual, transgender, and inter-sex people.* Brisbane, Australia: Anti-Discrimination Commission Queensland.

Arnott, J. (1994). *Gays* and lesbians in the criminal justice system. In Hendricks, J. & Byers, B. (Eds.), *Multicultural perspectives in criminal justice and criminology,* pp. 211–213. Springfield, OH: Charles, C. Thomas.

Barlow, D. E., & Barlow, M. H. (2000). *Police in a multicultural society: An American story.* Prospect Heights, IL: Waveland Press, Inc.

Bass, E., & Davis, L. (2008). *The courage to heal: A guide for women survivors of child sexual abuse (4E).* London: HarperCollins Publishers.

Belkin, A., & McNichol, J. (2002). Pink and blue: Outcomes associated with the integration of open gay and lesbian personnel in the San Diego Police Department. *Police Quarterly,* 5(1), 63–96.

Berrill, K. T., & Herek, G. (1992). Hate crimes: Confronting violence against lesbians and gay men. Newbury Park, CA: Sage.

Bloom, B., Brown, M., & Chesney-Lind, M. (1996). Women on probation and parole. In Lurigio, A. J. (Ed.), *Community corrections in America: New directions and sounder investments for persons with mental illness and codisorders* (pp. 51–76). Washington, DC: National Institute of Corrections.

Bloom, B., Owen, B., & Covington, S. (2003). *Gender-responsive strategies: Research, practice and guiding principles for women offenders.* Washington, DC: US.

Burke, M. (1994). Homosexuality as deviance: The case of the gay police officer. *British Journal of Criminology,* 34(2) (Spring), 192–203.

Carlson, P. M., & Garrett, J. S. (2013). *Prison and jail administration: Practice and theory.* Boston, MA: Jones and Bartlett.

Clear, T. R., Cole, G. E., & Reisig, M. D. (2009). *American corrections* (8th ed.). Belmont, CA: Wadsworth Publishing.

Comeau, M., & Klofas, J. (2010). *Women in policing: A history.* Rochester, NY: Center for Public Safety Initiatives.

Crawford, J. (2002). Alternative sentencing necessary for female inmates with children. *Corrections Today.* Retrieved from: http://www.aca.org/publications/ctarchivespdf/june03/commentary_june.pdf

Epigee Foundation. (2004). *Birth control guide on sexually transmitted diseases.* Epigee Foundation. Retrieved from: http://www.epigee.org/guide/stds.html

Fenton, J. (2009). 2 gay officers work for acceptance on force, in community. *The Baltimore Sun.* Retrieved from: http://articles.baltimoresun.com/2009-08-03/news/0908020076_1_gay-community-lesbian-liaison-liaison-unit

Garcia, V. (2003). "Difference" in the police department: Women, policing, and "doing gender". *Journal of Contemporary Criminal Justice,* 19(3), 330–344.

Grennan, S. A. (2000). The past, present, and future of women in policing. In Muraskin, R. (Ed.). *It's a crime: Women and justice* (pp. 383–398). Upper Saddle River, NJ: Prentice Hall.

Hartocollis, A. (2007). Claiming constant harassment, gay police officer in city files suit. *New York Times.* Retrieved from: http://www.nytimes.com/2007/09/29/nyregion/29gay.html

International Association of Women Police. (2010). *History of IAWP.* Retrieved from: http://www.iawp.org/history/historical.htm

Lawrence v. Texas, (2003) 539 U.S. 558.

Leavitt, N. (2003). *Legal globalization why U.S. courts should be able to consider the decisions of foreign courts and international bodies.* Findlaw: Thomson Reuters Business. Retrieved from: http://writ.news.findlaw.com/commentary/20031016_leavitt.html

Martin, S. E., & Jurik, N. C. (1996). *Doing justice, doing gender: Women in law and criminal justice occupations.* Thousand Oaks, CA: SAGE Publications.

Myers, K., Forest, K. B., & Miller, S. L. (2004). Officer friendly and the tough cop: Gays and lesbians navigate homophobia and policing. *Journal of Homosexuality, 47*(1), 17–37.

National Association of Women Judges. (2010). *The American bench: Judges of the nation—2010 Edition.* Dallas, TX: Forster-Long, Inc.

National Coalition of Anti-Violence Programs. (2009). *Hate violence against lesbian, gay, bisexual, and transgender people in the United States, 2008.* New York, NY: Author.

National Gay and Lesbian Task Force News. (2000, March 4). LGBT violence increase despite violence decrease. Washington, DC: National Gay and Lesbian Task Force Foundation.

Perry, B. (2001). *In the name of hate.* New York: Routledge.

Platt, Anthony M. (1969). *The child savers; the invention of delinquency.* Chicago: University of Chicago.

Price, B. R., & Gavin, S. (1981). A century of women in policing. In Schultz, D. O. (ED.), *Modern police administration* (pp. 109–122). Houston, TX: Gulf Publishing Company.

Rafter, N. H. (1985). *Partial justice: Women in state prisons 1800–1935.* Boston, MA: New England University Press.

Seiden, A. M. (1989). *Psychological issues affecting women throughout the life cycle.* In Parry, B. L. (Ed.), *The psychiatric clinics of North America* (pp. 1–24). Philadelphia: W. B. Saunders.

Snell, T. (1994). *Women in prison.* Washington, DC: Bureau of Justice Statistics.

Toth, R. C., Crews, G. A., & Burton, C. E. (2008). *In the margins: Special populations and American Justice.* Upper Saddle River, NJ: Pearson Prentice-Hall.

Cultural Competence and Intercultural Communication

LEARNING OBJECTIVES

After reading this chapter, students should be able to do the following:

1. Define and discuss cultural competence and intercultural communication.
2. Explain how cultural competence is important in the field of criminal justice.
3. Identify schemas, cross-racial and cross-linguistic issues associated with intercultural communication.
4. Identify examples of how cross-cultural communication skills and techniques can impact interviews, interrogations, and citizen relations.
5. Explain how cultural competence will be a continued area of emphasis in the criminal justice field indefinitely.

KEY TERMS

Agency Tokenism	Linguistic Competence
Categories of Acculturation	Cross-Linguistic Interrogation
Category Schemas	Cross-Linguistic Interview
Causal Schemas	Person Schemas
Cultural Blindness	Cultural Pre-Competence
Cultural Destructiveness	Role Schemas
Cultural Incapacity	Cultural Competence
Culturally Proficient	Schemas
Event Schemas	Top-Down Model
Freedom of Religion	Self-Construals
Intercultural Communication	Uncertainty Avoidance
Cultural Competence Continuum	Power Distance
Individualism versus Collectivism	Masculinity versus Femininity

INTRODUCTION

In this chapter, we will discuss the concepts of cultural competence and intercultural communication. Cultural competence is a term that emerged in the 1990s to describe the need to have skills and proficiencies in dealing with persons from various cultures. Although, on the one hand, an individual might be sensitive to diversity issues and the need for egalitarian treatment of persons in society, this does not necessarily mean that they are well versed and knowledgeable of the customs and mores of a particular group. In Chapter 2, we had noted that **cultural competence** describes the process of effectively attending to the needs of individuals by integrating the salient aspects of the culture to which they identify themselves. Furthermore, cultural competence refers *"...to the ability to honor and respect the beliefs, language, interpersonal styles, and behaviors of individuals and families receiving services, as well as staff who are providing such services..."* (DHHS, 2003, p. 12). Therefore, it is clear that when we discuss cultural competence, we are referring to more than mere sensitivity; rather, we mean that a person has specialized knowledge and fluency with specific minority groups so as to be able to converse and associate with individuals from these groups in a manner where both the practitioner and the individual in society are comfortable and where a rapport is easily built and maintained.

We would like to take a moment, at the beginning of this chapter, to address some key points related to our use of terms related to communication between different cultural, racial, or ethnic groups. We have used the work of Prosser (2012) as a reference in determining the specific vernacular for this text with regard to communication between persons of differing cultures who come into contact with one another in the United States and, due to necessity, must communicate with one another. Prosser (2012), based on the research of highly notable figures such as William Gudykunst (2003), distinguishes between intercultural communication and what many nowadays refer to as intercultural communication.

Prosser (2012) and others who study cultural linguistics and communication theory use the term **intercultural communication** to refer to communication that occurs between individuals from different cultures who engage in exchanges and discourse in interpersonal settings; these communications are usually one-on-one or consist of small groups who engage in informal communication settings rather than planned or organized settings. Cross-cultural communication, on the other hand, is more appropriately used when describing communication that takes place between persons of entire cultures or between representatives of these entire cultures; in essence, one entire cultural group is represented and talks with representatives of another entire cultural group. An example of intercultural communication might be a Caucasian customer who talks with a local store owner who is of Mexican descent about items for sale, whereas an example of cross-cultural communication might be representatives from different countries meeting each other at a professional conference.

Going further and being more specific to the point of this chapter and this text, intercultural communication is a process by which one person communicates with another who is from a different racial or ethnic group where language fluency, educational attainment, emotional affect, and nonverbal mannerisms are variables that impact the exchange of information between the two persons. Such forms of communication also consist of processes by which people express their openness to an intercultural experience (Prosser, 2012). In other words, intercultural communication consists of typical aspects of communication but entails persons of different cultures and, at the same time, that process of communication will convey whether persons are open to input from and dialog with the person's own cultural group.

The remainder of this chapter will address both of these concepts in depth, as they apply to the field of criminal justice. In doing so, this chapter will use terminology and definitions from other behavioral science disciplines that have explored these concepts in greater depth. The desire is to bring that rich literature on cultural competence and intercultural communication to the field of criminal justice in a way that is applicable and useful to both the practitioner and scholar in the criminal justice field.

THE SPECTRUM OF COMPETENCY: THE CULTURAL COMPETENCE CONTINUUM

To achieve cultural competence, agencies must do more than provide a glossy appearance of being politically correct or, as is the case with some agencies, ensuring that a person is designated as the diversity expert. Furthermore, cultural competence is not achieved through the simple translation of agency documents into other languages. Although multi-linguistic tools do aid in intercultural communication, they, too, have their limits, as we will see later in this chapter. Rather, cultural competence should be considered as a continual process of agency development that includes learning more about our own and other cultures, thereby altering our thinking and changing the ways in which we interact with others to reflect an awareness and sensitivity to diverse cultures.

The **Cultural Competence Continuum** as portrayed in Figure 5-1 is of our own design but integrates the stages of the continuum developed by Cross et al. (1989) for mental health professionals. We use this same continuum with criminal justice

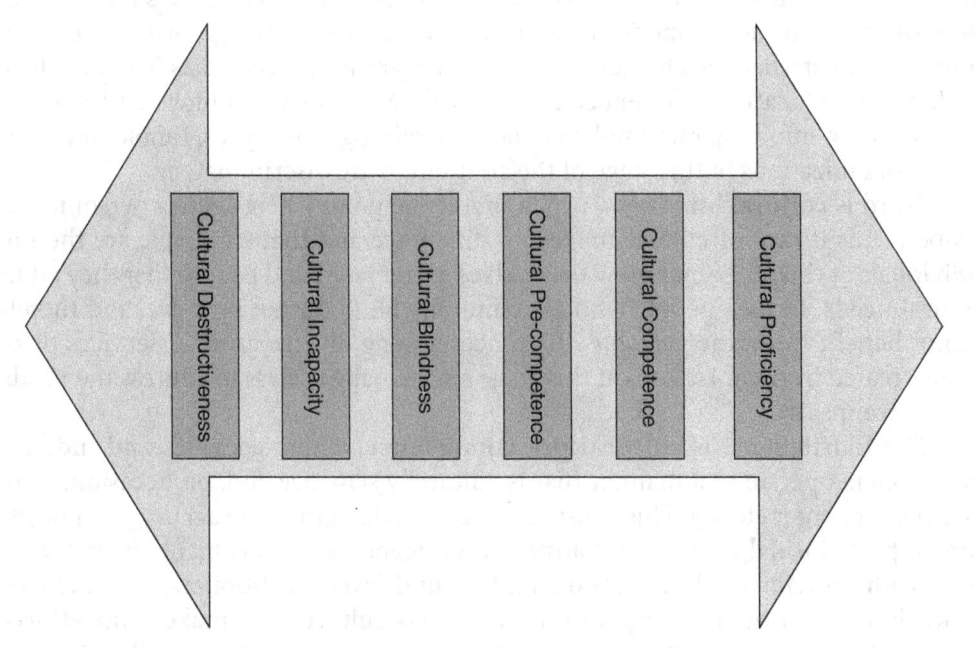

FIGURE 5-1 The Cultural Competence Continuum. *Sources:* Cross, T., Bazron, B., Dennis, K., & Isaacs, M. (1989). *Towards a Culturally Competent System of Care, Volume 1*. Washington, DC: CASSP Technical Assistance Center, Center for Child Health and Mental Health Policy, Georgetown University Child Development Center.

professionals, as well. This continuum is based on the idea that cultural competence is a dynamic process with multiple levels of achievement. It can be used to assess an organization's or individual's level of cultural competence, to establish benchmarks, and to measure progress. The continuum includes six stages: cultural destructiveness, cultural incapacity, cultural blindness, cultural pre-competence, cultural competence, and cultural proficiency (Cross et al., 1989). While cultural proficiency, according to Cross et al. (1989), is the ideal goal in achieving multicultural understanding and practice, it is not necessarily that well recognized in the literature as is cultural competency and, for many agencies, may be more of an ideal rather than a realistic policy-setting goal or directive. With this in mind, we now provide a brief discussion of each of the six stages of the cultural competence continuum.

An Overview of the Six States of the Cultural Competence Continuum

First is **cultural destructiveness**, which is, of course, at the negative end of the continuum; it is characterized by cultural destructiveness. Organizations or individuals in this stage view cultural differences as a problem and participate in activities that purposely attempt to destroy a culture. Examples of destructive actions include denying people of color access to their natural helpers or healers, removing children of color from their families on the basis of race, and risking the well-being of minority individuals by involving them in social or medical experiments without their knowledge or consent. Organizations and individuals at this extreme operate on the assumption that one race is superior and that it should eradicate "lesser" cultures.

Second is **cultural incapacity**, which is a point where organizations and personnel lack the basic ability to aid diverse communities due to inherent beliefs that their own racial or ethnic group is superior or more entitled than are other groups. The organizations have a paternalistic character toward other groups perceived as being of "lesser" intelligence, education, affluence, and so forth. Such agencies may reinforce social oppression by enforcing racist policies and maintaining stereotypes. Employment practices of organizations in this stage of the continuum are discriminatory.

Third is **cultural blindness**, which marks the point where agency personnel tend to operate as if race or culture makes no difference and that all people are the same. Individuals at this stage may view themselves as unbiased and believe that they address cultural needs. In fact, people who are culturally blind do not perceive, and therefore cannot benefit from, the valuable differences among diverse groups. Services or programs created by organizations at this stage are virtually useless to address the needs of diverse groups.

The fourth stage is **cultural pre-competence**, where agencies and individual practitioners operate in a manner that is culturally sensitive and, on occasion, centers on aspects of competency. This is usually due to leadership in the agency promulgating some type of formal training initiative and/or agency announcement. Such agencies, along with individual administrators and ground-level practitioners, will likely realize weaknesses in their attempts to serve various cultures and make some efforts to improve the services offered to diverse populations. These agencies will actively seek to hire staff from the cultures they serve, involve people of different cultures on their boards of directors or advisory committees, and provide at least rudimentary training in cultural differences. One potential drawback is the possibility of **agency tokenism**, where the organization may hire personnel from a racial or ethnic group to meet numerical specifications and, in the process, operate as if this, alone, ensures agency cultural competence.

The point of cultural competence occurs in agencies when personnel routinely accept and respect differences while, simultaneously, engaging in continued self-assessment regarding culture. Because the definition of cultural competence was provided in our previous subsection, we will not further belabor the point here. Needless to say, agencies that are culturally competent will strive to hire unbiased personnel and will be open to commentary on racial and cultural issues related to agency operations. In subsequent subsections, we will discuss in more detail how agencies can foster and maintain cultural competence through training and other forms of implementation.

Lastly, **culturally proficient** agencies will hold diversity as one of its highest ideals. Such agencies will seek to add to the base of knowledge on culturally competent practices through research, development of operations to enhance response to diverse populations, and publishing demonstration projects that hold the agency accountable for this agenda. The agency will have staff who are cultural experts in research and development of these agency practices. This is the highest and most difficult ideal to achieve in an agency.

CULTURAL COMPETENCE: COMMON ISSUES FACING DIVERSE MINORITY GROUPS

While there are certainly some differences between racial and ethnic groups, there are some common challenges and experiences that are shared by almost all of them, as well. It is important for criminal justice practitioners to recognize some of these similar experiences that may cut across or be common to all minority ethnic groups in the United States. Shusta, Levine, Harris, and Wong (2011) note the following considerations:

Generational status in the United States (first, second, and third generations), degree of acculturation and assimilation, comfort with and competence in English, religious beliefs and cultural value orientation, and family cultural dynamics—each of these five aspects are among the many others that can hinder the ability of practitioners to develop an effective rapport with minority populations. Some are more relevant than others to specific groups but almost all of these issues are relevant at one point or another when considering Latino American and Asian Americans. Naturally, these same issues, whether some or all of them, will also apply even to those groups (e.g., Native American and African American) where immigration is not a significant issue in the identity of that group. Certainly, religious beliefs and family dynamics will apply to every group that we discuss in this text.

Generational Status in the United States

A very substantial portion of Latino Americans and Asian Americans are born outside of the United States (Bennett, 2002; Shusta et al., 2011). Indeed, throughout the United States, the majority of both groups are born outside of the United States. Naturally, these two groups include a variety of countries ranging from Mexico to Central America and all the way throughout the continent of South America (for Latino American immigrants), including the Caribbean region as well as a number of countries along

the Asian Pacific Rim and other common locati
and so forth.

Likewise, this does not include person
increasingly immigrated to the United State
find themselves going through all of the same
ity groups experience. In fact, these groups a
Trade Center tragedy, 9-11, as well as wartim
affecting their ability to be easily accepted b
to wear traditional garb and/or speak their
among first-generation immigrants, distrust
enced all the more from others in their com

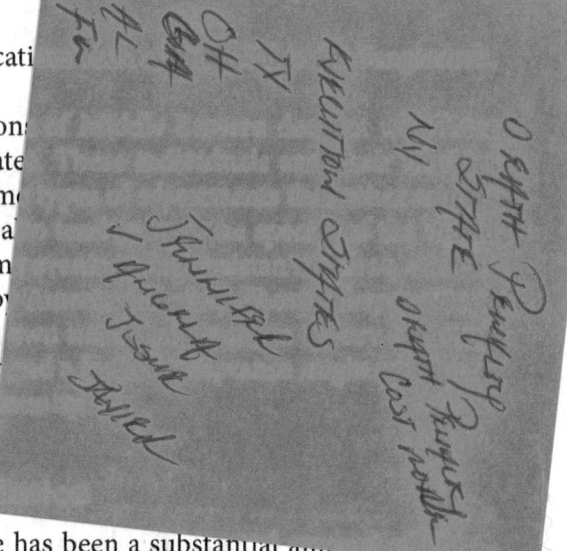

Degree of Acculturation and Assim

As we discussed earlier in Chapter 2, there has been a substantial am
ture on this issue, particularly among social science research. However, Shusta et al.
(2011) provide one of the clearest yet pragmatic descriptions of this process by providing several categories or points of acculturation that minorities may fall within. These
categories apply equally well to any minority group who has had a historically recent
migration to the United States. Thus, any immigrant family would likely experience
these categories of acculturation, but some groups may experience more challenges
than others, depending on language proficiency and various other characteristics that
can either ease the process or make it more difficult. These **categories of acculturation**
are adapted from Shusta et al. (2011) and are as follows:

1. Surviving—Includes individuals who have recently immigrated to the United
   States (within the last five years) and the majority of their socialization and experience will have been in their own nation-of-origin.
2. Preserving—This includes immigrants or refugees who have been in the United
   States for more than five years but who still had the majority of their socialization
   in their own nation-of-origin.
3. Adjusting—This will include the second-generation offspring of minority
   immigrants.
4. Changing—This group includes immigrants, but these immigrants will have had
   the majority of their experiences within the United States.
5. Choosing—This category consists of third-generation (or later) minorities.

When considering each of these categories, it is important to understand the individual perspective from which these individuals view the world. For instance, those in
the "surviving" category are typically in a survival mode and may have come from areas
where police and other authority figures were oppressive and abusive. This then will
tend to shape their frame of reference when dealing with criminal justice agents (especially police) in the United States. Likewise, individuals in the "preserving" category
seek to preserve their home culture and identity. Their own values and customs are
preserved and this can be the source of intergenerational conflict within their family
as youth become more "Americanized" and lose contact with their culture-of-origin.
Among the remaining categories (Adjusting, Changing, and Choosing), there is value
for the homeland but there is also a realistic understanding that changes will need to

be made (Shusta et al., 2011; Sue & Sue, 2007). This is particularly true for those in the Changing and Choosing categories, where decisions to include aspects of the old culture or to integrate aspects of the new culture are made. These individuals tend to be truly bicultural and it may be that many will use English as their primary language, allowing their proficiency with their native language to lapse (Sue & Sue, 2007). For these individuals, contact with the criminal justice system may be no different from that occurring between other citizens of the United States.

Comfort with and Competence in English

As previously noted, proficiency with the English language is a particular hindrance that can cause serious misunderstandings between practitioners and minority citizens (Shusta et al., 2011). This issue is somewhat tied to the generational status of the individual and their specific nation-of-origin, since groups that have immigrated most recently tend to be those with larger percentages that do not speak English. This is particularly true among the Southeast Asian groups. Indeed, nearly 38 percent of all Vietnamese Americans do not speak English (Shusta et al., 2011). In addition, it has been determined that an approximate 23 percent of Chinese Americans also do not speak English (Shusta et al., 2011). On the other hand, this is not typically an issue for Asian Indians owing to the fact that almost all people speak English as a result of prior subjugation during the reign of the British Empire (Almeida, 1996).

Another issue regarding minority proficiency with the English language may be important to note. In many cases, minority youth quickly learn the English language due to their mandatory involvement in the public school system (Sue & Sue, 2007). Therefore, it may be the case that in many immigrant households (whether Hispanic, Asian, Middle Eastern, or otherwise), the children are much more proficient in English than are the parental figures or any extended family members (Almeida, 1996; Sue & Sue, 2007). While this does allow these youth to aid their older family members, this can also lead to problems since the adult caretakers are generally at the mercy of their younger children when communicating with officials in society (Almeida, 1996; Sue & Sue, 2007). Naturally, this can (and sometimes does) lead to manipulation among children in minority households. In fact, of those minority youth who do become involved in delinquent activity, the parents are hard-pressed to adequately supervise these youth who become skilled at navigating around a system that cannot effectively communicate with the parents.

Police officers, juvenile caseworkers, truancy officers, juvenile probation officers, and school officials alike have grappled with this challenge in many areas of the United States from the West Coast to the East Coast. We will discuss in more detail regarding intercultural communication in later subsections of this chapter. For now, it is sufficient to point out that for some citizens, the English language may not allow for optimal communication flow and, with this in mind, agencies must be prepared to work around these challenges as part of their service delivery to the surrounding community.

Religious Beliefs and Cultural Value Orientation

Freedom of religion, secured by the 1st Amendment, is one of the core founding principles of the United States. Indeed, it is often touted that the desire for such freedom is what prompted the Pilgrims from England to sail for the Americas. Before this, however, is the fact that it was the Spanish who first settled in the Americas and, with them, they brought a new religion that was imposed upon the Native American populations of the Caribbean, the Southwestern United States, Central America, and South America: Catholicism. Throughout the history of the Spanish conquest of the Americas, Native populations were forced to "convert" to this religion and, in the process, their own indigenous religious beliefs were outlawed by the Church. The result was a total forced transformation in spiritual and religious orientation for the entire Hispanic population in these regions.

Today, it is common for any person in society to simply equate the Hispanic population with being Catholic; the fact that this religion was not, originally, their own indigenous religion has been lost. With this in mind, it is important for police officers to understand that Latino families will tend to be strongly influenced by the Catholic Church. Views on suicide, childrearing, the roles of husbands and wives, and so forth will be strongly influenced by this denomination of Christianity. However, there may be some groups who do still practice remnants of indigenous belief systems (such as Mexican shamans), particularly in interior Mexico, various areas of the Caribbean, and South America.

The presence of the church in African American culture and identity is also central to this community and is one that includes a religion that has been imposed upon a people. However, the imposition was done conversely to that of the Hispanic population in the Americas. Indeed, the ancestors of today's African American population were, of course, brought to the United States in bondage and, when being forced into slavery, were restricted from practicing their own native religious practices. As a result, these slaves from various tribes throughout West Africa, were forced to adopt Christian beliefs. The result is now that the Protestant Church has a major influence on the African American community and religious leaders in that community are typically afforded a high degree of respect.

Among Native Americans, religion is a varied concept depending on the particular tribe. In the Southwestern United States, groups such as the Hopi, the Navajo, and the Pueblo have maintained many of their indigenous religious traditions. The degree of commitment to these religious beliefs varies from tribe to tribe and from member to member, but generally these groups will tend to have a strong affinity to nature, the spiritual world, and the historical folklore that has been orally passed down from generation to generation. In many cases, these beliefs are coupled with ceremonies and the manufacture of crafts that retain commitments held decades, even centuries, back.

For Chinese and Vietnamese Americans, Buddhism, Confucianism, and Taoism tend to be honored. For Buddhist followers, the concepts of karma and reincarnation may be important considerations (Almeida, 1996; Sue & Sue, 2007). In addition, the reverence for ancestors may be honored as well. This practice may be found to be quite common in some areas, even among converts to Judeo-Christian traditions. On important anniversaries or family events, offerings to ancestors may be observed as a means of opening such festivities and celebrations (Almeida, 1996).

For Asian Indian Americans, it has been found that the higher the social class and the longer the time since immigration, the weaker is the allegiance to traditional gender roles and the greater the preference for individualistic rather than collective norms (Almeida, 1996; Sue & Sue, 2007). With this in mind, it has been said that Hinduism in the United States is more of a cultural tradition for Asian Indian

Americans than a religious doctrine (Almeida, 1996). Despite this, many Asian Indians may seek "purity" in their life, abstaining from bodily pleasures such as sex, alcohol, and other sensual pleasures with the view that these are "impure" and part of a polluted existence (Almeida, 1996). Likewise, even though there may not be rigid adherence to the caste system among Asian Indian Americans in the United States, "caste" is still seen as important and is considered part of one's *karma* (Almeida, 1996; Sue & Sue, 2007). Lastly, because Hinduism does not require regular worship at a temple, practice of the religion occurs mostly at home. Asian Indian families in the United States are left with no societal support and this has led to some deterioration in ardent Hinduism (Almeida, 1996).

Likewise, Middle Easterners and Asian Americans (particularly from India and Pakistan) may be Muslim and therefore follow the beliefs of Allah as recorded in the Qu'ran (Al-meida, 1996; Shusta, et al., 2011). How observant these Muslims will be often depends on their education, economics, societal influences, immigration patterns, and acculturation (Sue & Sue, 2007). Because of this religious affiliation, there have been documented incidents where police have misidentified Asian Indians for interrogation during the period shortly after the World Trade Center bombing in 2001 (Shusta, et al., 2011). It is with this in mind that it is important for police (particularly in the southern United States where police tend to lack exposure to many Asian groups) to effectively distinguish between Indian, Pakistani, and other racial groups. Over generalizations regarding attire and/or association can lead to erroneous conclusions and can also result in incidents of embarrassment for the police agency. This same misidentification (particularly among turban-wearing Sikhs) has been the basis for hate crimes against Asian Indians in various parts of the United States (Sue & Sue, 2007). Granted, hate crimes are equally abhorrent and punishable regardless of the group that is intended to receive the abusive treatment, but these incidents do demonstrate how the general public in the United States is ill equipped to distinguish between racial and ethnic groups among minority citizens (Shusta, et al., 2011).

Agency practitioners in many areas of the United States may not have a firm understanding of the religious dynamics associated with different groups because many of these religions (aside from Catholicism) are not commonly encountered and/or are not well represented in some areas of the United States. For these practitioners, it may serve them well to visit different religious institutions and, in a respectful manner, ask for insight on these belief systems. Naturally, reading about various religions can help but, as with anything written, there may be some discrepancies between what is read and what is reality in a given region of the nation. To use both tools in educating oneself on religious belief systems would likely be optimal.

INTERCULTURAL COMMUNICATION

Earlier in this chapter, we provided a definition of intercultural communication and hence will not repeat that definition. Rather, we will note that regardless of the knowledge that one may have of specific groups, there is no replacement for the ability to communicate effectively with persons from diverse origins. Thus, knowledge alone does not make us capable practitioners in a multicultural environment. Rather we must be able to talk and communicate effectively with persons from diverse backgrounds. We will, therefore, first turn our attention to some of the challenges associated with intercultural and cross-racial communication.

Intercultural Communication: Early Studies and Prospective Research

Prosser notes that there are multiple aspects of research on cultural variation and communication (2012), some of which are as follows:

1. **Power distance**: This refers to the degree to which cultures include status and power hierarchies vs. relative equality into their communication.
2. **Individualism versus collectivism**: This means the extent to which cultures value individual personal identity vs. community identity.
3. **Self-construals**: This referring to the means by which people see themselves and/or view their role in the world.
4. **Low and high context**: It is the degree to which a culture relies on unstated relational dynamics vs. direct verbal communication.

These various cultural dynamics are played out in the communication processes of members from various cultures along a continuum. They can also serve as the basis of how miscommunications can arise between members of two different cultures, even when both are completely fluent in the same language. For instance, as an example of power distance dynamics, consider a person from the nation of India may still hold on to cultural beliefs related to that culture's caste system and, when speaking with other persons, their ranking on that caste system may impact the way they communicate with people whom they meet.

When considering the above-listed dynamics, it is important to consider research that has been conducted because it is upon this research that we have based our own approach to issues of multicultural communication in this text. One landmark study by Hofstede (2001) examined national perceptions and values with 116,000 respondents. In this study, Hofstede developed and utilized four national cultural dimensions, which were (1) uncertainty avoidance, (2) power distance, (3) individualism vs. collectivism, and (4) masculinity vs. femininity. Prosser (2012) describes **uncertainty avoidance** as the level to which members of a national culture avoid or accept uncertainty, **power distance** as the extent to which less-powerful members of social groups accept unequal distributions of power, **individualism versus collectivism** as the means by which cultures emphasize personal autonomy over group cohesion, and **masculinity versus femininity** as a spectrum describing how gender issues are viewed within a national culture.

One early study conducted by Osgood et al. (1975) set out to determine if there were universal factors of meaning in communication in multiple cultures. In his research, Osgood asked participants from 50 different cultural backgrounds to assess terms for their understanding of good or bad, power or lack of power, and swift vs. slow speed. Osgood found support for his hypotheses, which held that, regardless of language or culture, people do have universal descriptive processes when conveying affective (meaning emotional) meanings of attitudes, feelings, beliefs, and even stereotypes. We will see more research that confirms these or similar findings later in the following subsection. The key point is that when it comes to emotional emphases in communication, people are similar regardless of their cultural orientation.

Prosser (2012) points out that early research on cross-cultural communication processes tended to focus on comparisons between American and Japanese, American and European, or American and Soviet cultural patterns. More recently, considerable research has emphasized contrasting cultural aspects of the Americans and Chinese or

Chinese and other Westerners. While these bicultural studies were and (to some extent) still are useful, they used Western research methods to deal with indigenous cultural patterns. This is an important observation because we cannot be certain whether these studies do not suffer from limitations related to ethnocentric views of the researchers, themselves, who regulated what would be studied and how it would be studied. Try as we might as researchers to avoid this, some of our own biases and views can still impact the studies we conduct.

Because of this potential bias, we contend that it is probably useful to have multiple researchers from various cultures, when possible and when studying these issues. Having multiple researchers from diverse backgrounds allows for more knowledge and familiarity with the participants who are studied and the cultural nuances associated with their communication patterns. Prosser (2012) notes the importance of research on these topics to use increasingly valid and reliable procedures. He notes that future studies should perhaps examine a multitude of cultures, noting that it requires at least 10 cultural groups when using standardized social science measurements. These processes of social science research include statistical measurements that are more sound, but require data that must meet minimal requirements. Thus, the information that we receive as feedback when examining whether agency staff effectively use intercultural communication in their day-to-day contacts is very important. As we will see later in Chapter 14, it is this information that will produce data to assess, evaluate, and refine training efforts of agencies in the future.

The Impact of Schemas on Intercultural Communication

Before discussing communication issues associated with intercultural, multilingual, and cross-racial groups, it is important to first note some common points regarding human perception. Much of the information that follows is derived from the field of cognitive psychology but serves as a good precursor to understanding how our memory, perception, and communication patterns are interlinked. Consider that the existence of cognitive schemas are relevant to all social groups around the world because every culture has a set of defined cognitive beliefs and structures that create the social bonds necessary for cultural and linguistic development. Likewise, these beliefs can affect how we perceive events that are processed through our sensory input systems.

Schemas are cognitive structures that represent knowledge about a given concept, including attributes associated with that concept and its relationship to the environment. A schema includes a dictionary definition of the concept, object, or event, along with a host of expectations concerning what it is like, how it behaves, what it should look like, and much more. To some extent, these schemas can lead to the development of stereotypes as we tend to categorize people based on these schemas, which are based on observations that we attribute to a group of people. Although this is not automatically the case, we must, on our own, constantly check our own perceptions and be alert for biases that may develop based on rigid schemas.

It is important to understand that humans possess a variety of schemas, including (a) **category schemas**, which tell us what the members of particular social group are like, (b) **person schemas**, which tell us what to expect of particular individuals, (c) **self-schemas**, consisting of how we think about ourselves, (d) **role schemas**, which tell us what individuals occupying particular social roles should be like and how they should behave, (e) **event schemas**, which include expectations for particular events or event categories, and (f) **causal schemas**, which tell us what tends to cause what, and how it does so (Davis & Follette, 2000, p. 39). From the description of each of these schemas, it is clear that the means by which we view ourselves, others, and the world around us are shaped by the narrations and expectations that we put in our own head. Thus, they are self-generated stories that we have crafted to make sense of our world and the behaviors of persons whom we know as well as those who are unfamiliar to us.

Without schemas, people could not understand and evaluate what they see or experience. Quite simply, schemas allow us to make sense of the world. Schemas are, quite naturally, a product of our socialization as well as our own unique experiences. From this point, it is clear that schemas are a natural by-product of one's cultural and/ or racial identity since each of these variables shape our perceptions of the world. As a result, schemas generate expectations of our environment concerning likely reactions from other people, outcomes in social circumstances, the mechanical characteristics of a given object, the laws of nature and/or physics, as well as other characteristics of our environment. Schemas also shape our interpretations of criminal behaviors just as they shape our interpretations of noncriminal behaviors. In short, schemas are learned beliefs that make sense of our world.

When we perceive certain events, our brains cannot always absorb all of the detailed information that is presented, at least not consciously. Instead, our cortical centers will essentially encode the "gist" of what is encountered and our minds "fill in" other details that are consistent with our prior learned schemas and expectations (Davis & Follette, 2000). It is in this manner that we generate beliefs and/or vague memories that we must have turned out lights before leaving home, locked car doors when parking and going to work, as well as a series of otherwise "mindless" behaviors. Research has demonstrated a tendency to remember both more and less than what is actually seen.

In reality, people do not remember schema-irrelevant information as well as schema relevant information, and people tend to add information that makes sense based on what they did see, and what their expectations and cognitive schemas would lead them to *expect* that they *should* have seen in a given situation (Davis & Follette, 2000). These schemas are likewise based on common stereotypes of one's given cultural or familial origins. For example, individuals may perceive the action of a member of one racial or cultural group differently than the exact same action by a member of another racial or cultural group. This is actually much more common than one might believe and is also common among cultures across the world.

Schemas are important to intercultural communication because they explain how we narrate our interactions with others and also provide a frame of reference for ourselves and from which we view others with whom we interact. In fact, we must remain mindful of our own schemas and consider those that are likely possessed by others if we are to be linguistically competent. This goes beyond simply being bilingual. Instead, this entails both knowing the language of the other person while, at the same time, being mindful of our own views and those of others as we talk in our own native tongue as well as other languages. Schemas also impact how we disseminate information throughout both an agency and a community and also impact how members of the community receive that information, including crime-fighting information. More will be discussed regarding linguistic competence and mass communication of crime-fighting information in the subsections that follow.

Intercultural Communication and Linguistic Competence

Language can be a major barrier to service delivery. Persons who are monolingual, limited in their English, or deaf or hard of hearing may be at a particular disadvantage. Criminal justice agencies, particularly those in small and midsized jurisdictions, generally have few or no staff trained to work with bilingual populations. This makes it difficult for these agencies to be linguistically competent. **Linguistic competence** ensures accurate communication of information in languages other than English. This capability enables an agency and its personnel to communicate effectively with persons of limited English proficiency, those who are illiterate or have low literacy skills, and individuals who are deaf or hard of hearing (Hanser, 2006). Elements of linguistic competence include the availability of trained bilingual and bicultural staff, translations of educational materials and documents, and sign-language and language-interpretation services. Although linguistic competence and cultural competence involve distinct skills, they are intrinsically connected (DHHS, 1999).

CURRENT EVENTS IN MULTICULTURAL CRIMINAL JUSTICE
The need for bi-lingual police officers is a continual problem—no end in sight

In 2011, an article in the Houston chronicle noted that on several occasions during any given week, police officers in Houston often rely on a variety of citizens to act as translators whenever bilingual officers cannot be found. Citizens utilized may be bystanders, witnesses, victims or their children, or even wrecker drivers and such (Pinkerton & Loucks, 2011). While this may sound bizarre, it would appear that the Houston Police Department is not alone, this is a national problem.

While Houston has over 1,000 bilingual officers who are given extra pay incentives for their language proficiency, these do not seem to be enough (Pinkerton & Loucks, 2011). This has caused problems in police-community relations and has also complicated crime-fighting efforts among police. In some cases, serious miscommunications occur where victims experience trauma that is misunderstood or where perpetrators are not found due to a lack of important testimony.

According to Shah, Rahman, and Khashu (2007), many agencies are still in need of developing a language access plan. These plans provide procedures for officers to access services of bilingual speakers in situations where an actual bilingual officer may not be available. In such cases, staff from the police department or other social service agencies may be available or, the agency may have a roster of volunteers. In either event, a protocol is established. However, Shah et al. (2007) do make the point to add that training must be provided to supervisors and patrol officers on the specific aspects of the protocol. Likewise, it is important to have dispatchers trained in this area, as well.

Another program, which will be discussed in more depth later, in Chapter 7, is the *Spanish Speaking Ride*

Along Program, which integrates the use of volunteers from the community that is being patrolled. These volunteers, many of whom may attend some type of citizen's police academy or similar training, assist the officer with routine issues where the Spanish speaking population is likely to be encountered. This program, started by the Tulsa, Oklahoma Police Department, was initially one of many problem-solving mechanisms that the agency implemented to fulfill a service need while staying within tight budgetary restraints (VIPS Newsletter, 2010).

Shah et al. (2007) make it clear in their research that the demand for bilingual police officers exists in various areas of the nation. Specifically, they examined the state-of-affairs in California, Nevada, and Ohio, when considering challenges that exist in meeting this demand. As is also seen previously in our example of the *Spanish Speaking Ride Along Program,* it would appear that the need for these services also exists in Oklahoma. Likewise, it is clear that this need exists in Houston, Texas. Thus, it would appear that police agencies will need to find innovative means to solve this problem and will need to be receptive to utilizing persons from social service backgrounds as well as volunteers from the community.

Going back to the first part of our discussion in which we showcased the challenges facing the Houston Police Department, we would like to make one additional point. Houston is a port town and this means, among other things, that it has a strong international focus in terms of commerce, influence, and population. Our point in mentioning this is to note that this means that Houston is not just a multicultural city, it is also an international city (Pinkerton & Loucks, 2011). Indeed, the same is true with numerous cities around the nation, such as Los Angeles, New York, and

Miami. We think that this is an important point because, as we have noted at the beginning of this text, in today's world, the study of multicultural issues is not complete unless it also considers international issues, simultaneously. No longer can the two areas of study and practice be presented as mutually exclusive, as can be seen by the challenges that face our law enforcement today.

References: Pinkerton, J. & Loucks, M. (2011, January 11). Some fear language barrier blocks HPD service. Houston Chronicle, retrieved from http://www.chron.com/news/houston-texas/article/Some-fear-language-barrier-blocks-HPD-service-1587827.php

Shah, S., Rahman, I., & Khashu, A. (2007). *Overcoming language barriers: Solutions for law enforcement.* New York: Vera Institute of Justice.

VIPS Newsletter (2010). *Bridging the Gap: Engaging Volunteers in Multicultural Outreach.* Alexandria, VA: International Chiefs of Police (IACP).

Availability of Trained Bilingual and Bicultural Staff

Ideally, criminal justice practitioners should be bilingual, bicultural, and be from the community that they serve. However, in some circumstances, personnel who are bilingual may not be from the culture and community that they serve. This may mean that, in such circumstances, the schematic views held by the practitioner and members of that community may be very different. In such situations, communication challenges may arise, even though personnel or interpreters speak the same language as those in the surrounding community. Thus, agency supervisors should be cautious when selecting bilingual personnel and interpreters. Those who are bilingual also must understand nonverbal and cultural patterns to communicate effectively. Bilingual staff members should demonstrate bilingual proficiency and undergo cultural competence training (DHHS, 2000a). Subsequent subsections of this chapter will demonstrate how important nonverbal communication and cross-racial issues can be in the communication process, even when both parties speak the same language.

Dissemination of Crime-Fighting Information

Written information should be translated into multiple languages, as appropriate for the community that is served. The literacy level of the target population must be considered when developing written materials. Any written materials should be supplemented with other forms of information (DHHS, 2000a). For example, messages may be conveyed by radio or through announcements at churches and other community centers. Most localities now have television stations that broadcast in the languages of various cultural groups. Although these communications media should be used, it is important to note that some people do not have access to television and may depend on radio broadcasts for information.

Criminal justice agencies, such as police departments, courthouses, and probation/parole agencies, should establish relationships with multicultural television stations, radio stations, and newspapers before a disaster occurs. In addition, the agency should invite television and radio station personnel to participate in the development of community crime prevention programs. The same is true for agencies that have victim-services bureaus or other similar units of operation. The key is to have media that encourages minorities in the community to utilize agency services as a means of building a positive rapport.

Lastly, as is workable, the information needs of people who are deaf or hard of hearing also must be considered. Closed-captioned television, for example, is a critical communication tool for this population. Crime information (i.e., crime stoppers, public

INTERNATIONAL FOCUS

Cross-Cultural Communication Misunderstandings in Hong Kong

As noted at the beginning of this section, there has been little research that addresses the use of cross-linguistic interviewing. Thus, multinational research related to cross-linguistic interrogation might prove beneficial as well. To illustrate this point, Broadhurst and Cheng (2005) discuss an example where a young Chinese American girl is detained at the border of Hong Kong and the People's Republic of China where she was accused of presenting a fake passport. The testimony given by the girl is not believed by border officials in Hong Kong at which point, the girl provides a confession claiming that her document was fake. As a result, she was jailed until, eventually, it was discovered that the passport was legitimate and that she should not have been arrested. This circumstance shows that it is difficult to determine truth from deceit in cross cultural settings around the world, not just in the United States (Broadhurst & Cheng, 2005).

Some research does exist related to cross-cultural differences and the detection of deception. For instance, O'Hair, Cody, Wang, and Choa (1990) examined vocal stress differences in truthful and deceptive messages among Chinese . They found that Chinese had higher levels of vocal stress when revealing negative emotions. Going further, Yeung, Levine, and Nishiyama (1999) provided research on cross cultural issues related to deception and the detection of deception. They note that there are substantial differences in what is referred to as 'Chinese ritual communication' (p. 4). In such cases with, for instance, with invitations, where Chinese may decline invitations when, in fact, in Chinese culture, these are not taken as actual denials but, instead, as a polite means of ensuring the sincerity of the invitation from the host. Among Westerners, such a decline might be perceived as a rude gesture. Often, these ritualistic strategies to communication are intended to 'save face' (p. 3) among Chinese communicators, an issue that is seldom of serious concern among Westerners, at least not to the extent that is found among Chinese.

As with the example by Broadhurst and Cheng (2005) of miscommunication and misinterpretation of deception that occurred among hong kong border officials, it could be that cross-cultural norms have much to do with misinterpretation of deception. Indeed, the young girl erroneously arrested for having a false passport was Chinese American, and was, therefore, somewhat Westernized. Likewise, persons in Hong Kong were more close in kinship and mannerism to their Chinese neighbors, though, they too, were more Westernized than their kin in the People's Republic of China. Though it is not clear if this situation was the result of primarily cultural differences and/or experiences in acculturation and assimilation, it is clear that this may, indeed, serve as the basis for many misunderstandings, both large and small. From the general police inquiry of a potential suspect or witness on the street, to larger-scale discussions among international leaders who come together to fight terrorism, the potential for misunderstandings and misattributions of deceit to others can undermine collaboration, productivity, and peaceful outcomes for crime-fighters and national security officials, alike.

Sources: Broadhurst, R.G & Cheng, K.H.W. (2005). The Detection of Deception: The Effects of First and Second Language on Lie Detection Ability. *Journal of Psychiatry, Psychology and Law, 12*(1), 107–118.

O'Hair, Cody, Wang, & Choa (1990). Vocal stress and deceptions detection among Chinese. *Communication Quarterly, 38*,158–169.

Yeung, Levine, & Nishiyama (1999). Information manipulation theory and perceptions of deception in Hong Kong. *Communication Reports, 12*(1), 1–11.

service bulletins, and soon) presented on television must be accessible to persons who are deaf or hard of hearing. Interpretation is the oral restating in one language of what has been said in another language. Translation typically refers to the conversion of written materials from one language to another (Goode et al., 2001).

Language and Sign-Language Interpretation

Language interpretation may be used when the language barrier is so great that communication between criminal justice practitioners and citizens is not possible or when no bilingual staff can be hired. Sign-language interpretation also must be considered when developing communication strategies. Here again, with the use of interpreters (whether verbal or sign-language) the schema of the sender and receiver in the communication process is important. Interpreters who are not culturally competent (or ideally, culturally proficient) in relation to those with whom they speak can make serious errors in relaying information.

In all cases, hiring bilingual personnel remains the preferred solution, as opposed to the use of interpreters. Indeed, Van der Veer (1995) notes that an interpreter's behavior may evoke certain feelings in a person. Factors such as the interpreter's gender, age, or level of acculturation may affect the citizen's willingness to speak openly. Consider also that some citizens may distrust interpreters who are from the same country and speak the same language, but who have different political or religious backgrounds (Van der Veer, 1995). Thus, the hiring of interpreters is not an instant panacea to problems associated with intercultural communication.

Lastly, interpreters should be trained to accurately convey the tone, level, and meaning of the information presented in the original language. Without adequate training, interpreters may interpret information inaccurately or incompletely. The most common problems include changing open-ended questions into leading questions, altering the content of questions, and adding comments. Problems in interpreting answers include leaving out part of the answer, adding something to the answer, and making mistakes because of limited understanding of English (Van der Veer, 1995). Obviously, this can have serious consequences for a citizen who is required to engage in legal proceedings during later stages of criminal justice processing of an incident.

Cross-Racial Issues

As we noted previously with schemas, individuals may be more prone to encode, interpret, store, and retrieve similar memories in a different manner when a person is of a different racial group than their own. Much of the reason for this difference in interpretation may simply be due to a lack of familiarity with the different racial group; this lack of familiarity therefore does not fit well with the preexisting cognitive maps that the person has to draw from when distinguishing important stimuli associated with the unfamiliar racial group. In fact, failure in the specificity of encoding has been noted as a causal factor for difficulties in cross-racial identification (Davis & Follette, 2000). It may be that individuals engage in more generalized processing of physical features, placing more attention on a person's race rather than on his/her individual features. In addition, certain racial groups may attend to less-effective features with other races due to the habit of using these same features to distinguish between members of their own racial group.

For instance, Caucasians may use eye and hair color to distinguish amongst themselves but have great difficulty with such distinctions between members of races where such characteristics tend to consist of dark hair and dark eyes. Thus, if these familiar strategies are used to encode facial features, the individual will be ineffective at relating details of that person's features. However, there has been some research that shows that such cross-racial identification is less difficult for people who spend more time with members of other races, thereby being more adept at discerning between features (Dunning, Li, & Malpass, 1998; Platz & Hosch, 1988). This demonstrates that a need exists for practitioners to be trained in nonverbal and facial recognition so as to ensure that they do not overlook important details when communicating with persons of racial groups other than their own. For those who interview and/or take reports from persons in the community (as will police), offenders in prison or on community supervision (as with correctional officers or probation officers), or even those in the judiciary (i.e., courthouse workers), it is imperative that these shortcomings not be allowed to create inconsistencies in the justice system.

To further illustrate the fact that racial recognition is a relevant issue to memory recall between races, Teitlebaum and Geiselman (1997) conducted a cross-racial recognition research to understand its impact on overall recall. These researchers examined cross-race facial recognition of Caucasian and African Americans with subjects from four distinct racial groups: Caucasians, African American, Latino American, and Asian Americans. Subjects in this study viewed sets of intermixed Black and White faces under varying circumstances. They found a strong cross-racial recognition effect between African American and Caucasian subjects, such that participants from either racial group were more likely to recognize faces of their own race and more likely to have a false recognition for faces of the other race. Latino and Asian Americans, on the other hand, were also less accurate in their recognition of African American faces than African American subjects, but they were no less accurate in their recognition of Caucasian American faces than African American ones (Teitlebaum & Geiselman, 1997). Thus, it is clear that cross-racial factors can be important in witness interviews, facial recognition processes, the reading of nonverbal cues, and perpetrator interrogation processes. By extension, it is easy to conclude that these issues probably affect the ability of criminal justice personnel to engage in effective communication with diverse community members in other contexts, as well.

Consider the research by Word, Zanna, and Cooper (1974) who had Caucasian men interview job applicants who were both Caucasian and African American in racial orientation. It was found that when the applicant was African American, the interviewers tended to sit further from the applicant, they ended the interview roughly 25 percent earlier than they did with the Caucasian applicants, and they made 50 percent more speech errors than when the applicant was Caucasian. However, these researchers were not sure whether these observed effects were, in fact, likely to be due to discomfort rooted in racial differences.

This is an important point to consider when addressing intercultural communications between criminal justice practitioners and citizens who are of differing racial groups. Indeed, practitioners can inadvertently contaminate the communication process as well as any testimony that they receive simply due to their own discomfort in interviewing individuals of a different racial or cultural group. This, when coupled with the difficulties that citizens may have when making cross-racial memory recollections of perpetrators or victims of crime, presents with compelling support for extensive training of personnel in intercultural communication dynamics.

Multi-Linguistic Issues in Interviewing and Interrogations

There is very little research that addresses interviewing techniques between interviewers and the interviewees who come from different cultures of origin. Because of the dearth of research on this specific issue, a number of studies are presented that address multi-linguistic issues associated with survey items as well as research on multi-linguistic interrogation techniques related to the detection of lies.

Recently, some studies have been conducted that use survey items to gather information regarding the subject's understanding of content within a given survey. Some of these studies have been conducted with multiple linguistic groups. One study in particular by Willis, Lawrence, Thompson, Kudela, Levin, and Miller (2005) focused on both Latino and Asian subjects and assessed the intercultural equivalence of survey questions. Specifically, Willis et al. (2005) explored the effectiveness of their questionnaire when translated from English to Spanish, Chinese (both Mandarin and Cantonese), Korean, and Vietnamese. During the process of translation, it was found that there were many more difficulties than initially expected in attempting to ensure that the intended meaning was extended to the person taking the survey. In fact, Chinese and Korean teams of translators suggested revisions to over 60 percent of the roughly 200 survey items, with even more extensive revision being needed for the Spanish and Vietnamese versions.

This alone demonstrates how difficult it may be to conduct **cross-linguistic interviews**, which refers to interviews that are conducted from written protocols that have been translated from English into another language. Willis et al. (2005) found reason to doubt the validity of interviews made during the study due to observation that the survey itself was administered improperly. For example, interviewers read items with no pauses, precluding any opportunity to answer each individual statement before the interviewer presented the next question from the structured protocol. Willis et al. (2005) concluded that these pitfalls helped demonstrate the difficulty researchers/investigators whose primary language is English might have in monitoring or conducting non-English communication. This research demonstrates the complexities that may be involved with any form of cross-linguistic communication.

Going beyond the study by Willis et al. (2005) and its examples of potential mishaps in translation, other researches have shown that respondents may face great difficulty with common interview probes and techniques. Specific to Asian populations, it has been found in one study by Pan (2004) that translated interview items did not work well with Chinese-speaking respondents (Pan, 2004; Potaka and Cochrane, 2002 & 2004). Pan even found that respondents with higher degrees of education experienced difficulties. Ultimately, Pan (2004) attributed this to a lack of familiarity with the social context of the survey interview as well as to various translation issues. Many English language interviews and surveys contain expressions specific to English and the literal translation of these expressions may not be linguistically or culturally appropriate.

These last few points are important to consider since, in many cases, expert interviewers may use protocols or other instruments to guide them through interviews and communication processes. This is even more likely to be the case when agencies cannot locate persons fluent in a specific language. This results in the use of quasi-fluent interviewers and/or translators who are not trained in effective interviewing or interrogation techniques. This can then hamper the effectiveness of intercultural communications where detailed information related to criminal offenses may need to be acquired. For the sake of clarity, the concern presented in this particular subsection of this chapter relates to interviewers who are fluent in the same language as their interviewees (i.e., Spanish-speaking interviewer with Spanish-speaking interviewee). There has been little research on the use of translated items and/or translators who conduct witness interviews or perpetrator interrogations who are not fluent in the language of the witness being interviewed. In countries like the United States, this can prove to be a fairly valid area of concern. This may be true in a number of situations, such as when translators are difficult to find or even when they may not be trustworthy (as with gang member interrogations or when interviewing witnesses of gang crimes). In fact, in some neighborhoods it may well be that witnesses will indeed lie even though they are not linked to a given crime. Often they may do so out of fear and feelings of intimidation from gang members in their community. This has been observed in both Latino American and Asian communities, and is especially problematic for newly immigrated persons (Valdez, 2005).

In addition, other research related to cross-linguistic interrogation might prove beneficial as well. **Cross-linguistic interrogation** is when an investigator seeks to gain evidence of deceit or criminal behavior from suspects who are of a minority racial or ethnic group. The research by Broadhurst & Cheng (2005) is largely centered around the ability to detect lies among suspects. Although interesting, it is not necessarily the ability to detect lies that is of central focus for this subsection—though such a skill can be useful when questioning witnesses who might employ deception for any number of reasons (i.e., a desire to not get involved, fear and intimidation, inconvenience, etc.). However, this study is relevant to this chapter because it specifically examines intercultural nonverbal communication patterns among persons speaking both a primary and a secondary language.

The work of Broadhurst & Cheng (2005) demonstrates that a person's ability to interpret nonverbal and verbal behavior is strongly linked to cultural variations embedded in language. At least two prior studies also seem to support these findings. For instance, Vinacke and Fong (1955) showed photographs to Japanese, Chinese, and U.S. subjects and found that there was greater agreement when judging the expression of emotional features among members of their own cultural group as opposed to persons from other groups. Another study by Joy and Casmir (1998) compared the ability of subjects to assess emotions by students. Subjects came from Japan, Germany, South Africa, and the United States. It was found that students who had engaged in foreign travel were more accurate in interpreting the facial nonverbal expressions in an intercultural context than were students who had not traveled abroad.

Broadhurst and Cheng (2005) found that observers did less well in identifying deceit in their first language but were more successful in identifying deceit when the person spoke in their second language. In addition, Broadhurst and Cheng (2005) noted that observers tended to rely on micro-expressions when predicting truthfulness and these types of nonverbal cues are not as easily manipulated as are more direct forms of nonverbal expression (Ekman, 1992). The observers in this study were not trained in facial recognition or micro-expression analysis. As such, Broadhurst and Cheng conclude that detection in judgment accuracy would likely be even further improved if such training were given to observers.

Though prior research has contended that there are universal facial expressions linked to basic emotional responses (joy, sadness, anger, disgust, fear, and surprise), this contention has not always held up to more recent research (Matsumoto, 2001). The work of Matsumoto (2001) has more recently found that intercultural emotional expression consists of a myriad of similarities and differences in how different cultural groups experience, express, and perceive emotions. Therefore, interviewers asking questions of a witness speaking a secondary language should exert extreme caution when making any kind of final determination regarding the emotional content of testimony. Indeed, one study of emotions found that a second language (English) served as a distancing factor among Chinese (who were primarily fluent in Cantonese), allowing speakers to be more emotionally neutral when discussing emotionally embarrassing issues (Bond & Lai, 1986). Again, this is particularly important for jurisdictions that may find the need to interview witnesses of an incident when these witnesses speak English as a second language and when the agency has no personnel who are fluent in the witnesses' primary language.

Intercultural Communication with Citizen Relations and Agency Operations

The previous subsections have dealt mainly with issues revolving around interviewing and interrogation processes in intercultural communications. While these two areas of information exchange are obviously important to criminal justice practitioners, it is also important to note that the average day-to-day communications with the general citizen are another primary consideration. Indeed, it is important for practitioners, namely police officers, to have effective interactions with citizens during routine encounters. In fact, community policing models, where citizen input and citizen volunteers in police agencies are common features, require that officers be effective in developing a rapport with members of the community, particularly the minority community.

Likewise, effective intercultural communications are important for leaders of criminal justice agencies, whether police, corrections, judicial, or juvenile. Leaders of any of these agencies will have personnel whom they manage who will likely come from a diverse array of backgrounds, whether they be racial, cultural, or some other type of minority status. This, in addition to the fact that their "clientele" with whom they routinely serve (citizens and victims) or process (offenders) are also likely to be a diverse population, necessitates that they be culturally competent and also that they engage in effective intercultural communication. Further, it is important that these leaders transmit the importance of these types of communication to other persons throughout the organizational hierarchy, establishing a top-down approach of implementation.

The **top-down model** of implementation exists when executive leadership makes mandatory the agency-wide adoption of culturally competent responses and inter-culturally effective techniques when dealing with people of various identities and backgrounds within the agency's jurisdiction. This is an important model of implementation that, in some cases, may require substantial organizational change. Even if these practices are adopted, it is important that top leadership emphasize their importance and provide recurring training and incentives for these practices. This ensures that such practices are understood by members of the agency who are new and by those who are long-term veterans. It also ensures that these aspects of agency operation do not become stale and outdated in their approach.

The day-to-day practitioner will benefit from being effective in intercultural communications because they will likely be more effective in gaining results that are positive in their daily interactions. Furthermore, as we have noted in the previous subsection, individuals who have experience with groups who are different from their own racial or ethnic group will likely be more effective in understanding individuals of other racial or cultural identities. This will likely lower the stress levels for the individual practitioner who will not be in a routine state of tension or conflict and will also likely allow them to develop more support from the community (if police) or compliance from inmates (if correctional personnel), which also improves effectiveness and lowers conflict within the organization. Such individuals will also be more adept at reading through communication patterns, both nonverbal and verbal, so that their effectiveness in addressing criminal processing of cases and/or resolving disturbances within facilities is optimized. This alone serves as sufficient support for why cultural competence and intercultural communication are so important in today's world of criminal justice.

CONCLUSION

In this chapter, we have gone to great lengths to explain cultural competence and provided an overview of the different levels of competency along a continuum of possibilities. We have also discussed, in detail, the means by which cultural competence can be implemented and maintained within criminal justice agencies. A willingness to understand the different levels of acculturation that immigrants experience is also important for agencies to provide effective services to those groups who may have differing generational levels of acculturation from the United States. Furthermore, religious diversity must also be considered if we are to be competent with many of the cultural groups that we will encounter in the criminal justice field. Through training, research, and evaluation, agencies can ensure that cultural competence is given the appropriate level of emphasis necessary, both internally within the organization and externally throughout the community.

Intercultural communication was another key aspect of this chapter. As a basis to understanding how cultural competence impacts intercultural communication processes, we presented an overview of different types of schemas that impact how we view ourselves, others with whom we communicate, the circumstances and roles of these interactions, and the value attached to those interactions. We likewise provide an overview of considerations regarding the use of interpreters as well as bilingual individuals.

Additional considerations regarding cross-racial communication were also provided. Lastly, we discussed important concepts with regard to intercultural interviews and interrogations.

It is clear that both cultural competence and intercultural communication are important to the agency's effectiveness within a diverse community. Agencies should strive to attain high levels of cultural competence, and effective means of providing intercultural communication within the community. With this in mind, practitioners and citizens can optimize the safety of their community and can also ensure that agency–community relations remain strong. This is, at the heart of it, the key desire of any service-oriented agency whose role is to protect its surrounding community.

Chapter 5 Learning Check

1. Which of the following is NOT a category of acculturation?
   a. **Maintaining**
   b. Surviving
   c. Choosing
   d. Adjusting
   e. Changing

2. _____, on the other hand, is the process by which one person communicates with another who is from a different racial or ethnic group where language fluency, educational attainment, emotional affect, and nonverbal mannerisms are variables that impact the exchange of information between the two persons.
   a. Intercultural proficiency
   b. Cross-linguistic communication
   c. **Intercultural communication**
   d. All of the above
   e. None of the above

3. Which of the following is NOT a stage of the cultural competence continuum?
   a. Cultural Blindness
   b. Cultural Destructiveness
   c. **Cultural Recognition**
   d. Culturally Proficient
   e. None of the above

4. **Schemas** are cognitive structures that represent knowledge about a given concept, including attributes associated with that concept and its relationship to the environment.
   a. **True**
   b. False

5. The terms intercultural communication and cross-cultural communication have the same definition.
   a. True
   b. **False**

6. Individualism vs. collectivism is a means by which cultures emphasize personal autonomy over group cohesion.
   a. **True**
   b. False

7. Linguistic competence ensures accurate communication of information in languages other than English.
   a. **True**
   b. False

8. Which of the following is NOT a type of schema discussed in this chapter?
   a. Self-Schema
   b. Role Schema
   c. Event Schema
   d. Causal Schema
   e. **None of the above**

9. _____ is when an investigator seeks to gain evidence of deceit or criminal behavior from suspects who are of a minority racial or ethnic group.
   a. Cross-linguistic inquiry
   b. Intercultural interview
   c. **Cross-linguistic interrogation**
   d. Cross-linguistic discussion
   e. None of the Above.

10. The _____ of implementation exists when executive leadership makes mandatory the agency-wide adoption of culturally competent responses and interculturally effective techniques.
    a. Executive Dissemination Model
    b. Collaborative Model
    c. **Top-Down Model**
    d. Agency Culture Change Model
    e. None of the above

Essay Discussion Questions

1. Explain why intercultural communication skills are so important to agencies. In your opinion, do you think that agencies can be culturally competent if their staff do not possess good skills in intercultural communication? Explain why or why not.

2. Explain the difference between assimilation and acculturation. How are each of these important when attempting to communicate with newer immigrants in the United States?

3. Identify and discuss the stages of the Cultural Competence Continuum, by Cross, Bazron, Dennis, & Isaacs (1989).

References

Almeida, R. (1996). Hindu, Christian, and Muslim families. In M. McGoldrick, M. Giordano, J. Pearce, & J. Giordano (Eds.), *Ethnicity and family therapy* (2nd ed., pp. 395–423). New York: Guilford Press.

Bennett, C. E. (2002). *A Profile of the nation's foreign-born population from Asia (2000 update)*. Washington, DC: U.S. Census Bureau.

Bond, M. H., & Lai, T. (1987). Embarrassment and Code-switching into a Second Language. *Journal of Social Psychology, 126*, 179–186.

Broadhurst, R. G., & Cheng, K. H. W. (2005). The detection of deception: The effects of first and second language on lie detection ability. *Journal of Psychiatry, Psychology and Law, 12*(1), 107–118.

Cheng, K. H., & Broadhurst, R. G. (2005). Detection of deception: The effects of language on detection ability among Hong Kong Chinese. *Psychiatry, Psychology and Law, 12*(1), 107–118.

Cross, T., Bazron, B., Dennis, K., & Isaacs, M. (1989). *Towards a culturally competent system of care, Volume 1.* Washington, DC: CASSP Technical Assistance Center, Center for Child Health and Mental Health Policy, Georgetown University Child Development Center.

Cultural Competence and Public Defense Michigan Workgroup. (2011). *Beyond diversity: The role of cultural competence in an effective Michigan public defense system.* Lansing: Michigan.

Dana, R. H., Behn, J. D., & Gonwa, T. (1992). A checklist for the examination of cultural competence in social service agencies. *Research of Social Work Practice, 2*, 220–233.

Dana, R. H., & Matheson, L. (1992). An application of the agency cultural competence checklist to a program serving small and diverse ethnic communities. *Psychological rehabilitation Journal, 15*(1), 101–105.

Davis, D., & Follette, W. C. (2000). Foibles of witness memory for traumatic/high profile events. *Journal of Air Law and Commerce, 22*(1), 2–174.

Dunning, D., Li, J. C., & Malpass, R. S. (1998). Basketball fandom and crossrace identification among european-americans: Another look at the contact hypothesis. *Redondo Beach, CA: American Psychology-Law Society.*

Ekman, P. (1992). An argument for basic emotions. *Cognition and Emotion, 6*, 169–200.

Ekman, P., & Friesen, W. (1975). *Unmasking the face.* Englewood Cliffs, NJ: Prentice Hall.

Fisher, R. P., & Geiselman, R. E. (1992). *Memory-enhancing techniques for investigative interviewing: The Cognitive Interview.* Springfield, IL: Charles C. Thomas Books.

Gudykunst, W. B. (2003). *Intercultural and intercultural communication* (Ed.). Thousand Oaks, CA: Sage Publications.

Hanser, R. D. (2006). *Special needs offenders.* Upper Saddle River, NJ: Prentice Hall.

Hofstede, G. (2001). *Culture's Consequences* (2nd ed.). Thousand Oaks, CA: Sage.

Joy, S., & Casmir, F. L. (1998). The impact of culture-sameness, gender, foreign travel, and academic background on the ability to interpret facial expression of emotion in others. *Communication Quarterly, 12*, 214–27.

Khashu, A., Busch, R., & Latif, Z. (2005). *Building strong police-immigrant community relations: Lessons from a New York City Project.* New York, NY: Vera Institute of Justice.

Law Enforcement Resource Center. (1997). *Community oriented policing: Facilitator's guide.* Minneapolis, MN: Law Enforcement Resource Center.

Lee, S. J. (1996). *Unraveling the "model minority" stereotype: Listening to Asian American youth.* New York: Teachers College Press.

Matsumoto, D. (2001). Culture and emotion. In D. Matsumoto (ed.), *The Handbook of Culture and Psychology.* New York: Oxford University Press.

McGoldrick, M., Giordano, J., Pearce, J. K., & Giordano, J. (1996). *Ethnicity and family therapy* (2nd ed.). New York: Guilford Press.

National Crime Prevention Council. (1995). *Lengthening the stride: employing peace officers from newly arrived ethnic groups.* Washington, DC: National Crime Prevention Council. Retrieved from: http://www.ncjrs.gov/txtfiles/stride.txt.

Olivo, A., & Avila, O. (2006). *Latinos Choosing Suburbs Over Cities*. Indiana: University of Notre Dame.

Osgood, C. E., May, W. S., & Miron, M. S. (1975). *Cross Cultural Universals of Affective Meaning*. Champaign, IL: University of Illinois Press, 1975.

Pan, Y. (2004). *Cognitive interviews in languages other than English: Methodological and research issues*. Paper presented at the American Association for Public Opinion Research conference, May 13–16, 2004, Phoenix, AZ. 2004.

Platz, S. J., & Hosch, H. M. (1988). Cross racial/ethnic eyewitness identification: A field study. *Journal of Applied Social Psychology, 18*(1), 972–1008.

Potaka, L., & Cochrane, S. (2002). Developing bilingual questionnaires: Experiences from New Zealand in the development of the 2001 Maori language survey. Paper presented at the International Conference on Questionnaire Development, Evaluation, and Testing Methods (QDET), Charleston, SC, November 14–17, 2002.

Potaka, L., & Cochrane, S. (2004). Developing bilingual questionnaires: Experiences from New Zealand in the development of the 2001 Maori language survey. *Journal of Official Statistics, 20*(2), pp. 289–300.

Prosser, M. H. (2012). Intercultural communication. In M. H. Prosser (Ed.), *Encyclopedia of Communication Theory* (pp. 248–52). Thousand Oaks, CA: Sage Publications.

Robbins, S. P. (2003). *Organizational Behavior* (10th ed.). Upper Saddle River, NJ: Prentice Hall.

Shaw, C., & McKay, H. (1942). *Juvenile delinquency in urban areas*. Chicago, IL: University of Chicago Press.

Shusta, M., Levine, D. R., Harris, P. R., & Wong, H. Z. (2011). *Multicultural law en-forcement: Strategies for peacekeeping in a diverse society* (5th ed.). Upper Saddle River, N J: Prentice Hall.

Singer, A. (2006). Skipping the city for the suburbs. *Urbanite Baltimore, 19*, pp. 47–49.

Sue, D. W., & Sue, D. (2007). *Counseling the culturally diverse: Theory and practice* (5th ed.). New York, NY: John Wiley & Sons, Inc.

Teitelbaum, S., & Geiselman, R. E. (1997). Observer mood and cross-racial recognition of faces. *Journal of Intercultural Psychology, 28*(1), 93–106.

U.S. Department of Health and Human Services. (2003). *Developing cultural competence in disaster mental health programs: Guiding principals and recommendations*. DHHS Pub. No. SMA 3828. Rockville, MD: Center for mental health services, substance abuse and mental health services administration.

U.S. Department of Health and Human Services. (2001). *Mental Health: Culture, race, and ethnicity—A supplement to mental health: A report of the Surgeon General*. Rockville, MD: U. S. Department of Health and Human Services, Substance Abuse and Mental Health Services Administration, Center for Mental Health Services.

U.S. Department of Health and Human Services. (1999). *Mental Health: A report to the Surgeon General*. Rockville, MD: Author.

United States Department of Justice. (2000). *Defense counsel in criminal cases*. Washington, DC: Bureau of Justice Statistics. Retrieved from: http://www.ojp.usdoj.gov/bjs/pub/pdf/dccc.pdf.

United States Department of Justice—Community Relations Service. (2005). *The Milwaukee agreement*. Chicago, IL: United States Department of Justice—Community Relations Service.

van der Veer, G. (1995). *Counselling and therapy with refugees, Psychological problems in victims of war, torture and repression*. New York: John Wiley and Sons.

Valdez, A. (2005). *Gangs: A guide to understanding street gangs* (4th ed.). LawTech Publishing. Retrieved from: http://www.LawTechPublishing.com.

Vinacke, W., & R. Fong. (1955). The judgment of facial expressions by three national-racial groups in Hawaii: Caucasian faces. *Journal of Personality, 17*, 407–29.

Willis, G., Lawrence, D., Thompson, F., Kudela, M., Levin, K., & Miller, K. (2005). *The use of cognitive interviewing to evaluate translated survey instruments: Lessons learned*. Paper presented at 2005 Conference of the Federal Committee on Statistical Methodology. November 14, 2005, Arlington, VA.

Word, C. O., Zanna, M. P., & Cooper, J. (1974). The nonverbal mediation of self-fulfilling prophecies in interracial interaction. *Journal of Experimental Social Psychology, 10*, 109–120.

Law Enforcement and Minorities: Specific Demographic Groups, Victims, and Offenders

LEARNING OBJECTIVES

After reading this chapter, students should be able to do the following:

1. Identify issues specific to African Americans, including the impact of slavery on African American identity formation, structural racism, racial profiling, and confidence in police.

2. Identify issues specific to Latino Americans, including differing nationalities, historical developments, and the impact of immigration issues.

3. Identify issues specific to Native Americans, including regional demographics, belief systems, and their unique legal status.

4. Identify issues specific to Asian Americans including generational issues, religious and cultural values, and family dynamics.

5. Identify issues specific to Middle Eastern Americans including differing nationalities, family dynamics, as well as hate crimes and discriminatory treatment after 9/11.

6. Discuss issues related to police response to victims and offenders of crime who are among various racial minorities

KEY TERMS

Arab Americans

Arab Anti-Discrimination Committee (ADC)

Bureau of Indian Affairs (BIA)

Civil Rights Movement

Creator or Great Spirit

Cuban Americans

Differential stops

Farsi

Historical victimization

Intra-racial

Iranians

Macro-level victimizations

Marginalization

Mexican Americans

Middle Eastern Americans

National Crime Victimization Survey

Puerto Ricans

Push factors

Racial profiling

Shi'ah sect

Structural racism

2010 Tribal Law and Order Act

Turks

Victim-Based selection bias

INTRODUCTION

In this chapter, we cover issues related to police–community relations with African Americans, Latino Americans, Native Americans, Asian Americans, and Middle Eastern Americans. For each group, we provide demographic and/or historical background. It is our intent to avoid rehashing the same material that has been covered on each group in previous chapters. Yet, at the same time, it is necessary to provide history in some circumstances if it relates to how police relations with a given group have developed over time and/or demonstrates how that group has been impacted in the past. Experiences in previous generations will be part of the social teaching that younger generations acquire today; hence, the historical context of policing with these groups can be very important. This is particularly true with African Americans.

Moreover, whether right or wrong, the weight of the content has been given to groups who are either larger and more commonly encountered minorities or minorities that have caught the public eye more frequently in the past few years. This is especially true with African Americans (excessive use of deadly force and portrayal as crime-prone), Latino Americans (border enforcement and immigration), and Middle Eastern Americans (the war on terror). For Asian Americans and Native Americans, we have included information that is relevant to policing but may have added less commentary on historical issues because information is provided in other areas of this text or because there is less relevancy to policing. In other words, each group is presented from the perspective of its relationship to police agencies and their experience with policing in their communities.

AFRICAN AMERICANS

Historically, a primary focus of police–community relations problems has involved the African American community. Much of this has to do with events that set the tone for discrimination and disparity over a hundred years back where, despite official programs to empower the African American community, unofficial resistance to the integration of African Americans into mainstream society resulted in years of disadvantaged opportunities that continued for generations. Thus, slavery is one key predecessor to explaining the long-term distrust of social services and criminal justice agencies that has existed for generations.

Historically and culturally speaking, there is no doubt that the institution of slavery left a lasting and profound impact on the African American psyche. Indeed, during the late 17th and 18th centuries, strict laws were imposed upon African Americans, both during the slave era and later. Blacks were punished harshly under these laws and law enforcement often acted as primary enforcers of these laws, being the bringer of harsh penalties that followed. In many areas of the nation, police were expected to continue enforcing biased and discriminatory laws including those setting curfews for African Americans and those that barred them from attending local functions.

Slavery has served as a source of historical trauma that has impacted the African American population throughout much of the history of the United States. Even though the practice of slavery ended over 100 years ago, there have been successive laws, policies, customs, and practices that were implemented which kept African

Americans from sharing an equal standard of life and liberty as Caucasian Americans. Indeed, many of the advances in civil rights gained by African Americans are the result of a fight from being slave, to freed person, to a people of equality. The origins of many of the disparities that exist between the African American population and the Caucasian American population lie in the early American practice of slavery and, because of this, we would be remiss if we did not provide a discussion of this aspect of African American history.

Slavery in the Colonies and Later United States

In the early to mid-1600s, the first legally recognized slaves in the United States began to appear (Frosch, 1997; Kolchin, 2003). This continued even after the American Revolution, in which the American Colonies obtained freedom from England. Despite America's rhetoric on freedom, slavery continued to be an important economic institution for southern states in the newly founded United States. During this time, most northern states passed emancipation acts from the 1780s to the early 1800s, but in the southern states slavery continued to expand in its implementation. By 1860, the U.S. Census recorded that approximately 8 percent of all U.S. families owned slaves, with a total of 3,950,528 slaves being owned in the United States. Approximately one-third of these were owned by families in the South (Frosch, 1997).

The practice of slavery was one that was cruel and harsh, with slaves being given no rights to family or other considerations. In fact, the southern system would commonly break up African slave families as a means of controlling the population and keeping them docile. Indeed, most slaves lived in fear of being transported away from their family and/or friends. This psychological tactic of gaining compliance impacted the entire population and intensified the historical trauma that African Americans would carry with them for generations after this practice was ended.

The working conditions were brutal and inhumane. Plantation owners engaged slaves in the cotton, tobacco, rice, and sugarcane fields of various states throughout the south, in hot and humid conditions. Most of the time, slaves throughout the south worked from dawn until dusk. However, some slaves worked under a task system where, if their work for the day had been completed, they might have some free time to tend their own gardens. Slaves might do both unskilled and skilled work, depending on their own personal ability and the needs of their owner. Most slaves conducted heavy physical labor, which included the clearing of land and the tending of crops. For those lucky enough to be household slaves, cooking, cleaning, and taking care of the slave owner's children were the usual chores.

For most slaves, especially the field hands, the standard of living was extremely poor and dietary standards were likewise inadequate. Despite this rough treatment and despite the cruel punishments inflicted on slaves who disobeyed their owners or tried to escape the plantation, the slave owner did have a vested interest in keeping slaves fit enough to continue work. However, this was usually the sole objective in maintaining the care of slaves in their stead.

Other forms of abuses were also inflicted on slaves. For instance, it was not uncommon for slave owners to sexually assault female slaves. This was especially true among the female household slaves who might be selected due to their superior physical features and/or some other attraction experienced by the slave owner.

Female slaves, regardless of whether they had children by other slave men and regardless of their own desires or affiliations with their families, could be taken into the slave owner's home and would be forced into sexual activity. This type of victimization was not entirely uncommon and, on some plantations, the offspring of the slave owner and female slave might be intermixed among the other slaves on the plantation.

The End of Slavery in the United States

Amidst the work of abolitionists who had long resisted the practice of slavery, it was the 1860 election of President Abraham Lincoln that provided the coordinated and organized reaction against this practice. Lincoln's official *Emancipation Proclamation*, given in 1863 during the American Civil War, was an official statement declaring that all slaves in the United States (both North and South) were officially free. This proclamation turned the official objective of the war from semantics related to state's rights to one geared toward freedom for all, including those who were held as slaves, within the borders of the United States. Upon the defeat of the Southern Confederacy and the victory of the Union, it was the passage of the Thirteenth Amendment in 1865 that officially ended the legal practice of slavery in the United States.

THE MODERN-DAY AFRICAN AMERICAN COMMUNITY

Nowadays, African Americans are more likely than other people in the United States to be the victims of crime. The **National Crime Victimization Survey (NCVS)** reveals that in 2001 and 2005 the overall violent crime victimization rate was higher than for any other racial group except Native Americans. Some of the reasons for this may be that African American women report crimes to the police at a slightly higher rate than do Caucasian Americans. For example, African American women reported 60.2 percent of all violent victimizations to police, compared to 47.1 percent of Caucasian women.

Because there is usually more crime in African American neighborhoods, police departments tend to assign higher levels of patrol to these neighborhoods when compared with others, resulting in disproportional enforcement. The combination of disproportional enforcement and more crime in these neighborhoods results in a higher number of contacts between police and citizens within African American communities. This is also thought to explain the higher arrest rate for African Americans and the higher rate of African Americans being shot and killed by the police.

It is because of the issues associated with historical slavery, potential bias within the criminal justice system, and the higher rates of violence experienced by this group that we would consider the topic of institutional racism and how it may relate to violence within the African American community. In the subsections that follow, we aim to demonstrate how the impact of structural racism on the African American population has affected rates of violence that has been committed against and has been committed by African Americans. It is both sad and ironic that, as a byproduct of structural racism, violence experienced by African Americans has been increased and tends to be intra-racial in nature, involving an African American perpetrator and an African American victim. The contention is that structural racism has had an insidious and debilitating undercurrent that has impacted the African American psyche so that, in its most covert and malevolent sense, African Americans now victimize themselves, further perpetuating what was originally set in motion by outside social rule makers who initially instigated this role of violence and victimization.

Structural Racism

The term **structural racism** implies that, within the very fabric of the structures of our society, there are both overt and covert forms of racism that exist in both official and informal relationships between different racial groups in our society. In particular, this term points toward a system where one racial group holds the majority of political, economic, and social power and that this group uses this power in a discriminatory fashion against another group based on the racial identity of persons involved (Lawrence & Keleher, 2004). This type of racism tends to be pervasive and exists within and among public and private organizations, agencies, institutions, and services in society (Lawrence & Keleher, 2004).

Marginalization of African Americans

As Kubisch (2006) notes, the term "structural racism" has been increasingly used in the past few years as a means of describing racial dynamics that are observed in our own 21st century. The study of structural racism has both academic and practical components. In the academic realm, this concept has tended to focus on race as a social and political concept that works to perpetuate the advantages that Caucasians typically have had in U.S. society while also identifying the challenges presented to people of color.

Within the practical realm of policy setting and law making, issues tend to focus on civil rights and issues related to social/economic justice. Kubisch (2006) has noted that for those who work in the social services and other similar areas, there has been an increased interest in research that addresses how poverty intersects with interracial issues, as well as racism. This is important because it is the economic disparity between Caucasians and African Americans that tends to perpetuate the other areas of discrimination within American society. In making this point, consider that one-fourth of all African Americans fall below the poverty line and continue to live in poverty in the United States (Mauk & Oakland, 2005, p. 239) and more than half of all African American children live in poverty (Jennings, 1997, p. 6).

Likewise, it is evident that prejudiced views of African Americans still persist in today's society. Research by Brown (2005, p. 41) shows that while most Caucasian Americans indicate that they have good intentions toward African Americans, they still have negative views of African Americans. Indeed, 34 percent of participants interviewed felt that most African Americans were lazy (Brown, 2005, p. 41). In addition, this same research found that 52 percent of Caucasian American participants believed that most African Americans were aggressive and violent. Research findings similar to these demonstrate that even among Caucasians who do not view themselves as biased or prejudiced, there are informal, perhaps even unintentional, but nonetheless real biases and negative stereotypes that serve to reinforce the **marginalization** of African Americans. As Riphagen (2008) states, "this continuing stigmatization of an entire race based on stereotypes of group attributes highly impairs African-Americans to develop their talents and makes it extremely difficult to be successful in the eyes of mainstream white Americans" (p. 3).

Historical Victimization

Though it is common knowledge that in America's past, African Americans were abducted, kidnapped, imprisoned, brought across the Atlantic under ghastly conditions, and systematically disjointed from loved ones and those who were familiar to them, enslaved and brutalized as a people, it is surprising and appalling that it is not understood how this **historical victimization** has impacted the psyche and cultural development of the African American community. The widespread, intentional, and total disintegration of the original African community once brought to the United States caused family and generational ties to be lost forever. Furthermore, throughout American history, the one-down position of African Americans has been taken as a norm in America. Consider, for instance, that even early American presidents owned African American slaves (Marable, 2002).

During this time, African American slaves lived under a set of laws known as the Slave Codes. These codes had some variation among the different states, but the general points were similar. Some of the common edicts of Slave Codes were that slaves were considered property, not people. Slaves did not have the legal standing to testify in court against a Caucasian, they could not form contracts, or leave the plantation without express permission (Public Broadcasting Service, 2008). To further demonstrate the severity of the historical victimization that African Americans endured as slaves, consider that the killing of a slave was seldom considered murder and the rape of a slave women was considered a simple form of trespass and nothing more (Public Broadcasting System, 2008).

Even years and generations later, it took the **Civil Rights Movement** of the 1960s to address the continued inequalities that persisted after the abolishment of slavery. These changes still did not result in substantial effort for wealth redistribution along racial lines, or help to provide cultural reorientation addressing race and racism (Winant, 2004, p. 21). Rather, racial injustices were simply seen as an outcome of prejudiced attitudes, which placed the outcomes of inequality as the responsibility of individual persons on a case-by-case basis, not a macro and structural bases. Naturally then, this left the gate open for persons to carry on a racially driven agenda, but on a covert rather than an overt basis. While official laws and Civil Rights may have been overtly established in the United States, very little stopped the covert practices of inequality in society that, while seeming to diminish slowly over generations, have taken an immeasurable toll on the African American population (Winant, 2004).

Impact of Structural Racism, Crime, Violence, and Criminal Justice

The impact of structural racism on the African American community has been profound and has poisoned many African American communities that are plagued with higher rates of violence and victimization (Middlemass, 2006). Oliver (2008) notes that there is a high rate of homicide and nonfatal violence that is committed against African American men. Further, this violence tends to be intra-racial and, proportionally speaking, more African Americans are victims of violent crime than any other racial group in the United States. According to the Bureau of Justice Statistics, in 2009, the rate of violent victimization against African Americans was 27 per 1,000 whereas the rate for Caucasians was 16 per 1,000, followed by an even lower rate for other races, being 10 out of 1,000. Furthermore, African Americans were victims of rape/sexual assault, robber, and aggravated assault at rates that were higher than those for Caucasians (BJS, 2009).

When considering the higher rates of victimization that are experienced by African Americans, on the one hand, coupled with the higher rates of violent crime that are committed by African Americans (most often against other African Americans), Oliver provides a clear reason for this observation. Oliver contends that structural pressures (i.e., institutional and cultural racism, restructured economic conditions) serve as independent variables whereas dysfunctional cultural adaptations (i.e., a lack of a coherent cultural identity and dysfunctional definitions of manhood) serve as mediating variables that aggravate the conditions, behaviors, and rationalizations that that lead to violent victimizations between African Americans (2008).

Oliver (2008) proposes that there are two specific dysfunctional adaptations that contribute to the high rates of violent offending and victimization common among African American men. These two dysfunctional adaptations, which were mentioned earlier—a lack of a cogent cultural identity and dysfunctional definitions of manhood—are adaptations produced by years (generations) of aversive **macro-level victimizations** such as racial segregation, violent acts against African American people, blocked access to educational and/or vocational opportunities, inadequate access to housing opportunities, and the cumulative effects of intergenerational institutional racism. These victimizations have further reinforced the macro-level historical trauma within the African American community and have been the basis of violent adaptations in reaction to the debilitating effects of structural racism upon that community.

AFRICAN AMERICANS AND LAW ENFORCEMENT

The results of a national survey, entitled "Police Attitudes Toward Abuse of Authority," showed race to be a divisive issues for American police. In particular, African American officers had significantly different views about the effect of a citizen's race and socio-economic status on the likelihood of police abuse of authority, when compared with officers of other racial groups (Weisburd & Greenspan, 2000). Indeed, throughout the African American community, there tends to be widespread belief that, in many cases, police do treat them differently, in terms of both the frequency with which they are questioned and the type of police service that is received. Indeed, the recent controversy related to the death of Trayvon Martin has highlighted issues relating to the treatment of blacks by local police departments, the state of race relations in the United States, and press coverage of African Americans. It is clear that due to these incidents, perceptions among the African American community of police agencies are less than flattering.

Consider research from the Pew Research Center (2012), where it was found that only 14 percent of African Americans said they had a great deal of confidence in local police officers to treat blacks and whites equally (see Table 6-1). More than twice as many whites (38 percent) had a great deal of confidence in the local police to provide equal treatment. More than three times as many blacks as whites said they had very little confidence in their local police to treat the races equally (34 percent vs. 9 percent).

TABLE 6-1 African American Confidence in Local Police

Confidence in local police to treat blacks and whites equally...	Total %	White %	Black %	B-W Diff
Great deal	33	38	14	−24
Fair amount	28	31	24	−7
Just some	18	16	22	+6
Very little	14	9	34	+25
Don't know	7	6	7	
	100	100	100	

Source: Pew Research Center. (2012). *Views of law enforcement, racial progress and news coverage of race.* Washington, DC: Pew Research Center.

Blacks' confidence in local police to provide equal treatment was changed little from 2007 or 1995.

Yet that survey showed that African Americans had a positive overall assessment of the state of race relations. About three-quarters of African Americans (76 percent) said blacks and whites got along "very well" or "pretty well." Majorities of both blacks (60 percent) and whites (70 percent) said that the values of the two groups had gotten more similar over the previous 10 years.

Furthermore, following the election of President Barack Obama, there was a sharp rise in perceptions of black progress. Nearly four-in-ten African Americans (39 percent) said that the "situation of black people in this country" was better than it had been five years earlier. In 2007, just 20 percent said the condition of blacks had improved in the previous five years. African Americans' concerns over racial discrimination had not decreased, however. More than four-in-ten (43 percent) African Americans said that there is a lot of discrimination against blacks, compared with just 13 percent of whites (see Table 6-2).

Whites were more likely to say that Hispanics than blacks faced a lot of discrimination (21 percent vs. 13 percent). Fully 81 percent of African Americans said "our

TABLE 6-2 African American and Caucasian Views on Racial Discrimination

How much discrimination against blacks?	Total %	White %	Black %	B-W Diff
A lot	18	13	43	+30
Some	51	57	39	−18
Only a little/None	27	26	16	−10
Don't know	3	3	2	
	100	100	100	

Source: Pew Research Center. (2012). *Views of Law Enforcement, Racial Progress and News Coverage of Race.* Washington, DC: Pew Research Center.

country needs to continue making changes to give blacks equal rights with whites." Just 36 percent of whites agreed, while a majority (54 percent) said "our country has made the changes needed to give blacks equal rights with whites."

RACIAL PROFILING, POLICING, AND THE AFRICAN AMERICAN COMMUNITY

Racial profiling has been recognized by the international community as a violation of human rights, with the United Nations defining **racial profiling** as *the practice of police and other law enforcement officers relying, to any degree, on race, color, descent or national or ethnic origin as the basis for subjecting persons to investigatory activities or for determining whether an individual is engaged in criminal activity* (United Nations, 2009). We adopt this definition for three key reasons. First, it is a comprehensive definition that is clear but encompassing of the concept. Second, this definition is provided by the world's premier and most far-reaching governing body, the United Nations. Third, the use of definitions from the United Nations reinforces points made in Chapters 1 and 2 regarding the fact that multiculturalism in the United States is juxtaposed against the broader changes associated with globalization; the two social phenomena are not mutually exclusive.

With the United States, the issue of racial profiling has drawn a substantial amount of attention that corresponds to all levels of law enforcement throughout the nation. For example, the Justice Department, acting on President George W. Bush's directive that racial profiling is "wrong and we will end it in America" campaign, issued a policy to ban federal law enforcement officials from engaging in racial profiling (Justice Department, 2003, p. 2). Thus, this social phenomenon was directly addressed by the Chief Executive Officer of the United States who has stated clearly that "it's wrong, and we will end it in America. In so doing, we will not hinder the work of our nation's brave police officers. They protect us every day, often at great risk. But by stopping the abuses of a few, we will add to the public confidence our police officers earn and deserve" (Justice Department, 2003, p. 12). The conviction of these political leaders further resonates with the final comments provided by Attorney General John Aschroft, who remarked that "this administration… has been opposed to racial profiling and has done more to indicate its opposition than ever in history. The President said it's wrong and we'll end it in America, and I subscribe to that. "Using race… as a proxy for potential criminal behavior is unconstitutional, and undermines law enforcement by undermining the confidence that people can have in law enforcement" (Justice Department, 2003, p. 12).

Research has shown that there are definite tendencies for some larger agencies to engage in **differential stops** of African Americans as compared to Caucasians (Joiner, 2005). These stops often result in no citation or a minor infraction. While this may seem good, on the exterior, as an outcome, it actually indicates that many of these stops are frivolous or based on reasons that cannot be sufficiently substantiated (Joiner, 2005). Joiner found statistically significant differences in the rate of stops and the types of outcomes observed between African Americans and Caucasians (Joiner, 2005). This study as well as others (Lamberth, 1997; Smith & Alpert, 2002) provides empirical support for many of the contentions that have been made by members of the African American community and also helps to show why African Americans may have little confidence in their local police department.

CURRENT EVENTS
Racial Profiling Still a Problem, both in Policing and in Private Sector

In November of 2013, numerous high-end retailers joined to form a council of members who will examine possibleracial profiling among employees within their collective places of business. At the heart of the issue is allegations leveled by the famous Reverend Al Sharpton as well as other civic leaders in New York City (Otis, 2013).

This issue has become known as the 'shop-and-frisk' scandal, which occurred in October of 2013 when two African American shoppers in Barney's department store were allegedly singled out and searched, the accusation being that they had shoplifted items of value from the store (Otis, 2013). During this incident, the New York Police Department was involved and helped to conduct the search. The shoppers, since that incident, have claimed that racial profiling served as the basis for the search. Another similar incident has been alleged at Macy's department store, months prior to this incident (Otis, 2013).

One example includes Kayla Phillips, 21, who while shopping at Barneys, bought a $2,500 handbag in February of 2013 (Green, 2013). After leaving the store, four plainclothes New York Police Officers stopped her for questioning, under suspicion for credit card fraud. According to Phillips, the officers were very rough, terse, and unprofessional in their conduct. As it turns out, Phillip's brother is also a New York Police Officer, so she knew to ask the detectives for their names and badge numbers, which she did, despite the harrowing incident. She currently has filed a $5 million notice-of-claim to alert the city of New York as to her intentions to file suit (Green, 2013).

Another example would be Trayon Christian, 19, who used his debit card to buy a $349 designer belt. After the purchase, police detained him for questioning, inferring that he was not likely to be able to legitimately afford the belt (Green, 2013). At this time, Christian has filed a lawsuit against both Barneys and the New York Police Department for violating his civil rights.

These incidents occur against the backdrop of a ruling recently handed down from a federal judge in August of 2013, holding that NYPD's stop-and-frisk practices were unconstitutional (Hanna, 2013). Judge Shira Scheindlin ruled on the class-action lawsuit (a class action lawsuit is one that is filed on behalf of numerous complainants or plaintiffs), and estimated that the NYPD, between the years of 2004 and 2012, had conducted nearly 200,000 stop-and-frisk maneuvers without having reasonable suspicion, thereby being a violation of these citizen's rights (Hanna, 2013). Judge Scheindlin also found evidence of racial profiling which also extended to violations of the 14th Amendment's requirement for equal protection under the law (Hanna, 2013).

As a result of these incidents, pressure from the African American community to address this issue, and a public image scandal, the task force of department store managers and civil rights advocates has examined policies of stores to clarify procedures and safeguard against potential bias that may exist. Further, the establishment of monitors and other features, in stores, to help document potential profiling was suggested at a recent meeting.

References: Green, T. (2013, October 24). Meet Kayla Phillips, Another Barneys Shopper Accused Of Credit Card Fraud For Buying Designer Handbag: Report. International Business Times. Retrieved from: http://www.ibtimes.com/meet-kayla-phillips-another-barneys-shopper-accused-credit-card-fraud-buying-designer-handbag-report

Hanna, J. (2013, August 12). Judge rules NYC's stop-and-frisk policy unconstitutional; city vows to appeal. CNN News. Retrieved from: http://www.cnn.com/2013/08/12/justice/new-york-stop-frisk/index.html

Otis, G. A. (2013, November 26). *New York racial profiling task force includes Macy's, Barneys,* executives. New York Daily News. Retrieved from: http://www.nydaily-news.com/new-york/retailers-leaders-racial-profiling-panel-article-1.1529145

LATINO AMERICANS

Overall, the Latino American population of the United States grew from 35.3 million in 2000 to 50.5 million in 2010, accounting for more than half of the nation's overall population growth during that decade (Passel, Cohn, & Lopez, 2011). Some 58 percent of this Latino population increase came from births rather than the arrival of new immigrants. However, for many non-Mexican-origin Latino groups in the United States, births accounted for less than half of their population growth in the past decade. For example, from 2000 to 2010, births accounted for just 38 percent of the growth of the Cuban-American population and just 39 percent of the growth of the population of U.S. Latinos of Central or South American origin. Latinos now comprise 16.3 percent of the total U.S. population. This share is projected to rise to 29 percent by the middle of this century, with the bulk of the future increase driven by births, many the descendants of today's immigration wave, rather than the arrival of new immigrants (Passel & Cohn, 2008).

Mexican Americans

During the early 1800s, the United States began its westward expansion through a process of annexations, settlement, purchase, and conflict. Indeed, the Mexican American war, which ended in 1848, ended with Mexico losing the land that now includes Texas, New Mexico, Arizona, and California. At this time, over 100,000 Mexicans lived in these territories. As one can see, it is clear that, in reality, these Mexicans, now called **Mexican Americans,** were the first to settle in these territories and are, therefore, the original inhabitants. Because of this and because of the family connections in these states and in Mexico, many Mexican Americans may envision these borders as artificial, to some extent. Though about a third of Mexican Americans can trace their ancestry to families living in the United States in the mid-1800s, the majority migrated into the United States after 1910 due to the economic and political changes that occurred because of the Mexican Revolution.

In 2007, Mexicans constituted 29.2 million, or 64.3 percent, of the Latino population, in the United States (Pew Research Center, 2009). Furthermore, Mexican births in the United States now account for this growth more than immigration (see Figure 6-1). This new trend is especially evident among Mexican Americans (Pew Hispanic Center, 2011). In the decade from 2000 to 2010, the Mexican American population grew by 7.2 million as a result of births and by 4.2 million as a result of new immigrant arrivals. This is a change from the previous two decades when the number of new immigrants either matched or exceeded the number of births (see Figure 6-1).

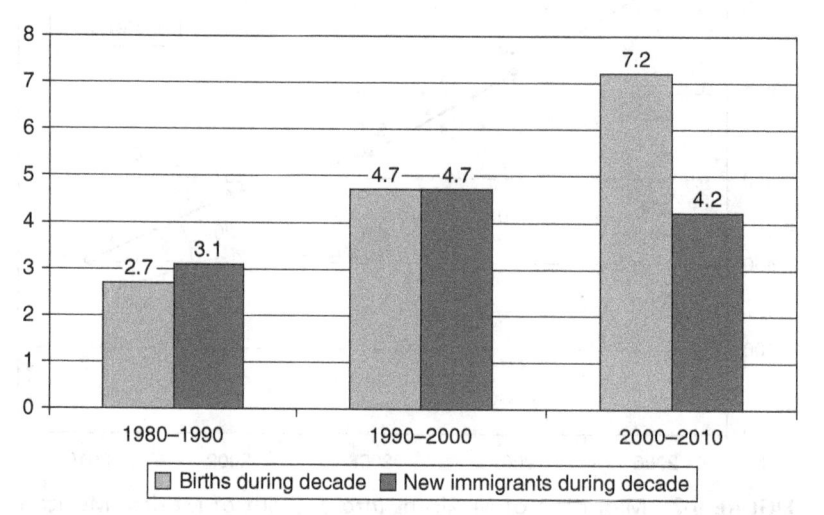

FIGURE 6-1 Mexican American Population Growth, 1980–2010. *Source:* Pew Hispanic Center. (2011). *The Mexican-American boom: Births overtake immigration.* Washington, DC: Pew Research Center. Retrieved from: http://www.pewhispanic.org/2011/07/14/the-mexican-american-boom-brbirths-overtake-immigration/.

The current surge in births among Mexican Americans is largely attributable to the immigration wave that has brought more than 10 million immigrants to the United States from Mexico since 1970. Between 2006 and 2010 alone, more than half (53 percent) of all Mexican American births were to Mexican immigrant parents. As a group, these immigrants are more likely than U.S.-born Americans to be in their prime child-bearing years. They also have much higher fertility rates (Pew Hispanic Center, 2011).

Meanwhile, the number of new immigrant arrivals from Mexico has fallen off steeply in recent years (see Figure 6-2). According to a Pew Hispanic Center analysis of Mexican government data, the number of Mexicans annually leaving Mexico for the United States declined from more than one million in 2006 to 404,000 in 2010—a 60 percent reduction (Passel & Cohn, 2009). This is likely a result of recent developments in both the United States and Mexico. On the U.S. side, declining job opportunities and increased border enforcement might have made the United States less attractive to potential Mexican immigrants (Pew Hispanic Center, 2011). In Mexico, recent strong economic growth may have reduced the **push factors** that often lead Mexicans to emigrate to the United States. This is likely a result of recent developments in both the United States and Mexico (Pew Hispanic Center, 2011). Students should examine Figure 6-2 for further details.

Interestingly, the period between 1970 and 2010 has witnessed one of the largest mass migrations in modern history—the net movement of more than 10 million Mexicans from Mexico into the United States. In 1970, there were fewer than one million Mexican immigrants living in the United States. By 2000, that number had grown to 9.8 million and by 2007 it reached 12.5 million. Since then, the Mexican-born population has remained roughly constant. Many Mexican immigrants are in

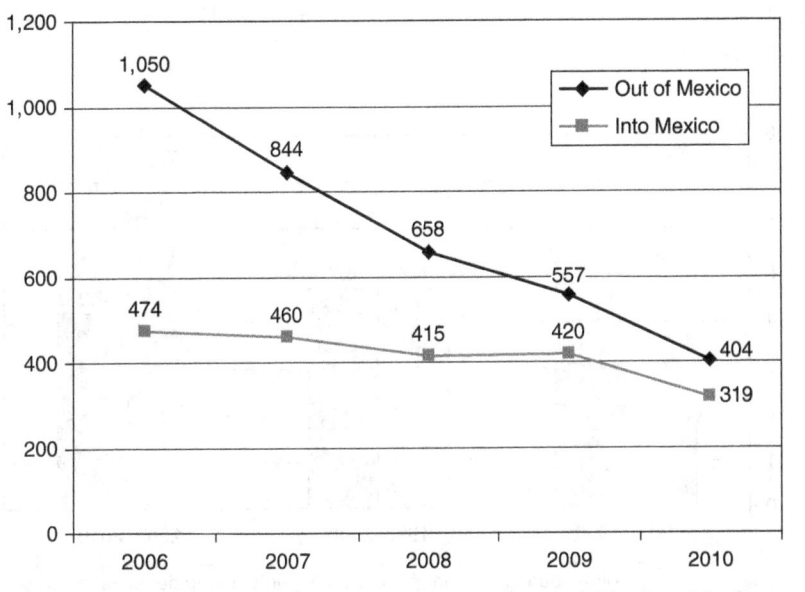

FIGURE 6-2 Migration of Mexicans into and out of Mexico, Mexican National Survey of Occupation and Employment, 2006–2010. *Source:* Pew Hispanic Center. (2011). *The Mexican-American boom: Births overtake immigration.* Washington, DC: Pew Research Center. Retrieved from: http://www.pewhispanic.org/2011/07/14/the-mexican-american-boom-brbirths-overtake-immigration/.

the United States without authorization. In 2010 some 6.5 million—more than half (52 percent) of all Mexican immigrants—were unauthorized immigrants. Among the nation's 11.2 million unauthorized immigrants from all parts of the world, the majority (58 percent) are from Mexico (Passel & Cohn, 2011). Many of these unauthorized immigrants have had children in the United States. Between March 2009 and March 2010, 68 percent of the 350,000 U.S. births to unauthorized immigrant parents were to Mexican unauthorized immigrants.

Mexican migration to the United States has long been characterized, at least in part, by a circular pattern. While many Mexican migrants enter the United States to settle permanently, a significant number come to the United States to work for a short time, often in seasonal jobs, and return to Mexico. According to a Pew Hispanic Center analysis of Mexican government data, there appears to be less of this return migration now than in the past, possibly because of the increased financial costs of migrating back to the United States and the increased danger of crossing the U.S.–Mexico border. In 2006 and 2007, more than 450,000 Mexican migrants returned from the United States to Mexico each year. Since then, the number of Mexicans returning to Mexico annually from the United States has declined, to 319,000 in 2010. From Mexico's perspective, a significant share of its population, especially its working-age population, is abroad. One-in-ten (10 percent) of everyone born in Mexico resides in the United States. Among Mexican-born men aged 30–44, one-in-five (20 percent) are in the United States. Among Mexican-born women in the same age group, more than one-in-seven (15 percent) are in the United States (Pew Hispanic Center, 2011).

Immigration Concerns

The media has been ablaze with issues related to the illegal immigration of Latinos into the United States, particularly regarding Mexican Americans. Indeed, laws in Arizona, California, and other states have recently increased penalties for illegal aliens and broadened the responsibilities of law enforcement to investigate if they have reason to suspect that a person may be in the United States illegally. One case that recently went before the Supreme Court (*Arizona v. United States*, 2012) upheld an Arizona statute known as S.B. 1070 to address pressing issues related to the large influx of unlawful immigrants in that state.

Puerto Ricans

Unlike Mexico, Puerto Rico was under the rule of Spain until 1897 when Spain allowed the tiny island nation to establish its own local government. The United States invaded Puerto Rico and annexed it as a result of the Spanish-American War in 1898. Although Cuba, which was also acquired by the United States during this war, was given its independence, the United States maintained control over Puerto Rico. In 1917, the Jones Act made Puerto Ricans citizens of the United States.

Today, Puerto Rico is still a territory of the United States with an elected governor.

Following World War II, an influx of Puerto Ricans into the United States was observed. With citizenship status already possessed, most could easily travel to areas of the nation where jobs existed. During this time, most jobs were on the East Coast or in the Northeast, with many settling in New York City. The estimated number of Puerto Ricans in the United States was about 4.6 million in 2009, according to the Pew

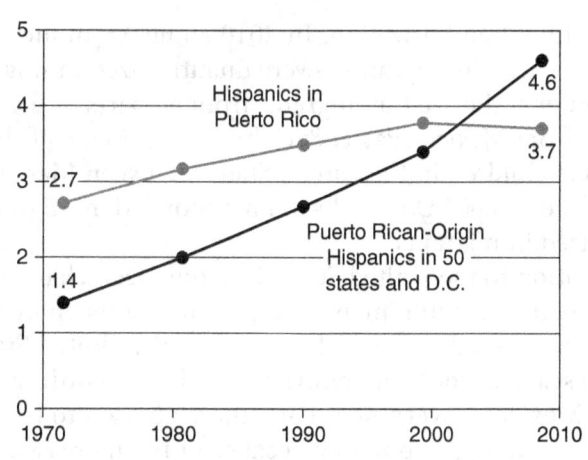

FIGURE 6-3   Puerto Rican Population Trends in the United States. *Source:* Pew Hispanic Center. (2011). *A demographic portrait of Puerto Ricans—2009.* Washington, DC: Pew Research Center. Retrieved from: http://pewresearch.org/pubs/2021/puerto-rico-statistical-profile-populations-trends.

Hispanic Center. That is a slightly greater number than the population of Puerto Rico itself in 2007, which was 3.7 million in 2009 (see Figure 6-3).

Nowadays, **Puerto Ricans** are the second-largest population of Latino origin residing in the United States, accounting for 9.1 percent of the U.S. Hispanic population in 2009. However, it would seem that, for the most part, Puerto Ricans do not fare as well as the remaining Latino population in the United States on some variables yet outpace Latinos on other variables. Consider some of the following facts, obtained from the 2009 American Community Survey by the Pew Hispanic Center, a project of the Pew Research Center:

Marital Status—Puerto Ricans are less likely than Latinos overall to be married—37 percent vs. 45 percent for other Latinos.

Marriage and Children—A majority (56 percent) of Puerto Rican women aged 15–44 who gave birth were unmarried. That was greater than the rate for all Latino women, which was 39 percent in 2009.

Homeownership—The rate of Puerto Rican homeownership (39 percent) is lower than the rate for all Hispanics (48 percent).

Puerto Ricans have lower levels of education and lower incomes than average for the U.S. population. They are less likely to be in the labor force, and among those in the labor force they have a higher rate of unemployment than either all Hispanics or the overall population. The rate of homeownership among Puerto Ricans is lower than the rate for Hispanics overall and the U.S. population overall.

As a group, Puerto Ricans are older than Hispanics on average but they are younger than the U.S. population. They are less likely to be married than either Hispanics overall or the U.S. population overall. Among Puerto Ricans aged 5 and older living in the United States, most do not speak only English at home. Some 20.5 percent of Puerto Ricans aged 5 and older report speaking English less than very well, compared with 38.8 percent of all Latino Americans. Puerto Ricans are concentrated in the Northeast, mostly in New York, and in the South, mostly in Florida.

INTERNATIONAL FOCUS

Police Abuses and Poor Community Relations in Puerto Rico

While Puerto Rico is, by definition, a commonwealth of the United States, its location and the police-community issues involved in this territory's jurisdiction, make it more than appropriate for consideration in this chapter's International Focus.

In late 2011, the United States Department of Justice (USDOJ) announced its findings from a long-term investigation into the Puerto Rico Police Department (PRPD), officially stating that the department had engaged in patterns of misconduct that were in violation of the United States Constitution as well as federal law. In its report, the USDOJ issued a report that found numerous problems with the Puerto Rico Police Department, providing at least 100 recommendations for improvement.

A little known fact is that the PRPD is the second-largest police department in the United States, with over 17,000 employees in its ranks (Catillo, 2012). The American Civil Liberties Union has followed up on the reports of widespread civil rights abuses that have been documented by the USDOJ, and has found that problems still persist (Catillo, 2012). Among the forms of misconduct that persist are displays of excessive force and other form of serious misconduct, usually directed at persons who are in lower socioeconomic levels of social standing, particularly those who were primarily of African descent or were immigrants from the Dominican Republic (Catillo, 2012).

To demonstrate the corrupt circumstances within the department, consider that between the years 2005 and 2010, there were over 1,700 officers who were arrested for a variety of criminal activities, including assault, theft, domestic violence, drug trafficking, and even murder (Catillo, 2012). Further, the violent crime rate on the island is very high, with a record-number of homicides recorded at 1,130 in the year 2011. In fact, despite lowering crime rates throughout the nation during the 2000's, from 2007 to 2009, violent crime in Puerto Rico increased by 17 percent (Civil Rights Division, 2011).

The USDOJ report noted that the PRPD's policies and procedures on use of force and searches and seizures were out-dated, disorganized, and omitted modern legal standards (Civil Rights Division, 2011). Further, it was found that officers were not provided with copies of PRPD's policies, or access to policies through other reliable means, to reference as they carried out their day-to-day activities… leaving officers to create their own informal practices of operation (Civil Rights Division, 2011).

Millions of dollars during the past few years have been spent to retrain the department. This is particularly important as the investigation determined that officers were not provided with post-academy field training to prepare them for the real world of policing, especially the world of policing in a jurisdiction as violent and dangerous as Puerto Rico (Civil Rights Division, 2011). Such training is particularly essential in developing the practical skills, judgment, and understanding necessary to lawfully employ force, effect arrests, treat all persons equally, and solve problems effectively as partners with the community. Instead, it was found that rookie officers were simply armed and released into the neighborhoods of Puerto Rico, with little or no follow-up guidance (Civil Rights Division, 2011).

It was further found that there was a lack of discipline within the department and that many specialized units had developed negative subcultural norms. All in all, the climate in the agency was one of "us against them," when facing the community, making the police seem to be the enemy of those whom they were sworn to protect.

Just recently, in July of 2013, the USDOJ entered into a formal agreement with Puerto Rico for official reformation of the PRPD (Bennett, 2013). This agreement requires the PRPD to develop and use a variety of policies and procedures to ensure ethical policing, use of force, searches and seizures, and community engagement (Bennett, 2013). Indeed, the USDOJ has committed $10 million from asset forfeiture funds obtained through the selling of property obtained in previous crime-fighting efforts (Bennett, 2013). This money is intended to defray the cost attributed to modernizing the PRPD. Since

Source: Bennett, K (2013, July 19). *DOJ reaches agreement with Puerto Rico police.* Pittsburg, PA: Jurist Legal News and Research Services, Inc. Retrieved from: http://jurist.org/paperchase/2013/07/doj-reaches-agreement-with-puerto-rico-police.php?edition=US

Catillo, M. (2012, June 19). ACLU report blasts Puerto Rico Police Department. CNN U. S., retrieved from http://articles.cnn.com/2012-06-19/us/us_puerto-rico-police-department_1_police-force-aclu-report-police-brutality?_s=PM:US

Civil Rights Division (2011). Investigation of the Puerto Rico Police Department. Washington, DC: United States Department of Justice.

Cuban Americans

Largely concentrated in Florida, New York, and New Jersey, **Cuban Americans** are now the third largest group of Latinos in the United States (Garica-Preto, 1996; Rochin, 1996; Romero & Stelzner, 1985). Cuban immigrants began to arrive in the United States in significant numbers during the 1960s, after the emergence of Castro's revolutionary government on the island of Cuba (Garica-Preto, 1996; Rochin, 1996). The United States opened its doors to migrating Cubans due to political obligations to many of the native Cubans who had resisted Castro. Those Cubans who first arrived were mainly Caucasian in origin, from the upper socioeconomic classes, being business savvy and with educational resources and financial clout (Garica-Preto, 1996; Rochin, 1996; Romero & Stelzner, 1985). Many of these immigrants settled in Miami, in what became known as "Little Havana." These immigrants originally viewed themselves as temporary exiles who would return when the revolution ended (Garica-Preto, 1996; Rochin, 1996; Romero & Stelzner, 1985).

Unlike other immigrant or exile groups in the United States, Cuban immigrants received the benefit of substantial assistance through government programs that provided direct financial aid (Garica-Preto, 1996). This has resulted in a belief among many fellow American Latinos that Cuban Americans are wealthy (Garica-Preto, 1996). However, this is a fallacy, particularly when the status of Cubans is compared to other Caucasian Americans. Even though Cubans are more affluent than most other Latinos, their family income still falls well below the national average (Garica-Preto, 1996; Novas, 1994; Rochin, 1996). This becomes especially true when the later Cuban refugees of the 1980s are factored into this picture (Rochin, 1996).

More recent immigrants differed from earlier Cubans, being of lower socioeconomic status and more racially mixed. These Cubans were given the label "Marielitos," which has a negative connotation in identifying the port and the incidents by which these immigrants arrived in America (Bernal & Shapiro, 1996; Rochin, 1996). This group of Cuban immigrants was not often given a warm welcome by their Cuban brethren within the United States because of fears in the Cuban American community that the new wave of immigrants would negatively influence the perception of Cubans among Americans (Bernal & Shapiro, 1998; Rochin, 1996).

Negative stereotyping has, in part, been a backlash to early Cuban immigrants who sought to separate themselves from more recent arrivals. Despite the fact that Cuban Americans are the third largest Latino group in the United States, there is a paucity of recent literature on the Cuban American experience within the American criminal justice system. This absence of research is thought to reflect the low Cuban American involvement in the criminal justice system prior to those who arrived during the 1980s (Romero & Stelzner, 1985). Earlier Cuban American immigrants came mostly from the wealthier, better-educated, and occupationally elite sectors of Cuban society (Rochin, 1996). One early study by Wilbanks (1980) does touch on the topic of Cubans and the American criminal justice system. This study reflected demographic changes in Dade County, Florida, between the years 1956 and 1978. This report described changing demographic patterns among Cuban immigrants to account for increases in violent crime (Wilbanks, 1980). These violent crime patterns have continued to be attributed to Cuban Americans, particularly within the drug trade. However, it is important to note that this connection is associated more with Cubans of lower social standing rather than those from the upwardly mobile elite (Rochin, 1996; Wilbanks, 1980). This study seems to provide some credence to contentions by early Cuban immigrants who held unfavorable views of Cuban immigrants arriving in the 1980s.

Other Groups

In addition to the three largest groups of Latino Americans in the United States, there are also exists a proportion of immigrants from 21 additional countries through Central America, the Caribbean, and South America (Shusta, Levine, Wong, Olson, & Harris, 2011). The arrival of many of these immigrants becomes noticeable in the 1980s due to turmoil and warfare that occurred in El Salvador, Nicaragua, and Panama. Some groups, such as those from the Dominican Republic, who are experiencing rapid growth in the Northeastern coast, are difficult to track due to the commonality of their undocumented entry into the United States (Shusta et al., 2011).

NATIVE AMERICANS

For police, there may be confusion in determining exactly who is an American Indian. Indeed, some individuals may claim to have "Indian blood", but it is the tribe itself that sets its criteria as to who is or is not a member. Because the determination of tribal membership is a fundamental attribute of tribal sovereignty, the federal government generally defers to the tribes' own determination when establishing eligibility criteria. Part of the confusion regarding genuine identity of Native Americans has to do with fraud, as there tends to be common instances of individuals claiming to be a member of a given tribe so that they can receive government benefits and/or tribal privileges. Investigators who have Native American communities in their jurisdiction routinely face this type of fraud.

Today, many Native Americans live on 283 reservations throughout the continental United States as well as roughly 200 Inuit, Aleut, and Native American communities in the state of Alaska. There are also some metropolitan areas where Native Americans are more commonly found, such as in Los Angeles, Tulsa, Oklahoma City, San Francisco, and Phoenix (Lester, 2003). Many Native Americans hold the belief that urbanization of their population has destroyed cultural roots for younger generations. The fact that many younger Native Americans do not speak their own native language and/or do not ever return to their tribal homes is seen as proof of this erosion of their cultural connection.

BOX 6.1 Definition of Native Americans (American Indian or Alaska Native)

Definition of American Indian or Alaska Native Used in the 2010 Census

According to OMB, "American Indian or Alaska Native" refers to a person having origins in any of the original peoples of North and South America (including Central America) and who maintains tribal affiliation or community attachment.

The American Indian and Alaska Native population includes people who marked the "American Indian or Alaska Native" checkbox or reported entries such as Navajo, Blackfeet, Inupiat, Yup'ik, or Central American Indian groups or South American Indian groups.

Source: United States Census Bureau. (2010). *American Indian and Alaska Native census.* Washington, DC: U.S. Census Bureau.

The 2010 Census showed that the U.S. population on April 1, 2010 was 308.7 million. Out of the total U.S. population, 2.9 million people, or 0.9 percent, were American Indian and Alaska Native alone (see Table 6-1). In addition, 2.3 million people, or another 0.7 percent, reported American Indian and Alaska Native in combination with one or more other races. Together, these two groups totaled 5.2 million people. Thus, 1.7 percent of all people in the United States identified as American Indian and Alaska Native, either alone or in combination with one or more other races.

The ten states with the largest American Indian and Alaska Native alone-or-in-combination populations in 2010 were California, Oklahoma, Arizona, Texas, New York, New Mexico, Washington, North Carolina, Florida, and Michigan (see Table 6-2). Among these states, three experienced substantial rates of growth in their American Indian and Alaska Native alone-or-in-combination populations from 2000 to 2010—Texas (46 percent), North Carolina (40 percent), and Florida (38 percent). In similar fashion, the American Indian and Alaska Native-alone population also experienced growth of at least 20 percent in Texas, Florida, New York, and North Carolina. Out of the ten states with the largest American Indian and Alaska Native alone-or-in-combination populations, eight also had the largest American Indian and Alaska Native-alone populations. The general population distribution of Native Americans, by region, in the United States can be observed in Figure 6-4.

Native American Values

Traditional Native American spirituality values harmony with nature and operates on the belief that land should be protected. The destruction of natural resources "in the name of progress" for commercial or industrial purposes is counter to traditional beliefs. Native Americans, regardless of tribe, tend to more often be present-oriented

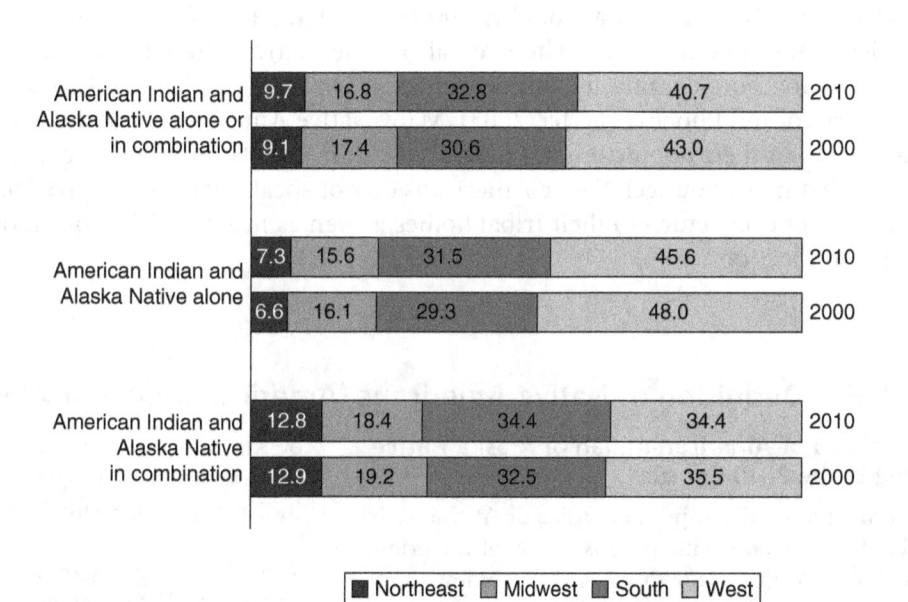

FIGURE 6-4 Percentage of Native Americans by Region of the United States. *Source:* United States Census Bureau. (2010). *American Indian and Alaska Native census.* Washington, DC: U.S. Census Bureau.

rather than future-oriented, and they believe that there is an interconnectedness of all things, both living and non-living. They place strong emphasis on extended family, particularly regarding the elders of the family. Likewise, truly traditional Native Americans view good health as being the result of four elements: the physical, the mental, the emotional, and the spiritual (Lester, 2003).

In general, Native Americans consider their traditional culture and spirituality to be interlinked. Spiritual beliefs are founded on the notion that all natural things are interconnected and that the land is the primary source of strength and life. Native spirituality is governed by what they may call **The Creator or Great Spirit** as the ultimate being, with all other living things possessing a spirit. Humans are viewed as being only one of the living things on Earth and are no more important than the other creatures they encounter. Each Native culture tends to use ceremonies, animals, symbols, or behavioral traits to demonstrate certain aspects of their tribal culture's spirituality.

Native American Victimization

A severe problem exists with regard to violent crime victimization among Native Americans. Between 2006 and 2010, according to the National Crime Victim Survey (NCVS), the violent crime victimization rate for Native Americans was twice the rate for Caucasians and African Americans (NCVS, 2011). This is, of course, alarming and curious to many observers but is not surprising when one considers the multitude of issues that impact Native Americans, particularly regarding drug and alcohol abuse and domestic violence issues.

Unique Legal Status

Native Americans have a very unique legal status that separates them from Caucasians and other minority groups in the United States, and this has a very important effect on their relations with police agencies. Indeed, Native American tribes are recognized as semi-sovereign nations that have many powers of autonomous government within the land that is allocated to them, usually as reservations. It is the **Bureau of Indian Affairs (BIA)** that is most often the policing authority on Native American grounds.

Nevertheless, there is competition for authority among tribal police agencies, whether county, municipal, or state, and this creates challenges in enforcing laws in these regions. Jurisdiction in "Indian territory" depends on where a crime was committed as well as the specific type of crime committed. A crime committed on reservation grounds by someone who is not a tribal member would be charged by the county sheriff. On the other hand, a member of the tribe would likely be charged by tribal authorities.

As to the state of affairs regarding policing on Native American lands, the United States Department of Justice (USDOJ) found that serious challenges exist for agencies on tribal grounds. Police agencies on tribal grounds tend to have budgetary problems, poor equipment, ineffective management, high levels of personnel turnover, and they also tend to be mired in local politics (USDOJ, 2013). Further still, the public safety challenges in Native American jurisdictions vary widely from district to district—and from tribe to tribe—depending on jurisdictional issues, geography, tribal cultures, and myriad other factors. The ratio of law enforcement officers to population served

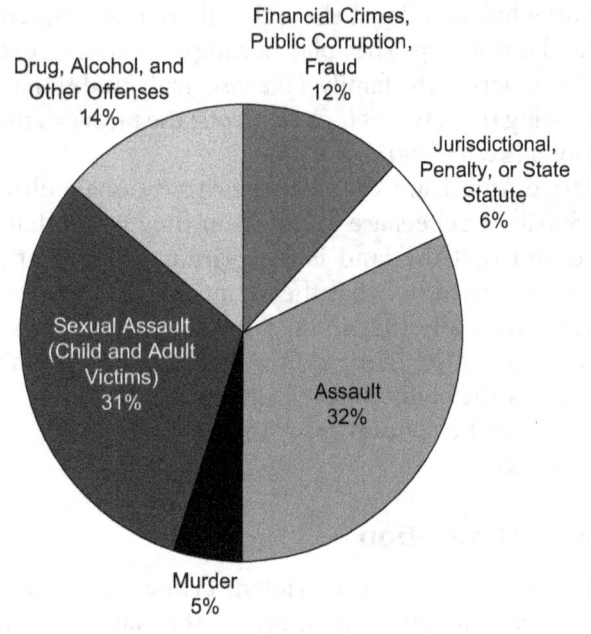

FIGURE 6-5 Declinations of Criminal Cases in Native American Jurisdictions, by Charge, in 2012. *Source:* U.S. Department of Justice. (2013). *Indian country investigations and prosecutions 2011–2012*. Washington, DC: USDOJ.

remains lower on Native American reservations than in other jurisdictions across the country (USDOJ, 2013). And, law enforcement agencies in Native American territories have the daunting challenge of patrolling large areas of sparsely populated land. These problems have resulted in a number of what are called *declined cases*, which are criminal incidents that ultimately, are not prosecuted for various reasons. Figure 6-5 provides a view of the various crime categories that were declined in 2012.

The majority of declined cases involve physical assaults or sexual assaults. Unfortunately, for myriad reasons, these types of crimes are very difficult to prosecute, regardless of whether they arise in Native American territories or other areas of the United States. Delayed reporting of the crime, inexperienced law enforcement officers untrained in how to effectively investigate a sexual assault case, or insufficient first-responder resources in tribal communities may further contribute to prosecutors' challenges to receiving a case referral where the guilt of the defendant can be proven beyond a reasonable doubt (USDOJ, 2013).

While these difficulties in prosecuting sexual assault and child molestation cases is unique to Native American communities, structural barriers in these communities may compound the challenges. This is especially true when outside federal law enforcement are required to be involved. For instance, victims and witnesses of these types of personal and sensitive crimes may be reluctant to travel long distances outside of their community to the federal courthouse to testify. In addition, federal or other outside investigators and prosecutors may not be able to build the rapport and trust needed to encourage a victim to see a case through, because they are not co-located in the community in the same way that a local law enforcement officer would be.

In response to these problems, Congress passed the **2010 Tribal Law and Order Act**. This law removed some of the sentencing restrictions placed on tribal courts (allowing more than one-year sentences for serious crimes), allowed greater crime data sharing between tribal, state, and federal agencies, and also provide assistance to tribal criminal justice agencies. The Department of Justice, through various federal law enforcement agencies (primarily the Federal Bureau of Investigation), work to strengthen relationships with federally recognized tribes, improve the coordination of training and information-sharing, and enhance tribal capacity, so that together the tribal and Federal governments can provide effective law enforcement and prosecutions in Native American territories (USDOJ, 2013).

ASIAN AMERICANS

As we have seen in Chapter 1, the term "Asian American" encompasses a broad array of diverse groups that tend to be combined as if the same. While many Asian Americans do experience similar challenges with the society of the United States, they naturally have numerous cultural differences. Despite this, the American public tends to be virtually ignorant of these differences (Shusta et al., 2011). Indeed, a high percentage of persons in the United States are not even aware of the geographical location of different nations throughout the world (including those in Asia) and are correspondingly less informed of the differences in cultures that may occur among various ethnic minorities. This is especially true with the Asian American population since this population has well over 40 distinct ethnic groups within its membership (McGoldrick, Giordano, Pearce, & Giordano, 1996; Shusta et al., 2011).

This same lack of cultural awareness extends to personnel in policing as well as other criminal justice arenas. Indeed, this is an important issue for police professionals, in particular, due to a variety of events that have occurred in differing parts of the nation during the last decade (Shusta et al., 2011). Media-catching incidents that have occurred across the United States make it clear that many law enforcement officers have difficulty understanding the diversity of customs, activities, behaviors, and values associated with different Asian American groups (Hanser, 2011). Likewise, these officers either do not know where to go for information about these groups or (and this is more likely the case in many instances) they may not have sufficient incentive to do so of their own accord. This is dually important for those agencies that do serve a substantial Asian American population but it is likewise important for those jurisdictions that do not have a substantial representation of Asian Americans. This is because a lack of understanding due to a lack of incentive will simply ensure that officers do not become competent with these citizens and, seemingly in defense of their apparent lack of motivation, this ensures that this group of citizens will continue to be on the periphery of the community, thereby being largely unnoticed. This is especially true in the southern region of the United States.

This lack of knowledge exists in many agencies despite the fact that throughout the past four decades, the Asian American population has experienced the largest proportional increase of any minority group in the United States (Shusta et al., 2011). In fact, it is estimated that the Asian American community, currently consisting of approximately 3.4 percent of the U.S. population, will grow to account for 9.3 percent of the overall U.S. population by 2050 (Centers for Disease Control, 2005). Likewise, it is fairly well known that this same population tends to be predominantly located in California, New York, Illinois (mainly Chicago), and various regions around the nation's capitol.

The fact that the Asian American population is growing at such a rapid rate underscores this population's emerging importance throughout the nation in general, and points toward the need for further accommodation within the regions of the United States where Asians may be newly arriving. Thus, law enforcement officers throughout the United States will increasingly need to have an understanding of Asian groups in their area. This alone demonstrates the need for training and attentiveness to community-relations issues and also makes it clear that there is a need for culturally competent law enforcement (specific to the Asian American groups in a given jurisdiction) in regions beyond the west and east coast, such as the Midwestern and Southern regions of the United States.

Difficulties and Challenges in Establishing a Rapport

It is important for law enforcement to recognize some of the differences that may cut across or be common to all Asian American ethnic groups. Shusta et al. (2011) note the following considerations:

- Generational status in the United States (first, second, and third generations)
- Degree of acculturation and assimilation
- Comfort with and competence in English
- Religious beliefs and cultural value orientation
- Family cultural dynamics

Each of these five noted factors is among the many others that can hinder the ability of law enforcement to develop an effective rapport with Asian Americans. Some are more relevant than others to specific groups, but mostly all of these issues are relevant at one point or another when considering Asian Indian Americans, Chinese Americans, and Vietnamese Americans.

Generational Status in the United States

A very substantial portion of Asian Americans are born outside of the United States, collectively comprising more than 25 percent of all the foreign-born citizens in the United States (Hanser, 2011). Indeed, throughout the United States, over 60 percent of all Chinese Americans, 70 percent of all Asian Indian Americans, and a full 90 percent of all Vietnamese Americans are not born in the United States. These percentages are likewise reflected among various states in the southern region of the United States. In fact, it is often the case that even more Asian Americans are foreign born within the southern region of the United States (Hanser, 2011).

Asian American Crime Victimization

Besides the fact that media reporting should be accurate, there are other concerns that arise from this "model minority" status. First, this creates the impression in the public eye that Asian Americans are not in need of assistance, assistance that is perhaps commonly provided to other racial groups. Second, this image has helped develop animosity from some members of other racial and/or ethnic groups (particularly among the African American and Caucasian American populations). Related to this animosity is the observance of hate crimes against Asian Americans (Shusta et al., 2011). In addition, there is a corresponding trend among some groups of offenders to single out Asian American businesses and/or persons for robberies and other utilitarian crimes due to the perception that these individuals will have substantial material wealth to make such criminal endeavors profitable (Shusta, 2011; Valdez, 2005).

Domestic Violence in Asian American Families

The customs and norms among many Asian households have typically adhered to a patriarchal system where women are expected to remain subservient. In these types of family arrangements, it may be socially proscribed that the male head of household maintains discipline over the house (McGoldrick et al., 1996). This can translate to the use of physical force to maintain the status hierarchy, thereby "normalizing" domestic violence within such households. Such forms of violence often emerge due to a value conflict between the traditional patriarchal values of husbands and the modern gender equality sought by wives (McGoldrick et al., 1996). Indeed, the prevalence of divorce has increased among many Asian American couples, including those born in their country-of-origin. Police should keep in mind that the reasons for underreporting might be linked to immigration issues and/or fear of the police. This makes these women vulnerable to manipulation, coercion, and abuse. As such, some abusive husbands may take advantage of their immigrant wives' status before they receive permanent residency (McGoldrick et al., 1996).

Furthermore, it may be that these women are simply not aware of the services and interventions that are available (Shusta et al., 2011). Indeed, it has been found that many Asian women simply use "self-help" forms of coping. In addition, Song (1996) found that roughly 70 percent of battered Asian women reported having little or no knowledge of the services available to them prior to the detection of the perpetrator's actions. As Shusta et al. (2011) note, "the role of the peace officers in detecting, assessing, and intervening in family violence situations within Asian/Pacific American communities is a critical one..." (p.147). This is particularly true when considering the social constraints against reporting, the fact that many of these women may not be fluent in English, and that they may have little understanding of the U.S. social service system given that their birthplace is likely to be in their own nation-of-origin.

Asian American Criminal Activity

Many of the crimes that are committed in Asian American communities are perpetrated by those not belonging to the Asian community (Hanser, 2011). This is especially true among first-generation and/or refugee Asian Americans. Hanser (2011) notes that it is often very difficult for law enforcement officers to gain victim or witness cooperation when investigating these crimes, which frequently include extortion, home robbery, burglary, theft, blackmail, and other crimes against persons (Shusta et al., 2011; Valdez, 2005). In fact, it would appear that home invasion robbery has been attributed as a specialty to many Southeast Asian (particularly Vietnamese) street gangs (Valdez, 2005). Consider that the Southeast Asian society inadvertently exerts a tremendous amount of pressure based on fear, intimidation, and shame not to report this type of violent crime to the police. As a result, law enforcement has a very limited database to track and prosecute some Southeast Asian gang members. To compound the problem even more, sexual assaults are almost never reported to the authorities, even whenthough robbery is (Valdez, 2005, p. 178).

Valdez (2005) adds that in cases of house robbery where sexual assaults occur, victims in the Asian American community almost never report them. The victims of sexual assault tend to lose face with their family and within the Asian community. When considering such cultural constraints, reporting sexual assault could be seen as disastrous to the victim (Valdez, 2005). In many cases, the victim may feel as if the assault is the result of their own inaction or wrongdoing (Valdez, 2005). Thus, the cultural pressures and self-blame tend to compound the trauma that such victims are bound to endure. Naturally, such victims will be even less likely to confide their victimization to law enforcement agents.

MIDDLE EASTERN AMERICANS

Issues related to criminal justice and Middle Eastern Americans are perhaps more relevant today than ever before in the history of the United States. Currently, the United States finds itself in the midst of conflicts that include Afghanistan, Pakistan, and Iraq, while other countries in the region, such as Libya and Syria, have experienced revolutions and serious internal upheaval. Because of these developments as well as other reasons, Middle Easterners have found immigration to the United States to be a favorable option. Some come to gain an education, others may come to invest in business with the hope of gaining citizenship, eventually, while others may follow other family members who have already settled in the United States.

Given that these populations are arriving in the United States at steady rates and given that there is strong public association with these populations and acts of terrorism, both in the United States and abroad, it is very useful and important for police to understand dynamics associated with Middle Easterners. They should especially be mindful of stereotypes that others in society may have of them and should also strive to stay abreast of world events in the Middle Eastern region. It is important to note that many of these immigrants know English and speak the language very well. Nevertheless, they may suffer from stigma related to the World Trade Center tragedy that remains on the minds of many Americans.

Within the American population, many people are not well versed in Arabic culture and do not really know about the diversity entailed therein. For instance, although most people believe that Iranians and Turks are of Arabic descent, this is actually not true. Indeed, Turkey has often had close ties with Europe throughout its history but this is seldom known by most persons in the United States. Furthermore, not all Arabs are Islamic; rather, there is a fair minority who are Christian. Likewise, Islam has numerous offshoots, similar to Christianity, and the world's Muslim population actually consists of dozens of differing ethnic groups. This is particularly true when one considers the even larger Islamic population that exists throughout Asia in countries such as Singapore, Thailand, India, and even China. In this section, we will focus primarily on refugees and immigrants from Arab countries in the Middle East because they are the primary group of new arrivals in the United States and because this is also the group where law enforcement could use additional training. We begin by differentiating between different groups, starting with Iranian and Turkish immigrants.

Iranians and Turks

Iranians use the Arabic script for their writing but tend to speak Persian, which is a different language from Arabic, and are from Iran. Persia is the ancient name of Iran. The current name for the Persian language is *Farsi*. People from the nation of Turkey speak Turkish, which is a completely different language from Arabic. In both countries, the majority religion is Islam. Though other religions exist, Islam is the prevailing religion, similar to Arabic nations, though both of these nations are not, in actuality, Arabic.

In Iran, the majority of the Muslim population belongs to the **Shi'ah sect** and this has been officially classified as that nation's primary religion. Shi'ah is a strict and conservative sect of the Islamic faith. Beyond religion, Persians form the largest ethnic group in Iran, who account for nearly 60 percent of the nation's population. Other non-Arabic populations include Kurds, Turkish, Armenian, and Assyrian groups.

In Turkey, the prevailing attitude toward the United States is much more favorable. Indeed, the author of this chapter has had the good fortune of encountering and befriending several Turkish police administrators who have studied in America. Further, **Turks** tend to be strongly affiliated with Eastern Europe and, as such, are more influenced by Western cultures than are persons from other countries in the Middle Eastern region. This means that, to some extent, Turks may seem to be more contemporary than Iranians. Many Turks who have come to America are from upper-class, professional groups, or are students in the United States. The same is true with Iranians.

Arab Americans

There are an estimated 4 million **Arab Americans** in the United States, who constitute nearly 2 percent of the population. Thus, their actual numbers are small. However, their numbers continue to grow as globalization and immigration patterns change with historical events around the world. As with Asian Americans, Arab Americans are a small but growing group. Unlike Asian Americans, this group of minorities draws a disproportionate amount of concern from the general public and is also greatly misunderstood by the general American public.

There is a great deal of diversity among Arab American groups. Understanding this will aid police officers who patrol jurisdictions where Arab Americans are present. Arabs from the Middle East come from over a dozen countries throughout the Middle East and Northern Africa. Arab visitors such as foreign students, tourists, and corporate people from the Gulf states are usually wealthy, in contrast to those from Jordan, Lebanon, and Palestine. Further, age and generational difference exist among Arabs. For example, older Arabic men may be found wearing their traditional headdress while younger Arabs are seldom seen doing so. Furthermore, younger Arab women are less likely to wear their head covering and the traditional long dress that older Arab women may wear.

Further still, it would appear that younger generations of Arabs are likely to disappoint their parents as they become more Westernized and less acquiescent to traditional Arabic norms. This is occurring both in the United States and in Arabic nations in the Middle East. Moreover, these generational differences are more pronounced among newly immigrated Arabs who have children who attend public school and, for the first time, are exposed to a new Western culture. This is in contrast to families who have been in the United States for several generations and where multiple generations have acculturated to Western styles and norms.

Even though there are differences in Arabic groups and individuals, whether due to socioeconomics, levels of traditionalism, the need to flee their homeland due to political change, and so on, there still remain some core values that tend to be consistent among mostly any Arabic group and/or individual. It is good for officers to be conversant on these customs and/or beliefs as a means of establishing rapport with Arabs in their jurisdiction. Among the various customs, the following three (Shusta et al., 2011) are perhaps the most prevalent:

1. *Personal Honor*: Traditional Arab society holds personal and family honor in high regard. The degree to which an Arab can lose face and be shamed publicly is not always understood by most Americans. Because of this, it is helpful if officers can handle calls-for-service in a manner that does not bring such disgrace on family members (especially the male head-of-household and his sense of authority or a female's need for modesty). Arab families are very sensitive to shaming and this is because in traditional Arab societies there could be serious consequences to the family and/or family member who is disgraced or found to be disgraceful (such as stoning to death or being ostracized).

2. *Family Loyalty*: Loyalty to one's family, in Arab culture, is more important than personal needs or desires. In Arab culture, family members are entwined to one another and there is no place for individualism. Protection for one another and privacy within the family from outside persons are important features of Arab family life and culture. Members of Arab families tend to avoid public displays of disagreement and, instead, prefer to handle issues among themselves with no outside observers.

3. *Courteous Communication*: Arabs emphasize harmony between individuals. Communication that is overly direct and candid is often seen as impolite. Most traditional Arab beliefs would also contend that it is not appropriate to be totally honest (i.e., the typical "brutally honest" approach that many Westerners are fond of using) if the person would experience a loss of face, especially if they did so personally or if this affected their family. In such cases, officers should attempt to work with families in their testimony to arrive at the truth through numerous points-of-view without, unless absolutely necessary, pushing members further, particularly if this would imply that they are dishonest. Among more Westernized Arabs, this aspect of communication is not considered as important an issue, so officers will generally encounter this mostly with persons who are new to America.

Victimization of Middle Eastern Americans

The terrorist attack on the World Trade Center on September 11, 2001, raised fears in the following months that discrimination against Arab Americans would increase and would include violent victimization. The **Arab Anti-Discrimination Committee (ADC)** has confirmed that this was the case, and show over 80 incidents where Arab Americans were pulled off airplanes solely because of their appearance rather than observation of illegal conduct. Thus, stereotyping of Arab Americans by exuberant officers was a problem that generated a host of concerns and resulted in the need for additional training to prevent racial profiling and discrimination.

The FBI Hate Crime Statistics has pointed out the surge in hate crimes against Arab Americans shortly after 9-11. Consider that in 2000, there were 36 victims of anti-Islamic hate crimes. In 2001, that number rose to 554 victims, more than a 1,500 percent increase. This initial spike in hate crimes during the immediate post 9-11 era declined quickly and significantly once community members and police worked together to quell the number of incidents. The key issue is to understand that discriminatory views and extreme hatred are directed at many Middle Easterners in the United States. Naturally, these communities of people are aware of this and are naturally wary. With this knowledge, continual work of government, police, and local community members has been observed, such as the May 2003 unanimously approved Senate resolution written by Senator Dick Durban (D-IL) that condemned violence and hatred toward Arab Americans, Muslim Americans, South Asian Americans, and Sikh Americans (Shusta et al., 2011).

It is interesting to point out that, though racial profiling does still seem to be an issue for Arab Americans, it is usually at the hands of federal agents, not local law enforcement. There were a number of incidents involving federal agents who showed discriminatory enforcement practices with Arab Americans attempting to board planes (ADC, 2008). Indeed, the 2003–2007 ADC report found relatively few instances of discrimination by local police and ultimately determined that the greatest threat for discrimination lay with the federal government's Joint Terrorism Task Force (JTTF), which consists of a number of federal enforcement agencies that work in collaboration to defend against terrorism in the United States. Since 9/11, practices among federal agencies have been revised and improved, particularly due to negative publicity such as with Guantanamo Bay, where Arab suspects were detained under rigid circumstances, drawing international attention.

MINORITY VICTIMS OF CRIME

In this section, we will examine some of the characteristics of crime victims who belong to minority groups. Data from the **National Crime Victimization Survey** (NCVS) show that African American, Asian American, Native American, and Latino Americans are more likely than Caucasians to be victims of household and personal crimes. African Americans (particularly African American males) are more prone to victimization and face a greater likelihood of homicide than do Caucasians. With this in mind, it should be clear that groups at greatest risk of becoming crime victims are those that belong to a racial or ethnic minority group.

Furthermore, it is important to remember that criminal victimization tends to be **intra-racial,** not inter-racial. In other words, crime victims are likely to have a crime perpetrated against them by a person of their own racial or ethnic orientation. Indeed, data from the NCVS shows that almost all violent crimes committed by Caucasian offenders were committed against Caucasian victims. The pattern can be seen in a wide variety of crimes, including robbery, sexual assault, aggravated assault, and simple assault. In other words, it is most common for white people to be victimized by other white people. This breaks away from many stereotypes that are reinforced by the media that consider white victims to typically have African American assailants.

Likewise, consider that this intra-racial pattern of violent crime is also reported by other racial victims. This then means that violent crimes committed against African Americans tend to be perpetrated by another African American. Thus, the same dynamic occurs in the victim–offender dyad that exists with Caucasians. The same is true with other racial groups, including Latino Americans, Native Americans, and Asian Americans.

To further illustrate how true this is, consider the victim–offender pairing for the crime of homicide. Longitudinal data from the UCR shows that homicide is an intra-racial event. For instance, in 2010, it was found that:

1. Nearly 4 out of 5 African American murder victims were slain by other African Americans.
2. Nearly 9 out of 10 Caucasians were slain by other Caucasians.

3. Over 6 out of 10 Asian Americans were victimized by other Asians.
4. Over half of Native Americans were victimized by other Native Americans.

Much of the reason for the above observations has to do with proximity and with relationship. Indeed, perpetrators of various racial groups will tend to go with what they know and who they know when committing crimes. This means that they will usually case victims who are familiar to them because they know them. Because racial groups tend to congregate with one another, the proximity of most victims to the offender will be high and this makes it likely that the offender will be of the same race as the victim. However, many homicides are also domestic in nature and, as such, given that most couples and/or family configurations are same-sex in composition, it stands to reason that these types of crimes will have victims and offenders of the same racial group.

Police response to victims of crime in minority communities should be very closely considered. The attitudes of police will prove crucial when responding to crime victims in minority communities. Smith, Graham, and Adams (2001) found that officers who are assigned to racial or ethnic minority communities, high-crime areas, and poverty-ridden neighborhoods felt that they received less respect from the public than did officers in other areas. This stands in contrast to a major concern among racial and ethnic minority communities that contend that police agencies do not care about their welfare and are also unwilling to admit when mistakes in policing practice occur which affect the community. The ability to mitigate these two opposing views between police and minority community members is one that requires attention to emotionally charged details and an empathetic approach.

MINORITY OFFENDERS AND THE POLICE

First, as we have seen, most crime is intra-racial. As a result, police in jurisdictions that have a large proportion of minority persons will tend to find that calls-for-service will also usually result in the report of an offender from the minority group that prevails in that region. Further, because of tense police–community relations in these areas, it is less likely that victims will call for service. However, when they do, racial bias is frequently cited to occur, arrests being made with more serious charges, a failure to provide services by some agencies, and slower response times from police officers. Indeed, racial and ethnic minorities are arrested, stopped and questioned, and shot and killed by police well out of proportion to their representation in the population. This implies that police responses are either too extreme or that they are, perhaps, many times lax due to apathy among police who patrol these areas.

Discussion regarding police response to minority offenders would not be complete without mention of the use-of-force in policing. Indeed, there is a great deal of controversy over the prevalence of police use of excessive force. Data from the 2005 BJS police–public contact survey indicate that African Americans are more than three times as likely to experience force than are Caucasian offenders. This is especially disturbing if one considers that this statistic had increased since the prior BJS report in 2002. The BJS police–public contact survey also collects data on Latino Americans and it found that Latino offenders were more likely to experience force than Caucasians, but not as much as African Americans. Naturally, these findings present the idea that police training in the use of force may need to emphasize more on discretion and uniform application of the use of force in arrests.

Research by Hindelang of victimization reports to the police revealed a pattern of differential reporting of offenses by victims. Specifically, Hindelang found that when the crimes of rape and robbery are concerned, those victimized by African Americans were more likely than those victimized by Caucasians to report the crime to police. Hindelang suggested that this is a form of selection bias, albeit **victim-based selection bias.** Hindelang concluded his comparison of the UCR arrest rates and victimization survey in 2008 by separating the elements of criminal justice systemic selection bias and victim-based selection bias, as well as differential offending rates. He argued that both forms of selection bias were present but that each was outweighed by the overwhelming evidence of differential involvement of African Americans in offending.

Other research using NIBRS arrest data was conducted by D'Alessio and Stolzenberg, which examined and compared effects from differential offending and differential enforcement by deriving research questions from the social threat hypothesis. They used racial composition of jurisdictions to approximate the social threat of racial minority populations to determine if law enforcement arrest practices varied by the racial composition of the jurisdiction that reported crimes. This allowed them to differentiate between differential arrest practices and differential offending practices. They found that the odds of arrest were actually higher for Caucasians than for African Americans in three-fourths of the crime categories that they examined. Thus, they concluded that the disproportionately high arrest rate for African Americans was most likely attributed to differential involvement in reported crime rather than racially biased policing techniques.

CONCLUSION

This chapter demonstrates that there is a wide degree of diversity between and among the various racial/ethnic groups discussed and this creates numerous opportunities and challenges for police as first responders. It is clear that training of police on customs and mores of various minority groups within the agency's jurisdiction should be routinely provided. This is becoming ever more the case as one considers news events related to allegations of extreme uses of force (including deadly force) by police, complications and legal battles related to immigration issues, the War on Terror, and other sensationalized events. Furthermore, as we have noted throughout this text, the United States is becoming a more diverse and globalized nation with each passing year. Policing an ever-diverse population has complications that require more understanding among officers than was true a couple of generations ago.

In this chapter, we have also learned that the relationship between the victim and the offender (especially with violent crime) tends to be intra-racial. This means that victims and offenders tend to be of the same racial group. This is counter to many of the stereotypes that the public may maintain regarding crime, particularly with African Americans, where the media has excessively portrayed the African American perpetrator and Caucasian victim association. This has created a false understanding of crime commission in the public mindset. It is the goal of this chapter to provide a deeper sense of context and a more accurate portrayal of crime commission to better demonstrate how police can and should operate when policing minority communities.

Chapter 6 Learning Check

1. _____ implies that, within the very fabric of the structures of our society, there are both overt and covert forms of racism that exist in both official and informal relationships between different racial groups in our society.
   a. Structural racism
   b. Structural disparity
   c. Cultural racism
   d. Cultural bias

2. When those victimized by African Americans are more likely than those victimized by Caucasians to report the crime to police, this is an example of _____ _____.
   a. Victim-perpetrator disparity
   b. Racial-based selection bias
   c. Victim-based selection bias
   d. Differential reporting bias
   e. None of the above

3. Nearly 4 out of 5 African American murder victims were slain by other African Americans.
   a. True
   b. False

4. Data from the **National Crime Victimization Survey** (NCVS) shows that minority groups are more likely than Caucasians to be victims of household and personal crimes.
   a. True
   b. False

5. _____ are the second-largest population of Latino origin residing in the United States.
   a. Cuban Americans
   b. Puerto Ricans
   c. Hondurans

   d. Mexican Americans
   e. None of the above

6. In Mexico, recent strong economic growth might have reduced the _____ that often lead Mexicans to emigrate to the United States.
   a. Desire
   b. Push factors
   c. Pull factors
   d. None of the above.

7. Farsi is the language that most Arabs speak.
   a. True
   b. False

8. Nearly 90 percent of Caucasians were slain by other Caucasians.
   a. True
   b. False

9. There are informal, perhaps even unintentional, but nonetheless real biases and negative stereotypes that serve to reinforce the _____ _____ of African Americans.
   a. Disparity
   b. Negative outcomes
   c. Marginalization
   d. All of the above
   e. None of the Above.

10. It was the _____ of the 1960s that addressed the continued inequalities that persisted after the abolishment of slavery.
    a. Malcolm X movement
    b. War on Poverty
    c. Martin Luther King, Jr., speech
    d. Civil Rights Movement
    e. None of the above

Essay Discussion Questions

1. In your own words, discuss how the experience of slavery has been linked to the general distrust of police by the African American population during the past 50–100 years?

2. Identify and discuss some of the factors that explain why differential reporting of offenders seems to occur in society.

3. Discuss racial profiling and how it has applied to Middle Eastern Americans after 9/11.

References

Almeida, R. (1996). Hindu, Christian, and Muslim families. In M. McGoldrick, M. Giordano, J. Pearce, & J. Giordano (Eds.). *Ethnicity and family therapy* (2nd ed., pp. 395–423). New York: Guilford Press.

Arab American Anti-Discrimination Committee. (2008). *2003–2007 Report on hate crimes and discrimination against Arab Americans*. Washington, DC: ADC. Retrieved from: www.adc.org.

Brown, R. H. (2005) *Culture, capitalism and democracy in the New America*. New Haven: Yale University Press.

Bureau of Justice Statistics. (2009). *Victim characteristics: Violent crime victims*. Washington, DC: Bureau of Justice Statistics. Retrieved from: http://bjs.ojp.usdoj.gov/index.cfm?ty=tp&tid=92.

Frosch, M. (1997). *Civil War Home Page*. Retrieved from: http://www.civil-war.net/pages/1860_census.html.

Hanser, R. D. (2011). Asian American populations and police relations in mid-sized communities of the Southern Region of the United States. In R. D. Hanser, S. Mire, A. Kualiang, S. Roh, & K. Unter (Eds.), *Readings in International Criminal Justice Issues*. New Delhi, India: Serials Publications.

Jennings, J. (1997) *Race and Politics: New challenges and responses for Black activism*. London: Verso.

Joiner, C. T. (2005). An examination of racial profiling data in a large metropolitan area. *Professional Issues in Criminal Justice, 1*(2), 1–14.

Justice Department. (2003). *Justice Department issues policy guidance to ban Racial profiling*. Washington, DC: United States Department of Justice.

Kolchin, P. (2003). *American slavery: 1619–1877*. New York: Hill and Wang.

Kubisch, A. C. (2006). Structural racism. *Poverty & Race, 15*(6), 1–7.

Lawrence, K., & Keleher, T. (2004). *Structural racism*. Queenstown, MA: Aspen Institute for Community Change.

Lester, D. (2003). Native Americans and the criminal justice system. In J. Joseph & D. Taylor (Eds.). *With justice for all: Minorities and women in criminal justice*. Upper Saddle River, NJ: Prentice Hall.

Marable, M. (2002). The political and theoretical contexts of the changing racial terrain. *Souls, 4*(3), 1–16.

Mauk, D., & Oakland, J. (2005) *American civilization: An introduction*. London: Routledge.

McGoldrick, M., Giordano, J., Pearce, J. K., & Giordano, J. (1996). *Ethnicity and Family Therapy* (2nd ed.). New York: Guilford Press.

Middlemass, K. M. (2006). America at the crossroads, *Souls, 8*(2), 1–6.

Oliver, W. (2008). The structural-cultural perspective: A theory of black male violence. In D. F. Hawkins (Ed.), *Violent crime: Assessing race and ethnic differences*. New York: Cambridge University Press.

Passel, J., & Cohn, D. (2008). *U.S. population projections: 2005–2050*. Washington, DC: Pew Research Center. Retrieved from: http://www.pewhispanic.org/2008/02/11/us-population-projections-2005-2050/.

Passel, J., Cohn, D., & Lopez, M. H. (2011). *Hispanics account for more than half of nation's growth in past decade*. Washington, DC: Pew Research Center. Retrieved from: http://www.pewhispanic.org/2011/03/24/hispanics-account-for-more-than-half-of-nations-growth-in-past-decade/.

Pew Research Center. (2012). *Views of law enforcement, racial progress and news coverage of race*. Washington, DC: Pew Research Center.

Public Broadcasting Service. (2008). *Africans in America: Conditions of Antebellum slavery*. Arlington, VA: PBS. Retrieved from: http://www.pbs.org/wgbh/aia/part4/4p2956.html.

Shusta, M., Levine, D. R., Wong, H. Z., Olson, A .T., & Harris, P. R. (2011). *Multicultural law enforcement: Strategies for peacekeeping in a diverse society* (5th ed.). Upper Saddle River, NJ: Prentice Hall.

Song, Y. I. (1996). *Battered women in Korean immigrant families*. New York: Garland.

Winant, H. (2004). *New politics of race: Globalism, difference, justice*. Minneapolis, MN: University of Minnesota Press.

United Nations. (2009). World conference against racism, racial discrimination, xenophobia and related intolerance, Aug. 31–Sept. 8, 2001. *Durban Declaration and Programme of Action*, § III(A)(1) 72, U.N. Doc A/CONF.189/12 (Sept. 2001). Retrieved from: http://www.un.org/durbanreview2009/pdf/DDPA_full_text.pdf.

U.S. Department of Justice (2013). *Indian Country Investigations and Prosecutions 2011–2012*. Washington, DC: USDOJ.

Valdez, A. (2005). *Gangs: A guide to understanding street gangs* (4th ed.). LawTech Publishing. Retrieved from: www.LawTechPublishing.com.

7

Law Enforcement and Minorities: Community Relations, Hiring, and Training

LEARNING OBJECTIVES

After reading this chapter, students should be able to do the following:

1. Discuss the importance of trust-building and community involvement.
2. Identify some typical community policing programs that aid police in building community rapport.
3. Identify how police can improve relations with minority and immigrant populations.
4. Discuss some of the challenges that face agencies when recruiting, hiring, and retaining minority police officers.
5. Evaluate the means by which police administrators can effectively provide diversity training to officers in their ranks.
6. Discuss some examples of how minority and immigrant community volunteers can be utilized to enhance the relationship between police and citizens.

KEY TERMS

Best practices in multicultural hiring

Best practices in police hiring

Citizen review panels

Citizen's advisory committee

Community leaders

Community Liaison Officer (CLO)

Community policing

Cultural liaison

Culturally specific training

Diversity training

Externally oriented diversity

Internally oriented diversity

Lesbian, Gay, Bisexual, & Transexual Program

National night out

Neighborhood watch

Organizational culture

Over-identification

Rebrand the training

Role-reversal experiences

Section 287(g) of the Immigration & Nationality Act

Spanish Speaking Ride-Along Program

Title VII of the Civil Rights Act of 1964

INTRODUCTION

This chapter will largely focus on police–community relations with the various racial and/or ethnic groups discussed in Chapter 6 as well as other diverse groups discussed in Chapters 3 and 4 of this chapter. The key point of this chapter will be to demonstrate how police agencies can benefit from positive relationships with the surrounding community that they serve and, at the same time, to provide some examples of how this might be achieved.

One important strategy that will be discussed is agency hiring of diverse officers who reflect the community that is served. There are many challenges that police agencies face with regard to hiring. The ability to hire qualified applicants and retain them is challenging enough and these challenges are magnified when agencies attempt to recruit officers from diverse racial and cultural backgrounds.

In addition, this chapter will address the current economic climate against which police agencies must operate. Although this might seem to be an unrelated issue to a discussion on police community relations, we contend that it is actually quite relevant for various reasons. Indeed, current economic challenges have led to innovative strategies among police agencies. One such strategy is the use of the community itself through the use of volunteers. This has turned out to be an effective means of aiding police agencies with a variety of functions, including administrative tasks and support tasks for police patrol functions.

Lastly, the use of volunteers has also been integrated into various crime prevention initiatives. Along the way, it has been discovered that the use of volunteers can also be instrumental in gaining assistance from diverse communities. This then translates to a rapport-building use of volunteers who come from these diverse populations whereby understanding between the police and citizens is developed. Just as important, these volunteers also, in turn, go back to their families and friends and provide supportive commentary and understanding about police operations, protocols, and means of response. The result is a win-win strategy for all involved, which increases understanding between police practitioners and community members.

TRUST-BUILDING AND COMMUNITY INVOLVEMENT

Community crime prevention efforts often occur through the education of citizens within a given police jurisdiction. In many cases, the provision of this type of public education falls under the umbrella of a community policing agenda (Hanser, Gallagher, Carlson, Kuanliang, & Lanham, 2012). While community policing tends to mean many things to many people, we will refer to the Department of Justice's Office of Community Oriented Policing Services, which defines **community policing** as follows:

> Community policing is a philosophy that promotes organizational strategies, which support the systematic use of partnerships and problem-solving techniques, to proactively address the immediate conditions that give rise to public safety issues such as crime, social disorder, and fear of crime. (2009, p. 2)

According to the Community Oriented Policing Services (COPS) office of the U.S. Department of Justice, collaborative partnerships between law enforcement agencies and the citizens or organizations that they serve work to develop solutions to problems and increase trust with the police. Law enforcement agencies, when embracing a community policing approach, should seek partnerships with community members and civic groups. Naturally, diverse members of the community should be included in these partnerships.

One of the best examples of community member participation in the community policing model is the use of **Neighborhood Watch**. This program was first created in 1972 by the National Sheriff's Association as a means of uniting law enforcement agencies, private organizations, as well as individual citizens into coordinated groups to reduce residential crime. Since its first inception, this program has grown and it is now used in numerous urban areas throughout the nation. Specifically, Neighborhood Watch is intended to bring citizens together to:

1. Make their own homes and families less-inviting targets for crime;
2. Cooperate with law enforcement through block and neighborhood groups to control crime throughout the community.

The premise behind Neighborhood Watch is the fact that police, regardless of how well trained, manned, or equipped, simply cannot be in every location and at every time that a crime might be committed. Rather, "the prevention of crime—particularly crime involving residential neighborhoods—is a responsibility that must be shared equally by law enforcement and private citizens" (Office of Community Oriented Policing Services, 2009, p. 5).

In building Neighborhood Watch programs, it is important that police agencies develop a good rapport with their community members. This means that networking in the community should be part and parcel to what law enforcement seek to do and this also means that law enforcement should be visible at both formal and informal community gatherings (Hanser et al., 2012). One such example, **National Night Out**, brings together local watch groups and crime prevention organizations while hosting a "block party" that consists of cookouts, dances, parades, and various other activities designed to foster community connectedness. These events involve local police and promote involvement in crime and drug prevention, and in essence build a sense of trust within these communities.

The development of programs like Neighborhood Watch and the hosting of functions like National Night Out can work wonders in building trust and rapport between the police and citizens of diverse communities. At the base of this discussion is the issue of trust. In most cases, community problems with police simply rest with a lack of trust among citizens, particularly those citizens and/or groups who have traditionally been marginalized.

Furthermore, it has been found that trust often develops from the bottom up, not the top down (National Crime Prevention Council, 1995). Relationships are more easily developed at the individual level and it is the personal interaction that ultimately bridges cultural gaps that may exist. Trust is a valued by-product when individuals, often from diverse backgrounds, collaborate on social and civic activities within their respective communities in an effort to solve local problems.

In addition to the typical actions that are part and parcel to a community policing orientation of peace keeping, there are other specific activities that can prove effective with minority communities. For instance, officers can develop relationships through various activities, including service as liaison between newcomer communities and law enforcement, providing assistance with language proficiency classes and interpreting services, and educating refugees about the American criminal justice system (National Crime Prevention Council, 1995). In addition, agencies and officers can support mutual assistance associations and refugee self-help groups that understand the needs of fellow refugees. All of these activities build trust, which can lead to further collaboration.

Partnerships between community members and the police agency are the most effective means of identifying areas and locations that are at risk. Shusta (2011) defines the term "at-risk" as those communities that have a high level of criminal activity or social disorganization, as well as the occurrence of civil rights violations and/or concerns (i.e., hate/bias crimes, discrimination allegations, racism, and so forth). The use of various community policing strategies will naturally mesh well with this type of policing and will facilitate the agency's efforts to empower minority communities as stakeholders and contributors to their own community.

Empowerment is the key word in this case, because it is the community that is likely to have the most information and intelligence regarding activities within the boundaries of the community and because the police agency cannot operate in a proactive (as opposed to reactive) manner on its own without the aid of the citizenry (Hanser et al., 2012). In short, the two entities, police and minority communities, must be partners, and the best means of establishing this partnership is through empowerment of the community itself. Indeed, an empowered community will also be one that will have less need for police intervention, thereby benefiting the agency and its personnel through a reduction in future calls for service.

CHALLENGES SPECIFIC TO IMMIGRANT COMMUNITIES

Although we have referred to the need for police agencies to be able to respond to diverse communities having various minority populations, specific attention has not been provided, in this chapter, to the influx of immigrants into various communities in the United States. As we noted in Chapter 1 of this text, multiculturalism now entails diversity from the internal racially and culturally heterogeneous nature of the U.S. population was well as external cultural and racial diversity as populations migrate into the United States. We refer to these types of diversity as internally oriented diversity and externally oriented diversity, respectively. **Internally oriented diversity** is associated with minority groups and/or individuals who have a long and extended history in the United States, with generational changes that have occurred within the borders of the United States and whose values, norms, and mores are primarily shaped by historical events on the North American continent (e.g., most African Americans, Native Americans, many but not all Latino Americans, and many Caucasian Americans tend to fit this definition). **Externally oriented diversity** is associated with minority groups who tend to be first- or second-generation Americans who have individually or as a family become located in the United States (e.g., Chinese Americans, Indians, or many newer immigrant Mexican Americans). With both types of diversity, a number of different groups and categories can exist.

Furthermore, with both types of diversity, the specific type of diverse group will vary by region. In some areas, one group may tend to migrate more frequently to that location than another. Regardless of the type of immigrant communities within a given jurisdiction, Lysakowski, Pearsall, and Pope (2009) note that most all police agencies tend to deal with some very similar challenges, as follows:

1. Large numbers of people who do not speak English fluently
2. Reluctance among immigrants to report crime
3. Immigrants' fear of the police
4. Effects of federal immigration enforcement actions
5. Confusion among immigrants over whether and to what extent local police enforce immigration laws
6. Misunderstandings based on cultural differences
7. Personal interactions between immigrants and police officers that damage goodwill and trust.

We will explain each of the above seven challenges in more detail as follows. In doing so, we would like to note that much of the material and content related to

Box 7.1 The Changing Demographics of the United States

Spotlight on Demographic Changes

It is clear that demographic changes are affecting law enforcement agencies across the nation. The Hispanic population, through immigration and a higher birth rate, is growing faster than other groups in the United States. In addition, internal migration, often in response to changes in local job markets, has resulted in rapid changes in the composition of communities across America. Historically, urban areas and border communities served as gateways for immigrants. Today, police chiefs and sheriffs in all parts of the country, including suburban and rural areas, find themselves serving burgeoning immigrant populations. As a result, law enforcement leaders in most areas are attempting to come to terms with cultural and language challenges, as well as the conflicts that arise between new immigrants and the established population. Demands for officers with language skills and cultural competencies has grown in these agencies, but law enforcement executives have often found it difficult to attract candidates who reflect and can serve the newly emerging communities.

Iowa, Minnesota, and North Carolina are among the states experiencing rapid growth in Hispanic populations. In Chaska, Minnesota, a suburban community about 25 miles southwest of Minneapolis, about 10 percent of the population is Hispanic. But according to Chief Scott Knight, none of Chaska's 23 officers is Hispanic, even though the department has made recruitment of Hispanic officers a priority.

Other immigrant groups also pose similar challenges for police chiefs and sheriffs. Hmong (an ethnic group from Southeast Asia) refugees have settled across Wisconsin and Minnesota, and Somalis are arriving in large numbers in places like Lewiston, Maine, a small mill town of with a population of 35,000, largely of French-Canadian heritage.

Given the intense competition for recruits among law enforcement agencies, local chiefs and sheriffs find it difficult to attract candidates of all backgrounds, including candidates from immigrant groups. Smaller cities with emerging minority and immigrant populations are at a competitive disadvantage because larger cities that are already ethnically diverse generally offer higher salaries and provide more opportunities for career advancement.

Source: Office of Community Oriented Policing Services. (2009). *Law enforcement recruitment toolkit.* Washington, DC: United States Department of Justice.

these challenges have been adapted from the work of Lysakowski et al. (2009). Though these challenges are very common throughout the United States, they do still vary from jurisdiction to jurisdiction as to their overall impact on police–community relations.

Language Barriers

In responding to calls for service, police have a difficult time knowing what to do or how to help if language barriers prevent them from understanding what has happened. As an example, consider a situation where police respond to a domestic violence call and cannot communicate with anyone on the scene, they may not be able to make an arrest. Community surveys have revealed that language barriers also prevent many immigrants from reaching out to the police for protection. Thus, an agency's lack of effective interpretation and translation services can be a significant barrier to communication with immigrants. Effective interpretation and translation require skill in communicating with proficiency, being specific to the geographic region or the country-of-origin differences that exist in how languages are written and spoken.

Reluctance to Report Crime

In conducting focus group research, Lysakowski et al. (2009) found that participants reported that when immigrants call police they may be taking a risk if they disclose their immigration status, or the status of their family members or neighbors, to authorities. Consider again, our example with a crime of domestic violence. In such a situation, a victim who does not have legal status may not call police for fear that she or her abuser will be deported. While it may seem odd that she might worry if the abuser is deported, immigrant women are often dependent on the men they are with and often, the livelihood of their children may be intertwined with his continued ability to provide for the family. Deportation, therefore, can spell economic doom for her and her children.

In addition, consider that criminals are also known to target immigrants because their reluctance to report crimes is known among perpetrators. Indeed, many of these perpetrators are minorities of the same ethnicity as their victims and, owing to their proximity and familiarity with the victims' households and lifestyles, they are even more shrewd and malicious in the crimes they commit. Thus, serious crimes, including murder and rape, are forms of victimization that might occur when, in other circumstances, the perpetrators might not be so emboldened.

For instance, in some Asian communities, Asian gangs may conduct "home invasion" robberies and, while there, may commit rape of the women as a crime that is incident to the robbery. In such cases, they know that the family is not likely to report the crime due to three key reasons. First, the traditional honor system that exists in many Asian communities will prevent them from coming forward due to the dishonor that is cast upon the victim and the family. Second, if some of the household members are illegal immigrants, then fear that reporting of the crime will lead to deportation from the United States can be a deterrent to seeking formal legal help. Third, individuals where such gangs operate tend to be afraid of retaliation from the gang members for reporting the crime and, because these gangs can be quite dangerous and willing to engage in any variety of harmful acts (i.e., kidnap kids from school, commit arson and burn down the family dwelling, or conduct drive-by shootings), the likelihood of reporting the crime is greatly reduced.

Lysakowski et al. (2009) conducted research that included members of a Latino community who explained that they knew who committed many of the crimes in their area, but citizens were not willing to come forward out of fear that their immigration status would be questioned.

Similarly, it was noted that some employers take advantage of undocumented immigrants' labor and refuse to pay wages, knowing that the workers will not report them to police or other authorities. As can be seen, there are a number of means by which the immigrant is victimized and this victimization is made worse by their failure to report these crimes. In essence, for some immigrants, they may feel trapped in a world where their own needs for safety are perpetually compromised, creating a bleak future picture for them and their families.

Fear of Police

Many immigrants—refugees, especially—come from places where police are corrupt and abusive. Take for instance, Lowell, Massachusetts, where there is a large Cambodian population. Many of the members of the region's Cambodian population had fled the Khmer Rouge, which was a regime in Cambodia that committed mass genocide. The circumstances were horrid and it was police in Cambodia that enforced and supported this process. Thus, we must remember that some immigrants have experienced civil war, genocide, and martial law and, as a result, they may have difficulty trusting that police in the United States really do intend to protect and serve.

Federal Immigration Enforcement Can Affect Local Trust-Building Efforts

Lysakowski et al. (2009) note that an immigration enforcement action by federal agents can seriously damage hard-won trust at the local level. Immigrants may not be able to distinguish between city, state, and federal law enforcement officers. Therefore, when a raid happens, they may incorrectly attribute the action to local police—even if local police have worked to build community trust for years. Complicating the matter, some local police are now authorized to enforce federal immigration laws under section 287(g) of the Immigration and Nationality Act, whereas others are not (Hanser & Gomila, 2012). More information on Section 287(g) can be found in Box 7.2 of this chapter.

Individual Officers Can Damage a Department's Efforts

This issue is one that is a result of both the individual officer's own biases and the organizational culture within the agency. We will discuss organizational culture in a later subsection of this chapter. However, the key point is that both the agency norms and the perceptions of the officer shape how individuals will respond to minorities, whether immigrant or not. In some cases, agencies may find that individual officers have racist views or that the officer is simply not culturally competent. This can lead to

Box 7.2 Section 287(g): A Tool for Local Police Enforcement of Immigration Law

During the past decade, growing concern over immigration issues has become a fixture within the news media, the public consciousness, and official policymakers alike. After 9/11, questions regarding entry into the United States were the source of serious scrutiny and this led to numerous changes in the organizational structure of federal government enforcement agencies. Amidst this and well after this catastrophic event, border security began to be a routine concern among policymakers and the lay public. Concern with border security was eventually dovetailed by persistent concerns related to illegal immigration into the United States. These two issues—concern over potential al-Qaeda operatives getting through the porous borders of the United States and the influx of Mexican illegal immigrants seeking work and coming into the southwestern parts of the United States—provided the impetus for numerous federal- and state-level developments that ultimately led to a renewed interest in having state and local law enforcement aid the federal government in enforcing immigration statutes.

While this may, in part, briefly explain how issues of internal security and immigration eventually became an area of enforcement for local and state police, this approach has nevertheless been very controversial. However, it should be pointed out that immigration issues have not, in fact, been beyond the purview of local police enforcement; though immigration is a federal issue, many states have required that their officers turn over information to federal officials when they have detected persons who are within the nation's borders illegally. However, this is rooted in **Section 287(g) of the Immigration and Nationality Act (INA)** and, according to Section 287(g), police possess an inherent authority to arrest illegal aliens who have violated *criminal* statutes. Once the person is arrested, local police officers are expected to contact federal immigration officials so that the illegal alien can be transferred to federal custody. As one my notice, this type of local police enforcement of immigration law is one that is incident to arrest but is not, unto itself, the basis for the initial arrest. While this tends to be generally true for all law enforcement, Section 287(g) also provides for more extensive broadening of police powers regarding immigration enforcement.

The opportunity for broadened immigration enforcement powers and responsibility among police agencies followed the events of 9/11 and the creation of the Department of Homeland Security in 2002. Subsequently, it is estimated that there are about 275,000 arrests and deportations made annually by the Department of Homeland Security, as well as the partnerships with state and local police that have signed formal agreements with ICE to grant them additional immigration authority, as authorized by Section 287(g) of the Immigration and Nationality Act.

Section 287(g) was established in 1996 to aid the outdated Immigration and Naturalization Service (INS) in enforcing immigration issues within the nation's interior. However, it is important to note that resources were much more limited for the INS than they are today for the modern federal agencies—Customs and Border Protection (CBP) and the Immigration and Customs Enforcement (ICE)—that are tasked with enforcing immigration issues. Importantly, the *Immigration and Nationality Act of 1996* broadened the types of crime for which immigrants could be deported and it restricted their right to appeal after being arrested (Espenshade, Baraka, & Huber, 1997). This act was the means by which the Section 287(g) program was established, as were many of the strategies that ICE currently uses in immigration enforcement.

It was not until 2002 that the first agreement between the federal government and a police agency was established when the states of Florida and Alabama signed agreements in 2003. Later, more agreements were signed during 2005 and 2006. However, the year 2007 is considered the primary year when Section 287(g) became more commonly implemented, with over 50 police agencies signing agreements by the close of 2008.

Capps (2010) notes that agencies adopting this policy are in states where immigration issues are perceived as problematic by the public and/or where immigration has seen a sharp increase in occurrence. Political fervor against illegal immigration has tended to weigh heavy on the agendas of elected city mayors who appoint police chiefs over their municipality and sheriffs who are directly voted into office by the public. As a means of currying favor from the public, governors, police chiefs, and sheriffs have found it prudent to adopt this concern as part of their own agenda, the public support being so great as to offset budgetary concerns within their agencies.

Source: Hanser, R. D., & Gomila, M. (2012). The enforcement of immigration law by police: Issues and challenges. In F. Reddington and G. Bonham (Eds.), *Flawed criminal justice policy: At the intersection of the media, public fear and legislative response* (pp. 39–59). Durham, NC: Carolina Academic Press.

situations where the officer treats minority and/or immigrant persons in a disrespectful or calloused manner. The act of one officer can seriously undermine the efforts of an entire agency. This problem is further magnified if it appears that the agency does not take such matters seriously.

Lysakowski et al. (2009) state that "no matter what their training and regardless of their department's policy, if line officers do not treat immigrants fairly and respectfully, the department's relationship with immigrant communities will suffer" (p. 5). It is important that incidents be dealt with in a thorough and transparent manner to demonstrate that the agency will take these issues seriously and that they will not hide facts from the public. One very good practice is to utilize **citizen review panels**, which allow citizens in the area to review circumstances that are reported. These panels provide an additional level of oversight to the agency's response to complaints of inappropriate actions by individual officers. Citizen review panels provide input from community members and help mitigate potential suspicion from minority/immigrant community members.

While we have talked about the means in which agencies can ensure that the community voice is heard in addressing individual officer behavior, we would like to add a word of caution on this issue. Although it is important that agencies be thorough in their investigation of complaints regarding individual officer behavior, the agency should not feel pressurized into coming to a quick answer or resolution; this can result in a number of negative and unfair outcomes for officers and can also impair an officer's ability to effectively enforce the law. Rather, these processes must be conducted in a manner that is realistic and untainted by public prejudice, yet, at the same time, open to the community and to citizen review panel oversight.

Lack of Awareness of Cultural Differences

It is important to note that it is common for misunderstandings to exist within new immigrant communities about the role of police and how police expect people to behave in routine encounters. When stopped by a police officer while driving, for example, Lysakowski et al. (2009) note that it is a normal cultural practice for people in El Salvador to get out of the car and approach the officer. In the United States, this is exactly the wrong thing to do and can lead to law enforcement using force on the person. As another example, consider that it is common for Cambodian immigrants to keep their wallet in their socks. Naturally, when asked by a police officer for identification, these individuals might reach down for the wallet. This is, of course, a movement that police officers—especially those not familiar with Cambodian habits—might interpret as reaching for a weapon.

While limited police understanding about cultural differences among people from different countries is a challenge, as the previous examples suggest, the likely language barriers that may exist between the officer and the citizen will further exacerbate these problems. Indeed, these misunderstandings can have dangerous or even tragic outcomes. In actuality, there is no limit to the number of examples that could be provided; the circumstances are endless. As such, it may well be that no officer can ever be truly conversant about all different minority and immigrant groups, but the genuine intent to provide respect, professionalism, and a willingness to develop knowledge about different groups will usually tend to be sufficient to allow relations between the agency and the community to flourish.

CURRENT EVENTS
Arizona v. United States (2012)

On June 25th, 2012, the United States Supreme Court handed down a ruling that upheld the practice of requiring immigration status checks during routine police stops in a 5-3 majority vote. However, this ruling was accompanied by cautionary commentary against detaining individuals for prolonged periods of time is they do not have their immigration documents and also warned against the potential for racial profiling to occur. As a result, HB 2162 limited the use of racial factors in effecting arrests state that police officials may not consider race, color, or national origin beyond what is currently permissible by prior case law.

Further, the Court pointed toward a legal doctrine known as *federal preemption*, in its rationale. In short, federal preemption maintains that when federal or state laws stand in contradiction to one another or when there is some challenge in maintaining or enforcing both sets of laws simultaneously, the federal law will preempt (or override) the state law. Article VI, Section 2, of the Constitution holds that the laws of the United States are to be the supreme law of the land, which has come to mean that, when the federal government exercises its rightful powers, the federal law must prevail over any conflict or inconsistency between state and federal exercise of power (Hoenig, 2002).

Further, when it is established that a federal law preempts a state law, the state law is automatically invalid (Hoenig, 2002). With this in mind, a state is not legally able to pass a law that is inconsistent with federal law. The High Court ruled that this is precisely what Arizona did when passing S. B. 1070 and, to make matters more clear, the lawmakers of that state understood, at the time of passage, that this law would contradict federal law.

Lastly, the Court did make note of the concern that S. B. 1070 would, through its provision of mandatory questioning of the citizenship by persons stopped by police would generate such a volume of immigration cases that it would overwhelm the ability of the Immigration and Customs Enforcement (ICE) agency's ability to process the demand. The state of Arizona was aware that the federal government would be forced to address the issue, as it was common knowledge in papers and other public sources that local politicians advocated that the federal government should be addressing the issue, rather than allowing state governments to be burdened with immigration issues in their jurisdictions. While the situation might seem unfair to states facing these challenges, the Court reasoned that it was not wise to mete out more grief and difficulty upon the federal system simply because state systems were beleaguered by the immigration issue; another, more reasonable solution would have to be found.

As a result, in *Arizona v. United States* (2012), the Supreme Court handed down a split decision regarding the legality of S. B. 1070. This split decision, in essence, ruled on the bill but had diverse rulings on various sections of the bill. Thus, the case was affirmed in part, reversed in part, and remanded back to the state of Arizona. In this case, the High Court ruled that:

1. In regard to Section 2, or more specifically §2(B), the Court noted that "…in practice, will require state officers to delay the release of detainees for no reason other than to verify their immigration status. This would raise constitutional concerns. And it would disrupt the federal framework to put state officers in the position of holding aliens in custody for possible unlawful presence without federal direction and supervision" (p. 4, 2012). However, the Court also noted that §2(B) could also be read to only require that state officers conduct status checks during the course of an authorized, lawful detention. If read within these limits, §2(B) does not conflict with federal law. Thus, *the Court did affirm this section, but provided very strong and limiting language to the use of this section of S. B. 1070.*

2. Section 3 of S. B. 1070 intruded on the field of alien registration as this was an area of executive control where Congress had not left room for individual states to regulate. Thus, the Court held that section to be invalid. In fact, the Court went on to clarify by stating that "because Congress has occupied the field, even complimentary state regulation is impermissible" (p. 2, 2012). *Thus, the Court reversed §3 of S. B. 1070.*

3. In regard to §5, making it a misdemeanor crime to seek work or to work without authorization to do so, the Court noted that the "…criminal penalty stands as an obstacle to the federal regulatory system" later followed with "Congress decided it would be inappropriate to impose criminal penalties on unauthorized employees. It follows that a state law to the contrary is an obstacle to the regulatory system Congress chose" (p. 3, 2012). *The Court, therefore, reversed §5 of S. B. 1070.*

4. Lastly, when considering Section 6, which authorized state and local officers to make warrantless arrests of certain aliens suspected of being removable, the Court held that §6 created an obstacle to federal law. The Court went on to add that §6 was intended to provide state officers with greater arrest authority on immigration issues, to be exercised without instruction or guidance from the federal government. This is clearly not consistent with the stipulations of §287(g) of the INA where parameters are laid out in formal MOA's between local police agencies and the federal government. With this in mind, the Court stated very

plainly that "...this is not the system Congress created" (p. 3, 2012), *and reversed §6 of S. B. 1070* mind, the Court stated very plainly that "...this is not the system Congress created" (p. 3, 2012), *and reversed §6 of S. B. 1070.*

From the discussion above and when considering the language of these decisions in *Arizona v. United States* (2012), it is very clear that the vast majority of S. B. 1070 was preempted by federal law. Though the state of Arizona was free to rewrite and significantly revamp the law, if desired, it did not withstand the legal scrutiny of preemption by the United States Supreme Court. The decision handed down by this case has impacted laws in other states, such as Alabama and Georgia, where the 11th Circuit Court. In this case, the 11th Circuit held that laws with imposed criminal sanctions for the transportation or harboring of illegal aliens within a state's jurisdiction would also likely be preempted. Thus, other aspects of illegal immigration seem to be impacted by this ruling, including issues related to human smuggling. Indeed, the 11th Circuit considered that federal

laws pertaining to alien smuggling included a comprehensive set of penalties for this illegal activity and, as a result, this framework of penalties precluded states from imposing their own criminal sanctions upon violators of these laws.

What is not known is how other circuit courts will rule in their respective regions, as interpretations can vary from circuit to circuit. What is certain is that criminalization of immigration activities is not likely to be considered legal and, states will be held under a great deal of scrutiny if they should take matters into their own hands. Like it or not, immigration issues are, according to the High Court, federal issues, and states will be forced to accept this reality.

References: *Arizona v. United States*, 576 U. S. 1 (2012).

Hoenig, M. (2002, Dec.). Supreme Court Teaches Preemption Lessons. *New York Law Journal, 1,* 228.

Manuel, K. M. & Garcia, M. J. (2012). *Arizona v. United States: A limited role for states in immigration enforcement.* Washington, DC: Congressional Research Service. Retrieved from: http://fpc.state.gov/documents/organization/198060.pdf

A Model Police Response to Immigrant Communities

Lysakowski et al. (2009) have identified several promising approaches that law enforcement agencies are using to overcome obstacles to community policing in minority communities. One of these model approaches is the development of a specialized unit within the agency that focuses on outreach and service to the minority and immigrant community as its primary purpose. Consider, for example, the Metropolitan Nashville Police Department's El Protector program, which has two dedicated officers who engage the Hispanic community in efforts that emphasize crime prevention and education about the role of law enforcement. El Protector also enlists the help of immigrant communities to solve crimes. For example, a crime videotaped in a Latino-owned store was once sent to one of the officers, who forwarded it to contacts in the community. The contacts remained vigilant for the perpetrator, both to protect themselves and to help identify the suspect. It can be seen how these efforts can lead to the apprehension of criminals.

Similar to citizen review panels, this program also utilizes a **citizen's advisory committee** that enlists prominent members of the Latino community, including politicians and business owners, to guide the program. Citizen's advisory committees provide input on crime prevention and crime-fighting programs as a means of enhancing the police agency's ability to keep their community safe. It is important that citizen advisory committees be diverse and representative of the community-at-large. Further, media attention on the role and membership of the citizen's advisory committee can showcase positive partnerships between the police and community leaders. We will discuss the value of including various community leaders in diverse communities, in greater detail, in a later subsection. For now, just understanding that community leaders serving on a citizen's advisory committee can enhance the development of a specialized police unit for minority and immigrant communities.

With all of this said, we do, of course, understand that the creation of a specialized unit is not always possible. Indeed, budgetary restrictions in today's world of agency

Box 7.3 The Impact of Immigration Enforcement on Police–Community Relations

Undoubtedly, if police are routinely questioning community members about their immigration status, there will be many more police–citizen contacts than would occur if they were not involved in this type of activity. Although this may not be a serious problem for persons who are legal citizens, it can become a bit of an inconvenience. This is particularly true if persons who appear to be of Latino, Middle Eastern, or Asian origin are disproportionately questioned. This can lead to allegations of racial profiling, which will be discussed later. Nevertheless, even if such persons, upon questioning, are found to be within U.S. borders legally, the experience is likely to be at least as inconvenient as it is to provide one's drivers license, proof of insurance, and automobile registration during a routine traffic stop. While this is considered a minor infringement on one's liberty, it can be a bit of a hassle nonetheless. Just this added inconvenience can add tension between police and citizens over time.

Consider also that most major urban areas throughout the nation consist of large immigrant communities. Indeed, in some communities, the immigrant population might be roughly 50 percent (or more) of the local population. Local police agencies are responsible for protecting the diverse members of their community and this includes both legal and illegal immigrants. With this reality, local police agencies have implemented community policing approaches that facilitate trust and cooperation with these diverse populations, including those with high proportions of first- and second-generation immigrants. In most larger agencies, as well as agencies in mid-sized communities, officers who are specially qualified to work with immigrant groups and specific minority communities may be given duty assignments that are intended to maintain a positive relationship between these community members and the police agency.

These types of community policing initiatives often allow officers to become familiar with persons in a community, both those who are law abiding and those who are not. This then means that these officers will be accurate in determining which suspects have likely committed a type of crime within the community due to their informal connections in the community and the knowledge that they gain from resulting informal contacts. This also means that victims will be more comfortable reporting crimes to these officers and that witnesses will be more inclined to talk with officers who are routinely present in their community and who also have a reputation of being trustworthy and knowledgeable of the community and its problems. Lastly and equally importantly, officers who have developed this rapport will also

have the ability to use their discretion (within legal and ethical bounds, of course) to resolve problems within the community. This may be especially important when incidents involve juvenile members of the community or persons who are related to respected families in the community. When complainants do not desire a formal criminal justice response, they will be hesitant to contact the police unless they know, in advance, that the responding officers are willing to consider other viable options as well (i.e., contacting parents, allowing individual citizens to work out petty issues, resolving disputes on the scene and de-escalating the circumstances, or integrating the services of other agencies or organizations when a criminal justice response is not specifically required). All of this will be prefaced with months of dialogue and discussion with community members who, during their contact with these officers (through informal talk, neighborhood watches, National Night Out programs, civic meetings, citizen police academies, and other formal and informal programs), will have become more comfortable than they would be with a complete stranger responding to the call.

The ability for officers to better identify among suspects those who are guilty of specific crimes, to gain more information from community members, and to utilize informal means of response should not be underestimated. Whether an immigrant member of these communities is documented or undocumented, their cooperation can be invaluable to achieving clearance of a case. Community cooperation is needed to prevent and solve crimes and maintain public order, safety, and security in the whole community. Thus, the cooperation of members living in the area is invaluable and this includes members who are legally in the country as well as those who are illegally within the United States. Obviously, immigration enforcement by local police can negatively affect and undermine the level of trust and cooperation between local police and immigrant communities and this would then impair local police agencies' ability to gain valuable information to prevent crime or threats to public safety. Thus, the concept of local police enforcing immigration laws appears to have some serious drawbacks, despite the seemingly logical alliance between local, state, and federal enforcement agencies.

Source: Hanser, R. D., & Gomila, M. (2012). The enforcement of immigration law by police: Issues and challenges. In F. Reddington and G. Bonham (Eds.), *Flawed criminal justice policy: At the intersection of the media, public fear and legislative response* (pp. 39–59). Durham, NC: Carolina Academic Press.

management may preclude the allocation of dedicated human resources to this aspect of operations. Nevertheless, the use of community liaison officers as well as citizen volunteers can provide some assistance with developing specialized responses to issues that might emerge. A **Community liaison officer (CLO)** meets with residential citizens and business owners to educate on crime awareness and crime prevention, assist in Neighborhood Watch Programs, develop and explain community policing approaches, distribute informational materials about crime prevention, and to conduct security surveys of residences and businesses to determine needed security measures in their community. As can be seen, these officers can be very useful in educating immigrant communities on their potential role when working in partnerships with the police.

We also suggest that agencies integrate their community liaison officer (CLO) with a volunteer coordinator who can integrate volunteers into the efforts of the CLO, thereby making the immigrant or minority volunteer an integral part of community crime prevention efforts. This then allows the CLO to intensify efforts to prevent crime and enhance neighborhoods while, at the same time, building relations with various members of the community who volunteer with the agency. We will talk in much more detail about the use of volunteers to aid police agencies, in general, and to provide effective policy–minority/immigrant citizen relations, in particular.

RECRUITMENT AND HIRING OF MINORITIES IN POLICING

This issue is one that has numerous facets that can be explored and could actually consist of an entire textbook of information, all by itself. However, we will provide a brief discussion that is more in line with the intended scope and function of this chapter. Although our discussion will be a bit short, in many respects, it is nonetheless a very important factor when considering police relations with diverse communities. A failure to acknowledge the demographic composition of the very personnel in a police agency would be completely remiss. Thus, we include this discussion here as a means of addressing this aspect of multiculturalism in today's world of policing. We begin with a section that provides a discussion of the benefits of diversity in police hiring. The information is taken from a government document by the Office of Community Oriented Police Services (COPS) entitled the Law Enforcement Recruitment Toolkit, published by the U.S. Department of Justice in 2009. We begin with that section, as follows.

Benefits of Diversity

"As a publicly funded service profession, law enforcement is ethically bound to serve the entire community. A commitment to diversity in an agency that reflects the community it serves sends a message of inclusiveness and equality and is consistent with fundamental notions of democracy" (COPS, 2009, p. 29). Accordingly, diversity in the workforce also helps build the trust and legitimacy to aid in effective police–community cooperation across all sectors of the community. Adding to our community policing perspective, diversity, helps police to better relate to the community and perform its crime-fighting missions. According to COPS (2009), police leaders have cited many benefits of a diversified workforce:

1. Helps police officers arrive at a broader array of solutions
2. Helps develop balanced, relevant, and culturally sensitive responses to community problems and critical incidents

3. Enhances mutual understanding between the department and the community
4. Reduces stereotyping of groups in the community by the police and stereotyping of the police by community groups
5. Inspires members of formerly underrepresented groups to support the police.

In recent years, the emergence of the community policing model has made it all the more clear why diversity should be emphasized. Mary Ann Viverette, a former chief of police and past president of the IACP, has argued that diversity is vital to law enforcement's continued success:

> We have learned that to be effective, police cannot operate alone; they require the active support and assistance of their communities. Central to maintaining that support is the recognition that law enforcement agencies must reflect the diversity of the communities they serve. Every day, our officers come into contact with individuals from different cultural backgrounds, socioeconomic classes, religions, sexual orientations, and physical and mental abilities. Each of these groups brings a different perspective to police-community relations and, as a result, our officers must be prepared to respond to each group in the appropriate fashion. Failure to recognize and adjust to community diversity can foster confusion and resentment among citizens and quickly lead to a breakdown in the critical bond of trust between a law enforcement agency and its community.

The bond Viverette describes can be challenging to develop, and it is much easier to break than it is to develop. Police administrators in jurisdictions grappling with rapidly changing demographics due to population growth and immigration patterns realize the need to earn and maintain the trust of new citizens who are vulnerable to criminals and who also tend to be underrepresented on the police force and in other city agencies (COPS, 2009).

Commitment to Hiring

The recruitment of minority, female, and same-sex preference candidates requires a good deal of commitment from police administrators who oversee agencies. This sense of commitment must be exhibited both inside and outside the agency. Internal to the agency, police chiefs and sheriffs must integrate values that promote diversity and affirmative action into every aspect of their agency, from the mission statement to basic operations such as training at shift-change. Externally, agency leaders should make public and delineate specific hiring and promotion goals of the department to community bodies through formal (such as the media) and informal (networking with diverse groups) methods of announcement. These leaders should also build relationships with their personnel officials to ensure that decisions reflect the goal of diversity in the department. Likewise, in regions that have workforce development task forces or other such labor and economic development workgroups, efforts should be made to ensure that attention is given to diversity. Figure 7-1 shows how police administrators in agencies of differing sizes view the importance of recruiting minorities. Figure 7-2, on the other hand, provides us with an understanding of the difficulties that have been experienced in recruiting various minority groups into the policing profession. We will discuss these issues in more depth throughout this section of the chapter, but find it interesting to note that the perceptions noted in both figures are based on nationwide data.

Agencies that are successful in building a diverse police force often involve the community in the recruiting process. Indeed, the community should have some type

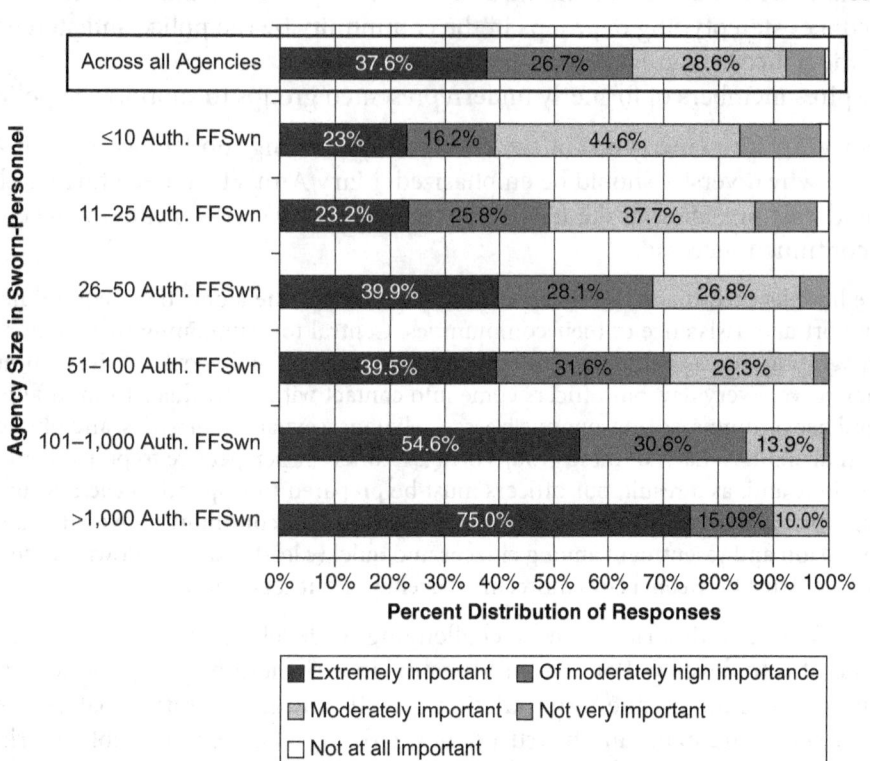

Question: "How would you describe the importance of diversity in your overall recruitment strategy and efforts?" Responses Across All Agencies and by Agency Size.

FIGURE 7-1 Police Administrators Rate Importance of Diversity in Their Agencies. *Source:* Office of Community Oriented Policing Services. (2009). *Law enforcement recruitment toolkit.* Washington, DC: United States Department of Justice.

of involvement early in the process of recruiting candidates. Representatives from different ethnic and racial backgrounds should be involved in preliminary meetings where recruitment campaigns are initially developed. These persons can assist in selecting the best marketing methods for the demographic groups that they represent and they can help by making personal contacts with highly qualified candidates from within those groups. This can help overcome any barriers that may exist and that might otherwise discourage these individuals from applying to the agency. One key example of an agency that embraces diversity is the Federal Bureau of Investigation (FBI). Students should refer to Box 7-4 for examples of several programs that embrace hiring of minorities.

Legal Considerations

Although police chiefs and sheriffs may be earnest in their efforts to promote diversity within their agency, their support for programs such as affirmative action can have some legal implications. As such, these executives must ensure that their policies and procedures do not violate **Title VII of the Civil Rights Act of 1964**. Title VII

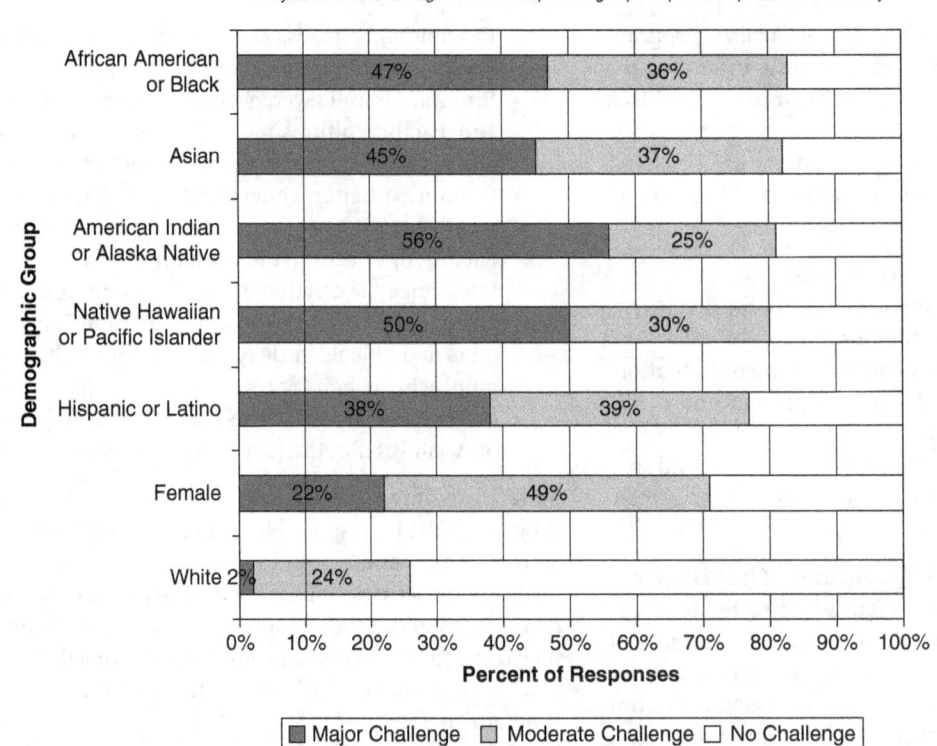

FIGURE 7-2 Recruitment Challenges for Police Agencies Seeking Minorities. *Source:* Office of Community Oriented Policing Services. (2009). *Law enforcement recruitment toolkit.* Washington, DC: United States Department of Justice.

basically holds that it is an unlawful employment practice for an employer to do either of the following:

1. Fail or refuse to hire or to discharge any individual, or discriminate against any individual with respect to compensation, terms, conditions, or privileges of employment because of that individual's race, color, sex, or national origin, or
2. Limit, segregate, or classify employees or applicants for employment in any way that would deprive or tend to deprive an individual of employment opportunities or adversely affect their status as an employee, because of that individual's race, color, sex, or national origin.

Although this may seem to be common sense, it is nevertheless clear that these practices do, sometimes, occur and that despite today's widespread acceptance of diversity, these types of discrimination under Title VII do still occur. However, while direct and blatant forms of discriminatory candidate selection may be rarer, it is the use of biased hiring practices based on race, color, religion, sex, or national origin that is more common and is also more difficult to prove. When we say a disparate impact, we mean that repetitive practices have, as a whole, resulted in officer demographic compositions that are uniquely different from the surrounding region and also seem to have a particularly

Box 7.4 Minority-Specific Programs in the FBI

Black Affairs Program: The Black Affairs Program encompasses all persons having origins in any of the Black racial groups of Africa, and assures that all Black Americans enjoy and are given a chance to experience the full measure of employment opportunities in the federal workforce. The goals and objectives of the Black Affairs Program are to:

- Eliminate discriminatory practices
- Assure that Black Americans are appropriately represented throughout the workforce
- Enhance the recruitment, employment, retention, and advancement of Black employees and applicants within the FBI
- Identify employment barriers and recommend specific actions to remove these barriers or minimize their impact on Black employees

Hispanic Employment Program: The Hispanic Employment Program was established to focus attention on the needs of Hispanic Americans in the area of federal employment. Hispanic Americans and/or Latinos are persons of Mexican, Puerto Rican, Cuban, Central or South American, or other Spanish culture or origin, regardless of race. The Hispanic Employment Program's primary goals and objectives are to:

- Eliminate discriminatory practices
- Assure that Hispanic Americans are appropriately represented throughout the workforce
- Increase the representation of Hispanic Americans in key occupational categories throughout the grade levels and in policymaking positions (particular attention will be focused on increasing representation in the Senior Executive Service)
- Modify and/or change policy to increase opportunities for all employees to advance to their highest potential
- Provide advisory services including: informational programs, training sessions, and counseling

Asian American/Pacific Islander Program: The Asian American/Pacific Islander Program encompasses all persons having origins in the Far East, Southeast Asia, the Indian subcontinent, or the Pacific Islands. These areas include, for example, China, India, Japan, Korea, the Philippine Islands, and Samoa. The Program provides a focus for over 30 ethnically distinct groups from Asia and the Pacific regions. The primary objectives of the Asian American/Pacific Islander Program are to:

- Promote and establish effective and equitable participation of Asian Pacific Americans in the workforce
- Promote overall awareness of the impact of Asian and Pacific cultures, contributions, work ethics, and behavior as related to government employment
- Promote a better understanding of, and to seek solutions for, the particular problems of Asian Pacific Americans in the workforce
- Encourage the creation of effective communication and goodwill between Asian Pacific Americans and other individuals in the government and the community in general
- Promote the career development and advancement of Asian Pacific Americans in the workforce

Federal Women's Program: The Federal Women's Program (FWP) is responsible for improving employment and advancement opportunities for women in the federal service. The activities of the FWP focus on the employment needs and issues of special concern to women as they relate to federal personnel policies and practices.

The primary objectives of the Federal Women's Program are to:

- Eliminate discriminatory practices
- Assure that women are appropriately represented throughout the Federal workforce

The Office of the Federal Women's Program in the Office of Affirmative Employment Programs, U.S. Office of Personnel Management (OPM), provides policy guidance and program leadership for the government-wide FWP. Agency FWP Managers assist women as they advance by identifying barriers to career development, devising solutions, and drafting plans for implementation by the agency head. The major objectives of the FWP Manager are to:

- Educate and work toward the elimination of sexual harassment in the workplace
- Identify problems and solutions in the recruitment and retention of women in the workplace
- Discuss ideas and present proposals to improve employment opportunities and working conditions for women in the workplace

Source: Federal Bureau of Investigation. (2013). *Diversity: Fostering an environment that values individuality.* Washington, DC: United States Department of Justice. Retrieved from: www.FBIJobs.gov.

negative outcome for a select group of applicants identified by Title VII of the Civil Rights Act of 1964. In order to make such a claim, the

> Complaining party must demonstrate that a respondent used a particular employment practice that caused a disparate impact on the basis of race, color, religion, sex, or national origin and the respondent must, in turn, fail to demonstrate that the challenged practice was job related for the position in question and consistent with agency necessity. (United States Equal Employment Opportunity Commission, 2013)

Thus, discrimination can be demonstrated against a single individual, based on minority status, or can be demonstrated as a result of aggregate outcomes if these outcomes are considered to be due to deliberate practices to marginalize a group of candidates.

It is important to point out that agencies are not required to grant preferential treatment to any individual or group based on race, color, religion, sex, or national origin on account of an imbalance that does exist in the percentage or number of persons from each group who are employed by the agency. This includes circumstances where such percentages may vary considerably from the community or workforce in the area. With this in mind, we would like to ensure that students understand that we consider it a **best practice in multicultural hiring** to have agency personnel demographics that are reflective of those in the broader community that it serves, but we do not want to imply that this is a legal obligation for such agencies.

Planning and Techniques

When hiring, police agencies often utilize a strategic recruitment plan that includes advertising and public notice mechanisms to solicit for qualified applicants. The hiring process in police agencies is rigorous and there are a number of aspects (background checks, physical fitness, financial stability, entry testing) that are included in determining if an individual is qualified and fit for law enforcement duty. The inclusion of diversity as a consideration can seem, in these cases, to just make matters more difficult. However, this may seem as such because it can often be that minority groups may not identify with the role of law enforcement and/or they may initially shy away from this type of potential employment.

Shusta, Levine, Wong, Olson, & Harris (2011) note that any strategic recruitment plan should include an advertising campaign that will target the following:

1. Colleges and universities, especially those that are known to have diverse campuses.
2. Military bases and reserve units.
3. Churches, temples, synagogues, and other religious institutions.
4. Minority community centers in minority neighborhoods.
5. Gymnasiums, fitness clubs, and martial arts studios.

These and other locations have a high likelihood of having a diverse population and also, at the same time, environments where people with aptitudes and talents needed for police work are more likely to be found.

Besides the venue, the timing and means by which agencies approach the recruiting process are important, as well. For instance, rather than the typical 8–5, Monday through Friday, routine for law enforcement hiring events, agency leaders should consider hosting these events on the weekend or during evening hours so that individuals who are already employed during the day can more easily attend. At these types of events, the use of role-model panels of officers who are from various minority categories could be showcased in which these individuals would answer questions from persons potentially interested in policing. This type of process would first answer questions that potential applicants might have about the policing field and, second, would also show that minorities (including women, same-sex preference populations, and individuals with disabilities) are welcomed into the agency. This technique works even better if the individual is a high-ranking or well-decorated officer.

Lastly, almost all agencies utilize the power of the internet, nowadays, as a means of posting job openings. Even the use of YouTube and Craiglist has been seen with some agencies, including the simple announcement of positions on the agency website. This technology is inexpensive and easily reaches thousands of potential applicants. When attempting to recruit from diverse populations, agencies can feature biographies and photos of their own staff. This naturally allows agencies the ability to provide a face to the community, which can mirror their surrounding area and/or can attract other applicants from diverse backgrounds in other regions of the United States. According to Shusta et al. (2011), the internet is now the primary means by which candidates learn of job openings in police agencies.

Community Involvement

Successful police agencies involve the community in recruiting and hiring minority and female applicants. In this section, we provide many suggestions for **best practices in police hiring**, as a means of providing specific suggestions that should be considered if agencies truly seek to have a diverse staff composition. Some of these best practices are as follows:

1. The community should have some involvement early in the effort to recruit candidates as this will ensure that their input impacts the formative process when decisions about hiring needs are initially made.
2. Representatives from different racial and cultural backgrounds can provide useful information regarding the needs for recruitment in the area.
3. Utilize community leaders as consultants on the best means of marketing for the groups they represent. In some cases, these individuals can even assist in contacting candidates.
4. Community leaders should be involved in the selection process, including participation on oral boards for applicants.

These **community leaders** are individuals who have influence with specific groups of people in their community with whom they identify and they can prove crucial in bridging agency efforts with community needs and desires.

Community leaders representing the diversity of the community should be provided with recruitment information such as brochures and posters, which they can disseminate at religious institutions, civic centers, community organizations, schools, and/or recreational events. Shusta et al. (2011) note that agencies may encourage their officers to join community-based organizations where they will interact with community members because this will allow them to involve these groups in recruiting efforts of the agency.

We would like to note that, in any and all cases, it is a smart strategy to develop a strong rapport with community leaders, whether this be for recruiting purposes or

Box 7.5 An Example of Minority and Female Officers Bridging Police–Community Relations in a Diverse Community

In their research on police and immigrant community relations, Lysakowski et al. (2009) conducted focus groups with immigrant citizens and police. In one instance, they recall when one immigrant business leader invited a police representative to talk to his employees and their families—more than 100 people—while they ate dinner together at a restaurant. In this informal setting, he said, employees got the message that the police were there to help. When a police officer stood up, spoke a few words in Spanish, and announced she was from El Salvador, everyone cheered. "She made people feel part of the police department and part of the policing effort" said the business owner. This is an excellent example of how police–community relations can bridge understanding between police and minorities and, thereby, increase their crime-fighting ability in their jurisdiction. Furthermore, these types of experiences can also aid in the successful recruitment of qualified police candidates from these minority backgrounds.

Source: Lysakowski, M., Pearsall, A. A., & Pope, J. (2009). *Policing in immigrant communities.* Washington, DC: Office of Community Oriented Police Services, United States Department of Justice.

otherwise. Very often, these leaders can mobilize members of the community to help them in achieving the desired outcomes. Furthermore, the use of these community members in the hiring process can convey to the community concern that its own personnel come from the grassroots of the surrounding region. Having support from community leaders in this process can help facilitate community acceptance of the agency and those it hires. Lastly, insight from the community and its leaders is also likely to identify persons from the region who are not only well suited for the job, but also can help identify persons who are easier to retain owing to their connections with the community that they police. It is this last point, minority retention, that we will next discuss.

Broadening the Recruiting Age Pool—Hiring the Young and Old

Besides racial and immigrant minority status, police departments should not forget that another category of diversity includes age. For members of all racial or ethnic groups, agencies should consider modifying their hiring standards in a manner that will not lower quality but will allow both younger and senior applicants to compete for jobs. So long as these applicants are qualified (both physically and mentally) for the job, age may be an unnecessarily limiting factor.

Some agencies have modified their personnel employment rules to permit hiring applicants before they reach the minimum hiring age, which commonly is 21. Young hires are often enrolled in the police academy with a scheduled graduation date that coincides with their age requirement, allowing them to be commissioned as police officers. Other agencies find non-sworn support positions where a qualified applicant can work, earn, learn, and be readily available to continue in the selection process.

Laws and regulations in many jurisdictions bar agencies from hiring entry-level police officers beyond a specific age. We agree with the COPS office in noting that police chiefs and sheriffs in those jurisdictions should use their influence and collective voice to bring about a change in those laws if they exclude potential candidates for reasons that are not warranted. It is our stance that, if an older worker is able to perform all of the physical and mental aspects required at the training academy (i.e., physical fitness, mental exams, paper tests, driving qualifications, and shooting qualifications), then they should be considered qualified to be a police officer. A denial of this opportunity should be made clear along with a rationale for not being included in the selection process.

Minority Retention in Policing

It is important to first point out that police training is, for many agencies, a very serious expenditure in terms of both time committed and monetary resources that are allocated. This is particularly true in today's economy and, as we will see in a later subsection of this chapter, agencies find the need to utilize volunteers and other innovations as a means of filling the gap in their ability to hire personnel for required positions. However, when an agency does hire, the officer will need to stay for at least a couple of years in order for their investment to pay for itself in terms of cost-effective budgeting. This is also true with police officers who are minorities. Moreover, the ability to retain diverse personnel is preferable since, as we have discussed previously, community relations (and crime fighting) are improved when personnel reflect the diversity of the neighboring region.

Part of the ability to retain officers from minority backgrounds will have to do with opportunities that exist for officers in general and for minority officers in particular. The ability of minority officers to promote and/or options for career development and enhancement will likely determine whether they stay with the agency on a long-term basis. In addition, the lack of promotions of protected classes to supervisory positions has been cited as one of the most severe problems during the past three decades of police research. An international example of this problem can be found in this chapter's *International Focus insert*, which shows that the problem of low minority hiring and promotions exist among many police agencies in England.

In addition to hiring and promotion of minorities, it is important that agencies develop an open and trustworthy organizational culture. Indeed, when agencies are viewed as fair, they are more likely to retain their employees. Thus, ethical processes based on equality and merit will help agencies retain their personnel. Furthermore, the organizational culture of the agency will determine how well minorities feel that they "fit" within the organization. One means of improving this "goodness of fit" is through top-down support for diversity and using training that emphasizes the benefits and value of diversity. In other words, the reputation of the agency among minority personnel and, invariably, throughout the community will be impacted by the organizational culture of the agency, which is shaped and enhanced by the messages that managerial leadership provide, in terms of both training and operation. Despite this, it is not necessarily guaranteed that minority representation in a law enforcement agency will be reflective of the population that is served. Table 7-1 shows that despite the FBI's efforts to recruit minority members into its organization, the percentages for various minority groups are fairly low overall in the FBI when compared with similar demographic groups throughout the entire United States.

Regardless of the hiring circumstances that an agency encounters with the minority or immigrant population, the need for diversity training will be an ongoing theme in all levels of law enforcement. It is with this in mind that we now turn our attention to the role of diversity training and organizational culture in police agencies.

TABLE 7-1 Diversity by Race/Ethnicity in the Federal Bureau of Investigation

Diversity Employment Report
SPECIAL AGENTS
as of 1/31/2012

RACE/ETHNICITY	Total Group	Percent of Total	Number of Men	Percent of Total	Number of Women	Percent of Total
Am. Indian/Alaska Native	55	0.40	46	0.33	9	0.07
Asian	576	4.18	463	3.36	113	0.82
Black/African American	652	4.74	505	3.67	147	1.07
Hispanic/Latino	983	7.14	759	5.51	224	1.63
White	11,431	83.04	9,307	67.61	2,124	15.43
Hawaiian/Pac. Islander	13	0.09	12	0.09	1	0.01
Multi-Racial	55	0.40	38	0.28	17	0.12
Unknown (no race)	1	0.01	0	0.00	1	0.01
TOTALS	**13,766**	**100.00**	**11,130**	**80.85**	**2,636**	**19.15**
ALL MINORITIES	2,334	16.95	1,823	13.24	511	3.71

PROFESSIONAL STAFF EMPLOYEES INCLUDING WAGE BOARD
as of 1/31/2012

RACE/ETHNICITY	Total Group	Percent of Total	Number of Men	Percent of Total	Number of Women	Percent of Total
Am. Indian/Alaska Native	111	0.51	48	0.22	63	0.29
Asian	923	4.22	407	1.86	516	2.36
Black/African American	3,881	17.75	968	4.43	2,913	13.32
Hispanic/Latino	1,283	5.87	466	2.13	817	3.74
White	15,541	71.08	7,090	32.43	8,451	38.65
Hawaiian/Pac. Islander	22	0.10	6	0.03	16	0.07
Multi-Racial	101	0.46	32	0.15	69	0.32
Unknown (no race)	1	0.00	1	0.00	0	0.00
Other (no race & gender)	0	0.00	0	0.00	0	0.00
TOTALS	**21,863**	**100.00**	**9,018**	**41.25**	**12,845**	**58.75**
ALL MINORITIES	6,321	28.91	1,927	8.81	4,394	20.10

EMPLOYEES WITH DISABILITIES
as of 1/31/2012

Employee Type	Total	Disability	Percent of Total	Targeted Disability	Percent of Total
Special Agent	13,766	160	1.16	11	0.08
Support Personnel	21,517	1096	5.09	131	0.61
Wage Board	346	24	6.94	2	0.58
TOTAL	**35,629**	**1,280**	**3.59**	**144**	**0.40**

Source: Federal Bureau of Investigation. (2013). *Diversity: Fostering an environment that values individuality.* Washington, DC: United States Department of Justice.

DIVERSITY TRAINING IN POLICE AGENCIES

Implementing diversity training should not be a process whereby another box is checked on a list of items that must be completed by the end of the year. Rather, this type of training should be conducted with passion and commitment with the objective of creating long-lasting transformative change among employees. According to Keesee and Nela (2011) **diversity training** must have the following demonstrated elements:

1. Focus on considering all others as people with value and worth and deserving of unconditional respect
2. Contribute to personal development and self-mastery
3. Be challenging, current, and relevant to policing
4. Expand the intellect while touching the hearts of officers—they must learn and "feel" in the educational experience
5. Be experiential in nature as adults learn best by doing and participating in an experience
6. Provide tools and skills that can be practiced and applied to daily work
7. Make educational sessions one part of a continuing process of learning that reinforces a philosophy ultimately leading to a culture shift
8. Encourage all levels of leadership in the organization to experience, understand, and embrace the training and continually reinforce the cultural shift

Diversity training is a function of police agency operations that should be ongoing and should be integrated into the promotion of the officer ranks. When agencies make this part of the means by which their staff are evaluated, it becomes clear that this is an important issue. However, as Keesee and Nela (2011) note, this training should be grounded in the feelings and sense of connection among staff as it is in the actual content of the training. In other words, diversity training should not be allowed to be sterile and it should not isolate demographic groups from the majority culture of the region. This can be a delicate balance to maintain, but it is the very essence of inclusiveness that is a key goal of diversity training. The point should be to bring officers together, not to separate them. In developing this sense of inclusion, the organizational culture of the agency is impacted so that diversity becomes second nature to the agency and to its personnel.

When we discuss **organizational culture**, we are referring to a set of operating principles that guide how personnel operate within an organization's contextual identity that is shared by its members, both internally with employee-to-employee relations and externally when facing the public. The means by which groups of personnel (whether they be formal groups such as a section of a patrol unit, an investigative unit, or informal groups, such as with a group of friends during off-duty hours) behave affirms and reaffirms what is defined as acceptable or "normal" behavior and that which is considered "unacceptable" or atypical behavior (Keesee & Nela, 2011). These boundaries on behavior are determined by the culture within the organization and are linked to the agency's personnel and the values and beliefs that they maintain.

This concept is important as the culture of police agencies have undergone many changes in the past few years. Take, for instance, the representation of the gay/lesbian population in the ranks of law enforcement. Nowadays, it is more common to have agencies specifically address their personnel who are LGBT in an inclusive manner. Nevertheless, this aspect of inclusiveness is still in a formative stage. Students should refer to Box 7.6, which presents the **Lesbian, Gay, Bisexual, & Transexual Program** for the FBI.

As can be seen from the *Question-and-Answer* content of this insert, some aspects of inclusion readily exist whereas others, such as the extension of benefits to partners of same-sex couples in the FBI, are limited because of federal laws and regulations. This showcases an organization that, in good faith, seeks to include their LGBT personnel but, at the same time, faces limitations to this inclusion owing to the outdated legal

---

Box 7.6 Lesbian, Gay, Bisexual, and Transgender Program in the FBI: A Reflection of the Agency's Progressive Organizational Culture

The Sexual Orientation Program was established to address employee diversity issues and concerns of sexual orientation in the FBI workforce. Its primary goals are to ensure equal employment opportunity, promote effective and equitable participation, enhance career development opportunities for gay, lesbian, bisexual, and transgender employees of the FBI, and to better educate all employees on sexual orientation issues as well as other diversity matters affecting the FBI workforce.

Questions & Answers for Applicants

Q: Can you be gay and work at the FBI?

A: *Yes. The FBI does not discriminate against a person's sexual orientation with regard to hiring decisions. To be sure, the FBI has open lesbian, gay, bisexual, and possibly transgender employees, as well as an LGBT Advisory Committee. The FBI welcomes and appreciates the contribution of its LGBT employees.*

Q: Can you be gay and be an FBI Agent?

A: *Yes. In fact, you can be gay in any position within the FBI.*

Q: When I go through my background investigation, will I have to disclose my sexual orientation (i.e. I'm not "out" openly at work.)?

A: *The FBI will not discriminate against you because of your sexual orientation. The most important thing about the background investigation is honesty. A lack of candor is one of the top reasons why candidates do not pass their background investigations. This best policy is to be open and honest with the investigators as they complete your*

background. A background investigation will not specifically ask questions about your sexual orientation.

Q: Does the FBI recognize same-sex marriage?

A: *Yes and No. First, the FBI cannot legally recognize same-sex marriage because of the Defense of Marriage Act of 1996 (DOMA). This law only recognizes marriages between a man and a woman. Furthermore, DOMA denies most federal benefits to same-sex partners. However, this law does not prevent the FBI from accepting and welcoming employees who are in committed same-sex relationships or who are married in states that legally recognize same-sex marriage. In addition, same-sex partners of FBI employees may be eligible for certain benefits where eligibility for the benefit is not based on being the employee's spouse. Furthermore, as you may be aware, President Obama and various congressional members have expressed a desire to repeal DOMA.*

Q: Will my partner receive medical benefits?

A: *No. Because of the DOMA law, the FBI is not able to extend medical benefits and coverage to same-sex partners.*

Q: What benefits am I or my partner eligible for?

A: *As a federal employer, the FBI is prohibited by the Defense of Marriage Act (1 U.S.C. § 7) from recognizing same-sex marriages or from providing spousal benefits to same-sex couples. This prohibition, however, only applies to benefits that are limited by federal statute or regulation to the employee's spouse. Consistent with President*

Box 7.6 Continued

Obama's June 17, 2009, memorandum and with the DOJ's policy (28 C.F.R. § 42.1) "to eliminate discrimination on the basis of ... sexual orientation ... in employment within the Department," the FBI will provide qualified same sex domestic partners with certain benefits that are not barred by statute or regulation. Finally, in response to President Obama's June 17, 2009, memorandum, the Office of Personnel Management and the State Department are revising federal regulations to extend additional benefits to qualified same-sex domestic partners of Federal employees. The FBI is prepared to implement any such new regulations when they become effective.

Q: Does the FBI celebrate PRIDE?

A: *Yes. The FBI recently held an informal reception at FBI Headquarters and was proud to have Congressman Barney Frank as its speaker. Also, individual field offices are encouraged to have their own celebrations, educational presentations, or participate in LGBT community events.*

Q: Does the FBI have an LGBT Advisory Committee?

A: *Yes. The FBI recently formed the LGBT Advisory Committee under the Office of Equal Employment Opportunity Affairs. The committee is composed of both Special Agents and support employees and is represented by gay, straight, and lesbian employees. The purpose of the committee is to listen to the voices of the FBI LGBT employees and communicate concerns, policies, and ways in which the FBI can recognize its LGBT employees.*

Q: I'm not out at work, but I want to be. Does the FBI provide assistance with coming out?

A: *The LGBT Advisory Committee, as well as the employee assistance programs and counselors, are available to employees who need assistance with coming out or adjusting to being openly gay at work.*

Source: Federal Bureau of Investigation. (2013). *Diversity: Fostering an environment that values individuality.* Retrieved from: https://www.fbijobs.gov/428.asp.

parameters. This is reflective of an organization culture that is still developing in the FBI, having internal top-down support but being subject to external limits of society's legal process of change.

Follow-up from top executives to ensure that messages related to multiculturalism, diversity, and cultural competence are, in fact, provided as was intended. This means that these executives should take a close interest in diversity training and they should follow up to see how well the training is provided and how well it is received among members of the agency. The use of some type of clear evaluation system can aid them in this process. If this is implemented, then the culture of the organization will be one where diversity is a central component. As Keesee and Nela (2011) note, "police executives require a truthful understanding of the organization's culture in order to manage personnel, direct crime reduction initiatives, and develop community relationships" (p. 37).

From the previous quote, it can be seen that an emphasis on diversity is important for crime reduction initiatives and in the development of community relationships. Thus, multiculturalism is, in itself, part of our crime-fighting toolbox and agencies should identify it as such. When we hire diverse staff and when we follow up with diversity training we are, in actuality, improving our ability to interact with the community that surrounds the agency and, in the process, we are enhancing our ability to gain assistance from that community in detecting crime and apprehending criminal offenders. All good police executives will understand these connections and will, therefore, support efforts to enhance an officer's understanding of diversity issues.

Immigrant-Specific Diversity Training

Lysakowski et al. (2009) found that law enforcement leaders have noted that training in cultural competence is no longer a "new idea" but they still tend to agree that it is essential for good police relations with immigrant minorities. However, one of the drawbacks of this training is that it can be ineffective if the training is not specific to the communities in their agency's jurisdiction or if the trainers were not aware of the various challenges associated with the policing profession. Both of these points are very important observations that diversity trainers should seriously consider if they wish for this training to be truly useful for police professionals.

It is because of this that we suggest to our readers that diversity training needs to refrain from being generalized with police because, as many police administrators have noted (Lysakowski et al., 2009; Shusta et al., 2011), the idea that the United States is diverse is no longer a new one. Also true is the fact that most police administrators understand that the world has been impacted by globalization and that, in the United States, the population is heterogeneous due to both the *internally oriented diversity* that is historic to the United States and the *externally oriented diversity* that has occurred due to immigration patterns in the past two or three decades. We suggest that diversity training should focus on being culturally specific in focus when provided to specific agencies. When we use the term **culturally specific training**, we mean that diversity training should identify the specific nationality or demographic group or groups that are the focus of this training and these groups should be those that are highly represented in the agency's jurisdiction. This should include specific, real-world examples from that local area where these minority groups are located and where the police agency has been involved and with which they can readily identify.

The next issue regarding trainers of diversity is the need to, at least on a general level, truly understand the world of policing. While it is, of course, perfectly fine to have police officers as trainers, this can have problems if they are from the same agency because their colleagues may or may not be as receptive to their message as they would from an outside expert. Furthermore, there may be some tendency among fellow cops to not challenge one another due to concerns of loyalty and due to over-identification between officers. **Over-identification** is a term we use to describe when professionals have such a strong tie of loyalty to one another, due to a professional calling, that their ability to be receptive to messages from individuals outside of the profession is seriously compromised. This can especially exist when the topic is diversity and when the individual who is a trainer does not have a policing background or identity.

Going further, there are other suggestions that have been provided by police administrators that can help make diversity training more attractive to officers who might consider the training as "fluff." If officers are given reasons to view this training as applicable and useful, rather than simple feel-good, we-are-one, we-are-the-world, type of training, it will likely be much more effective at impacting the police culture of the agency. Two suggestions, in particular, from Lysakowski et al. (2009) will be provided as follows:

1. **Rebrand the Training**: This suggests that agencies should consider using diversity-related content that is needed for their personnel but could provide a name for the training that makes it seem, initially, as if the purpose of the training

entails some other agenda. A seminar called "Maintaining Tactical Advantage" that teaches officers about ways immigrant and minorities may behave in encounters with police may be more appealing than one titled "Cultural Diversity," even though they cover the same material. Furthermore, it is suggested that cultural training be connected to other law enforcement training workshops or conferences because they tend to already be well attended.

INTERNATIONAL FOCUS

Challenges to Diversity in Police Agencies in England

In England, there has been a noticeable lack of upper police administrators who are of African descent, as well as rank-and-file officers. Further, it would appear that among police agencies, there is, in general, a lack of diversity (i.e. Asians, Middle Easterners, as well as women) within the policing field throughout the country, as a whole (Laville,2013).

The circumstances are so serious, that some, have suggested that England should implement a policy that favors hiring police from minority groups, particularly those of African descent (Laville,2013). This has been touted as a radical idea that would change the policing landscape significantly. It would also help to make the police force more reflective of the populations that are served.

At the heart of the problem, is the fact that the overwhelming majority of chief police officers are Caucasian and the same is true for middle-ranking officers who will later compete for the rank of chief officer. The British policing system has a regimented and strict process for promotion and, when adhering to these protocols, it is very likely.

Further still, the poor economy that has impacted nations around the world, along with reductions to middle management positions, indicates that diversity problems will simply persist (Laville,2013). Given these challenges, it would seem that the only way any type of quick and long-term solution will occur is if it is made a legal requirement.

What is important, according to many police administrators in England, is to understand that the need for more diversity is an operational need, it is a matter of police effectiveness. The desire is to be viewed as legitimate by the community, to be accepted as the law not because of the power that can be wielded over citizens, but by consensus and acceptance throughout the community. The issue, then, is one of cultural competence, as evidenced by the requirement that police be able to resolve disputes in communities to derive at informal and peaceful outcomes; this requires in-depth knowledge and appreciation of diverse communities and persons who come different walks of life (Laville,2013).

The issue is now being examined and is considered worrisome given that middle management positions have suffered a 40% reduction in force, thereby lowering the overall number of candidates for high-ranking positions, such as chief constable. Thus, it is likely that if legal interventions are not put into place, the state-of-affairs in British policing will remain the same, indefinitely.

In a report by the Association of Chief Police Officers (ACPO), entitled *Equality, Diversity, and Human Rights Strategy for the Police Service*, when addressing issues related to policing in a diverse community, the ACPO has committed to implementing the following (p. 11):

1. Identify services and strategies that may have a disproportionate effect on diverse communities.
2. Build equality, diversity, and human rights into policing services which focus on citizens.
3. Make sure that police operations to prevent terrorism promote community cohesion and have the confidence of diverse communities.

To further show the serious-minded nature of policing policy-makers in the United Kingdom, consider that, in this report, a chapter entitled People and Culture, explores another strategic theme in developing police operations throughout the country. According to this report, "evidence shows that a diverse workforce and a culture that includes and supports everyone within the…" organization leads to many positive results (2010, p. 11). Among these, according to the Association of Chief Police Officers (ACPO) are the following (p. 13):

1. A reduction in absences from work.
2. A reduction in grievances and complaints.
3. Access to broader ranges of skills and experience.
4. Efficiency, creativity, and growth.

From these statements, it is clear that the importance of diversity and cultural competence in police services is understood in England, both in terms of how the community is impacted and how the agency operates. Whatever means that are implemented, the process is sure to be challenging. Indeed, there has a number of reports conducted during the past three decades that have acknowledged problems with diversity among police in the United Kingdom (John, 2005).

In fact, one report by the Commission for Racial Equality (CRE) generated 125 recommendations back in 2005 (John, 2005). Nevertheless, problems with diversity and community relations have seemed to persist as far back as the 1980's, with the Scarman Report that was released after the 1981 riots that occurred in Brixton, London. Another report in 1999, known as the MacPherson report, concluded that the London police operated in a culture of institutional racism (John, 2005).

Though problems have long existed, progress has been made with more being possible with each passing day. The first step is to acknowledge the issue, followed by plans for change that lead to implementation. The specific means of implementation are where the challenges rise and this is precisely why some advocate for legal mechanisms to be put into place that will enact and mandate this need for change.

Source: Association of Chief Police Officers (2010). *Equality, diversity, and human rights strategy for the police service.* London, UK: Association of Chief Police Officers.

John, C. (2005, March 8). *Chequered history of police diversity.* BBC News. Retrieved from: http://news.bbc.co.uk/2/hi/uk_news/4329415.stm

Laville, S. (2013, Jan. 27). Call for new law to force police to tackle diversity crisis at top. The Guardian. Retrieved from: HYPERLINK "http://www.guardian.co.uk/uk/2013/jan/27/law-police-%09diversity"http://www.guardian.co.uk/uk/2013/jan/27/law-police-diversity

2. Implement **Role-Reversal Experiences**: This entails a process where police officers are paired with a community member and each person is asked to spend a day observing what the other's routine is like. This has been called the "walk a mile in the other's shoes" concept in some agencies that have adopted this technique, which helps in educating officers about minority members in their community and educates the minority community on police officer experiences. We vehemently agree with Lysakowski et al. (2009) that having each person spend time learning what the other person's life is like will often leave a more lasting impression than the standard lecture format of training.

MULTICULTURALISM AND VOLUNTEERISM IN POLICING

According to the 2008 U.S. Census American Community Survey, of the 304 million persons in the United States, 12.5 percent were foreign born. This rapid growth in immigrant populations is expected to continue to increase. With this changing cultural landscape, many law enforcement agencies are building trust and preventing crime by reaching out to immigrant communities. In connecting with the minority population, the agency must place a priority on having culturally competent means of public response. Volunteers can be a key resource for law enforcement in building relationships with diverse communities and helping to empower immigrant groups to overcome their apprehension and possible distrust of law enforcement. Volunteers are also a resource that can help provide culturally competent service response, when appropriate. We provide three specific programs as examples of how volunteers can aid law enforcement agencies in providing culturally competent responses in the communities that they serve.

Bilingual Volunteer Assistance

As an example, consider the *Spanish Speaking Ride Along Program,* which was developed by the Tulsa, Oklahoma Police Department (VIPS Newsletter, 2010). This program was developed amidst budget cuts and departmental reorganization, which left one Tulsa police sergeant in charge of both the Volunteers in Police Service (VIPS) program and the Hispanic Outreach program. Recognizing the potential for crossover, the **Spanish Speaking Ride-Along Program** was developed both to build trust in the Spanish-speaking community and to bring new volunteers with valued language skills into the VIPS program. This program provides Spanish-speaking citizens with an opportunity to assist Tulsa police officers in better communicating with the Hispanic community. Bilingual citizens or legal residents who volunteer for this program ride with on-duty officers and utilize their language skills as needed.

Importantly, volunteers who work with the *Spanish Speaking Ride Along* quite often live right in the communities where they assist law enforcement. Thus, they are recognized by others in the community, which helps diffuse tension and prevent misunderstandings. In addition, these volunteers, in tandem with patrol officers, provide presentations to Spanish-speaking groups in the city as a means of cultivating positive police–community relations while also providing the Spanish-speaking community education on basic crime prevention. These presentations also serve as very effective tools for recruiting other volunteers for the *Spanish Speaking Ride Along* program.

Cultural Liaisons

In Westbrook, Maine, a growing African American and Middle Eastern refugee population has led to the development of volunteer programs designed to be culturally specific to these diverse citizen groups (VIPS Newsletter, 2010). Rapid demographic changes in many neighborhoods led to increased misunderstandings and challenges. With the goal of preventing and avoiding conflict, this agency began to recruit volunteers to act as *cultural liaisons.* **Cultural liaisons** are volunteers who provide on-call support to officers with language and cultural interpretation. Volunteers go through a selection process where they must provide an application, driver's license, and criminal background check. Likewise, the police department makes a point to check with members of cultural organizations to ensure the volunteers are well-respected members of their communities. In the past, cultural liaison volunteers have effectively translated police department brochures into numerous different languages. These brochures outline the services available to residents to foster knowledge and understanding of police services. Full-time officers carry these brochures and interpreter lists while on patrol, so that the services can be accessed during a traffic stop or at the scene of a call. These volunteers have provided help in various capacities related to public safety and human service issues.

Immigrant Communities and Ethnic-Specific Responses

During the early 1990s, the City of Delray Beach, Florida, experienced a large influx of immigrants from Haiti. This immigration trend continued through to the 2000s and, today, approximately 13 percent of the city's population is of Haitian ethnicity. Many of these immigrants arrived with little understanding of law enforcement in the United States and, due to experiences in their home country, distrusted the police of Delray Beach. Likewise, during these years of transition, the area saw a rise in the rates of crime victimization experienced throughout the Haitian community, much of this being due to intra-ethnic feuding and conflict. As a result, the Delray Beach Police Department sought out leaders in the Haitian community and also visited Haitian churches to build partnerships and enhance communication between the police and this community.

Over time, the Delray Beach Police Department developed a volunteer program known as the Haitian Roving Patrol, which is used to supplement patrol efforts of the police and enhance the relationship between the Delray Beach Haitian population and the local police. All volunteers are carefully screened and each must meet requirements established by the agency, which are identical to those of fully sworn officers on patrol. Volunteers patrol in pairs every evening. Those vehicles used by volunteers are clearly distinguished from typical departmental patrol vehicles by an amber light bar and large-face decals identifying these personnel as volunteers.

In Sacramento, California, one particularly unique program exists that addresses diversity in the community and the need for culturally competent police response has been developed. It is important to note that Sacramento is one of the most diverse cities in the United States. Indeed, this city is home to persons from approximately 48 different cultures, including Hmong, Vietnamese, Slavic, and Mien. Because of the diversity of this city, the Sacramento Police Department, as a means of showing understanding and responsiveness to the city's demographic features, transformed its standard police academy into one that is well suited for a variety of different cultures. This academy, named the Cultural Academy, has been hosted for a number of ethnic groups, including the Mien, the Hmong, and Slavic communities. These cultural academies are held one evening a week over a six-week period. The academy includes a field trip of the communications center and the training academy. The inclusion of these types of observation field trips allows citizens to see their police department at work besides demystifying the agency and its role in the community. Rather than standing apart from the surrounding community, the agency is transformed into one that is actually part of the community, including the diverse minority and/or immigrant population.

The process for application is made deliberately simple to encourage and welcome interested individuals to the cultural academies that are offered. In addition, it is important to note that these academies do not include a background check. Food is provided at each academy session to help bring individuals together, build trust, and facilitate a relaxed atmosphere of open communication. The Sacramento Police Department has up to 50 participants per academy session and it is held in a very large community room at the agency's headquarters that is fully equipped with audiovisual equipment. This equipment is important because, with the use of headsets, participants can hear simultaneous interpretations of the English version of the presentation in their own primary language.

CONCLUSION

As can be seen, police–community relations are an important aspect of any good crime-prevention and crime-fighting strategy. This is true in general and also when police work in diverse communities. Furthermore, it is clear that diversity is just that— it is diverse. This includes demographic distinctions, national origin, sexual orientation, religious identity, language proficiency, and other varied characteristics. The wide degree of diversity between and among the various categories of diversity discussed creates numerous opportunities and challenges for police as first responders. This is true for minorities of both immigrant and non-immigrant populations.

In meeting the challenges of policing in a diverse community, agencies have found opportunities that might otherwise have gone underutilized. Among these opportunities is the benefit of hiring diverse officers that reflect the population within the agency's jurisdiction. This benefits the agency with regard to organization culture and also enhances the rapport that is likely developed with the surrounding community. While this is true, there are many considerations involved with the recruiting, hiring, and retention of officers from minority or immigrant backgrounds.

Although the hiring practices and outcomes of agencies can help address some of the issues associated with multiculturalism and policing, this alone cannot address these challenges. This is particularly true when considering today's tough economic times. Owing to financial challenges, many police agencies have increased their use of volunteers to help address gaps in service delivery that might occur due to fewer resources, including personnel and equipment. Amidst this, agencies have learned to utilize volunteers from diverse backgrounds as a means of aiding general agency functions but also to aid in building awareness and understanding between ethnic communities and the police. We have provided numerous examples of how the integration of volunteers has aided agencies in bridging gaps in rapport between those served and the police.

Lastly, it is clear that globalization and immigration have impacted diversity in the United States and police contend with this change on a daily basis.

Police must be able to work with minorities whether they be first, second, or third generation or whether, like Native Americans, they were the first group to locate on the North American continent. As the world continues to become a smaller and smaller place and as the world's population continues to soar, so too will the need for police to be competent in working with a multicultural population. The need for this will not decline but will, instead, be a feature of operations that will continue to be required throughout the future of the policing profession, both in the United States and elsewhere.

Chapter 7 Learning Check

1. _____ refers to the organization's contextual identity that is shared by its members, both internally with employee-to-employee relations and externally when facing the public.
   a. Agency identity
   b. Organizational culture
   c. Police culture
   d. Agency diversity culture

2. _____ are volunteers who provide on-call support to officers with language and cultural interpretation.
   a. Cultural liaisons
   b. Police diversity response personnel
   c. Diversity liaisons
   d. All of the above
   e. None of the above

3. _____ entails a process where police officers are paired with a community member and each person is asked to spend a day observing what the other's routine is like.
   a. Trading Places Program
   b. The Switch Program
   c. Exchanging Roles
   d. Put Yourself in My Shoes Program
   e. Role-Reversal Experiences

4. Citizen review panels allow citizens in the area to review complaints pertaining to police behavior that are reported by community members.
   a. True
   b. False

5. This suggests that agencies should consider using diversity-related content but provide a different name for the training.
   a. Training renewal
   b. Rebrand the training
   c. Mix-it-up training
   d. Diversity retooling
   e. None of the above

6. _____ is associated with minority groups who tend to be first- or second-generation Americans who have individually or as a family become located in the United States.
   a. Internationally oriented diversity
   b. Externally oriented diversity
   c. Globally based diversity
   d. Both b and c, but not a
   e. Both a and c, but not b

7. Which group is reflective of one who is, in contemporary times, an example of internally oriented diversity?
   a. African Americans
   b. Caucasian Americans
   c. Native Americans
   d. All of the above
   e. None of the above

8. One of the best examples of community member participation in the community policing model is the use of _____.
   a. Neighborhood Watch
   b. National Night Out
   c. Citizen Swap
   d. Both a and c, but not b
   e. Both b and c, but not a

9. The use of YouTube and Craiglist has been successful with some agencies when disseminating job announcements.
   a. True
   b. False

10. _____ describes when professionals have such strong ties of loyalty to one another that their ability to receive messages from individuals outside of the police profession is seriously compromised.
    a. Blue loyalty
    b. Police confidentiality
    c. Us-and-them syndrome
    d. Over-identification
    e. A and c, but not b or d

Essay Discussion Questions

1. Discuss the concept of community policing and explain why this model is considered optimal for developing effective police relations with minority and/or immigrant communities. Provide some specific examples.

2. Explain the difference between internally oriented diversity and externally oriented diversity. Explain how one is the "typical" meaning of diversity to many whereas the other accounts for the impact of globalization upon the face of the U.S. population.

3. Discuss some examples of how minority and immigrant community volunteers can be utilized to enhance the relationship between police and citizens. Provide at least two specific examples from the chapter.

References

Capps, R. (2010). Local enforcement of immigration laws 5 evolution of the 243(g) program and its potential impacts on local communities. In Anita Khashu (Ed.), *The role of local police: Striking a balance between immigration enforcement and civil liberties.* Washington, DC: Police Foundation. Retrieved from: www.policefoundation.org.

Hanser, R. D., Gallagher, C., Carlson, C., Kuanliang, A., & Lanham, B. D. (2012). Community crime prevention initiatives, collective efficacy, and criminal investigations. *Journal of Sociology Studies, 2*(4), 278–291.

Hanser, R. D., & Gomila, M. (2012). The enforcement of immigration law by police: Issues and challenges. In F. Reddington and G. Bonham (Eds.), *Flawed criminal justice policy: At the intersection of the media, public fear and legislative response* (pp. 39–59). Durham, NC: Carolina Academic Press.

Keesee T., & Nila, M. J. (2011, March). Fairness and neutrality: Addressing the issue of race in policing. *The Police Chief, 78,* 34–39.

Lysakowski, M., Pearsall, A. A., & Pope, J. (2009). *Policing in immigrant communities.* Washington, DC: Office of Community Oriented Police Services, United States Department of Justice.

Office of Community Oriented Policing Services. (2009). *Law enforcement recruitment toolkit.* Washington, DC: United States Department of Justice.

Shusta, M., Levine, D. R., Wong, H. Z., Olson, A .T., & Harris, P. R. (2011). *Multicultural law enforcement: Strategies for peacekeeping in a diverse society* (5th ed.). Upper Saddle River, NJ: Prentice Hall.

United States Equal Employment Opportunity Commission. (2013). *Title VII of the Civil Rights Act of 1964.* Retrieved from: http://www.eeoc.gov/laws/statutes/titlevii.cfm.

Viverette, M. A. (2005 Dec.). President's message: Diversity on the force. *The Police Chief, 72,* 1–2.

VIPS Newsletter. (2010). *Bridging the Gap: Engaging volunteers in multicultural outreach.* Alexandria, VA: International Chiefs of Police (IACP).

The Courts and Minorities

LEARNING OBJECTIVES

After reading this chapter, students should be able to do the following:

1. Understand the concepts of impartiality and implicit biases and how they affect the judicial system.
2. Identify experiments and methods used to test implicit biases and explain how implicit biases distort judgments.
3. Identify how the basic Federal and state court structures operate.
4. Understand the selection processes for the courts and be able to identify disparities that exist for minorities.
5. Identify noteworthy minority judicial figures and understand that minority inclusion is only a recent phenomenon.

KEY TERMS

Appellate courts

Brown v. the Board of Education of Topeka Kansas

Chambers v. Florida

Civil

Clark and the Doll Experiments

Colorblindness

Commissions

Court of Appeals

Criminal

Delinquency

Dependency

Ex parte Crow Dog

Explicit stereotyping and attitudes

Federalism

Formalist model

Furman v. Georgia

Gubernatorial appointment

Impartial justice

Implicit Association Tests

Implicit biases and stereotypes

Indian Reorganization Act

Individual adoptions

Joint/Second parent adoption

Legislative appointment

Major Crime Act of 1885

Merit selection

Murray v. Pearson (1936)

Nonpartisan election

Partisan election

People v. Kimura

Plessey v. Ferguson

Problem solving courts (PSCs)

Race of the victim effect

Realist model

Sentencing circles

Shelley v. Kraemer

Smith v. Allright

Special courts

Supreme courts

Sweatt v. Painter McLaurin v. Oklahoma State Regents

Trial courts

Tribal courts

*Our experiences instantly become part of the lens through which
we view our entire past, present, and future, and like any lens, they shape
and distort what we see.*

—GILBERT, 2006

INTRODUCTION

Since the 15th century, the blindfolded statue of "Lady Justice" has adorned the halls of courts. Her symbolism is understood by all that view her as a representation of the impartial judge. She is prevented from seeing the accused and holds her scales in order to carefully weigh out evidence. She represents "justice," which means to objectively sort through facts, without consideration for fame, fortune, gender, race, or sexual orientation. The ideals cast in her symbolism represent the highest level of discernment available to the judgeship—which concedes that all are equal in the right to pursue justice. As is true with most ideals, **impartial justice** may not be afforded to everyone. Largely, this is related to the fact that judges, though they may strive to remain impartial, bring their own histories and perceptions into the cases that they decide.

There are two models of thought regarding judicial decision making as it relates to impartiality—the **formalist model** and the **realist model**. The formalist model concludes that the characteristics and experiences of the judge (e.g., race, cultural background, etc.) in no way affect the outcome of decisions and that judges apply objective and neutral legal principles and interpretations. In contrast, the realist model asserts the personal characteristics of the judge meaningfully affect the outcomes of judicial decisions. The realist model arrives at this conclusion, particularly as it relates to race and ethnicity, because it is understood that persons of different backgrounds often have different viewpoints. Once more, the judges' "social location" within any social system affects their experiences and consciousness beyond the legal setting.

Part of the promise of the U.S. court systems is equal representation for all. This idea effectively links diversity to the concept of equal justice. One way to achieve a more impartial judiciary as a whole is to recruit individuals who have varied racial, ethnic, and experiential backgrounds. Although a diverse judiciary does not assure impartiality, it does increase the probability that judges will be more likely to have attributes and backgrounds that have commonalities with those accused.

THE MYTH OF COLORBLINDNESS

Colorblindness refers to the act of being able to separate the personal characteristics of the person in judgment from the facts of the case. To claim colorblindness in the courtroom is to assert that the judge does not see the race, gender, or social status of the defendant but, rather, is only interested in impartial judgment of the facts surrounding the case. The question that remains for legal scholars and social psychologist alike is, "Does claimed colorblindness actually shield those making judgments from their own personal biases?" There are numerous experimental researches studying the phenomenon of colorblindness and what has become convincing is though we may not believe that we have biases toward others, we almost certainly do. These unconscious biases are referred to as **implicit biases and stereotypes**.

Implicit stereotyping is the perceptual phenomenon where persons unconsciously hold biases toward groups or persons based on their previous experiences. Juxtaposed to implicit stereotyping is **explicit stereotyping and attitudes**, where the person is consciously aware of biases and attitudes that a person holds for a person or group. As expected, when biases are consciously known (explicit) persons act on those biases. Social-cognitive research has also shown that even when biases are unknown, persons still take actions toward the group or person that support the implicit bias. An example of this can be seen through the use of criminal justice "shooter experiments." In these experiments, video simulations of law enforcement officers in "shooter situations" were conducted. The experiment forced the participating officer to make a split-second decision about whether to shoot his weapon in situations where he perceived an imminent threat. These studies showed that law enforcement officers were more likely to make shooting errors (i.e., were more likely to shoot a person holding a harmless object) when the person was an African American.

Much of the research concerning implicit biases and stereotyping has occurred through a multi-university team of researchers that include Tony Greenwald (University of Washington), Mahzarin Banaji (Harvard University), and Brian Nosek (University of Virginia). The theory of implicit bias notes that persons have unconscious biases toward other persons and objects that largely are outside of conscious thought. To test this theory, the **Implicit Association Test (IAT)** was developed by Greenwald in 1998. This test uses a computer platform in which a word is placed in the center of the screen and the respondent is asked to choose between words displayed on the periphery that are best associated with the central word. For example, perhaps the word in the center of the display is the word "good." The respondent would then be asked to choose between two words on the periphery such as "black" and "white." Through the series of word/group choices that occur in rapid succession, researchers are better able to understand how participants unconsciously group concepts in order

Box 8.1 Kenneth and Mamie Clark and the Doll Experiments

Kenneth and Mamie Clark were a pair of African American psychologists who were known for their 1940s experiments using dolls to ascertain children's attitudes about race. In these experiments, the Clarks introduced dolls to children that were identical with the exception of their skin and hair color. The children in the study came from both segregated and integrated schools. The children in the study were asked questions about preferences for each of the dolls such as, "Which one of these dolls is the nice doll?," "Which one looks bad?," and "Which one has the nicer color?" In this experiment, most children showed a clear preference for white dolls. The Clarks used this experiment as the indication that African American children experienced internalized racism as a result of societal views. The Clarks further asserted that this self-hatred amongst African American children was more pronounced for children attending segregated schools. This experiment was used as part of the expert testimony that occurred during the *Brown v. Board of Education*—the 1954 case that ended racial segregation of schools.

In 2005, Kiri Davis repeated the experiment in her film "A Girl Like Me." In this experiment, Davis finds that the truisms of the 1940s still hold true for today's African American youth. Much like the experiment of the Clarks, Davis' participants identify the black dolls as being the "bad ones" and the white dolls as being "good." From this experiment we can conclude that society holds implicit biases that value some persons over others. This is particularly true related to black and white race relations in the United States.

Source: Kira Davis' 7 min video "A Girl Like Me" can be viewed at: http://www.understandingrace.org/lived/video/.

to better understand implicit biases. As expected, researchers have been able to show conclusive evidence of implicit biases that necessarily result in differential treatments of minorities.

IMPLICIT BIAS WITHIN THE COURTROOM

It has been shown that implicit bias affects many different areas of the courtroom process. Implicit biases likely alter the views of judges, jurors, prosecutors, and defense attorneys, rendering outcomes that likely disfavor minorities. In one study of judges, in which the IAT was given, white judges were shown to have a strong preference toward

Box 8.2 Price Waterhouse v. Hopkins (1989)

The Price Waterhouse Supreme Court decision is an important case as it relates to implicit biases. In this case, the plaintiff, Ann Hopkins, brought suit claiming that she had been postponed promotion to partnership two years in a row related to sex-stereotyping related to gender non-conformity. Hopkins was known to display personality characteristics that are more commonly associated with male attributes (e.g., aggression, foul language, demanding) and was reprimanded by her supervisor for her "less than feminine" behavior. Hopkins was told that if she hoped to obtain partner status that she would need to "walk more femininely, dress more femininely, wear make-up, have her hair styled, and wear jewelry." Hopkins was granted a *writ of certiorari* and the case was heard before the Supreme Court. She would eventually prevail in her sex-discrimination suit.

Price Waterhouse v. Hopkins case was important for two reasons: first, it established that gender stereotyping was actionable as sexual discrimination under Title VII of the Civil Rights Act of 1964; second, it affirmed that even though the defendant's actions did not constitute intentional discrimination (related to implicit biases) the plaintiff only needed to show disparate treatment and adverse employment actions. As stated in the decision, "unwitting or ingrained bias is no less injurious or worthy of eradication than blatant or calculated discrimination."

"Whites" (87.1 percent of the sample). In contrast, African American judges were not shown to have a clear preference toward either race. It was also revealed by this and similar experiments that judges often have the "illusion of objectivity," which allows them to feel overly confident about their ability to remain unbiased. In a somewhat stunning fashion, when judges were asked about their ability to avoid racial prejudice, 97 percent of the sample rated themselves as having a strong ability not to be affected by biases. This figure stands in contrast to the 87 percent sample of judges who showed a strong preference for "Whites" on the IAT. Ironically, research has also shown that persons who hold most firm that they are able to remain unbiased are often those who most readily fall victim to group-based biases, thus further affecting their decision-making abilities.

Jurors also fall victim to their own implicit biases. In general, jurors tend to show bias against defendants of different races (Kang et al., 2012). In one experiment that tested IAT biases among jurors, research participants were presented a slideshow in which an equal number of dark-skinned and light-skinned perpetrators were shown. In this experiment, participants were more likely to consider evidence to be indicative of criminal guilt and more likely to assert that the defendant was in fact guilty when the defendant had darker skin (Levinson, Cai, & Young, 2010). In a similar experiment with jurors, Levinson (2007) noted that when mock jurors were told that defendants had the name "Tyronne" jurors were more likely to remember facts about the aggressiveness of the defendant. Of this, Levinson (2007) found that jurors have a way of misremembering facts due to their own implicit biases. Furthermore, implicit biases affect not only the way information is perceived, but also the outcome of the jurors' decisions. Levinson et al. (2010), in their test of jury outcomes, noted that there was a relationship between mock juror's implicit biases toward African Americans and their presumptions of guilt.

Sentencing is also affected by implicit biases. "Black" and more "Afrocentric" traits (e.g., darker skin, wide noses, full lips) are known to illicit perceptions of increased criminality (Eberhardt, Goff, Purdie, and Davies, 2004) and overall negativity. In one study that examined the implicit biases related to "Afrocentric" features, Blair, Judd, and Chapleau (2004) explored Florida Department of Corrections databases to determine if there were differences between "White" and "Black" sentences. The researchers found that inmates from both groups were given similar sentences based on equivalent criminal records. However, when "Black" inmates were sorted based on the degree of "Afrocentric" features displayed (with criminal records held equivalent), the more Afrocentric inmate was found to receive significantly longer sentences. The researchers noted that inmates with more Afrocentric physical features were likely to garner sentences that were seven to nine months longer than their less Afrocentric black counterparts. This implies that although judges have become skilled at not discriminating in sentencing between races, they continue to be more punitive to ethnic minorities with more stereotypical racial features.

This stereotypical bias toward racial features has also been shown to exist in death penalty cases. Eberhardt, Davies, Purdie-Vaughns, and Johnson (2006), in their study of death-eligible cases between 1979 and 1999, found that black physical traits increased the likelihood of being sentenced to death. It is noteworthy that this general trend of producing the harshest of sentencing held true in most cases, with the exception being when the victim of the crime was black. This may be attributed to the **race of the victim effect**, which is discussed in more detail in Chapter 9.

Finally, prosecutors are known to be susceptible to implicit biases. These are found in all phases of prosecution (e.g., charging decisions, pretrial strategy, and trial strategy) (Smith and Levinson, 2012). These biases affect the way prosecutors charge crimes, often leaving the defendant with a more difficult legal arrangement. For example, prosecutors may seek the death penalty vs. imprisonment, adult charges vs. juvenile charges, or imprisonment vs. diversion or some lesser plea deal based on their own implicit biases. African Americans, in particular, have been stereotypically labeled to be lazier, less trustworthy, and dangerous. This stereotype may trigger the prosecutors' implicit biases and may affect their ability to receive plea bargains. Furthermore, prosecutors can paint a picture of the defendant that allows the jurist to activate their own implicit biases surrounding minorities. Goff, Eberhardt, Williams, and Jackson (2008) noted that many persons maintain implicit biases of African Americans that liken them to apes, thus having subhuman features. Prosecutors can deliberately or unintentionally taint arguments with references to subhuman, apelike, or animalistic behavior, which has been shown to increase a jury's likelihood of rendering a death sentence.

OVERVIEW OF THE AMERICAN COURT SYSTEM

The U.S. court system (see Figure 8-1) is unique in that it consists of two separate levels of state and Federal courts. These two subsystems largely operate independent of one another and coexist under the principle of **federalism**. The court that is deemed to have jurisdiction to hear a particular case depends on the type of law that is alleged to be violated. Those cases that allege violation of state law are typically heard in state courts whereas the alleged violation of Federal law is heard in the Federal court system. Within both state and Federal systems, there are two types of cases that are heard within the courts—**civil** and **criminal**. Civil trials are those cases that involve disputes between two persons, whereas criminal trials are those cases

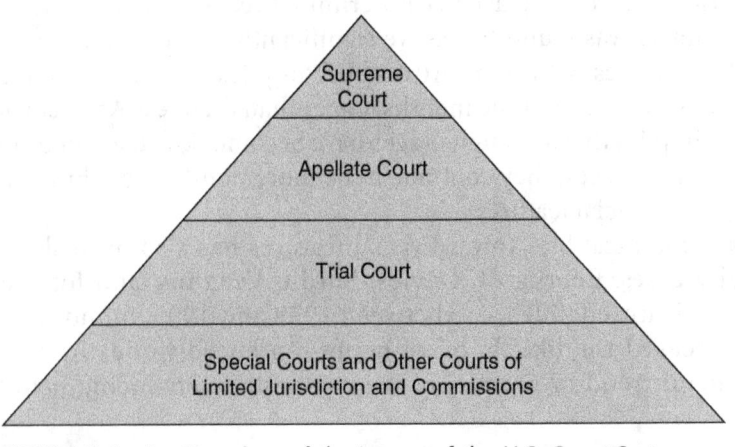

FIGURE 8-1 An Overview of the Layers of the U.S. Court System.

that violate state or Federal criminal laws. It is understood that criminal offenses are of greater seriousness and are seen as acts committed against society at large or the government itself. Likewise, the penalties for crimes are steeper, commonly resulting in fines and potential jail time. Furthermore, in criminal proceedings, defendants are able to present their testimony to a jury of peers, whereas civil trials are more typically arbitrated by judges.

In most states, the court structures are set up in a similar fashion. At the bottom of the tier of the court system are special courts and other courts of limited jurisdiction and commissions. Each of the lowest level courts is designed to achieve some special outcome of narrow scope. Examples of these courts include municipal courts, juvenile courts, drug courts, mental health courts, family courts, and tax courts. **Special Courts** make up the bulk of the courts within the U.S. court system. **Commissions** are quasi-judicial bodies usually in the form of a tribunal that hears cases related to a particular area. These bodies observe powers and procedures familiar to a court of law through objectively determining facts and drawing conclusions. They are also able to impose legal penalties or else affect privileges and rights of special parties (e.g., civil service commissions, etc.). The next tier of courts includes the **trial courts**. Trial courts mark the beginning of the judicial process where initial claims of violation of state law are heard. In these courts, parties present evidence in order to establish the facts of the case. Once testimony is heard, a decision is rendered. If either party involved feels that the trial judge made an error, then the party that alleges the error can appeal the case to the second tier of courts known as **appellate courts. Courts of appeals** determine whether or not the correct trial procedure was followed. A previous decision can be appealed if the trial court judge: (1) misapplied the law, (2) came to an incorrect finding of the facts, (3) acted outside of proper jurisdiction, (4) abused powers, (5) was biased, and/or (6) failed to properly include or exclude evidence or testimony. Once a case is heard in the court of appeals, the original decision of the trial court is either affirmed, reversed, remanded, or modified. If either party feels that the ruling was unjust, then a final appeal can be made to the final tier of the court system—the **Supreme Court**.

METHODS FOR SELECTING JUDGES

Federal judges on District Courts, Appellate Courts, and the Supreme Court are nominated by the President and confirmed by the Senate as prescribed in the Appointment Clause in Article II of the U.S. Constitution. State judges are appointed by a more complex and diverse set of methods that include: (1) **merit selection**, (2) **gubernatorial appointment**, (3) **legislative appointment**, (4) **partisan election**, (5) and **nonpartisan election**. Merit selection is usually performed through establishing an expert panel to nominate the most qualified candidates. Typically, these committees are formed by lawyer and non-lawyer members that evaluate all potential candidates and send a list of candidates to the Governor who will select the final candidate. Merit selections have gained popularity over the last 50 years related to the need to eliminate political interference in the judicial nominating process. Gubernatorial and Legislative appointments most resemble that of the Federal appointment process in which judges are nominated by the governor and confirmed by the state legislature. The drawback to straight gubernatorial appointment processes is that frequently politics determines who will assume a judgeship vs. some other merit-based process.

Box 8.3 "State's Rights"—a Ploy from the Past? Does the Politics of Race Still Affect the Appointment of Minority Judges to the Highest State Courts?

Both racial/ethnic minorities and women occupy seats in the judiciary in proportions that are far below their percentage of makeup in the general population. For example, women make up roughly 50 percent of the population, yet are known to occupy less than 32 percent of the seats available in the state judiciary. Similarly, racial/ethnic minorities make up roughly 20 percent of the U.S. population yet only maintain 12.5 percent of seats available in the state judiciary. This has led many to believe that racial/gender politics come into play when deciding judicial appointments.

One case that illustrates the struggles of minority judges is that of Bernadette Johnson in her rise to become Louisiana's first African American Chief Justice. In Louisiana, Chief Justices are selected based on who has seniority within the Supreme Court. Despite Judge Johnson's tenure on the courts, her bid to become the Louisiana Chief Justice was stalled by fellow justices and the governor of the state. The dispute in her seniority arose because part of Johnson's initial service to the court was called into question. The controversy involved the fact that Ms. Johnson assumed her position on the state Supreme Court following the Federal *Chisolm v. Roemer* decision. *Chisolm v. Roemer* was a Federal court case in which the plaintiff alleged that the residents of New Orleans were predominately African American and were not being properly represented due to how the districting of elections occurred. Because of the Federal case, an additional temporary seat was created on the Louisiana State Supreme Court. Bernadette Johnson would be elected to this newly formed seat. Those opposed to Johnson's ascendancy to the Chief Justice position claimed that the initial six years for which she occupied the *Chisolm Seat* (because it was a temporary appointment) should not be counted in her tenure. A contentious battle was waged in which the Federal courts would have to decide Johnson's claim to the Chief Justice position. U.S. District Judge Susie Morgan ruled in favor of Judge Johnson noting that she was the rightful heir to the Chief Justice position.

Following the affirmation of the U.S. District Court in favor of Johnson, Gov. Bobby Jindal stepped into the fray. The governor, assisted by his legal counsel, vowed to appeal the U.S. District Court's ruling based on his assertion that this was a matter for the state courts to decide. The lawyer for Johnson (attorney James Williams) claimed that Gov. Jindal's proclamation of "state's rights" served as a smokescreen for blatant racism. James Williams is quoted as saying, "That's what the proponents of slavery said during the Civil War—it's an age-old excuse."

Finally, partisan (those that involve political parties) and nonpartisan elections are ways in which the citizens decide the judicial makeup. Some view this process as being the most democratic in that the citizenry is allowed to choose the judges for their given locality. Critics of elections note that frequently special interest money is involved in the election of judges and that most citizens lack information and understanding of the qualifications of elected officials.

With respect to diversity of the courts, merit-based selection is frequently cited as the most favorable way to increase diversity in the judiciary. This is because nominating committees can observe all aspects of a judge's qualifications and consider aspects related to diversity. According to the Reddick et al. (2009), racial/ ethnic minorities and women are most commonly selected by merit selection (54.3 percent and 48.5 percent, respectively). Conversely, minorities and women are less likely of being selected when elections or gubernatorial processes are involved. This is because politics comes into play and judges are selected based on their affiliations. Democratic regimes have been found much more likely to nominate and elect minorities than Republican regimes, particularly as it relates to the court of last resort (state Supreme Court). Given this, minorities are less likely to be selected in years in which Republican regimes are in power. In contrast, nonminorities have a strong likelihood of being appointed while either political party is in power.

CURRENT EVENTS
City of New York seeks to Increase Minority Held Seats in Court System

In 2012, the City of New York had numerous city court personnel retire, some as expected, others as a result of early retirements. According to court statistics, 12 out of the 21 positions went to individuals who were minorities (Storey, 2012). This recent set of promotions increases the city's overall diversity in the municipal judicial system. This means that 45.5% of all upper level court positions in the city - 20 out of 44 seats - are held by minorities (Storey, 2012). This was observed as a result of a citywide initiative that began in the late 1980's after a report indicated that minorities were less likely to be appointed to upper level court positions than Caucasians with similar qualifications.

Since that time, the Minorities in the Courts Committee, as a state-wide committee in New York, was developed to focus on the treatment of litigants, as well as minority lawyers and court personnel in the state of New York as well as the federal courts with jurisdiction in that state (New York City Bar Association, 2013). The specific charge of the committee is to assist in the development of minority attorneys and court personnel and to examine the experiences of minority litigants in the court systems of the state of New York (New York City Bar Association, 2013). This committee has released numerous reports regarding minority representation and involvement in the court system of the State of New York, in general, as well as the City of New York, in particular. As a result of numerous reports and studies on these topics, a variety of recommendations or 'best practices' have been developed. Among them are the following:

- Court Systems should Integrate Diversity Efforts into All Organizational Initiatives:

This includes the establishment of a ranking diversity committee that has executive privileges to support and monitor diversity efforts. This would include oversight of hiring processes to ensure that diverse professionals are attracted and retained. This would also include the integration of diversity into other aspects of operation, "including recruitment, professional development, marketing, and performance management efforts" (2010, p. 1).

- Courts should have Proportionate Representation

This recommendation includes the employment and retention of minorities that is similar in demographic composition to racial/ethnic minorities throughout the state of New York. In addition, this would also require that minorities be in high-profile leadership positions within the organization, rather than lower level or entry-level positions.

- Courts Must Offer Mandatory and Elective Diversity and Inclusion Education

This standard calls for "mandatory ongoing education on racial/ethnic diversity, including inclusion, discrimination, subtle bias, stereotyping, and the interplay between race-based stereotypes and performance perceptions" (2010, p. 2).

Given the outcomes that were presented by Storey (2012), it is clear to see that these recommendations have been given heed and that the impact of the Minorities in the Courts Committee is quite substantial. We present this recent development as an example of how court systems are changing; with state systems taking specific and focused efforts to address the issues associated with minority representation in the judicial system. Though recent successes cast light on the efforts of this committee, they also reflect a change in culture within the judicial system of New York as well as a change in consensus and expectations among the citizens of the state of New York, as well.

References: Committee on Minorities in the Profession (2010). *Best practices standards for the recruitment, retention, development, and achievement of racial/ethnic minority attorneys.* New York: New York City Bar Association. Retrieved from http://www.nycbar.org/pdf/report/Minorities_Professions.pdf

New York City Bar Association (2013). *Minorities in the courts committee.* New York: New York City Bar Association. Retrieved from http://www.nycbar.org/minorities-in-the-courts

Storey, J. (2012). *More minorities were promoted to top positions in New York City courts after early retirements.* New York: New York City Bar Association. Retrieved from http://www.nycourts.gov/careers/diversity/pdfs/minorities-article.pdf

TRIBAL COURTS

Tribal courts are courts operated by Indian tribes under laws and procedures that the tribe has enacted. As such, these courts operate separately from the state and Federal court systems having separate laws and procedures. Most tribes receive funding from the Department of Interior as well as through their own funding mechanisms. In addition to local jurisdiction courts, Tribes also have a separate Federal court system known as the Courts of Indian Offenses, which are operated by the Department of Interior, Bureau of Indian Affairs, on certain reservations. These courts operate under Volume 25 of the Code of Federal Regulations, and thus are sometimes referred to as "CFR" courts. All total, there 150 tribal and 20 CFR courts in operation in the U.S.

TABLE 8-1 Summary of State Judicial Selection Methods by State

Merit selection through Nominating Committee	Gubernatorial or Legislative Appointment without Nominating Committee	Partisan Election	Nonpartisan Election	Combined Merit Selection with Other Methods
Alaska	California (G)	Alabama	Arkansas	Arizona
Colorado	Maine (G)	Illinois	Georgia	Florida
Connecticut	New Jersey (G)	Louisiana	Idaho	Indiana
Delaware	Virginia (L)	Michigan	Kentucky	Kansas
District of Columbia	S. Carolina (L)	N. Carolina	Minnesota	Missouri
Hawaii		Ohio	Mississippi	New York
Iowa		Pennsylvania	Montana	Oklahoma
Maryland		Texas	Nevada	S. Dakota
Massachusetts		W. Virginia	N. Dakota	Tennessee
Nebraska			Oregon	
New Hampshire			Washington	
New Mexico			Wisconsin	
Rhode Island				
Utah				
Vermont				
Wyoming				

Source: American Bar Association. Retrieved from: http://www.americanbar.org/content/dam/aba/migrated/publiced/lawday/schools/lessons/pdfs/judicialhandout3a.authcheckdam.pdf.

The tribal court system began in 1883 following the Federal case known as ***Ex parte Crow Dog.*** In this case, Crow Dog, a Lakota on the Rosebud Indian Reservation in South Dakota, allegedly killed another Lakota named Spotted Tail. Due to the fact that there was not a formal court procedure on the reservation at the time, members of the tribe settled the alleged murder in a traditional way that resulted in Crow Dog paying restitution to the family of the victim. The Federal Territory, when they learned of the settlement, intervened because they felt Crow Dog had not been punished sufficiently. Crow Dog was tried through the Federal system and eventually would be exonerated for the offense by the Supreme Court due to the Courts' claim that they did not have jurisdiction to prosecute crimes on the reservation and that this ability could only be had if Congress authorized the ability to prosecute tribal matters. As a result, the Congress passed the **Major Crime Act of 1885**, which placed serious crimes under Federal jurisdiction if committed on tribal territories (See 18 USC § 1153).

18 USC § 1153—Offenses committed within Indian country

a. Any Indian who commits against the person or property of another Indian or other person any of the following offenses, namely, murder, manslaughter, kidnapping, maiming, a felony under chapter 109A, incest, a felony assault under section 113, an assault against an individual who has not attained the age of 16 years, felony child abuse or neglect, arson, burglary, robbery, and a felony under section 661 of this title within the Indian country, shall be subject to the same law and penalties as all other persons committing any of the above offenses, within the exclusive jurisdiction of the United States.

b. Any offense referred to in subsection (a) of this section that is not defined and punished by Federal law in force within the exclusive jurisdiction of the United States shall be defined and punished in accordance with the laws of the state in which such offense was committed as are in force at the time of such offense.

In addition, The State Department of Interior set up "Courts of Indian Offenses," which were designed to handle less-serious disputes between tribal members. The judges of these courts were typically non-Indian Bureau of Indian Affairs representatives. Related to this, early Courts of Indian Offenses were not seen by Tribes persons as being helpful in that they frequently were used to punish activities that interfered with the integration of Indians into the non-Indian world.

It was not until 1934 with the **Indian Reorganization Act** (IRA) that Tribes were allowed to institute their own courts. The IRA, also known as the Indian New Deal, allowed for the return of self-governance to tribal lands. The goal of the act was to reestablish sovereignty and self-government and allow the Native people to return to economic self-sufficiency. It was during this time of the IRA that many tribes decided to develop their own constitutions and court systems. Some smaller tribes, because of their lack of resources, maintained the CFR courts that were operated by the Bureau of Indian Affairs. Furthermore, some tribes did not choose to operate courts at all and chose to fall under state jurisdiction as indicated by Public Law 280. The tribes that did choose to set up their own constitutions and courts chose traditional models. These models typically employ dispute resolution models that were part of Native American traditions before non-Native interference such as Peacemaking and/or Sentencing Circles.

Current tribal courts operate much like state and Federal courts procedurally. Many of the judges that operate Tribal courts are attorneys whereas some are not. Also similar to state and Federal courts, judges of Tribal courts are either elected or appointed. Tribal attorneys or non-attorneys who are familiar with Tribal law may represent clients in court. Each tribe may set up different parameters of who can practice law and some may require attorneys to take the bar exams along with being mandated to study Tribal codes and constitution.

AN OVERVIEW OF SENTENCING CIRCLES

A sentencing circle is a community-directed process, conducted in partnership with the criminal justice system, to develop consensus on an appropriate sentencing plan that addresses the concerns of all interested parties. Sentencing circles—sometimes called peacemaking circles—use traditional circle ritual and structure to involve the victim, victim supporters, the offender, offender supporters, judge and court personnel, prosecutor, defense counsel, police, and all interested community members. Within the circle, people can speak from the heart in a shared search for understanding of the event, and together identify the steps necessary to assist in healing all affected parties and prevent future crimes.

Sentencing circles typically involve a multi-step procedure that includes: (1) application by the offender to participate in the circle process; (2) a healing circle for the victim; (3) a healing circle for the offender; (4) a sentencing circle to develop consensus on the elements of a sentencing plan; and (5) follow-up circles to monitor the progress of the offender. The sentencing plan may incorporate commitments by the system, community, and family members, as well as by the offender. Sentencing circles are used for adult and juvenile offenders with a variety of offenses and have been used in both rural and urban settings. Specifics of the circle process vary from community to community and they are designed locally to fit community needs and culture.

Sentencing circles have been developed most extensively in Saskatchewan, Manitoba, and the Yukon and have been used occasionally in several other communities. Their use spread to the United States in 1996 when a pilot project was initiated in Minnesota.

GOALS

The goals of sentencing circles include the following:

- Promote healing for all affected parties.
- Provide an opportunity for the offender to make amends.
- Empower victims, community members, families, and offenders by giving them a voice and a shared responsibility in finding constructive resolutions.
- Address the underlying causes of criminal behavior.
- Build a sense of community and its capacity for resolving conflict.
- Promote and share community values.

IMPLEMENTATION

A successful sentencing circle process depends upon a healthy partnership between the formal justice system and the community. Participants from both need training and skill building in the circle process, peacemaking, and consensus building. The community can subsequently customize the circle process to fit local resources and culture. It is critically important that the community's planning process allow sufficient time for strong relationships to develop among justice professionals and community members. Implementation procedures must be highly flexible, because the circle process will evolve over time based on the community's knowledge and experience.

In many communities, direction and leadership are provided by a community justice committee that decides which cases to accept, develops support groups for the victim and offender, and helps conduct circles. In most communities, circles are facilitated by a trained community member, who is often called a "keeper."

Sentencing circles are not appropriate for all offenders. The connection of the offender to the community, the sincerity and nature of the offender's efforts to be healed, the input of victims, and the dedication of the offender's support group are key factors in determining whether a case is appropriate for the circle process. Because communities vary in health and in their capacity to deal constructively with conflict, representatives of the formal justice system must participate in circles to ensure fair treatment of both victims and offenders.

The capacity of the circle to advance solutions capable of improving the lives of participants and the overall well-being of the community depends on the effectiveness of the participating volunteers. To ensure a cadre of capable volunteers, the program should support a paid community-based volunteer coordinator to supply logistical support, establish linkages with other agencies and community representatives, and provide appropriate training for all staff.

Tribal courts have limited jurisdiction over the types of crimes and civil matters that it can prosecute. For example, Tribal Courts cannot prosecute crimes that are committed by non-Indians on reservations. Crimes involving non-Indians would be under the jurisdictional authority of state and Federal courts. In civil matters, Tribal courts have broader jurisdictional authority and hear a broad range of cases that occur on the reservation between both non-Indians and Indians alike. In this regard, Tribal courts

Box 8.4 Lessons Learned with Sentencing Circles

Very little research has been conducted to date on the effectiveness of sentencing circles. One study conducted by Judge Barry Stuart (1996) in Canada indicated that fewer offenders who had gone through the circle recidivated than offenders who were processed by standard criminal justice practices. Those who have been involved with circles report that circles empower participants to resolve conflict in a manner that shares responsibility for outcomes, generate constructive relationships, enhance respect and understanding among all involved, and foster enduring, innovative solutions.

Source: The National Institute of Justice. (2007). Retrieved from: http://www.nij.gov/topics/courts/restorative-justice/promising-practices/sentencing-cricles.htm.

look very much like state civil courts hearing similar cases related to marriage, adoption, child custody, and personal injury.

SPECIAL COURTS THAT AFFECT MINORITIES

There are a number of special courts that are exclusively set up for or else have a significant impact on minorities. These courts have the potential to impact minority issues, thus improving the quality and inclusiveness of the court system. The following sections will provide an overview of prevalent structures.

Juvenile Courts

Juvenile courts are a form of special courts that have limited jurisdiction over under-aged defendants who are charged with crimes. These courts routinely process cases involving those under the age of 18 and will frequently enlist the assistance of social workers, counselors, and probation officers in order to prevent the defendant from committing further crimes. It is noteworthy that juvenile courts do not have jurisdiction in cases where the defendant is over 18 or else where the minor defendant is being charged with an adult offense. Juvenile courts are said to handle cases that involve **delinquency** or **dependency** issues. Delinquency refers to crimes that are committed by minors. The term delinquency is used instead of criminal to show that juvenile courts are not criminal courts and is more representative as a quasi-civil court. Dependency refers to issues regarding who will maintain guardianship in the event a non-parental person is chosen to care for the minor.

Family Courts

Family courts are a number of specialized courts of limited jurisdiction that decide matters and produce orders related to family law. Commonly, these courts address issues related to divorce, child custody and support, guardianship, adoption, and the issuance of restraining orders in domestic violence cases. These courts are usually presided over by a single judge and only hear cases involving family civil matters.

One area of growing interest involving minorities and these courts is the adoption of children by same-sex couples. The adoption laws in most states support what is known as **individual adoptions.** *Individual adoptions* allow for one person to petition the courts to adopt a child. In theory, this affords any single LGBT person to adopt a child in any state. However, there is some legal controversy that exists when LGBT couples attempt to adopt a child. This is related to the fact that in order for the non-custodial parent or couple to adopt the child, they must participate in what is known as a **joint** or **second**

parent adoption. Traditionally, married persons could petition the court to either adopt a child together or become the legal guardian of a child in concert with the current custodial parent. This form of adoption has many benefits for the child, including giving the child the emotional and legal security that is afforded by having two parents as well as entitling them to certain financial benefits (e.g., tort damages, Social Security, child support, etc.). Despite the obvious advantages, there is still some ongoing debate in states whether LGBT couples should be allowed to adopt, particularly where LGBT marriages are not recognized. The states that have enacted LGBT marriages allow LGBT couples to adopt just as opposite-sex couples. Other states have enacted procedures where "stepparents" can adopt and LGBT couples can adopt under these procedures. However, it appears that there are no uniform procedures that apply to LGBT cases in these states and therefore it is determined based on a case-by-case basis. Advocates of LGBT adoptions note that sexual preference should never be included in the adoption determination and only the fitness of the parent should be considered.

Elder Courts

One fairly recent addition to the court system is that of the "Elder Court." Started in 2008 in the Contra Costa Superior Court of California, these courts work to address elder-related cases including criminal, conservatorship, probate, financial abuse, physical abuse, civil cases, restraining orders, small claims, etc. In addition to having a specialized court, there are a number of added features that are meant to assist elderly persons. One such addition is that of a Senior Peer Counseling program that assigns volunteers to assist petitioners during the court procedures. These volunteers will meet with the seniors before the hearings and explain the procedures of the court in simple terms (e.g., showing them where to sit, when to speak, and what documents will need to be provided to the judge). After the court procedures, these same volunteers will make follow-up calls to the seniors to offer reassurance and review what transpired within the courtroom. Another service offered by the court is a Senior Self-Help Center. These centers assist the senior with free legal assistance, translation services, and other assistances that may be critical for the senior to participate in the judicial process. Furthermore, the court proceedings adjust to the optimal times for senior by preparing a later calendar of events that considers when elders may be at their optimal mental alertness. Instead of the 8 AM start to court proceedings, elder courts frequently have a delayed start of 10 AM to assure that elderly participants are alert and prepared.

Drug Courts

Drug courts are a number of specialized courts that are developed to treat nonviolent offenders. These courts are considered **problem solving courts (PSCs)**, meaning that they attempt to solve the underlying problem that has resulted in the criminal behavior. These courts have only been in use since approximately 1989 and were established to prevent the revolving door from court to prison that was a result of not addressing the underlying problems of addiction. Traditionally, drug courts have included supervision, drug testing, substance abuse treatment, and vocational training.

Mental Health Courts

Mental Health Courts, much like drug courts, are PSCs. These courts aim to proactively work with offenders that would otherwise be prison-bound or would reside in long-term residential care. Eligible candidates for these specialized courts are offenders who have been diagnosed with a DSM IV diagnosis and who have no history of violent crime. Participants frequently agree to a set term of treatment, which may include drug therapies, counseling, case management, and community supportive interventions.

DIVERSITY AND THE COURTS

A judiciary that is diverse is a likely ideal of the U.S. citizenry. This is because a diverse set of judges (within both the state and Federal courts) goes further to assuring that once disenfranchised groups have representation within all branches of government and that person have access to equal justice. One might assume that cultural, racial, and generative differences add viewpoints to the court that would not otherwise exist. It is assumed that diversity ultimately adds to the quality of decisions in that it offers a broader perspective related to the varied backgrounds of judges. Torres-Spelliscy, Chase, and Greenman (2008) provide five reasons why a diverse bench is critical: (1) a more diverse bench inspires confidence in the judiciary, (2) it is more representative of the broader community, (3) it promotes justice, (4) it promotes equality of opportunity for historically excluded groups, and (5) it promotes judicial impartiality.

Despite the fact that increasing diversity in the courts has been a priority over the last several years, minorities and women are still inadequately represented on the bench. As can be seen in Tables 8-2, 8-3, and 8-4, minorities lag behind in representation at every level of both state and Federal courts. It is important to note that of all minority groups, women have fared the best on whole of moving toward parity on the courts. Largely, this is related to the fact that white women (unlike most ethnic minorities) participate in the Republican party (unlike a majority of racial/ethnic minorities) and as such have a greater likelihood of being appointed to the courts.

There are numerous structural barriers preventing women and ethnic/racial minorities from obtaining judgeships. These include that judge positions within state and Federal courts do not support the salary that is obtainable for minorities within the private sector; appointment commissions, historically, have been made up of all-white male members, resulting in all-white male appointments; and judgeships infrequently come open, thus few candidates (including diverse candidates) apply.

JUDICIAL PROFESSIONALS AND CULTURAL COMPETENCE

Because so little attention is typically provided to cultural competence among judicial staff and, because this chapter has a strong emphasis on police and correctional agencies, we believe it is important to consider some issues related to the judicial system. The research of Perlin and McClain (2009) provides some excellent insight on cultural

TABLE 8-2 Minority Judges at Differing Levels of Federal Court System						
Type of Court	African American Men	African American Women	Hispanic Men	Hispanic Women	White Men	White Women
Supreme Court	11% (1)	0% (0)	0% (0)	11% (1)	55% (5)	22% (2)
Court of Appeals	4%	2%	4%	1%	71%	17%
District Courts	7%	2%	4%	2%	69%	15%

Source: American Bar Association. (2010). Retrieved from: http://apps.americanbar.org/abanet/jd/display/national.cfm.

TABLE 8-3   Minority Judges in Special Courts of the Federal System

Type of Court	African American	Asian/Pacific Islander	Hispanic American	Native American	Other	Total
Court of Last Resort	9% (32)	1% (4)	3% (10)	0% (0)	0% (1)	47
Immediate Appellate Level Court	8% (75)	1% (13)	4% (34)	0% (1)	1% (8)	131
Trial Court of General Jurisdiction	7% (662)	2% (140)	4% (364)	0% (12)	1% (80)	1258
Total	769	157	408	13	89	1436

Source: American Bar Association. (2010). Retrieved from: http://apps.americanbar.org/abanet/jd/display/national.cfm.

TABLE 8-4   Representation by Race/Ethnicity of Minority Groups

Race/Ethnicity	Percentage of the U.S. Population
White	78.1
Black	13.1
Asian American	5.0
Native American	1.2
Native Hawaiian and Other Pacific Islander	0.2
Persons of two or more races	2.3

Source: US Census Bureau. (2011). Retrieved from: http://quickfacts.census.gov/qfd/states/00000.html.

competence within this arena of the criminal justice system. They explain how it is important for defense attorneys to develop strategies that will best ensure that a comprehensive picture of the defendant be painted for the fact-finder. Research has shown that available psychological and forensic tests lack the normative database that would permit cross-cultural comparisons. Most standardized tests used by Western clinicians have been designed for use in Caucasian populations and those with Euro-American backgrounds (on potential bias of personality tests, see McCurley, Murphy, & Gould, 2005). They point out that the use of these tests in clients with non-Western cultural backgrounds requires utmost caution and discretion.

Just as the acquisition of multicultural competency is considered a "necessary prerequisite" in providing mental health services to clients from diverse cultural backgrounds (D'Andrea & Daniels, 2001, p. 432), so is such acquisition a prerequisite in providing evaluation services in the criminal trial context (see Kavanaugh, Clark, Mason, & Kahn, 2006, discussing the clinician's responsibility to be aware of potentially relevant cultural factors). Cultural competence is an integral aspect of comprehensive mitigation efforts in criminal capital crimes. (on nurturing and fostering multicultural competence and its relationship to social justice, see Vera & Speight, 2003). As established in ***Furman v. Georgia*** (1972, p. 274), a thorough life history involves a careful search into the defendant's background. We argue here that cultural competence in interview and testing strategies will lead to a more robust approach and ultimately more successfully humanize the client and their context. A team approach by psychologists (or other mitigation specialists) and lawyers may be more effective for both legal strategizing and gathering effective mitigation information. Potential pitfalls in communication can more easily be assessed when an integrated effort is made to utilize the strengths of the defense team in laying a roadmap to humanize the client.

By way of example, consider the case of ***People v. Kimura*** (1985). There, a Japanese American woman in her 30s—a wife and mother of two children (a 4-year-old son and 6-month-old daughter)—had the intention of committing parent–child suicide (oyako-shinyu) after learning that her Japanese-American husband had been keeping a mistress for many years. The children drowned but she was rescued by a passerby. The prosecution charged her with first-degree murder. However, the Japanese-American community petitioned the court to reduce the charge, emphasizing that parent–child suicide was at the root of her culture directing her to act and behavior should be judged within the context of Japanese standards. Three psychiatric experts opined she was temporarily insane at the time and one protested that she was suffering a "brief reactive psychosis." As a result of both the experts' and community input, the homicide was reduced to voluntary manslaughter and the defendant was sentenced to one year in custody and five years probation with psychiatric counseling recommended.

Minority Legal Representation: Minority Public Defenders

The issue of cultural competence for public defenders is particularly relevant when one considers that public defense attorneys represented 77 percent of African Americans and 73 percent of Latinos who ultimately served time in state prisons (Harlow, 2001). However, most public defense systems employ a lower percentage of minority attorneys compared to the percent of people of color in their state or county populations (see Table 5-1). Indeed, the majority of jurisdictions do not have recruitment programs that target people of color. Some states, such as Ohio, may conduct moderate attempts to gain applicants of color by attending job fairs, and talking with Black/African American law student associations at major state universities. Others may also attend career fairs, conduct visits to law schools, and give early offers to top law students of color.

Given that minorities are disproportionately represented in the American criminal justice system and also considering that many are in the lower economic strata and therefore use public defender programs, we recommend that states with 10 percent or more of a minority population should implement specific recruitment policies and strategies to attract minority attorneys. Communities with immigrant populations should also work to recruit attorneys of color, especially those with immigrant backgrounds. Emphasizing the recruitment of attorneys of color from the client communities could improve the quality of representation. Furthermore, improved communication between attorneys and clients may lead to better representation, as will increased community confidence in the public defense system.

NOTABLE HISTORIC MINORITY JUDICIARY FIGURES

The story of diversity on the courts cannot be complete without understanding the historical figures and their struggles to become members of what was once a traditional all-white male judiciary. The following figures consist of notable firsts and well-known historic personalities that have shaped the public view of the current court system. Attention should be paid to the fact that although the court system is well over 200 years old, it was only in the last century that minorities and women were allowed to participate in the judicial process as judges.

William Henry Hastie, Jr.

William Henry Hastie, Jr. was the first of many distinguished titles. He was the first African American to serve as Federal judge, Federal appellate judge, and Governor of the United States Virgin Islands. Hastie received his Doctor of Laws from Harvard Law School in 1933, and he became a race relations advisor to President Franklin Roosevelt. In 1937 he was appointed by President Roosevelt to the U.S. District Court in the Virgin Islands, thus becoming the first African American Federal judge. He served as a Federal judge for two years and then resigned to become Dean of Howard University Law School. During his time at Howard University, Hastie once again became involved in governmental affairs as he served as Civilian Aid to Secretary of War, Henry L. Stimson, where he was to focus on race relations in the army. He was not pleased with the segregated training facilities for Air Force pilots and technicians and the lack of black superiors in the armed forces with only seven black colonels out of 5,220 colonels and only one black general out of 776 in 1946. After protesting to no avail, Hastie resigned from his post, which gained national attention. In 1943, Hastie was awarded from the NAACP the Spingarn Medal, which was awarded to an individual who made outstanding progress in the standing of blacks in society. After resigning from his post, Hastie's attention turned again to the Virgin Islands, and in 1946, he was elected governor of the islands. Three years later, President Harry Truman nominated Hastie to serve on the Third Circuit Court of Appeals. Because of racial tension, the Senate did not approve his nomination readily, and it was not until 1950 that the Senate confirmed his nomination. In 1971, after two decades on the Federal bench, he resigned, but he remained active in bettering society for all people. At the 62nd annual convention of the NAACP, he shocked the crowd with his criticism of the separatist movement, claiming, "black society that is no better in its aping of white materialism, and its accommodation of hucksters, hustlers, and other operators as predatory and cynical as their white counterparts; in its spawn of sick, violet men who murdered Malcolm X just as viciously as whites murdered Dr. King, and who continue to disfigure the black community with sporadic homicidal guerilla strife among rival separatists groups."

Thurgood Marshall

Thurgood Marshall is known as being the most prominent African American to have ever practiced law. Marshall held a number of distinctions including being named the first African American U.S. Solicitor General and the first African American to ever sit on the Supreme Court. Marshall's legacy included creating a modern movement where minority lawyers would have the opportunity to aspire to benches in the highest courts.

Thurgood Marshall was born in Baltimore Maryland (July 2, 1908). It is noteworthy that both his grandfather and his great-grandfather were slaves. His introduction into law began in 1936 when he went to work for the National Association for the Advancement of Colored People (NAACP) in Baltimore. He won his first major civil rights case in *Murray v. Pearson*(1936), which was the first case of its kind to challenge the separate but equal doctrine that was part of the *Plessey v. Ferguson* decision. At age 32, Marshall won his first U.S. Supreme Court case—*Chambers v. Florida*. The same year he was appointed chief counsel for the NAACP. He went on to argue several civil rights cases successfully, including *Smith v. Allright*, *Shelley v. Kraemer*, and *Sweatt v. PainterMcLaurin v. Oklahoma State Regents*. The seminal case that made Marshall famous was *Brown v. the Board of Education of Topeka Kansas*. In this case the Supreme Court ruled that separate but equal public education, as established in *Plessey v. Ferguson*, could never be truly equal. This case began the desegregation of public schools.

In 1961, John F. Kennedy appointed Marshall to the U.S. Court of Appeals for the Second Circuit. In 1965, President Lyndon B. Johnson appointed Marshall to be the first African American U.S. Solicitor General. Just two years later on June 13, 1967, Johnson nominated Marshall to the Supreme Court following the retirement of Justice Tom C. Clarke. Marshall was confirmed as an associate justice by the Senate by vote of 69–11. Marshall would then go on to serve the court for the next 24 years, compiling a record of strong support for the constitutional protections of individual rights, especially for minority defendants.

Frank Howell Seay and Michael Burrage

Frank Howell Seay (left) is the first Native American appointed to the Federal bench. He was confirmed to the bench in 1979 and assumed senior status in 2003. It is noteworthy that Seay did not learn of his Native American heritage until he had assumed the Federal bench.

Michael Burrage is the second (and only other) Native American appointed to the Federal bench. Before his appointment, he was an active member of the Choctaw Nation having served on the tribal counsel. He was appointed to the Judgeship by President Bill Clinton in 1994, serving until his departure in 2001.

Florence Ellinwood Allen

Florence Ellinwood Allen (March 23, 1884–September 12, 1966) was the first woman to serve on a state Supreme Court and one of the first to serve as a Federal judge. She attended Western Reserve's University in Ohio where she received her master's degree in political science, but she could not continue her studies in law as she desired because Western Reserve's Law School did not admit women. She transferred to New York University and in 1913 graduated with a law degree. As an attorney, Allen became committed to the cause of women's suffrage to a great extent; hence, she fought for the women of East Cleveland for the right to vote in municipal elections before Ohio's Supreme Court. In 1919, Allen, a Democrat, became the first woman appointed assistant prosecuting attorney, but not without great opposition from the Democratic Party. By 1920 she tried nearly 900 cases as she was elected to Common Pleas judge. Allen quickly rose to success, and in 1922 she was elected to the Ohio Supreme Court. In her reelection in 1928, she was the only Democratic representative. Allen continued to educate and encourage women to fight for equal rights and was determined to utilize her position to improve women's legal rights. In 1934, President Franklin D. Roosevelt appointed her to the United States Court of Appeals for the sixth circuit, making her one of two women to hold such a position. She was not promoted during Harry S. Truman's presidency for his was not a proponent of women filling the seats of the highest courts in United States. In 1958, Allen was the first woman to serve as chief judge of the U.S. Court of Appeals.

Sonia Sotomayor

Sonia Sotomayor was the first Hispanic and the third female justice nominated to the U.S. Supreme Court. Sotomayor was born in the Bronx New York—the daughter of Puerto Rican immigrants. Sotomayor completed her undergraduate degree from Princeton University in 1976 and her Juris Doctor from Yale Law School in 1979. While at Princeton, Sotomayor develop the necessary educational skills that would eventually propel her through her career. It is noteworthy that because of her disadvantaged background, she had not fully developed her vocabulary and other general academic skills on arrival at Princeton. Sotomayor also began an activist role while at Princeton, lobbying for the hiring of Hispanic minorities to the University faculty.

Her early career was spent as an assistant district attorney in New York County, beginning in 1979. In this role, she prosecuted every imaginable crime including those that occurred in the most impoverished and diverse communities. From this experience, Sotomayor established the belief that low-level crimes were largely the result of the socioeconomic environment in which offenders lived.

In 1991, Sotomayor was nominated to the U.S. District Court for the Southern District of New York by the then-President George HW Bush. As a notable first, Sotomayor became the youngest judge in the Southern District and also the first Hispanic Federal judge in New York State. She was also the first Puerto Rican woman to serve as a judge in the U.S. Federal court system. While on the District Court, Sotomayor was known to give heavy sentences, particularly for those who committed white-collar crimes.

In June 1977, Sotomayor was nominated by President Clinton to a seat on the U.S. Court of Appeals for the Second Circuit. This appointment would be held up in confirmations until October 1998 because of legislative wrangling over Sotomayor's political beliefs. Of this, Sotomayor would remark that she believed that members of the Republican Party assumed that, because she was a Latina, she must hold certain liberal beliefs. She noted that she believed this stereotyping was the most insidious of all problems in our society today.

On May 26, 2009 upon the retirement of Justice David Souter, President Barack Obama would nominate Sotomayor to the U.S. Supreme Court. In an attempt to block the confirmation, a controversial statement would be highlighted by Republican Senators in which Sotomayor, in a Berkeley law lecture, stated, "I would hope that a wise Latina woman with the richness of her experience would more often than not reach a better conclusion that a white male who hasn't lived that life." Of this statement, Sotomayor would eventually remark, "I do not believe that any ethnic racial or gender group has an advantage and sound judgment." On August 6, 2009, Sotomayor was confirmed by the full Senate. In her appointment, Sotomayor became the first Hispanic and the third woman to serve on the court. Sotomayor has also been credited as the being the first person to be appointed with a disability to the High Court, noting that she suffers from diabetes.

Sandra Day O'Conner

On July 7, 1981 Sandra Day O'Connor was nominated as the first female associate justice of the Supreme Court. This fulfilled a promise that President Ronald Reagan pledged in his 1980 campaign. With almost no opposition, O'Connor was confirmed by the Senate 99 – 0.

O'Connor was born in El Paso Texas (March 26, 1930), and grew up on her family's Arizona cattle ranch. She went on to attend Stanford University, graduating in 1950 with a degree in economics. She later went on to attend Stanford Law School, completing her law degree in 1952. In her early years as an attorney, O'Connor struggled to find work and even worked as a volunteer with California's San Mateo County Attorney's Office. O'Connor later went on to work as a civilian attorney in Frankfurt Germany and with the Arizona state Attorney General's office. In 1969, O'Connor went into politics, being named a State Senator for Arizona. She would be reelected twice to the state Senate. In 1979, O'Connor was appointed to serve on the states Court of Appeals until being named to the Supreme Court in 1981.

Despite being the first woman nominated to the court, O'Conner's voting record on the court was very conservative. O'Conner generally agreed with more conservative justices on issues of segregation, affirmative action, and the death penalty. Despite being conservative, O'Conner generally believed that abortion was a fundamental right of women supported by the Due Process clause of the 14th Amendment.

Lance Ito

Judge Lance Ito received national appeal for being the judge who presided over the OJ Simpson trial. Although Ito is not a notable first, he certainly became the most famous Asian American judge to serve on the bench. His popularity is important because Asian Americans are one of the least represented minority groups among both Federal and state judiciaries.

Judge Lance Allan Ito was born on August 2, 1950 in Los Angeles California to parents Jim and Toshi Ito. Jim and Toshi Ito were both held in Japanese American Internment camps during World War II. Ito procured his J.D. degree from the University of California in 1975, and went to work for the LA District Attorney's office in 1977. With the LADA office he worked mostly with the organized crime and terror unit. In 1981 he married Margaret Ann York, who was the first woman to attain the rank of Deputy Chief of the Los Angeles Police Department. Ito would later go on to become the most famous Asian American judge of the 20th century because of his involvement with the OJ Simpson trial.

Reynaldo Guerra Garza

Reynaldo Guerra Garza (July 7, 1915–September 14, 2004) was the first Latino appointed to a federal court and to any circuit of the U.S. Court of Appeals. He received his L.L.B. from the University of Texas School of Law in 1939. He had to leave his private practice from 1942 to 1945 to serve in the Army Air Force during World War II. In 1961, Garza was appointed by President John F. Kennedy as the first Latino Federal district judge. In 1976 President Carter asked Garza to serve as Attorney General to the United States, which would have made him the first Mexican American Attorney General, but refused the offer because he felt the move to Washington D.C., would be too burdensome for his family. In 1979, President Carter nominated Garza for the Fifth Circuit Court of Appeals in New Orleans, where he served until his service was terminated by his death in his hometown of Brownsville, Texas, in 2004.

Herbert Young Choy

Herbert Young Choy (January 6, 1916–March 10, 2004) was the first Asian American to serve as U.S. Federal judge. Judge Choy was born on January 6, 1916 on Kauai, Hawaii, as the son of Korean immigrants. He earned his J.D. from Harvard Law School and was the first person of Korean ancestry to be admitted to practice law in the United States. From 1942 to 1946, Choy served in the U.S. Army and in 1946 he served in the U.S. Army Judge Advocate General's Corps. Choy became Attorney General for the Territory of Hawaii, and in 1971 President Richard Nixon appointed him to the U.S. Court of Appeals Ninth Circuit.

Constance Baker Motley

Constance Baker Motley was the first African American woman Federal court judge. She was born in 1921 to parents who immigrated to America from the Caribbean, and she was the ninth of twelve children. Motley procured a law degree from Columbia University School of Law in 1946, and she was hired by the NAACP Legal Defense and Educational Fund as a law clerk, who worked her way up to a civil rights lawyer. It was here she worked beside future U.S. Supreme Court Justice, Thurgood Marshall. Motley was dedicated to the civil rights movement and was known to visit black churches that were bombarded by racist oppositionist and even visited the legendary Rev. Martin Luther King in his jail cell. Her dedication to civil rights derived from her own experiences with racism and that her mother was the founder of the New Haven NAACP chapter. As a civil rights lawyer, Motley was the first to write a complaint in the case of *Brown v. Board of Education*, in which the Court declared state laws establishing separate public schools for black and white students unconstitutional. She was the first African American female to argue before the Supreme Court; she was actually successful in nine of the ten cases she presented before the Supreme Court, with one of her most notable being *Meredith v. Fair*. In this case, she successfully won James Meredith's case of being the first African American student to enter the University of Mississippi. Motley was the first of many: the first woman elected to the New York State Senate and to the Manhattan Borough President. In 1966, her ultimate title of Federal court judge was delivered by President Lyndon B, Johnson, making her the first African American woman to fill that position, which she held until her death in September 2005. One of Motley's most current and memorable breakthrough decisions as a Federal court judge was the allocation of female reporters in sports broadcasting entrance into Major League Baseball's locker rooms, which was granted in 1976.

Eric Hampton Holder

Eric Himpton Holder, Jr. (born in January 21, 1951) is the first African American to serve as U.S. Attorney General. Holder received his J.D. from Columbia Law School and after graduating, joined the U.S. Justice Department's new Public Integrity Section, which investigates and prosecutes official corruption on the local, state, and federal levels. In 1988, President Ronald Reagan appointed Holder as a judge of the Superior Court of the District of Columbia and with the election of President Bill Clinton in 1993, Holder was appointed as U.S. Attorney for the District of Columbia, making him the first African American U.S. Attorney. In 1997, Holder was elevated to the position of Deputy Attorney, where he was instrumental in advising department heads on such issues as Clinton's Lewinsky affair, bribery in the 2002 Winter Olympics in Salt Lake City, and the Matthew Shepard and James Byrd, Jr. hate crimes cases in which he was a proponent of implementing hate crime laws. Holder experienced criticism with his involvement with the pardoning of the fugitive and Democratic contributor Marc Rich during the last minutes of Clinton's administration. A fugitive had been allowed a pardon, and Holder leaned approvingly to Clinton's pardon; however, he later conveyed regret about his judgment, claiming he was unaware of certain details. When Clinton's presidential term ended, Holder returned as an Attorney General in 2001 at Covington & Burling in Washington D.C.

One of his most familiar cases during this period was when he represented the NFL throughout its dog-fighting investigation of Atlanta Falcons quarterback, Michael

Vick. Holder acquired the spotlight again in 2008 when he positioned himself with U.S. Attorney General, Janet Reno, in urging the Supreme Court to uphold Washington, D.C.'s handgun ban because he believed that the overturning of a 1976 handgun law put more guns on the streets. It was on January 20, 2009 that Eric Holder made history again by becoming the first African American Attorney General of the United States under the President Obama administration.

As Attorney General, Holder has been praised and criticized for his management of different issues. One of Holder's greatest causes is voting rights. He is a staunch advocate in defending the Voting Rights Act of 1965, and has assertively fought against new voting laws that redistrict communities in states such as Texas, Alabama, and Florida, which ultimately weaken political representation for minority communities. He has also stated the Department of Justice does not defend the Defense of Marriage Act that Congress passed in 1996. He has advocated for over 36,000 same-sex partnerships in which Americans are in relationships with non-U.S. citizens.

Johnnie L. Cochran, Jr.

Johnnie Cochran is one of the most famous trial attorneys of the 20th century. The most famous trial that Cochran worked was the OJ Simpson trial. Even before the OJ Simpson case, Cochran was known for being one of the top attorneys for the rich. Cochran was born in 1937 in Shreveport, Louisiana. His mother sold Avon products and his father sold insurance. In 1949, they relocated to Los Angela California. Cochran would go on to graduate from the University of California in Business Administration and earn his Juris Doctor from Loyola Marymount School of Law in 1962. Cochran started his early legal practice working for the Los Angeles District Attorney, but ultimately would work exclusively in private practice. Cochran would eventually open the Cochran Firm and open 26 offices in 15 states. Although the OJ Simpson case was the most famous case in which Cochran was involved, he was involved in representing a number of famous persons. These figures included Michael Jackson, Jim Brown, Snoop Dogg, Riddick Bowe, Sean Combs, and Marion Jones.

DIVERSITY AND THE BENCH: SOME ADDITIONAL COMMENTS

We have presented a number of iconic figures from the legal profession who are also racial/ethnic minorities. We have done this to showcase some of the contributions that various minority members have provided to the judiciary. We do this betwixt a concern that minorities are still underrepresented on the bench and in various official capacities in the American judicial system. This is a problem that impacts the welfare of the nation because, with this underrepresentation, issues related to discrimination, disparity among adult and juvenile offender processing, and extension of Civil Rights to various groups of minorities based on any variety of categories cannot be truly ensured because it is the judicial system that serves as the arbiter between the legislative and executive realms of government. It is, therefore, the judicial practitioner who holds the critical role of protecting the rights of all, equally and without prejudice. To fail to represent these minority groups on a large-scale basis is problematic for all of us, including the Caucasian minority. Indeed, as we will discuss in future chapters, the Caucasian majority is becoming the new minority. It is, therefore, important for all of us that a precedent of representation and non-disparity be set. Besides these facts,

INTERNATIONAL FOCUS

In Canada, Lawyers Call for More Diversity and More Gender Equality on the Bench

It would appear that diversity and gender equality have been an issue of debate among lawyers and laypersons in Canada. Indeed, recent news media and even the Canadian Bar Association have highlighted this issue in a number of forums. Given that these issues continue to catch the eye and ear of the Canadian public, it would appear that there is, indeed, some sort of disparity that is noticeable.

In an article by the Toronto Star, James Morton makes the point of sharing a well-known legal and philosophical saying that goes as follows: "not only must justice be done; it must also be seen to be done" (2012, p. 1). His primary point is that it is not just good enough to have sound legal processes; those processes must also actually reflect the general mores, views, and opinions of the people whom they are designed to serve. We think that this is an important point for this entire text in general, and for this chapter, in particular.

Law and legal processes are tools created for human beings and are designed to serve human beings. In order for this to be the case, they must also be created, utilized, and maintained by those humans upon which they are binding. Thus, the point is that if we are to expect legal systems to adequately reflect the population for which they are designed, then the legal personnel responsible for their creation, maintenance, and enforcement should represent the population upon which they are to apply. In Canada, it would seem that this is not the case, at least according to a number of legal scholars, news media, political pundits, and special interest activists.

In Morton's (2012) article, he notes that while we like to think that the personalities and idiosyncrasies of judges, justices, and other legal professionals are unbiased and unaffected by personal views, they are not. Thus, it is important that the views, opinions, and beliefs of minority groups also be represented in this system. To further illustrate his case, he notes that a substantial number of pollsters in Canada do not feel comfortable with the current means by which judges are selected.

Neubauer (2007) points out that laws are shaped and modified, over time, by the changing mores and customs of a society. Though this may happen in the legislator, it also happens through rulings made by independent judges and juries who, collectively and over time and with each decision, contribute to the slow but sure evolution of law that is adopted throughout the nation. If either judges, juries, or both are not reflective of the population, the result is law that does not, in reality, reflect the mores and attitudes of the people involved.

Morton (2012) notes that the current system in Canada, through the Judicial Appointments Commission, does not seem to take diversity into consideration and that this, in turn, severely impairs the quality of justice that is the result. He notes that the appointment of minority judges is much lower than minority representation in the broader population.

It would appear that Morton is not alone. Krystle Gill and Alycia Shaw also wrote an article for the Canadian Bar Association in which they contend that there is also a lack of gender balance on the Canadian bench. Roughly speaking, it would appear that, at best, about one-third of the various federal and territorial judgeships in Canada are female, and in many cases the proportion is lower. Obviously, racial or ethnic minorities women are also even less represented.

From the information provided by these sources, we can see that it is not just the United States that struggles with diversity issues in the legal system. Canada is often portrayed as a progressive nation with more liberal viewpoints than the United States. It is, therefore, interesting to note that this nation also struggles with minority diversity and gender equality among their judiciary. It is with this in mind that we conclude that multiculturalism in judicial settings is not just an issue relevant to the United States but is, instead, likely to be relevant to the entire global community.

Sources: Gill, K., & Shaw, A. (2013, March). Representing Canada on the bench: On gender balance, equality, and judicial appointments. The Common Room, CBA Women Lawyers Forum *Newsletter*. Retrieved from: http://www.cba.org/CBA/conf_women/Women_Newsletters2013/bench.aspx.

Morton, J. (2012, Jan. 08). Diversity bypasses the bench: Judges' decisions are influenced by their identity and personal history. *Toronto Star*. Retrieved from: http://www.thestar.com/opinion/editorialopinion/2012/01/08/diversity_bypasses_the_bench.html.

Neubauer, D. W. (2007). *America's courts and criminal justice system* (5th Ed.). Belmont, CA: Wadsworth.

we contend that this is, if nothing else, simply a matter of fundamental fairness, which holds merit in its own right in any free and enlightened democratic society.

CONCLUSION

Undoubtedly, the best judiciary system is one that is made up of a diverse set of judges. Unfortunately, to date, minorities have not been appointed or elected to judgeships in a representative fashion. One might assume from this disparity that courtrooms have not gone far enough to represent the views of all and thus do not provide representative justice. Furthermore, those majority judges who do sit on the bench likely decide cases based on their own implicit biases, biases that were greatly influenced by their upbringing in a majority society. This probably indicates that even though most majority judges believe they afford impartial justice, the opposite is likely true.

In order for our justice system to become more representative and impartial, a representative judiciary is required. Although there has been much progress toward this objective in the last 30 years, more work needs to be done. This means that special attention needs to be paid to appointment commissions (ensuring that commissions are representative), more minorities need to be recruited into the law profession, and judgeships should provide the financial rewards and prestige to attract minority attorneys.

Chapter 8 Learning Check

1. _____ refers to the equal application of the law for all citizens regardless of race, gender, or status.
   a. Impartial Justice
   b. Implicit Bias
   c. Fairness
   d. Representative Justice

2. The _____ of decision making presents that judges can be impartial when deciding cases.
   a. Realist model
   b. Formalist Model
   c. Federalism Model
   d. Implicit Bias Model

3. The _____ of decision making presents that judges make decision based on their personal histories and biases.
   a. Realist model
   b. Formalist Model
   c. Federalism Model
   d. Implicit Bias Model

4. The _____ selection method refers to when the governor or legislature assigns the justice to the bench.
   a. Merit selection
   b. Appointment
   c. Partisan Election

   d. Nonpartisan Election
   e. Combined

5. The _____ selection method refers to when a commission chooses the most appropriate candidate for the bench.
   a. Merit selection
   b. Appointment
   c. Partisan Election
   d. Nonpartisan Election
   e. Combined

6. The _____ selection method refers to when an election is held based on political party in order to determine the next judge.
   a. Merit selection
   b. Appointment
   c. Partisan Election
   d. Nonpartisan Election
   e. Combined

7. The _____ selection method refers to when both a commission and an appointment are rendered to select the judge.
   a. Merit selection
   b. Appointment
   c. Partisan Election
   d. Nonpartisan Election
   e. Combined

8. The _____ selection method refers to when an election is held that is not party based to elect the judge.
   a. Merit selection
   b. Appointment
   c. Partisan Election
   d. Nonpartisan Election
   e. Combined

9. Thurgood Marshall was the first African American appointed to a Federal Court.
   a. True
   b. False

10. Sonia Sotomayor has been called the first Supreme Court justice to suffer from a disability.
    a. True
    b. False

Essay Questions

1. Describe the reasons why minorities have not been promoted to the bench in a representative fashion. Using what you know about implicit biases and structural racism, explain how historical treatments of minorities come into play.

2. Describe how Tribal Courts differ from state and Federal courts. Do you believe tribal courts should have more independence in prosecuting criminal offenses? Why or why not?

3. Describe the different methods by which judges are selected for the bench. Which of these methods do you believe improves the diversity of the courts? Why?

References

Blair, I. V., Judd, C. M., & Chapleau, K. M. (2004). The influence of afrocentric facial features in criminal sentencing. *Psychological Science, 15*(10), 674–679.

D'Andrea, M., & Daniels, J. (2001). Expanding our thinking about White racism: Facing the challenge of multicultural counseling in the 21st century. In J. G. Ponterotto, J. M. Casas, L. A. Suzuki, & C. M. Alexander (Eds.), *The handbook of multicultural counseling* (2nd ed., pp. 289–310). Thousand Oaks, CA: Sage.

Eberhardt, J. L., Davies, P. G., Purdie-Vaughns, V. J., & Johnson, S. L. (2006). Looking deathworthy: Perceived stereotypicality of black defendants predicts capital-sentencing outcomes. *Psychological Science, 17*(5), 383–386.

Eberhardt, J. L., Goff, P. A., Purdie, V. J., & Davies, P. G. (2004). Seeing black: Race, crime, and visual processing. *Journal of Personality and Social Psychology, 87*(6), 876–893.

Gilbert, D. (2006). *Stumbling on happiness.* New York: Vintage Books.

Goff, P. A., Eberhardt, J. L., Williams, M. J., & Jackson, M. C. (2008). Not yet human: Implicit knowledge, historical dehumanization, and contemporary consequences. *Journal of Personality and Social Psychology, 94*(2), 292–306.

Harlow, C. W. (2001). *Defense counsel in criminal cases.* Washington, DC: Bureau of Justice Statistics. Bureau of Justice Statistics.

Kang, J., Bennett, M., Carbado, D., Casey, P., Dasgupta, N., Faigman, D., & Mnookin, J. (2012). Implicit bias in the courtroom. *UCLA Law Review, 59*(5).

Kavanaugh, A., Clark, J., Mason, T., & Kahn, B. (2006). Obtaining and utilizing comprehensive forensic evaluations: The applicability of one clinic's model. *Nevada Law Journal, 6,* 890–910.

Levinson, J. D. (2007). Forgotten racial equality: Implicit bias, decisionmaking, and misremembering. *Duke Law Journal, 57*(2), 345–424.

Levinson, J. D., Cai, H., & Young, D. (2010). Guilty by implicit racial bias: The guilty/not guilty implicit association test. *Ohio State Journal of Criminal Law, 8,* 187.

McCurley, M. J., Murphy, K. J., & Gould, J. W. (2005). Protecting children from incompetent forensic evaluations and expert testimony. *Journal of the American Academy of Matrimonial Lawyers, 19,* 277.

Perlin, M. L., & McClain, V. (2009). "Where souls are forgotten": Cultural competencies, forensic evaluations, and international human rights. *Psychology, Public Policy, and Law, 15*(4), 257.

Reddick, M., Nelson, M. J., & Caufield, R. P. (2009). Racial and gender diversity on State Courts: An AJS Study. *Judges' Journal, 48,* 28.

Smith, R. J., & Levinson, J. D. (2012). The impact of implicit racial bias on the exercise of prosecutorial discretion. *Seattle University Law Review, 35*(3), 795–826.

Torres-Spelliscy, C., Chase, M., & Greenman, E. (2010). *Improving Judicial diversity.* Brennan Center for Justice at New York University School of Law http://brennan.3cdn.net/96d16b62f331bb13ac_kfm6bplue.pdf.

Vera, E. M., & Speight, S. L. (2003). Multicultural competence, social justice, and counseling psychology: Expanding our roles. *The Counseling Psychologist, 31*(3), 253–272.

Minorities in the Court System

LEARNING OBJECTIVES

After reading this chapter, students should be able to do the following:

1. Discuss due process and the historical subversion of equal protections for minorities.
2. Identify landmark cases responsible for the modern indigent defense.
3. Identify racial disparities that occur in bail setting procedures.
4. Identify prosecutorial discretion points and discuss how they influence minority disparities.
5. Discuss jury selection and how these procedures affect the outcome of trials.

KEY TERMS

Bail setting

Change of venue

Charge reduction

Conditions of release

Contextual discrimination

Direct

Direct discrimination

Discrimination

Dismissal

Disparity

Due process

Equal Protection Clause

Filing of formal charges

Fourteenth Amendment

Indirect discrimination

Individual discrimination

Initial screenings

Institutional discrimination

Interaction

Interaction effect

Intra-racial phenomenon

Judicial discretion

Jury nullification

Justice

Los Angeles Riots of 1992

Perpetrator

Plea bargaining

Powell v. Alabama

Preemptory challenges

Prima facie

Prosecutorial death discretion outcome

Protective orders

Pure justice

Race of the victim effect

Strain theory

Subtle

Victim

Voir dire

INTRODUCTION

The court system of the United States is set up to ensure due process for all those charged with criminal conduct. **Due process** is a term that means persons are assured all fundamental rights given through the constitution, which include fairness, justice, and liberty for all. This right is asserted in the Fifth Amendment and later reasserted in the Fourteenth Amendment of the Constitution. The intent of due process is that all persons, regardless of race, creed, and color, be treated fairly in all phases of participation in life as a citizen.

Even with these protections existing, due process has not been equally applied to all citizens. In fact, history is littered with examples of minorities being denied fundamental fairness as it relates to the court system. One such example lies in the historical account of the South in the post Civil War Era. During this time period, despite a reaffirmation of individual rights that extended to all persons (expressly to minority groups), states passed constitutional amendments that essentially disenfranchised poor whites and African Americans. In this political climate, minorities were not given fair trials by a jury of peers, were not allowed to serve on juries, and were often subjected to vigilante justice in the form of lynchings (that were not only tolerated but encouraged). Arguably, justice did not begin to prevail for minorities until the Civil Rights movement of the late 1960s.

Despite the further development of minority rights that occurred in the Civil Rights Era, there are remnant disenfranchisements that still greatly impact the courts system. One only need to view the symbols of Southern oppression in the form of confederate flags that are draped in front of many Southern courthouses to know that equal justice within the court system has still not been actualized. These symbols hint at the remnant values and practices that still affect the lives of minorities today. The following chapters will explore the current court system to examine the ways in which minorities remain disenfranchised.

MINORITY DEFENDANTS AND LEGAL REPRESENTATION

The Sixth Amendment of the Constitution states that, "in all criminal prosecutions the accused shall enjoy the right to … have the assistance of counsel for his defense." The framers of the Constitution inserted the right to counsel in the Sixth Amendment in order to avoid the unfair practices of England in which persons were known to be prosecuted for felonies without the benefit of being able to defend themselves. Unfortunately, despite the fact that the actual right to council was authorized, many indigent defendants still were unable to hire representation and the Sixth Amendment makes no explicit provision for indigent defense. As one might imagine, minorities disproportionately were the group most affected by not allowing for indigent defense. All this changed in 1932, with the introduction of the Scottsboro ruling.

Historical Precedence: Scottsboro Case

In 1932, a landmark case would forever decide the fate of indigent defense requirements. The case, formally known as ***Powell v. Alabama***, involved nine African Americans who were accused and subsequently sentenced to death for raping two white women. The details surrounding the alleged rape involved the nine African American men, seven white men, and two white women who were all hoboing on a train bound from Chattanooga to Memphis, TN. Somewhere during the passage, the group of men began fighting, which resulted in all of the white men exiting the train. The white men went to the local sheriff, who immediately assigned a posse to arrest the African American men and rescue the two girls. When the sheriff arrived, the women accused the men of having raped them. The *Scottsboro Boys* were arrested and detained until they faced trial. On the day of the trial, court-appointed attorneys arrived to defend the case. The attorneys had not previously met with the young men or discussed the details of the case. Consequently, eight of the nine men were sentenced to death penalty for their involvement with the alleged rape. The lone juvenile among the men was given life in prison owing to the fact that juveniles could not be sentenced to death.

Powell v. Alabama marked the first time that the Supreme Court ruled on due process (the rights that are attributed to citizens) of sentencing. In the decision, the court ruled that in capital offenses, defendants must be given the right to counsel. As the court found:

> "The right to be heard would be, in many cases, of little avail if it did not comprehend the right to be heard by counsel. Even the intelligent and educated layman has small and sometimes no skill in the science of law. If charged with a crime he is incapable, generally, of determining for himself whether the indictment is good or bad. He is unfamiliar with the rules of evidence. Left without the aid of counsel he may be put on trial without a proper charge, and convicted upon incompetent evidence, or evidence irrelevant to the issue or otherwise inadmissible. He lacks both the skill and knowledge adequately to prepare his defense, even though he has a perfect one. He requires the guiding hand of counsel at every step in the proceedings against him. Without it, though he be not guilty, he faces the danger of conviction because he does not know how to establish his innocence."

Despite the ruling of *Powell v. Alabama*, the right to counsel for indigent defenders would have to wait for more than 30 years until the *Gideon v. Wainwright* decision. This is related to the fact that *Powell* only established the rights of defense in *capital cases*. *Gideon v. Wainwright* would open this right to all criminal cases involving those who could not otherwise afford legal counsel.

Historical Case: *Gideon v. Wainwright*

The facts of the case involved a drifter by the name of Clarence Gideon who had been accused of breaking into a pool hall. A witness was said to have observed Clarence Gideon breaking into the pool room and leaving with money that he had stolen from a cigarette machine. When he presented to the court, Gideon was told that under the state laws of Florida, counsel would not be provided. Gideon, doing the best that he could, defended himself in court only to be sentenced to five years imprisonment. Gideon appealed the decision, noting that his constitutional rights had been violated. The court affirmed this noting that all persons who have been charged with a crime, regardless of education, class, and wealth, have the right to face their accusers with the benefit of counsel.

THE CURRENT INDIGENT DEFENDER SYSTEM

Powell, Gideon, and the subsequent case law created the modern indigent defender process as we know it. Despite the fact that defense is provided for all those who cannot afford their own counsel, there is a litany of problems related to the public defense system that ultimately disadvantages many minorities. First, the public defense system experiences an overall lack of resources. This causes the public defender to be poorly paid (as compared to both the prosecutors and private defense) and to practice without the proper resources in order to research the case. Furthermore, because of the low wages that are paid to public defenders, the office lacks prestige and respect. It is assumed that due to this lack of respect, prosecutors and judges often push around public defenders like "step-children." Low wages also attract newer attorneys who lack experience or else attorneys who lack the skill (having graduated lower in their law school class) of more formidable private attorneys. Second, caseloads of public defenders are excessive to seek justice for defendants adequately. Owing to this, public defenders are assigned late in the trial process and often have too many cases to address the charges lobbied against their clients adequately. The fact that defendants do not meet their attorney until after they have languished in jail for some time (owing to the fact that indigent defendants often cannot post bail) encourages that guilty pleas are accepted.

Minority defendants are more likely than white defendants to enlist the aid of a public defender. It has also been shown in many studies that there is a substantial benefit to enlisting the aid of a private attorney, noting that those with private attorneys are frequently given more lenient sentences. Given the bias of the system, minority defendants know not to trust court-appointed attorneys. This distrust can be found in the various slang names given to the attorneys such as "public pretenders," "dump trucks" (because of their tendencies to dump cases), and "prison delivers/ plea deal" (from the acronym PD for public defender). This perception of inadequate representation is not without merit. For example, it is not uncommon for the attorney not to know the facts of the case when they enter the courtroom, not having had time to review the client's record. As one defendant noted of this process, "My lawyer asked me my name and what I did right when we went up before the judge. I knew I was screwed." Another defendant declared, "The system is a joke. My lawyer just told me to plead guilty when I didn't even do it!"

The empirical evidence of differential treatment of minorities related to indigent counsel is somewhat sketchy. This is because of the numerous confounding variables that are related to the kind of defense enlisted. Some social scientists contend that there is not much difference between a private and public attorney and that public perception does not accurately portray what occurs within the courtroom. These researchers note that public defenders are often more skilled than they are given credit for and that they have the opportunity to forge relationships within the courthouse (because of the time spent within the court confines), which other private attorneys do not have.

CURRENT EVENTS
Racial Disparity in Bail Setting Still Persists

In early 2013, public schools in Atlanta, Georgia revealed that widespread fraud in testing processes had been uncovered, involving 35 teachers throughout the school system (Soave, 2013). Specifically, these teachers were alleged to have changed test scores and to have provided students with correct answers to test questions as a means of improving data related to their teaching performance. Among these educators was the alleged leader of the scam, the school system's superintendent, Dr. Beverly Hall, a long-time educator and African American woman in her 60's, who has a history of correcting broken school systems in New York and New Jersey (Soave, 2013).

As a result of her conduct, Dr. Hall faces up to 40 years in prison (Soave, 2013). The other defendants have been accused of a variety of crimes and face a variety of sentences of differing severity. Further, the bond set for many of these are considered exorbitant, including bond amounts of $1 million for some accomplices and an alarming $7.5 million for Dr. Hall (Chiles, 2013). Because most of the educators are African American and because the bond amounts set are so ridiculously high, some people have accused the court system of racism.

While some might wish to discount these claims of racism, there is evidence of serious disparity in the bail/bond setting process, leading many to perceive this as evidence of racism. Indeed, during the past decade, numerous studies have found that there are significant racial disparities in bail-setting and that these disparities have remained stable over time (Devers, 2011). Likewise, it has been found that bail decision-makers are less likely to trust African American defendants than they are Caucasian defendants, and it is clear that African Americans are much less likely to be released from pre-trial detention than are Caucasian defendants (Devers, 2011; Free, 2002). Further, ethnicity has been found to be related to pretrial release decisions and bail determinations. This is especially true with drug offenses, where Latino Americans are detained much more frequently than are African American or Caucasian defendants (Devers, 2011; Demuth, 2003).

Recent research conducted by the Department of Justice's Bureau of Justice Assistance, found the following:

1. *Judges possess a great deal of discretion in pretrial release / bail decisions.*
2. *For defendants who are not granted pretrial release or whose bail too expensive, there are adverse effects for the defendant on the eventual sentencing outcome.*
3. *The bail decision can and does affect all future stages of the criminal justice process.*
4. *Race, ethnicity, and to a lesser degree gender, have been found to influence decisions related to pretrial release.*

What is interesting about the case of Dr. Beverly Hall is that she is not a typical defendant and, if convicted, is not the typical offender. Indeed, it is highly unlikely that the 66 year old woman would be dangerous to others or that she would be a flight risk (Soave, 2013). Afterall, she does not have a background of violence or criminal activity – she has over 40 years history as a teacher (Soave, 2013). Thus,

it seems absurd to think that she would need to be jailed for a prolonged period of time. Further, she is educated and would know that flight presents no logical options for evading the criminal justice system for any long period of time; the attempt would essentially be silly. Lastly, she is an African American female and is in a system that, according to our previously presented research by the Bureau of Justice Assistance (Devers, 2011) and others, has been proven to have very negative outcomes for minority defendants, namely African Americans. This research (Devers, 2011; Demuth, 2003; Free, 2002) has found this disparity in bail/bond pretrial release processes to be serious for minorities among typical criminal defendants; making it even more suspicious when this same disparity exists for a non-violent, 66 year old, female, African American, school teacher-turned-administrator.

It is perhaps for this reason that, ultimately, at the request of her attorneys, she was released from Fulton County jail with bond set at $200,000 – much lower than the $7.5 million initially recommended by prosecutors (Chiles, 2013). Why such an exorbitant amount had initially even been considered is perplexing. The risks the court faced of having a suit where excessive bail/bond would likely be seen as cruel and unusual punishment, a violation of the 8th Amendment, was at least in part, a likely incentive to lower the amount to something much more reasonable.

References: Devers, L. (2011). Bail decisionmaking: Research summary. Washington, DC: Bureau of Justice Assistance.

Demuth, S. (2003). Racial and ethnic differences in pretrial release decisions and outcomes: A comparison of Hispanic, black, and white felony arrestees. Criminology 41: 873–908.

Free, M. (2002). Race and presentencing decisions in the United States: A summary and critique of the research. Criminal Justice Review 27:203–232.

Chiles, N. (2013, April 01). Beverly Hall to surrender to jail Tuesday in Atlanta cheating scandal. *Atlanta Blackstar.* Retrieved from: http://atlantablackstar.com/2013/04/01/beverly-hall-must-turn-herself-in-by-tuesday-in-atlanta-cheating-scandal/

Soave, R. (2013, April 03). Atlanta teachers' scandal prompts allegations of racism. The Daily Caller. Retrieved from: HYPERLINK "http://dailycaller.com/2013/04/03/atlanta-teachers-scandal-%09prompts-allegations-of-"http://dailycaller.com/2013/04/03/atlanta-teachers-scandal-prompts-allegations-of-racism/

RACIAL MINORITIES AND BAIL-MAKING DECISIONS

Bail setting refers to the process in which the defendant is allowed to be released based on various conditions while awaiting trial. It is the understanding in the bail setting agreement that the defendant will return for trial or else be penalized in some way. At the very least, the defendant failing to return for trial can expect to be charged with the new offense of failure to appear. Frequently, when establishing bails, there are monetary conditions, non-monetary *conditions of release*, and victim *protective orders* assigned. Non-monetary conditions of release involve restrictions of freedom that would assure the court that no further harm occurs to society or else that the person is likely to present for the court date. Examples might be that a person is restricted to a certain

Box 9.1 Terms Related to Court Bail/Bond Setting

Released on Recognizance (ROR) is when one is released on their own recognizance, he or she promises to attend to all of the required judicial proceedings and will not engage in illegal activity or other prohibited conduct. With this form of bail a monetary amount is frequently named, but not collected unless the court orders it to be forfeited. The monetary amount attached to an ROR is sometimes referred to as an *unsecured appearance bond*.

Citation Release (*cite out*) refers to the arresting officer issuing a citation denoting when the defendant must appear in court. This process typically occurs directly after someone is arrested and no monetary bond is required. Typically, citation releases are associated with minor infractions and traffic stops.

Surety Bond—a surety bond is where a third party agrees to be responsible for the debt or obligation of the defendant. In most localities this services is provided by a private commercial bail bondsman. Typically, the bail bonding agency will require 10 percent of the bail amount up front and will retain that amount as a payment regardless if the defendant presents to court or not. In return

for payment, the court agreed to pay the amount of the original bail if the defendant does not show up for court.

Property Bond—this form of bond is set by the defendant pledging real property that has a value in excess of the amount of the monetary bail (often twice the amount of the monetary bail). If the defendant fails to present to trial, the state can institute foreclosure proceeding in order to collect the amount associated with the monetary bond.

Immigration Bond—is a Federal bond in which an illegal alien is the defendant. In this form of bond, 15–20 percent of the original bail is posted in order to be released. These persons usually deal directly with the Department of Homeland Security and the Bureau of Immigration and Custom Enforcement.

Cash Bond (*cash only*)—is a bond in which persons are only allowed to issue bail with cash funds. This form of bail making is often reserved for persons who are at high flight risk. If the person completes all required appearances, then the amount of the bond is refunded to the defendant.

geographic location or else is not allowed to use drugs or alcohol while awaiting trial. Protective orders refer to conditions designed to protect the alleged victims of crimes from further injury. Examples may include an order issued in a domestic violence case that does not allow the defendant to have contact with the alleged victim. There are several different forms of bail conditions for which a defendant may be allowed to be released (see Box at 9.1).

According to the Eighth Amendment of the U.S. Constitution, no defendant should be required to make an excessive bail. In the attempt to ensure that no excessive bails are set (particularly for minority defendants), many jurisdictions use fee schedules and are built around the type of offense, prior history, and risk for continued harm to the community. Other times, judges exercise judicial discretion. *Judicial discretion* means that judges are afforded the opportunity to take in multiple sources of information in order to make decision rather than to be bound by guideline and rules. It is when judicial discretion is applied that the opportunity for racial bias enters into bail setting decisions.

The exercise of judicial discretion in bail making has found that race affects the outcome of decisions, causing minorities to be treated unfavorably. One hypothesis about why minorities suffer disparate treatment in bail setting is that judges may stereotype these defendants believing that they are more threatening or at greater risk for flight. However, considerations of threat to the community are primarily dealt with through crime considerations and prior history. Even when these factors are removed from the equation, racial disparities still exist. Concomitantly, minorities have been shown to be at reduced risk for flight as compared to whites. Despite this, when judicial discretion is involved, minorities experience bail-determination discriminations.

BAIL DISCRIMINATIONS

There are essentially two ways in which race can impact the bail-making decision, these are related to (1) who is allowed to have an ROR bond and (2) the amount of monetary bail required. Being granted an ROR bond provides the defendant a significant advantage, in that no monetary bail is required up-front and the defendant is free pretrial. Being released pretrial gives the defendant a significant advantage in being able to defend him/herself at trial. Released defendants have better opportunities to prepare for the trial and are more likely to be seen in a favorable light by the judge and jury. Because of this, released defendants have been known to receive more lenient sentencing. Conversely, detained defendants suffer what is known as a detention penalty.

If one is not afforded the opportunity to ROR, then a monetary bail comes into play to decide whether the defendant achieves release pretrial or not. The amount of bail set can be a main determinant in whether a person achieves release, in that they may not have the resources to make bail. Minorities, because of their increased likelihood of experiencing poverty, frequently have difficulty making bail. This difficulty is compounded when the amount of bail is inflated beyond what might be an affordable level for the defendant (Ayres & Waldfogel, 1994). In some jurisdictions, African Americans are known to have 70 percent higher bonds set than white defendants (some of the difference may be related to severity of the crime and other factors). Even when controlling for type of crime and prior history, racial minorities are known to receive higher bail amounts, thus increasing dramatically their chances of experiencing pretrial detainment.

Hispanic groups are known to suffer the harshest treatments of all races as it relates to bail setting. Research has shown that Hispanics experience disparities on two points: first, Hispanics (like African Americans) are more likely than whites to be denied release. Second, Hispanics are less likely than either whites or African Americans to be released on ROR conditions. Compounding the fact that Hispanics are more likely than whites or African Americans to be released on monetary bail is the fact that, when bail is set, the amounts are frequently higher than other racial groups. This makes the likelihood of pretrial detention much greater than other racial groups.

INTERNATIONAL FOCUS

The Courts and Religious Offenses around the World.

According to the United States Commission on International Freedom (USCIF), many countries around the globe have laws that punish – what are alleged to be - blasphemous actions. The USCIF also points out that these laws are incompatible with international human rights standards adopted by the United Nations. The UN Human Rights Committee has chastised these nations and asked that they repeal these laws, in some cases, to no avail.

Around the world, incidents related to religious freedom of expression have resulted in court decisions, even in countries that are considered industrialized. For instance, consider that in Poland, during a concert by heavy-metal rock musician, Adam "Nergal" Darski, the Supreme Court of that country, in 2012, reversed an acquittal on criminal charges for "offending religious feelings" by destroying a Bible and speaking against the Catholic Church during a performance (USCIF, 2013). The lower trial court had found him not guilty, contending that he had engaged in artistic expression during the concert – the Polish prosecutors appealed the trial court's decision. As a result, the Supreme Court agreed to rule on the case and held that an individual may be convicted of offending religious sentiments – even if this was not their intent – in circumstances where it is reasonable to think that they should have known that their actions might be offensive to others, regardless of their intent. This case will be re-examined at the trial court level, again, with penalties being potential fines, other sanctions, and even 2 years in prison.

In Pakistan, the enforcement of blasphemy laws have resulted in the detention of a Christian girl who is accused of burning several pages of the Quran (Sayah & Habib, 2012). A Muslim cleric accused the 14 year old girl of desecrating the Quran, contending that she should be punished, regardless of her age (Sayah & Habib, 2012). The penalty for blasphemy is death in Pakistan.

The young girl was initially jailed but Judge Muhammad Azam Khan, ordered her to be released on bail after hearing arguments from both the prosecution (who carried forward the Muslim cleric's accusation as if they were fact) as well as arguments provided by the defense (Sayah & Habib, 2012). Upon her release, armored cars and helicopters were used to return her home due to concerns for her safety.

Though multiple nations, including Canada, Italy, and the United States have offered temporary refuge, the family of the accused has decided to stay in their native Pakistan.

A neighbor had accused the girl of burning the pages but did not actually observe the occurrence (Sayah & Habib, 2012). Rather, the girl had used paper as fodder to start a fire for cooking, but the paper was not necessarily pages from the Quran. Once word got out in the community, rumors persisted that the girl had, as a fact, burned pages from the Quran and an angry mob gathered at the family's house; the girl was then jailed (Sayah & Habib, 2012).

However, the case turned out to consist of conspiracy and intrigue... as it was later revealed that the pages were not from the Quran and that, upon receiving the neighbor's report, the local Muslim cleric, Khalid Jadoon Chishti, was concerned that insufficient evidence would exist; he then decided to include a few pages of a Quran with the charred remnants of paper used as evidence against the girl (Sayah & Habib, 2012). This obvious act of deceit and the filing of untrue charges is illegal according to Muslim law and, as a result, the imam is now facing blasphemy charges for taking pages out of the Quran when attempting to frame the young girl (Sayah & Habib, 2012).

In Pakistan, as with many Middle Eastern countries, religion serves as the basis of the nation's legal system. This system of law, known as Sharia, extends the precepts of the Quran into all matters of law, including business deals, health and safety, as well as criminal law (Dammer & & Albanese, 2012; Reichel, 2012). Sharia law comes from a number of sources with the Quran being the most important source. Sharia governs all aspects of a Muslim's life, including day-to-day routine interactions at home and at work. There is no separation of church and state in countries governed under Sharia, making theses nations theocracies (governments whose basis resides upon a religious system). Thus, the intermixing of religious condemnation and criminal prosecution is a routine and normal process in these nations, unlike nations where secular systems are maintained (Dammer & & Albanese, 2012; Reichel, 2012).

References: Sayah, R. & Habib, N. (2012, September 9). Pakistani Christian girl accused of blasphemy released on bail. CNN News Pulse, retrieved from http://www.cnn.com/2012/09/08/world/asia/pakistan-girl-blasphemy/index.html?iref=storysearch

United States Commission on International Freedom (2013). Annual report 2013. Washington, DC: U. S. Commission on International Freedom.

Dammer, H. R. & Albanese, J. (2012). Comparative Criminal Justice Systems (5th Edition). Publisher: Wadsworth.

Reichel, P. (2012). Comparative Criminal Justice Systems: A Topical Approach (6th Ed.). Upper Saddle River, NJ: Prentice Hall.

PROSECUTORIAL DISCRETION

There is perhaps no single place in the legal process that has a greater opportunity for creation of disparities and discrimination than that of the **filing of formal charges**. The prosecutor of a crime (frequently known as the district attorney or attorney general) has the sole discretion in deciding whether a case will have criminal charges brought and what charges will be pursued in a case. With this authority, prosecutors have the discretion to reject charges outright if they feel that there is a lack of evidence, the case

Box 9.2 Jena Six and the Filing of Excessive Charges

The prosecutor is perhaps the most influential person in a criminal case. The prosecutor determines whether to bring charges and the severity of those charges. Once more, the prosecutor acts alone in making these initial decisions. Owing to the powerful role played by the prosecutor and the lack of checks and balances, the possibility for racism entering into decisions is great.

One example of where race was alleged to have entered into the filing of formal charges was that of the Jena Six Case. The Jena Six were six black teenagers from Jena, Louisiana, convicted of beating Justin Barker, a white student, on December 4, 2006. The events that led up to the beating were filled with racial conflict, noting that tensions had mounted due to white students not allowing black students to sit under a certain tree on the Jena High School campus. Jena High School (represented by 90 percent white students and 10 percent African American students) students observed a tradition where African American students sat on the bleachers whereas white students sat under the "white tree" or "prep tree." According to reports, an African American student requested the principal to sit under the "white tree."

Following this request, nooses were hung from the white tree left as a threatening sign to black students. Tensions escalated further when two physical altercations broke out between white and black students, finally culminating with the assault of Barker.

In response to the assault of Barker, the DA in the case charged the ringleader of the Jena Six—Mychal Bell, and his codefendants with attempted murder. Once more, the then 16-year-old Mychal Bell was charged as an adult assuring that, if convicted, the teen could receive over 100 years in prison. The severity of these charges, combined with the known racial conflict, amounted to what many described as a "modern-day lynching."

In response to the severity of charges, 20,000 protestors descended on Jena. The result of these protests was that the charges against the Jena Six (except for Bell) were eventually reduced to simple battery. Mychal Bell, who was initially convicted on aggravated battery and conspiracy to commit battery, later had his conviction thrown out by an Appellate Court, who noted that Bell should have been tried as a juvenile. Bell ultimately received the simple battery charge as his codefendants.

is trivial, or if they feel that it would not be in the interest of justice to pursue the case. The prosecutor also has the ability to change the formal charges from a felony and prosecute the defendant under a misdemeanor offense.

The ability to charge is especially relevant as it relates to crimes that have minimal sentencing guidelines. Prosecutorial discretion allows the prosecutor to charge a crime with a minimal standard, therefore taking the ability to sentence away from the judge. This, in essence, allows the prosecutor to have a greater role in judicial outcomes than either the judge or the jury.

The rules that govern a prosecutor's discretion, although broad, are not limitless. Before charges are filed, the prosecutor must establish probable cause that the defendants committed the offense for which they are accused. In addition, the Supreme Court has established protections regarding the decision to prosecute, observing that it may not be "deliberately based upon an unjustifiable standard such as race, religion, or other arbitrary classification." In other words, the prosecutor cannot use race as a reason to pursue charges or as a way to determine the seriousness of those charges to be filed.

There are essentially five discretion points in which prosecutorial bias could affect the outcome of a criminal prosecution. These are: (1) initial screening, (2) dismissal, (3) charge reduction, (4) plea bargaining, and (5) sentencing. These points make up a continuum (see Figure 9-1), where decisions are made that can affect the outcome of sentencing, and therefore cannot be understood in isolation. In other words, one simply cannot look at the outcome of whether one racial group was charged with a crime or not, because it is possible that at a later time, the charge that was made was reduced to a lesser penalty. The following chapters will explore the prosecutorial continuum and discuss the effects of racial bias on each of the decision points.

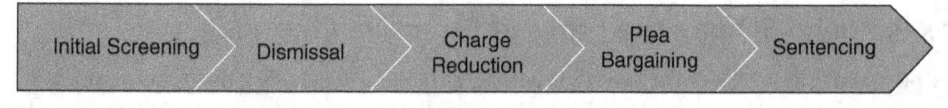

FIGURE 9-1 Prosecutorial Discretion Points

Initial Screenings

The **initial screening** is when the prosecutor screens the case and decides whether to accept the case for prosecution and, in some instances, how to charge the offense. As one might imagine, this is a critical place where, if discrimination were present on the part of the prosecutor, race would affect whether the crime was charged or dropped. Interestingly, in the majority of studies where purport racial differences occurred as it relates to the initial screening, being part of a minority racial group actually enhanced the likelihood of charges being dismissed or receiving a more favorable charge (Wooldredge, 2011). The exception to this is when the victim was from a nonminority group. The *race of the victim effect* is said to be responsible for both the decision to charge and the severity of the charge as it relates to racial minorities committing and offenses against whites. It is noteworthy, however, that many of these studies that measured the race of the victim effect were performed in the mid- to late 1970s, where there were more distinct racial divisions. Some researchers have concluded that the race of the victim effect, as it relates to the initial screening process, is no longer as pronounced or else does not exist at all given today's more accepting view of minorities.

Dismissal

At any point in the prosecution of a case, charges can be dismissed against a defendant. **Dismissal** of charges may be viewed on a continuum in which the severity of criminal involvement is reduced through the cancelation of one or multiple charges. Dismissal of the case would mean completely dropping charges filed against the defendant.

The significance of this process as it relates to minority defendants is that there is potential for giving white defendants more favorable dismissal conditions. However, even though one might expect that white defendants might be treated preferentially with regard to the dismissal of charges, actually the opposite is true. Wooldredge and Thistlewaite (2006), in their study of domestic violence, found that African Americans and those from low-income neighborhoods were less likely than whites to have their cases fully prosecuted. The exception to this seems to be in the southern United States where African Americans are less likely to have their cases dismissed than whites.

Charge Reduction

Charge reduction refers to the process by which a prosecutor can reduce charges to a more favorable set of charges. This frequently involves the reduction of felony charges to misdemeanor charges. This process is highly desirable for defendants in that their likelihood of facing a prison sentence is likely nullified.

Of the studies available that examined charge reduction for minority defendants, results have been mixed. For example, Farnworth, Teske, and Thurman (1995) found that whereas blacks were somewhat less likely than whites to have charges reduced, even greater disparities were found between Hispanics and whites. Similarly, O'Neill-Shermer and Johnson found that minority defendants were less likely than white defendants to have charges reduced. This was particularly true when examining weapon charges for minorities, noting that black and Hispanic defendants were less likely than whites to have charges reduced when weapons were involved.

Hispanic defendants were more likely to have charges reduced as related to drug offenses. Although this may appear contrary to what had been initially asserted that Hispanics receive the least-favorable charge reductions of all racial groups, researchers have concluded that reduction of drug charges might have been related to the severity of the original charge. Under this reasoning, Hispanics only received more favorable charge reduction because of the particular severity of the initial drug charge.

Other studies have found no effect of race and ethnicity on charge reduction procedures. Albonetti (2009) found that a suspect's race did not affect charge reduction decision for 400 burglary and robbery suspects between 1979 and 1980.Similarly, Spohn and Horney found that a victim's race did not affect the decision to reduce the severity of the defendant's sexual assault charges.

Plea Bargaining

Plea bargaining is the step in the prosecution of the case where a defendant has the opportunity to reduce or drop charges in exchange for a guilty plea. To date there are few studies examining the racial characteristics of offering and accepting plea bargains. Moreover, of those few studies that do exist there is controversy as to how race and ethnicity play into those decisions. One such study that examined 683,513 criminal cases in California noted that "Whites were more successful at getting charges either reduced or dropped, in avoiding enhancement or extra charges, and in getting diversion, probation or fines instead of incarceration."

JURY SELECTION AND MINORITIES

"Almost every case has been won or lost when the jury is sworn."
—CLARENCE DARROW

The swearing-in of the jury is perhaps the most critical time during any trial. Prosecutors and defending attorneys alike understand that the juror's life experiences and circumstances have great bearing on the verdict. Given this acknowledgment, there is great scrutiny on the actual selection of the jury. Jury selection begins with choosing a jury pool from the jurisdiction in which the trial will occur. This pool of potential jurors will be selected from a reasonably random method of selecting residents from the community. Trials are generally held in the jurisdiction where the crime occurred; however, there can be arguments held to move the trial to a different location—known as a **change of venue**. Changes of venue are generally performed because of fear that a fair and impartial jury could not be selected in the current venue. This is particularly true when the case is a high-profile one, in which a majority of the residents know the details of the case and may have already formulated their belief about guilt or innocence. It is important to consider the particular venue in which trials are held because minority defendants may be not be represented on the jury, thus altering the outcome of the case.

One such case is that of the famous Rodney King police brutality trials. Rodney King was an African American man who was a victim of police brutality filmed by an amateur photographer. Four police officers were eventually charged and stood trial for the assault. On April 29, 1992 when the verdict was read, despite there being videotaped evidence, all four police officers were acquitted. The acquittals of the police officers provoked the **Los Angeles Riots of 1992**.

Changes in venue allowed for the police officers to be tried in the Simi Valley rather than Los Angeles where the crime occurred. Simi Valley is predominantly white and, consequently, all known jurors selected were white. Following the reading of the verdict, *Time Magazine* produced a survey questioning the public what they thought of the trial verdict. Sixty eight percent of respondents believed that officers were guilty and 89 percent of African Americans polled believed that if any jurors had been African American then the verdict would have been different.

Similarly, the famous OJ Simpson Trial rendered an equally flawed verdict, which also seemed to be based on racial biases of the jury. OJ Simpson, famous athlete and movie star, was charged with the deaths of his ex-wife and her lover (Nicole Brown and Ron Goldman). In the OJ trial, a change of venue was requested from Santa Monica (where the crime occurred) to downtown Los Angeles. Santa Monica is predominantly white whereas downtown Los Angeles has a more diverse minority population. The result was a jury makeup that had 60 percent minority representation versus a jury that would have likely been all white. Arguably, given the breadth of evidence available in the trial and because OJ was actually held liable for the deaths of Brown and Goldman in a civil suit, OJ would likely been found guilty by a predominantly white jury. Many legal scholars agree that the change of venue secured by OJ's attorneys was the single most significant event that insured his acquittal. The research similarly concludes that African American defendants are more likely to receive acquittals when African American representation is present and more likely to be charged in all-white juries.

It is of little doubt that the geographic region in which a trial is held, because of its inherent racial and ethnic makeups, affects the outcome of trials. Location, however, is not the only way that the racial makeup of the jury can be affected. The formal process of jury selection through questioning of potential jurors can also influence who sits on a jury.

Voir Dire

The questioning of potential jurors occurs through a legal process known as *voir dire*. The term *voir dire* comes from the Latin phrase (verum dicere) meaning "to tell the truth." *Voir dire* originally referred to the oath that jurors took before listening to the arguments. *Voir dire*, in the common use, refers to the selection process by which jurors are questioned in order to determine certain biases. Through this process, both the prosecutor and the defendant attorneys are allowed to question potential jurors and eliminate a set number of jurors from the selection pool. The process of eliminating potential jurors is initiated through the use of **preemptory challenges**. A set equal number of preemptory challenges are given to both the prosecution and defense in order that potential jurors can be eliminated from the selection pool for perceived biases that they may hold. In this manner, both the prosecution and defense teams have an equal opportunity to influence the final jury in order to ensure a fair verdict.

As one might imagine, in order "to stack" juries to have more favorable outcomes, racial minorities have often been the target of preemptory challenges. In jurisdictions where there was a very light distribution of minority groups, the likelihood of selection for a jury pool would have been equally low. Prosecutors could use preemptory challenges to negate these minority participants, and therefore ensure a more likely verdict with an "all-white jury."

Before 1986 and the landmark case, *Batson v. Kentucky*, there were few protections to ensure that racial stacking did not occur in the jury selection process. *Batson v. Kentucky* (1986) was a case settled by the Supreme Court that asserted that a prosecutor exercising a preemptory challenge could not be used to dismiss jurors solely related to race. In this case, James Batson, the defendant, appealed a burglary conviction, noting that jurors had been dismissed from the jury pool based on racial grounds, thus denying fair representation as asserted by the **Equal Protection Clause** of the **Fourteenth Amendment**. A previous Court ruling, *Swain v. Alabama* (1965), had ruled that the burden of proof remained with the defendant to show that there was a systematic attempt to deny minority representation through the use of preemptory challenges, thus making claims of racial stacking very difficult to prove. Batson overturned this ruling, noting that the defendant could make a **prima facie** case (as seen on face value) that purposeful racial discrimination occurred during the jury selection process. The result of *Batson v. Kentucky* sparked the most common grounds for appeals known as the "Batson challenge." Batson challenges assert that due to unfair jury selection, the outcomes of trail decisions are invalid. Since the 1986 ruling, Batson has also been applied to gender claims but it was not affirmed in sexual orientation claims (*J.E.B. v. Alabama ex rel. T.B., U.S. v. Blaylock*).

JURY NULLIFICATION

In reaction to the corruption that existed in jury selections as well as the disparity in African American sentencing, some individuals who were tasked to serve on a jury began to engage in acts of jury nullification. **Jury nullification** is when jurors collectively decide to ignore the technicalities of the law when coming to a verdict in a criminal case and, instead, vote with their conscience, owing to a belief that the law or the punishment being considered is inappropriate, unfair, or extreme. Jury nullification has actually existed throughout history, even dating back to the days of old England prior to the founding of the United States colonies. However, in America, it was during alcohol prohibition that this process became a widely known concept, when juries commonly refused to enforce laws outlawing alcohol. For example, in New York between 1929 and 1930, 60 percent of alcohol-related prosecutions ended in acquittal (Parmenter, 2007). Indeed, the refusal of juries to convict in alcohol cases helped hasten the prohibition's repeal.

During the 1960s and the 1970s, America again found itself in the midst of controversies that inspired acts of jury nullification. Even in the absence of nullification instructions or argument, juries in the South too often refused to convict whites accused of violence against blacks and civil rights workers. However, the judiciary and public gave more attention to efforts made at promoting nullification in a number of cases involving Vietnam War protests. These cases, sometimes called "the Vietnam War resister cases," usually had similar facts. The government would prosecute antiwar activists who had violated the law in acts of civil disobedience. The defense would request a nullification instruction, and the court would refuse to give one. These instructions were often given in response to creative defense tactics that sought to encourage the jury to use their conscience to acquit the defendant (Parmenter, 2007).

Box 9.3 Racism and Jury Selection: The Supreme Court Case of *Miller-El v. Cockrell*

In the 2003 Supreme Court case *Miller-El v. Cockrell*, the Supreme Court ruled by a vote of 6–3 in favor of Miller-El that he should have the opportunity to prove that his death sentence was the result of discriminatory jury practices. Such practices included the so-called "Texas shuffle" to limit or eliminate African American jurors. Other practices included disparate questioning of potential jurors based on race, and a training memo instructing prosecutors on ways to skew juries based on race. In choosing a jury to try Miller-El, a black defendant, prosecutors struck 10 of the 11 qualified black panelists. The Supreme Court said the prosecutors' chosen race-neutral reasons for the strikes were suspicious and concluded that the selection process was replete with evidence that prosecutors were selecting and rejecting potential jurors because of race.

Justice Souter, writing for the majority, set out the evidence that race governed who was allowed on the jury, including disparate questioning of white and black jurors, jury shuffling, a culture of bias within the prosecutor's office, and the fact that the prosecutor's race-neutral explanations for the strikes were so far at odds with the evidence that the explanations themselves indicate discriminatory intent.

Prior to this, in 2002, the Court had reversed a ruling from the lower federal court of appeals (the 5th Circuit) that concluded that Miller-El had not provided sufficient evidence to obtain a habeas corpus appeal (habeas corpus, as students may recall, is an appeal that inmates can file after they are convicted and while in jail or prison). In this earlier ruling, the High Court voted 8–1 that the lower court had implemented a "dismissive and strained interpretation" of critical facts that ensured that claims of discrimination could not be sufficiently supported by Miller-El. In other words, the Supreme Court pointedly held that the 5th Circuit Court of Appeals had been unrealistic and biased in its decision. Therefore, the Supreme Court reversed this ruling with the issue revolving around standards for obtaining a habeas corpus appeal under the Anti-Terrorism and Effective Death Penalty Act of 1996. According to the 5th Circuit, this act required that the inmate provide clear and convincing evidence (about an 80 percent likelihood) of a Constitutional violation before a Certificate of Appeal would be granted. However, the Supreme Court ruled that courts of appeal should limit their examination to a simple threshold inquiry (perhaps around a 25 percent likelihood), much less than the clear and convincing standard.

Consistent with prior rulings, the High Court noted that inmates must only demonstrate "a substantial showing of the denial of a constitutional right" in order to obtain an appeal. Providing a substantial showing only requires that the inmate demonstrate that jurists of reason could disagree with the lower court's decision regarding his constitutional claims. In considering the merit of Miller-El's claims of racial discrimination, the Supreme Court noted that Miller-El's criticism of the prosecution's use of jury shuffling had merit. This practice permitted parties to rearrange the order in which potential jurors were examined so as to increase the likelihood that visually preferable candidates would be selected. With no information about the prospective jurors other than their appearance, the party requesting the procedure literally shuffled the juror cards, and the members were then reseated in the new order. This shuffling process affected jury composition because any prospective jurors not questioned were dismissed and a new panel of jurors appears the following week. Thus, jurors who were shuffled to the back of the panel were less likely to be questioned and hence are less likely to serve on the jury.

On at least two occasions the prosecution requested shuffles when there was a predominate number of African Americans in the front of the panel. On yet another occasion the prosecutors complained about the purported inadequacy of the card shuffle by a defense lawyer but lodged a formal objection only after the post-shuffle panel composition revealed that African American prospective jurors had been moved forward.

Furthermore, the Court seemingly contradicted its own prior rulings in *McClesky v. Kemp* (1987) by pointing toward statistical data to support its concern with the practices of prosecutors in the Texas court system. The Court said that:

In this case, the statistical evidence alone raises some debate as to whether the prosecution acted with a race-based reason when striking prospective jurors. The prosecutors used their peremptory strikes to exclude 91 percent of the eligible African-American venire members, and only one served on petitioner's jury. In total, 10 of the prosecutors' 14 peremptory strikes were used against African-Americans. Happenstance is unlikely to produce this disparity.

The Court stated that the Texas courts' finding of no discrimination smacked of reality and was both unreasonable and erroneous. The facts and circumstances of the case determined that the Texas courts were, indeed, racially biased, resulting in a reversal of the lower court's rulings and granting Miller-El legal relief and a new trial.

Source: Miller-El v. Cockrell (01-7662) 537 U.S. 322 (2003). Cornell University Law School. Retrieved from: http://www.law.cornell.edu/supct/html/4.ZO.html.

During the 1990s, racial tensions, controversial verdicts, and harsh criminal laws swirled together, forming a storm of media and academic attention focused on jury nullification (Parmenter, 2007). The storm began in January 1990, when the FBI conducted a drug sting on the enormously popular black mayor of Washington, D.C., Marion Barry. Prosecutors charged Mayor Barry with conspiracy to possess cocaine, possession of cocaine, and perjury for lying to a grand jury. Before his trial, Mayor Barry proclaimed the prosecution racist and declared his hope that he would be acquitted in an act of jury nullification. The trial drew an enormous amount of media attention. Although Barry was convicted on one count of perjury, the public widely viewed his acquittal on the cocaine charges as an act of jury nullification by a jury composed of a majority of African Americans.

In 1995, the most famous and recent alleged act of jury nullification occurred when a predominantly black jury returned a not guilty verdict in the O.J. Simpson trial (Parmenter, 2007). During the closing arguments of Simpson's defense, his attorney, Johnnie Cochran, seemed to implore the jury to flex their nullification power, arguing:

> You ... police the Police. You police them by your verdict. You are the ones to send the message. Nobody else is going to do it in this society. They don't have the courage. Nobody has the courage. They have a bunch of people running around with no courage to do what is right, except individual citizens. You ... are the ones in war; you are the ones on the front line.

While we can probably never determine, for a fact, whether the jury acquitted Simpson to send a message against police bias and corruption as opposed to the possibility that the prosecution did not prove its case beyond a reasonable doubt, it was nevertheless a verdict that drew sensational attention and serious criticism throughout the United States. Critics of the outcome implied that African American jurors had tainted the justice system by allowing their biased distrust of the police and prosecutors into their decision-making or that they were, at the very least, overly sympathetic to African American defendants (Parmenter, 2007).

There has, during the past decade, been a backlash from the judiciary, against jury nullification (Parmenter, 2007). Allegations that judges have omitted options for jurors exist (Parmenter, 2007). In addition, there are some cases where jurors who engage in this process are, themselves, given legal sanctions by some courts. Some legal scholars believe that this is inappropriate and unconstitutional, citing historical precedent of this practice and its continued use (albeit rare) in court cases. Whether this practice is a means of correcting an unfair system and whether this approach does more harm than good is a matter of debate. It does, nevertheless, show how the courtroom has served as a war field regarding racial issues and the judiciary.

DISPARITY AND DISCRIMINATION IN SENTENCING PROCEDURES

When exploring the differential treatment that many minorities experience with regard to sentencing, two terms are used to describe that dissimilar treatment—disparity and discrimination. Although they may be used interchangeably at times, the terms have two very different and distinct meanings. A **disparity** refers to an unequal accounting in a sentencing category that can be distinguished by minority status. A common disparity that is known to exist is the number of African Americans who receive prison sentences. This means that African Americans, as compared to their makeup in the general population, are sentenced more often to prison than any other race. Examining these differences helps researchers begin to parse out the reasons for the differential treatment with regard to sentencing.

Disparities may or may not be attributed to preferential or detrimental treatments by the judicial system; in fact, they could be related to the offender behavior rather than to some overt prejudice of the system. For example, one reason why African Americans are disproportionately imprisoned is related to the types of offences committed and the history of criminal offense prior to sentencing. Sometimes referred to as "double trouble," having a criminal history and committing a more severe crime (e.g., violent crime involving a weapon) increase precipitously the likelihood of being imprisoned. In this vein of thinking, one cannot understand disparities as existing simply related to unfair treatment that is built into the system, but through a number of mutually supporting effects that increase the likelihood of imprisonment.

Juxtaposed, **discrimination** is the preferential or detrimental treatment of the defendant, based on race, ethnicity, or gender. Discrimination can be present in institutional practices or can be overt favoritism based on the biases of the judge. Discrimination of the institutional kind is related to laws, systems, and rules being put in place that favor or disfavor one group over another. For example, the Federal government prescribes different sentencing guidelines for persons found to be in possession of crack cocaine as compared to those possessing powder cocaine. Chemically, powder and crack cocaine are identical and the only difference is the route of administration for each substance. Crack cocaine is frequently smoked and inhaled, whereas powder is frequently snorted. Related to the route of administration, cocaine has a faster action than powder cocaine; however, each affects the brain in very similar ways (e.g., increased production of dopamine). Crack cocaine, because of its relatively low street value and concentrated drug effects, is more often sold in poor minority communities. Because of its prevalence in these communities, the net effect of the Federal guideline governing crack cocaine is that minorities (frequently African Americans) are sentenced to longer sentences. Arguably, although perhaps not intentional, this differential treatment of the same substance equates to discrimination.

DISCRIMINATION CONTINUUM

Walker et al. (2007) noted that discrimination occurred on a continuum. The beginning point of the continuum is known as **pure justice** (See Figure 9-2). Pure justice represents the ideal for sentencing practices, noting that it is the point in which all sentencing practices are devoid of discriminatory practice. It is seen as the point where all societies should strive. The second point on the continuum is known as Institutional Discrimination.

Institutional discrimination represents the point on the continuum that represents the difference in outcomes or treatment based on the different policies and procedures that have been established. For example, North Carolina sentencing guidelines allow for the consideration if a defendant is gainfully employed. This special

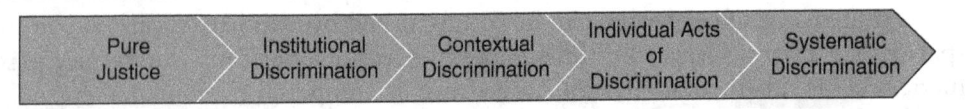

FIGURE 9-2 Pure Justice and Types of Discrimination

consideration invariably will affect minorities differently due to structural differences that are common to many minority communities (e.g., heightened unemployment, lack of employment, lack of employable skills). The third segment of the continuum is known as **contextual discrimination**.

Contextual discrimination refers to discrimination that is not systematic in that it differs depending on regional characteristic stages of the decision-making process, type of crimes, or defendants with particular characteristics. For example, assigning death penalty for murder when controlling for type of crime, prior criminal history occurs seemingly as often for minorities as for whites. This is not true when considering the race of the victim. When a minority kills a white victim, the odds of receiving the death penalty become inflated. Individual discrimination occurs when particular criminal justice officials insert their own racial bias into the case. For example, if a particular judge were to punish persons of a particular race more harshly, this would be a case of **individual discrimination**. In the case with individual discrimination, the acts themselves seem to be isolated from the judicial system at large. Given this, one could expect that the cases of discrimination would be isolated and limited in scope. The final form of discrimination involves the use of discriminatory practices that occur at all stages of sentencing across all times. Unlike contextual and individual discriminations, the act of discrimination is more pronounced, and not limited to nuanced parts of a particular practice, and across multiple jurisdictions. An example of this form of discrimination lies in the once-held laws that allowed for the death penalty in cases of rape. Of the 453 men executed for rape in between the years of 1930 and 1976, 405 were African American.

Walker, Spohn, and DeLone (2007), further distinguish between **direct**, **subtle**, and **interaction** effects in discriminatory practices. **Direct discrimination** refers to when the discriminatory act can be directly related to race. An example of this is that Black and Hispanic Americans have a higher probability of being incarcerated than do white Americans, even when all parameters involved in crime are matched. **Indirect discrimination** refers to race, ethnicity, and gender affecting the sentencing outcome through some third factor. An example of indirect discrimination is that minorities are frequently held in jail before trial because of an inability to post bail. The fact that one is detained pre-sentencing becomes an indirect discriminatory factor that affects the outcome of sentencing. The final form of discriminatory effect is called the **interaction effect**. This effect accounts for severity of sentencing, that is some factor that interacts with race. For example, African Americans are known to use illegal substances at roughly the same rate as whites. However, when being sentenced for drug crimes, African Americans ultimately get harsher sentences.

CRIME AS AN INTRA-RACIAL PHENOMENON

Victims of crime disproportionately come from poor communities. Although whites outnumber all other groups of the "poor," minorities disproportionately experience poverty and thus disproportionately are victims of crime. Because of this, both African Americans and Hispanic Americans are more likely than whites to become the victims of property and violent crimes.

When crimes are committed against victims, it is most often by a person from the same race. This has led criminologists to conclude that crime is mostly an *intra-racial phenomenon*. This stands to reason because people from similar racial, ethnic, and economic backgrounds frequently live in close proximity to persons from like backgrounds. Crime, as asserted by the **strain theory**, results from structural problems such as poverty, lack of employment, and lack of education or opportunity, thereby increasing the likelihood for minority involvement (both as offender and as victim).

A fallacy when examining defendant treatment within the criminal justice system is to assume that just because minority defendants receive a more favorable outcome within a stage of prosecution, that there was in fact no disparity present. This is a one-sided argument, in that it does not consider outcomes for both the **perpetrator** and the **victim** of the crime. The race of the victim of the crime has been shown ultimately to have a greater influence on the decision to charge and the outcome of sentences than the defendant's race. One might assume that this means prosecutors and judges often align themselves with the victim and thus carry out justice on their behalf. The question remains whether minority victims receive **justice** as do white victims. The research seems to conclude that minority victims are not defended as thoroughly as white victims.

The value of human life: One might argue that the reason for this differential treatment of minority victims as compared to white victims is the perceived value of human life that society has imposed. People of white skin color, as imposed by institutional racism, are seen as being more valuable than people of dark skin color. Given this context, is society less concerned about crime that occurs in minority communities because they are seen as having less value? An argument could be made that law enforcement and the judicial system only get involved in minority communities in order to prevent the spread of crime to more valuable nonminority communities. In addition, if the crime rates that exist in minority communities were somehow transplanted to nonminority neighborhoods, society would find an answer for these problems. It might be concluded that society's lack of answers for crime problems in minority neighborhoods is a silent agreement that nothing needs to be done.

MINORITY SENTENCING ISSUES

There is clear evidence of disparities in minority sentencing. The first form of evidence of disparity sentencing lies in the distinction between who is sentenced to prison and who ultimately afforded a lesser punishment. The second form of evidence comes from the multiple studies of judicial sentencing practices. What has been revealed in both cases is that Black and Hispanic offenders receive harsher sentencing than white offenders. Black offenders, on average, received almost double the length of sentences as did whites, and Hispanics received lengths of sentences that were almost 1.5 times those of whites.

There have been four identified reasons for the disparities in sentencing. First, minority offenders are more likely than whites to commit more serious offenses and have a more extensive criminal history than those of white Americans. Minorities are more likely to be involved in violent crimes that involve weapons and therefore are more likely to receive mandated sentences regarding these factors. Second, there are differences that are a result of economic discriminations. These discriminations involve not being able to afford a private attorney, not being able to afford bail, or taking a charge in order to avoid lengthier prison sentencing. Judges are also known to look more favorably on defendants who are employed and have resources. Third, there is evidence of direct discrimination on the part of judges. Once all factors of type of crime and prior history are controlled for, discrimination still exists simply because of bias that the judge may have against the defendant. Finally, it is possible that discrimination in judicial ruling is different for different types of crimes. For instance, some types of crimes may afford minorities favorable or equal rulings whereas other crimes likely find the minority in a distinctly more disadvantaged situation. This is known as contextual discrimination, in that it is dependent on the context of the actual criminal offense.

Minorities as group are more likely than whites to receive harsher treatments within the court system. This is particularly true related to convictions regarding substance abuse, noting that even though there are few differences in drug-use patterns between racial groups, African Americans and Hispanics are several times more likely than other racial groups to be charged for a substance abuse crime. The reason for this pronounced disparity lies in the differential sentencing guidelines for powder and crack cocaine as well as the fact that minorities are typically stereotyped as being drug users and ultimately the source of a society's "drug problems." It has been noted that in society's efforts to focus on minority neighborhoods and to prevent the spread of drug contamination to other neighborhoods, frequently African Americans are implicated, and as a result, punished more harshly. Evidence of the perception that whites are less menacing to society can be possibly found in the differential treatment of African Americans with regard to plea bargaining. Whites, as compared to African Americans, ultimately receive plea bargains more often, and consequently maintain lighter sentencing. The results of plea bargaining allow whites to disproportionately benefit by having charges reduced or dropped, and/or receiving diversion, probation, or fines instead of incarceration (Tarver, Walker, & Wallace, 2002).

DEATH PENALTY CONVICTIONS

In addition to disparities found in substance abuse sentencing, death penalty convictions are more frequently handed out to African Americans. The obvious reason why African Americans are disproportionately represented on death row is that African Americans disproportionately commit murders—the crime for which all death sentences are attached. When the rate of murders is controlled for, African Americans actually receive death penalty sentences at rates lower than whites (Blume, Eisenburg, & Wells, 2004). This is most true in the South where one would least expect favorable treatment for African Americans.

Despite African Americans receiving death penalty sentences at a lower rate when controlling for murder rates, this might lead one to draw the conclusion that this is a "favorable" treatment with regard to race. In fact, this reduced rate of the number of death penalties handed out to African Americans may represent just the opposite, a devaluing of minority races in the system. This is because the majority of murders committed by African Americans are same-race murders. When considering how to prosecute a crime, prosecutors are less likely to seek death penalty when the victim is an African American. When the victim is white, prosecutors are more likely to seek death penalty. The reason for this disparate treatment, known as the race of the victim effect, is said to exist because of a societal undervaluing of certain races and as a consequence, certain victims.

Race of Offender and Victim in Death Penalty Cases

A primary source of controversy related to death penalty relates to perceptions of racial bias in its application. Statistics such as those from Figure 18-6 show that approximately

56 percent of all persons who are executed are Caucasian and 35 percent are African American. While the argument can be made (particularly among those who are not familiar with demographics in the United States and/or are neophytes in research) that most persons executed are Caucasian, this still reveals disparity in the application of executions. When one considers that African Americans account for approximately 13 percent of the population, it would then seem that the percentage who are on death row and the percentage who are executed are disproportionately high. Conversely, when one considers that Caucasians account for around 70–75 percent of the population (depending on classifications of Hispanic Americans), it would seem that the percentage of those given the death penalty and those who are executed are disproportionately.

Because of these and other observations, some contend that death penalty is administered in a racially and class-biased manner. Although it was true that outright racism existed in the system during the early to mid-1900s, oversight by the Supreme Court helped mitigate this a bit. Now, the issue of discriminatory application has shifted to the race of the victim who is killed. Students can see in Figure 18-6 that over 75 percent of murder victims in cases resulting in an execution of the offender were Caucasian. This is despite the fact that only 50 percent of those victims were Caucasian. Simply put, if you murder a Caucasian, you are more likely to be executed but if you murder an African American, you have lower odds of being executed (See Figure 9-3).

This is an important observation because it does perhaps underlie some bias in the justice system regarding the value of persons who are victimized. Where the race of the defendant may matter to some extent due to socioeconomics and the inability to obtain effective legal counsel, this should not matter with regard to victims. The prosecutor is the body responsible for seeking a death sentence and, after this, it is the appeals process that generally determines how quickly the execution will follow. Because the number of resources available for district attorneys is often plentiful and because the same is true with the state (at least compared to the resources available to most offenders and their legal counsel), it would be expected that executions would not be influenced by the race of the defendant. All of this is mentioned because as an overall general economic demographic, Caucasians tend to have more affluence and property ownership in the United States than do most minority groups. The question is then, what is it that makes it so that persons who kill Caucasians are more likely to be executed than if they kill African Americans?

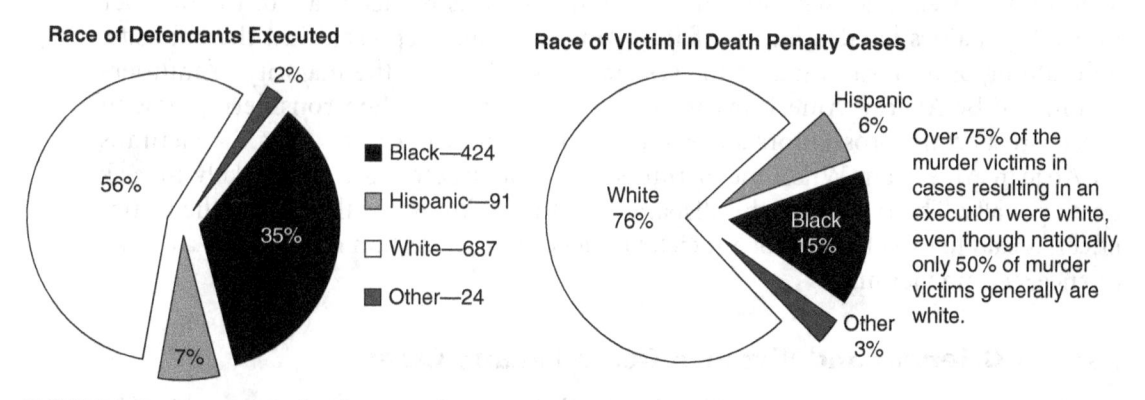

FIGURE 9-3 Race of Defendants and Race of Victims in Death Penalty Cases *Source:* Death Penalty Information Center. (2010). *Facts about the death penalty.* Washington, DC: Death Penalty Information Center.

Before answering this question, let us further consider research that supports the notion that persons who kill whites are more likely to get the death penalty than are those who kill blacks. One study conducted by the General Accounting Office (1990) of the federal government evaluated 28 other studies, which covered homicide cases for different time periods throughout several states that had the death penalty. This meta-analysis of prior studies included different geographic regions of the United States. They found a pattern of evidence that indicated racial disparities in death penalty processing after the Furman decision.

In fact, in 82 percent of those studies, the race of the victim was found to influence the likelihood of being charged with capital murder or receiving the death penalty, i.e., those who murdered whites were found to be more likely to be sentenced to death than those who murdered blacks. It was amazing that these findings were remarkably consistent across data sets, states, data collection methods, and analytic techniques. The finding held for high-, medium-, and low-quality studies that the Government Accounting Office analyzed (1990).

Thus, when we ask the question—what is it that makes it so that persons who kill Caucasians are more likely to be executed than if they kill African Americans?, our answer has been provided, at least in part, by the research just presented. That answer has to do, at least in part, with prosecutorial discretion at earlier stages of the criminal justice process. However, is this issue truly this simple or is there perhaps some other factor at play? In this chapter, the contention will be that there is indeed another set of issues to explain this phenomenon. But before explaining, we will name this phenomenon the *prosecutorial death discretion outcome*. The **prosecutorial death discretion outcome** basically observes that prosecutors are overwhelmingly Caucasian and that, when determining whether to seek the death penalty, they tend to do so disproportionately more often when the victim is also Caucasian than when they are African American. The reasons for this, however, are not as likely to be due to racism as they are to be due to politics.

Almost all district attorneys (prosecutors) hold their positions by public election. This means that they are voted into office and, as such, their communities must generally be happy with their performance. In many cases, it is the affluent within a community who tend to have more political power in that community and they also tend to vote more. Prosecutors may be tempted to ensure that the affluent members of their community remain satisfied with decisions that are made or, at the very least, they may try to ensure that they do not upset this socioeconomic strata of citizens too greatly. In addition, when members of this group have someone who is killed, their families tend to have more influence and likely will more effectively ensure that their case is prosecuted with more vigor, or to the maximum extent of the law. On the other hand, minority communities (particularly African American communities) tend to have fewer resources and less political clout. This does not mean that crimes of murder against members of this community will not be prosecuted, but it does mean that there will be a stronger likelihood for plea bargains and life sentences without parole to be given. This is even truer when one considers that most crimes are intra-racial, with black offenders tending to kill black victims. The general incentive to prosecute for death rather than to plea out of court is perhaps not as strong.

In addition, their voting potential tends to be less due to lower numbers in most jurisdictions and other factors. In inner-city jurisdictions that are largely African American, crime rates may be higher and, stereotypically, violent crime tends to correlate. Given this observation, the fact that most crime is intra-racial, and that drugs and gangs may be associated with these areas of the United States, the impetus behind a long and drawn-out legal prosecution may not be as strong, particularly if the crime involved offender-on-offender violence, such as with rival gang members or drug dealers.

All of these factors—more affluence (on the average) among families of Caucasian victims, the lack of socioeconomic power among much of the African American community, and crime dynamics in many African American urban communities—tend to impact courthouse dynamics. Discretionary decisions made at the time of plea bargaining tend to favor those with more clout and not to be as favorable as those who do not. If the victim's family has substantive influence, then this too affects the overall total outcome of who is prosecuted to the fullest, up to and including death penalty.

CONCLUSION

There is a history of disparate treatment within the U.S. court system for minorities. At extreme points in history, racial minorities were not afforded any due process rights. Gradually, over time, minorities have gained an equal access to procedural process used to ensure fairness. Despite these advances, minorities still receive disparate treatment within the courts related to biases that are inherent to the system. Researchers and policymakers must continue to examine racial disparities and work to eliminate those barriers that prevent equal justice for all.

In this chapter, we have examined the various stages of the court system and processing of criminal cases, all the while maintaining a focus on this process and disparate and/or discriminate experiences of minority populations in the judicial system. From bail setting to initial prosecution, to plea bargain and conviction, through sentencing, we have shown different means by which minorities have been disproportionately given less-than-equal treatment. The historical, social, and legal aspects of these observations have been presented.

Chapter 9 Learning Check

1. The Supreme Court case referred to as _____ _____ noted that, "The right to be heard would be, in many cases, of little avail if it did not comprehend the right to be heard by counsel. Even the intelligent and educated layman has small and sometimes no skill in the science of law. If charged with a crime he is incapable, generally, of determining for himself whether the indictment is good or bad."
   a. *Gideon v. Wainwright*
   b. *Powell v. Alabama*
   c. *McClesky v. Kemp*
   d. *Brown v. Board of Education*

2. Crime is largely an interracial phenomenon.
   a. True
   b. False

3. _____ refers to the process by which a trial is relocated to another locality.
   a. Change of court
   b. Change of venue
   c. Voir dire
   d. Dismissal

4. Voir Dire refers to:
   a. Having charges formally dropped
   b. A change of venue
   c. Dismissal of a case
   d. Procedures for jury selection

5. *Disparity* and *Discrimination* are terms with synonymous meanings.
   a. True
   b. False

6. ROR is the abbreviation used in bail-setting which means:
   a. Released on Recognizance
   b. Released on Recommendation
   c. Released on Rights
   d. Right to Release
7. If OJ Simpson's trial location had not been changed, he would have likely been tried by an all-white jury.
   a. True
   b. False
8. The race of the victim seems to impact sentencing more than the race of the defendant.
   a. True
   b. False
9. _____ was the Supreme Court case that provided for indigent defense.
   a. *Gideon v. Wainwright*
   b. *Powell v. Alabama*
   c. *McClesky v. Kemp*
   d. *Brown v. Board of Education*
10. More favorable sentencing outcomes for minorities compared to those for whites prove that racism in sentencing does not exist.
    a. True
    b. False

Essay Discussions

1. What is the race of the victim effect? Why is it important in sentencing outcomes?
2. Detail how discriminations can occur with regard to being charged with a crime. How have minorities been effected by these discriminatory practices?
3. Explain the reason why a lawyer might request a change of venue. How might this change affect the outcome of the case?

References

Ayres, I., & Waldfogel, J. (1994). A market test for race discrimination in bail setting. *Stanford Law Review*, 987–1047.

Bales, W. D., & Piquero, A. R. (2012). Racial/Ethnic differentials in sentencing to incarceration. *Justice Quarterly*, DOI: 10.1080/07418825.2012.659674

Blume, J., Eisenberg, T., & Wells, M., (2004). Explaining death row's population and racial composition. *Journal of Empirical Legal Studies, 1*(1), 165–207.

Death Penalty Information Center. (2010). *Facts about the death penalty*. Washington, DC: Death Penalty Information Center.

Krivo, L. J., & Peterson, R. D. (2000). The structural context of homicide: Accounting for racial differences in process. *American Sociological Review, 65*, 547–559.

Farnworth, M., Teske, R., & Thurman, G. (1995). Gender differences in felony court processing. *Women and Criminal Justice, 6*(2), 23–44.

General Accounting Office. (1990). *Death penalty sentencing research indicates a pattern of racial disparities*. Washington, DC: Author.

Parmenter, A. J. (2007). Nullifying the jury: The judicial oligarchy declares war on jury nullification. *Washburn Law Journal, 46*(1), 379–428.

Tarver, M., Walker, S. D., & Wallace, H. (2002). *Multicultural issues in the criminal justice system*. Boston: Allyn and Bacon.

Walker, S., Spohn, C., & DeLone, M. (2007). *The color of justice*. Belmont, CA: Wadsworth.

Wooldredge, J. (2011). Distinguishing race effects on pretrial release and sentencing decisions. *Justice Quarterly, 29*(1), 41–75.

Wooldredge, J., & Thistlethwaite, A. (2006). Changing marital status and desistance from intimate assault. *Public Health Reports, 121*, 428–434.

10

Corrections, Classism, Poverty, and Minority Groups

LEARNING OBJECTIVES

After reading this chapter, students should be able to do the following:

1. Define and understand the context by which the corrections and poverty may be interlinked.

2. Explain the formation of certain historical institutions and how they preempted the modern correctional system.

3. Identify the themes of minority exclusion, detainment, reform, punishment, and exploitation.

4. Explain some of the commonalities between serfdom, peasantry, slavery, and modern correctional populations.

5. Identify the current most prevalent minority groups represented in correctional settings.

6. Explain the precedence for the current mass incarceration phenomenon.

7. Identify some key case laws related to religious practices, minorities, and correctional practices.

KEY TERMS

Bearden v. Georgia

Behavioral illnesses as a minority status

Blue Laws

Bourgeois

Class

Convict transportation

Cooper v. Pate

Cruz v. Beto

Cutter v. Wilkinson

Debt bondage

Debtor's gaols

Deinstitutionalization

Dominant group

Dual employment rates

Establishment Clause

Ethnic succession

Feudalism

Free Exercise Clause

Fulwood v. Clemmer

Indentured servants

Indentured servitude

Institutions of confinement

Majority

Mariel boatlift

Minority group

O'Lone v. Estate of Shabazz

Peasants

Poor Laws of 1388

Prison

Proletariats

Serfdom

Slavery, Chattel

Theriault v. Carlson

Trial by Jury of One's Peers

INTRODUCTION

As described in Chapter 2, the United States holds a unique position historically as it relates to minorities and their treatment within the criminal justice system. On the one hand, the United States was created by minorities for minorities. Diverse people from socially ostracized disparate groups (e.g., Protestants, indentured servants) came to the country with hopes of improving their social lot. Through revolution, these groups formed the "free" and "independent" democracy known as the United States of America. The personal freedoms that could be enjoyed in the United States were unique as it related to other world governments that had existed up to this era.

In stark contrast to the personal liberties that were available to the majority, were the historically poor treatment received by non-Protestant, ethnic minority groups. Irish-Catholics, Italians, Chinese, Native Americans, and African Americans maintained a lesser status, and therefore did not receive the complete entitlements of a free society. Of all minority groups, none suffered as much as African Americans, who were relegated to the lowest social order through slavery. Slavery, as a racially organized institution, would create a long-lasting legacy for race-based relations in the United States that continues to the present day.

To understand the present-day correctional system, one must appreciate the changing beliefs about crime and punishment that occurred over the last 1,000 years. Largely, the philosophy about the nature of crime and its required punishment evolved through changes in cultural values. How we think about crime cannot be simply reduced to "right" and "wrong" behavior but must be placed in a socio-cultural-economic framework. For instance, in ancient Judaic culture, breaking the Sabbath was a capital offense. For modern people, even those of Jewish faith, receiving the death penalty for not observing the Sabbath is extreme and does not fit into a current worldview. However, despite the fact that penalties for breaking the Sabbath no longer exist, remnants of those cultural beliefs linger (carryover laws).

An example of modern carryover law is that of the **blue laws**. Blue laws are laws designed to enforce religious standards (particularly as it relates to the sale of alcohol). Despite the fact that many blue laws have been found to be unconstitutional, some still remain such as the prohibition of Sunday sale of alcohol in certain jurisdictions.

These remnant laws are in place because of the once-held values and customs of the past. These laws were socially constructed and based on the norms and values of the culture at the time. Once more, punishments and corrective actions that were used to enforce violations of laws were also socially constructed and culturally based. Because culture is ever changing, laws as well as prescribed forms of punishment are also perpetually changing. Current practices cannot be understood without historical references to the past because many features and carryover practices are grounded in the historical past.

Another factor that must be considered when attempting to understand the cultural relevance of crime and punishment is the acknowledgment of what group is making the law. In each culture there is a **dominant group** and **minority groups**. The dominant group is the one that maintains the dominant control over the society's power, wealth, and prestige. It is often this group that is in a place of power and can dictate "What is a crime?" vs. "What is not a crime?" As an act of virtue, laws can be constructed to ensure equality and freedoms that allow minorities equal access to society's resources. Unfortunately, many laws have been constructed with the opposite goal in mind.

Codified Law and the Reinforcement of Social Structures
What has been will be again, what has been done will
be done again; there is nothing new under the sun.

—SOLOMON THE WISE

Perhaps one of the most universal pieces of the historical past (that is relevant to the modern correctional system) is that social minorities have always received disparate treatments in the legal system. Throughout history, each generation and culture has seen distinctions between how the law treated those in the majority vs. those in the minority. Examples may include how different cultures have treated women, ethnic populations, the poor, the infirmed, etc. The inequalities of the modern system of crime and punishment can be traced back to ancient history, and the first legal codes. Arguably, the earliest codified law came into being to draw divisions between those who had property, wealth, and prestige and those who did not. This practice of protecting the privileged through legal traditions became important because it worked to create and maintain social structures. Some might argue that the legal system came to protect the rights of those who were of lesser social standing; however, this truth seems to be a mere byproduct of the law.

Under most traditional legal systems, persons were granted varying degrees of personal freedoms based on their social standing. An example of this is that of the slave who occupied the lowest rung of the social ladder. The slave (in most cultures) could not own property or participate in government. The slave also had limited control of his own body and personal welfare. Slaves were often seen as property and therefore were subjugated to the desires of their owners. Conversely, nobility were traditionally not subjected to the same laws as the commoner. Regarding civil matters, nobles frequently were exempt from paying taxes, could levy fines, and create their own tax structures. Regarding criminal penalties, nobility were once again exempt from the crimes typically charged to commoners and peasants. For example, a slave would be executed for killing a noble, yet a noble killing a slave would hardly go noticed. To a degree, whether overt or not, class distinctions still exist that create preferential treatments within the criminal justice system.

The importance of social status and freedoms permitted through the law is relevant when considering the institution of modern corrections. It is through *legal structures that those with power, wealth, and prestige maintain power by limiting the freedoms of those without power.* Traditionally, over a number of historical legal systems, limitations of personal freedoms vary, ranging from limiting of financial acquiescence (e.g., ownership of land and other property) to a complete lack of freedom that can be associated with forced slavery or other similar institutions. Incarceration, as a practice,

Box 10.1 The American Myth

Freedom and democracy were not always the case for America. In fact, a majority of immigrants who arrived during the Colonial Period arrived in some form of bondage. The main driving force behind this phenomenon was the demand for cheap labor that the colonial plantation system required. Out of all of the immigrants who came to the colonies between 1609 and 1755, nearly 75 percent were bonded.

How they arrived:

(1700–1755)

Slave   46 percent

Free   26 percent

Indentured   19 percent

Prisoner   9 percent

With this view of "American Bondage" in mind, it is easier to understand the historical precedence for the American carceral system that has its traditions set in an older European system. North American legal tradition was established by English settlers and therefore transplanted many of the ideas and premises of incarceration that were practiced in England. To this day, many of the euphemisms that are associated with modern prisons (e.g., "the clink," "the po-house") are "carry-overs" from English penal practices.

takes all societal freedoms that were once available to that person, rendering him/her essentially a slave. Arguably, the penal system, in part, evolved to replace historical institutions that worked similarly to limit minority group freedoms. The following sections outline how the traditional values and beliefs of Americans are rooted in the cultural past. Once more, it provides a framework to begin to think about minority groups and how these groups continue to be disenfranchised through the mechanisms of the law.

Institutions of Confinement

The modern western prison system is historically rooted in a continuum of restrictive social mechanisms termed by Foucault as "institutions of confinement" (Foucault, 1965; Goffman, 1961; Rothman, 1971). According to Foucault (1965), the original **institutions of confinement** were the leper houses that sprung up around Europe during the Middle Ages. Toward the late Middle Ages, as leprosy was being eradicated in Europe, these homes took on new purposes that frequently served those that were "poor vagabonds, criminals and the mentally ill." As noted by Foucault, even though these homes shifted focus away from the treatment of lepers, the core values and meanings of the treatment of lepers did not diminish—namely that society could be protected through the exclusion of social minorities.

In addition to the formation of the idea that the public could better be protected by the exclusion of minority groups was the notion that teaching and forcing labor were

Box 10.2 The Use of Forced Labor

According to Karl Marx, throughout history, the ruling class has always found ways to exploit the labor of the working class. Marx divided the class warfare that occurred in society into two classes—the bourgeois and the proletariats. The **bourgeois** refers to those in society who own property (and consequently the rights to production), whereas the **proletariat** are the workers who are constantly at odds with the bourgeois to prevent themselves from being exploited for labor. Class warfare involving labor is important as it relates minority issues because minorities are always at the lowest order of class system and, consequently, often are the group most exploited for labor. The exploitation of minority groups for labor is a key feature of many institutions of confinement.

important features of a perfect culture. Thomas More in his book *Utopia* (1516) wrote about how everyone in the perfect culture would be engaged in some form of labor. Public sentiment of this time was one that would have emphasized the need for the role of work in the betterment of society and the need to segregate the fringe of society. Consequently, a theme of many institutions of confinement would be to force labor for those who were not inclined to work. The following sections outline the various institutions of confinement that evolved over the last millennia—all of which contribute to our current ideas common to western views of incarceration, confinement, and forced labor.

THE RATIONALE BEHIND THE USE OF JAILS

Jails or "gaols" (derived from Latin *gavioli*, which means little cell) became common to England during the late Middle Ages (1100 A.D. to 1300 A.D.). This was largely in response to the creation of a jury system by the Assize of Clarendon in 1166 A.D., which, over time, led to trial by jury of one's peers. **Trial by jury of one's peers**, as is common in today's legal system, afforded a person the opportunity to present testimony to others who were of the common cloth and not necessarily the rich, affluent, or politically powerful. Commoners as well as other members of society could and would be represented on these juries and, therefore, helped eliminate bias in the justice system. One issue of key importance in the development of the trial by jury of one's peers is that judicial corruption is, at least partially, put in check because jurors are drawn equally from the common cloth that likely reflects the background of the accused.

Jails became common because trial by jury, as a process, took considerable time to occur and therefore the accused needed a place to be held while awaiting trial. Early

Box 10.3 The "Clink," Peasants, Poverty, and Debtor Incarceration

One example of a typical jail facility of late-medieval times is that of "The Clink." The Clink (the name is still viewed as a synonymous to the term jail) was perhaps the oldest jail in England. The Clink was initially a facility close to the Bishop of Winchesters' resident where heretics would be detained. In 1144, the original structure was enlarged in order to house both male and female prisoners. It was during this same time period that brothels were regulated by the church and therefore "The Clink" would have serve the dual purpose of prison and brothel.

Jailers who worked in "The Clink" would have been paid low wages and therefore would have required that prisoners and prostitutes pay for better treatment. Jailers, if afforded bribes, would loosen leg irons, provide extra bedding, allow prisoners to beg for food, or work. Common amenities, such as basic food and drink, required payment at twice the outside rate. Those who could not afford the exploitive rates would be forced to beg through the grates that looked into the street for pieces of food and drink.

Facilities like "The Clink" became more prominent in the late 1300s to the 1500s related to the establishment debtor's prisons and enactment of Poor Laws. Debtor's prisons became prominent during the decline of **feudalism**. Feudalism was the principal social system that dominated England from the 9th to 15th centuries in which those with landholders exchanged the benefits of land for labor. **Peasants**, in this system, were the laborers of the land who worked on the land in exchange for food and shelter. Most of the production of the land went back to the landowner while the peasant had a meager existence. Those members of society who could not pay their debts would be held in prison until debts were paid or else would be placed on a debtor's lien becoming a de facto slave of a feudalistic manor. Society's debtors would be locked up in jails and have to repay debts through labor. In families where the father was in a debtor's prison, women and children were often subjected to further poverty and debt and would be placed in debtor's prison alongside the primary wage earner. Poor laws also influenced the crowding of prisons by offering mechanisms by which poor vagrants (essentially the homeless of the era) would be placed in prisons.

jails were no more than holding facilities and torture was a primary form of punishment once a person had been found guilty of a crime. Common punishments included cutting off the hands of thieves, cutting off ears of poachers, hanging, drawing and quartering, public floggings, etc. Each town would have likely had a gibbet (a small hanging cell that would have been hung from a tree outside of the city gate in full public view) in which those convicted of serious crimes would have been left to die and rot as a public spectacle.

The living conditions in jails were so harsh that starvation, disease, and death were common. Compounding the living conditions was that most jails were privately operated and funded through charging those held within its confines. Jailers would have been poorly paid, thus encouraging further exploitation of prisoners. By the time cost associated with paying for prison and the many exploitive items required to survive prison were achieved, there was little left to repay debts (as related to debtors' house in jails). In some cases, those in jails would be allowed to enter into debt bondage or serfdom in turn for release from jail (medieval period). **Debt bondage** is the practice of forfeiture of freedom as a result of failure to repay debts.

Debtor's Gaols

The **debtor's gaols** were essentially holding facilities where a person was kept until they could repay an unpaid debt. Medieval times also saw the emergence of housing debtors in jails due to the **poor laws of 1388**, which restricted the migration of the poor and required each district (known as a hundred) to alleviate its own poverty problems. In this time period, the decline of the feudal system displaced agriculture laborers as well as deteriorated the feudal justice system that had been in place for centuries. The result was the need for a civil judiciary marked by civil punishments. One such punishment was to place persons in debtor's prisons until they could repay debts. It would not be uncommon for the head of the household to be locked up in a debtor's prison until the family would have been able to repay the debts. The resultant of this practice was that the debtor would be held for indefinite periods of time until debts were repaid.

The concept of seizing one's freedoms for failure to repay debts was not a new concept, in that it dated back to ancient times. In ancient Greece, pledging oneself as collateral for a loan was a common occurrence. This pledging of oneself as security usually occurred because those who had no land needed permission to farm in order to survive. The agreement, between the rich landowner and the poor worker, would have required repayment of living expenses plus interest, which would have been exorbitant. When the debtor failed to repay the loan, the debtor and his family could be sold into slavery (debt bondage), losing all rights to ever live free again. The reality in Greece and in the rest of the ancient world was that most persons lived in some social status between total *freedom* and total *slavery*. Solon, the great Greek lawgiver, is said to have abolished the act of debt bondage, or total and permanent enslavement for failure to repay debts, with his legal proclamation know as the Seisachtheia (c. 638 B.C.).

The feudal system in England, similarly, had a prescribed social system by which persons were afforded varying levels of freedom. This caste system was known as **serfdom**. Serfs were the lowest order of the feudal system. A freeman was the highest order of serf whereas the lowest order was a slave. Slaves had no rights and privileges whereas freemen were essentially tenant farmers. Freeman would frequently be relegated to a lower status and loss of freedoms related to debts due to crop failures or some other misfortunes. Debtors prisons, which came about at the end of the feudal period, would have acted on the principal of limiting freedoms based on indebtedness.

Workhouses, Poorhouses, and Houses of Correction

Workhouses (also known as poorhouses and houses of correction) emerged in the 16th century and would have been extensions to existing jail structures. The earliest known workhouse in England was known as the Bridewell (c. 1553). *Bridewell* became a term that would become synonymous with the English workhouse. The original Bridewell consisted of a jail, workhouse, hospital, and orphanage. This principal structure was designed to house, punish, and reform social minorities. The minorities of that time period included the poor, those who were mentally and physically infirmed, prostitutes, criminals, and orphans. The predominant view was that poverty was created by idleness and therefore the workhouse was implemented in order to teach the virtue of hard labor. The "corrective action" taken in these houses of correction was the teaching of labor. Persons housed in workhouses were typically forced to pick oakum (hemp used in shipbuilding), perform spinning or weaving, or carry out some other menial task.

Transportation

The colonial period in English history saw the emergence of penal colonies for those who committed petty crimes or else could not repay even small amounts of debt. Also referred to as **convict transportation**, the colonies became places where indigent people were sent, usually in an inhospitable frontier country, as a way to repay debts. These convicts would be used cheap labor to operate the agrarian pursuits that were common to the Colonial Americas and other British colonies (e.g., Australia). It is noteworthy that many of the crimes or claims against debtors were sometimes of very small amounts, thus lending credence to the idea that the government and landholder conscripted persons to perform cheap labor through false or insignificant charges. It is estimated that roughly 9 percent of all of the settlers immigrating to the American colonies between the years of 1700 and 1775 were transported convicts, most of who arrived in the states of Virginia and Maryland.

Box 10.4 Oliver Twist: Charles Dickens's Activist Tale of a Poor House Orphan

In 1838, Charles Dickens published his famous novel, *Oliver Twist*. The novel was designed to bring attention to the "poor laws" in England that established debtor's prisons and workhouses. Under these laws, young orphans were labeled as criminals and exploited for child labor in workhouses. Oliver Twist, the hero of Dickens's novel, is a child who almost from birth (with the death of his mother) finds himself interned in a "baby farm" or debtors prison for infants. Oliver's early life consists of a meager existence marked by extreme poverty and desperation. At age nine, Oliver is moved to the adult workhouse where he will continue to pay off his debt to society. On one fateful day, Oliver is taken from the poorhouse as an apprentice to an undertaker. Oliver finds a new life as a mourner at children's funerals. This life with his new family is cut short when a feud ensues with his master. Oliver is forced to run away and become a street dodger to avoid the terrible possibility of returning to workhouse.

Dickens, perhaps better than any author of the era, accurately depicts the social inequalities, poverty, the inability to escape poverty, and the unjust laws that were common to this era. Dickens's novel portrays how those with social power and resources can be unjust to those born without resources. The minorities of Dickens's tale were orphans and debtors who could not escape their lifestyle or social status largely because of forces beyond their control.

Box 10.5 Georgia: The American Penal Colony?

One popular fabled penal colony in the Americas was the Georgia Colony. There was never an actual penal colony in Georgia and the myth was probably born out of Georgia Colony's founder, James Oglethorpe's idea to alleviate debtor's prisons in England. James Oglethorpe, the founder of the Georgia, established the land grant in order to carry out his social reformist ideas. Through all accounts, Oglethorpe was appalled by the debtor's prison and developed a plan for the poor to relocate them to the new world in the Georgia Colony. The Georgia Colony, as a grand experiment, outlawed slavery and encouraged debtors to relocate to her shores for a "fresh start." Unfortunately, the experiment was abandoned 1734 by the board of trustees because, as one journalist of the time period wrote: "as many of the poor who had been useless in England were inclined to be useless likewise in Georgia" (~London Life in the 18th Century, Mary George).

THE PRISON

The modern conception of a **prison** refers to a facility used to house someone convicted of a crime that serves the dual purpose of protecting the public from the person's criminal conduct as well as serving as a punishment/reformatory for the offender. The concept of incarceration, the modern method of punishing crime, was not always the preferred way to administer justice in the West. Before 1770, persons were placed in jails to assure the repayment of debts or else to await trial or sentencing. Early America and Europe, up to this time, relied on other forms of punishment and crime deterrence. Among these were physical punishments, the death penalty, imprisonment in debtor's prisons, and exile. It is noteworthy that the most common penalties were public corporal punishment displays such as flogging, the pillory, and other forms of torture. The death penalty was common and used for crimes as small as larceny. The colonial period in the Americas and England punished crime so harshly that this period (1688–1815) is sometimes referred to as the era of the *bloody code*.

Although early American society did not rely on imprisonment as a primary form of punishment, the precedence for its use existed in forms of torture that restricted freedom and movement. Imprisonment, as a physical punishment, belongs to a larger class of punishments that sought to inflict physical harm on a person's body through the restriction of movement. Often, the restriction of movement was accompanied with an attempt to degrade or else make a public spectacle. An example of this is the use of the *pillory*. The pillory was a post (usually elevated above the crowd) where a criminal would be shackled and put on public display in place common to public gatherings. The punishment associated with the pillory was designed to humiliate through the restriction of physical movement in public spectacle. The *stocks*, a slight deviation from the pillory, forced the criminal into a bowing position, which was seen as a further degradation. Institutions and social conventions were also used to limit freedoms and movement. For example, slavery was a common practice for most premodern cultures. In part, slavery and similar institutions were used to limit power acquiescence on the part of minority groups. There can be little doubt that modern incarceration techniques have supplanted the institution of slavery and other social institutions (e.g., asylums, indentured servitude) that limit freedoms. It can be clearly concluded that with increased societal freedoms came counterbalanced institutions that limited freedoms. From this perspective, it is little wonder why the United States, the freest country in the world, incarcerates more persons per capita than any other country.

This is an important fact as it relates to the study of corrections in the United States because the politics of social inequalities between the rich and the poor have always weighed heavily on who was free and who was in bondage. There is a clear history of laws that have disenfranchised minority groups so as to support the ambitions of the ruling class. At the very heart of the correctional system is a history of disenfranchisement and continued policy that disproportionately impacts social and ethnic minorities.

HOSPITALS AND ASYLUMS

Another historical institution that paved the way for the modern-day correctional system was that of the hospital, and as an extension, the "madhouse." Most medical care in the medieval period onward was provided within the home. Hospitals of this era would have been organized solely to provide medical care to the impoverished or insane. These hospitals would invariably become more specialized to care for the mentally ill exclusively.

The original English insane asylum was known as Bethlehem Hospital and commonly referred to as *Bedlam*. *Bedlam*, the term that originated from its association with the hospital, means related to uproar and confusion. The original use of the hospital at Bedlam was not to treat patients (in our common sense of psychiatric care) but rather to house "beggar lunatics." These "lunatics" were commonly said to suffer from "moral insanity." During the early formation of the hospital, the prevailing belief of society was that mental infirmity was the result of improper moral choices. All those deemed immoral could have been sentenced to Bedlam. Bedlam was made famous through a series of painting by William Hogarth known as Rake's Progress. In the paintings, Tom Rake is a spendthrift son of a wealthy merchant who spends all of his money on prostitution and gambling. He is pronounced to have fallen into "moral insanity" and sent to Fleet Prison and later Bedlam.

Modern Asylums

Before the 1840s in the United States, there existed few distinctions between those who were criminal and those who suffered from mental/behavioral illnesses (e.g., substance dependency issues, mental retardation, autism, schizophrenia). In fact, jails of this era frequently housed *beggar lunatics* in order to purge the society of unwanted persons (Finzch & Jutte, 1997). Despite the advent of the penitentiary system and purported "more humane forms of penalty," those with behavioral health issues continued to dominate jail systems as they had for centuries before.

To understand this practice, one must first understand the cultures' orientation to disease and the appropriate cures. As is today, the general society was largely uninformed about the nature of behavioral illnesses and their appropriate treatments. Given that the culture was very fervently religious, both criminal activity and disease were thought to stem from immoral behavior. As one can easily imagine, diseases such as schizophrenia and drunkenness were lumped together with other immoral behaviors such as theft and murder. There is little doubt that a person's hearing of voices or else strange behaviors would likely be linked to demon possessions and immoral lifestyle that persons brought on themselves. Through the religious lens, the cure for one's sinful nature was to show remorse and abate from a wicked lifestyle. Society facilitated this

Consider This:

Over 65% of inmates in both Federal and state prisons suffer from mental disorders or substance abuse disorders. Both sets of disorders have been shown to be largely heritable and chronic. Modern science has conclusively demonstrated that these conditions are not determined by morality but rather by biology. Should we continue to place persons in prisons for having these illnesses?

"cure" by sentencing the offender to pay "penance" in the prison system. Probably more influential than seeking an actual cure was the act of hiding persons who were seen as being defective. Prisons and jails achieved this goal well.

The 1840s brought with it a wave of reform for prisons led by Dorthia Dix. Dix championed the creation of the asylum system for those characterized as the *indigent insane*. Dorthia Dix began her career as a volunteer at the East Cambridge Jail as a Sunday school teacher. To her dismay, she witnessed prostitutes, drunks, criminals, retarded individuals, and the mentally ill all housed together in unheated, unfurnished, and foul-smelling quarters (Viney & Zorich, 1982). When she inquired about why the jails allowed these unsavory conditions, the jailers responded "the insane do not feel hot and cold." This episode prompted Dix to become one of the greatest reformers of the 19th century, bringing about the modern mental hospital system (asylum system) for many states.

SLAVERY

Although not classified as an institution of confinement by Foucault, the practice of slavery doubtlessly had a profound effect on the establishment of the modern prison system. No institution so clearly delineates the loss of freedom through confinement as does the practice of slavery. In the United States, because of the racial nature of slavery, this historic institution continues to have a profound effect on the modern prison system.

The roots of slavery for the colonies began early with the discovery of tobacco at the Jamestown colony in 1611. Pressed with a great demand for laborers, **indentured servants** were first used to meet the work demands of the newfound crop. **Indentured servitude** was, in design, the voluntary contracting to perform labor for a set period of time. Once the time period had elapsed, the servant would receive freedom dues, which consisted of clothing, land, and provisions along with their actual freedom. As a real practice, indentured servitude was very similar to slavery. First, those who volunteered for indentured servitude were often coerced (due to crimes committed or unpaid debts) or kidnapped and forced to enter into servitude. Second, once a person signed into servitude, they were treated as property, often punished violently with no legal recourse. It is believed that much of the violence and harsh treatments afforded to slaves were first present in the servitude system. Finally, there were no guarantees that a servant would ever live to see freedom. Many servants died at the hand of their masters due to the harsh treatments and poor living conditions.

Many of the first Africans were not slaves but rather indentured servants. It is noteworthy, however, that black indentured servants were not treated equally as their white counterparts. One example of this is the fact that many African American indentured servants were indentured for life. It is estimated that by 1650, 70 percent of all African American indentured servants were indentured for life, setting up a de facto form of slavery.

Over time, colonial plantations moved away from the use of indentured servants and adopted slavery as the preferred way to provide labor. This occurred largely due to the fact that indentured servants were becoming rarer due to an improved economy and also because, after a number of years of practicing servitude, there was a swell of poor white underclass that threatened the property owners' holdings. The pivotal event that likely turned toward the adoption of **chattel slavery** as the primary labor force of the plantation system was Bacon's Rebellion in 1660.

Bacon's Rebellion, named after its organizer by Nathanial Bacon, was a rebellion that pitted poor whites, indentured servants, and slaves against the Governor of Virginia. After this revolt was quelled, wealthy landowners feared the idea that poor whites and African slaves could ban together and potentially overthrow the ruling class. To prevent this, landowners increasingly began engaging in the slave trade and drawing the distinction between races as it relates to slavery. It is widely accepted by historians that this event helped hasten the recognition of *chattel slavery*—a term that refers to the most common form of slavery in which one person owns another as property.

Race-Based Slavery: The Myth of Inferiority

To justify the cruel disenfranchisements of slavery and gain public acceptance of the practice, slave owners had to first establish palatable rhetoric. For the English forbearers of the colonies, the idea that blacks were inferior already fit into their worldview. More so than other European ethnic groups, the English believed that blacks were primitive and subhuman. This belief system emerged because of manifold social realities that were unique to England in this time period. First, England was geographically isolated from other cultures. For the most part, between the 15th and 17th centuries England would have been a very homogenous ethnocentric culture. This degree of isolation from people of other cultures led to the most rigid form of race ideology. Second, race-based slavery had existed in Europe since the mid-15th century when Portugal first entered into the African slave trade. This would have predisposed the English to think about racial differences through a lens of slavery. Many historians conclude that the idea of a "black race" was invented during this time period in order to justify enslaving the African people. This invented concept of a "black race" led to the counter-reality of a "white race." The English naturally believed that they were part of the superior white race. Finally, the English were of the Protestant faith and viewed non-Protestants as being inferior and unworthy. A stark comparison can be drawn between Catholic slave owners of South America and Protestant slave owners. Catholics, in contrast to Protestants, afforded more freedoms to slaves, were more open to the intermixing of race, and were more likely to view slaves in human terms (as opposed to property). On the contrary, English Protestants developed a cultural view that regarded the black race as pagan savages who were not human. The term "black," for the English, became associated with "filth, disease, malignancy, and crime," whereas "white" was associated with "purity, innocence and goodness." It is through ethnic propaganda that an American social caste system was established that persists until modern times. At the heart of this system, albeit highly invisible, is the presumption of privilege that exists for all those belonging to the dominant "white" race.

Historically, the raced-based caste system, which pits African Americans at the very bottom of the social ladder, can be seen to be played out in every domain of social life. Criminal justice is the beginning of the African American experience, in that, African Americans were initially deemed to be outside of the law, thus not being afforded any protections of the law.

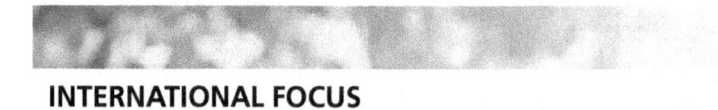

INTERNATIONAL FOCUS

Pussy Riot's Nadezhda Tolokonnikova, Russia and International Slave Labor Camps.

Pussy Riot is an all-female punk rock band that was begun in Moscow Russia in 2011. The original band consisted of 11 women that adorned themselves in brightly colored ski masks and produced music advocating for feminist rights and LGBT issues while protesting Vladimir Putin, the Russian President, whom they regarded as a dictator.

The band is best known for what is known as the *Punk Prayer* incident that occurred on February 21st 2012. On this day, the members of the band stormed into the Cathedral of Christ the Savior in Moscow and performed musical renditions laced with obscenities that shouted lines such as "Holy Mother – send Putin Packing!". The band was carrying out these stunt performances around the city in public places in the months leading up to the presidential election to protest, what they viewed as, the Russian President's dictatorial regime. The Cathedral of Christ the Savior was chosen as a site of protest because the performers believed that the church supported Putin's bid to the presidency (Makey &Kates, 2012). Following the actual performance, band members released a video on You-Tube that captured the event.

In the weeks following the incident, Nadezhda Tolokonnikova, one of the band members, was arrested for *hooliganism*. Although first denying being a member of the group, Tolokonnikova was eventually sentenced to a two year prison sentence. It was during the serving of this sentence that Tolokonnikova made the world more aware of the inner workings of the Russian penal system.

On September 23, 2013, while serving out this sentence, Tolokonnikova went on a hunger strike protesting the conditions of her imprisonment. In an open letter to *The Guardian*, Tolokonnikova described her imprisonment at Mordovia Penal Colony No. 14 as being a modern slave labor camp. Of the working conditions, Tolokonnikova (2013) described them as being 16 to 17 hours a day, 7 days a week, working in a sewing shop. Despite Tolokonnikova's tragic circumstances, she described her treatment as being better than most because of the public scrutiny given to the case. She describes the lot of other prisoners as being worse, describing all types of inhumane forms of treatment.

Although Tolokonnikova's case gathered much attention, cases like these (around the world) are in reality probably not that uncommon. In one such case, Qatar's World Cup Stage, forty-four Nepalese workers died during a three month span of working on the arena. The Guardian newspaper's investigation of the incident found that there was evidence where Nepalese workers had been denied wages, had passports confiscated, and were denied free drinking water in brutal desert conditions (Pattison, 2013). Moreover, these Nepalese men frequently had huge recruitment debts that they could not repay due to the denied wages (Pattison, 2013).

It is estimated that 27 million persons around the world are subjected to forced labor conditions (Gould, 2012). The highest percentage of slave labor is anticipated to be in South and Southeast Asia, China, Russia, and former Soviet states but is also prevalent in Western society. Modern slavery is organized and highly mobile making it truly an international phenomenon. An example of this can be found during the 2010 Haitian earthquake where opportunist quickly overran the island searching for children that could be forced into the sex and labor slave trade (Gould, 2012).

References: Gould, J. (2012). Slavery's Global Comeback. The Atlantic. Retrieved from: http://www.theatlantic.com/international/archive/2012/12/slaverys-global-%09comeback/266354/

Makey, R. and Kates, G. (2012). Russian Riot Girls Jailed for 'Punk Prayer'. The New York Times. Retrieved from: http://thelede.blogs.nytimes.com/2012/03/07/russian-riot-grrrls-jailed-for-punk-prayer/?_r=0

Pattisson, P. (2013). Revealed: Qatar's World Cup "slaves". The Guardian. Retrieved from: http://www.theguardian.com/world/2013/sep/25/revealed-qatars-world-cup-slaves

Tolokonnikova, N. (2013). Pussy Riot's Nadezhda Tolonnikova: Why I Have Gone on a Hunger Strike. The Guardian. Retrieved from: http://www.theguardian.com/music/2013/sep/23/pussy-riot-hunger-strike-nadezhda-tolokonnikova

Modern Minorities within the Prison System

As the previous sections detailed, the modern prison system was built on a foundation of institutions that had previously been used to exclude and isolate social and ethnic minorities from the culture at large. If one were to take a cross-section throughout modern history of who received prison as a punishment, it would not take long to discover that social and ethnic minorities have always filled prisons. The following sections will provide an overview of the social and ethnic minorities who have dominated prison makeup. It is important to note that many of these groups overlap, meaning that offenders often belong to multiple minority classifications.

BEHAVIORAL ILLNESSES AS A MINORITY STATUS

Behavioral illnesses consist of a number of mental health and substance use, brain disorders in which a person's normal voluntary responses have been changed in relation to their illness. These illnesses are considered medical conditions (they are largely heritable, progressive and chronic in nature) that prevent persons suffering from these illnesses from a normal level of societal functioning. Behavioral illness accounts for significant levels of health disability and is ranked the 5th leading cause of disability in the United States overall (CDC, 2009). The following sections will explore how persons with these disabilities are impacted through incarceration.

PERSONS WITH ADDICTIONS

Addiction is defined as a chronic, relapsing brain disease that is characterized by compulsive drug seeking and use, despite harmful consequences. It is considered a brain disease because drugs change the brain—they change its structure and how it works. These brain changes can be long lasting, and can lead to the harmful behaviors seen in people who abuse drugs.

—National Institute on Drug Abuse, 2007

Perhaps the most distinguishing feature of a modern prison is that it is populated with persons that suffer from addictions. It has been estimated that substance use illnesses

Box 10.6 The Conundrum of Addictive Illnesses

The current U.S. policymakers have yet to adopt policies in dealing with addictive diseases that are consistent with what is known to be true medically about these illnesses. This, in part, has been caused by the public's outdated view that all persons use drugs through voluntary choices. This is evidenced through policy that fails to recognize addictions as a cause of disability (42 U.S.C. §423(d)(2)(C)) as well as laws that criminalize the use of addictive substances. The U.S. Policy regarding drugs implies that drug users are morally bad, should not be afforded care, and should be punished as a way to deter the behavior. There has been a substantial body of research that has conclusively shown that addictions are acquired brain disorders as a result of prolonged substance use. Those suffering from addictions have been determined to have permanent neurological changes in which vital reward centers of the brain have been "high jacked" by the effects of mood-altering substances (e.g., drugs, alcohol, tobacco).

As a result, rational decision making becomes impaired. Once these changes occur, persons who suffer from these illnesses have limited ability to make rational decisions regarding drug use. Persons continue to be criminally involved because of the poor decision-making process that occurs as a result of having the disease, the psychogenic effects of drugs/alcohol, and their effect on behavior (increased violence and aggression), as well as the prolonged exposure to criminal elements (as is common to many illicit substances). Some controversy exists in the criminal justice arena as to how to properly intervene with persons with these illnesses. It is clear that current drug-enforcement strategies (supply-side strategies) have done very little to limit the current supply of drugs entering into the United States. Once more, this enforcement strategy is the defining policy that has led to the United States lead the world in incarcerating its citizenry.

are a primary factor in the commission of crime as well the most likely reason for recidivism. Approximately 65 percent of incarcerated individuals in U.S. prisons meet DSM-IV criteria for some type of substance abuse and/or substance addiction whereas another 20 percent were arrested for substance-involved offenses. The most prevalent crime-linked drug, alcohol, has being implicated in the commission of 80 percent of all crimes (Belenko, 1998). More than half of all state prisoners admit to being under the influence of alcohol or drugs at the time they committed their crime and nearly one in five prisoners admitted to performing a crime in order to get money to buy drugs (Mumola, 1999).

The Substance Addiction–Crime Connection

Crime and addiction are intimately linked on multiple levels. For the layperson, the most obvious reason for the link between crime and substance abuse is the psychogenic effects of substances. Stimulant drugs (e.g., cocaine and methamphetamines) and alcohol both have properties that predispose persons to violence as well as other criminal acts. Impulsivity, increased violence, sexual deviance, and impaired judgment are related to the chemical effects of certain drugs and, therefore, these drugs lend themselves to certain crimes (e.g., homicide, domestic violence, sexual crimes). In addition, when a person becomes addicted to the reward mechanisms of the drug, rational judgment is suspended and much effort goes into resuming use. This ongoing process of drug seeking and relapse places users at increased probability of committing a crime.

A second reason for the link between crime and substance abuse is the illegal nature of many substances of abuse. The United States, since prohibition, has embarked on a policy of making mood-altering substances illegal. The net result of this is that people suffering from addictions have been increasingly approached with criminal sanctions when caught with these substances. Since 1970, the U.S. Drug policy known as the "War on Drugs" has created an eight-fold increase in the number of persons incarcerated. It is estimated that 65 percent of all persons behind bars meet the clinical criteria for a substance disorder (CASA, 2010). Drug policy is the prime reason for the United States garnering the highest incarceration rate per capita in the world.

The criminalization of substances also has the added effect of creating black-markets and surrounding drug distribution with criminal elements. As was true with the prohibition period, increased crime is a result of the illegal markets created by illicit substance sales than is directly related to the properties of the chemical itself. These black-markets often develop in impoverished minority communities where few opportunities for societal advancement exist. Youth in these neighborhoods, through integrating the values of the community and peers, learn that selling and using drugs are socially acceptable and a route toward success that had been otherwise denied. Once more, as compared to non-minority neighborhoods, these communities are more likely than not to be exposed to a heightened law enforcement presence. This, in part, accounts for the disparate number of minorities who become criminally involved compared to whites.

Compounding policy issues is the fact that incarceration of substance abusers, as a practice, has a tremendously negative effect on those incarcerated, their families, and the communities in which they live. While incarcerated, a person's emotional and physical health often worsens. Offenders are at heightened risk for communicable diseases as well as other health concerns. Prisons are known for incidences of violence, which often lead to traumatic illnesses for offenders. The stresses felt by family and communities of incarceration fuel a climate in which the cycle of incarceration continues. Those incarcerated have few ways to acquire resources for themselves or their families while incarcerated. This limits the offender's ability to care for his/her family or prepare for the post-incarceration period. The offender's family, often headed by a single caregiver, may struggle under the weight of financial hardships owing to the lack of contribution by the offender. Moreover, the single caregiver, in an attempt to earn a livable wage for the family, may neglect the children's supervisory needs. Communities, by their very nature, attract persons of like backgrounds. Because of this, whole disadvantaged minority communities struggle with the same issues of crime, incarcerated parents, lack of supervision, and poverty. According to America's Cradle to the Prison Pipeline Report, "the most dangerous place for a child in America to grow up is where poverty and race intersect."

Despite the fact that there is a high prevalence of substance abuse illness within the prison system, virtually no treatment exists within prisons. It has been estimated that fewer than 10 percent of prisoners who need substance abuse treatment ever receive it while incarcerated. Once released, there is little in the way of transitional substance abuse care and community follow-up. It has been estimated that as many as two-thirds of all substance abusers will relapse within three months of release (Wexler, Lipton, & Johnson, 1998).

PERSONS WITH MENTAL ILLNESSES

"There are now more than three times more seriously mentally ill persons in jails and prisons than in hospitals"

—Torrey et al. (2010)

As described in the previous section, Dorthia Dix was a seminal figure in the creation of state asylums that began in the 1840s. Dix pushed for the creation of the asylum system because of her recognition that the mentally ill deserved to be humanely cared for in hospital settings. Through her avocation, most states built hospitals that were dedicated to the care of the mentally ill.

This period of mental hospital reliance continued until approximately the 1950s when a new period know as the **deinstitutionalization** era began. The deinstitutionalization era was a well-intended response to overcrowding and deterioration of asylum facilities. Medical advances in the form of antipsychotic medications (the first of which was Thorazine that was introduced in 1952) had been developed that restored some level of functioning for those that were most impaired by schizophrenia or other forms of thought disorders. This led reformers to believe that those who had previously been cared for could now be maintained in the local communities where they hailed from and that this was the most appropriate and humane setting. Fiscally conservative politicians seized on the opportunity to initiate the changes because it also meant considerable savings could be had on both the Federal and state levels.

The deinstitutionalization process had almost an immediate effect on local jails, in that many formerly institutionalized patients were now being arrested and placed in local jails. Early studies on the effects of deinstitutionalization found that there was a 36 percent increase in the number of mentally ill prisoners confined to county jails and a 100 percent increase in the number of detainees who were deemed incompetent to stand trial. One prison psychologist of the early 1970s noted of the effects of deinstitutionalization, "We are literally drowning in patients…. Many more men are being sent."

Lastly, it has been estimated that between 16 and 20 percent of current offenders meet the diagnostic criteria for a major mental disorder (Broner, Borum, & Gawley, 1997)

IMMIGRANTS

Immigrants have always fared poorly with regard to ending up behind bars. Starting with the very first large wave of immigrant influx that occurred in the 19th century, immigrants have always disproportionately entered into the correctional system. Immigrants, because of their varying cultural backgrounds, have always been perceived as different, and consequently, were labeled as "criminal, defective, or retarded." Related to these labels, it became common for the newest immigrants to be found in institutions of confinement. There were essentially two periods in which immigrants were likely to be imprisoned—on arrival and post arrival.

Detainment on Arrival

During the first wave of U.S. immigration (early 1900s), thousands of European and Asian immigrants made their way to America. The immigration policy of that period required that new immigrants pass through immigration processing centers—the largest of which were located at Ellis Island, New York, and Angel Island, California. Both of these facilities were used to house and detain immigrants. However, Angel Island was notorious for holding persons in detainment for years. This was largely due to the Chinese Exclusion Act of 1882, which prevented Chinese immigration unless the person immigrating was related to someone who was already a legal citizen. Because of the ethnic/racial sentiment that existed in California in that period, Angel Island was used as a means to dissuade immigration through processes of interrogation and detainment.

Detainment of immigrants ended in 1954 with the closure of Ellis Island, only to be reinvented in 1981 in response to the influx of Cubans into South Florida. The immigration of Cubans from the port city of Mariel (known as the **Mariel boatlift**) saw the migration of 100,000 persons to the United States within a period of a couple of months. In response to this influx, the Immigration and Naturalization Service identified several prisons to house detainees awaiting decisions regarding their immigration or repatriation cases. One such facility was the Houston Processing Center, owned by Corrections Corporation of America (CCA). This facility was contracted through the U.S. Department of Justice and brought about the modern private prison system in the United States.

Currently, over 40,000 immigrants are detained every year. These immigrants are held for both civil and criminal detentions. There is virtually no difference in criminal and civil detention centers, noting that many civil detainees are held in jail structures. Criminal detainees are held frequently for misdemeanor offenses. This practice has prompted many advocacy groups to declare that racial profiling is the key impetus for immigrant detainment.

Post-Arrival Arrest/Imprisonment

The term used to describe the plight of immigrants into the correctional system is sometimes referred to as **ethnic succession**. This term was used to describe the exchange of one group of ethnic immigrants with a newer group of ethnic minority; one wave of immigrants would populate the prisons, only to be followed by a "newer"/"poorer" wave of immigrants that would follow.

The reasons for ethnic succession were the poor living conditions garnered by new immigrants combined with discriminatory practices. Most new immigrants had very little in the way of resources. Hence, they would likely find housing in the worst part of the city where there already existed a strong criminal presence. This would encourage their introduction into criminal activity. The newest waves of immigrants have always received harsher treatments by the **majority** as compared to more established groups. An example can be seen with the Irish prejudice that was felt during the great Irish wave of immigration during the 1840s. Frequently, shop-owners and other business would hang signs in the window front that would read, "NINA," short for "No Irish Need Apply." Other discriminatory practices such as dual employment rates for ethnic minorities made life more difficult. **Dual employment rates** refer to being able to pay different

Consider This:

During the Irish Immigration period of the 1840s, 55 percent of all those arrested in New York City were Irish. Irish were also disproportionately represented in poorhouses, hospitals, and prisons.

rates for the same work just because of the ethnic background of the person delivering labor. This discriminatory practice forced those who were already poor toward criminal activity because legitimate work could not be found. Currently, the practice of dual employment rates can be found in the hiring of illegal Mexican immigrants as migrant workers and other unskilled laborers throughout the United States.

The Newest Immigrants: Hispanic Americans

Hispanic Americans, both legal and illegal immigrants, are the largest ethnic group to immigrate to the United States of recent. Arguably, this group has filled the ethnic succession void of earlier immigrants and now fall victim to the many ethnic and racial biases of the past. Of the 1.44 million Americans behind bars, 345,900 are Hispanic (Guerino, Harrison, & Sabol, 2010). Compared to the representation in the population at large, Hispanics represent 24 percent of the prison population, whereas they only account for 16 percent of the population (Guerino et al., 2010; US Census Bureau, 2010). Hispanics have a particularly high representation in the Federal prison system, noting that they compose the largest racial group (40 percent). The disparity in the Federal system can mostly be attributed to the fact that a majority of those Hispanics held in Federal prison were illegal immigrants and a majority of the offenses were immigration offenses. Hispanic Americans are more than four times likely to be incarcerated than white males and are incarcerated at a rate nearly twice that of whites. Hispanic Americans, despite using drugs at rates very similar to other ethnic groups, are charged with drug crimes twice as often. Once entering prison, Hispanics are less likely than other ethnic groups to receive substance abuse treatment, therefore diminishing their opportunity to mitigate the illness. Hispanic Americans have unique issues related to poverty and assistance, noting that they have less education than other ethnic groups, they are more likely to experience poverty, and less likely to receive public support. In addition, where there is the view that Hispanic communities are riddled with violence, usually the opposite has proven to be true—that in fact Hispanic communities have lower incidences of crime than the general population. This view of the "criminal immigrant" may, in part, explain the disparities that Hispanics share in the prison system.

Middle Eastern Muslims

Since September 11, 2001, with the bombing of the World Trade centers, Middle Eastern immigrants have been under great scrutiny for their potential links to Islamic terrorism. One measure taken to thwart terrorism was the National Security Entry–Exit Registration System (NSEERS, INS Special Registration). NSEERS was developed to track non-citizen activities in the United States. The program targeted immigrants from Iran, Sudan, Libya, Syria, and Iraq register on arrival. Those non-citizens already residing in the United States (only from Iran, Iraq, Libya, Sudan, Syria, Afghanistan, Algeria, Bahrain, Eritrea, Lebanon, Morocco, North Korea, Oman, Qatar, Somalia, Tunisia, the United Arab Emirates, Yemen, Pakistan, Saudi Arabia, Bangladesh, Egypt, Indonesia, Jordan, and Kuwait) were also required to come forward and register. As a result of entry into the program, it is estimated that 16 percent of all those registered with the program (82,581) were detained and placed on the deportation list.

This has led many to claim that the U.S. "National security" measures taken after 9-11 have targeted almost exclusively people from the Middleeast and Southeast Asia and that this targeting has invariably resulted in incarceration, deportation, and interrogation of numerous individuals who had nothing to do with 9-11. It is noteworthy that of the 25 countries named in this mandate, 24 are predominantly Muslim countries. This has led many to decry that NSEERS (and the subsequent US-Visit program) amounts to another exclusionary set of laws targeting immigrants.

Asian Americans

As noted in prior chapters, these racial groups include Filipinos, Chinese, Japanese, Chinese, as well as Indo-Chinese groups (Vietnamese, Laotians, Cambodians, and Thais). Asians as a collective group have been stereotyped as the "model minority" because of the perceived economic success of Asians in America. Related to the "model minority" stereotype is the relatively low crime involvement experienced by Asians. One suggested theory for the low involvement with crime is that Asians identify with the label and therefore emulate attitudes and behaviors perceived to fulfill the stereotype. Asian communities also prefer to resolve problems within the family unit and therefore are less likely than other minority groups to report crimes.

Owing to low crime involvement, Asians likewise have low rates of incarceration. Asians constitute approximately 4 percent of the population but respectively only contribute to 1 percent of the prison population. Asian Americans also live up to the model minority stereotype behind bars. Asian Americans are the least likely ethnic/racial group to be involved in prison violence and the most likely to exhibit good behavior (Berg & DeLisi, 2006).

African Americans

Related to a number of historical and sociological reasons, African Americans are the ethnic minority group most severely affected by incarceration practices. It has been estimated that:

- 49 percent of prison inmates are African American, compared to their 13 percent share of the overall population.
- African American males have a 29 percent chance of spending time in prison at some point in their lives as compared to white males, who have a 4 percent chance (Bonczar & Beck, 1997)
- One in fourteen (7 percent) of African Americans is behind bars one any given day (Warren, 2008)

Incarceration, as a final destination of the criminal justice process, sees the cumulative effect in ethnic disparities, assuring that imprisonment is more pronounced for African Americans. Although the main reason for the disparities in incarceration rates for African American lies in the rate of arrest for serious felony (76 percent), 24 percent of the disparity is related to criminal histories, racial bias, and other factors (Blumstein & Beck, 1999). Elliot (1994) concluded through his longitudinal analyses that African American males, as a group, are more likely to be viewed as being aggressive than their

CURRENT EVENTS
Pelican Bay State Prison's Racial Based Classification System

In April of 2013, several California state prisons made national headlines for racially segregating inmates. Although not an official policy of the California Department of Correction (CDCR), many prisons operated a coding system by which certain racial/ethnic attributes were used to segregate offenders (Gottesdiener, 2013). The reason for this racial segregation policy, as acknowledged by the facilities, was to curtail gang violence which was perceived as being raced based. According to CDCR, the coding system labels were to "provide visual cues that allow prison officials to prevent race-based victimization, reduce race based violence, and prevent thefts and assaults" (Thompson, 2013).

Despite CDCR's rationale for implementing this coding system, everyone was not in agreement. Legal scholars weighed in by acknowledging that multiple cases brought before the courts have established that racial segregation is a violation of an offender's civil rights that is counterproductive. Further, critics such as the ACLU pointed out that California is the only state that continued to permit race based segregation, further demonstrating the dubious nature of the practice.

The issue of racial segregation was brought into the view of national media through the ruling of the California Appeals Court on **re Jose Morales habeas corpus** that occurred in January of 2013. Jose Morales, the defendant in the case, was an offender at Pelican Bay State Prison that was placed into one of the five racial classification categories (i.e., White, Black, Northern Hispanic, Southern Hispanic, and Other). He filed the writ of habeas corpus due to being denied privileges (e.g., yard recreation, visits, phone calls, etc.) because of his classification. Morales had been classified in the Southern Hispanic racial category and, because of violence that had occurred before his arrival to the facility, was placed on "lock-down" with other Southern Hispanics (Janquart, 2013). Morales claimed that, not only was he being denied privileges based on his classification, but he was never afforded the opportunity to choose which ethnic group he would prefer to be associated. In fact, Morales had noted during the classification process that he "could live with anyone" and did not care which ethnic group he was housed.

The ruling re-established offenders' individual protections afforded through the Constitution noting that – "Prison walls do not form a barrier separating prison inmates from the protections of the Constitution" (*Turner v. Safley*) - segregation that is prohibited outside of prison is also prohibited with prisons. Moreover, the court reaffirmed protections of a previous California Appeals case, **Escalera V. Terhune** which noted that, although ethnic grouping may be used as a short-term measure to curb violence, it should not be used as an ongoing solution. The court found that practices employed at Pelican Bay were not sufficiently tailored narrow enough to further the prison security, noting that race/ethnicity alone was the sole determinant of who would receive reduced privileges. The court noted that gang-affiliation and proclivity towards violence should be explored rather than the broad generalization of race/ethnicity.

It may be assumed that raced based classifications will continue in California despite the Morales case. The security benefits of this classification system are likely to be seen as outweighing the potential to deprive civil liberties. However, it is expected that Pelican Bay and other state facilities will take appropriate steps to ensure that civil liberties are honored despite the classification system employed. It is likely that these prisons will adopt policies such as requesting that offenders choose their ethnic classification or else interview offenders post-violence in order to better understand a prisoner's gang affiliations as well as their proclivities towards violence.

References: Gottesdiener, L. (2013) California's Prisons Face Allegations Of Race Discrimination. Huffington Post. Retrieved from: http://www.huffingtonpost.com/2011/05/25/california-prisons-race-discrimination_n_866948.html

Janquart, P. (2013). Pelican Bay Slammed for Housing Groups by Race. Courthouse News Service. Retrieved from: http://www.courthousenews.com/2013/01/29/54368.htm

Thompson, C. (2013). Are California Prisons Punishing Inmates Based on Race? ProPublica. Retrieved from: http://www.propublica.org/article/are-california-prisons-punishing-inmates-based-on-race

white counterparts despite the fact that African Americans were only slightly more prone to violence than whites (Mauer & Hyling, 1995). This public perception of ethnic attributes, in part, explains the harsher treatments initiated through the criminal justice system. Given the perception of threat that surrounds African Americans, black males are more likely to be arrested than whites for similar offenses.

Perhaps the most salient reason for the disparities in African Americans behind bars lies in the difference of arrest rates that are the result of the War on Drugs. African Americans and Hispanic Americans, as compared to whites, are at heightened risk of being arrested for drug offenses (Kubrin, Squires, & Stewart, 2007). One reason for this disparity is the result of differential sentencing guidelines for crack cocaine compared to powder cocaine (as discussed in Chapter 11). Moreover, in fighting the War on Drugs, enforcement has increasingly created a presence in minority neighborhoods (Boyum & Reuter, 2005). This presence invariably has led to higher drug-related arrest rates.

THE POOR/UNDEREDUCATED

One of the most distinguishing features of the modern criminal justice system lies in the fact that it is constructed along class lines. For all practical purposes, **class** is defined as a person's ability to earn income. What class a person belongs to in the United States can be simply reduced to how much income they earn. Income can be further correlated to a person's level of education. Those who are incarcerated, on average, lack education and consequently lack any real ability to earn a greater income (Western & Pettit, 2010). As can be seen in Figure 10-2, as education increases, the likelihood of being incarcerated decreases.

For ethnic minority groups, class and education are multigenerational events and are profoundly influenced by the current criminal justice system. Incarceration, as a practice, has a tremendously negative financial effect on those incarcerated, their

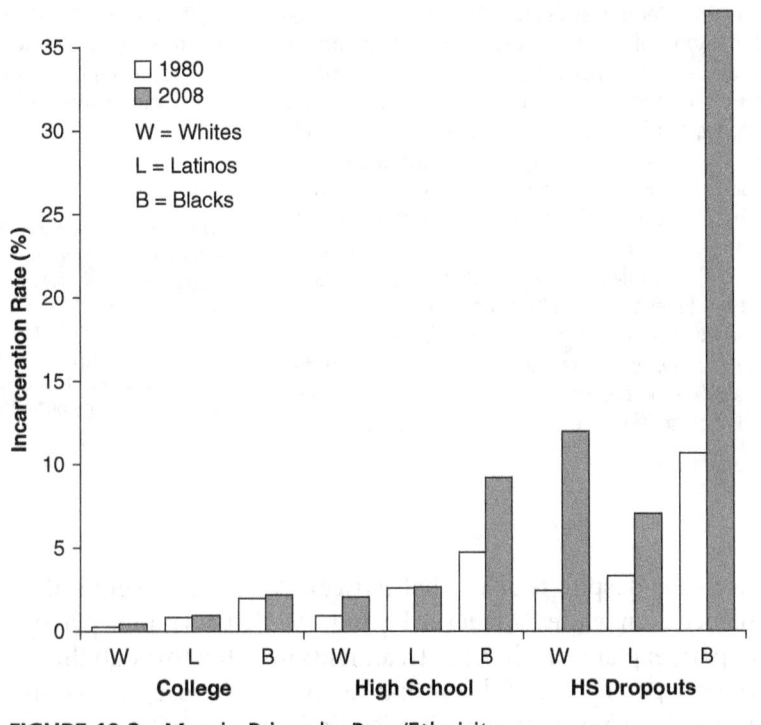

FIGURE 10-2 Men in Prison by Race/Ethnicity.

Box 10.7 Rise of the New Debtors Prisons?

The majority of incarcerated offenders are from lower classes, meaning that they are on average less educated, earn less income, and are more likely to suffer from poverty than someone of higher-class standing. However, increasingly, there has been a strong emphasis on offenders paying requisite fines and fees associated with criminal justice involvement. This has led to a practice where larger numbers of offenders are being incarcerated related to a failure to pay fines. This led the American Civil Liberties Union to declare that this practice is the modern day version of the "debtor's prison," despite the fact that the Supreme Court ruled in *Bearden v. Georgia* that persons could not be incarcerated simply because they were poor.

Bearden v. Georgia is the Supreme Court case that held that courts must take into consideration the reasons why a defendant failed to pay a fine before they could mandate imprisonment (Bannon, Nagrecha, & Diller, 2010). The defendant in the case, Danny Bearden, was sentenced to three years probation. Almost immediately after receiving his sentence, he was mandated to pay a $750. Mr. Bearden initially made payments of the fine, but soon after, his ability to pay changed because of a loss of employment. Owing to the fact that Mr. Bearden was illiterate, he had difficulty resuming employment and consequently could not pay off the fine. Because of not being able to pay the fine, Mr. Bearden's probation term

was revoked and he was forced to finish his sentence behind bars. The courts found that Mr. Bearden's failure to pay the fine was of no fault of his own and found it fundamentally unfair to imprison someone because of poverty.

Despite the protections and principles established in *Bearden v. Georgia* 20 years ago, courts routinely incarcerate persons for failure to repay debts that they could not be realistically be expected to manage. The cost associated with criminal involvement mount at all phases of criminal proceeding. An application fee for a public defender and a jail fee assessed during the preconviction phase are not uncommon. During sentencing, there are fines, restitution charges, fees for administrative costs, fees for designated funds (e.g., libraries, prison construction), public defender reimbursement fees, and prosecutor reimbursement fees. If one remains in jail while awaiting trial, there are frequently fees associated with that confinement. Once someone is placed in supervision (probation or parole) there is a possibility of probation and parole supervision fees, drug testing fees, vehicle interlock device (other monitoring devices), and mandatory treatment fees. If the offender fails to make payments or needs to be set up on a payment plan, there could be charges such as recovery of interest, late fees, payment plan establishment fees, and collection fees (Bannon et al., 2010).

families, and the communities in which they once lived and will return (Hairston, 2002). The stresses felt by family and communities of those incarcerated fuel a climate in which the cycle of incarceration continues. Those incarcerated have few ways to acquire resources for themselves or their families while incarcerated. This limits the offender's ability to care for his/her family or prepare for the post-incarceration period. The offender's family, often headed by a single caregiver, may struggle under the weight of financial hardships due to the lack of contribution by the offender. In addition, the single caregiver, in an attempt to earn a livable wage for the family, may neglect the children's supervisory needs. Communities, by their very nature, attract persons of like backgrounds. Because of this, whole disadvantaged minority communities struggle with the same issues of crime, incarcerated parents, lack of supervision, and poverty. Once offenders are released and return to these disadvantaged communities, they are further confronted with challenges to obtain adequate housing, pay requisite fines and penalties, and well as find adequate employment. As a result, minority offenders returning to the communities are more likely to recidivate, further damaging their own possibility at class advancement as well as contributing to the community's damaged class profile. According to America's Cradle to the Prison Pipeline Report, "the most dangerous place for a child in America to grow up is where poverty and race intersect."

RELIGION IN CORRECTIONS: GENERAL RIGHTS TO MINORITY RELIGIOUS BELIEFS

The 1st Amendment of the U.S. Constitution protects the freedom of religion as a fundamental right; this extends to inmates. In essence, regardless of whether someone is locked up, they still have a right to practice the tenets of their religious beliefs without obstruction. The right to religion in prison was not an issue that had been identified as requiring court intervention until the 1960s and 1970s. During this time a handful of cases emerged in Federal courts that directly addressed religious practice within the prison setting. Most notable among these cases were *Fulwood v. Clemmer* (1962), *Cooper v. Pate* (1964), and *Cruz v. Beto* (1972). In the **Fulwood v. Clemmer (1962)** case, the U.S. District Court for the District of Columbia ruled that correctional officials must recognize the Muslim faith as a legitimate religion and not restrict those inmates who wish to hold services. Although this is not a Supreme Court case, this case was decided in the U.S. Capitol district (the District of Columbia) and is therefore considered a decision that is universally agreed throughout the nation. Two Supreme Court cases that addressed religion include **Cooper v. Pate** (1964), where the courts recognized that prison officials must make every effort to treat members of all religious groups equally, unless they can demonstrate reasonableness to do otherwise. In the case of **Cruz v. Beto** (1972), it was ruled discriminatory and a violation of the Constitution to deny a Buddhist prisoner his right to practice his faith in a comparable way to those who practice the major religious denominations.

These cases demonstrate support for the practice of religious observance from Federal courts. However, the Federal courts are receptive to the potential challenges that can emerge due to inmate manipulation of religious safeguards. Later, the 5th Circuit Court of Appeals ruled in **Theriault v. Carlson** (1977) that the First Amendment does not protect so-called religions that are obvious shams, that tend to mock established institutions, and whose members lack religious sincerity. Though this was not a Supreme Court ruling, there are other legal precedents in state and Federal courts that indicate that, generally speaking, the judiciary does not expect prison officials to be foolish in their efforts to respect the religious rights of inmates; requests for religious consideration must be valid and sincere among inmates.

Furthermore, though inmates have protected rights to exercise their faith, prison staff do have the right to regulate religious practices within prisons to ensure that the safety and security of the institution are not compromised. In addition, *Turner v. Safley* established the ability of correctional officials to limit or curtail Constitutional rights of inmates as long as there is a legitimate penological interest. However, another case also emerged that further reinforced the ruling in *Turner* but was also specific to religious issues in prison. In the cases of **O'Lone v. Estate of Shabazz (1987)**, it was ruled that depriving an inmate of attending a religious service for "legitimate penological interests" was not a violation of an inmate's 1st Amendment rights. This fully affirms the fact that ultimately the safety and security of the institution is the paramount priority in prisons.

Thirteen years later, a significant piece of legislation emerged that has weathered the tests of litigation—the Religious Land Use and Institutionalized Persons Act of 2000 (RLUIPA). The RLUIPA has helped refine and clarify inmate's religious rights under the 1st Amendment. The primary intent of this law is to further safeguard (not restrict) the rights of inmates to practice their religious tenets in state and Federal facilities. Specifically, this law prohibits the government from restricting inmates' opportunities to practice their religion unless there is a compelling government interest and only if the interference is the least restrictive means of securing that interest.

Legality of "Non-traditional" Religions

In 2005 the Supreme Court issued a ruling in *Cutter v. Wilkinson*, addressing the constitutionality of the RLUIPA and its application to nontraditional religions. In this case, the plaintiffs who filed were inmates of prison facilities in the state of Ohio's Department of Rehabilitation and Correction. These inmates asserted that they were adherents of "nonmainstream" religions, namely the Satanist (typically the Church of Satan, which opposes Christian churches), Wicca (nature worship that includes witchcraft), and Asatru (the name for a Nordic-based religion that reveres Odin) religions. In addition, some of the plaintiffs in this lawsuit included members of the Church of Jesus Christ Christian (CJCC), which has ties to an extremist group and criminal gang, the Aryan Nation. These inmates complained that Ohio prison officials, in violation of the RLUIPA, failed to accommodate their religious exercise "in a variety of different ways, including retaliating and discriminating against them for exercising their non-traditional faiths, denying them access to religious literature, denying them the same opportunities for group worship that are granted to adherents of mainstream religions, forbidding them to adhere to the dress and appearance mandates of their religions, withholding religious ceremonial items that are substantially identical to those that the adherents of mainstream religions are permitted, and failing to provide a chaplain trained in their faith" (p. 713).

The Court unanimously decided in favor of the inmates and found that the state of Ohio had violated the rights of the inmates and that Ohio's objections to several issues regarding the RLUIPA were mistaken. The state of Ohio had reasoned that, among other things, the RLUIPA: (1) violated the Establishment Clause of the 1st Amendment, (2) gave religious inmates more rights and protections than nonreligious inmates, and (3) prevented prisons from enforcing appropriate security measures.

When addressing the Establishment Clause claim, the Court noted that the Religion Clauses of the First Amendment provide: "Congress shall make no law respecting an establishment of religion, or prohibiting the free exercise thereof" (p. 719). The first of the two Clauses are commonly called the **Establishment Clause**. The second, the **Free Exercise Clause**, requires government respect for, and noninterference with, the religious beliefs and practices of our nation's people. Although the two Clauses express complementary values, they often exert conflicting pressures. The Court has struggled to find a neutral course between the two Religion Clauses, both of which are cast in absolute terms, and either of which, if expanded to a logical extreme, would tend to clash with the other. In deciding the Cutter case, the Court noted that, "our decisions recognize that "there is room for play in the joints" between the Clauses (p. 719). With this in mind, the Court concluded that the RLUIPA neither established or promoted any specific religion (indeed, the plaintiffs represented several separate religions, two of which—the Satanists and the Church of Jesus Christ Christian—philosophically opposed one another) nor interfered with religious observance, including the right to *not* observe a religion or belief system. Thus, the Court reasoned, the RLUIPA did not violate the Establishment or the Free Exercise Clauses.

In addition, because inmates are free to choose their religion and because they are also free to choose no religion, the Court did not determine that religious inmates were afforded more rights than nonreligious inmates. Rather, if inmates wished to have a certain prescribed set of rights to activities that are part of a bona fide religion (not an obvious sham), then they had the unobstructed right to join that particular religion; the sincerity of their belief might be questionable, but was not the legal issue of argument and therefore was not addressed. Lastly, the Court rejected the notion that prisons could not provide sufficient security while respecting religious observances, again deferring to the prior ruling in *Turner v. Safley* whereby a balancing test should be utilized to ensure that neither the rights of inmates nor the security of the institution are compromised in an unreasonable fashion.

Religious Diets and Holy Days

Inmates of various religious groups will request specialized diets that are required for their particular faith. In most instances, prison staff can and do ask inmates to document that such a diet is a required part of their faith, in advance. Legitimate requests, based on recognized religious tenets, must be accommodated (Van Baalen, 2008). Rulings related to the Religious Land Use and Institutionalized Persons Act of 2000 (RLUIPA) suggest that prison systems should refrain from requiring inmates to prove that their dietary regimens are part-and-parcel of their religious tenets, so long as the dietary requests are not so onerous as to require substantive budget challenges and/or provided that the safety and security of the institution are not compromised.

Vann Baalen (2008) notes that many religious observances for even traditional faiths may require the consumption of particular foods (such as with Jewish Passover) and some religions may require that food not be consumed at specific times during the day or night (i.e., Muslim Ramadan). Prisons around the United States routinely accommodate these dietary modifications based on religion. There are even some occasions where a religious group may require the setting of a group meal as part of a ceremony; such types of request should be accommodated as long as appropriate notice is given to prison administrators (Vaan Baalen, 2008). In these cases, the chaplain or another religious expert will aid security staff in providing the accommodations to ensure that misunderstandings are minimized.

CONCLUSION

Since the beginning of human history, those in power have used the mechanisms of the law to restrict the personal freedoms and movements of those with less power. These restrictions of freedoms and movements through the law worked to galvanize class and caste roles within the society. Over the last millennium, institutions of confinement such as poorhouses, asylums, workhouses, jails, and prisons have been used to exclude, reform, and punish ethnic and social minorities.

The modern period of mass incarceration is yet another rewrite of the age-old script that tales the exclusion of minorities. Once incarcerated, caste roles of poverty, under-education, and ethnic criminality are further set for the offender and the community from which he/she hails. In fact, this tendency toward incarceration has been so widespread as to lead to considerations of religious freedoms in prison, addressing religions that might be considered nontraditional by many persons in the United States, religions that the original framers of the Constitution may not have even considered.

In order to live in a truly free society, new forms or criminal sanctions must be created that consider the personal and environmental factors that contribute to the stagnation of human potentials. Although civilization may never reach an apex where violent crime is eradicated—and thus prisons may always be a necessary evil—better options should be pursued that work to improve minority standing within society.

Chapter 10 Learning Check

1. Congress shall make no law respecting an establishment of religion, or prohibiting the free exercise thereof, refers to which of the following?
   a. Freedom of Religion
   b. The Establishment Clause
   c. The Free Exercise Clause
   d. None of the above

2. The issue of key importance in the development of the Trial by Jury of One's Peers is that judicial corruption is, at least partially, put in check because jurors are drawn equally from the common cloth that likely reflects the background of the accused.
   a. True
   b. False

3. _____ is the Supreme Court case that held that courts must take into consideration the reasons why a defendant failed to pay a fine before they could mandate imprisonment.
   a. *Turner v. Safely*
   b. *Cutter v. Wilkinson*
   c. *Cruz v. Beto*
   d. *Bearden v. Georgia*
   e. None of the above

4. One key contention of this chapter is that, in the field of corrections, persons with addictive disorders should be viewed as a specialized group in need of specialized care and treatment.
   a. True
   b. False

5. From your readings in this chapter, we have learned that the _____ refers to those in society who own property (and consequently the rights to production), whereas the _____ _____ are the workers who are constantly at odds with the bourgeois to prevent themselves from being exploited for labor.
   a. Haves; Have-nots
   b. Proletariat; Bourgeois

   c. Bourgeois; Proletariat
   d. Affluent; Downtrodden
   e. None of the above

6. Dual employment rate refers to being able to pay different rates for the same work just because of the ethnic background of the person delivering labor.
   a. True
   b. False

7. Behavioral illnesses are presented in this chapter as a form of minority status within the field of corrections.
   a. True
   b. False

8. African Americans represent _____ _____ of the prison population whereas they only account for _____ of the population.
   a. 49 percent; 13 percent
   b. 38 percent; 14 percent
   c. 32 percent; 15 percent
   d. 24 percent; 16 percent
   e. None of the above

9. The deinstitutionalization era was a well-intended response to overcrowding and deterioration of asylum facilities that ultimately added to the current state of jail and prison overcrowding that we see today.
   a. True
   b. False

10. Hispanics represent _____ of the prison population whereas they only account for _____ of the population.
    a. 49 percent; 13 percent
    b. 38 percent; 14 percent
    c. 32 percent; 15 percent
    d. 24 percent; 16 percent
    e. None of the above

Essay Discussion Questions

1. Explain how poor laws, indentured servitude, chattel slavery, economics, and incarceration practices are linked throughout the history of corrections.
2. Identify how mental/behavioral illnesses, substance abuse addiction, and deinstitutionalization are related to minority groups in corrections. Also, explain whether you think, in your own opinion, if these areas of correctional treatment should be considered a minority status.
3. Provide a discussion on how and why African Americans and Latino Americans (Hispanics) are overrepresented in the correctional population. Be sure to include economic factors in your discussion as with the intent of this chapter.

References

Bannon, A., Nagrecha, M., & Diller, R. (2010). *Criminal justice debt: A barrier to re-entry*. Brennan Center for Justice at New York: University School of Law. Retrieved from: http://www.brennancenter.org/content/resource/criminal_justice_debt_a_barrier_to_reentry/.

Belenko, S. (1998). *Behind bars: Substance abuse and America's prison population*. New York: National Center on Addiction and Substance Abuse at Columbia University.

Berg, M. T., & DeLisi, M. (2006). The correctional melting pot: Race, ethnicity, citizenship, and prison violence. *Journal of Criminal Justice, 34*(6), 631–642.

Blumstein, A., & Beck, A. (1999). Population growth in U.S. prisons, 1980–1996. In Tonry, M. & Petersilia, J. (Eds.), *Crime and justice: A review of the research, Vol. 26, Prisons* (pp. 17–61). Chicago, IL: University of Chicago Press.

Bonczar, T. P., & Beck, A. J. (1997). *Lifetime likelihood of going to state or federal prison*, Table 9. Washington, DC: Bureau of Justice Statistics.

Boyum, D., & Reuter, P. (2005). *An analytic assessment of U.S. drug policy*. Washington, DC: AEI Press.

Broner, N., Borum, R., & Gawley, K. (2002). Criminal justice diversion of individuals with co-occurring mental illness and substance use disorders: An overview. In G. Landsberg, M. Rock, L. Berg, & A. Smiley (Eds.), *Serving mentally ill offenders and their victims: Challenges and opportunities for mental health professionals* (pp. 83–106). New York: Springer.

Center for Disease Control. (2009). Prevalence and Most Common Causes of Disability Among Adults—United States. *Morbidity and Mortality Weekly Report, 58*(16), 421–426.

Elliott, D. S. (1994). Serious violent offenders: Onset, developmental course, and termination—the American Society of Criminology 1993 Presidential Address. *Criminology, 32*(1), 1–21.

Finzch, N., & Jutte, R. (1997). *Institutions of confinement: Hospitals, asylums, and prisons in Western Europe and North America, 1500–1950*. Cambridge, England: Cambridge University Press.

Foucault, M. (1965). *Madness and civilization: A history of insanity in the age of reason*. New York: Pantheon Books.

Goffman, E. (1961). *Asylums: Essays on the social situation of mental patients and other inmates*. Garden City, NY: Anchor Books.

Guerino, P., Harrison, P., & Sabol, W. (2010). Prisoners in 2010. Bureau of Justice Statistics. Retrieved from: http://www.bjs.ojp.usdoj.gov/content/pub/pdf/p10.pdf.

Hairston, C. F. (2002). Prisoners and families: Parenting issues during incarceration. Paper prepared for the *From Prison to Home: The Effect of Incarceration and Reentry on Children, Families, and Communities* national policy conference convened by the U.S. Department of Justice and the Urban Institute, Washington, DC, January 30–31.

Harcourt, B. (2009). From the asylum to the prison: Rethinking the incarceration revolution. Retrieved from: www.law.uchicago.edu/files/files/institutionalized-final.pdf.

Kubrin, C., Squires, G., & Stewart, E. (2007). Neighborhoods, race, and recidivism: The community-reoffending nexus and its implications for African Americans. Sage Race Relations Abstracts. Retrieved from: https://webfiles.uci.edu/ckubrin/Neighborhoods,%20Race%20and%20Recidivism.pdf?uniq=fn1t83.

Mauer, M., & Hyling, T. (1995). *Young black americans and the criminal justice system: Five years later*. Washington, DC: Sentencing Project.

Mumola, C. J. (1999). Substance abuse and treatment, state and federal prisoners, 1997. *Alcohol, 21*, 8.

National Center for Addiction and Substance Abuse at Columbia University—CASA. (2010). *Behind Bars II: Substance abuse and America's prison population*. Retrieved from: http://www.casacolumbia.org/articlefiles/575-report2010behindbars2.pdf.

National Institute on Drug Abuse, National Institutes of Health, & United States of America. (2007). *Drugs, Brains, and Behavior: The Science of Addiction*. Bethesda, MD: National Institute on Drug Abuse.

Rothman, D. (1971). *The Discovery of the asylum: Social order and disorder in the new republic.* Boston: Little Brown Co.

Torrey, E., Kennard, A., Enslinger, D., Lamb, R., & Pavle, J. (2010). More mentally ill persons are in jails and prisons than hospitals: A survey of the states. Retrieved from: www.treatmentadvocacycenter.org/.../final_jails_v_hospitals_study.pdf.

United States Census Bureau. (2010). *The hispanic population: 2010.* Retrieved from: http://www.census.gov/prod/cen2010/briefs/c2010br-04.pdf.

Van Baalen, S. M. (2008). Religious programming. In P. M. Carlson & J. S. Garrett (Eds.). *Prison and Jail Administration: Practice and theory.* Sudbury, MA: Jones and Bartlett Publishers.

Viney, W., & Zorich, S. (1982). Contributions to the history of psychology XXIX: Dorothea Dix. *Psychological Reports, 50,* 211–218.

Warren, J. (2008). One in 100: Behind bars in America 2008. The Pew Charitable Trust, Retrieved from: http://www.pewtrusts.org/uploadedFiles/wwwpewtrustsorg/Reports/sentencing_and_corrections/one_in_100.pdf.

Western, B., & Pettit, B. (2010). Incarceration and social inequality. *Daedalus,* 8–19.

Wexler, H. K., Lipton, D. S., & Johnson, B. D. (1998). *A criminal justice system strategy for treating cocaine-heroin abusing offenders in custody.* Washington, DC: National Institute of Justice, U.S. Department of Justice.

Corrections and Minorities: Minorities, Gang Affiliation, Gender, and Staff Issues

LEARNING OBJECTIVES

After reading this chapter, students should be able to do the following:

1. Identify key legislative acts that have impacted minorities in the prison environment.
2. Discuss how minority groups have been treated throughout the history of corrections in the United States.
3. Identify key features of the prison subculture.
4. Discuss how the prison subculture impacts the behavior of both inmates and staff.
5. Assess the current state of employee recruitment and training within a diverse correctional population.

KEY TERMS

1972 Gates v. Collier Prison Reform Case
1986 Anti-Drug Abuse Act
Affirmative Action Policies
American correctional association
Anti-Drug Abuse Act
Aryan Brotherhood
Barrio Azteca
Black Guerrilla Family
Bloods
Brennan v. Farmer
Chain gangs
Comprehensive Drug Abuse Prevention Act (1970)
Convict Lease system
Crips
Deliberate indifference
Equal employment opportunity

Fag
Federal prisons
Industrial prison complex
Institutional racism
Jailhouse turnouts
Jails
Mass incarceration
Mexican Mafia
Mexikanemi
Nazi Low Riders (NLR)
Ñeta
Pig Laws
Prison Rape Elimination Act of 2003 (PREA)
Prisonization
Private correctional facilities
Punk

State prisons

Symbiotic prison relationship

Texas Syndicate

Trusty system

Turning out

United Blood Nation

War on Drugs

Wolf

INTRODUCTION

Ironically, in a country that purports to be one of the freest in human history, more persons are behind bars than in any other place in the world (2.29 m). Closely tied to the actual number of persons locked up is a staggering percentage of the population that is incarcerated (as compared to the rest of the world), which is also the highest in the world (754 persons per 100,000 thousand). In contrast, only China and Russia, two countries know for very punitive criminal justice systems, come close to incarcerating as many of its citizens as does the United States. Collectively, the United States (2.29 m), China (1.57 m), and Russia (0.89 m) house nearly half of all those behind bars in the world (Walmsley, 2008). As relative to a population size, Russia is the only country that even remotely comes close to incarcerating as many of it citizenry as does the United States (629 persons per 100,000). In contrast to other world nations, the incarceration rate in the United States is nearly five to eight times that of most developed countries (See Figure 11-1). This reliance on incarceration as a primary form of societal deterrence and punishment has prompted many to term the practice as mass incarceration.

Since the early 1970s, the United States has experienced an expansive increase in the number of individuals incarcerated. It has been estimated that over the last 40 years, there has been a six-fold increase in the number of individuals confined in the United States. The reasons for this dramatic shift in incarceration rates are manifold. Perhaps the most simplistic reason for the increased reliance on incarceration is the prevalence of crime. The United States, when compared to other countries, has similar non-violent

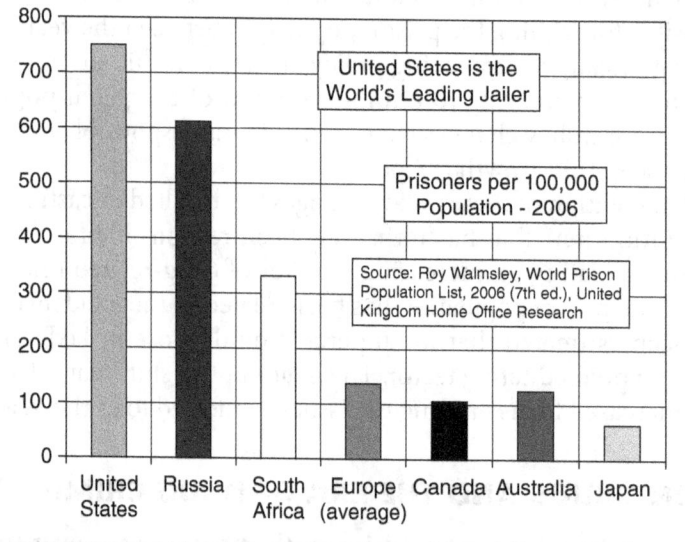

FIGURE 11-1 The United States Rate of Incarceration. *Source:* Walmsley, R. (2006). *World Prison Population List, 2006.* United Kingdom: UK Home Office Research.

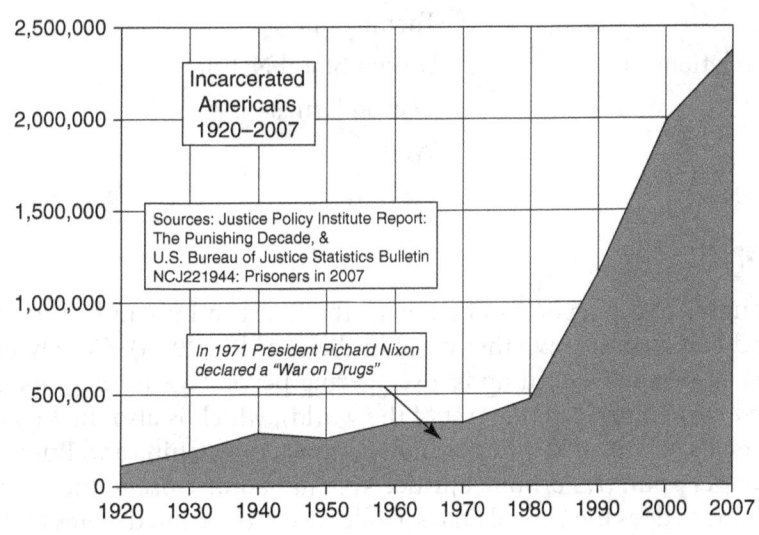

FIGURE 11-2 Incarcerated Americans. *Source:* Bureau of Justice Statistics. (2009). *Prisoners in 2008.* (OJ Publication No. NCJ 228417) Washington, DC: U.S. Government Printing Office.

crime rates; however, violent crime rates are exponentially higher. It is noteworthy that over 50 percent of all those incarcerated are for a violent crime offenses. It has been estimated that despite recent trends of decreases in homicides, the United States still maintains a rate that is four times higher than most countries in Europe. Largely, this difference in homicide rates is fueled by the prevalence of firearms in the United States. It is widely accepted that industrialized nations without strong gun control policy naturally have disparate murder rates.

Although an increase in the violent crime rate may explain some of the increase in the rise of incarceration rates, it however does not come close to being a driving force of this movement. Alfred Blumstein and Allen Beck (1999) concluded that of all the factors responsible for tripling the prison population between the years 1980 and 1996, none were as significant as sentencing policy changes. In this study, changes in crime rates were seen as contributing to a minor amount of the penal population growth (12 percent) whereas policy changes were seen as being responsible for the overwhelming amount of rise in this growth (88 percent).

The implementation of these policy changes has resulted in casting an increasingly wider "incarceration net" that has ultimately been responsible for criminalizing and subsequently incarcerating an increasing number of drug-related offenses. The greatest expansion of the prison population has been related to the incidence of drug-related crime. It has been estimated that in 60 percent of all those in Federal custody, drug involvement was a premeditating factor. The major policy shift that is largely seen as the reason for the increased focus on drug use issues is referred to as the **War on Drugs**.

THE WAR ON DRUGS AND THE ERA OF DRUG CRIMINALIZATION

The predominate reason for the expansion of the penal system over the last 30 years can be directly attributed to the creation of governmental infrastructure and policy whose focus was to stem the use and distribution of drugs. Before this modern era, incarceration was viewed as a community protection measure whose primary mandate was to house violent offenders. Fueled by the emergent public opinion of the late 1960s (that drugs were causing increased criminality and a decadence of society in general) a political groundswell formed that focused its attention on drug use and distribution issues.

The 1960s set the stage for reform measures that would be implemented in the subsequent decade. The 1960s were defined by a dramatic cultural shift that involved civil rights issues, the war in Vietnam, and the recreational use of drugs by teens. In addition, there was a perceived heroine epidemic that had been brought back from the War in Vietnam. The 1960s represented a cultural upheaval that threatened the more conservative views of previous generations. Capitalizing on conservative backlash, Richard Nixon, in his 1969 Presidential campaign, highlighted the country's illicit drug use problem and promised to alleviate crime related to drug use. In keeping with his campaign promises, once elected, President Nixon declared a "War on Drugs" in which illicit drugs were "public enemy No. 1." Implicit to this concept of the "War on Drugs" was that it was to be fought with subsequent policy changes and governmental interventions that had not previously existed. In order to carry out this so-called war, the administration needed a legal framework as well as a governmental policy-enforcing agency. These came in the form of the **Comprehensive Drug Abuse Prevention Act of 1970** and through the creation of the Drug Enforcement Agency (DEA).

The Comprehensive Drug Abuse Prevention Act (CSA) of 1970 was a Federal legislation that required, among other things, that pharmaceutical companies maintain physical security and strict record keeping of certain types of drugs. The CSA mandated that controlled substance be divided into five schedules based on potential for abuse, accepted medical use, and the accepted safety of the drug given through proper medical supervision. As it still exists today, Schedule I drugs have the highest potential for abuse, whereas Schedule II—VI drugs have a decreasing potential for abuse.

The trend toward a tough stance on drug-related crime has persisted until the present time. The only changes in the efforts have mostly centered on the kinds of drugs being targeted. In 1986, following the death of Boston Celtic star Lin Bias in a cocaine-related death, a renewed public interest spawned the eventual adoption of the **Anti-Drug Abuse Act**. One of the key provisions of this act, mandatory minimum sentencing, ultimately led to an explosion of the penal population as well as wide racial disparities.

The specific provision that has been showed to target minorities is mandatory sentencing guidelines for crack cocaine. Under these sentencing guidelines, possession of crack cocaine brings a mandatory five-year sentence. In contrast, 100 times the amount of powder cocaine is required to garner a five-year sentence. According to Boyum and Reuter (2005), this sentencing guideline has resulted in a racially disparate outcome, noting that African Americans are much more commonly charged with crack distribution whereas whites are more commonly charged with powder cocaine distribution.

Although on the surface, the rhetoric that still surrounds the War on Drugs seems noble and worthwhile, upon closer examination the whole premise behind the need for criminalization of drug use is faulty. First and foremost, many of those involved in drug sales and use are actually physically addicted to substances. The physiological and psychological processes involved with addictions are due to permanent brain alterations that have been caused by prolonged use of substances. In a sense, the neurologic functioning of the brain has been hijacked, thus accounting for the erratic, illogical, and sometimes criminal actions of many drug abusers. Even after the substances have been removed, it is well known that erratic thought processes persist. The criminalization of addictive diseases has resulted in attempting to solve a medical problem through rational-moralistic means. The resultant failure of this approach is obvious because addiction is not an illness that responds to punitive measures alone—treatment is needed. Unfortunately, substance abuse treatment within prison settings is a rarity. Second, the emphasis in the War on Drugs has been on supply-side control in the form of enforcement. At best, enforcement has had marginal success at making drugs cost prohibitive by decreasing supplies (Boyum & Reuter, 2005).

Finally, the War on Drugs has arguably made living conditions for many minority groups worse. The realities of drug use and sales are that average Americans experience very little risks for death, injury, or property loss, as related to direct consequences of drug use. As was the case in the Prohibition Era, the "black market" that has developed around drug trafficking and sales has more societal consequences than the substances alone. Minority communities, those communities that are most affected by the use of illicit substances, are the ones most affected by punitive enforcement strategies. These enforcement strategies have further eroded minority culture that was already struggling under the weight of impossible societal disadvantages. Poverty, crime, lack of education, and lack of employment are all greatly worsened when 40 percent of the working male population is removed from the community through incarceration.

MINORITIES AND INCARCERATION

As stated previously, the United States incarcerates nearly 754 persons per 100,000. This is an astonishing number when compared to the average world incarceration rate, which is 158 per 100,000 (Walmsley, 2008). Even more shocking is the disparities that exist between whites and ethnic minorities. As compared to whites, Hispanics are three times more likely than whites to be incarcerated and African Americans are six times more likely to be incarcerated (Carson & Sabol, 2011). There are numerous reasons for the disparities in incarceration rates that exist for minority offenders. Among them are policy issues that affect minorities disparately, targeting of minority communities as a result of increased crime rates and drug problems, access to substance abuse treatment services, economic disadvantages experienced by many minorities, the psychogenic effects of culture-specific drugs of abuse, and institutional racism.

As previously mentioned, policy issues have had a profound impact on the 40-year surge of offenders incarcerated; it should be noted that before these policies, many offenders might have otherwise been placed on supervised release. The Federal policy of the War on Drugs is a three-tiered approach that focuses on enforcement, prevention, and treatment. Of these three methods of tackling the U.S. drug problem, enforcement, also known as a supply-side intervention, has been the prevailing strategy, receiving 65–69 percent of all funding. Demand-side approaches that focus on treatment and prevention have received significantly less attention and funding. Ironically, of all approaches, enforcement seems to be the most expensive, with the least amount of return on investment (Boyum & Reuter, 2005). State approaches have similarly followed Federal policy, noting that mandatory minimum sentencing guidelines are prevalent. These sentencing policies have disproportionately affected racial minorities, thereby causing many to conclude the presence of **institutional racism**.

In addition to policy issues, societal issues that surround minority communities are seen as precipitants to the increased rates of incarceration. Disadvantaged minority communities, particularly African American communities, are more likely to experience increased incidences of crime, drug sales, and poverty as well as a greater law enforcement presence than does the other communities. Other coalescing social ailments may include a lack of meaningful employment opportunities, a lack of educational opportunities, and limited access to healthcare and treatment. In communities

FOCUS TOPIC 11-1

Native Americans Experience Disparate Rates of Incarceration

Rising prison population continues to be a problem throughout the United States. This is so true that many prison systems in the United States have begun mass-release programs where they emphasize reentry programming and community supervision to alleviate their problems of overcrowding. Although this is a fairly well-known development in prison operations and while we have shown that minorities are over-represented in prisons in the United States, these minority offenders are most often African American or Latino American.

However, in states like South Dakota, this racial and ethnic dynamic is different because in this state, it is the Native American inmate who is disproportionately represented in that prison system. Indeed, in South Dakota, the Sioux Native American Tribe has numerous members who are currently behind bars. The Sioux community is one that suffers from poverty in this state, with a large proportion of its primary aged potential breadwinning population (males between the ages of 18 and 30) being locked up in South Dakota. This has had a devastating effect on the Sioux community.

Similar patterns of over-incarceration are seen in other states with substantially sized Native American populations. States like Montana, Wyoming, and New Mexico share similar problems. This has, of course, drawn attention and led to anti-prison activism among various Native American tribes in these states. Furthermore, this has also placed renewed attention on the poor standard-of-living that is common to many Native American communities. In addition, Native tribes are increasingly showcasing rates of disparity and also alleging discrimination from the justice system, noting that when left to their own justice system (i.e., the tribes' own court system in Indian Country), the likelihood of severe sanctions that are disproportionate to the crime is much less.

It should be noted that this is similar to what we see when examining incarceration among other minorities. However, the Native American population is unique owing to historical circumstances and legal distinctions. Furthermore, the Native American population is a very small population compared to other minority groups. Likewise, their unique citizenship status would seem to mitigate, not aggravate, these numbers. Thus, many contend that, like other minority groups, the Native American population's over-representation is, of course, due to a multitude of factors; however, amidst these, there is a likelihood that institutional racism and biased outcomes are also part of the equation in determining why rates of incarceration are so high. This is certainly the view of many Native tribes who provide examples of disparity between Caucasians in these states who commit similar crimes but are given lighter sentences. Naturally, socioeconomic variables also impact this outcome, but the overall results are quite compelling and should be quite disturbing to persons working in the justice system.

Sources: Desjardins, L., & Lacey-Bordeaux, E. (2012, August 10). Problems of liberty and justice on the plains. CNN Justice, retrieved from http://www.cnn.com/2012/08/10/us/embed-america-tribal-justice/index.html. Hanser, R. D. (2013). *Introduction to corrections.* Thousand Oaks, CA: Sage Publications. Shusta, M., Levine, D. R., Wong, H. Z., Olson, A .T., & Harris, P. R., (2011). *Multicultural law enforcement: Strategies for peacekeeping in a diverse society* (5th Ed.). Upper Saddle River, New Jersey: Prentice Hall.

where there is a lack of opportunity for societal advancement, crime is regarded by many as a legitimate enterprise. A criminal lifestyle is often regarded as an opportunity to escape the trappings of poverty. Many youth living in these communities lack education or employable skills, thus making them targets for drug sales involvement. Once ensnared, these youth often start using drugs themselves. In a spiral of behaviors, actions that once were used toward the promise of "getting ahead," turn into a means of supporting addictive behaviors. This perpetuates a scene in these disadvantaged minority communities where hard drugs are sold in open view around an increased law enforcement presence. It is this climate of drug use and sales that led researchers Boyum and Reuter (2005) to conclude that heavy concentrations of drug sales in minority communities is perhaps the principal explanation for criminal justice disparities.

Coinciding with drug-related criminal activity that occurs in disadvantaged minority communities are the psychogenic effects of cocaine, an overall lack of treatment services, and a lack of financial resources that increases the likelihood of harsher sentences. Crack cocaine, the most prevalent drug found in many minority communities (because of its relatively low street value), is attached to a violent trade economy. In addition, it has psychogenic effects that promote violence. Consequently, the incidences of violent crimes in minority communities have flourished corresponding with the crack cocaine epidemic that began in the early 1980s. One example of the increase of violence associated with the crack cocaine epidemic is the increased homicide rate for African American males between the ages 14 and 24 that doubled in the years between 1984 and 1994 (Fryer, Heaton, Levitt, & Murphy, 2005).

Consequently, as the crack cocaine epidemic wanes (through the aging out of many crack cocaine users), the disparity gap continues to decrease for African Americans. Treatment alternatives are also limited for many minorities. Minorities are less likely to have health insurance or be able to afford treatments for substance abuse condition. Furthermore, in many states, Medicaid funds, which are used as an indigent healthcare resource, do not pay for substance abuse treatments. The only option for many of these individuals is to seek treatment at state-funded facilities or through local non-profit organizations. Thus, it is a widely held belief that minority communities have a disparate unmet treatment need (OAS, 2009).

CURRENT EVENTS

America is Waking up from the Mass Incarceration Nightmare: Political Opponents Unite for a Common Goal

As emphasized elsewhere in the text, the United States leads the world in the rate at which its citizens are incarcerated. No other country, (including known human rights violating countries such as North Korea) house more persons per capita than does the United States. Moreover, it is estimated that there has never been a country in human history to incarcerate person at the rate of the United States.

The reason for this mass incarceration of citizens is manifold, but most significantly is caused by the misguided War on Drugs. Since 1980, the number of persons incarcerated has quadrupled. Further, it has been acknowledged that, like no other time in history, human behavior has been criminalized leading to more punitive/longer sentences (Bloom, 2012). Further, upon release, offenders often experience a heavy-handed, pricey control issued form the criminal justice system which follows them for years to come (Bloom, 2012). Felons often are barred from fully participating in society lacking the ability to vote, obtain public housing, or else receive education through a variety of student loan programs. This overbearing system has created a spiral of behaviors for offenders that have, all too often, resulted in a re-offense.

Ironically, recent interest in reforming our current prison dilemma has not stemmed from the human rights concern, but rather, come from the Federal, State, and local budgetary concerns. Prison costs have, as of recent, been crippling to State, Federal, and local budgets, where, in some case, more money is spent on housing offenders than is spent on any other civic program – including education.

Reformers on a state, Federal, and local levels are continuing to see the need for prison reform. In one such example, Texas governor, Rick Perry has instituted changes reducing the sanction for non-violent drug offenses. In recent years, the State of Texas has passed legislation to that mandated probation for drug possession convictions for less than a gram. Further, Texas allocated more funding to substance abuse treatment and alternatives to prison ($241m) for non-violent offenders (The Economist, 2013).

In August of 2013, there seemed to a renewed effort to remedy the mass incarceration issue through unlikely alliances in Congress. Political players from both sides of the aisles joined in with embracing the philosophy that something must be done to reduce the current rate of incarceration. Eric Holder, the current Attorney General of the United States commented with the following statement, "Too many Americans go to too many prisons for far too long, and for no truly good law enforcement reason". One recent bill for 2013, the Smarter Sentencing Bill, introduced by Congressmen Raul Labrador (R-ID) and Bobby Scott (D-VA), aims to reduce mandatory minimum sentencing requirements of drug offenses (Drug Policy Alliance, 2013). In addition, it also will mitigate the disparity between crack cocaine and powder cocaine convictions experienced by African Americans. As noted by Jasmine Tyler, Deputy Director of National Affairs for the Drug Policy Alliance (from Drug Policy Alliance, 2013), the use of mandatory minimum sentences is costly and ineffective, being too costly for us to further ignore the deficiencies inherent in this sentencing approach.

References: Bloom, L. (2012). When Will the U.S. Stop Mass Incarceration? CNN. Retrieved from: http://www.cnn.com/2012/07/03/opinion/bloom-prison-spending/index.html

Drug Policy Alliance (2013). Bipartisan Bill to Reform Mandatory Minimums Introduced in U.S. House. Retrieved from: http://www.drugpolicy.org/news/2013/10/bipartisan-bill-reform-mandatory-minimums-introduced-us-house-companion-bipartisan-sena

The Economist (2013). An Unlikely Alliance of Left and Right. Retrieved from: http://www.economist.com/news/united-states/21583701-america-waking-up-cost-mass-incarceration-unlikely-alliance-left-and

WOMEN AND INCARCERATION

The number of women in state and Federal prisons continues to grow at a rate that is faster than that for male inmates, with the incarceration rate for women increasing at nearly twice that of men (U.S. Department of Justice, 1994). Further, a substantial portion of the female inmate population is held in three states. Data from 2005 shows that these three states are (1) California, which held 21,601 women in prison and jail, (2) Texas, which held 21,344 female inmates in prison and jail facilities and, (3) Florida, which had 14,094 women behind bars throughout the state (Hartney, 2007).

In 2009, there were over 106,000 women in prisons, which is substantially more than were locked up at the beginning of the millennium. While the total number of female offenders incarcerated has seen a steady growth, in 2009 there was a slight downturn in this growth. The reasons for this are not clear, but may be due to a combination of factors related to more emphasis on reentry, treatment, and community-based sanctions. Furthermore, though the female population continues to grow in prison, they are, in fact, a small proportion of the overall prison population, pushing perhaps 8 percent of the entire U.S. prison population. To ensure that the numbers are kept in perspective, consider that at the end of 2003, U.S. prisons held 1,368,866 men. This means that in 2003, one in every 109 men was in prison. For women the figure was one in every 1,613.

Because of the War on Drugs, and because of the extended sentences associated with that era, many women were incarcerated for lengthier sentences and this has helped fuel the growth in the female inmate population. Given the rates of drug use among female offenders, the growth in their numbers behind bars is not surprising. Currently, the United States incarcerates more women than any other country in the world.

INSTITUTIONAL RACISM AND CORRECTIONS

Institutional racism, also known as structural or systemic racism, is defined as racism that occurs in public government bodies, corporations, and institution. At the core of institutional racism are preferential or discriminatory policies that create disparities in access to societal affluence. In the United States, there is a long history of prejudicial and racial discriminatory practices that have been present in almost every facet of American life including employment, societal benefits, access to healthcare and education, and housing. It is widely held that race-based slavery created a social underclass in the United States.

Despite the fact that slavery was abolished, a racial underclass has persisted through policies that discouraged access to societal wealth and prominence. Specific examples of these policies include the convict lease system, Jim Crow laws, and the one-drop rule (as previously mentioned in Chapter 2). Many scholars believe that present disparities in incarceration rates are created by yet another form of institutional racism. As indicated previously, policy decisions are the single greatest cause of the high rate of incarceration in the United States. The War on Drugs, which coincidentally began at the end of an era that represented newfound rights and freedoms for African Americans, targeted African American communities where drugs were most likely to be sold. Once more, Federal sentencing guidelines (for which states frequently pattern laws) reinstated mandatory sentencing guidelines, and saw fit to make punishments for crack cocaine possession (a form of cocaine of low street value, therefore being more common in minority communities) more severely than that of powder cocaine possession (a form of cocaine commonly associated with affluence because of its relatively high street value). There is little doubt that African Americans, because of specific policies, have been the group most affected by the War on Drug's policies. As shown in Graph 5.3, the practice of incarcerating drug offenders has disproportionately most affected African Americans, particularly in the years following the passage of the **1986 Anti-Drug Abuse Act** (See Figure 11-3). This dramatic increase following the passage of the 1986 Anti-Drug Abuse Act has lead the NAACP to title this particular provision as one of the most discriminatory laws in U.S. history.

The terms mass incarceration and prison industrial complex are used to represent this capitalistic system that feeds on the underclass of American society. Arguably, African Americans (as well as other minority groups) have been the main targets of a capitalistic system, which uses the circumstances and disadvantages of minorities to fuel a complex bureaucratic machine. One could deduce through logical conclusion, by following the historical record, that **mass incarceration** and the **industrial prison complex** are tools of subjugation that have replaced outdated forms of societal repression through policies of institutional racism.

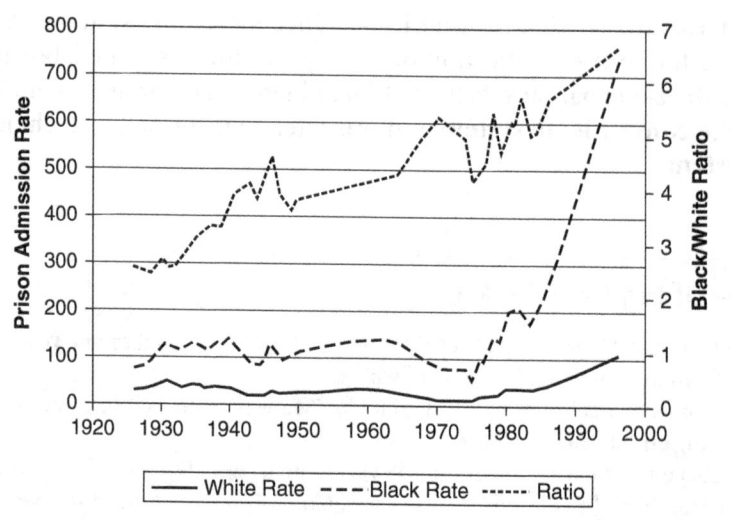

FIGURE 11-3 Minority Disparities Increase. *Source: Presentation by pam oliver*, University of Wisconsin. Retrieved from http://ssc.wisc.edu/~oliver/RACIAL/Disparities%20slidesNov2001.pdf

A HISTORY OF MINORITY TREATMENT IN IMPRISONMENT

The history of modern-day corrections has a sordid past that is littered with abuses. Many of these abuses directly involved minority groups and can be linked to a common theme of the exploitation of minorities that is part of our historical past. Indentured servitude, for example, was an exploitation of those of lower socioeconomic standing for the provision of cheap labor. Likewise, race-based slavery was an exploitation whose aim was to fill the labor void created by the plantation system. Although the provision of labor was the primary reason for these exploitations, this system ensured that a largely raced-based social stratification occurred that persists until the present time.

The emergence of the prison system, particularly as it relates to minorities, can be traced back to practices employed in the South following reconstruction. The South is of particular interest because the majority of ethnic minorities living in the country were from the South, noting that African Americans had not begun to migrate to the North and West until about 1910 (1910–1930 is known as the first great migration period). In many ways, the prison system in the South became a legal mechanism by which to reinstitute the practice of slavery.

Following the Civil War in the South, there was widespread belief that African Americans were prone to criminal activity, particularly larceny (Curtin, 2000). To stem perceptions of larcenist blacks, as well as to regain political power that was lost during the reconstruction era, draconian laws were put in place known as "**Pig Laws**." Pig Laws made theft of small animals or any property valued at $10 or more to be punishable by five years in prison. Under these laws, frequent abuses occurred that targeted young black men, who committed seemingly "petty" crimes of theft. It was not uncommon for these laws to apply to children as young as eight years old with crimes as small as stealing loose change from dry goods stores.

The resultant of these laws was a disparate increase in the number of African Americans incarcerated during this period. For example, in Mississippi three years after the Pig Laws were instituted (1874), the prison population quadrupled—the majority of the new arrests being African Americans. Once locked up, systems were instituted that resembled the former institution of slavery—filling the same labor niche as well as employing the same barbaric tactics of forced labor. The progression of this system began with the **convict lease system** and was later transformed into **chain gangs** and the **trusty system**.

Examples of Pig Law Arrests

- Green Country Alabama—"Three little Negro Boys" Sentenced to one year in jail for the theft of "three oranges and a bottle of wine".
- Rause Echols—"a colored" of Lauderdal Co., MS was sentenced to three years in prison for stealing an "old suit of clothes".
- Lewis Luckett "a Negro" of Canton, MS was sentenced to two years for the theft of a hog.
- Robert Hamber—"a colored" of Chicksaw, Co., MS was sentenced to five years for the theft of a horse

---

The Convict Lease System (1865–1910)

The convict lease system was a form of prison labor instituted in the American South following the abolition of slavery. In this system, states would lease out their prisoners to private companies in return for paying the state a fee. As a whole, the system represented a means of financial profit through the use of subjugated labor—much like its predecessor institution—slavery. States where the convict lease system was used made large profits for states and private enterprises alike. Conditions working in the convict lease system were seen as deplorable—much like conditions that were common to slavery.

With the institution of the convict lease system, African American representation in the criminal system grew exponentially. This involvement in the prison system grew primarily for two reasons: (1) emancipation released a largely unskilled undereducated labor force into areas where there were few employment opportunities and (2) policy enactments that targeted freedmen increasing the number of arrests (e.g., Pig Laws).

The Trusty System (1910–1975)

The convict lease system lost the appeal of the public not because of the moral dilemma that it created, but rather because of the economic inequalities that it created. Businesses could not compete with the inexpensive labor offered by many prison institutions, and therefore opposed the measure. To replace the convict lease system, a system that had been very profitable to many Southern states' bureaucracies, a new system was instituted that was a variation of convict leasing. Instead of selling labor to private enterprises, a kind of "work-farm" was created that sold various crops and products. In addition to the selling of goods, the prison limited the number of state employees hired and supplemented the staff numbers with inmate trusties. These inmate trusties were responsible for administering and controlling the inmate population—often times with very physical forms of punishment.

INTERNATIONAL FOCUS

North Korean Prison Camps

North Korea, a country known for human rights violations, has recently been exposed for expanding its largest prison camps. The tyrannically ruled nation is suspected of housing over 100,000 prisoners – some of which are most certainly political dissidents. The North Korean government has always denied the existence of these camps despite overwhelming evidence that they in fact exist. Following the death of Kim Jong Il (father), the world looked on with anticipation hoping the brutalities of the former leader would be ended. Kim Jong Un (son) ascended to the throne and, unfortunately, it appears as if the current leader intends to continue the abuses of the past.

In the recent investigation (December 2013) conducted by Amnesty International, satellite images found that new buildings had been constructed in one of the largest compounds – kwanliso 16. With the recent growth of the compound, the total land mass occupied for housing prisoner is three times that of Washington D.C. It is estimated that 20,000 prisoners are held in this facility alone.

As one might expect, abuses are common in North Korean compounds. In the same investigation, former inmates and security guards were interviewed and asked to recall the conditions of the compounds. These informants noted that compounds often housed women and children, and that rape and murder were commonplace. One security officer described abuses as requiring women to perform sexual favors for men throughout the evening, only to then be put to death because the captors did not want the secret to get out through word-of-mouth from the victim (Fox News, 2013).

In addition, it has been reported by prior prison staff that it was not uncommon for detainees to be forced to dig their own graves and then be killed with hammer strikes to the back of the neck. He also recounted memories of prison officers strangling detainees and then beating them to death with wooden sticks.

Corroborating the abuses reported by Lee are similar accounts by detainees such as Kim Young-soon. Kim Young-soon, a former detainee of North Korean compound of Yodok, was imprisoned for gossiping about the former leader Kim Jong Il. Like most North Korean prisoners, no trial was afforded and his family members were also imprisoned due to guilt by association.

Similarly, a UN report, published in September of 2013, detailed similar abuses. In this report, compounds were said to produce "unspeakable atrocities" comparable to those of Nazi concentration camps (Wiener-Bronner, 2013). Some interviewed were said to have been forced to eat lizards and rodents to survive. Others recalled accounts of women that were forced to kill their babies due to the unsustainable conditions of the compounds.

References: Fox News (2013). Satellite Images Reveal Scale of North Korea Prison Camps, Group Says. Retrieved from: http://www.foxnews.com/world/2013/12/05/satellite-images-reveal-scale-north-korea-prison-camps-group-says/

Smith, A. (2013). North Korea Expands Prison Camp Where Inmates Dig Own Graves: Amnesty International. NBC News. Retrieved from: http://worldnews.nbcnews.com/_news/2013/12/05/21768325-north-korea-expands-prison-camp-where-inmates-dig-own-graves-amnesty-international

Wiener-Bronner, D. (2013). North Korea is Still Expanding its Largest Prison Camps. The Wire. Retrieved from: http://www.thewire.com/global/2013/12/north-korea-prison-camp/355876/

In the trusty system, white and black camps were frequently segregated. From the segregated groups, a hierarchy of prison status was formed. At the top of the hierarchy were "trusty shooters" who would essentially carry guns and control day and night work crews. The second level of trusties was the unarmed trusty who would care for janitorial, clerical, and other menial tasks. A third level of trusty included inmates known as "hallboys." Hallboys would carry out simple tasks that needed to be performed.

The trusty system ended in the years following the **1972 *Gates v. Collier Prison Reform Case*.** This case involved civil rights advocates that for many years had complained about the abhorrent conditions of the Mississippi State Penitentiary at Parchman. In this case, four Parchman Penitentiary inmates, represented by lawyer Roy Haber, brought suit against the superintendent of the prison alleging that their rights had been violated by being subjected to cruel and unusual punishment. The court sided with the Parchman inmates, noting a number of abuses against the inmates. These abuses were decided to be a violation of prisoners' First, Sixth, Eighth, and Fourteenth amendments rights and brought a rapid closure to the trusty system, bringing about a much-needed change to the American prison system.

Chain Gangs

Chain gangs were an extension of the convict lease system and became prominent in the Southern United States following the Reconstruction Period. For many who lived in the South, chain gangs were unmistakably a reminder of days of old, noting that the majority of convicts working on the chain were African Americans. For those who would witness the work of chain gangs, there was perhaps the feeling that the rigid caste system that saw fit to relegate African Americans to the lowest rungs of society was still intact. Slavery as an institution had officially been abolished, but the chain gang would accomplish the same end—forced labor performed by African Americans. Although the widespread use of chain gangs ended in 1955, in 1995 there was a resurgence of their use in Alabama and Arizona as part of a "get tough on crime campaign." Alabama's reinstitution of the chain gang as a method of reform was short lived, lasting less than a year, whereas Arizona's Maricopa County Jail still relies on chain gangs to provide public labor. Dubbed as "America's Toughest Sheriff," Sheriff Joe Arpaio brags on his website that, "Of equal success and notoriety are his [the sheriff's] chain gangs, which contribute thousands of dollars of free labor to the community. The male chain gang, and the world's first-ever female and juvenile chain gangs, clean streets, paint over graffiti, and bury the indigent in the county cemetery."

Old School Corrections, Prison Reform, and LSP Angola during the Trusty System

In the summer of 1943, a former Angola prisoner by the name of William "Wooden Ear" Sadler wrote a series for Collier's Magazine entitled "Hell on Angola." Sadler was given the name "Wooden Ear" because he had been deafened on one side by the brutal attack from a prison guard. In the "Hell on Angola" series, Sadler described a conversion of Angola that had occurred in the 1930s that turned the prison into a government entity that would pay for itself. In Sadler's description of this process, he stated that it brought with it an "era of murder, graft, corruption, maimings and brutality, all to the end that Angola might become self-supporting." Sadler described life at Angola as being "worse than the darkest days [of slavery] before the war." Armed with a new general manager, who Sadler coined as "Smith," Angola was to become a "place of profit [for the state of Louisiana] not loss." Smith, the general manager, used the expression "make it go!" which meant whether by "blood, flesh, or tears" "put more dollars in the bank"—"profits must continue!"

In his narrative, Sadler described barbarities that are difficult to comprehend. During this time, inmates of Angola were relegated to a life of slavery. Like the historical beginnings of Angola, that was once a 18,000-acre slave plantation, men are forced to tend crops and work the farm in order to make profits. Life in the prison was unbearable. Prisoners were commonly fed a piece of cornbread and tomato stew consisting of tomato base with a piece of meat no larger than a person's thumb. Dessert consisted of "the last-run molasses" from the Angola sugar refinery that was full of "roaches, rats, and sundry filth" that had never been screened out during the refining process. Death related to heatstroke was a common occurrence.

Abuses by the Wardens of Angola were commonplace. The Head Warden, who was called "Bad Eye" behind his back (because of his left eye being out of focus), was a sadist who held the power of life and death of every inmate at Angola within his hands. When inmates failed to live up to the expectations of "Bad Eye," "the bat"—a three-feet-long leather strap that is double near a two-feet wooden handle, was brought into action. One subsequent beating with the bat was described as follows:

> Placing his foot on the naked man's neck, "Bad Eye" asked: "So you can't pick Mistah Brown's tomatoes? You sorry, good fo' nuthin! You want to just go in the field and talk, eh? I'll l'arn you about workin', you heah?" The "bat" is first "curled" under the shoe... the tip must be well sanded. It must bite and tear flesh. "Bad Eye" raised it over his head, with both hands, and brought it down with a sharp pop like a pistol shot on the naked man's back. One... two... three...twenty; the count goes beyond thirty... the man moans, pleads for mercy, calls on God. The captain tells him: "you bettah call on someone closer to you- someone who kin help you!" The man then pleads with "Bad Eye": "Captain... please captain... please! I'll work, captain sir! I'll work and never fall out! Please captain!"

Men were not alone in suffering the horrors of "the bat"—women prisoners also were commonly beaten across the "breast" or "stomach." These vicious beatings of inmates sometimes continued until 170 lashes were given. This often left a "man's back a bloodied pulp" that would bleed into his clothes and stick. In addition to the "biting pain," these men and women endured a feeling of "helplessness" that encompassed them. Of this, Sadler states, the victim either "endured or died."

Angola in this period was also known to be a murderous place. Wardens, guards, and trusties alike could shoot an inmate "if they thought he was trying to escape." Sadler noted: "Bad Eye" had been personally responsible for several deaths. In one account, "Bad Eye" was thought to have shot his trusty chauffeur after a brief agreement. In yet another incidence, "Bad Eye's" houseboy was found floating in the Mississippi River with gunshot wounds to the abdomen.

TYPES OF MODERN PRISON FACILITIES AND AFFIRMATIVE ACTION

The incarcerated population in the United States is supervised in structured environments on four levels. These incarcerating facilities include: **jails**, **state prisons**, **Federal prisons**, and private correctional settings. Jail is a term used to refer to localized structures whose primary purpose is to house pretrial detainees or offenders with minimal sentences of a year or less. Jails are typically viewed as local holding facilities where arrested offenders can be housed until bond can be posted or until a court proceeding can occur. In some cases, offenders with short terms are allowed to serve those sentences in a local jail where conditions might be more favorable for the inmate

FOCUS TOPIC 11-2

Clovis Tillery: An Interview with One of Angola's First African American Guards

In the Spring of 1971, the then 25-year-old Clovis Tillery was returning from the battlegrounds of Vietnam to accept his first job as a civilian at Angola Prison. Little did Tillery know at the time that his combat experiences in Vietnam would pale in comparison to what would become a 20-year career at "America's Bloodiest Prison."

Tillery was brought into Angola at a time of transition. The pending *Gates v. Collier Case* had drawn attention to the Southern prison system. This unwanted attention of the case would bring about a gradual change that would preempt the eventual *Gates v. Collier* ruling. Tillery would be those among the first hired to replace "trusty guards," also known as "khaki backs." "Khaki backs" manned the majority of posts in the prison, including armed guard posts. Tillery's hiring was unique not only because of his service that would replace the khaki backs, but also because he was one of the first African Americans to work as a guard at Angola. Tillery's first days on the job were marked by his introduction to a "khaki back" at Camp F who told Tillery, "All you need to do is just be here. I'll take care of things. I'll protect you." It was understood that inmates ran the prison.

Tillery described the scene when he arrived at Angola as "living up to its name as America's Bloodiest Prison." Unlike the war that he had left a year previously, his first days of his newfound employment were filled with apprehension and dread. "I had been in fire-fights in Vietnam, but I never got as scared as I did my first days at Angola," "You never knew what to expect when working in Angola," Tillery noted. "There were generally two to three stabbings a week" and "sexual enslavement was common practice." Tillery described that the prison as being "survival of the fittest," noting that only the "strong survived" Angola.

One of Tillery's earliest experiences while on his first shifts at the prison was witnessing the murder of an inmate. The incident that led up to the murder was that the newly arrived inmate had been claimed as a sex slave by one of the camp's "toughest" inmates. According to Tillery, it was a common practice at Angola during this period for inmates to claim other inmates as sexual slaves. Tillery stated, "On the walk leading from reception, the inmates all use to line up to greet the newly arrived inmates. They were pointing at the new inmates to claim them as the sexual slaves. If the new arrivals declined the sexual advancement of long-time inmates, the long-time inmates would 'turn them out' or force them into sexual acts." In the incident that lead up to the inmate's death, another inmate had claimed him as a sexual slave. In an attempt to get away from the long-timer's abuse, the other inmate went to the guards and asked to be removed from the dormitory setting. "No sooner than had the abused inmate walked out the door of the dormitory, the long-timer rushed up behind him and stabbed him to death." "This was my introduction to Angola." Of this incident, Tillery noted that, "because of how the prison was run under the trusty system, guards had very little control over the population. It was not uncommon for there to be 'one guard to 200 inmates.'" A year later, Tillery recalled, "a guard was stabbed to death which reminded me of how dangerous Angola could be."

On race relations, Tillery stated that when he first arrived at Angola, blacks and whites were still segregated. Tillery noted that approximately 85 percent of Angola's prison population at the time was African American. When asked of the reasons of the high numbers of African Americans at Angola, Tillery stated, "At the time, if you went to prison you went to Angola. Today Angola primarily houses long-term and violent offender. Back then, everybody went to Angola. Blacks at Angola seemed to be convicted of petty crimes at a higher rate than whites." When asked what it was like being an African American in a place predominated by white guards, he stated, "I didn't have much trouble, but fortunately I worked with a Warden that was open to the situation." As for inmate relationships, "half liked it and half didn't." "Half of the inmates thought an African

American guard would work out in their favor because he might be more lenient while the other half didn't like it because it represented change." When asked about desegregation of Angola, Tillery commented, "The day arrived when we finally did it and there was a lot of talk about what might happen. People thought it was gonna be bad. Then, nothing happened!"

In 1980, Tillery was stabbed in the arm by an inmate armed with a shank. Of this experience, Tillery noted, "I guess it didn't bother me too much, I continued working there for ten more years after that happened." This, as well as many other horrors of Angola, now recedes into the back of Tillery's mind. Tillery now is as battle-hardened and resolute as any combat veteran. Despite his experiences, he is still as energetic, hopeful, and vibrant as ever. He currently stays active through his employment at Richwood Correctional Center in Monroe, Louisiana, where his experience serves him well in his role as Warden.

Source: Personal interview with Clovis Tillery in 2010.

(e.g., local family support, release to local community). State prisons are correctional facilities that house those who have been sentenced to prison for the violation of a state law. Federal prisons are reserved for offenders who have been prosecuted in violation of Federal laws. Jails, state prisons, and Federal prisons are all generally staffed by public employees and paid for through local, state, and Federal tax revenues. The fourth category of prisons is **private correctional facilities**. These correctional facilities are private for profit facilities that are often contracted through local, state, and Federal agencies. Private correctional facilities can house local, state, and Federal offenders, often within the same facility. Fewer than 3 percent of all inmates are currently incarcerated in private facilities, noting that the vast majority of offenders are housed in public institutions.

Because of the public nature of most correctional facilities, there are a number of employment guidelines that encourage the hiring of minority applicants. It is perhaps because of these hiring principles that correctional institutions have seen a dramatic diversification of staff over the last 20 years. Among these measures are equal employment opportunity laws and **affirmative action policies**. **Equal employment opportunity** laws ensure that employers cannot discriminate against employees on the basis of age, sex, race, or ethnic origin. Affirmative action policies are designed so that hiring practices favor underrepresented minority groups. Affirmative action policies are designed in order to redress disadvantages that minorities have encountered as a result of institutional racism.

CORRECTIONAL WORKERS

Before the 1980s, prisons tended to be in rural areas and hired staff from within the same locality. Consequently, staffing patterns in those institutions largely reflected the local demographic. Overwhelmingly, the racial and gender makeup of staff before the 1980s was Caucasian males whereas the offender population has been disparately African American. Women and minorities who did happen to be employed in corrections during this period were considered a threat to the cohesion of the correctional workgroup. These disparate groups of women and minorities were often not treated fairly in the working environment, being subject to discrimination and harassment. Likewise, stereotypically, white male prison guards were viewed as "rednecks" whose attraction to the job was "a love for inflicting punishment" (Wittmer, Lanier, & Parker 1976). The lack of diversity experienced in corrections only worked to reinforce stereotypical characterizations.

The Racial Composition of Correctional Officers

The demographics of correctional staff in the United States have changed greatly from the late 1980s to the current time. Increasingly, minority officers have been included in the staffing patterns of correctional institutions in order to reflect the racial makeup for society at large as well as the correctional population. Currently, minorities contribute 29 percent the racial makeup of correctional officers. Of this 29 percent, African Americans are overwhelmingly the most prominent minority group to work within corrections (noting that only 7 percent of correctional officers are a minority other than African Americans). In contrast to the population at large, African American representation in the field of corrections is nearly double that of the U.S. population (12.9 percent). Although at first glance this inclusion of minorities represents progress toward a more diversified workforce, it must be viewed through the lens of the inmate racial makeup of correctional facilities. African Americans, for example, account for 45 percent of the incarcerated population, yet only 23 percent of prison guards are African Americans. This lack of parity only works to reinforce negative stereotypes and promotes racial discord. Although much progress has been made toward racial parity within correctional institutions, a greater level of racial parity should be established to continue to improve facility and community relations.

The Gender Composition of Correctional Officers

The correctional field has traditionally been one that has been stereotyped as a male-dominated area of work. Women are increasingly becoming represented within the field of corrections. Although women have had a long history of conducting prison work, they have typically been placed in clerical positions, teaching roles, support services, or the guarding of female offenders—they have not historically worked in direct supervision of male offenders. It was not until the late 1870s and/or early 1980s that women were routinely assigned to supervise male inmates (Pollock, 2004). The introduction of women into the security ranks has greatly impacted the organizational culture of many prison facilities and the subculture within them.

Women tend to not have the same aggressive social skills that men in prison tend to exhibit. Furthermore, the prison environment tends to emphasize the desire to 'be a man' and also denigrates the role of women as inferior. This means that women were not widely accepted among correctional officers and/or inmates. Since women have become integrated into the correctional industry, the male-oriented subculture has been weakened. The introduction of women into the security ranks, along with the inclusion of diverse minority groups, the professionalization of corrections, and the proliferation of prison gangs, has eroded the influence of the male-dominated and male-oriented convict code. Although the convict code still exists and has its adherents, it is no longer considered a primary standard of behavior in many prison facilities, but instead has become more of an ideal.

The Need of Bilingual Workers

Increasingly, because of the influences of globalization, communities are becoming more culturally diverse. Consequently, the racial and ethnic makeup of the offender population is becoming equally diverse. Perhaps the group that has most contributed to increasing diversity of the U.S. over the last 20 years has been persons born of Latin American decent. It is estimated that 12 percent of the U.S. citizenry speaks Spanish within the home (28 million persons). Hispanic Americans are incarcerated at a rate nearly three times that of white Americans. Consequently, especially in the Southwestern portions of the United States, prison populations have high concentrations of Spanish speakers.

Spanish-speaking inmates in facilities with high concentrations of Hispanic offenders often speak in Spanish slang, creating their own prison language. Correctional officers working in these facilities need to be able to comprehend inmate languages in order to assist the inmate, as well as enhance the security of the prison. Due to an overall lack of Spanish-speaking officers, there is a great demand for bilingual workers.

Diversity Training Programs in Corrections

Increasingly, correctional administrations have begun to understand the need for culturally competent employees from diverse racial and ethnic backgrounds. This reflects the shift in prison operations where the primary purpose of prison is to simply respond to problematic behavior with force. Rather, the use of effective communication skills as a means of preventing problems and addressing issues in a more professional manner requires a sense of cultural competence among agencies and certainly among staff. One means of improving agency cultural competence is through the hiring of diverse workers who can relate to the inmate population's own diversity. Having officers of similar racial groups, proficient in various languages that are spoken in the facility, and from similar customs and beliefs, enhances the ability of the agency to address problematic issues related to racial and/or cultural barriers. Thus, diverse workgroups can mitigate many of the negative effects of the prison subculture as well as gangs that tend to be structured along racial lines.

RACE AND PRISON

Race may be the greatest socially dividing factor in prisons. Because of the disparate number of social minorities who are incarcerated, often a role reversal occurs related to who constitutes racial majorities in prison. The social dynamics of many prisons are created by factions divided along racial lines. Perhaps the most prominent display of this fictionalization is through the allegiances to rival gangs within the institution. Rival gangs are overwhelmingly responsible for incidences of violence, including murder, in many institutions. It is for these reasons that many facilities have opted for segregation of inmates along racial lines until an inmate's threat level can be accessed appropriately.

Racial Segregation Case Law

Until the 1970s, most U.S. prisons were segregated based on race. The reasons for this segregation were related to the cultural atmosphere of the time as well as fears of racial violence. It was not until the case of *Gates v. Collier* that the practice of segregating inmates based on race, as the only consideration, ended. In the *Gates v. Collier* case, the courts ruled that segregating inmates based on the sole consideration of race violated the inmates' Constitutional rights because segregation amounted to unequal treatments.

Despite the ruling in *Gates v. Collier*, some prisons still segregate based on racial considerations particularly as it relates to the potential for racial violence and inter-gang violence. Gang violence is known to be the main contributing factor to murders within prison, the murder rate of which is five times higher than that happening in society at large. One of the distinguishing features of prison gangs is that they are usually organized around racial groups. Many prisons have opted to segregate prisoners for a period of time to ensure that violence is reduced. This practice of segregation of inmates based on race has drawn controversy as to inmates' Constitutional rights and possible violations.

In 2003, the U.S. Court of Appeals for the Ninth Circuit delivered a ruling in *Johnson v. California* that clarified the constitutional rights of inmates as it relates to the act of segregating in order to prevent violence. In California, state prisoners are classified and housed with prisoners of like racial backgrounds for the first 60 days of internment to deter threats of rival gangs (that are often race based). In *Johnson v. California*, the plaintiff Garrison Johnson, an African American, alleged that the state of California had violated his constitutional rights through the consideration of race as a policy of correctional receptions. Johnson argued that this policy violated the Equal Protection Clause of the Fourteenth Amendment. The court sided with the state of California, noting that the prison's policies were appropriate because they were designed to protect the welfare of the inmates.

PRISON GANGS: STRUCTURED ALONG RACIAL LINES OF ALLEGIANCE

During the 1950s and the 1960s, there was a substantial amount of racial and ethnic bias in prisons. This was true in almost all state prison systems, but was particularly pronounced in the Southern United States and in the state of California. During the late 1950s, a Chicano gang formed, known as the Mexican Mafia (National Gang  Intelligence Center, 2010). This gang was drawn from street gang members in various neighborhoods of Los Angeles and, while in San Quentin, began to exercise power over the gambling rackets within that prison. Other gangs soon began to form as a means of opposing the Mexican Mafia. Among the earliest to form were the Black Guerilla Family, the Aryan Brotherhood, La Nuestra Familia, and the Texas Syndicate.

This section provides a brief overview of some of the major prison gangs found throughout the nation. As accurately as possible, these gangs are presented in a manner that is historically correct, capturing the basic feeling of the time and context during their development. Because the Federal government produces accurate resources and data on justice-related topics, information regarding most of these gangs has been obtained from the National Gang Intelligence Center, a think-tank group of the Department of Justice. Much of the information presented has been obtained from a recent document titled the National Gang Threat Assessment 2009. Though not fully inclusive, this is a comprehensive listing of the major prison gangs that exist today. Each gang is presented in the order in which they were formed, starting with the late 1950s and continuing through the early 1990s. It is important to point out that each gang tends to consist of one racial group or another, usually to the exclusion of other groups.

The **Mexican Mafia** prison gang, also known as La Eme (Spanish for the letter M), was formed in the late 1950s within the California Department of Corrections. It is loosely structured and has strict rules that must be followed by the 200 members. Most members are Mexican American males who previously belonged to a southern California street gang. The Mexican Mafia is primarily active in the southwestern and Pacific regions of the United States, but its power base is in California.

Black Guerrilla Family (BGF), originally called Black Family or Black Vanguard, is a prison gang founded in the San Quentin State Prison, California, in 1966. The gang is highly organized along paramilitary lines, with a supreme leader and central committee. The BGF has an established national charter, code of ethics, and an oath of allegiance. BGF members operate primarily in California and Maryland. The gang has 100–300 members, most of whom are African American males.

Aryan Brotherhood (AB) was originally formed in San Quentin in 1967. The AB is highly structured with two factions—one in the California Department of Corrections and the other in the Federal Bureau of Prisons (BOP). Most members are Caucasian males, and the gang is active primarily in the southwestern and Pacific regions. Some AB members have business relationships with Mexican drug traffickers that smuggle illegal drugs into California for AB distribution. The AB is notoriously violent and is often involved in murder for hire. Although the gang has been historically linked to the

BGF Term	Meaning
Annette Brooks	Aryan Brotherhood
Bobby G. Foster	BGF
Central High	mainline
Compton	hole or segregation
D.C.	decision or deciding
kiss	marked for death
Mary Mitchell	Mexican Mafia
Nelson Franklin	Nuestra Familia
Paula	police officer
record shop	hospital
salt	hacksaw
Sammy Davis, Jr.	bootlicking
Supermarket	killed or dead

Sample Black Guerrilla Family (BGF) code

California-based prison gang Mexican Mafia (La Eme), tension between AB and La Eme is increasingly evident, as seen in recent fights between Caucasians and Hispanics within the California Department of Corrections.

Crips is a collection of structured and unstructured gangs that have adopted a common gang culture. The Crips emerged as a major gang presence during the early 1970s. Crips membership is estimated at 30,000–35,000; most members are African American males from the Los Angeles metropolitan area. Large, national-level Crips gangs include 107 Hoover Crips, Insane Gangster Crips, and Rolling 60s Crips. The Crips operate in 221 cities in 41 states and can be found in several state prison systems.

Bloods is an association of structured and unstructured gangs that have adopted a single-gang culture. The original Bloods was formed in the early 1970s to provide protection from the Crips street gang in Los Angeles, California. Large, national-level Bloods gangs include Bounty Hunter Bloods and Crenshaw Mafia Gangsters. Bloods membership is estimated to be 7,000–30,000 nationwide; most members are African American males. Bloods gangs are active in 123 cities in 33 states and they can be found in several state prison systems.

Ñeta is a prison gang that was established in Puerto Rico in the early 1970s and spread to the United States. Ñeta is one of the largest and most violent prison gangs, with about 7,000 members in Puerto Rico and 5,000 in the United States. Ñeta chapters in Puerto Rico exist exclusively inside prisons; once members are released from prison, they are no longer considered part of the gang. In the United States, Ñeta chapters exist inside and outside prisons in 36 cities in nine states, primarily in the Northeast.

Constitution of the Mexikanemi

1. Membership is for life ("blood in, blood out").
2. Every member must be prepared to sacrifice his life or take a life any time.
3. To achieve discipline within the Mexikanemi brotherhood, every member shall strive to overcome his weaknesses.
4. Members must never let the Mexikanemi down.
5. The sponsoring member is totally responsible for the behavior of new recruit. If the new recruit turns out to be a traitor; it is the sport soring member's responsibility to eliminate the recruit.
6. When insulted by a stranger or group, all members of the Mexikanemi will unite to destroy the person or other group completely.
7. Members must always maintain a high level of integrity.
8. Members must never relate Mexikanemi business to others.
9. Every member has the right to express opinions, ideas, contradictions, and constructive criticism.
10. Every member has the right to organize, educate, arm, and defend the Mexikanemi.
11. Every member has the right to wear a tattoo of the Mexikanemi symbol.
12. The Mexikanemi is a criminal organization and therefore will participate in all activities of criminal interest for monetary benefits.

The **Texas Syndicate** originated in Folsom Prison during the early 1970s. The Texas Syndicate was formed in response to other prison gangs in the California Department of Corrections, such as the Mexican Mafia and Aryan Brotherhood, which were attempting to prey on native Texas inmates. This gang comprises predominately Mexican American inmates in the Texas Department of Corrections. Though this gang has a rule to only accept members who are Latino, they do accept Caucasians into their ranks. The Texas Syndicate has a formal organizational structure and a set of written rules for its members. Since the time of its formation—largely as a means of protection for Texas inmates in the California Department of Corrections—the Texas Syndicate has grown considerably, particularly in Texas.

The **Mexikanemi** prison gang (also known as Texas Mexican Mafia or Emi) was formed in the early 1980s within the Texas Department of Criminal Justice (TDCJ). The gang is highly structured and is estimated to have 2,000 members, most of whom are Mexican nationals or Mexican American males living in Texas at the time of incarceration. Mexikanemi poses a significant drug trafficking threat to communities in the southwestern United States, particularly in Texas. Gang members reportedly traffic multikilogram quantities of powder cocaine, heroin, and methamphetamine; multiton quantities of marijuana; and thousand-tablet quantities of MDMA from Mexico into the United States for distribution inside and outside prison.

The **Nazi Low Riders (NLR)** evolved in the California Youth Authority, the state agency responsible for the incarceration and parole supervision of juvenile and young adult offenders, in the late 1970s or the early 1980s as a gang for white inmates. As prison officials successfully suppressed Aryan Brotherhood activities, the Brotherhood appealed to young incarcerated skinheads, NLR in particular, to act as middlemen for their criminal operations, allowing Aryan Brotherhood to keep control of criminal undertakings while adult members were serving time in administrative segregation. Through their connections to Aryan Brotherhood, NLR was able to become the principal gang within the Youth Authority and eventually to move into penitentiaries throughout California and across the West Coast. NLR maintains strong ties to Aryan Brotherhood and, like the older gang, has become a source of violence and criminal activity in prison. Aryan Brotherhood still maintains a strong presence in the nation's prison systems, albeit less active, while NLR has also become a major force, viewing itself as superior to all other white gangs and deferring only to Aryan Brotherhood.

Barrio Azteca emerged in 1986 in the Coffield Unit of TDCJ by five street gang members from El Paso, Texas. This gang tends to recruit from prior street gang members and is most active in the southwestern region, primarily in correctional facilities in Texas and on the streets of southwestern Texas and southeastern New Mexico. The gang is highly structured and has an estimated membership of 2,000. Most members are Mexican national or Mexican American males.

United Blood Nation (UBN) is a universal term that is used to identify both West Coast Bloods and United Blood Nation. UBN started in 1993 in Rikers Island GMDC (George Mochen Detention Center) to form protection from the threat posed by Latin Kings and Ñetas, who dominated the prison. Although these groups are traditionally distinct entities, both identify themselves by "Blood," often making it hard for law enforcement to distinguish between them. UBN is a loose confederation of street gangs, or sets, that once were predominantly African American. Membership is estimated to be between 7,000 and 15,000 along the U.S. eastern corridor.

RELIGION AND PRISON

The freedom to religion is a fundamental constitutional right guaranteed by the First Amendment. While it is implicit that religion is a fundamental right, there are limits to how religion is practiced within prisons. Prisons, because of safety concerns and other administrative functions, may not be able to meet the demands of all religious groups. Once more, as is often the case in prison, inmates may use this First Amendment right as a way to subterfuge special rights and privileges void of any sincere religious conviction.

The Black Muslims Movement is perhaps the event most responsible for bringing about the greatest changes to the practice of religion in the penal system. At the core of this movement was the African Americans' search for individualism, self, dignity, and identity that was closely associated with the Civil Rights movement. During the Civil Rights Era, prisoners gained substantial abilities to practice their faith, including access to resources (i.e., literature, prayer rugs, space), equal representation of clergy, and certain allowances including specialty diets, etc.

Recently, there has been further clarification of an inmate's rights to religious practice through the Religious Land Use and Institutionalized Persons Act (RLUIPA). RLUIPA, adopted in 2000, was crafted to fix the problems of the 1993 Religious Freedom Restoration Act (RFRA). RLUIPA, among other areas, addresses prisoners' freedom to worship in that it prohibits undue burdens being placed on prisoners to exercise free practice of religion (Section 3.). The law states that "no government shall impose a substantial burden of the religious exercise of a person confined to an institution, as defined in section 2 of the Civil Rights of Institutionalized Persons Act (42 U.S.C. 1997), even if the burden results from a general applicability, unless the government demonstrates that imposition of burden on that person—(1) is in furtherance of a compelling governmental interest, or (2) is the least restrictive means for furthering a compelling governmental interest."

STAFF AND INMATE DYNAMICS: PRISON CULTURE AND PRISONIZATION

Within most prison systems, there are various norms and mores that impact the routine day-to-day life of the agency. Perhaps one of the most interesting dynamics within prison is that which occurs between the inmates and the prison staff. This area of discussion is both complicated and paradoxical, in many respects. The paradox involved with this dynamic is that, while on the one hand, inmate subculture restricts inmates from 'siding' with officers and officer culture restricts officers from befriending inmates, there is a natural give-and-take that emerges between both groups. In fact, there is usually a symbiotic relationship that emerges between prison security staff and the inmate population. The **symbiotic prison relationship**, exists between correctional staff and inmates as a means to develop mutually compliant and informal negotiations in behavior that is acceptable within the bounds of institutional security, yet, at the same time, allow inmates to meet many of their basic human needs. This relationship is grounded in the reality of the day-to-day interactions that prison security staff have with inmates who live within the institution.

Because prison is a very intense environment that has a very strong psychological impact on both inmates and staff, it is only natural that this type of relationship would often emerge. **Prisonization** is the process of being socialized into the prison culture. This process occurs over time as the inmate or the correctional officer adapts to the informal rules of prison life. Unlike many other texts, the author of this text believes it is important to emphasize that correctional officers also experience a form of prisonization that impacts their worldview and the manner in which they operate within the prison institution. Within his text on prisonization, Gillespie (2002) makes the following introductory statement:

> Prison is a context that exerts its influence upon the social relations of those who enter its domain (p. 1).

The reason that this sentence is set off in such a conspicuous manner is because it has profound meaning and truly captures the essence of prisonization. However, for this chapter, students should understand that the influence of the prison environment extends to *all* persons who enter its domain, particularly if they do so over a prolonged period of time. Thus, prisonization impacts both inmates and staff within the facility. While the total experience will, of course, not be the same for staff as it is for inmates, it is silly to presume that staff who are routinely exposed to aberrant human behavior will not also be impacted by that behavior.

Indeed, to some extent, prison is a traumatizing experience, even for those who work there. For security staff who must be involved in altercations (i.e., uses of force, the need to contain riots, observing and responding to inmate-on-inmate assaults) the impact of prisonization can be particularly traumatizing. The impact that prisonization has upon staff as well as on inmates is an important consideration since it does, in part, dictate the

While the individual behaviors, beliefs and values may differ greatly, the culture of the prison community is that expressed through the *prevailing* or *predominate* behaviors, beliefs, and values of that community.

contours of the guard subculture, which stands in competition with the inmate subculture. The prison experience can and often does impact relationships that guards have with persons who do not work in the prison setting, such as their spouses and/or children.

With respect to inmates, Gillespie (2002) found that both the individual characteristics of inmates and institutional qualities affect prisonization and misconduct. However, he found that individual-level antecedents explained prisonization better than did prison-level variables. This means that experiences of inmates prior to being imprisoned were central to determining how well inmates would adapt to the prison experience. For this text, this contention will also be extended to prison guards as well; their prior experiences and their individual personality development prior to employment within the prison will dictate how well they adapt to both the formal and informal exchanges that occur within.

The Prison Subculture and Women in Corrections: Both Inmate and Staff Subculture

As noted in Chapter 4, the problem of sexual harassment affects the prison worksite. Although this issue impacts police and judicial agencies as well as the broader society, it is much more pronounced and pervasive in prisons. Harassment can include behaviors such as cussing, intimidation, or inappropriate humor. In the prison or jail setting, male staff as well as inmates may present challenges to women through an atmosphere that is demeaning to women. For instance, a male staff member may say to a group of male inmates working in the field "Okay, c'mon ladies, let's get back to work," which implies that women are less accepted and respected than are men. The fact that the guard is referring to the male inmates as "ladies" is meant to be demeaning and reinforces the notion that women have lesser stature within the prison. In cases where inmates 'punk one another out' or say "you just got punked out," the implication is that the person holds a sexual role that is passive or subservient; this is typically equated to female behavior and/or a nonaggressive (and therefore weak) person. All of these biases toward women and anything that is effeminate exist in many prison environments and are juxtaposed against an environment of hyper-masculinity.

In order that women can be integrated more fully into the world of prison operations, it is necessary that sexist opinions, beliefs, and informal exchanges be minimized by administrators. However, higher-level supervisors must do more than craft a policy and act punitively to enforce the policy; this will likely breed resistance to the idea. Rather, upper-administrators should ensure that positive accomplishments of female staff and supervisors are showcased and rewarded within the agency. At the same time, administrators should ensure that these rewards are balanced with those given to male employees as well. The key is to change the image of the agency by demonstrating support for female officers and supervisors while doing so within the framework of acknowledging, showcasing, and rewarding *all* officers within the agency. This will be particularly effective if women who perform difficult duties that are in close contact with inmates are specifically noted within the agency. Such showcasing will counter stereotypes among inmates and other staff and will empower other women who might also wish to work among the direct security ranks rather than separated areas (i.e., count room, camera stations, or call centers), support services (i.e., food, laundry, or recreational programs), or auxiliary functions (such as security in protective custody, visitation, or religious services).

Furthermore, it is important that female supervisors be present and represented in male facilities, not just female facilities. Although this can lead to some complications in certain situations, agencies must be committed to working around and through legal issues related to cross-gender searches, privacy issues for male inmates in shower areas and/or locations where strip searches may occur, and so forth. Ultimately, this acknowledgment of women in corrections is healthy for the sexist subculture that tends to exist among inmates and some correctional officers. Providing training on sexual equality, sexual harassment, and other similar topics is also important and should not be made optional but should be mandatory.

SEXUAL ORIENTATION AND CORRECTIONS

The stereotype of the U.S. prison system is that it is rampant with homosexual behavior and sexual violation. The reasons for these stereotypes include the history of corrections, which is littered with sexual abuses, as well as the conditions of prisons, which encourage deviant sexual practice. It is the very act of confining men together for prolonged periods that brings about both the myths and the realities of sexual behavior and exploitation in prison.

In prisons, there are distinct differences between those who engage in homosexual activities because of considerations of "sexual identity" vs. those who engage because of "situational conditions." In fact, Ibrahim (1974), one of the pioneers in studying prison sexual behaviors, noted that most same-sex sexual behavior that occurs in prisons is not related to social identity, but rather the external realities of living in a prison. He noted that there were six reasons why inmates chose same-sex sexual activities, which are as follows:

1. Prisons are a uni-sex communities; thus, inmates are inclined to act out sexual gratifications with each other.
2. Deviant sexual behavior is often tolerated by prison officials even though its official policy may restrict these activities. This allows for stronger inmates to intimidate weaker inmates, thus forming status roles. Allowing this behavior is seen as a necessary means of controlling the population. Once more, addressing the behavior often opens the facility up to public scrutiny.
3. Inmates often remain idle throughout the day. Lack of programming and work opportunities make the likelihood of sexual engagement more likely. It has been noted that as many as 90 percent of all inmates have no opportunity to work.
4. Overcrowding produces a situation in which prison officials are greatly outnumbered and incapable of monitoring all behaviors. This lack of observation as well as an overall lack of privacy that inmates share makes sexual encounters more likely.
5. A lack of appropriate classification system also encourages sexual behaviors. Most prison systems do not separate those convicted for sexual crimes or those who are gay from the general population. This lack of separation allows the inmate to continue sexual behaviors as they once did in society.
6. And lastly and perhaps most importantly, prisons isolate individuals from the rest of society. Because of this, many societal norms are readily discarded in favor of sexual behaviors that include other inmates.

Male Prison Hierarchies and Sexual Victimization

Prison social hierarchy is largely developed around sexual identity and behavior. As was noted in Chapter 4, this has the unfortunate effect of increasing the likelihood of victimization of the Gay, Lesbian, Bisexual, Transgender (GLBT) population in prison. However, it is not just the GLBT population that is sexually assaulted in prison, some heterosexual inmates are also assaulted. Prison social structure, being organized around male identity, rewards those individuals possessing the most masculine traits. Sexual behavior works in concert with the sexual social hierarchy of the prison, noting that dominant masculine males sexually control non-dominant males.

Essentially, social roles engaged by those who participate in homosexual activity can be divided into three categories. These are the roles of **wolf**, **fag**, and **punk** (Donaldson, 1993; Kirkham, 1971; Sagarin, 1976; Sykes, 1958). "Wolves," in the prison hierarchical structure, are viewed as those who are the most masculine, and are thus of the highest prison order. Their sexual roles are seen as exploitive, powerful, active, and aggressive. If a prison rape were to occur, it would be expected that "a wolf" would have perpetrated the rape. Wolves take advantage of the lower social orders known as "fags" and "punks." A wolf's domination separates him from being known as homosexual, in that it is he who commits the sexual offense to another who is weaker. Conversely, "Fags" and "Punks" are of a lower submissive order.

Fags are those individuals who entered into prison as gay men. Fags are known to accentuate their feminine qualities and embrace the fact that they are gay. Although not as respected as wolves, fags are someone respected for fulfilling their "natural role." Fags provide a feminine counterpart by which Wolves form their identity. In the jailhouse culture, fags do not have "assholes," they have "pussies." Fags are often seen as "wives." Because of this feminine role, they are not allowed to shower facing the other inmates; they may wear clothes in a feminine way and are also expected to sit to urinate like women. Fags are willing participants in homosexual acts and therefore retain some control and power and are thus seen as "more masculine" than punks.

Punks, also known as **jailhouse turnouts**, are of the lowest order. Punks are those men who could not fulfill their role as men, due to their physical weakness or lack of courage, and thus were "turned out" into a submissive role. **"Turning out"** means to sexually enslave another by the use of forcible rape. Commonly, these men consist of smaller, middle class, white males who are first-time offenders. They are not homosexual nor do they adopt feminine characteristics, yet they often perform sexual favors as a way of obtaining material items.

Prison Rape Elimination Act of 2003

Although sexual encounters in prison are strictly forbidden, given the fact that the most distinguishing characteristic of humans is their sexual nature, sexual acts do occur. In the recent decade, of great concern regarding prison sexuality (both internationally and domestically) is the issue of prison rape. The Federal Bureau of Prisons has estimated that between 9 and 20 percent of all those incarcerated have been subjected to sexual violation. This startling fact combined with public awareness of involuntary sexual activity within prison institutions prompted the **Prison Rape Elimination Act of 2003 (PREA)**. PREA adopted a "zero tolerance" policy as it relates to prison rape in Federal institutions. A separate provision of PREA is that states must likewise show vigilance in the deterrence of rape or else lose access to Federal funding. As a consequence of

PREA, a new vigilance has emerged in the field of corrections that has undoubtedly reduced the occurrences of prison rape.

In concert with PREA is the idea that those with different sexual orientations need protections from sexual exploitation and violation while incarcerated. In a U.S. Supreme Court ruling *Farmer v. Brennan*, a transsexual petitioner claimed that he was sexually assaulted as a result of not being carefully segregated from the general population. In keeping with past decisions initiated by the U.S. Supreme Court, the Court ruled that prisoners have rights guaranteed under the Eight Amendment that prohibit cruel and unusual punishments. Specifically, prisoners are guaranteed the right to "humane conditions of confinement" and that these conditions must include "food, clothing, shelter, medical care, and must protect prisoners from violence at the hands of other prisoners." In this case, the Court stated that prison officials acted with **"deliberate indifference"** and thus allowed the plaintiff to be harmed. "Deliberate indifference," as defined by the Courts, refers to reckless behavior on the part of prison officials to ensure an inmate's safety.

Implementing Organizational Change to Counteract the Prison Subculture

Wardens and senior administrators must establish a vision of a successful correctional operation. In developing this sense of vision, administrators must be able to sell their goals to those within the organization so that all persons provide earnest commitment. The best way to do this is through an understanding of the organizational culture that exists within an agency. Supervisory staff play a critical role in shaping and forming organizational culture and it is the emphasis on the midlevel and lower-level supervisory staff that upper administrators can best disseminate their vision plan for the future. This vision plan should entail the development of an organizational culture that emphasizes professionalism and works against the cliquish nature of the prison subculture, both for inmates and for correctional officers. This can be done by placing a priority on transparent operations among inmates and custodial staff. This is also best done by placing more emphasis on rewards for staff rather than punishments and sanctions.

One aspect of traditional prison operations is the continued adherence to the paramilitary model of organization. As is feasible, the paramilitary aspects of facility management should be minimized and a participative model should be encouraged. This will reduce the inherent distrust and fear-based style of management that often exists within prison facilities. Ensuring that supervisory staff are trained on effective communication techniques and that they are also skilled in human relations will equate the most well-spent of money within an agency's budget. Couple this with a largely decentralized approach and it will soon be discovered that many of the problems that occur throughout an institution—particularly the recurring and routine problems— will eventually diminish and perhaps even disappear altogether.

CROSS-RACIAL INMATE AND STAFF SUPERVISION ISSUES

During the times prior to the 1980s, prisons tended to be in rural areas and tended to hire staff from within the local area. The demographics of correctional staff in the United States have changed greatly from the late 1980s to the current time. This change toward a more multicultural setting is reflected in broader society and in almost all criminal justice agencies. This trend toward multiculturalism and diversity will only continue, both with the staff who are employed and with the inmate population who are supervised.

The diversity that has developed in the correctional workforce has followed, in step, with the move toward professionalization of the correctional profession. Indeed, in times prior to this shift, women and minorities were considered a threat to the cohesion of the correctional workgroup. During this time, women and minorities were often not treated fairly in the working environment, being subject to discrimination and harassment. Many African American and Latino American correctional staff reported bias in the workplace and this was even more pronounced among women in corrections. However, the professionalization of corrections has opened the door for more fair and balanced work environments and correctional staff have become more sensitized to different perspectives in the workplace.

Furthermore, administrators of correctional facilities have made attempts to hire persons from diverse backgrounds since it has become increasingly clear that this is a benefit when contending with a diverse inmate population. This reflects the shift in prison operations, where the primary purpose of prison is to simply respond to problematic behavior with force. Rather, the use of effective communication skills as a means of preventing problems and addressing issues in a more professional manner requires a sense of cultural competence among agencies and certainly among staff. One means of improving agency cultural competence is through the hiring of diverse workers who can relate to the inmate population's own diversity. Having officers of similar racial groups, proficient in various languages that are spoken in the facility, and from similar customs and beliefs enhances the ability of the agency to address problematic issues related to racial and/or cultural barriers. Thus, diverse workgroups can mitigate many of the negative effects of the prison subculture as well as gangs that tend to be structured along racial lines.

Education and Training of Staff

During the 1970s, amidst the increase in hiring that began to take place, concern arose regarding the training and competency of correctional officers. Indeed, in 1973 the National Advisory Commission on Criminal Justice Standards and Goals encouraged state legislators to take action to improve the education and training of correctional officers. Furthermore, correctional administrators cited the need for security staff to study criminology and other disciplines that could aid in working with difficult populations. The National Advisory Commission on Criminal Justice Standards and Goals also indicated that "all new staff members should have at least 40 hours of orientation training during their first week on the job, and at least 60 hours additional training during their first year" (1973, p. 494). This represents some of the first national-level attempts to mandate professional training and standards for correctional officers. Though these first steps were certainly headed in the correct direction, progress was slow. In 1978, it was determined that only half of all states were actually meeting the 40 entry-level training requirement and even fewer were meeting the recommended 60 hours of training during the officer's first year.

The **American Correctional Association** has, throughout the past decade, placed a major push for professionalization of the field of corrections. This has resulted in a pattern of steadily increasing entry-level educational requirements to be consistent with a broader trend toward correctional officer's professionalism. However, the term professionalism itself has been touted about by various correctional systems with much of an attempt to articulate what this specifically means. While corrections are pointed in a progressive direction, there is definitely much more work to be done. Furthermore, given the widespread budget cuts common in many states throughout the nation, it would seem that money and resources for improved training and educational standards may be lacking. Yet, this is at a time when it is needed the most. How well prison systems fare in the future is yet to be seen, but one thing is clear—a failure to train and educate this workforce will only ensure that the potential corrective efforts of prison systems are minimized and this then creates a potential risk to the public safety of society as a whole.

CONCLUSION

This chapter has provided a historical overview of corrections in America with emphasis on the prison environment, because it is this environment that is most intensive and it is this environment where most of the racial, gender-based, and religious-based disparity and discrimination have occurred. Various topics related to the development of these circumstances have been provided. Throughout early corrections, historical circumstances and social norms led to discriminatory treatment within correctional systems. This was reflected through the passage of various discriminatory laws, such as Pig Laws and other mechanisms, that unfairly sentenced minority groups, particularly African Americans.

In more recent times, laws related to drug offending have had similar effects on the demographics of the American prison population. The War on Drugs was presented as one of the key occurrences that dramatically increased the number and proportion of minorities who were incarcerated during the later 1980s and 1990s due to targeted focus on specific drugs, such as crack cocaine. Indeed, this single agenda resulted in serious and disproportionate arrests and sentencing practices that caused enormous growth in prison building and swelled the numbers of offenders in the correctional populations of most states and the Federal system. The focus of crack cocaine, typically a drug-of-choice among minority groups, resulted in disproportionate sentencing (both in numbers of offenders and in the length of their sentences) for African Americans and, to a lesser extent, Latino Americans.

Lastly, the means by which employees have been recruited and trained in correctional agencies have greatly impacted the organizational culture within prison systems. The informal subculture within prisons has typically been paramilitary and male-dominated. More frequent integration of female staff and the intentional diversification of staff have ameliorated some of the negative aspects of this strict and often oppressive internal culture. Likewise, training and professionalization of the field of corrections have helped develop a more progressive, ethical, and fair-minded system of operation.

Chapter 11 Learning Check

1. Compared to Caucasians, Hispanics are _____ _____ times more likely than whites to be incarcerated and African Americans are _____ times more likely to be incarcerated.

   a. 5; 10
   b. 10; 20
   c. 3; 6
   d. 2; 8
   e. None of the above

2. The reliance on incarceration as a primary form of societal deterrence and punishment has prompted many to term the practice as mass incarceration.
   a. True
   b. False

3. There has been further clarification of an inmate's rights to religious practice through the _____ _____.
   a. The Civil Rights Act of 1964
   b. Americans with Disabilities Act of 1990 (ADA)
   c. Religious Land Use and Institutionalized Persons Act (RLUIPA)
   d. Right to Free Speech in Public Areas of Prison Act (2010)
   e. None of the above

4. Punks, also known as jailhouse turnouts, are of the lowest order in the prison subculture.
   a. True
   b. False

5. Which organization has, throughout the past decade, placed a major push for professionalization of the field of corrections?
   a. The National Prison Reform Council
   b. The American Correctional Association
   c. The Child Savers
   d. None of the above

6. The case of *Gates v. Collier* ruled against the practice of segregating inmates based on race as the only consideration.
   a. True
   b. False

7. In the U.S. Supreme Court case of _____ _____, a transsexual petitioner claimed that he was sexually assaulted as a result of not being carefully segregated from the general population. The Court ruled, in this case, that prison officials acted with "deliberate indifference" and thus allowed the plaintiff to be harmed.
   a. *Atkins v. Virginia*
   b. *Grutter v. Bollinger*
   c. *Farmer v. Brennan*
   d. *Miller-El v. Cockrell*
   e. None of the above

8. The sentencing policies associated with the War on Drugs have disproportionately affected racial minorities, causing some to equate this to a form of institutional racism.
   a. True
   b. False

9. According to the text, biases toward women and anything that is effeminate exist in many prison environments and are juxtaposed against an environment of hyper-masculinity.
   a. True
   b. False

10. The Prison Rape Elimination Act of 2003 (PREA) adopted a "zero tolerance" policy as it relates to prison rape in Federal institutions.
    a. True
    b. False

Essay Discussion Questions

1. Fully discuss how minority groups have been treated throughout the history of corrections in the United States.
2. Discuss how the War on Drugs exacerbated the incarceration of various minority groups.
3. Provide a detailed discussion on how the prison subculture impacts the behavior of both inmates and staff.

References

Blumstein, A., & Beck, Allen J. (1999). Population growth in U.S. prisons, 1980–1996. In M. Tonry & J. Petersilia (Eds.), *Crime and justice: A review of the research, Vol. 26, Prisons* (pp. 17–61). Chicago, IL: University of Chicago Press.

Boyum, D., & Reuter, P. (2005). *An analytic assessment of U.S. drug policy.* Washington, DC: AEI Press.

Bureau of Justice Statistics. (2009). *Prisoners in 2008.* (OJ Publication No. NCJ 228417) Washington, DC: U.S. Government Printing Office.

Carson, E. A., & Sabol, W. J. (2012). *Prisoners in 2011.* Washington, DC: Bureau of Justice Statistics.

Curtin, Mary (2000). *Black prisoners and their world: Alabama, 1865–1900.* Charlottesville: University Press of Virginia.

Donaldson, S. (1993). A million jockers, punks, and queens: Sex among male prisoners and its implications for concepts of sexual orientation. Retrieved from: www.igc.apc.org/spr/docs/prison-sex-lecture.html.

Fryer, R., Heaton, P., Levitt, S., & Murphy, K. (2006). Measuring crack coaciane and its impact. Retrieved from: http://www.freshman.umb.edu/engl101/fall06/sec23/LevittCrackCocaine.pdf.

Gillespie, W. (2002). *Prisonization: Individual and institutional factors affecting inmate conduct.* LFB Scholarly Publishing.

Hartney, C. (2007). *The nation's most punitive states for women.* Oakland, CA: National Council on Crime and Delinquency.

Ibrahim, A. (1974). Deviant sexual behavior in men's prisons. *Crime and Delinquency, 20*(1): 38–44.

Kirkham, G. L. (1971). Homosexuality in prison. In J. M. Henslin (Ed.), *Studies in the sociology of sex* (pp. 325–349). New York: Appleton-Century-Crofts.

Office of Applied Studies. (2009). *Results from the 2008 National survey on drug use and health: National findings* (DHHS Publication No. SMA 09-4434, NSDUH Series H-36).

National Gang Intelligence Center. (2010). *National Gang Threat Assessment 2009: Prison Gangs.* Washington, DC: Federal Bureau of Investigation.

Pollock, J. (2004). *Prisons and prison life: Costs and consequences.* Los Angeles: Roxbury Publishing.

Sagarin, E. (1976). Prison homosexuality and it's effect on post-prison behavior. *Psychiatry, 39,* 245–257.

Sykes, G. (1958). *The society of captives.* Princeton, NJ: Princeton University Press.

U.S. Department of Justice, Bureau of Justice Statistics. (1994). *Special report. Women in prison.* Washington, DC: U.S. Department of Justice, Bureau of Justice Statistics.

Walmsley, R. (2006). *World prison population list, 2006.* United Kingdom: UK Home Office Research.

Walmsley, R. (2008). *World prison population list* (8th ed.). United Kingdom: UK Home Office Research.

Wittmer, J., Lanier, J.E., & Parker, M. (1976). Race relations with correctional officers. *Personnel & Guidance Journal, 54,* 302–306.

Wooden, W., & Parker, J. (1982). *Men behind bars: Sexual exploitation in prison.* New York: Plenum.

Juvenile Minority Wellness and Health Disparities, Gender, Sexual Identity, Youth Culture, and Social Class

LEARNING OBJECTIVES

After reading this chapter, students should be able to do the following:

1. Identify issues related to the youth subculture.
2. Discuss issues related to gender, sexual activity, and sexual preference.
3. Identify and discuss challenges associated with sexual minority youth.
4. Assess disparities in wellness among minority youth.
5. Discuss how social class and poverty disproportionately impacts minority youth.

KEY TERMS

Acculturation

Assimilation

Blended families

Broken homes

Criminal subculture

Externalizing behaviors

Internalizing behaviors

Juvenile as minority

Learning disabilities

Macro-system effects

Micro-system effects

Outing

Protective factors

Sexual minority youth

Social factors

Social inequality

Social Justice Approach

Socialization process

Troubled female youth

Risk factors

Youth culture

Racial discrimination

"Victim-turned-offender-hypothesis"

INTRODUCTION

In this chapter, we provide an examination of examine some key aspects for juveniles, in general, because the juvenile population is, in itself, a minority group population. The **juvenile as minority** refers to the fact that youth are a distinct class and category of individuals in society who share a common characteristic (age) and also have specific challenges that they face that are unique between them and other groups. Likewise, the *juvenile as minority* also indicates that rights and access to resources for these individuals are less than those for adults in society.

Furthermore, we will discuss a number of issues associated with youth that are related both directly and indirectly to their potentially being processed through the juvenile system. In addition, many of the variables that lead to a youth being in contact with the juvenile system have to do with aspects of their development, such as family life, educational access and achievement, sexual activity and pregnancy, as well as health and wellness indicators. Some of these initial discussions will address youth, in general, while others will address minority youth, in particular. In all cases, we address these issues from the perspective of the practitioner and provide guidance on what one should consider and how one should address challenges that these youth face.

In this chapter, we pay specific attention to the effects of discrimination on the development of youth, including potential health effects as well as the psychological impact of discrimination. We also devote attention to the importance of peer groups and socialization of youth. Likewise, this chapter (and this text, for that matter) is unique because it provides specific attention to sexual minority youth, or youth who have same-sex preferences. This population has grown among the younger generation and we consider our coverage of this aspect of diversity in the juvenile population to be quite progressive. Lastly, we discuss the impact of social class and poverty on youth, particularly minority youth, because minority youth are disproportionately represented among the lower income strata of the population.

HEALTH AND WELLNESS AMONG JUVENILES

As youth grow older, they are exposed to various social factors that can affect their personality development and life-course opportunities in the future. **Social factors** include both risk factors and protective factors that are associated with a youth's eventual proclivity for aberrant or pro-social behavior. While growing, **risk factors** (see Table 12-1) can accumulate and exacerbate the likelihood that youth will engage in delinquent acts. **Protective factors** (again, see Table 12-1), on the other hand, are those factors that insulate youth from engaging in delinquency or reduce the likelihood of delinquent behavior. In general, there are a number of each that may coalesce together to protect youth from (i.e., a strong family system, support for education, and good nutrition) or encourage youth toward delinquent behavior (i.e., drug abuse, teen pregnancy, and poor grades in school).

To prevent delinquency, practitioners must understand the risk factors that lead to such behavior. This is important from a multicultural perspective, as well, because this means that the juvenile practitioner (i.e., juvenile probation officer, juvenile court judge, social worker, police officer who works with youth) must be familiar with different cultural aspects of the community as well as beliefs within the family. Importantly, risk factors may be found in the individual, the environment, or the individual's ability to respond to the demands or requirements of the environment. Research has indicated a number of factors that have a high likelihood of leading to delinquent behavior (McCall, 1994). Furthermore, each of these factors, when added together, can have a cumulative effect on the likelihood of future delinquency (Cheng, 2004; McCall, 1994). For instance, while poor parenting is a risk factor, this becomes more pronounced

TABLE 12-1   **Risk Factors for Delinquency**

Type of Domain	Risk Factors Early Onset (age 6–11)	Risk Factors Late Onset (age 12–14)	Protective Factors Early & Late Onset (ages 6–15)
Individual	1. General offenses 2. Substance use 3. Male gender 4. Hyperactivity 5. Antisocial (problem) behavior 6. Exposure to TV violence 7. Low I.Q. 8. Dishonesty	1. General offenses 2. Risk taking 3. Aggression 4. Being male 5. Antisocial attitudes 6. Crimes vs. persons 7. Low I.Q. 8. Substance abuse	1. Intolerant attitude to criminality 2. High I.Q. 3. Female gender 4. Positive social orientation 5. Perceptions of sanctions
Family	1. Low socioeconomic status 2. Antisocial parents 3. Harsh, lax, or inconsistent discipline 4. Separation from parents 5. Abusive home 6. Neglectful home	1. Harsh or lax discipline 2. Poor adult supervision 3. Low parental involvement 4. Low socioeconomic status 5. Abusive home	1. Warm relationship w. adult caretaker 2. Peer group accepted by parents 3. Parental monitoring
School	1. Poor attitude or performance	1. Poor attitude or performance 2. Academic failure	1. Commitment to school 2. Recognition for conventional activities
Peer Group	1. Weak social ties 2. Antisocial peer group	1. Weak social ties 2. Antisocial peer group	1. Friends who engage in conventional behavior
Community	1. Neighborhood crime and drugs	1. Neighborhood crime and drugs	1. Crime, delinquency, and drug-free neighborhood

Note: Table adapted from the Surgeon General Executive Summary. (2002). entitled "Youth violence: A report of the Surgeon General." Available online at: http://www.mentalhealth.org/youthviolence/surgeongeneral/SG_Site/chapter4/sec1.asp.

when it is coupled with a child's poor academic performance. Furthermore, the environment can serve to compound this, such as when a child attends a school where rules of conduct are lax and teachers are dissatisfied. In such cases the chances of the child engaging in delinquency increases (McCall, 1994).

Family

Regardless of racial or ethnic demographics, one of the most important factors influencing the behavior of youth is the family setting. It is within the family system that youth are taught basic beliefs, values, attitudes, and patterns of behavior that guide them through life. The family is, in most cases, the group that provides for the socialization of the youth during the initial formative years. The **socialization process** is how youth learn cultural beliefs, religious views, and refine personality formation and development. There has been an abundance of research on the impact of the family on delinquent youth (Cheng, 2004; Thornberry, Smith, Rivera, Huizinga, & Stouthamer-Loeber, 1999).

There is substantial research that shows a relationship between delinquency and the marital quality of youth's parents. Juvenile delinquency tends to be more commonly found in homes with marital discord, a lack of family communication, parents who are not affectionate, and in homes where parents do not present a united front and/ or undermine one another (Cheng, 2004; Wright & Cullen, 2001). When family circumstances are unhappy, it is likely that parents do not experience much reward from their responsibilities in childrearing. In fact, it is likely that such activities are stressful for the parents. In addition, these types of homes are likely to be inconsistent in rule-setting and in the use of corrective discipline. In some cases (particularly if the parents are divorced or are considering divorce), there may be a tendency to use the child against the other parent. This may occur through manipulation or through contests of loyalty from the child as a means of sparking jealousy or creating distance with the other parent (Simons, Simons, Burt, Brody, & Cutrona, 2005). Many youth who come from these types of experiences later present with trust issues, conduct problems, and substance abuse.

One issue that is often attributed to juvenile delinquency is the increased occurrence of **broken homes** (homes disrupted through divorce, separation, or desertion) that have been seen in the past 40–50 years. Despite rhetoric related to lifestyle choices and other such politicized points of contention, homes where there are fewer caretakers for children tend to have fewer protective factors and are more susceptible to risk factors. At the least, we can easily say that one-half of the potential socializing and control team is separated from the family in these circumstances. The belief that one-parent families produce more delinquents is supported both by official statistics and by numerous studies. Consider that, according to the Forum on Child and Family Statistics (2006), when children live with two parents who are married to each other, they tend to have more favorable life-course outcomes. This point is particularly important for the African American community where there is a disproportionate amount of single head of household families.

In addition, the increase of **blended families**, in which each parent brings children of his or her own into the family setting, may result in conflicts among the children or between one parent and the children of the other parent. When we consider blended families, we would like to note that there is research that shows that over time, as youth experience increased changes and transitions in family structure, they tend to be more likely to engage in substance abuse and other forms of delinquency. We present research by Thornberry et al. (1999) to demonstrate this point. Their research examined the effect of the number of family structure transitions on youth outcomes for delinquent behavior and substance abuse in four major cities in the United States (see Figure 12-1) and found clear evidence that these transitions (i.e., divorce, death of parent, remarriage) can work in a cumulative fashion to increase the likelihood of problematic behaviors for youth.

In addition, there is research that indicates that, in multiple instances, the difference between placing juveniles in institutions and allowing them to remain in the family setting depends more on whether the family is intact than on the quality of life within the family. This also can be an important factor to consider in explaining (as we will see later, in Chapter 13) the disproportionate likelihood of African American youth being institutionalized; because there tends to be a higher rate of single-motherhood within this group, it could be that the justice system, at least in part, reacts differently to this variable, thereby creating disparity in likelihood of detention for African American youth.

Lastly, we would like to close on the note that concentrating on the broken family as the major or only cause of delinquency fails to take into account the vast number of

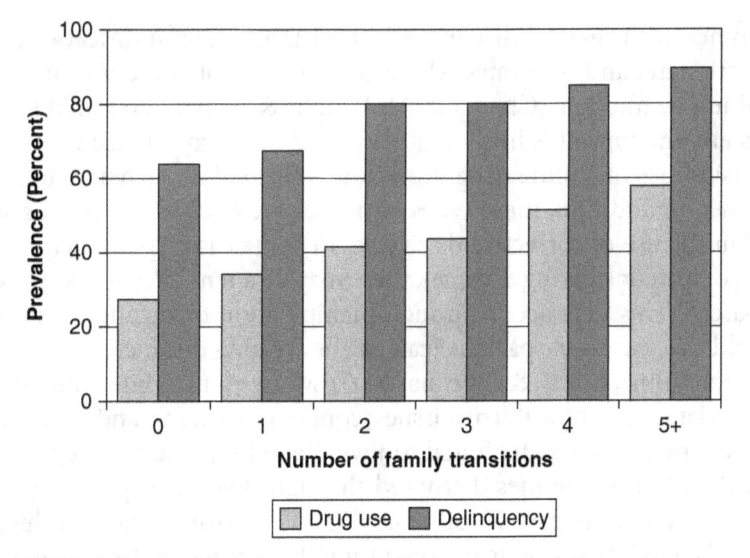

FIGURE 12-1 Prevalence of Delinquency and Drug Use by Number of Family Transitions. *Source:* Thornberry, T. P., Smith, C. A., Rivera, C., Huizinga, D., & Stouthamer-Loeber, M. (1999). *Family disruption and delinquency.* Washington, DC: NCJRS.

juveniles from broken homes who do not become delinquent as well as the vast number of juveniles from intact families who do become delinquent (Krisberg, 2005, p. 73). In addition, we would like to note that among families who do have one primary caretaker, there often are additional extended family members who assist, particularly in the African American and Latino communities. These family systems are often warm and nurturing; nevertheless, it may be that the justice system tends to not respect this family configuration as much as it does the traditional nuclear family composition.

Education

Parents often hope that their children will succeed in life, but for youth who are from families of poverty, or from families whose values may not comport with the stereotypical white middle class family image, many may encounter difficulties in school. Studies have shown that youth who are from middle class family backgrounds tend to internalize competitiveness, deferred gratification, and other characteristics that often equate to success in school. In addition, there is research that shows that teachers in public schools tend to have lower expectations for youth who come from lower socioeconomic backgrounds or belong to minority groups (Alwin & Thornton, 1984; Hayes, 2008). Furthermore, this tendency persists during early childhood on toward adolescence.

Numerous studies show that although some difficulties may be partially attributable to early experience in the family and neighborhood, others are created by the educational system itself. The label of low achiever, slow learner, or learning disabled may be attached shortly after, and sometimes even before, entering the first grade based on the performance of other family members who preceded the child in school. In these cases, teachers may expect little academic success from these students. The resulting inattention can often lead the youth to feeling shutout, distant, and frustrated about the school experience. In such cases, the likelihood of delinquency among these youth is increased.

One good description of the relationship between learning disabilities and delinquency is provided by The National Center on Education, Disability and Juvenile Justice (2007), as follows:

> Educational disability does not cause delinquency, but learning and behavioral disorders place youth at greater risk for involvement with the juvenile courts and for incarceration. School failure, poorly developed social skills, and inadequate school and community supports are associated with the over-representation of youth with disabilities at all stages of the juvenile justice system. (p. 1)

When we discuss **learning disabilities**, we are referring to a set of problems that result from difficulties in the way information is received and processed to the brain. Learning disabilities are usually associated with neurological disorders such as physical disorders of the brain or nervous system. Learning-disabled persons are almost always born with their disabilities, although most of these disabilities do not become obvious until the individual reaches school age and has to learn to read, write, or compute. Learning disabilities tend to be permanent conditions. However, individuals can develop strategies that allow them to compensate and work around the disability.

Another notion regarding the link between learning disabilities and delinquency proposes that differential treatment occurs between non-learning-disabled and learning-disabled delinquent youth. According to this notion, teachers, social workers, and other juvenile justice officials treat these youth differently (and unfairly), which increases the likelihood of arrest and adjudication of learning-disabled youth. The differential arrests are purported to occur because learning-disabled youth are more likely to be apprehended by the police because they lack the abilities to plan strategies, avoid detention, interact appropriately in encounters with the police, or to comprehend the justice system process (Rutherford, Griller-Clark, & Anderson, 2001).

Violence in Schools as Wellness Indicator

In the past 20 years, society has seen increased media portrayals of school violence that occurs throughout the nation. Certainly, when we discuss health and wellness among today's youth, safety and risk of violence at school are relevant topics. In today's world, for some youth, the question is not whether a child can learn in school but rather whether he or she can get to school and back home alive. Armed security guards, barred windows, and metal detectors have given many schools the appearance of being the prisons that some children have always found them to be. Although student fears of being attacked at school have declined (the percentage of children who feared attack at school or on the way to and from school decreased significantly from about one in eight in 1995 to about 1 in 20 in 2007), statistics vary among racial groups (Child Trends DataBank, 2010). As Figure 12-2 shows, larger percentages of African American and Hispanic students feared attacks than did Caucasian students. This may be a direct result of the geographic area in which these schools are located, an impersonal school atmosphere, and/or a lack of support or understanding that African American and Hispanic students feel in the school environment.

In another survey of American schoolchildren, it was found that improvements in school safety have occurred over the past two decades. While 10 percent of students reported being victims of at least one crime at school in 1995, 4 percent of students reported at least one victimization at school in 2005. In 1995, 7 percent reported being victims of theft and 3 percent reported theft in 2005. Three percent of students reported being victims of violent crime in 1995 and 1 percent reported being victims of violent

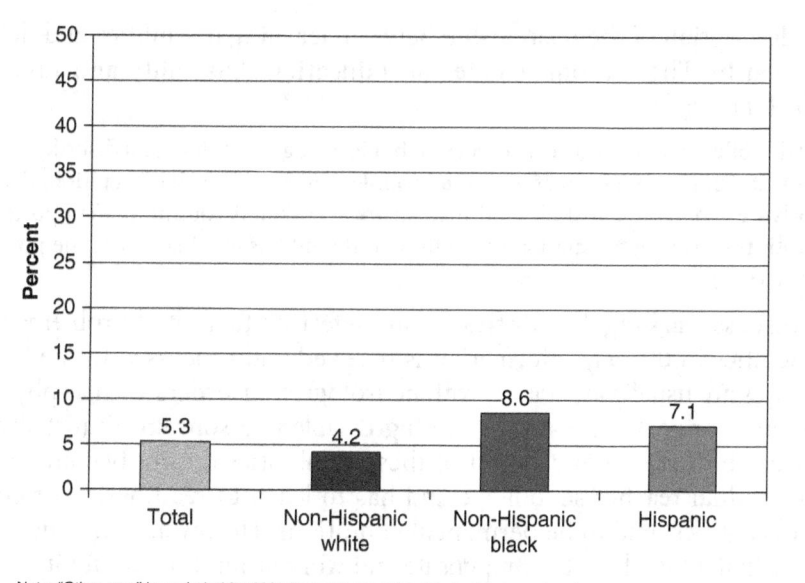

Note: "Other race" is excluded for 2007 because reporting standards were not met.
Source: Bureau or Justice Statistics. (2009). Table 17.1 Percentage of students ages 12–18 who reported being afraid of attack or harm, by location and selected student and school characteristics: Various years, 1995–2007, U.S. Department of Justice and U.S. Department of Education. Washington, DC: U.S. Government Printing Office.

FIGURE 12-2 Caucasian, African American, and Latino Youth Who Fear Attack at School.

crime in 2005. In both 1995 and 2005, less than 1 percent of students reported a serious violent crime (Bauer et al., 2008, p. 4). The violent crime victimization rate declined from 48 per 1,000 students in 1992 to 28 per 1,000 students in 2003. Despite the decrease, violence, theft, bullying, drugs, and weapons are still widespread in some schools, and events of the past few years have raised national concern about school safety.

Sexual Activity and the Juvenile Population

When teachers or other practitioners talk with youth on sex-related issues, it is important to keep in mind that many youth will already have a good idea about sex and sex-related topics. In fact, many will have been sexually active and even on a routine basis. However, many will not be conversant on specific anatomical issues associated with sexual activity and with the transmission of sexually transmitted diseases. In many cases, juvenile males will be much less informed than juvenile females.

Importantly, juvenile workers (teachers, social service personnel, juvenile probation officers) should provide pertinent and accurate information regarding sexuality, sexual health, and reproduction. Juvenile workers in this role should work to demystify sexual myths, provide accurate and precise science-based information on sexuality, and provide practical strategies for the young person to act on the new information and skills learned. It is important to develop rapport and trust through appropriate self-disclosure while maintaining confidentiality. Lastly, it is very important that the juvenile worker use age-appropriate language that the juvenile population will understand. The use of jargon and clinical terminology is to be avoided.

Juvenile workers (i.e., probation officers, court personnel, case workers, and so forth) should keep the following points in mind when working with youths:

• Youth often have different terminology for, and understanding of, sexual terms. In many cases there may be terms and slang that are used. It is recommended that the practitioner be well versed on this terminology. Though the juvenile worker may know the terminology, it is not necessarily recommended that they incorporate the terminology in their own feedback and/or questions. Indeed, if their usage seems artificial and/or if the youth seem uncomfortable with such informality, then this technique should be avoided. On the other hand, if youth respond with additional dialog and do not give indication that the use of common verbiage is not respected, then this can be a good means of joining and rapport building.

- Unlike many adults who seek counseling and testing for STDs and/or HIV, juveniles may actually be more interested in obtaining information than in being tested. Youth who may not have initiated sex might be seeking support in making informed decisions about their sexual and reproductive health.
- Youth may not always be candid about their sexual experiences out of fear of stigma and labels. For instance, some youth may have engaged in sexual activity with the same sex (minority status based on sexual identity will be discussed later in this chapter). Due to any number of reasons, these youth may not wish to divulge these experiences. Another example might be a youngster who had consensual sex with a sibling and/or another family member. Owing to self-consciousness of the taboo about incest, they may not wish to admit to the activity.
- Addressing these issues often takes more time than working with adults, because youth often know less about their sexual health than adults do. Moreover, it should be remembered that for some youth, particularly young males, some of the issues discussed may elicit humor and jokes, particularly jokes that are macho or male-dominated in nature. The juvenile practitioner should never join in on such humor and should ensure that all topics are addressed in a serious and respectful manner.

GENDER AS A MINORITY STATUS AMONG JUVENILES

During the past few decades, arrest rates for male juveniles were seen to be three to four times higher than those for female juveniles. Thus, as with adult offenders, it can be seen that males are much more likely to be involved in delinquent or criminal behavior. However, during the years 2004–2008, this ratio changed considerably so that juvenile females now account for roughly one-third of arrests of those under 18 years of age. The reasons for this may be many, but we speculate that much of this has to do with more liberalization between both genders among the younger population and also to a less patriarchal view among courthouses toward female youth. It would seem perhaps that the justice system is less protective of female youth and is now willing to process female offenders just as it would male offenders, even those who are underage.

As we have noted, female youth have been largely overlooked by those interested in juvenile justice (Chesney-Lind, 1999), and indeed many of their survival mechanisms (e.g., running away when confronted with abusers) have been criminalized. The juvenile justice system has often ignored the unique needs of female juveniles, often because of their smaller numbers when compared to male offenders (Holsinger, 2000). Still, the number of girls engaging in problematic behavior is increasing, and it is becoming clearer that gender-specific interventions are necessary. For example, a study conducted by Ellis, O'Hara, and Sowers (1999) found that troubled female youth have a profile distinctly different from that of males. **Troubled female youth** are characterized as abused, self-harmful, and social, whereas the male group was seen as aggressive, destructive, and asocial. The authors concluded that different treatment modalities (more supportive and more comprehensive in nature) may need to be developed to treat troubled female adolescents.

Practitioners in child protection agencies often observe that many girls who flee from abusive parents are eventually labeled as runaways. Krisberg (2005, p. 123; see also Zahn et al., 2010, p. 3) concluded, "Research on young women who enter the juvenile justice system suggests that they often have histories of physical and sexual abuse. Girls in the juvenile justice system have severe problems with substance abuse and mental health issues" (p. 123). If they are dealt with simply by being placed on probation, the underlying causes of the problems they confront are unlikely to be addressed. To deal with these causes, counseling may be needed for all parties involved, school authorities may need to be informed if truancy is involved, and further action in adult court may be necessary. If, as often happens, a girl's family moves from place to place, the process may begin all over because there is no transfer of information or records from one agency or place to another. According to Krisberg, "There are very few juvenile justice programs that are specifically designed for young women. Gender-responsive programs and policies are urgently needed" (p. 123). The notion that female youth may respond better to gender-specific interventions is supported by Zahn et al. (2010, p. 12), who found the following eight variables to be related to female delinquency:

1. negative and critical mothers,
2. harsh discipline,
3. inconsistent discipline,
4. family conflict,
5. frequent family moves,
6. multiple caregivers,
7. longer periods of time with a single parent, and
8. growing up in socioeconomically disadvantaged families.

Although some of these factors are significantly related to male delinquency as well, the lack of gender-specific programming for girls caught in the juvenile justice system requires more serious attention. To further this point, consider that female youth are also becoming more violent in nature, as well, lending further to the need for more attention to female delinquency and criminal activity. As noted with other types of delinquency, the heightened involvement of females in violent offenses has also been attributed to prior victimization of females (Bloom, Owen, & Covington, 2003). This has been referred to as the "**victim-turned-offender hypothesis**" by some researchers (Hanser, 2007c). From an abundance of literature, it is clear that female offenders are often victims of sexual abuse and physical abuse during early childhood and tend to be victims of sexual assault and/or domestic abuse during adulthood (Bloom et al., 2003; Hanser, 2007c). The suggestion is that females become violent perpetrators in response to their own victimization, although substance abuse, economic conditions, and dysfunctional family lives have also been linked to violent offending by females (Zahn, 2010).

Teenage Mothers and Unwanted Pregnancies

The United States has the highest rates of teen pregnancy and births in the western industrialized world. Teen pregnancy costs the United States at least $7 billion annually. Indeed, 34 percent of young women become pregnant at least once before they reach the age of 20, which amounts to roughly 820,000 pregnancies a year by girls or young women. Roughly 80 percent of these teen pregnancies are unintended and 79 percent are to unmarried teens. Furthermore, the younger an adolescent girl is when she first has sex, the more likely it is that this first sexual experience was actually unwanted or non-voluntary in nature. Lastly, almost 40 percent of girls who first had intercourse at the age of 13 or 14 report that the sexual activity was not wanted. In addressing teen sex, young girls, and potential pregnancy, consider the following:

- Approximately one in five youth has had sexual intercourse before his or her 15th birthday.
- Approximately one in seven sexually experienced 14-year-old girls report having been pregnant. This translates into about 20,000 pregnancies each year and 8,000 births. (For those aged 15–19, the numbers are about 850,000 pregnancies and 450,000 births.)
- Teens 15 and older who use drugs are more likely to be sexually experienced than are those teens who do not use drugs—72 percent of teens who use drugs have had sex, compared to 36 percent who have never used drugs.
- Teens who have used marijuana are four times more likely to have been pregnant or to have gotten someone pregnant than teens who have never used marijuana.

From the above information, it is clear that adolescents' early life-course sexual activity is leading to pregnancy and it is also clear that much of the sexual activity occurs in tandem with drug use. Indeed, it would seem that some drug use further facilitates the likelihood of a future pregnancy. Given this, it is important to consider that in many families in which a daughter acts out sexually, the parents tend to be non-communicative or they may be in constant conflict and turmoil with one another. In such cases, these teens do not feel comfortable talking with their parents due to the added strain and burden that the pregnancy is likely to add to the family household.

In trying to limit the amount of teen pregnancy, abstinence should be presented as one choice. Indeed, the primary reason that teenage girls who have never had intercourse give for abstaining from sex is that having sex would be against their religious or moral values. Other reasons cited include desire to avoid pregnancy, fear of contracting a sexually transmitted disease (STD), and not having met the appropriate partner. When educating juvenile girls on peer pressure and sexual activity, practitioners should provide these youth with suggestions on how they can be assertive in resisting sexual advances from young men. Facts should be made clear to girls (i.e., three-fourths of all girls at 14 who report having had sex state that it is mainly because their boyfriends want them to). Practitioners should ensure that young girls are aware of these facts and that they are aware of their own right to refuse such advances.

When attempting to prevent undesired pregnancies among juvenile girls, it may be useful to note that teens who have strong emotional attachments to their parents are much less likely to become sexually active at an early age and are therefore at a lower risk for teen pregnancy. In addition, contraceptive use among sexually active teens has consistently increased. This is a good trend since it has been found that sexually active teens who do not use contraception have a 90 percent chance of teen pregnancy within one year.

While it may be the view of the juvenile worker that these youth should simply abstain, the fact of the matter is that many will not. With this in mind, alternative safeguards against pregnancy should be discussed with juvenile girls, particularly if the young girl notes her intent to be sexually active. When juvenile workers talk with juvenile girls, the use of contraceptives and decisions to engage in sexual activity can

CURRENT EVENT
Teenage Pregnancy and Intervention Programs

During the last few years, teen pregnancies have gone down and some speculate that this is due to the combined efforts of various social activist groups as well as efforts of the federal government. For instance, the President's Teen Pregnancy Prevention Initiative (TPPI), has made teen pregnancy a priority public issue to be addressed. The Centers for Disease Control (CDC) have outlined their goals from 2010–2015, to reduce teenage pregnancy and address disparities in teen pregnancy and birth rates. Among the five key components associated with this strategy is the objective of working with the diverse community. The CDC aims to raise the awareness of community partners regarding the link between teen pregnancy and social determinants of health, to ensure that culturally and linguistically appropriate programs and reproductive health care services are available to youth. Through this process, the CDC seeks to do the following:

1. Engage and recruit a diverse group of community partners, including those not typically engaged in the target community, to collaborate in teen pregnancy prevention efforts.

2. Identify and implement best practices that address the social determinants of teen pregnancy among diverse youth.

3. Ensure that prevention efforts are inclusive of both male and female youth.

4. Ensure that clinical providers provide culturally competent and adolescent-centered clinical reproductive health services, assess appropriately for social determinants, and link youth to needed social services.

5. Identify and educate a diverse group of community stakeholders on strategies that have an impact on teen pregnancy prevention and related social determinants.

Further still, it is clear that, when working with the teen population, the CDC understands that the means by which communication might occur is an important consideration. Indeed, the use of social media by teens is important and is a central feature to this campaign. The creation of referencing guide for the use of social media in teen prevention programs has been developed by the CDC, and gives pointers on using podcasts, facebook, and other social media to disseminate information on assistance to sexually active teens.

Some of these techniques are meant to counter observations that some social media and tabloid sources were glamorizing teen pregnancy. Henson (2011) points toward shows like MTV's Teen Mom and 16 and Pregnant as chief examples. She points out that while the producers likely had good intentions, the end result has been one where the girls have become celebrities and they are on headline tabloid articles with front page photo appearances. She contends that these shows are irresponsible and that they misportray the lives of these moms. She states that "MTV chooses to focus on the girls' volatile relationships with the babies' fathers or their new body piercings and tattoos," rather than focusing on more serious issues (Henson, 2011, p. 1).

Others disagree with Henson's view and there is some research that demonstrates that, despite the tabloid sensationalism, teens around the nation do heed the intended warnings that these shows provide. For instance, the National Campaign to Prevent Teen and Unplanned Pregnancy (2010) conducted a survey in 2010 of over 1,000 teens and they found that among the teens surveyed, 82 percent thought that shows like MTV's Teen Mom and 16 and Pregnant helped them to better understand the challenges involved with parenting. Further, only 15 percent thought that the shows glamorized teen pregnancy. Lastly, many also indicated that media portrayals also opened the door for conversations with adults regarding issues with love, sex, and parenting.

Regardless of how one views the issue, it is clear that teen pregnancy is on a downward trend. Efforts to make this a reality have been ongoing since 1981, when the federal government enacted the Adolescent Family Life (AFL) program, which has two key components, the the "care" component and the "prevention" component (Solomon-Fears, 2013). AFL care d projects focus on comprehensive health, education, and social services, including life and career planning, job training, safe housing, decision-making and social skills. These care services for parenting teens include pre- and post-natal care, nutrition counseling, continuing education, and vocational services (Solomon-Fears, 2013). This aspect of intervention is intended to address issues that currently exist, while the prevention components of the President's Teen Pregnancy Prevention Initiative (TPPI) are intended to tackle the issue on a longer-term basis by decreasing likely statistics in the future.

These programs, in order to be youth-specific and individualized, reflect the age, sexual experience, and culture of youth who are in these programs (Moore, 2010; Solomon-Fears, 2013). In addition, cooperation with teens and experts can be an effective feature while helping teens to develop coping skills, values, and goals, as well as attending to psychological risks and cultivating protective factors such as those listed in Table 12-1 of this chapter (Moore, 2010; Solomon-Fears, 2013). The combination of care and prevention approaches that consider these various aspects of intervention, it would seem, are producing good results and, in the process, improving the lives of those who currently contend with this issue or are born into these circumstances, reducing social ills and disparity among minority youth and non-minority youth, alike; creating a better tomorrow for the nation's youth of today.

References: Centers for Disease Control and Prevention (2013). *Teen Pregnancy Prevention 2010–2015.* Atlanta, GA: Centers for Disease Control and Prevention. Retrieved from: http://www.cdc.gov/TeenPregnancy/SocialMedia/index.htm

Henson, M. (2011). MTV's 'Teen Mom' glamorizes getting pregnant. CNN Opinion. Retrieved from: http://www.cnn.com/2011/OPINION/05/04/henson.teen.mom.show/

Solomon-Fears, C. (2013). *Teenage Pregnancy Prevention: Statistics and Programs.* Washington, DC: Congressional Research Services.

Moore, K. A. (2010). *What If We took Research Seriously: What Would Teen Pregnancy Programs Look Like?*, Baltimore, MD: Presentation to the Healthy Teen Network.

National Campaign to Prevent Teen and Unplanned Pregnancy (2010). Fast facts: **Does the Media Glamorize Teen Pregnancy?: New Polling Data on What Teens Think.**

be very emotional for the young girl. Furthermore, male juvenile practitioners may experience some degree of discomfort discussing these issues. In cases where a female is available, it may be useful to have same-gendered practitioners discuss sex and pregnancy issues—but this should not at all be considered mandatory.

If the juvenile girls are not uncomfortable with the male staff's input and if the male correctional counselor is professionally adept with such topics, then there is an opportunity for the male practitioner to provide some very effective and pro-social modeling. In fact, male juvenile workers can demonstrate genuine care and consideration for the young girl's future and health.

On the other hand, male staff working with juvenile girls should be careful to not seem "fatherly" or as if they are "lecturing" the youth. This is important because this is common among many father–daughter relationships and this can have an opposite effect than what is intended.

Lastly, when and where the opportunity exists, the use of both male and female practitioners is highly recommended. In addition, group interventions with young juvenile girls can allow the youth to discuss issues of sexual activity and pregnancy. The inclusion of peers can help facilitate the intervention and create a stronger set of reinforcements for the young girl. The feedback that juvenile girls gain from supportive peers can be very useful in providing the support and encouragement required so that the girl can make her own independent choices regarding her own sexual behavior.

IMPACT OF RACIAL DISCRIMINATION ON HEALTH AND WELLNESS OF JUVENILE MINORITIES

At this point in the chapter, we begin to focus less on general topics relevant for the juvenile population, in general, and more on issues relevant to racial, ethnic, or other demographics for specific groups of juveniles who present with identities that are considered minority status for adults as well as youth. Thus, this subsection will address issues related to socialization for minorities based on race and ethnicity while the next subsection will address issues related to same-sex preference youth. Each of these specific areas of focus is relevant to the juvenile justice system and demonstrate that diversity and multiculturalism include a number of perspectives that go beyond simple race and ethnicity.

Currently, minority youth who identify as being African American, Latino, Asian/Pacific Islander, or Native American constitute about 30 percent of the entire U.S. population. These groups are also minority groups that have suffered from generations of social inequality and disparate opportunity. **Social inequality** is a term for circumstances of disparate treatment and opportunity for groups of people based on ethnicity, gender, or other characteristics. **Racial discrimination**, for this chapter, is a form of social inequality that includes experiences that result from legal and/or non-legal types of discrimination based on the racial identification of the individual. Racial discrimination can occur at both the personal and institutional levels. We have discussed, in prior chapters, how racism can exist at the institutional level where norms and processes throughout society collectively work against the individual who is the subject of discrimination.

Indeed, it is institutional discrimination that is the primary reason for group differences in material wealth and living conditions (such as poverty, education, employment, and access to medical care) and political power (control of the media, political influence, and community finances). Exposure to both individual and institutional discrimination is stressful and leads to frustration and feelings of hopelessness for many racial minorities. This stress and these feelings of frustration are related to negative health outcomes among minority groups.

Phillips, Settles-Reaves, Walker, and Brownlow (2009) provide research in which they examine a theory on racial inequality and social integration that examines social factors where racial discrimination is associated with negative mental and physiological health outcomes. They note that, as youth detect contradictions between opportunities in broader society and the lack of opportunity in their own lives, stress and frustration are often experienced. Racial discrimination increases frustrations, reinforces perceptions of unfairness (inequality), and further limits options to achieve life goals.

In the education system, African American and Latino youth, especially males, are highly likely to report negative encounters where their access to education is diminished. On the other hand, Asian youth have indicated higher levels of racist treatment from their peer group at school (such as racial epithets, social rejection, and physical threats). African American female youth tend to report negative racially based treatment more than any other female racial group in the school setting. Lastly, African American youth of both genders tend to report racial discrimination as they grow older, on into adulthood. As can be seen, many minorities tend to report racially based discrimination that begins early in life and continues throughout their lifespan.

The ability to adaptively cope with racial discrimination is a very important developmental challenge for many minority youth. These youth, like non-minority youth, must build a healthy self-concept, work through psychological stress, and make life-course adjustments that entail periods of storm and stress. Unlike their non-minority counterparts, they also must develop effective coping skills when faced with racial discrimination—over which they have no power and little influence. Further, they must deal with persons who undermine their ability to achieve goals for reasons that have no logical basis. During their teens, these youth often have good understanding about social power and are often greatly impacted by experiences, whether direct or vicarious, where racial discrimination has been inflicted against them, their friends, or their family. In many instances, prolonged feelings of anger and bitterness may exist due to these injustices.

For minority parents, their ability to socialize their own children is usually impacted by their own past experiences with racial discrimination. Indeed, in some communities where parents have experienced racial discrimination from law enforcement, they may instruct their children to not trust Caucasian police officers. While their own previous experiences may be valid, this type of message being given to youth instantly creates friction between the child and police officers, in general, and between the child and Caucasian officers, in particular. In addition, this obviously sets a racist tone that permeates the neighborhood, wherein multiple children are given the same message.

The same circumstances may exist within school systems, where minority parents who have experienced racism may instruct their children not to trust teachers of a given color or cultural background. There is research that some African American mothers report vicarious experiences of racism when they sense or observe racial discrimination that has been leveled at their children. Often, these parents will socialize their children to not trust certain racial groups of teachers. With this said, we also would like to point out that the opposite of this is also equally true; some Caucasian families may instruct their children not to trust minority teachers, thereby reinforcing prejudice and racism.

From a juvenile justice and delinquency perspective, one of the more relevant findings is that between experienced racism and aggressive behavior. For African American youth, both those who are victimized and those who perpetrate incidents of violence have histories of reported discrimination and attribute their use of violence as a necessity for their survival. Furthermore, it has been found that exposure to racial discrimination is associated with a lowered sense of empathy and also can stunt moral development—thereby increasing the ability for these youth to engage in injurious behaviors.

It is with this previous thought that we would like to offer some additional explanation. We are not trying to provide excuses for violent behavior and we are not attempting to rationalize violence based on prior discrimination that youth experience. However, we are noting that environmental variables such as the surrounding community, peer groups, family, and social circumstances are risk factors for delinquency (refer again to Table 12-1), which are also the social mechanisms by which racism and racial discrimination are experienced or perpetuated.

These **micro-system effects** (family and peer groups) and **macro-system effects** (community, school, and social environment) impact a youth's socialization (see Figure 12-3). In social environments where a sense of injustice is conveyed to youth, both in personal relationships at the micro-level and through media and public messages at the macro-level, the stage is set for youth to become desensitized to the feelings of others and to develop a worldview where they believe that the only form of justice is through victimizing others or, perhaps, that the wrong they commit in harming others is no worse than what is generally experienced by themselves and others whom they observe. Essentially, toxic social environments at the micro- and macro-levels produce circumstances where violence and victimization become rational options for youth.

Lastly, exposure to racial discrimination by minority youth has consistently been found to correlate with higher rates of anxiety, depression, and substance abuse. These are **internalizing behaviors,** which are self-destructive means of coping with the stress, abuse, and trauma of racist environments. Other behaviors such as displays of loud anger and

Micro System Effects	Macro System Effects
Young experiences of racial discrimination	Media and Social Environments
Observation of family and peer experience of discrimination	Schools
Racial socialization	Police and Courts

FIGURE 12-3 Potential Effects of Racial Discrimination on Health Outcomes of Minority Youth. *Source:* Phillips, K. S., Settles-Reaves, B., Walker, D., & Brownlow, J. (2009). Social inequality and racial discrimination: Risk factors for health disparities in children of color. *Pediatrics, 124,* 176–186.

aggression, as well as violent actions, have also been correlated with racial discrimination among minority youth. These are **externalizing behaviors**, which are destructive to others and are also considered maladaptive forms of coping with the pain of racist environments.

Perhaps, as we will see in Chapter 13 that follows, many of the reasons that minority youth join gangs in impoverished areas might be to address these internal and external pulls and pushes upon youth, providing them with a sense of security and a sense of belonging that can supplement or even replace micro- and macro-effects on youth. Furthermore, internalizing behaviors that were previously mentioned as well as externalizing behaviors are easily assimilated into gang culture as adaptive behaviors that are shared among members and where a member is rewarded and gains respect. Thus, the gang family ameliorates much of the pain that these youth experience and also provides a reward system where violence, substance abuse, and maladaptive coping are rewarded. The fact that gangs are often aligned along racial membership and loyalty (as we will see in Chapter 13) provides further support for this notion.

Lastly, research shows that the negative effects of social inequalities and racial discrimination can be mitigated through intervention. Indeed, many youth programs in the juvenile system address various aspects of micro- and macro-effects upon youth to help in their reformation from delinquent to non-delinquent behavior. However, it is our contention that, in order to be truly culturally competent for minority youth, juvenile programs must directly address racial discrimination experienced by youth.

Box 12.1 Caucasians as the Upcoming Minority among Youth

There is indication that by 2019 the population who is under 18 years of age will be mostly non-Caucasian youth. Much of this rapid change in demographics is due to higher birth rates among Latino Americans, Asian Americans, and biracial persons. This trend in the demographic statistics is similar to, but more rapid than, the move toward the Caucasian population being a minority among the adult population, which is anticipated to occur sometime around 2040. To make this point clearer, consider that there was a decrease in Caucasian youth by 4.3 million from 2000 to 2010, in contrast to a total increase of 5.5 million youth who were either Latino or of Asian American descent.

Latino Americans are the fastest growing minority with birth rates that exceed all other racial/ethnic groups in the United States. Further, in two states, California and New Mexico, the majority of youth are of Latino (mainly Mexican) origin. In eight other states (Nevada, Arizona, Texas, Mississippi, Georgia, Florida, Maryland, and Hawaii), Caucasian youth are a minority when compared with other racial and ethnic categories. This demonstrates that immigrant communities are becoming increasingly influential in various areas of the United States, as we have seen in prior chapters.

As noted in many other chapters of this text, there is often a language barrier that exists, which hinders the ability of many criminal justice practitioners to communicate with many immigrant groups. However, what is being observed among Latino and Asian American youth is fluency in the English language. In fact, not only do these minority youth from immigrant communities tend to be fluent in English, many do not even learn their native languages. Thus, over time the language barrier for these immigrant groups is expected to disappear, as English becomes the adopted language among youth of these different groups.

Further still, there is a broadening gap between the older populations and the younger populations. Among minorities who have higher birthrates, adults within those groups tend to be younger than Caucasian adults. This means that, within the next 20 years, the majority population will be younger. This is likely to affect the social and political landscape of the United States significantly. This also means that as we consider juveniles as a separate category in our study of diversity, we are examining a group that is growing in size, relevance, and influence but, at the same time, consists of ever more intra-group diversity than ever before.

Source: Little, C. J. (2011, Apr. 6). Study: Whites becoming the new youth majority. News Max.

This means that these programs must treat these experiences as valid and true and provide youth with means of coping and overcoming these obstacles in a manner that leads to productive outcomes for minority youth and that minimizes or prevents negative outcomes. As Phillips et al. (2009) state:

> Intervention and prevention programs can foster empowerment and behavioral change in youth of color by acknowledging the consequences of social inequalities such as racial discrimination and helping children address these inequalities on the basis of the principles of social justice and social action. (p. 180)

It is through a process similar to what Phillips et al. (2009) advocate that minority youth who have experienced the abuse of racial discrimination can be helped. The **social justice approach** to intervention is one that is community based and requires that persons be active in countering toxic social norms through advocacy, public announcements, and activism within political, economic, and financial spheres of government and private society to effect a change in prevailing norms and beliefs related to circumstances of injustice that exist. This is the process that was initiated during the Civil Rights Movement of the 1960s and is an approach that continues today, both in the United States and in other areas of the world where discrimination and unfair treatment exist for marginalized groups in a given society.

SEXUAL MINORITY YOUTH

Students will recall that in Chapter 4, we introduced populations based on same-sex preference as a minority group of focus in this text. Likewise, in other chapters, we have continued to address issues related to gender and/or sexual orientation as aspects of diversity that are encountered within the criminal justice system. In some cases, this area of diversity is introduced in relation to practitioners and their rights to employment in agencies (Chapters 4 and 11), in other cases, we have addressed these issues among the offender population (see Chapter 11), and in other cases we have included same-sex preference populations as victims of crime in Chapter 4, and in now, in this current section of Chapter 12. We consider our emphasis on the gay-lesbian-bisexual-transgender (GLBT) population to be one aspect of this text that is truly progressive in nature and relevant to the world of practitioners in the criminal justice system. In fact, as we see in society, this is becoming truer with each passing day.

There is little doubt that, among today's teens, the acceptance of same-sex couples is much greater than with teens from generations past. This is particularly true in larger metropolitan areas of the nation, with more commonplace occurrences of same-sex and bisexual youth being represented and where there is less stigma attached to this orientation than in other areas of the United States. Nevertheless, media portrayals and obvious changes in public sentiments toward these sexual orientations make it clear that tolerance is much more improved today than even just 20 years ago. Legal decisions and changes in legislative enactments make it all the more clear that these sentiments are becoming codified and serve as official acknowledgment that these individuals are entitled to rights and privileges extended to any other minority group in the United States. It is with these points that we proceed to address the topic of youth who we refer to as sexual minority youth. In doing so, we provide research from the Centers for Disease Control and Prevention (2011) on sexual identity and health-risk behaviors among middle school and high school students in seven different locations.

For this subsection, we refer to **sexual minority youth** as those who adopt sexual identities described as being part of the gay, lesbian, or bisexual population or those who indicate that they are unsure of their sexual identity. Nevertheless, we would be remiss if we did not note that youth who identify themselves as heterosexual, gay, lesbian, or bisexual may not have actually had sexual contact. To add further to the complexity, youths who have only had sexual contact with persons of the same sex or with both sexes might identify themselves as heterosexual, and youths who have only had sexual contact with persons of the opposite sex might identify themselves as gay, lesbian, or bisexual. Some youths who eventually identify themselves as a sexual minority or only have sexual contact with persons of the same sex or both sexes might not identify themselves as a sexual minority and might not have had any sexual contact. There is a substantial amount of research documenting these different and dissonant perspectives on sexual identity among youth in today's world (Centers for Disease Control and Prevention, 2011). We mention this but, for the sake of simplicity, will focus on our own, more limited definition of sexual minority youth for this subsection.

The research by the Centers for Disease Control and Prevention (2011) examined a number of risky behaviors that seem to be disproportionately represented among sexual minority youth. We present these behaviors separately and distinctly because we believe that these results from this research, along with their corresponding data charts, provide a compelling argument that this group of youth is subjected to circumstances where they are discriminated against by persons at school, including their peers. This means that, while there is more acceptance of GLBT youth in today's youth culture, these youth are subjected to discrimination and victimization from other youth just as adult members of the GLBT population suffer similar forms of victimization in the broader population. With this in mind, we now proceed to our presentation of problematic behaviors associated with sexual minority youth who struggle to cope with their identity formation and levels of acceptance among youth and the community around them.

Sexual Minority Youth Who Carry a Gun to School

Based on the Centers for Disease Control and Prevention research, it is clear that sexual minority youth do not feel as safe as heterosexual youth because they tend to carry a weapon for protection much more frequently than do their heterosexual counterparts. Only three of the seven sites associated with this study provided data on this particular issue. Among those three that did (Delaware, Maine, and Massachusetts), it is clear that heterosexual youth carry guns to school much *less* often than do gay/lesbian youth, bisexual youth, and youth who are uncertain about their sexual identity (see Table 12-2).

From the data in Table 12-2, we can see that regardless of the state, gay/lesbian youth and those who are unsure of their sexual orientation are much more likely to bring a firearm to school. Bisexual students are more likely as well, particularly in the state of Maine. The key point we would like to make is that these youth must feel less safe at school than their heterosexual counterparts due to their desire to bring firearms to school for protection. Adding to this, it is our contention that even though the GLBT population is more commonly accepted in youth culture, there still exists a strong degree of homophobia within society (including youth) and there are also many youth who may bully and abuse others—the GLBT population may simply be easier targets for bullies.

TABLE 12-2 Percentage of Youth who Carried a Gun to School by Sexual Identity, 2001–2009

State Surveyed	Sexual Identity of Youth Surveyed				
	Number of Participants	Heterosexual Percentage	Gay/Lesbian Percentage	Bisexual Percentage	Not Sure Percentage
Delaware	10,323	5.3	15.7	8.4	13.0
Maine	1,297	3.8	16.5	20.7	23.5
Massachusetts	16,577	2.9	17.4	5.1	13.9

Source: Centers for Disease Control and Prevention. (2011). Sexual identity, sex of sexual contacts, and health risk behaviors among students in grades 6–12—Youth risk behavior surveillance, selected sites, United States, 2001–2009. *Morbidity and mortality weekly report, 60.* Atlanta, GA: Centers for Disease Control and Prevention.

Sexual Minority Youth and Reports of Physical Fights at School

It has also been found that sexual minority youth also tend to be engaged in physical fights more often than are heterosexual youth. Students can see in Table 12-3 that for all five states included in the study, gay/lesbian and bisexual students, as well as students unsure of their sexual identity, all had higher reports of being in a physical fight at school. Because it is very unlikely that these youth, who are a smaller minority of students, would initiate the majority of these fights, we must conclude that, in general, heterosexual students are often picking fights with sexual minority youth, resulting in their experiencing fights at school more often than do other students. It is quite interesting to observe that in every state and for every category, the prevalence of being in a physical fight was greater among sexual minority youth than with heterosexual youth.

Sexual Minority Youth and Sexual Assault

As with other forms of negative life experiences, it would seem from the Centers for Disease Control and Prevention study that sexual minority youth are also sexually victimized much more often than are heterosexual youth. Indeed, as seen in Table 12-4, data from the three states involved in this study clearly shows that gay/lesbian and bisexual youth, as well as those who are not sure about their sexual orientation, all report much

TABLE 12-3 Percentage of Youth who were in a Physical Fight by Sexual Identity 2001–2009

State Surveyed	Sexual Identity of Participant Youth				
	Number of Participants	Heterosexual Percentage	Gay/Lesbian Percentage	Bisexual Percentage	Not Sure Percentage
Delaware	10,213	31.1	43.6	43.9	45.1
Maine	10,057	23.5	38.0	41.6	48.1
Massachusetts	16,520	29.0	48.1	45.2	36.6
Rhode Island	5,226	24.0	40.3	42.8	32.1
Vermont	22,840	24.2	41.8	41.9	33.9

Source: Centers for Disease Control and Prevention. (2011). Sexual identity, sex of sexual contacts, and health risk behaviors among students in grades 6–12—Youth risk behavior surveillance, selected sites, United States, 2001–2009. *Morbidity and mortality weekly report, 60.* Atlanta, GA: Centers for Disease Control and Prevention.

TABLE 12-4 Percentage of Youth who were Ever Physically Forced to have Sexual Intercourse by Sexual Identity, 2001–2009

State Surveyed	Sexual Identity of Participant Youth				
	Number of Participants	Heterosexual Percentage	Gay/Lesbian Percentage	Bisexual Percentage	Not Sure Percentage
Delaware	10,281	6.4	31.0	32.1	22.5
Maine	10,134	8.0	25.5	30.3	25.3
Rhode Island	5,296	7.2	21.8	22.6	21.8

Source: Centers for Disease Control and Prevention. (2011). Sexual identity, sex of sexual contacts, and health risk behaviors among students in grades 6–12—Youth risk behavior surveillance, selected sites, United States, 2001–2009. *Morbidity and mortality weekly report, 60.* Atlanta, GA: Centers for Disease Control and Prevention.

greater prevalence of being forced to have sexual intercourse. From this study, it is not clear whether these youth were forced by other students or, perhaps, by persons within their family or in other environments. This study did not distinguish this when the survey was conducted. Nevertheless, given that sexual minority youth tend to present with higher rates of depression, anxiety, and other mood and adjustment disorders, it may be that noxious experiences like sexual assault serve as the etiology to these other diagnosable problems.

To further clarify, it is very common for persons who have been sexually assaulted to have higher rates of substance abuse, depression, trauma, anxiety, and other issues that impair coping. Likewise, many youth and adults who grapple with sexual identity issues also present with similar challenges. Our contention is simply that for sexual minority youth who have been forced to engage in sexual intercourse, they are likely to suffer from a host of other corollary problems that are further compounded both by the trauma of sexual assault as well as the stress and by the anxiety that is involved with their sexual identity development. Even more problematic is the fact that their sexual assault experience may become intertwined with their sexual orientation, leading to self-doubts, questions about their self-worth, and other indications of a damaged sense of self-esteem and heightened sense of shame.

Sexual Minority Youth and Attempted Suicide

From the data in Table 12-5, it is clear that at five different sites, gay/lesbian and bisexual youth, as well as those who are uncertain about their sexuality, have suicide attempts that are much more prevalent than that experienced by heterosexual youth. In fact, when one looks at the data provided, it is clear that in every state and in every category, sexual minority youth have rates that are much higher than those of heterosexual youth. This is very disturbing, in its own right, because this means that these youth are depressed and feel miserable about their life circumstances. The fact that suicide rates are so much higher with these youth, alone, make this population a worthwhile population to examine. However, as noted when discussing sexual minority youth who have been forced into sexual intercourse, many of the symptoms associated with being sexually victimized and many of the challenges that are experienced by persons who struggle between keeping their sexual orientation secret and/or coming forward with their sexual orientation are similar. However, youth who experience both of these are

TABLE 12-5 Percentage of Youth who Attempted Suicide by Sexual Identity, 2001–2009

State Surveyed	Sexual Identity of Participant Youth				
	Number of Participants	Heterosexual Percentage	Gay/Lesbian Percentage	Bisexual Percentage	Not Sure Percentage
Delaware	9,062	5.7	27.0	29.3	26.7
Maine	10,165	5.1	22.3	20.6	20.7
Massachusetts	14,734	6.4	33.1	28.0	20.9
Rhode Island	4,632	6.3	25.8	32.0	16.1
Vermont	22,068	3.8	25.4	26.7	16.9

Source: Centers for Disease Control and Prevention. (2011). Sexual identity, sex of sexual contacts, and health risk behaviors among students in grades 6–12—Youth risk behavior surveillance, selected sites, United States, 2001–2009. *Morbidity and mortality weekly report, 60.* Atlanta, GA: Centers for Disease Control and Prevention.

doubly likely to suffer from trauma, which lead to negative emotional states where suicide might seem like an option where they can get relief from their negative emotional experiences.

As noted previously in prior subsections, sexual minority youth experience challenges in just coming to terms with their sexuality and in feeling accepted by others, including family and friends. Furthermore, many will struggle with what they refer to as **outing**, where members of the GLBT community who have kept their orientation secret make the decision to become open to their family, friends, in their work environment, and with the public at large. The decision to do this can be anxiety-provoking, whereas, on the other hand, not doing so can be very troubling to youth who keep their sexual orientation secret and live the life of a lie. The distress that is caused for these individuals should not be underestimated.

Lastly, we noted in the first part of this subsection that in today's youth culture, there is greater acceptance of same-sex preference populations or sexual minorities. While this is true, it is also clear that these youth still suffer from a great deal of discrimination and that they are victimized much more frequently than their heterosexual counterparts. This simply reflects the fact that our society is still in a state of transition, particularly in relation to same-sex couples and freedom in sexual orientation. Things have improved, to be sure, in the past 30–50 years; in times past, youth simply would not be able to admit to these diverse sexual orientations owing to the stigma and social ostracism that they would receive, as well as even more intense victimization that would have, in the past, probably have been condoned by the individual's peers.

Therefore, we do note that despite the higher levels of victimization for sexual minority youth when compared to heterosexual youth, tolerance and acceptance of these youth from within today's youth culture are much higher. As we have seen elsewhere, the transition toward acceptance of diverse groups can be quite a process that takes a very long time to come to realization. For sexual minority youth, identity acceptance from other peers is still in transition and, amidst this, there is a great deal of risk to their health and well-being that we can observe from the different types of victimization that we have seen in the study by the Centers for Disease Control and Prevention

INTERNATIONAL FOCUS

Teen Suicide Around the World

Around the world, it is estimated that nearly 100,000 teens, aged 15–19, commit suicide per year. Among this age group, suicide is the third leading cause of death. This number is, in actuality, underestimated due to data not being available in a number of countries and/or due to misreporting of suicides as a means of protecting families from grief. Indeed, there may be a number of reasons why, depending on the culture, that suicides may not be counted as such.

According to the International Association of Suicide Prevention (IASP, 2013), nearly 90 percent of all teen suicides occur in conjunction with some type of psychological disorder, most often this being a mood disorder or substance abuse disorder and, in most cases, this problem had persisted for more than two years. This organization notes that suicide usually is preceded by a history of other risky behaviors, such as binge eating, binge drinking, tobacco smoking, unprotected underage sexual activity, and/or carrying firearms (IASP, 2013). What is interesting about these observations, for this chapter, is that these same dynamics are observed among youth in the United States, as we have seen in our readings from this chapter. This means that there may be much benefit in international information exchange between different nations when addressing this social ill. This is the contention of the IASP and, judging by the research, it would seem that this is a valid point for consideration.

When considering suicidal behaviors around the world among youth, the research by Wasserman, Cheng, & Jiang (2005) shows that suicide rates tend to be higher for male youth than female youth, which is a dynamic that seems to be true in the United States, as well. However, for some countries, the reverse was true, namely in China, Cuba, Ecuador, El Salvador and Sri Lanka, where the female suicide rate was higher, but usually only marginally so. Their research examined data from the World Health Organisation (WHO) and took into account suicide data from over 90 countries, giving a very good global view on juvenile suicide around the world and, amidst issues related to cultural differences and views, providing a good baseline on different dynamics related to youth suicide.

Colucci and **Hjelmeland** (2013) have written and directed research on behalf of the IASP on issues related to culture and suicide. They have noted the importance of cultural settings to implementing prevention programs and have also pointed to the importance of spirituality and religion when addressing suicide in various areas of the world. Likewise, having gender-based programs that deal, not only with suicide but also with potential antecedent problems such as sexual assault and domestic violence, can be very important. Issues related to poverty and suicide have also been advocated by **Colucci** and **Hjelmeland** (2013). The goal, then, for these two and for the IASP, is to increase awareness around the world and to advocate for culturally competent interventions to suicidal behavior.

Perhaps it is De Leo (2009) who best explained the importance of having both a multicultural and a multinational lens when considering juvenile suicide. He notes that, in a world of increasing globalization and migration, the failure to attend to cultural differences can be very detrimental to those whom we wish to assist (De Leo, 2009). With this in mind, it is important that international programs, protocols, and processes not be grounded in European or United States design. Rather, a truly international approach should include pluralism and should involve earnest efforts to approach evaluation and research in such a manner as to include cultural comparisons in a functional and usable manner to benefit practitioners throughout the world who work in the field, day-to-day, to save lives and minimize the risk of suicide in the future.

References: Colucci, E. & Hjelmeland, H. (2013). *Special Interest Group: Culture and Suicidal Behaviour.* International Association of Suicide Prevention. Retrieved from: http://iasp.info/culture_and_suicidal_behaviour.php

International Association of Suicide Prevention (2013). *Special Interest Group: Suicidal Behavior in Adolescents.* Retrieved from: http://www.iasp.info/suicidal_behaviour_in_adolescents.php

Wasserman, D., Cheng, Q., Jiang, G. (2005). Global suicide rates among young people ages 15–19. *World Psychiatry, 4(2):* 114–120.

De Leo, D. (2009). Cross-Cultural Research Widens Suicide Prevention Horizons. *Crisis, 30(2),* 59–62.

(2011). Over time, we anticipate that circumstances will improve for sexual minority youth but, at this time, juvenile practitioners must be willing and able to consider the various challenges that these youth face and they must be able to provide effective care and consideration for these youth.

PEER GROUPS, SUBCULTURE, MINORITY ISSUES, AND SOCIALIZATION

Peer groups are important for youth and, when discussing with youth, the correctional counselor should keep this in mind. The peer group will likely be the primary source of socialization aside from the youth's family. Indeed, if the family was seriously dysfunctional, it is likely that the youth only identifies with his or her peer group. Among youth who are processed in the juvenile justice system and/or the criminal justice system, there exist a number of subcultural groupings that will be important reference points for youth seen by the counselor. In particular, it should be noted that the "gangsta" movement has had a particularly strong impact on youth culture, particularly among delinquent youth. The "thug" look and/or genre of music is fairly common among youth who are processed throughout the juvenile system. Although other subcultural groups exist (i.e., Goths, alternative, etc.), they are not as well represented among the hardcore juvenile offender population. This is not to say that knowledge of such groups is not relevant to correctional counseling, but it is to say that these groups will not be as prevalent, largely because they are simply not as widespread in popularity among today's youth and the public media.

Furthermore, a disproportionate number of minority youth are processed through the justice system. Thus, in many juvenile systems, youth will tend to congregate along racial lines just as they might along subcultural lines. African American and Latino American youth are particularly represented, and these youth will likely affiliate with their own racial categories. In many cases, the youth from these minority groups will also come from families who are not affluent, with economic challenges being common to their background. These factors will tend to impact the socialization process that has been experienced by these youth and this is likely to be quite different from the backgrounds of many counselors. Hence, the juvenile worker must also understand the cultural backgrounds common to youth in their intervention programs. Knowledge of the locale from which youth may have been raised can also be helpful for the correctional counselor.

Culturally Relevant Considerations

The cultural identity will be important for many youth that the correctional counselor may encounter within the juvenile and/or criminal justice system. This then requires that the correctional counselor be culturally competent in providing therapeutic services. With this in mind, there are several points that should be made about the content of culturally competent intervention services for juveniles. Certain key themes and issues should be included in these interventions when dealing with minority clients. Among these issues are those of acculturation, assimilation, migration history, race and institutional racism, and socioeconomic classism. These issues are likely to be directly relevant to most juvenile minorities who are processed within the formal system. Furthermore, Caucasian youth should likewise be encouraged to explore their cultural roots, particularly with family-of-origin issues, for all the same reasons that minority youth would do so. In fact, there should be no distinction, as cultural beliefs are transmitted through all families, and all youth can benefit from drawing on their cultural strengths and from learning about how issues such as racism and classism affects us all.

When working with minority youth who are from immigrant populations, juvenile workers should likewise discuss the importance of **acculturation** and **assimilation**, the former referring to the abilities and actions of the individual in adapting to the host culture and the latter referring to the permeability of the host culture (Smart & Smart, 1997). With respect to acculturation, minority youth should be encouraged to discuss how maintaining their own original culture and language can place them at cross purposes with the criminal justice system and the American ideal of appropriate functioning. This should be compared with issues pertaining to assimilation, in which the minority juvenile is coerced to become more like the mainstream culture. The benefits and drawbacks to both options should be discussed openly in the group and youth should be given homework that allows them to reflect on these issues.

In addition, some juvenile youth may come from families that have lived in the United States for only a handful of years. Migration issues should be discussed as well, with difficulties in the adaptation process being discussed openly. Issues pertaining to first-generation immigrants and the generations that follow should be discussed. Youth in intervention programs, whether school-based or otherwise, should be encouraged to engage in homework assignments to discuss immigration issues and cultural belief systems that were maintained or discarded by their families. In covering these topics, the self-efficacy of the youth is improved through the strengthening of their self-identity and understanding of the development of their family-of-origin in the broader society.

In addition, issues of classism should be brought squarely into focus for the juvenile client. The effects of poverty on family relationships should not be overlooked. Economic levels affect the type and amount of service delivery that different populations receive in educational, medical, and political arenas. The effects of poverty can likewise affect feelings of power over one's environment, feelings of self-worth, and perceptions of victimization. Minority youth should be made aware of this and provided an environment where these issues can be openly discussed. There should be explorations into how social class can shape a youth's reactions to their sense of powerlessness, so that juvenile can readily identify with the social structures that put them at heightened "risk" of turning delinquent.

SOCIAL CLASS, POVERTY, AND THE UNDERCLASS

At this point, we conclude this chapter with a subsection on issues related to social class and poverty among youth. We think this is important for several reasons. First, for minority youth, there tends to be a disproportionate number who come from economically marginalized backgrounds when compared to Caucasian youth.

While this is not to say that many Caucasian youth do not also come from backgrounds of deprivation, the proportion of those who do tends to be much less than that observed among minority populations. Second, money and status are concepts that are not lost on youth and, in many cases, we see cliques that form amongst youth that are based on the economic background of the youth's family-of-origin. Third, the socioeconomic status of youth often impacts the region in which they are raised and affects the likely life chances that they may experience. The impact that this can have on youth, in terms of both overall development and being delinquent, is obviously important.

In continuing this discussion, we would like to note that there is research that shows that youth whose families-of-origin are in the middle-class bracket of income commit delinquency more than may typically be suspected. Often, middle-class delinquents adhere to specific patterns of activities, standards of conduct, and values different from their parents (Cox, Allen, & Hanser, 2013). In fact, we would contend that youth of today tend to be influenced by a youth culture that stands apart from and in opposition to adult values and norms. When we use the term **youth culture**, we refer to a culture where juveniles are much more open to messages of influence from their own peers than they are to other sources, especially adults. The trends, activities, media messages, social contexts, etc. of these youth tend to be distinct and apart from the world of adults and this is intentional on the part of these youth.

Activities such as attending parties, drinking, joyriding, smoking cannabis, listening to common music, and engaging in various types of sexual behavior are all reflective of youth culture. By participating in and conforming to the youth culture, status and social success are achieved through peer approval. Indeed, we contend that the bulk of middle-class delinquency occurs in the course of customary non-delinquent activities but moves to the realm of delinquency as the result of a need to "be different" or "start something new." Likewise, many people note that adolescence is a time of storm and stress. Amidst this period of volatility and change, various types of relationships and activities (i.e., family, education, employment) are also in states of change as the youth assumes new roles and identities. Although more males than females are arrested for delinquency, the number of female delinquents has increased significantly during recent years.

Accessibility to social objects for participating in the youth culture is an important part of delinquent behavior. Social objects, such as cars, the latest styles, alcoholic beverages, and drugs, are frequently part of the delinquent youth culture. Peer recognition for young males may be a reason for acts of property destruction or even acts of violence. In addition, these youth who engage in high-risk behaviors and/or exhibit a sense of bravado tend to gain a sense of respect among their peers. This serves as reinforcement for these behaviors and once the tone is set, the replication of these behaviors among a given peer group is increased in likelihood.

Moreover, there are often differences in how aberrant behaviors are manifested between middle-class youth and those who come from impoverished areas. For instance, acts of vandalism in which one's bravery can be displayed for peer approval are somewhat different from the violent behavior often seen in lower-class youth, who may demonstrate their bravery by gang fights/shootings, muggings, robbery, and other crimes against people. This tends to be the case for youth of any racial or ethnic background who come from impoverished areas. However, as minorities are disproportionately represented in lower socioeconomic circumstances (when compared with Caucasians), it is more common that media portrayals will cast these trends in the light that they are a minority issue rather than one of social class, as well.

Wooden and Blazak (2001) indicated that suburban youth are often told to act like adults but are not given the privileges of adulthood, forcing them into a subculture characterized by delinquency-producing focal concerns (p. 19). Some end up in trouble-oriented male groups, and they sometimes get involved in violent crime to conform to group norms. More typically, those in middle-class coed groups get involved in petty theft and drug use. This tends to be true of Caucasian youth and minority youth who come from middle-class backgrounds rather than those from backgrounds of poverty.

We would like to take a moment to comment on another circumstance that may be observed when discussing socioeconomics, geographical location, and delinquent behavior. We have put a significant amount of emphasis on juvenile behavior in metropolitan and suburban areas but have not mentioned delinquency in rural areas. In many cases, youth also exhibit behaviors that are 'autonomy seeking' and risky in nature. However, there are fewer means of detecting their activity; hence, many activities are not reflected in official counts. Nevertheless, even in rural areas drug use among youth is problematic and other activities, including high rates of sexual activity, partying, and so forth, are also common among rural youth. If nothing else, these youth may engage in activities that are idealized by media and youth culture portrayals from city and suburban settings. Essentially, the culture and the trends are simply transmitted to youth in more rural areas.

Although most evidence indicates that juveniles from all social strata and locations may become delinquent (Elrod & Ryder, 2005), we would like to focus attention on the notion of a criminal subculture that tends to develop in many impoverished, inner-city areas. A **criminal subculture** develops when juveniles are encouraged and supported by persons in their lives who engage in criminal activities or are in routine contact with criminal institutions. In noting how criminal subcultures may form in neighborhoods and communities, we will refer to the classic tenets of Miller (1958) who, during his study of lower- and middle-class norms, values, and behavioral expectations, concluded that a delinquent subculture is inherent in lower-class standards and goals. The desirability of the achievement of status through toughness and smartness, as well as the concepts of trouble, excitement, fate, and autonomy, is interpreted differently depending on one's socioeconomic status. Miller concluded that by adhering to lower-class norms, pressure toward delinquency is inevitable and is rewarded and respected in the lower-class value system. Miller believed that lower-class youth who become delinquent are primarily conforming to traditions and values held by their families, peers, and neighbors. As indicated earlier, Wooden and Blazak (2001) used this same approach to describe middle-class delinquency during the 21st century, demonstrating how Miller's initial work is still applicable to today's world of youth from the spectrum of socioeconomic strata.

CONCLUSION

This chapter presents juveniles in the criminal justice system as a minority group, all unto themselves. The rationale for this is because youth are, in fact, a specialized population with regard to police response, legal proceedings, and correctional placement and treatment. Their Civil Rights status in society is unique from other groups and, similar to older persons in the community, we consider youth a diverse group that is based on age. Furthermore, as noted, several commonalities (along with differences) are shared in the youth culture, which are often different from the priorities and norms of most adults.

In addition, there are a number of risk factors and protective factors that come into play for youth of all racial and ethnic groups. Among these are the influences of family and peers, educational quality and access, the quality of life in the community, as well as various individual factors. Each of these areas of influence can either increase or decrease the likelihood of future aberrant behavior among youth, resulting in delinquent or even later criminal behavior. Thus, juvenile workers must be adept at addressing these various issues for youth of all cultural backgrounds, paying special attention to specific racial, ethnic, or socioeconomic factors that impact youth.

Further, we have shown how family-of-origin issues as well as problems related to school safety are uniquely important for juvenile populations. The state of the family in contemporary society has greatly impacted youth, and youth who come from unstable or negative home environments are at greater risk to develop various physiological and psychological reactions. Likewise, school environments where youth are concerned about their safety and well-being are also negatively impacted and will present with traumatic responses. Some may resort to carrying weapons to school and/or engaging in other means of defensive but potentially violent behaviors. The likelihood of delinquent behavior for youth who have toxic family systems or educational environments is also likely to increase, in terms of both frequency and severity, for these youth.

We have also discussed how racial discrimination negatively impacts minority youth in terms of health and wellness. A number of adverse effects are observed among minority youth who experience racial discrimination. Furthermore, the mental health of youth is detrimentally impacted, besides physiological health. Micro- and macro-effects on youth can work independently or together to aggravate the healthy development of minority youth. The means by which these youth cope, in terms of internalizing and externalizing behaviors, are important because self-sabotaging acts and acts of aggression toward others both may have some of their genesis in the injustices and frustrations that these youth experience in a discriminatory environment.

We have also discussed gender diversity among juveniles, providing an overview of the various types of crimes that delinquent girls tend to commit and also providing several factors that are likely to contribute to their delinquency. The need for gender-responsive programs was also presented in this chapter. Furthermore, we have noted how sexual activity impacts the juvenile population. Indeed, sexual development and experimentation begin at young ages for many juveniles who are in the juvenile or criminal justice systems. With this comes exposure to unhealthy practices that result in various health complications and/or early pregnancies. Issues related to teen pregnancies generate an entirely new set of dynamics that lead to challenges for female juveniles, who must not only find a way to support themselves, but must also support their newborn. For those involved with young male juveniles, economic autonomy is not likely to be realized, and whether with help of the father or without, these youth also experience a host of unique stresses and challenges to obtaining a lifestyle of independence and self-sufficiency.

Likewise, we have also discussed sexual minority youth as a specific element of diversity within the juvenile population. This is a very unique aspect of diversity to be included in most texts and we consider this both an appropriate and progressive addition to this chapter. It has been noted that today's youth are much more comfortable with the GLBT population than did prior generations. Despite this, tolerance and acceptance of this population are still in a state of transition. As a result, these youth experience higher prevalence rates of various forms of victimizations and also suffer from negative mental health and wellness factors because of the discrimination and abuse they receive. Naturally, school systems and juvenile workers must strive to provide safe and effective interventions for these youth.

Lastly, we have discussed the need for culturally relevant interventions as well as attention to social class, socioeconomic status, and poverty. Programs must obviously be culturally competent for different minority groups if they are to be effective. This means that programs must ensure that diverse groups are given specific attention. In addition, the impact of socioeconomic demographics must be considered as these tend to have similar effects on youth, regardless of their racial or ethnic characteristics. In such cases, all youth can be impacted (for worse or for better), including both Caucasian and minority racial groups, if they suffer from poverty or are fortunate enough to have been born into wealth or affluence. Regardless, we see juvenile delinquency and criminality that emerges at all points along this spectrum.

Chapter 12 Learning Check

1. _____ is a culture where juveniles are much more open to messages of influence from their own peers than they are to other sources, especially adults.
   a. Criminal subculture
   b. Youth culture
   c. Minority youth group
   d. None of the above

2. Outing is a term for when members of the GLBT community who have kept their orientation secret make the decision to become open to their family, friends, their work environment and with the public at large.
   a. True
   b. False

3. _____ are those who adopt sexual identities described as being part of the gay, lesbian, or bisexual population or those who indicate that they are unsure of their sexual identity.
   a. Gay, Lesbian, Bisexual youth
   b. Same-sex preference
   c. Sexual minority youth
   d. None of the above

4. Assimilation refers to the ability and actions of the individual to adapt to the host culture.
   a. True
   b. False

5. Macro-system effects include which of the following?
   a. Media
   b. Schools
   c. Police and courts
   d. All of the above
   e. None of the above

6. Externalizing behaviors are self-destructive means of coping with the stress, abuse, and trauma of racist environments.
   a. True
   b. False

7. _____ are families in which each parent brings children of his or her own into the family setting, which may result in conflicts among the children or between one parent and the children of the other parent.
   a. Blended families
   b. Broken families
   c. Transitional families
   d. Families-of-divorce
   e. All of the above

8. According to research in this chapter, it has been found that, in actuality, heterosexual youth have been forced

to have sexual intercourse more often than sexual minority youth.
a. True
b. False

9. Troubled female youth are characterized as abused, self-harmful, and social, whereas the male group was seen as aggressive, destructive, and asocial.
a. True
b. False

10. _____ is a term for circumstances of disparate treatment and opportunity for groups of people based on ethnicity, gender, or other characteristics.
a. Racial discrimination
b. Economic discrimination
c. Racial disparity
d. Social inequality
e. None of the above

Essay Discussion Questions

1. Discuss how social class and poverty disproportionately impact minority youth.
2. Identify sexual minority youth and provide a detailed explanation of some of the challenges that are disproportionate to this group when compared to heterosexual youth.
3. Provide a discussion on the characteristics of troubled female youth and explain how female delinquency has occurred in the recent past. In addition, discuss some of the issues that female juveniles face that are unique from male juveniles.

References

Alwin, D. F., & Thornton, A. (1984). Family origins and the schooling process: Early versus late influence of parental characteristics. *American Sociological Review, 49,* 784–802.

Bauer, L., Guerino, P., Nolle, K. L., Tang, S. W., & Chandler, K. (2008, October). Student victimization in U.S. schools: Results from the 2005 School Crime Supplement to the National Crime Victimization Survey. Retrieved from: http://nces.ed.gov/pubs2009/2009306. pdf.

Bloom, B., Owen, B., & Covington, S. (2003). *Gender responsive strategies: Research, practice, and guiding principles for women offenders.* Washington, DC: National Institute of Corrections.

Centers for Disease Control and Prevention. (2011). Sexual identity, sex of sexual contacts, and health risk behaviors among students in grades 6–12—Youth risk behavior surveillance, selected sites, United States, 2001–2009. *Morbidity and mortality weekly report, 60.* Atlanta, GA: Centers for Disease Control and Prevention.

Cheng, T. (2004). The impact of family stability on children's delinquency: An implication for family preservation. *Journal of Family Social Work, 8*(1), 47–60.

Chesney-Lind, M. (1999). Challenging girls' invisibility in juvenile court. *Annals of the American Academy of Political & Social Science, 564,* 185–202.

Child Trends DataBank. (2013). *Unsafe at school.* Retrieved from: http://childtrendsdatabank.org/?q=node/323.

Cox, S. M., Allen, J. M., & Hanser, R. D. (2013). *Juvenile justice: A guide to theory and practice* (8th ed.). Thousand Oaks, CA: Sage Publications.

Ellis, R. A., O'Hara, M., & Sowers, K. (1999). Treatment profiles of troubled female adolescents: Implications for judicial disposition. *Juvenile and Family Court Journal, 50*(3), 25–40.

Elrod, P., & Ryder, R. S. (2005). *Juvenile justice: A social, historical, and legal perspective* (2nd ed.). Sudbury, MA: Jones & Bartlett.

Hanser, R. D. (2007c). *Special needs offenders in the community.* Upper Saddle River, NJ: Prentice Hall.

Hayes, L. (2008). *Teachers' expectations affect kids' grades, student-teacher relationships.* EduGuide. Retrieved from: www.eduguide.org.

Holsinger, K. (2000). Feminist perspectives on female offending: Examining real girls' lives. *Women & Criminal Justice, 12*(1), 23–51.

Krisberg, B. (2005). *Juvenile justice: Redeeming our children.* Thousand Oaks, CA: Sage.

McCall, R. B. (1994). *Preventing school failure and antisocial behavior in the U.S.A.* Pittsburgh, PA: University of Pittsburgh Office of Child Development.

Miller, W. B. (1958). Lower class culture as a generating milieu of gang delinquency. *Journal of Social Issues, 14*(3), 5–19.

Phillips, K. S., Settles-Reaves, B., Walker, D., & Brownlow, J. (2009). Social inequality and racial discrimination:

Risk factors for health disparities in children of color. *Pediatrics, 124,* 176–186.

Rutherford, R. B., Griller-Clark, H. M., & Anderson, C. W. (2001) Treating offenders with educational disabilities. In J. B. Ashford, B. D. Sales, & W. H. Reid (Eds.), *Treating adult and juvenile offenders with special needs.* Washington, DC: American Psychological Association.

Simons, R. L., Simons, L. G., Burt, C. H., Brody, G. H., & Cutrona, C. (2005). Collective efficacy, authoritative parenting, and delinquency: A longitudinal test of a model integrating community- and family-level process. *Criminology, 43,* 989–1030.

Smart, D.W., & Smart, J. F. (1997). DSM-IV and culturally sensitive diagnosis: Some observations for counselors. *Journal of Counseling and Development, 75,* 392–397.

Thornberry, T. P., Smith, C. A., Rivera, C., Huizinga, D., & Stouthamer-Loeber, M. (1999). *Family disruption and delinquency.* Washington, DC: NCJRS.

Wooden, W. S., & Blazak, R. (2001). *Renegade kids, suburban outlaws: From youth culture to delinquency.* Belmont, CA: Wadsworth.

Wright, J. P., & Cullen, F. T. (2001). Parental efficacy and delinquent behavior: Do control and support matter? *Criminology, 39,* 677–705.

Zahn, M. A., Agnew, R., Fishbein, D., Miller, S., Winn, D., Dakoff, G., et al. (2010, April). *Causes and correlates of girls' delinquency.* Girls study group: Understanding and responding to girls' delinquency. Washington, DC: Office of Juvenile Justice and Prevention. Retrieved from: www.ncjrs.gov/pdffiles1/ojjdp/226358.pdf.

Types of Juvenile Offending, Gang Affiliation by Race and Gender, and Disproportionate Minority Contact in the Juvenile System

LEARNING OBJECTIVES

After reading this chapter, students should be able to do the following:

1. Identify issues related to differences in male and female juvenile offending.
2. Discuss disparities in offending by racial and ethnic groups.
3. Assess the problems with gang offending among various minority and non-minority youth.
4. Discuss the issue of disproportionate minority contact with the juvenile justice system.
5. Identify effective programming considerations for minority youth who are in confinement.

KEY TERMS

Assessment–training–evaluation cycle

Community Mediation Agreement

Culturally competent activities

Culturally competent objectives

Culturally competent policy

Evaluative transparency

Evidence-based practices

Failing forward concept

Goals of cultural competence

Ill-structured problem

Implementation evaluation

Learning organizations

Outcome evaluation

Pre-service training

Problem-based learning approach

Process evaluation

Stakeholders

INTRODUCTION

This chapter will continue forward with information that was presented earlier in Chapter 12 of this text. In that chapter, we discussed the juvenile as a minority group simply due to age and the diminished legal status that youth possess. Going further, we then discussed a number of issues that put youth of minority racial and ethnic groups at risk of being involved in the juvenile justice system. We also discussed how girls in the juvenile system have additional considerations that require additional specialized gender-specific intervention. These themes will be further explored in this current chapter, as well. While Chapter 12 also discussed sexual minority issues among youth, this aspect will not receive as much focus because the themes of disproportionate minority contact and gang offending, two primary foci of this chapter, seldom note this aspect of diversity as being directly relevant.

In this chapter, we will focus on minority youth based on racial and/or ethnic group and we will provide an overview of disproportionate contact at multiple points in the justice system, which ultimately result in the disparities in confinement and detention of minority youth that we see today. The key point is to showcase a term that has come into vogue during the last decade of juvenile justice studies—disproportionate minority contact (DMC). We will officially define DMC later in this chapter. Issues related to DMC are routinely noted in the juvenile justice research literature and we would be remiss if we did not make this a large part of our discussion on multiculturalism and juvenile justice.

We also will further address issues related to female youth in the justice system. We have identified women and, just as correctly, young girls, as a minority group worthy of exploration when addressing diversity and the need for gender-appropriate knowledge and response in the justice system. Issues related to concerns for females caught in the juvenile system are gaining attention because female representation has increased in recent years. Thus, we provide additional information on females in the juvenile system but, in this case, we focus more specifically on the trends in offending that are found among female juveniles with discussion as to the reasons for this offending.

Lastly and very importantly, we include an extensive discussion on juvenile gang activity, particularly among racial and ethnic minority youth, as well as gang activity among female juveniles. There are many reasons for this, which include the fact that often, due to media portrayals and public perceptions, gangs are thought to consist of minority juveniles. Furthermore, as we will see, most gangs have loyalty lines that are based on racial or ethnic identity, presenting a need for practitioners to be culturally competent when responding to these groups of youth. Moreover, gang violence and gang culture are often epitomized in youth culture (as seen in Chapter 12) and this means that we would be remiss if we did not acknowledge and address this facet of juvenile offending. Even female juveniles have received increased attention in gang research as their numbers have increased in the past decade. Thus, our decision to provide in-depth attention to gangs and juvenile offending is, in actuality, an aspect of multiculturalism in the juvenile justice system that is necessary and very relevant for practitioners who desire to work with diverse youth. We now turn our attention to the rates and types of offending seen among the juvenile population.

RATES AND TYPES OF OFFENDING BY AGE AND GENDER

Although there are numerous characteristics and aspects of juvenile offending that could be analyzed as points of interest, we will tend to restrict our analysis of rates and types of juvenile offending to issues related to the age (age being an aspect of

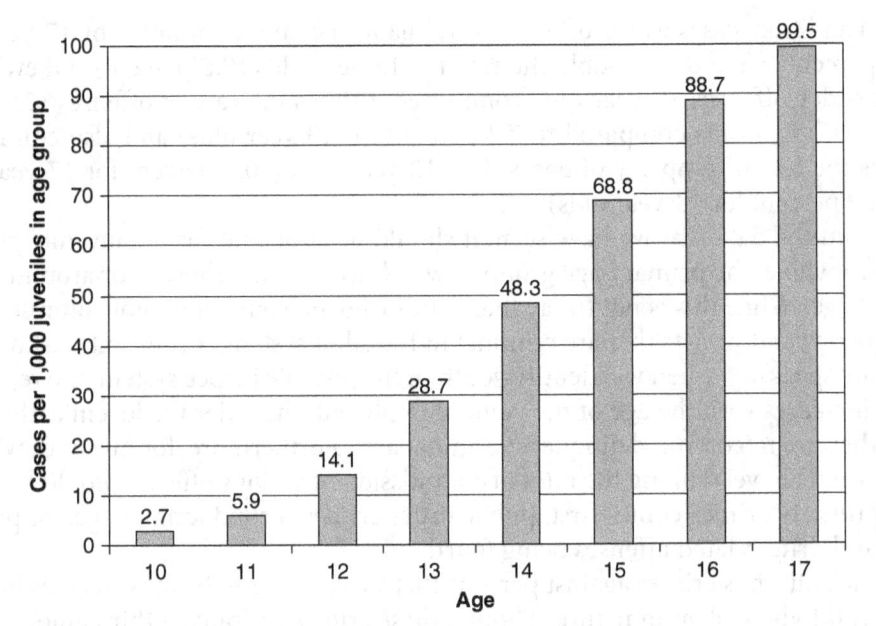

FIGURE 13-1 Delinquency Cases Increase with the Referral Age of the Juvenile. *Source:* Puzzenchera, C., Adams, B., & Hockenberry, S. (2012). *Juvenile court statistics 2009*. Washington, DC: National Center for Juvenile Justice.

diversity), race/ethnicity (this also obviously being associated with diversity), and/or the gender of youth who offend. This is because this is the focus of this text and this chapter. We simply want to acknowledge that a comprehensive analysis of juvenile crime would include a much broader discussion than what we provide here. In fact, entire books are written on this subject. It is our goal, in this section, to simply discuss offending as it relates to various categories of diversity that we have previously identified.

When considering the age of delinquent youth, we can see from Figure 13-1 that as youth get older, the rates of referral to the juvenile court system increase. It is important to note that this data is from the national juvenile court statistics, which means that these consist of cases that are disposed. The fact that a case is "disposed" simply means that a definite action was taken as the result of the referral. As we can see from the data in Figure 13-1, the highest rate of referrals come from youth who are aged 16 and 17 years old. Indeed, in 2009 the delinquency case rate for 17-year olds (112.5) was more than twice the rate for 14 year-olds (53.8) and more than 3.5 times the rate for 13 year-olds (31.4). Much of the reason for this is because delinquency does become more common among youth as age progresses. However, an additional reason is that there is a tendency to defer very young children out of the justice system for all but the most extreme of cases.

According to Puzzenchera et al. (2012), the largest rate of increase for youth between 13 and 17 years of age was related to drug offenses. Further, it can also be seen that the rate of drug offending is highest for 17 year old juveniles (18.0 out of 1,000 juveniles in same age group), which was 9 times higher than the rate for 13 year olds (2.0 out of 1,000 juveniles in same age group).

In addition, cases where offenses were against persons committed by 17-year olds (22.6 percent) were over double the rate for 13-year olds (9.8 percent). Likewise for public order offenses 17-year olds committed 4 times the rate of offenses (31.1 percent for 17-year olds compared to 7.3 percent for 13-year olds) and also committed 3 times the rate of property offenses than 13-year olds (40.8 percent for 17-year olds and 12.2 percent for 13-year olds).

From the data that we have seen, it should be clear that for the juvenile population, as a whole, the primary age group to which we refer are those at or around 16–17 years of age. While this is not to say that youth who are younger do not commit acts of delinquency and/or acts that are criminal in the adult system, it is meant to show that, generally speaking, when we identify youth in the juvenile justice system, the representation increases with the age of the youth. Simply put, the older the juvenile, the more likely they are to commit delinquent/criminal acts. Furthermore, for juveniles who are aged 15 and above, ranking the rates of commission of various offenses would be as follows: property crimes comes first, public order crimes second, crimes against persons third, and drug-related offenses being fourth.

Naturally, it is crimes against persons that we consider to be most serious because these tend to be violent in nature. Though these crimes are ranked third among youth who are 15 and above, it is interesting to point out that for both male and female youth, crimes against persons increased more than any other category between the years 1985 and 2009.

As seen in Figure 13-2, female cases have remained constant from 2000 to 2009 while male cases, overall, have declined during the same period.

Lastly, as we can see in Figure 13-3, it remains consistently true that, regardless of the year we examine, male juveniles commit many more offenses than female juveniles. We have noted this earlier in this chapter and have indicated that this is one of the reasons why female juveniles garnered such little attention among juvenile researchers

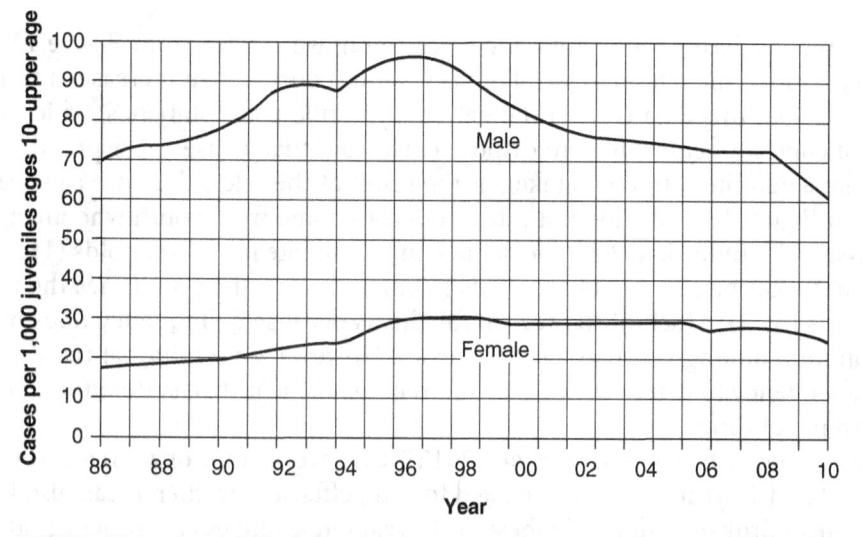

FIGURE 13-2 Delinquency Rate Higher for Male Juveniles but Female Rate of Offense Increased More than Male Rate of Offense between 1985 and 2009. *Source:* Puzzenchera, C., Adams, B., & Hockenberry, S. (2012). *Juvenile court statistics 2009.* Washington, DC: National Center for Juvenile Justice.

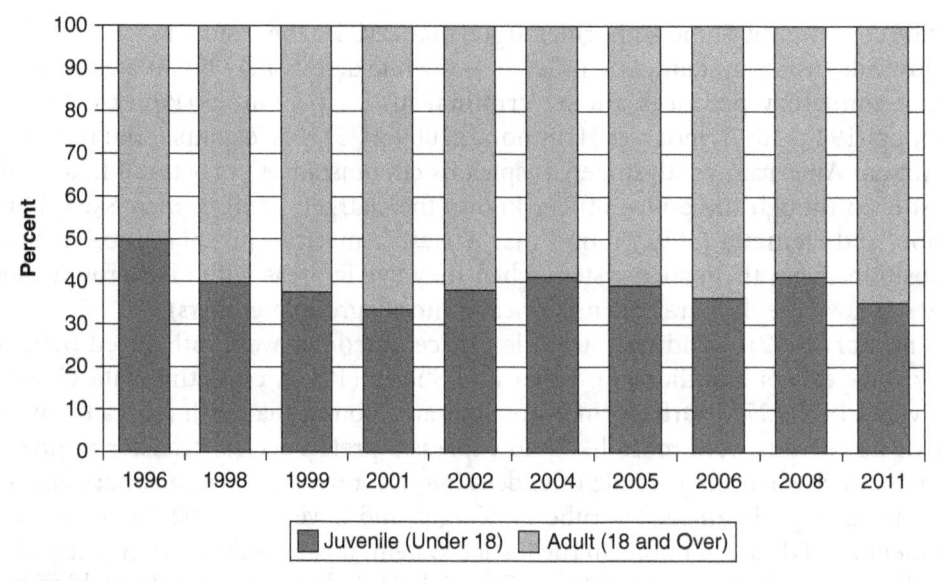

FIGURE 13-3 Proportion of Gang Membership who are Youth vs. Adult.
Source: National Gang Center. *National Youth Gang Survey Analysis.* Retrieved [September 20, 2013] from: http://www.nationalgangcenter.gov/Survey-Analysis.

in decades past. Indeed, this essentially makes the female juvenile a minority group within the juvenile minority group (thus, female juveniles are a double minority, in this respect) and, if they are a racial/ethnic minority, as well, they are a triple minority. This further accentuates the fact that more attention should be given to juvenile females, particularly because female juveniles have numerous gender-specific challenges (i.e., more concerns with esteem needs, teen pregnancies, and so forth) and because many of these girls are racial minorities, as well.

Figure 13-3 demonstrates that while male juveniles commit more offenses, per capita, the rate of offending for males in 1985 was 4 times greater than the rate of female juveniles. However, in 2009, the rate of offending for male juveniles was only 2.5 times greater than the rate of offending for female juveniles. Students examining Figure 13-3 can see that in 2009, approximately 69 cases per 1,000 juveniles (aged 10 and more) were identified compared to about 28 cases per 1,000 juveniles for female offenders. Thus, what we can determine from this figure and the previous tables and figures is that the gap between female juvenile offenders and male juvenile offenders is closing. Furthermore, the closure of this gap is reflected more in offenses against persons, which is a category of offense that is considered more serious in nature than the others that we examined previously. In conclusion, female youth are committing more offenses, per capita, than in the past and these offenses tend to be more serious in nature, as well.

DMC IN THE JUVENILE JUSTICE SYSTEM

Four our purposes, we will define **disproportionate minority contact (DMC)** as the tendency for the justice system to process minority youth at rates that exceed, out of expected proportions, their representation in broader society. In other words, DMC means that more minorities, per capita, are behind bars than exist, per capita, in the outside community. Some authorities argue that DMC is the result of racial bias within the juvenile justice system. Any index of nonwhite arrests may be inflated as a result of discriminatory practices among criminal justice personnel (Benekos & Merlo, 2004, pp. 194–210; Armour & Hammond, 2009, p. 5). For example, the presence of an African American youth under "suspicious circumstances" may result in an official arrest even though the police officer knows the charge(s) will be dismissed. Frazier, Bishop, and Henretta (1992) found that African American juveniles receive harsher dispositions from the justice system when they live in areas with high proportions of whites (i.e., where they are true numerical minority group members).

Kempf (1992) found that juvenile justice outcomes were influenced by race at every stage except adjudication. Feiler and Sheley (1999), collecting data via phone interviews in the New Orleans metropolitan area, found that both African American and white citizens were more likely to express a preference for transfer of juveniles to adult court when the juvenile offenders in question were African Americans. Even more disturbing, Huizinga, Thornberry, Knight, and Lovegrove (2007) note that DMC is evident at all decision points in the justice system. It is with this notion that we focus on information from a key study by Carmichael, Whitten, and Voloudakis (2005), which provide strong support for Kempf's (1992) and Huizinga et al.'s (2007) contentions that DMC exists at all levels of the juvenile justice system.

DMC at All Stages of Justice System

According to Carmichael, Whitten, and Voloudakis (2005), the term **disproportionate minority confinement** (DMC) first gained nationwide attention in 1988 through a report that had been submitted to Congress by the Coalition for Juvenile Justice. During that same year and in reaction to this report, Congress amended the **Juvenile Justice and Delinquency Prevention Act of 1974** and made it a requirement for states to develop plans to reduce the rate of minority juvenile detention within their juvenile systems (Hsai, 2004b). The thinking was (and still is) that the proportion of minority youth in detention in the juvenile justice systems of each state should not exceed the proportion of a minority group's representation in broader society.

The Juvenile Justice and Delinquency Prevention Act of 1974 was again modified in 2002 to further drive home the need for states to avoid overrepresentation of minority youth within their secure facilities. These modifications went further, however, and expanded concern to total contacts for minority youth with the justice system. Essentially, there was a shift in terms to *disproportionate minority contact*, which examined various points-of-contact for minority youth with the juvenile justice system.

During this time, research in many states demonstrated that offense-oriented reasons (not racially oriented considerations) determined procession of juveniles, except at the detention stage (Carmichael at al., 2005). However, many skeptics were not satisfied with these results and continued to question why minorities remained overrepresented among juvenile offenders. In response to this skepticism, the state of Texas conducted additional research that surveyed practitioners who worked with juvenile offenders. When asked their opinion as to why there was so much minority overrepresentation in the justice system, it was found that most of these practitioners noted that minority youth tended to have more family, social, economic, and environmental risk factors, which increased their tendency to engage in delinquent behavior (Carmichael et al., 2005).

This is important because these opinions, expressed by several hundred juvenile practitioners of various levels and capacities, expressed reasons for minority delinquency that were similar—if not identical—to those that we have read about in Chapter 12 of this text. It is, therefore, clear that there is a good deal of congruence between the research findings and the views of practitioners. We consider this important because, as we have noted before, this text is intended to provide both an academic and a practitioner-oriented perspective on multiculturalism. This is important because it ensures students are not provided with a largely theoretical presentation but are also provided with information that is grounded in the day-to-day world of criminal justice.

Carmichael et al. (2005) noted that, in Texas, a comparison of minority proportional representation in the juvenile justice population initially showed few, if any, disparities in contact. Rather, it was initially found that most all disparate treatments were attributed to African American juveniles. However, upon using multivariate analyses (a more sophisticated form of data analysis than simple rendering of pie charts, bar charts, and other more descriptive statistics), they found that, when certain risk factors are taken into account, they found that Latino Americans were just as likely and, perhaps more likely, to be referred than African American youth. The distinguishing factor that tended to exist between both groups was related to the number of disciplinary cases in the school environment.

We think that this is, again, very important as a finding because, as we have seen in Chapter 12, African Americans report a much higher level of discriminatory treatment than most other minority groups. Furthermore, as we have seen, this can and does negatively impact the wellness and self-esteem of African American youth. Moreover, the social environment is one of the many risk factors noted in Chapter 12 that can impact whether youth are brought into the juvenile system. Certainly, the school environment is important for these youth and, if it were to be that school personnel were biased against African American youth, this would likely have a serious and negative impact on their development and behavior; behavior that may be further singled out due to the perceptions of officials in the school environment.

During this period of research, a number of other factors were examined to provide a comprehensive investigation as to those factors that might be responsible for DMC in the juvenile justice system of Texas. The research by Carmichael et al. (2005) examined how these factors impacted decisions and turning points in the justice system during four key points of processing. These four points-of-contact are (1) during the initial juvenile justice system contact (i.e., school official, police officer, or other person), (2) at the point at which the prosecutor reviews the case, (3) when charges are initially filed in court, and (4) during the sentencing phase where court action is taken.

Generally, the severity of the offense still seems to be the most important factor that determines if a case goes forward through the system. In addition, urbanicity of the community from which the juvenile has been raised turns out to be a very important variable. The term **urbanicity** is essentially an indicator of how metropolitan-like a region may be, along with the attendant juvenile departments, district attorney's offices, as well as the area court system. It has been found to be true that youth who enter large metropolitan juvenile systems tend to receive more aggressive prosecution. Thus, the area in which one is charged can significantly augment the outcome.

In the next section, we will discuss the social contexts that are common to many juvenile minorities. Most of these youth, regardless of racial/ethnic background, do not usually do well in academics, tend to be economically disadvantaged, and often have some type of mental or emotional disability. Regarding these various risk factors, Carmichael et al. (2005) note the following:

> Most justice involvement among minorities can be explained because they possess one or more of these risk factors. Race-ethnicity plays a relatively small role in justice contact. This information is essential to know in order to develop and target solutions capable of truly eliminating disproportionality. (p. 5)

Although it is nice to believe that, for the most part, racial variables do not seem to be at the basis of why disparate minority contact is observed, it is nevertheless disturbing to find that the multitude of issues that confront these youth coalesce, disproportionately, for minority youth. The disparity in life quality that is experienced by minority youth apparently takes its toll. With this in mind, we now take a closer look at the social contexts that impact many minority juveniles in the section that follows.

SOCIAL CONTEXTS ASSOCIATED WITH JUVENILE MINORITIES

Many minority group members live in lower-class neighborhoods in large urban centers where the greatest concentration of law enforcement officers exists. Because arrest statistics are more complete for large cities, we must take into account the sizable proportion of African Americans found in these cities rather than the 13 percent statistic derived from calculating the proportion of African Americans in our society. It is these same arrest statistics that lead many to believe that any over-representation of African American and other minority juveniles in these statistics reflects racial inequities in the juvenile and criminal justice networks. For example, African-Americans, Latino Americans, Asians, Pacific Islanders, and Native Americans comprise a combined one-third of the nation's youth population. Yet they account for over two-thirds of the youth in secure juvenile facilities (Armour & Hammond, 2009, p. 4).

As indicated previously in Chapter 12, social–environmental factors, exposure to racial discrimination, and disparities in health and wellness variables can all have an important impact on delinquency rates (Cheng, 2004; Huizinga et al., 2007; Phillips, Settles-Reaves, Walker, & Brownlow, 2009). Race and ethnicity as causes of delinquency are complicated by social class (Huizinga et al., 2007; Phillips et al., 2009). A disproportionate number of African Americans are found in the lower socioeconomic class with all of the correlates conducive to high delinquency. Unless these conditions are changed, each generation caught in this environment not only inherits the same conditions that created high crime and delinquency rates for its parents but also transmits them to the next generation.

It is interesting to note that, according to research, when ethnic or racial groups leave high crime and delinquency areas, they tend to take on the crime rate of the specific part of the community to which they move. It should also be noted that there are differential crime and delinquency rates among African American neighborhoods, providing further credibility to the influence of the social–environmental approach to explaining high crime and delinquency rates (Armour & Hammond, 2009, p. 4). It is unlikely that any single factor can be used to explain the disproportionate number of African American juveniles involved in some type of delinquency. The most plausible explanations currently center on environmental and socioeconomic factors characteristic of ghetto areas. Violence and a belief that planning and thrift are not realistic possibilities may be transmitted across generations. This transmission is cultural, not genetic, and may account in part for high rates of violent crime and gambling (luck as an alternative to planning).

Whatever the reasons, it is quite clear that African American juveniles are overrepresented in delinquency statistics, especially with respect to violent offenses, and that inner-city African American neighborhoods are among the most dangerous places in America to live. Because most African American offenders commit their offenses in African American neighborhoods against African American victims, these neighborhoods are often characterized by violence, and children living in them grow up as observers and/or victims of violence. Such violence undoubtedly takes a toll on children's ability to do well in school, to develop a sense of trust and respect for others, and to develop and adopt nonviolent alternatives. The same concerns exist for members of other racial and ethnic groups growing up under similar conditions.

Youth Composition of Gangs and Reasons for Joining

Currently, it is thought that some 756,000 gang members are active in more than 29,400 gangs across the United States in 2010 (Egley & Howell, 2012). Approximately 40 percent are also thought to be juvenile members. As can be seen in Figure 13-1, youth have consistently represented less than half of all gang members since 1996. While juvenile membership composition in gangs has varied since 1996, it has, nonetheless, consistently stayed at or under 40 percent, indicating that the majority of gang members are actually adult offenders. We make a point to demonstrate the juvenile and adult composition of most gangs in the United States because many laypersons seem to envision street gangs as primarily a problem associated with youth. In reality, most youth who join gangs are exploited by members of gangs and manipulated into committing offenses such as theft and burglary to benefit the gang as part of their initiation or rite of passage. However, as members become older, they tend to move away from street crime and move up in stature within the gang hierarchy. The younger members maintain the turf-oriented activities, and the adults move into more organized and sophisticated activities such as drug trafficking.

While many have speculated as to how and why these youth join gangs, it is our contention that many youth join gangs for a number of reasons but, among all others, the primary reason is to have some sort of need met. Indeed, for many younger juveniles, adult gang members serve as role models whose behavior is to be emulated as soon as possible to become full-fledged gang-bangers because of the prestige, respect, and sense of belonging that the gang-banger role provides them. There has been considerable research that has demonstrated that gangs provide

Box 13.1 A Myriad of Factors that Impact Juvenile Delinquency for Minority and Non-Minority Youth

Federal Advisory Committee on Juvenile Justice

The numbers of youth in the juvenile justice system who have behavioral health involvement issues remain high. Increasingly, data from regional and national studies document the extraordinarily high rates of children and youth who progress through the juvenile justice system with behavioral and/or emotional problems of diagnostic severity (Coalition for Juvenile Justice, 2000).

Strong research over the past 10–15 years confirms that the majority of youth who formally enter the juvenile justice system often exhibit a wide array of conduct, affective (e.g., depression), anxiety, and developmental disorders; substance use/abuse; and/or learning disabilities. These mental health/developmental disability/substance abuse issues typically occur in multiple forms, or what behavioral health professionals term *comorbidities*. The problems usually evolve over many years and are difficult to resolve using short-term interventions. Furthermore, children from non-Caucasian origins (African-American, Latino American, and multiracial youth in large measure) are diagnosed with disproportionately higher clinical levels of disturbance in many categories, especially the externalization disorders (e.g., conduct disorder, attention-deficit hyperactivity disorder, oppositional defiant disorder), and learning problems. They also are prone to failing and dropping out of school at substantially higher rates than their Caucasian counterparts.

What is not known is why the prevalence rates among those at risk of and those who actually enter the juvenile justice system are so high. Many theories have been suggested, including but not limited to (1) genetic or familial patterns of criminal tendencies in repeat generations of offenders; (2) better use of mental health/substance abuse screening and diagnostic tools across systems; (3) institutional patterns of social stress, exclusion, and culturally inappropriate treatments or interventions, including the absence of culturally appropriate screening and assessment tools; (4) complex environmental and social patterns impinging on children in vulnerable situations (e.g., poverty, availability of guns/drugs, overcrowded schools, etc.); (5) the rise of violence and gangs, and the effects of the media on young, impressionable children; and (6) food additives or changes in the biology or processing of the food chain, resulting in metabolic differences among children.

Another notable dynamic evident in the public school system is that significantly more minorities are labeled exceptional and placed in exceptional children's services programming classes or conditions, often viewed as a precursor to school expulsion and an expedited pathway into the juvenile justice system. (*Exceptional children* are those identified by the Education for All Handicapped Children Act of 1975 and the Individuals with Disabilities Education Act as requiring free and accessible public education and other services as a result of having a disability diagnosed through observation, evaluation, and assessment of academic performance.) It is also not known why so many children in the general population (regardless of juvenile justice involvement) are now treated with psychopharmacology when compared to rates of even 10–20 years ago (Olfson et al., 2006).

In addition to the startling numbers of youth presenting with diagnosable and treatable behavioral health problems (including substance abuse), the dynamics associated with disparities among recipients of behavioral healthcare are also unclear (Elster et al., 2003). It is clear, however, that children and youth in the United States appear to be under a high level of stress, exacerbated by a diverse and complicated set of risk factors, and receive treatment at highly disparate rates.

Source: Federal Advisory Committee on Juvenile Justice. (2006). Annual Report. 3–4.

many youth with basic **human needs** related to belonging. Some of these needs might include security, acceptance, friendship, food, shelter, discipline, belonging, status, respect, power, and money (Valdez, 2005; Hess & Drowns, 2004). Thus, gangs and gang membership likely results from any variety of personal, social, or economic factors.

In some cases, youth may be pressured into gangs. This is particularly true where rivalries are rampant and the need to recruit members exists. Peer pressure and intimidation may be the causal factor for some youth. Likewise, protection from victimization at the hands of other gang groups in the community might be another motivator. In addition, there may be expectations from older siblings and/or family members who have also joined a given gang. This is an important consideration because gangs in some areas of Chicago, Los Angeles, and New York have family memberships that may span three or more generations. Indeed, some neighborhoods in these metropolitan areas may have members throughout who are current members or, now well into adulthood, were once members before settling down. In such cases, it is not uncommon for that neighborhood to sympathize with the gang and to provide it with support.

These types of **neighborhood dynamics** can result in community-wide socialization that promotes gang membership. Hess and Drowns (2004) note that it is common among many underprivileged youth to experience frustration and feelings of deprivation from the predominantly middle-class values that pervade throughout broader society (Hess & Drowns, 2004). These youth are not afforded the same opportunities and privileges that more affluent families may have. Underprivileged youth eventually become aware of this and feel the stings of poverty that other middle-class youth avoid. To youth socialized in poor communities that are rampant with vice, crime, and violence, delinquency may not appear to be anything abnormal or undesired (Hess & Drowns, 2004).

Amidst these neighborhood social conditions, the internal influences of the gang membership also work on the youth's development. The youngster may grow up knowing older gang members prior to himself becoming a member. He may learn to admire these members. Over time, an informal familiarization with the gang may develop. Eventually, the gang psyche is taught via the gang formal indoctrination process. This transformation of a youth into a gang member involves a slow process of assimilation (Hess & Drowns, 2004). Once these youth reach an age at which they are able to prove their worth to the gang leadership, they are required to engage in some sort of ritual. In most cases this may consist of getting "jumped in," which is when the gang members beat the youth and the youth is expected to fight until they cannot continue to do so; it may consist of getting "sexed in," in which some females may be required to have sex with male members to obtain affiliate status. Other cases may not require such ceremonies, particularly when the recruit is highly desired by the gang. In addition, these forms of initiation are typical of male juvenile gangs but female gangs may not use the same types of initiation rites.

Minority Youth, Gang Involvement, and Reasons for Joining

As seen in Figure 13-4, when examining the national demographics of juvenile gangs, about 50 percent of all gang members were thought to be Latino American, 32 percent to be African American, 10 percent Caucasian, and 8 percent Asian or "other" (National Gang Center, 2012). More than one-third of all youth gangs were thought to have memberships including members of two or more racial groups (McGloin, 2005).

Among Latino and Asian juvenile gang members, the structure of their family-of-origin may consist of numerous immigrant members. In such cases, the parents

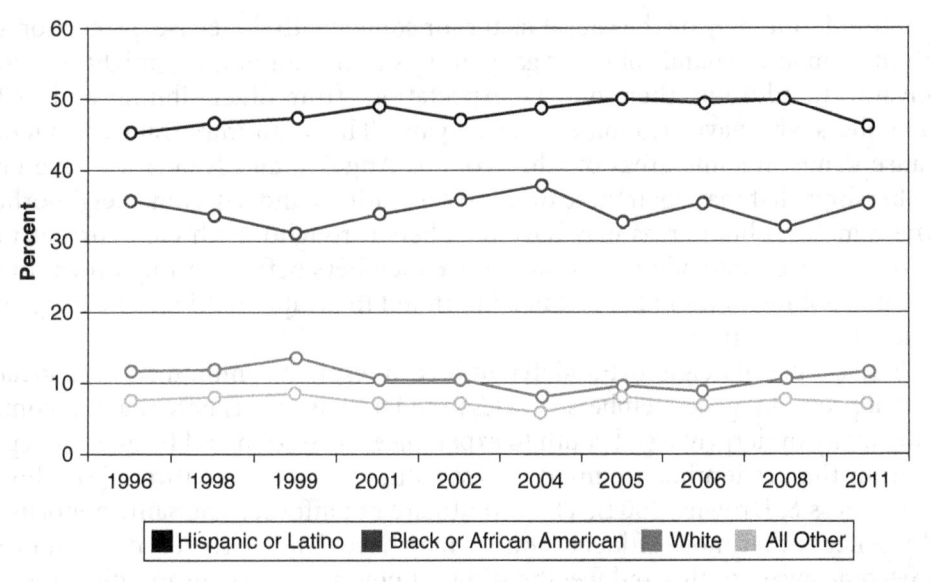

FIGURE 13-4 Race/Ethnicity of Gang Members, 1996–2008. *Source:* National Gang Center. *National Youth Gang Survey Analysis.* Retrieved [September 20, 2013] from: http://www. nationalgangcenter.gov/Survey-Analysis.

may not speak English. Youth in these families learn the language and, owing to school influences, become quickly comfortable with American society. In the process, some may lose respect for their parents and/or may seek to divest themselves of their cultural roots. In these cases, they quickly become experts at manipulating their parents and the parents lose the ability to regulate the behavior of their child. In such cases, it is very difficult to obtain any genuine reform of these youth unless they are separated out from any of their old influences prior to adjudication.

In these circumstances, the use of some type of family therapy is highly recommended. This is typically because the parents have little support and also because the structure of the family is being undermined. In such cases, the correctional counselor will find that the parents are more than willing to assist in regulating their youth; however, they just are not able to, given the linguistic and cultural limitations. It should be pointed out that these types of interventions require a correctional counselor who is either fluent in the client's primary language or an interpreter will be needed. One of the authors of this textbook has conducted therapy concerning similar issues using an interpreter and found the process to be quite productive.

Consider further that many hardcore juvenile offenders come from abusive and/ or neglectful homes. This is one key motivator for youth from these homes to join gangs. This motivation holds true for both male and female juvenile gang members. As was noted earlier in this chapter, the family-of-origin is the primary source for developing the youth's sense of belonging and self-worth. If these youth do not get this support at home, they are likely to seek this support from some other source; gangs provide that source (Hess & Drowns, 2004).

Certain commonalities exist with many families that have hard-core gang members. A family that has members who are also gang members is quite often a racial minority with underprivileged economic resources (Hess & Drowns, 2004). In many cases, the male role model may have a criminal history and/or may actually be incarcerated at the time that the youth obtains gang affiliation. Thus, the gang becomes a surrogate family, of a sort. Within the gang family, violence toward others is commonplace. Hess and Drowns (2004) note that "one reason for this is that gang members were often neglected or abused as children" (p. 194).

Naturally, the previous point dovetails with points made earlier in Chapter 12 regarding the socioeconomic status of many juvenile offenders. The issues related to economic deprivation and the desensitization toward gang affiliation and gang violence that may occur illustrate one reason why it is important to discuss issues related to classism and poverty with these youth. Thus, it is clear that many points made throughout Chapter 12 may serve as genuine causal factors for gang membership and for the maintenance of that affiliation over the span of years. As noted earlier, this may even become an intergenerational affiliation as entire families become enmeshed within the gang and neighborhood identity. Here again is an opportunity for family systems techniques, when and where some adult members do not wish to support a criminogenic lifestyle for their children. In some cases, even older members of a family who were gang members may not wish the same for their own offspring or kin. In such cases, it may be worthwhile to engage multiple family members into the intervention process, so long as these members do not seek to encourage delinquent or criminal activity among family members.

Gangs and Racial Affiliation

Many gangs throughout the United States have developed along racial or ethnic lines. This was true during the early historical development of gangs when ethnic immigrant groups formed gangs in early American history. This has continued to be the case throughout generations and, as we have noted, many gangs are multi-generational, with family membership extending back to multiple generations. In these cases, neighborhoods where ethnic and racial groups predominate and where gangs have their homes, there will be a tendency for future members to be drawn from the same racial/ethnic backgrounds of which the gang initially was composed. This process, therefore, gets replicated throughout generations. Furthermore, gangs in prisons tend to be aligned on racial loyalties, which also is true in most juvenile institutions. As youth exit these facilities and rejoin youth on the streets, they "stick with their own" both on the inside and on the outside of institutions. In addition, adult members of these gangs also continue this very same tendency and, of course, pass this form of loyalty on to more junior gang members.

In Chicago, for example, major street gangs include the **African American Disciples**/African American Gangster Disciple Nation/Brothers of the Struggle (BOS) who are collectively known as **folks**. They are in competition with the **Vice Lords**, also known as the Conservative Vice Lord Nation, who have aligned themselves with other groups such as the **Latin Kings** (Main, 2001; Main & Spielman, 2000). These gangs are collectively referred to as **people** (Babicky, 1993a, 1993b; Dart, 1992). Splinter gangs of "people" and "folks" have been found in Minneapolis, Des Moines, Green Bay, and the Quad Cities area of Illinois. Activities include extortion, drug trafficking, and violent crime in the form of homicide, robbery, drive-by shooting, and battery.

Latino gangs exist in every major urban area and many suburban areas as well. Indeed, Latino gangs have spread to various areas of the United States, including cities in the Southwest, Florida, New York, and the city of Chicago. In fact, the National Criminal Justice Reference Service (2005), estimated that nearly 47 percent of all gang members are Latino in racial orientation. Furthermore, in states such as Arizona, it is reported that fully 62 percent of gang members are Latino in demographic orientation. Other areas of the Southwest report similar levels of Latino gang activity (National Criminal Justice Reference Service, 2005).

Among gangs in general, including Latino gangs, there has been an emergence of gang nations (Attorney General of Texas, 2002; MCTFT, 2010). The term **gang nation** is an informal name for a very large gang that may have several affiliated subsets of members, sometimes stretching across vast areas of the United States (Attorney General of Texas, 2002; Multijurisdictional Counterdrug Task Force Training, 2010). Increasingly, law enforcement officials are considering the Surenos and Nortenos in California, as well as the **Mexican Mafia** in California and Texas, to be gang nations (Hanser, 2007b). These two Latino gang nations are made up of smaller "sets" that share certain symbols and loyalties. These gang nations have become so large that different sets of the same gang might not even know each other except by recognition of some common sign or insignia (Attorney General of Texas, 2002; MCTFT, 2010). In fact, these sets, although belonging to the same nation, may develop rivalries among themselves while also rallying against a common enemy (Attorney General of Texas, 2002; Hanser, 2007b).

Although Asian gangs exist, they are much less numerous than those consisting of African American or Latino American members. Asian gangs are located mostly in California (particularly Los Angeles), New York, Virginia, and Philadelphia and consist of mainly Chinese, Vietnamese, Cambodian, Korean, and Hmong communities and are involved in a variety of illegal activities such as extortion, protection of illegal enterprises, and summary executions of members of rival gangs (Valdez, 2005). Often, these gang members victimize their own ethnic groups and/or communities (Abadinsky, 2003; Valdez, 2005).

Groups like the **Hmong Nation Society** are located in major cities, in some suburbs of California, and in some areas of the East Coast. This gang's adopted color is deep red (symbolic of blood) and this gang was particularly noted for its violence during the late 1990s. In particular, this gang has been known to commit gang-related sexual assaults of women in Hmong communities, establishing extortion rackets of Asian businesses, and being active in the drug trade. It is important to note that Hmong culture is very patriarchal in nature; boys are much more prized than are girls in Hmong families. The honor system among the Hmong holds that men drive the wealth of the family, preside over functions, and hold predominant social clout. Thus, members of Hmong and also other Laotian descent will tend to be very macho in their beliefs. Often, the acts of sexual assault committed by the Hmong Nation Society of young Hmong women is one that asserts their superiority and is designed to disrespect and dishonor families who are aligned against their gang.

CURRENT EVENT
Youth Gangs and Social Media as a Gang Tool

As we have seen, earlier in Chapter 12, social media is a central feature in the current youth subculture. We noted, in that chapter, that the use of social media has also been used in teen pregnancy prevention programs. It is clear from that discussion that social media can be used for good and bad purposes, and now, it would appear that juvenile gangs have incorporated social media into their routine operations.

In Chicago, two teen gangsters were in a gang war with one another that ultimately escalated in the murder of one of these youth. Both Chief Keef of the Black Disciples Gang and Lil JoJo of the Gangster Disciples, posted songs on YouTube that served as battle anthems for their respective gangs (Austin, 2013). Often, these songs included threats to rival gang members and also provided hidden messages to their own gang members. A series of posted threats and insults were posted on various social media until Lil JoJo was murdered by members of the Black Disciples (Austin, 2013). What ensued afterwards was a series of back-and-forth deaths as retaliation for actions from prior actions of enemy gang members. All the while, on Facebook, Twitter, Instagram, and YouTube the gang war was 'fought' through online insults and 'outing' of members, being easy for all to observe, both in the neighborhood concerned and throughout the entire city (Austin, 2013).

In fact, this mode of insult has escalated violence because, unlike in the past when a member 'dissed' a rival, only those in the vicinity usually were aware (Austin, 2013). Now, due to the online posting technology, the 'diss' is openly public for a broader audience to see. The rival member who is 'dissed' has no choice, in the gang subculture, but to confront the violator of their honor; usually this is through an act of violence, often resulting in death.

Aside from events like those between the Black Disciples and Gangster Disciples in the Chicago area, it has become increasingly more common for criminal gangs to utilize computers and to also use the internet as a means of furthering their criminal activities. The level of sophistication can vary from the type of gang and the specific use of the electronic media. For instance, some gangs may simply use web pages as a means of communication, using blogs, uploading pictures, and providing coded messages that, while secretive in nature, do not have content that is criminally incriminating (Pyrooz, Decker, & Moule, 2013)

In other circumstances, gangs may use the online world as a recruiting ground and have been known to solicit youth via Youtube and other social networks. Indeed, the internet has become an avenue ripe with opportunity for gangs such as the Bloods and Crips. The practice of recruiting online has been referred to as "Net Banging" by many gangsters in the United States. Through internet websites, gangs post information that glorifies the 'thug lifestyle' as a means of enticing youth as young as 8 years old into the gang life. The types of gangs using the internet are not restricted to the Bloods and Crips but include MS-13, international gangs, outlaw motorcycle biker gangs, as well as local street gangs.

In many instances, gang members may post videos of their crimes openly. Much of the reason for this is the desire to gain prestige and status among their peers (Austin, 2013; Pyrooz, Decker, & Moule, 2013). In addition, members of gangs may watch the events as a form of entertainment and will sometimes use certain incidents as warnings to competing gang members (Austin, 2013; Dominguez, 2011). In some cases, the identities of these offenders may be disguised or hidden from camera view and/or a variety of code phrases and hand signs may be used as warnings or methods of covert communication to other gang members, both those allied with and, opposed to, the gang member who posted the video. In some instances, police agencies may identify crimes committed by gang members who post a variety of videos on YouTube. These videos may be viewed by hundreds prior to their discovery by law enforcement (Dominguez, 2011)

One case in San Diego, California, the United States District Court indicted numerous gang members who worked together to recruit prostitutes by targeting young girls who came from vulnerable backgrounds (Graham, 2011). In this case, approximately three dozen members of the Crips street gang worked with two motel owners and operated a prostitution ring through a variety of social networking sites that included MySpace, Craigslist, Twitter, and Facebook. The operation extended to various areas of the United States and was not restricted to San Diego. In this case, gang members kidnapped most of the girls and then trafficked them to different locations, using Craigslist and Backpage.com, to place orders Graham, 2011). Though this incident involved mostly adult gang members (though not exclusively) it does show how social media have aided gangs in committing a variety of crimes.

From these incidents, it is clear that gang-related cybercrime flourishes throughout the United States and it is clear that juvenile and adult gang members have exploited cyberspace. While examples exist where gangs have used the internet to commit various crimes, most juvenile members are using these media to gain prestige and to research other rival gang members (Pyrooz et al., 2013). Much of this is thought to be due to the fact that most juvenile gang members, while being conversant in using applications, they are not truly tech-savvy to use encryption devices and other more sophisticated technology that is often used by more complex organized criminal syndicates.

References: Austin, B. (2013, September 13). Public Enemies: Social Media Is Fueling Gang Wars in Chicago. Wired. Retrieved from: http://www.wired.com/underwire/2013/09/gangs-of-%09social-media/

Dominguez, V. (2011, April 18). Greeley gang members post videos online. Greeley Gazette. Retrieved from: http://www.greeleygazette.com/press/?p=8774.

Graham, M. (2011, April 18). Gang members indicted in online prostitution ring. Reuters U.S. Edition. Retrieved from: http://www.reuters.com/article/2011/04/19/us-prostitution-online-idUSTRE73I06J20110419.

Pyrooz, D. C., Decker, S. H., & Moule, R. K. (2013). Criminal and Routine Activities in Online Settings: Gangs, Offenders, and the Internet. Justice Quarterly, 30(5), 192–210.

Gangs and Juvenile Females

Typically, female gang members have been described in the literature primarily as sex partners for male gang members or as members of auxiliary groups to male gangs (Campbell, 1995). Yet as we have indicated throughout this book, involvement in crime, including violent crime, among juvenile females has clearly increased over the past decade. In fact, a study by Bjerregaard and Smith (1993) found that rates of participation in gangs are similar for males and females.

As noted in Chapter 12, researchers have generally failed to examine female delinquency to an extent that is similar to their male counterparts. This is particularly true with regard to female juvenile gang members. From the research that does exist, there has been a focus on Latino females (known as *Latinas*) and African American females in gangs (Hanser, 2007b; with Valdez, 2005, 2007). Research by Harper and Robinson (1999) found that involvement of African American juvenile females in sexual activity, substance abuse, and violence was clearly related to membership in gangs. Thus, the research on female youth in gangs has also examined racial and ethnic allegiances and has also found that activities of these female youth are similar to other female juveniles who are not gang members, as was discussed in Chapter 12.

As with points that we made in Chapter 12 regarding social class, minority youth, and delinquency, Campbell (1995) has argued that, to account for female gang membership, we must consider the community and class context within which these girls live, the problems that face poverty-class girls, and the problems for which they seek answers in gangs. Among these problems are the following:

1. A future of meaningless domestic labor with little possibility of escape
2. Subordination to the man of the house
3. Sole responsibility for children
4. The powerlessness of underclass membership

Furthermore, Wolf and Gutierrez (2012) note that for many girls in gangs, there is a history of sexual and physical abuse in the home, which is a gender-specific risk factor that leads girls to join gangs. Many of these girls come from very abusive homes and seek gang membership as a way out, whereas others join to seek a sense of family. Unfortunately, there can be additional abuse (particularly sexual abuse) that follows them into the gang life. Likewise, females who are active in the gang lifestyle may become pregnant. In such cases, this often makes their ability to be effective contributing members of the gang impossible. This, in turn, may be a reason that is acknowledged by the gang to end their obligation as a member but, at this point, they are also

INTERNATIONAL FOCUS

Gang Resistance Education and Training in Central America

G.R.E.A.T. Initiative in Central America

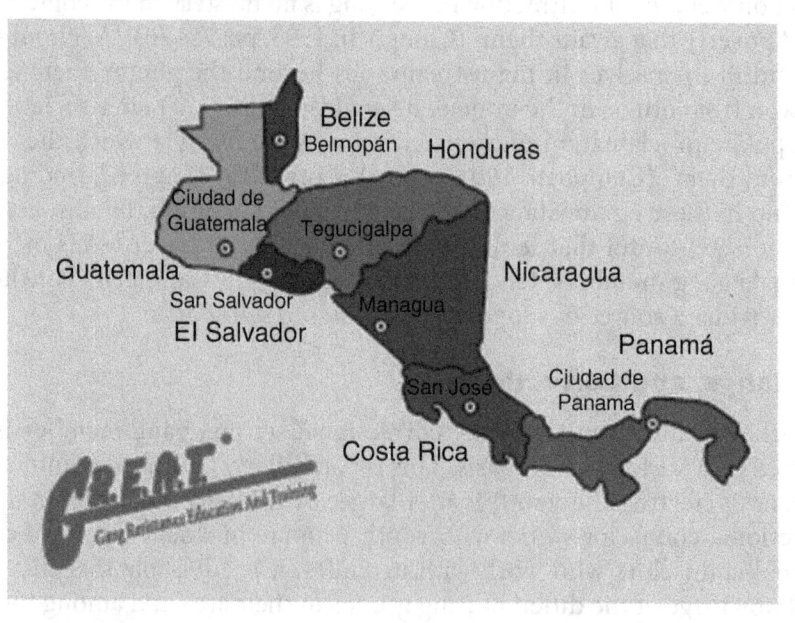

In November 2009, the Gang Resistance Education And Training (G.R.E.A.T.) Program broke ground in its international efforts by piloting a training in Central America. Since that successful pilot, the Regional Gang Initiative, funded by the U.S. Department of State, has provided G.R.E.A.T. Officer Trainings, G.R.E.A.T. Families Trainings, G.R.E.A.T. Officer In-Service Trainings, and a bilingual Web site.

To date, 135 officers from six Central American countries have been certified to teach the G.R.E.A.T. curriculum in middle and elementary schools, and around 12,000 students have graduated from the Program. A seventh country—Costa Rica—is slated to join the initiative in the spring of 2012.

Jim Rose, Regional Gang Advisor for the Bureau of International Narcotics and Law Enforcement Affairs, U.S. Department of State, recently reported that G.R.E.A.T. is quickly becoming a success, and with its current progress in the region, he foresees a day when every student in Central America will be exposed to the Program during elementary and/or middle school.

Commissioner Pedro Rodriguez Arguetta, the Second Chief of the Juvenile Affairs Division of the Nicaraguan National Police, reported that he has completed teaching at two public schools and provided curriculum to 133 students in Granada, Nicaragua. Commissioner Rodriguez stated, "We believe that the kids have learned skills to say no to violence. We know that drugs and violence are linked to organized crime." He said that G.R.E.A.T. is a way to work on the serious problem of juvenile violence "not with a heavy hand, or a soft hand, but with an intelligent hand, to continue getting safer cities in Nicaragua."

According to a recent BBC News article, "Central America drug gang violence at 'alarming levels.'"

There are currently 900 street gangs and 70,000 members in Central America.

Source: National Gang Center. (Spring, 2012). *G.R.E.A.T initiative in Central America*. Tallahassee, FL: National Gang Center.

not given support or assistance by gang members. This can leave these girls in a doubly vulnerable position. Regardless, they are usually left to fend for themselves and their newborns on their own, many of whom have broken ties with their families-of-origin and/or come from homes that would not be good options for them to return (Wolf & Gutierrez, 2012).

In addition, many of these girls will be arrested, "and the vast majority will be dependent on welfare. The attraction of the gang is no mystery in the context of the isolation and poverty that awaits them" (Campbell, 1995, pp. 75–76). "Without the opportunity to fulfill themselves in mainstream jobs beyond the ghetto, their sense of self must be won from others in the immediate environment.....Their association with the gang is a public proclamation of their rejection of the lifestyle which the community expects from them" (Campbell, 1997, p. 146). Curry (1998) agreed, finding that gang membership in these circumstances can be a form of liberation. Finally, Esbensen and colleagues (1999) found that female gang members have lower levels of self-esteem than do male gang members, lending further support to Campbell's conclusions that the gang provides a source of support and feelings of self-worth.

Youth, Gangs, and Corrections

When working with juveniles in the correctional setting, gang membership will be encountered on a fairly frequent basis. This is particularly true if the community supervision agency referring the youth is in a larger or mid-sized metropolitan area or if the correctional counselor works with youth who are in a state-operated facility. For correctional counselors who work with juveniles, it is advisable that they develop a working knowledge of the different gang groups in their area and among their juvenile population. An understanding of the tenets of a particular gang, how leadership structures operate, and gang alliances can be important in rapport building and can also provide the counselor with an understanding of the youth's world, which will, undoubtedly, be influenced by the activities of their gang. This basic knowledge—and the correctional counselor should strive to learn more of the basic information—will provide the counselor with the bare basics to competently provide services to these youth.

It is advisable that the correctional counselor have sufficient training with gangs and gang offenders if they plan to work with the offender population (both juvenile and adult) on a long-term basis. An excellent source of training and information for correctional counselors would be the **National Gang Crime Research Center (NGCRC)**. The NGCRC is a nationally based non-profit organization of recognized gang experts from around the nation. This organization hosts an annual training conference where information regarding juvenile and adult gang issues is covered comprehensively. Organizations such as NGCRC should be consulted by correctional counselors if they have little or no experience with gang offending because a wealth of information may be available to enhance one's effectiveness when dealing with gang offenders.

FEMALE JUVENILES IN CUSTODY

As with adult female offenders, the needs of female juvenile offenders differ from those of males, as do the services they receive. As can be seen in Figure 13-5, female juvenile offenders in placement have more mental health and substance use problems and worse abuse histories (Hanser, 2013; Sedlak & McPherson, 2010). Higher percentages of females report an above-average number of mental or emotional problems and

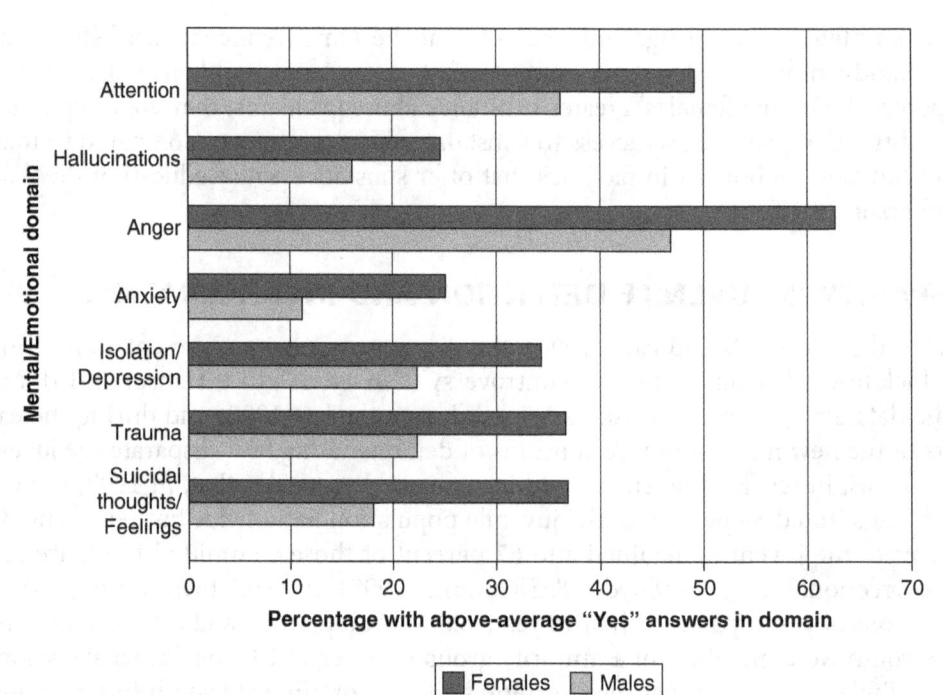

FIGURE 13-5 Percentage of Males and Females With Above-Average Numbers of "Yes" Responses to Mental and Emotional Survey Questions. *Source:* Sedlak, A. J., & McPherson, K. S. (2010). *Youth's needs and services: Findings from the survey of youth in residential placement.* Washington, DC: Office of Juvenile Justice and Delinquency Prevention.

traumatic experiences, compared to male juveniles. The work of Sedlak and McPherson (2010) has been integrated into this section to illustrate some of the differences between male and female juveniles. According to their research, females reveal nearly twice the rate of past physical abuse (42 percent vs. 22 percent), more than twice the rate of past suicide attempts (44 percent vs. 19 percent), and more than four times the rate of prior sex abuse (35 percent vs. 8 percent) as males. As we have seen in earlier sections of this chapter and as we saw in Chapter 10, prior childhood abuse (particularly sexual abuse) produces long-term damage to female offenders; often this translates into long-term criminality for the most severely troubled girls and women who are victimized.

Female juvenile offenders are more commonly placed in residential treatment programs (compared to other types of programs), and nearly all youth in residential treatment programs are in facilities that provide onsite mental health services (Hanser, 2013). Among these female youth, more receive individual counseling (85 percent vs. 67 percent) and fewer receive group counseling. Females also give their counseling less positive ratings (Hanser, 2013; Sedlak & McPherson, 2010). This last point is a bit troubling and indicates the need for correctional programs to improve services for young female offenders, just as is needed for adult female offenders.

Lastly, female juvenile offenders report significantly more drug experience than males, with 91 percent saying they had used at least one of the drugs listed (including marijuana, cocaine/crack, ecstasy, meth, heroin, inhalants, and an "other illegal drug" category) compared to 87 percent of males. More females than males report using nearly every substance listed and 47 percent (compared to 33 percent of males) report having ever used four or more of the listed substances (Hanser, 2013). Although males and females use drugs and/or alcohol at the same frequency just before entering custody, more females report recent substance-related problems (71 percent vs. 67 percent). Despite females' greater substance abuse problems, they are often housed in facilities that provide less access to substance abuse treatment. Compared to males, fewer females are housed in facilities that offer substance-abuse education (Sedlak & McPherson, 2010).

DISPARITY IN JUVENILE DETENTION AND INCARCERATION

During the late 1980s and early 1990s, the disparate minority representation in juvenile lockdowns became a topic of controversy (Cox et al., 2013; Hanser, 2013). Most of the data available on this issue emerged during the late 1990s and during the early parts of the new millennium. As a means of demonstrating how disparate the juvenile system was, in terms of detention and incarceration, consider that, in 1997, minority youth constituted 34 percent of the juvenile population nationwide but represented 62 percent of the juveniles detained and 67 percent of those committed to secure juvenile correctional facilities (Snyder & Sickmund, 1999). In 1997, there were 7,400 new admissions of youth younger than 18 years old to adult prisons, and three out of four of these youth were members of a minority group (Hanser, 2013; Poe-Yamagata & Jones, 2000). Table 13-1 shows that the overrepresentation of minority youth in secure juvenile detention and correctional facilities increased between 1983 and 1997, although it decreased slightly between 1995 and 1997.

Overrepresentation of African American youth occurs at all stages of the juvenile justice system, and African American youth are overrepresented more than any other minority group. In 1996–1997, African American youth constituted about 15 percent of the nationwide juvenile population but represented 26 percent of all juveniles arrested, 45 percent of those who were detained, and 40 percent of those in residential placement. However, for all stages of juvenile justice processing, except arrest and delinquency cases involving detention, the African American proportion of the national totals was smaller in 1996–1997 than in 1990–1991 (Hsia, 2004).

The number of Latino American youth in the United States has increased faster than the number of youth of any other racial or ethnic group, growing from 9 percent of the juvenile population in 1980 to 16 percent in 2000 (Hsia, 2004). State studies show

TABLE 13-1 Percentage of Minority Youth in Secure Detention and Correctional Facilities in the United States for Selected Years From 1983 to 1997

Year	Total Youth Year Population (%)	Minorities(%)	
		Secure Detention	Secure Correction
1983	32	53	56
1991	32	65	69
1995	32	68	68
1997	34	62	67

Sources: Hsia, H. M. (2004). *Disproportionate minority confinement 2002 update.* Washington, DC: Office of Juvenile Justice and Delinquency Prevention.

overrepresentation of Latino American youth at arrest and other decision points in some states (DeJong & Jackson, 1998). Colorado is one example. Although Colorado does not have arrest data for Latino Americans because they are included as white, the state's data for July 1998 to June 1999 show that Latino Americans were overrepresented at all later decision points in the juvenile justice system (Hsia, 2004).

The Census of Juveniles in Residential Placement showed that Native American youth aged 10–17 constituted 2 percent of the youth in secure correctional facilities nationwide but were only 1 percent of the national youth population (Snyder & Sickmund, 1999). Although national data suggest that Native American youth are placed in correctional facilities at twice the expected rate, state data give evidence of an even greater overrepresentation. For example, North Dakota's 1998 data indicate that Native American youth made up 8 percent of the state's total juvenile population but accounted for 13 percent of arrests, 21 percent of the secure detention population, and 33 percent of secure correctional placements (Hsia, 2004).

Asians and Pacific Islanders are the least studied racial groups. Research from the Census of Juveniles in Residential Placement revealed that Asian youth constituted 4 percent of the national juvenile population but represented only 2 percent of youth in secure correction. The available state data for Asians alone or Asians and Pacific Islanders combined also show, for the most part, that these youth are underrepresented in the population of confined juveniles at the state and even at the county levels. In cities with high concentrations of Asian youth, however, indications of overrepresentation exist. For example, a study of juvenile transfers to adult court in California showed that, in 1996, the composition of Los Angeles County's juvenile population aged 10–17 was 25 percent white, 51 percent Latino American, 13 percent African American, and 11 percent Asian and other races (Hsia, 2004).

From the above information, it is clear that minority youth are disproportionately represented, regardless of the group examined. Even more telling is the fact that, in those states where a given minority group might tend to be more commonly represented, the proportional difference in the rate of confinement is increased. This basically implies that, in jurisdictions that find it necessary to work with minority groups, the disproportionate use of confinement is exacerbated—particularly when this is compared with jurisdictions that have marginal representation of a given group of minority youth.

FACTORS THAT CONTRIBUTE TO DISPARATE MINORITY CONFINEMENT

The reasons for the disparity in juvenile confinement are many. Most published literature on this issue notes that these statistics are not likely to be due to a racist system. While we cannot possibly answer this question within the scope of one discussion within one section of a single textbook, it should have become clear to students that, throughout the history of corrections in the United States, African American men and women have been disproportionately incarcerated. Given the various historical precedents associated with the civil rights era and other indicators that our society held minorities in a weakened position, and given the common knowledge regarding the existence of institutional racism that officially existed until the 1960s, it is not unreasonable to presume that, in some cases, racism may be part of the explanation.

Recent research by Huizinga et al. (2007) investigated the often-stated reason for disparate minority confinement—that it simply reflects the difference in offending rates among different racial/ethnic groups—and they found no support in their rigorous study examining disparate minority contact with the justice system. Huizinga et al. (2007) note that "although self-reported offending is a significant predictor of which individuals are contacted/referred, levels of delinquent offending have only marginal effects on the level of DMC" (p. i). They found these results in terms of both total offending and more focused data that examined violent offenses and property offenses separately. Thus, it would appear that minority youth are no more delinquent than Caucasian youth.

The work of Hsia (2004) is a compilation of surveys and official investigation into the juvenile correctional systems of all 50 states. Hsia notes the following reasons for why such disparities existed in many state systems:

1. **Racial stereotyping and cultural insensitivity:** Eighteen states identified racial stereotyping and cultural insensitivity—both intentional and unintentional—on the part of the police and others in the juvenile justice system (e.g., juvenile court workers and judges) as important factors contributing to higher arrest rates, higher charging rates, and higher rates of detention and confinement of minority youth. The demeanor and attitude of minority youth can contribute to negative treatment and more severe disposition relative to their offenses. The belief that minority youth cannot benefit from treatment programs also leads to less-frequent use of such options.
2. **Lack of alternatives to detention and incarceration:** Eight states identified the lack of alternatives to detention and incarceration as a cause of the frequent use of confinement. In some states, detention centers are located in the state's largest cities, where most minority populations reside. With a lack of alternatives to detention, nearby detention centers become "convenient" placements for urban minority youth.
3. **Misuse of discretionary authority in implementing laws and policies:** Five states observed that laws and policies that increase juvenile justice professionals' discretionary authority over youth contribute to harsher treatment of minority youth. One state notes that "bootstrapping" (the practice of stacking offenses on a single incident) is often practiced by police, probation officers, and school system personnel.
4. **Lack of culturally and linguistically appropriate services:** Five states identified the lack of bicultural and bilingual staff and the use of English-only informational materials for the non-English-speaking population as contributing to minorities' misunderstanding of services and court processes and their inability to navigate the system successfully.

Based on the research by Hsia (2004), it is our general contention that much of the reason the disproportionate confinement exists among minority youth has to do with a confluence of issues that plague members of society who have suffered from historical trauma and, generation after generation, have had restricted access to material, educational, and social resources. Indeed, issues such as poverty, substance abuse, few job opportunities, and high crime rates in predominantly minority neighborhoods place minority youth at higher risk for delinquent behaviors (Cox et al., 2013). Moreover, concerted law enforcement targeting of high-crime areas yields higher numbers of arrests and formal processing of minority youth. At the same time, these communities have fewer positive role models and fewer service programs that function as alternatives to confinement and/or support positive youth development.

Furthermore, it has been found that a disproportionate number of youth in confinement came from low-income, single-parent households (female-headed households, in particular) and households headed by adults with multiple low-paying jobs or unsteady employment (Cox et al., 2013). Family disintegration, diminished traditional family values, parental substance abuse, and insufficient supervision contribute to delinquency development. Poverty reduces minority youths' ability to access existing alternatives to detention and incarceration as well as competent legal counsel (Cox et al., 2013). Thus, all of these factors, associated with historical deprivations over time, have contributed and culminated in the state of affairs that we now witness among minority juveniles in the United States.

Because of past research on juvenile detention and juvenile treatment outcomes, many researchers and advocates now call for a comprehensive strategy aimed at eliminating all risk factors for further delinquency, including gang involvement (Carmicheal et al., 2005; Hanser, 2007c; Valdez, 2005; Wolf & Gutierrez, 2012). This strategy called for a wide spectrum of services and sanctions to be used to protect potential and current delinquents from the womb to school and beyond (Hanser, 2007c; Wolf & Gutierrez, 2012).

A Model Program to Respond to Minority Juveniles in Secure Environments

When we consider that minority youth are so heavily represented in the juvenile justice system, it becomes clear that juvenile systems must strive to provide services that are culturally appropriate and competent. One model program that we have identified is the **Minority Youth Transition Program** in the state of Oregon. In Oregon, numerous needs for their overrepresented African American population were identified and addressed and, as a result, reductions in future confinement of these youth were observed in that state.

In responding to minority youth in the Oregon Youth Authority, emphasis was placed on culturally specific and language-appropriate programming. This included a wide array of services such as mentoring, drug and alcohol treatment, family interventions, anger management classes, grief and trauma counseling, conflict resolution, gang intervention/mediation, transportation and clothing assistance, educational assistance, and 24-hour per-day crisis response (Armstrong & Jackson, 2012).

Moreover, the organization adopted a set of cultural competency principles to guide decision making, staff perceptions and behavior, and program activities as they related to issues of race, ethnicity, and culture (Armstrong & Jackson, 2012). These efforts helped to more clearly define what it means to provide culturally specific services, to refine policies and procedures related to those services, and to incorporate issues of culture that are relevant to the youth involved, thus meaning it must be age-appropriate, as well. According to Armstrong and Jackson "cultural competency derives from a set of personal values and enhanced skills internalized and inculcated from treatment, enabling each youth to interact and cope more successfully in a variety of community contexts and situations" (2012, p. 19).

It has been noted that one of the key challenges for juvenile corrections practitioners is the need to be knowledgeable about and skilled in addressing issues related to dress, language, beliefs, history, and daily life experiences in culturally diverse settings (Armstrong & Jackson, 2012). This is consistent with what we have noted in Chapter 12 when we discussed the youth subculture. Practitioners who work with these populations will need to possess effective means of communication that will likely mirror that used by the youth with whom they work. While practitioners should blend their communication mannerisms to be compatible with youth, the attempt must not be artificial and must not be patronizing to the youth. Thus, training in these areas of expertise will likely be needed. It is up to the agencies and their administrators to address this and ensure that such training is provided if they are to become culturally specific, language appropriate, and address the various special needs being exhibited by these youth (Armstrong & Jackson, 2012).

PREVENTION AND INTERVENTION EFFORTS NEEDED IN THE FUTURE

Community programs aimed at alleviating the causes of juvenile offending as well as providing opportunities for those inclined to juvenile offending will need to be given priority if we hope to confront juvenile offending, gang affiliation, and issues related to DMC. Support for the police is essential, but so is support for myriad community programs directed at high-risk youth. The best efforts of school personnel, social-services professionals, non-profit organizations, and the community at large will also be necessary. Only by producing our best efforts in this regard can we hope to maintain the integrity of the juvenile justice network while providing appropriate alternatives for juveniles who cannot, or will not, be helped through education, treatment, care, concern, and opportunity.

This is more important than ever because, as one can tell, these youth will need a complete range of services that are likely provided on a continuum that addresses the multiplicity of problems that these youth present. One issue tends to compound the severity of another, making the entire treatment process difficult to unravel. As seen from Figure 13-6, the various aspects of juvenile processing all work together, at multiple stages of the juvenile system, to address various needs. As we have seen in Chapter 12 and in research provided in this chapter related to DMC, there are numerous issues at various stage that must be addressed if offending among juveniles is to be reduced; this is particularly true for minority juveniles.

Furthermore, issues related to substance abuse will likely continue to be correlated with almost all of the other acts of delinquency and crime that we associate with juvenile offenders. This is what some have defined as the **juvenile drug–crime cycle** (Cox et al., 2013; VanderWaal, McBride, McElrath, & VanBuren, 2001). In addition, these youth will be highly likely to have a number of co-occurring disorders such as depression, anxiety, as well as learning disabilities and cognitive deficits. We have seen this in Chapter 12 when examining the health and wellness of youth who have suffered from racial discrimination and we have seen this among sexual minority youth, as well. In addition, in this chapter, we have seen similar problems develop for female juveniles who are placed in detention or long-term incarceration.

When combined with their young age and the disparities in health and wellness (again, consider Chapter 12), it becomes clear that this issue is one that is impacted both my macro and micro systemic issues. As a result, these youth will tend to be less healthy both physically and emotionally, as time goes on. We predict, just as Maghan (1999) did

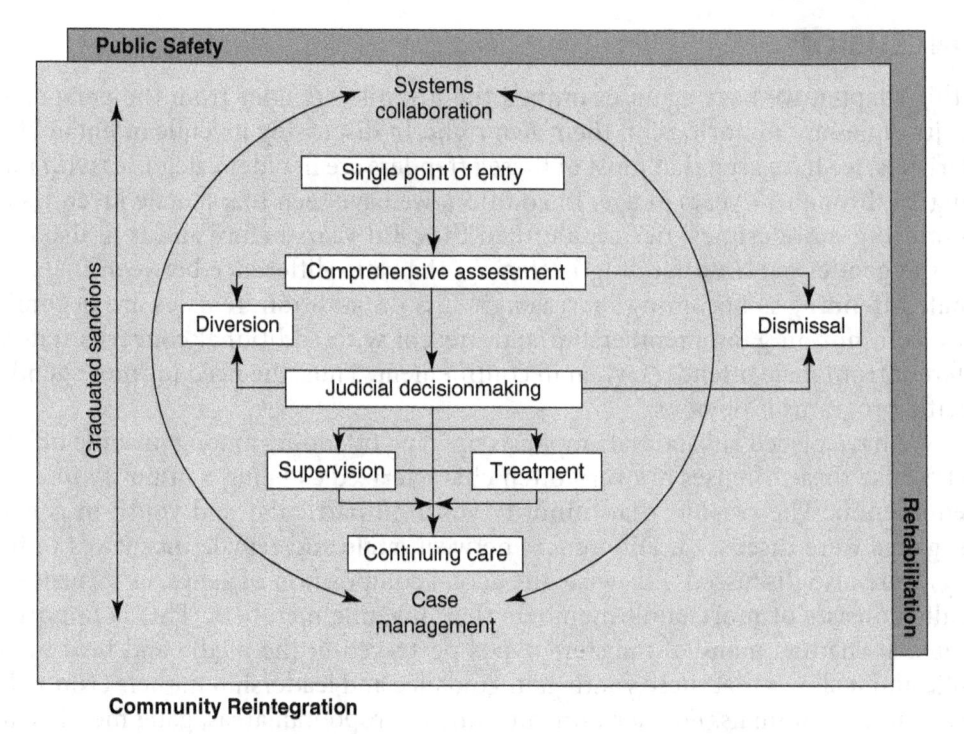

FIGURE 13-6 Elements of a Model Juvenile Intervention System. *Source:* VanderWaal, C. J., McBride, D. C., Terry-McElrath, Y. M., & VanBuren, H. (2001). *Breaking the juvenile drug-crime cycle: A guide for practitioners and policymakers.* Washington, DC: National Institute of Justice.

regarding adult offenders, that future juvenile offenders will tend to have the following characteristics:

- Members of racial minority groups
- Unhealthy (average of 10 years older than physical age)
- Infected with sexually transmitted diseases, HIV, or tuberculosis
- Overly emotional and lack impulse control
- Having children of their own
- Gang affiliated
- Unmarried
- From single-parent households

As we have seen in this chapter and in Chapter 12, Maghan (1999) has been correct in his prediction, even though that prediction was made almost 15 years back. Although his observations are important, it is equally important to note that the characteristics just listed have been observed among juvenile offenders around the world (Cox et al., 2013). Indeed, youth in various industrialized nations are all exhibiting similar demographic and lifestyle trends. The effects of urbanization (and urbanicity) upon family systems have been detrimental, and problems with high rates of poverty have exacerbated these negative effects upon youth. We have shown this to be true from research presented in this chapter and in Chapter 12. In reaction to these changes, youth (both minority and non-minority youth) are engaging in behaviors that place them at greater risk for detrimental health effects.

CONCLUSION

In this chapter, we have again examined the juvenile offender from the perspective that juveniles are minorities, in their own right. In discussing juvenile offender characteristics, we have seen that most of these offenders are in older categories with most being 15 through 17 years of age. In addition, we have seen that female juveniles are committing more crimes, per capita, than they did years before and it is also clear that the gender gap in offending is closing; the ratio difference between male and female offending is becoming increasingly less. In addition, females are becoming more common in gang membership and present with additional concerns that are different from male offenders when in confinement. Thus, the need for more gender-specific programs is obvious.

We have placed substantial emphasis on gang offending among juvenile offenders because these offenses are very often characterized as being a minority offender phenomenon. The reasons that minority youth in particular and youth in general join gangs were discussed. Differences between male and female incentives to join gangs were also discussed. Likewise, the actual composition of gangs, as it turns out, usually consists of more adult members than juvenile members. This is important because it shatters many of the stereotypes portrayed in the media and held by the public and it shows that these youth gain guidance and leadership in their criminality from veteran criminals. Furthermore, in some metropolitan areas, gang membership may extend across multiple generations of a family. When coupled with many of the socioeconomic variables, racial/ethnic allegiances, and historical/cultural considerations of a given area, it is easy to see why these youth might find gang membership appealing.

This chapter has also provided extensive discussion on various social issues that impact offending among minority youth. A variety of individual, family, school, and social factors impact the outcomes that we see in the data. These observations are very similar to what was presented earlier in Chapter 12 and show consistency in the results that the research produces. Indeed, practitioners in the field have, from their own anecdotal perspective, also provided input that confirms that a number of socioeconomic, educational system, and neighborhood variables tend to impact the behavior and options that these youth possess. Thus, as noted in Chapter 12, these various risk factors all coalesce in certain areas of the United States and among many minority groups (particularly those who are in poverty-level income brackets) to all but ensure we have the results that we currently see in today's juvenile justice system.

Lastly, we have also placed considerable attention on minority youth based on racial and/or ethnic characteristics and we have discussed how minority youth are overrepresented at multiple points in the justice decision-making process with the intent to showcase a term that has come into vogue during the last decade of juvenile justice studies—disproportionate minority contact (DMC). Students have been provided a definition of DMC and we have presented information on confinement and detention rates of minority juveniles. Recommendations for culturally competent programming with minority youth in confinement were provided and one model program was also discussed, as an example of how others might be tailored to address DMC in their jurisdictions.

Chapter 13 Learning Check

1. In 2009, females had higher rates of _____ _____ types of crimes than their male counterparts.
   a. Person
   b. Public order
   c. Property
   d. Both a and c, but not b
   e. Both a and b, but not c

2. The Minority Youth Transition Program is a model program to respond to minority juveniles in secure environments.
   a. True
   b. False

3. _____ are related to belonging and might include security, acceptance, friendship, food, shelter, discipline, belonging, status, respect, power, and money.
   a. Family needs
   b. Human needs
   c. Low-level needs
   d. None of the above

4. Generally speaking, minority juveniles are placed in secure confinement at rates that are proportionally higher than those for their Caucasian counterparts.
   a. True
   b. False

5. According to Campbell (1995), the community and class context that influence girls to join gangs include which of the following?
   a. A future of meaningless domestic labor with little possibility of escape
   b. The powerlessness of underclass membership
   c. Sole responsibility for children
   d. All of the above
   e. None of the above

6. Characteristics of juvenile offenders, as predicted by Maghan in 1999, do not greatly resemble those of the juvenile population of today.
   a. True
   b. False

7. Major street gangs that include the African American Disciples, African American Gangster Disciple Nation, and the Brothers of the Struggle (BOS) are collectively known as _____.
   a. People
   b. Gang Nation
   c. Folks
   d. a and c, but not b
   e. None of the above

8. Between the years of 1985 and 2009, the ratio difference between male juvenile offending and female juvenile offending went from being 4 times higher for males than females to being only 1.5 times higher for male offending when compared to female offending.
   a. True
   b. False

9. The term disproportionate minority confinement (DMC) first gained nationwide attention in 1988 through a report that had been submitted to Congress.
   a. True
   b. False

10. _____ _____ was NOT found to be a factor in predicting minority youth contact with the juvenile justice system.
   a. The possession of a learning disability
   b. Limited English proficiency
   c. Violence between siblings
   d. Urbanicity
   e. None of the above

Essay Discussion Questions

1. Discuss some of the differences that were noted between female juvenile and male juvenile offending. Also discuss some of the issues noted with female juveniles who are kept in confinement.

2. Discuss some of the reasons why minority youth may join gangs. What are some of the reasons for female juveniles, in particular, to join gangs? Lastly, provide some examples of how juvenile gangs have loyalties along racial lines.

3. Discuss the issue of disproportionate minority contact (DMC) and explain what the research has found when exploring this phenomenon. Be specific and be organized in your response.

References

Abadinsky, H. (2003). *Organized crime* (7th ed.). Belmont, CA: Wadsworth/Thomson Learning.

Armour, J., & Hammond, S. (2009). *Minority youth in the juvenile justice system: Disproportionate minority contact.* National Conference of State Legislatures. Retrieved from: www.ncsl.org.

Armstrong, T., & Jackson, L. (2012). Overrepresentation of minorities in youth correctional confinement in the United States: A promising aftercare approach for ameliorating this problem. In N. Queloz, R. Brossand, F. Butikofer, B. Meyer-Birsch, & D. Pittits (Eds.), *Migrations in ethnic minorities: Impacts on youth crime and challenges for the juvenile justice and other intervention systems.* Brussels, Belgium: International Association for Research in Juvenile Criminology.

Attorney General of Texas. (2002). *Gangs in Texas 2001: An overview.* Retrieved from: www.oag.state.tx .us/AG_Publications/pdfs/2001gangrept.pdf.

Babicky, T. (1993a). *Gangs fact sheets: A reference guide.* Springfield: Illinois Department of Corrections.

Babicky, T. (1993b). *Gangs and gang activity.* Springfield: Illinois Department of Corrections.

Benekos, P. J., & Merlo, A. V. (Eds.). (2004). *Controversies in juvenile justice and delinquency.* Cincinnati, OH: Anderson.

Bjerregaard, B., & Smith, C. (1993). Gender differences in gang participation, delinquency, and substance abuse. *Journal of Quantitative Criminology, 4,* 329–355.

Campbell, A. (1995). Female participation in gangs. In M. W. Klein, C. L. Maxson, & J. Miller (Eds.), *The modern gang reader* (pp. 70–77). Los Angeles: Roxbury.

Campbell, A. (1997). Self definition by rejection: The case of gang girls. In G. L. Mays (Ed.), *Gangs and gang behavior* (pp. 129–149). Chicago: Nelson-Hall.

Carmichael, D., Whitten, G., & Voloudakis, M. (2005). *Study of minority over-representation in the Texas juvenile justice system.* College Station, TX: Public Policy Research Institute.

Cheng, T. (2004). The impact of family stability on children's delinquency: An implication for family preservation. *Journal of Family Social Work, 8*(1), 47–60.

Coalition for Juvenile Justice. (2000). 2000 Annual report-handle with Care: Serving the mental health needs of young offenders. Retrieved from: http://www.juvjustice. org/resources/fs002.html.

Cox, S., Allen, J., Hanser, R., & Conrad, C. (2013). *Juvenile Justice: A guide to theory, policy, and practice* (8th Ed.). Belmont, CA: Sage Publications.

Curry, G. D. (1998). Female gang involvement. *Journal of Research in Crime and Delinquency, 35,* 100–118.

Dart, R. W. (1992). *Street gangs.* Chicago: Chicago Police Department.

Egley, A. & Howell, J. C. (2012). *Highlights of the 2010 National Youth Gang Survey.* Washington, DC: Office of Juvenile Justice and Delinquency Prevention.

Elster, A., Jaroski, J., VanGeest, J., and Fleming, M. (2003). Racial and ethnic disparities in health care for adolescents: A systematic review of the literature. *Archives of Pediatric and Adolescent Medicine, 157,* 850–851.

Esbensen, F.-A., Deschenes, E. P., & Winfree, L. T. (1999). Differences between gang girls and gang boys: Results from a multisite survey. *Youth & Society, 31,* 27–53.

Feiler, S. M., & Sheley, J. F. (1999). Legal and racial elements of public willingness to transfer juvenile offenders to adult court. *Journal of Criminal Justice, 27*(1), 55–64.

Frazier, C. E., Bishop, D. M., & Henretta, J. C. (1992). The social context of race differentials in juvenile justice dispositions. *Sociological Quarterly, 33,* 447–458.

Hanser, R. D. (2007a). *Special needs offenders in the community.* Upper Saddle River, NJ: Prentice Hall.

Hanser, R. D. (2007b). Gang crimes: Latino gangs in America. In F. Shanty (Ed.), *Organized crime: An international encyclopedia.* Santa Barbara, CA: ABC–CLIO.

Hanser, R. D. (2013). *Introduction to Corrections.* Thousand Oaks, CA: Sage Publications.

Harper, G. W., & Robinson, W. L. (1999). Pathways to risk among inner-city African-American adolescent females: The influence of gang membership. *American Journal of Community Psychology, 27,* 383–404.

Hess, K. M., & Drowns, R. W. (2004). *Juvenile Justice* (4th ed.). Belmont, CA: Wadsworth.

Hsia, H. (2004a). *A Disproportionate Minority Contact (DMC) Chronology: 1988 to Date.* Washington, DC: Office of Juvenile Justice and Delinquency Prevention.

Hsia, H. M. (2004b). *Disproportionate minority confinement 2002 update.* Washington, DC: Office of Juvenile Justice and Delinquency Prevention.

Huizinga, D., Thornberry, T., Knight, K., & Lovegrove, P. (2007). *Disproportionate minority contact in the juvenile justice system: A study of differential minority arrest/referral to court in three cities.* Washington, DC: U.S. Department of Justice.

Jackson, L. (2002). *The Oregon Youth's Authority's Gangbusters Program and Office of Minority Services.* Longham, MD: American Correctional Association.

Kempf, K. L. (1992). *The role of race in juvenile justice processing in Pennsylvania.* Shippensburg, PA: Center for Juvenile Justice Training and Research.

Maghan, J. (1999). Corrections countdown: Prisoners at the cusp of the 21st century. In P. M. Carlson & J. S. Garrett (Eds.), *Prison and jail administration: Practice and theory* (pp. 199–206). Gaithersburg, MD: Aspen Publications.

Main, F. (2001, January 16). Gangs go global. *Chicago Sun-Times,* 3.

Main, F., & Spielman, F. (2000, October 5). Gang battles terrorize schools: Students locked inside after series of shootings near campuses. *Chicago Sun-Times,* 1.

McGloin, J. M. (2005). Policy and intervention considerations of a network analysis of street gangs. *Criminology and Public Policy, 4,* 607–636.

Multijurisdictional Counterdrug Task Force Training. (2010). *Criminal street gangs overview training course.* Pearl, Mississippi: Multijurisdictional Counterdrug Task Force Training.

National Criminal Justice Reference Service. (2005). *Gangs: Facts and figures.* Washington, DC: U.S. Department of Justice. Retrieved from: www.ncjrs.org/spotlight/gangs/facts.html.

Olfson, M., Blanco, C., Linxu, L., Moreno, C., & Laje, G. (2006). National trends in the outpatient treatment of children and adolescents with antipsychotic drugs. *Archives of General Psychiatry, 63,* 679–685.

Phillips, K. S., Settles-Reaves, B., Walker, D., & Brownlow, J. (2009). Social inequality and racial discrimination: Risk factors for health disparities in children of color. *Pediatrics, 124,* 176–186.

Poe-Yamagata, E., & Jones, M. (2000). *And justice for some: Differential treatment of minority youth in the justice system.* Washington, DC: Youth Law Center.

Pope, C. E., Lovell, R., & Hsia, H. M. (2003). *Disproportionate minority confinement: A review of the research literature from 1989 through 2001.* Washington, DC: OJJDP.

Puzzenchera, C., Adams, B., & Hockenberry, S. (2012). *Juvenile court statistics 2009.* Washington, DC: National Center for Juvenile Justice.

Sedlak, A. J. & McPherson, K. S. (2010). *Youth's needs and services: Findings from the survey of youth in residential placement.* Washington, DC: Office of Juvenile Justice and Delinquency Prevention.

Snyder, H. N., & Sickmund, M. (1999, November). *Juvenile offenders and victims: 1999 national report.* Washington, DC: U.S. Department of Justice.

Valdez, A. (2005). *Gangs: A guide to understanding street gangs.* San Clemente, CA: LawTech Publishing.

Wolf, A. M., & Gutierrez, L. (2012). *It's about time: Prevention and intervention services for gang-affiliated girls.* The California Cities Gang Prevention Network, Bulletin 26. Los Angeles: Institute for Youth, Education, & Families.

14

Cultural Competence Training, Assessment, and Evaluation of Cultural Competence, and Evidence-Based Practices in Culturally Competent Agencies

LEARNING OBJECTIVES

After reading this chapter, students should be able to do the following:

1. Apply the assessment–training–evaluation cycle as related to culturally competent services in criminal justice agencies.
2. Identify and discuss effective training techniques to develop cultural competence in criminal justice agencies.
3. Identify the process of evaluative research and distinguish between process and outcome measures.
4. Be able to explain how evaluative research contributes to agency effectiveness in implementing culturally competent service delivery.
5. Identify and discuss the use of evidence-based culturally competent practices in criminal justice agencies.

KEY TERMS

Assessment–training–evaluation cycle
Community Mediation Agreement
Culturally competent activities
Culturally competent objectives
Culturally competent policy
Evaluative transparency
Evidence-based practices
Failing forward concept

Goals of cultural competence
Ill-structured problem
Implementation evaluation
Learning organizations
Outcome evaluation
Pre-service training
Problem-based learning approach
Process evaluation
Stakeholders

INTRODUCTION

This chapter will provide students with information on how agencies can assess and implement practices that are culturally competent. This is an important aspect of this text because while many texts (including this one) illustrate the need for cultural competence, they do not usually explain exactly *how* one determines if the agency is culturally competent and *how* one can implement the tools to improve cultural competence. As seen in Chapter 5, cultural competence and intercultural communication are very important in our increasingly multicultural society. This is also true considering the globalized nature of crime fighting; immigrant populations entering the United States present challenges to the criminal justice system that require continued training to meet these challenges.

This chapter first begins with a discussion of how one might assess the cultural competence of an agency and also provides understanding of how agencies can develop policies that encourage, establish, and sustain cultural competence throughout. Beyond this, the next step, after first determining a baseline as to where the agency sits in terms of culturally competent service delivery, is the implementation of initiatives to improve or, if already sufficient, to maintain a level of competence that is acceptable for the agency. Furthermore, the agency must then be evaluated, over time, to determine whether these initiatives have been effective and to determine where improvements can be made.

In this chapter, we then note how effective research and evaluation of cultural competence can inform agencies as to whether they have sound policies and procedures. To not effectively research and evaluate these initiatives is, in essence, either quasi-negligent or a weak attempt to feign ignorance that agencies should put a focus on culturally competent services. The question then becomes, how do we effectively evaluate cultural competence in agencies and how do we know when programs are working? In response to this question, we begin this chapter with an explanation of the specific function of evaluation research, which can be described as a form of explanatory research. We then discuss Evidence-Based Practices as the standard-of-choice among agencies when using data-driven results to guide agencies in selecting solidly verified methods of operation that are culturally competent. Lastly, we discuss some implications to training staff in culturally competent operations that are intended to use our data-driven results as a guide in determining diversity-related training needs in an agency. We use the term **assessment–training–evaluation cycle** to describe this process of assessing the agency, providing training, evaluating the impact of training, and ultimately adopting those practices that are based on data-driven evidence as best practices.

ASSESSING AGENCY CULTURAL COMPETENCE

A number of researchers have examined cultural competence within agencies (Dana, Behn, & Gonwa, 1992). Typically, evaluations of agency cultural competence have involved the use of checklists as well as surveys of practitioners and persons in the community who use an agency's services. Any effective evaluation of an agency's cultural competence will be multi-faceted in scope and should include an evaluation at the practitioner, consumer, agency, administrative, and policy levels. Issues related to bilingual representation, diversity training, access to public transportation (for disadvantaged minority families and such), racial and ethnic identity of practitioners and supervisors, specialization of services, and location of the agency within the minority community are some examples of issues that should be considered. Figure 14-1 provides an example of an agency self-assessment tool, developed by the U.S. Department of Justice, to measure, track, and document the cultural competence of a given agency.

Instructions for the Agency Cultural Competence Self-Assessment Tool:					
First, please rank each Standard (from 1 to 15) in order of importance to your program. Second, please indicate the date(s) that each Standard is assessed as "Achieved," "In Progress," "Not Yet Addressed," or "N/A" (Not Applicable). You can use the rankings later to help plan your implementation of those Standards that are "In Progress" or "Not Yet Addressed." Then you can indicate the reassessment date(s) without erasing the earlier assessment date(s) to help you keep track of your progress over time.					
Standard	**Rank This Standard in Order of Importance (from 1 to 10)**	**Indicate Date(s) Assessed as...**			
		Achieved	**In Progress**	**Not Yet Addressed**	**N/A**
1. When possible, *locate* offices near public transportation and/or near diverse populations. If this is not possible, explore partnerships with other agencies for outreach space.					
2. Acknowledge that *variation exists* among individuals within cultures, and that these variations may influence service needs.					
3. Participate in cultural competency *plan development and review* to continue improving the workplace environment and client services.					
4. Learn and use *proper pronunciation* of clients' surnames and words of greeting from the cultures of immigrant, refugee, and native populations.					

FIGURE 14-1 Determining Whether an Agency is Culturally Competent. *Source:* Braeutigam, B., & Greenman, N. (2006). *Cultural competency standards for programs serving victims of domestic violence and sexual assault and other crimes in Oregon.* Washington, DC: United States Department of Justice. Retrieved from: http://www.doj.state.or.us/victims/pdf/cultural_competency_standards.pdf.

Standard	Rank This Standard in Order of Importance (from 1 to 10)	Indicate Date(s) Assessed as...			
		Achieved	In Progress	Not Yet Addressed	N/A
5. Understand and allow for *cultural differences in communication*, including culturally appropriate levels of eye contact and physical contact.					
6. Use *oral, written, and visual communication styles* as appropriate. Notice reading and writing abilities of clients. Provide additional assistance to clients who have difficulties.					
7. Use *language translation and interpretation* services whenever possible when staff do not speak the same primary language as a client.					
8. *Confirm that clients understand* and accept all aspects of the services being provided.					
9. Be aware that clients from some cultures may be uncomfortable with *answering questions*. Limit the number of questions asked of clients upon initial intake to gather only the most essential information needed to determine service needs. Gather additional information after a positive rapport is established.					
10. Approach cultural competency *trainings* as opportunities for personal and professional growth and for improving relationships.					

(continued)

Standard	Rank This Standard in Order of Importance (from 1 to 10)	Indicate Date(s) Assessed as...			
		Achieved	In Progress	Not Yet Addressed	N/A
11. *Partner* with diverse individuals and agencies to further understanding of how client backgrounds affect perceptions of victimization, protection, and support.					
12. *Provide services jointly* or partner through referrals to existing organizations in the community that have been identified as serving specific cultures.					
13. Develop multiple *strategies for outreach* to the culturally diverse populations in the community.					
14. *Provide specialized services* or adapt services to respond to diverse needs. Use culture-relevant assessments of client problems and deliver culture-relevant services.					
15. *Acknowledge clients' abilities and rights* to draw strength from their cultures and make their own decisions. Acknowledge that clients may desire varying degrees of acculturation to the dominant culture.					

FIGURE 14-1 Continued

IMPLEMENTATION OF AGENCY CULTURAL COMPETENCE

The idea of cultural competence is one that came into vogue during the last 15–20 years. Prior to this, it was more common for cultural *sensitivity* be touted as being important among practitioners. Cultural competence goes beyond mere sensitivity or awareness and focuses on the need to have actual knowledge and skills related to interactions with persons from cultures that are different from our own. Cultural competence is an aspect of agency operation that is best infused throughout the entire process of service provision, as these considerations are relevant to criminal justice agencies. The New York State Office of Mental Health (2008) lays out an excellent set of objectives for agencies that wish to implement culturally competent services. These objectives are as follows:

1. Develop a written strategic plan to address disparities.
2. Know and understand the various cultural groups present in the community served.
3. Recruit and retain a diverse array of staff that are representative of the community.
4. Plan to include readily accessible bilingual/bicultural staff or translators.
5. Provide language assistance at all points of contact as needed.
6. Provide translated vital service documents, program documents, and rights and grievance information.
7. Provide ongoing training about the cultural groups served, and assure strategies employed are effective across cultures.
8. Include assessment of cross-cultural interactions as part of the employee evaluation and supervisory processes.
9. Consider various methods and media for information exchange, education, and awareness of issues related to multicultural services.
10. Collect demographic data about the community at large and service recipients to determine future directions for program development.
11. Develop partnerships with community leaders, cultural brokers, and natural networks to facilitate increased service access and to provide feedback that will guide service design.
12. Examine agency and individual outcomes to determine whether specific groups within the service population are over- or underrepresented, to track consumer satisfaction, and to promote consumer-driven services.

Students should understand that this list is not topical, but actually addresses the various components of a culturally competent program. If agencies make a good-faith effort toward completing each of these objectives, they will be sure to deliver appropriate services that are recordable and accountable. Further, this will invariably improve rapport with communities and can have a healing effect upon communities that have not typically been the focus of improved service delivery. For probation and parole agencies, effective integration of these objectives will improve the rapport that develops between the supervision personnel and offenders on their caseload. Likewise, it is also likely to improve the general experiences of police officers who enter communities where a large number of citizens are of minority origin. The easing of this social tension can be good for the agency and the community. This also allows for more effective integration of community members and further reinforces partnerships with community groups that may be influential in the area.

Finally, there is of course a need to demonstrate whether such practices do indeed reach the appropriate clientele and whether they have the intended effects. Thus, some form of accountability and measurement is required. The New York State Office of Mental Health (NYSOMH) again speaks to this issue in a very clear way. According to the NYSOMH (2008), the process of connecting cultural competency with evidence-based practices entails the following objectives:

1. Cultural competence activities need to be imbedded within all stages of development, implementation, and evaluation of evidence-based practices.
2. Implementation should ensure that agency practices are tracked in a manner that yields a rubric or other evaluation scheme that can produce clear outcomes.

3. Attention should be paid to the effectiveness of evidence-based practices across cultural groups with data tracking maintained throughout.
4. Cross-culturally relevant strategies should be identified and defined in measurable terms, whenever possible.
5. Dissemination of "what works" should be a priority, with performance measures taken to determine how well interventions seem to be working.

The above objectives provide guidance so that culturally competent approaches may impact on the overall success rates in agency response to citizen requests. This is actually a very important component of any culturally competent program, since it ensures that agencies are refining the process and that they are conducting their day-to-day operations in a manner that integrates such approaches to service delivery. Over time, agencies can use their outcome data to continually refine their approach, just as they would with any other issue of importance where a measurement of one sort or another is necessary. It is important that cultural competence not escape similar measurements lest it ultimately be ignored and forgotten over time.

Cultural Competence Training in Large and Small Agencies

It should be noted that it is quite natural that an agency's cultural competence educational format will be specific to minority groups in that jurisdiction. In other words, if the community encounters a large population of immigrants from El Salvador (but not from Mexico) then the training will of course be most applicable and most useful if it is tailored around issues specific to El Salvador or, in not practical, Central America. Beyond this, Herbert Z. Wong—a leading diversity expert on minority issues—notes that many of the exercises that can be used in teaching multicultural approaches can be quite simple, regardless of the specific racial or ethnic group that is represented (Johnson, 2006).

With this point made, the specific length and timing of the training should be given careful consideration. Although it is always good for agencies to provide multicultural training to cadets during the pre-service stage of training, this is not likely to have sufficient results in and of itself. **Pre-service training** is any of the initial training that employees receive prior to their working in their specific job duty. Often, this term refers to police, jailer, prison staff, or probation and parole officer training given to agency personnel prior to their actual work in the field. In many cases, such training will typically consist of a small 2–4-hour block of training that is generic in presentation. Therefore, academy training should not be considered the stopping point in this process (Shusta et al., 2011). Rather, such training should be provided with the explicit intent and understanding (communicated to the cadets themselves) that such training is an introductory segment that will later lead into further culturally specific in-service training within the first year of service (Dana, Behn, & Gonwa, 1992).

It is recommended that agencies provide such in-service training as early as possible once cadets have graduated from their basic level of training (Shusta et al., 2011). The reasons for this should be obvious and self-explanatory; simply put, new practitioners should be culturally competent as early as possible to ensure effective policing in jurisdictions that contain diverse minority populations. Likewise, any such in-service training must address diversity within the organization itself as well as diversity external to the agency (Dana et al., 1992; Robbins, 2005). This is important because the agency itself must develop an organizational culture that is supportive of diversity and the need for cultural competence (Robbins, 2005). This must come from within the agency and must also be emphasized by top leadership within the agency (Robbins, 2005). Thus, diversity training within the department should be seen as an internal mirror of the culturally competent external services provided from within the department to the outside community. It is in this manner that the police or correctional agency will become a culture-based learning organization.

In designing training for cultural competence with immigrant populations, several recommendations and guidelines should be implemented. The guidelines that follow are adapted from the United States Department of Justice Community Relations Service (2005) mediation agreement between the Milwaukee Police Department and several cultural and social service agencies in Milwaukee. A **community mediation agreement** is a process to assist disputants in arriving at a consensual agreement to settle their conflict. These types of agreements may be required by Federal courts or may be a voluntary initiative on the part of police agencies to enhance community relations and to demonstrate a genuine desire to foster those relations.

In the case of Milwaukee, the mediation agreement that we reference was voluntary. As was desired by the Milwaukee Police Department, the process resulted in a proposal that was directed at improving interaction between the Milwaukee Police Department personnel and citizens in the greater Milwaukee area. This is perhaps one of the most effective "first steps" when implementing culturally competent services to any minority group. It is important for smaller agencies to take heed of this and to also implement guidelines that are both broad and specific (appealing to a wide variety of populations and providing in-depth knowledge and/or services when needed). Because the proposal has received Federal oversight and approval, is comprehensive yet specific in scope, and because this proposal is a very good example of how diversity issues can be addressed in a good-faith manner by a criminal justice agency, these guidelines are likely to be ideal for smaller agencies faced with an influx of diverse populations. These modified guidelines are as follows:

- Cultural competency training should operate within the structure and guidelines of the traditional in-service training schedule and should specifically include elements relevant to minority populations within the jurisdiction that is served.
- The agency should provide sufficient training hours in cultural competency. Preferably two days (sixteen clock hours) or more should be provided each year.
- The agency staff providing cultural competency training shall be well-versed in Asian cultures. Staff shall be skilled in diverse group facilitation and should be specific to the Asian communities that are served.
- When possible, personnel from the local community should provide or at least assist in the training. This provides an added personal link between the agency and members of the community.
- Cultural Competency training should be broad and in-depth, and address issues such as race, ethnicity, gender, age, disability, religion, gender expression, and sexual orientation.
- Scenario-based training should include topics of racism and racial profiling.
- Scenario-based training shall be reflective of actual incidents or situations that have occurred between the community and the agency. It is important that these specific incidents be overtly addressed and worked upon since this will provide the opportunity for rapport and since this will make the training relevant and practical rather than theoretical.

- In addition, the agency should implement policies and procedures that contribute to citizen satisfaction and that assist the department in managing its interactions with residents of the minority community.
- The agency should provide all agency personnel with citizen service training that includes techniques that have proven effective in professional service delivery with relevant minority communities.
- When and where appropriate, agencies should encourage officers to learn a second language that is used by primary minority groups in the region. Agencies should make a point to provide tuition assistance for such efforts and should provide promotional incentives to employees who pursue such educational options.

The agency training program should include a component devoted to individual professionalism independent of personal beliefs or attitudes. In this instance, the need to maintain professional and ethical decorum should be emphasized, regardless of individual, religious, or cultural orientations. The program should also include police officer safety, customer service, minority youth/police relations, cultivating positive cross-cultural relationships, mediating and negotiating conflict and life-threatening situations. Furthermore, cultural competent services must be dynamic and must change as the need arises. This requires the following:

1. Review of training curriculum.
2. Observation and evaluation of training sessions.
3. Periodic evaluation of training outcomes.
4. Periodic meetings with agency staff involved in the development of the training program to discuss the content, status, and direction of the program.

Lastly, Herbert Wong points out that many techniques, even those that are very simple to implement, can be very powerful in revealing the discomfort for agency personnel receiving such training. For instance, in one exercise called "guess the facilitator," Wong frequently exposes participants to their own biases by asking three simple questions: What kind of car do you think I drive? What is my favorite food? And what do you think my hobbies are? As Wong notes, the answers are often very unorthodox and even illogical. Wong notes that "people bend over backwards to not be stereotypical. They will not even say Asian food or Chinese food…" when guessing an Asian instructor's favorite cuisine (Johnson, 2006, p. 2). Wong notes that these incongruent responses are often given because the persons in training do not wish to offend the instructor (Johnson, 2006). But, according to Wong, "…that creates as much a problem as it does otherwise. To be over-sensitive is not to be sensitive." (Johnson, 2006, p. 2).

It is precisely because of situations described by Wong that we wish to again emphasize that cultural sensitivity is not the same as cultural competence. Indeed, as it turns out, some commonalities among racial and cultural groups *do* tend to be true. To ignore these tendencies, trends, and commonalities is foolish. However, by the same token, to immediately presume that a person, due to appearances or otherwise, automatically prescribes to any of these commonalities should not be considered as a matter of fact. In addressing this, the instructor of any type of course on cultural competence cannot shy away from these topics, both those of over-categorizing groups and those ignoring obvious social trends. To do this in a manner that is educational and not abrasive can be a challenge but is very necessary in today's multicultural environment.

From this it can be determined that the particular instructor who provides training on cultural competence is instrumental to its success. While agencies can generate guidelines and curricula that "appear" to address cultural competency, it is the specific skill and technique of the instructor that are likely to translate the information from "written theory" to insight that actually affects the day-to-day practice and routine of the officer. Thus, agencies should carefully select instructors who provide such training. It is perhaps best that the instructor be a member of one of the cultural groups that are represented in the jurisdiction and it is even more ideal that the person come from the same region or locale.

Having instructors from the same region is sometimes counter-intuitive to some training administrators since some may think that police familiarity with the individual can diminish respect for the credentialed qualifications (or at least the novelty) of the instructor. In other words, officers may see the training as much more informal when the instructor is personally known—directly or indirectly—by the officers (Robbins, 2005). Because of this, the official in-service training should not be conducted by officers within the agency (though they should be encouraged to augment such training when and where they desire). On the contrary, persons outside the agency who have impeccable credentials in providing such training should be selected, even if they are known locally by officers in the agency. The quality of the instructor will typically override the perceived informality that officers may perceive, and if such credentials are indeed known and respected in the community, this can enhance officer receptiveness to such training. If a given community has no suitable training personnel to provide cultural competency training, then agencies should enlist the aid of a trainer from areas outside the jurisdiction.

TRAINING BEYOND THE CLASSROOM AND USING ILL-STRUCTURED PROBLEMS IN DEVELOPING CULTURAL COMPETENCE

Besides the various suggestions that we have just presented in the prior subsection related to diversity and cultural training of personnel, there is a specific training modality that we would like to present as a preferred means of training agency practitioners. This approach to training was originally developed for police training but we have decided to extend this training out to all criminal justice practitioners because we think that it can be successfully utilized with other types of staff and because we believe this is a superior approach to training personnel beyond the pre-service level. This modality of training is referred to as the **Problem-Based Learning Approach** (PBLA), and we will elaborate on this approach and two associated concepts used with this mode of training: the Ill-Structured Problem and the Failing Forward concepts of PBLA.

The PBLA is grounded in the notion that most problems that practitioners will encounter do not lend themselves perfectly to textbook descriptions and/or to the parameters of specific and often sterile policy. Thus, the PBLA trains staff to utilize their own sense of professional discretion, ethical bearing, and sound judgment to address scenarios

INTERNATIONAL FOCUS

International Peacekeeping and Cultural Views on Gender-Based Exploitation and Abuse

The United Nations is typically seen as the primary organizational body tasked with maintaining peace in unstable regions of the world. In many cases, the armed peacekeepers are tasked with protecting civilians in areas that are war-torn and otherwise troubled. Unfortunately, it is the United Nations peacekeeper who may present a danger to this population. More specifically, there has been a long-term off-and-on occurrence of sexual exploitation and abuse that has occurred at the hands of U.N. Peacekeepers who have victimized women of the local population.

The work of Lutz, Gutmann, and Brown (2009) is focused specifically on this aspect of United Nations peacekeeping. These anthropological researchers examined the cultural, political, and socio-economic issues at the base of this problem, demonstrating how cultural issues can greatly contribute to the onset of gender-based violence and abuse. While conducting their research, they focused on the relationship between beliefs and attitudes of peacekeepers about culture, gender, sexuality, and peacekeeping and the onset of sexual exploitation and abuse.

Back in late 2005, the United Nations created a Conduct and Discipline Team whose charge was to investigate and uncover inappropriate behavior among U.N. peacekeeping forces (United Nations System Staff College, 2013). Between 2005 and 2009, fourteen Conduct and Discipline teams were established covering 19 United Nations peacekeeping locations (Lutz et al., 2009). These groups investigate actual and attempted abuses that take advantage of a citizen's vulnerability, differential power, or trust, for sexual purposes, including the profiting from sexual exploitation of citizens (United Nations System Staff College, 2013).

Examples abound where young teen girls in developing or war torn nations, hungry and alone, have been given food in exchange for sexual favors (Lutz et al., 2009). In other instances, full-fledged forcible rape has occurred. In other cases, peacekeepers may have genuine relationships with locals and may wish to give "gifts" and money to help their lovers out economically; some may do political favors as well, related to immigration and obtaining other benefits not available in the person's nation-of-origin. All of these acts are unauthorized but have occurred in a variety of locations, such as in Afghanistan, Bosnia–Herzegovina, the Congo, East Timor, the Ivory Coast, Haiti, Lebanon, and the Sudan (Rubenstein, Keller, Sherger, 2008). What is disturbing about these actions is that follow-up information reveals that in most the overwhelming majority of these cases, the ultimate sanctions against perpetrators seem to be very light (i.e. demotions in rank, being barred from future peacekeeping work, marginal economic sanctions, very short jail stints, and so forth) in comparison to what would be given in similar criminal actions in the perpetrator's own nation-of-origin.

It is clear that cultural beliefs of individual peacekeepers and those from specific regions of the world impact these outcomes. Beliefs, particularly about race, sexuality, and gender can impact both how U.N. personnel react to citizens in a given region and it can impact how they relate to one another (Lutz et al., 2009). Further, among the various participating countries, there are many different cultural standards around sexuality and gender represented within peacekeeping contingents and their individual members. The legality of prostitution, the age of consent and the age of legal marriage vary considerably around the globe. Despite this, U. N. workers are required to adhere to the United Nation's standards on these matters, not those of their own nation.

Among some peacekeepers, there has been documented disagreement that sex with local citizens is a problematic occurrence. Consider, as an example, that members may not believe that sex with adult members of a peacekeeping region is problematic, so long as it is consensual (Higate, 2007; Rubenstein, 2008). Further, in some regions, claims that women are overbearing and persistent in developing a relationship with male peacekeepers have been noted… and there is even the claim that in truly impoverished areas, mothers are angry that they are not able to capitalize on circumstances by prostituting their daughters with peacekeepers (Lutz et al., 2009).

Thus, cultural views on sexuality and its legality are aggravated by socioeconomics of a given region. Further, in some participating countries, the culture believes in the rights of male entitlement, referred to as masculine privilege. Masculine privilege maintains that men ought to be able to dominate women and have what they want; the needs of men come first (Higate, 2007; Lutz et al., 2009). Often, this belief is coupled with one in which the culture believes that male sexuality is biologically beyond a man's control, that he will, in essence, engage in this behavior, simply because he is a man and because he has little or no control over these drives (Higate, 2007).

These two beliefs, those of male privilege and those related to the "boys will be boys" mentality, are common in much of the world, particularly in the non-industrialized or developing nations (Higate, 2007). They are but two examples of how cultural issues come into play in exacerbating gender-based violence in the international scene. It is clear, then, that in the context of peacekeeping, problem-solving should involve issues of culture and cultural competence because it is the basis upon which people generate options for structuring their actions and creating solutions to problems (Rubenstein et al., 2008). Further, culture is that it gives a frame of reference from which people gain an initial sense of their reality and develop their ideas about what is proper behavior in a given situation or in a particular region of the world. Culture, then, influences what peacekeepers believe to be true, and like it or not, it shapes their emotional reactions. This includes their emotional reactions to sexuality, legalities, and view on fundamental fairness.

References: Higate, P. (2007). Peacekeepers, Masculinities and Sexual Exploitation. *Men and Masculinities, 10* (1), 99-119.

Lutz, C., Gutmann, M. & Brown, K. (2009). *Conduct and Discipline in UN Peacekeeping Operations: Culture, Political Economy and Gender*. Providence, RI: Watson Institute for International Studies.

Rubenstein, R. A., Keller, D. M. Sherger, M. E. (2008). Culture and Interoperability in Integrated Missions. International Peacekeeping, 15(4), 540–555.

United Nations System Staff College. (2013). Gender & cross-cultural training. Retrieved from: http://www.unssc.org/home/category/themes/gender-cross-cultural-training-0; United Nations Institute of Training and Research.

where there is no absolutely clear response. In using this approach, trainers will give personnel an **Ill-Structured Problem**, which is reflective of the following characteristics:

- The problem is not easily solved
- Staff in training initially lack and must obtain information to solve the problem
- Staff in training must consider a variety of facts and issues
- All learning occurs through the problem-solving process
- Learning that occurs has a real-life context
- Staff in training learn a process that he or she can apply to future problems

When using the PBLA, staff who are in training will confront circumstances that are familiar and unfamiliar to them. Using this approach, diversity/cultural competence trainers will require that these staff ask questions, conduct research, conduct role-plays and responses that are observed by others, and allow their peers to determine the effectiveness of their actions. The following steps are the basis of the problem-solving style:

- The diversity trainer presents the trainees with a real-life problem
- Staff in training work with the problem and consider initial ideas
- Staff in training identify what they know about the problem
- Staff in training identify what they need to know about the problem and seek information from available resources, including relevant community sources
- Staff in training develop an action plan based on their research
- Staff evaluate their own performance as well as that of their peers and learn to transfer the new knowledge to future problems

Lastly, we also would like to introduce the concept of Failing Forward, which is also a component of the PBLA. The **Failing Forward Concept** is founded on the idea that many of our greatest learning moments occur when we fail to achieve something, particularly when that failure either has consequences or leaves a long-term impression upon us. When using problem-based approaches, we ideally wish to avoid mistakes and instead provide effective responses. However, along the way, we also inevitably discover some approaches that simply do not work as well, if at all; this is considered a healthy learning lesson under the Failing Forward Concept. Essentially, "we learn from our mistakes," as the old adage goes; thus, productive learning can also occur when we "fail forward."

Rather than viewing our mistakes as a step backward, we view them as one more step closure to moving forward. In summary, allowing staff to explore ideas and make non-critical mistakes help further encourage an environment of exploration and enjoyable learning. However, it is important that training personnel ensure that they intervene before staff encounter serious mistakes or come to truly erroneous conclusions. While it is unlikely that most training situations related to cultural competence will lead to dangerous outcomes, there is the potential for off-hand joking and/or misunderstandings that can offend or hurt staff, intentionally or unintentionally. In such cases, trainers must safeguard the welfare of their trainees from noxious or toxic training circumstances.

BEYOND THE TRAINING: INDIVIDUAL STAFF RECOGNITION FOR UTILIZING CULTURALLY COMPETENT PRACTICES

Once training is complete, it is important that staff not just receive continued support for integrating culturally competent techniques in their daily duties, but this should also be linked to their supervisory appraisal of performance. When performance information is used to reward individuals, these measures can hold individuals accountable for certain work activities and related goals and, as a result, create an incentive for achieving results (GAO, 2006). A greater focus on performance results can be achieved by creating a cascade from an organization's goals and objectives (see Box 14.1) down

---

Box 14.1 Culturally Competent Policies, Activities, Goals, and Objectives in Criminal Justice Agencies

Culturally Competent Policy: A governing principle of cultural competence that is reflected in the goals, objectives, and/or activities of the agency. It is a decision on an issue not resolved on the basis of facts and logic only. *For example, the policy of expediting bilingual assistance in the courts might be adopted as a basis for reducing the average number of days from arraignment to disposition.*

Culturally Competent Activities: Services or functions carried out by a program (i.e., what the program does) that are effective in responding to diverse populations. *For example, agencies might quickly determine issues specific to the community's demographic makeup, utilize tailor-made units to respond to special needs, etc.*

Goals of Cultural Competence: A desired state of affairs that outlines the ultimate purpose of a program. This is the end toward which program efforts are directed and, in achieving this end, culturally competent

approaches are specifically included. *For example, the goal of many criminal justice programs is a reduction in criminal activity; this might be done, in part, through improved community relations (via better minority/immigrant community connections) so that crime fighting can be more effectively implemented in the agency's jurisdiction.*

Culturally Competent Objectives: Specific results or effects of a program's activities that must be achieved in pursuing the program's ultimate goals. *For example, a diversity program may expect to change staff attitudes about diversity with the GLBT population (objective) to ultimately improve citizen perceptions of police in GLBT communities (goal).*

Source: Author. Bureau of Justice Assistance, Center for Program Evaluation. (2007). *Reporting and using evaluation results.* Washington, DC: Bureau of Justice Assistance. Retrieved from: http://www.ojp.usdoj.gov/BJA/evaluation/sitemap.htm.

Box 14.2 Employee Performance Evaluation Designed to Encourage and Reward Cultural Competence among Agency Staff

- Has the department considered bringing culturally representative residents in to recruit training to work with recruits on real-life problem-solving exercises?
- Are performance evaluations based on job descriptions that reflect the principles of diversity and the development of cultural competence?
- Do performance evaluations emphasize taking action to make a positive difference in the community as the yardstick of success?
- Did the process of developing performance evaluations reflect broad input from inside and outside the organization?
- Are performance evaluations written from the customers' point of view (the diverse public who are the recipients), rather than serve the department's bureaucratic needs?
- Do performance evaluations for managers and supervisors reflect the shift from controller to facilitator, as well as the roles of model, coach, and mentor?
- Do performance evaluations for managers and supervisors reward them for developing collaborative partnerships with individuals and groups outside the organization?
- Do performance evaluations for managers and supervisors reward them for efforts to generate internal support for diversity and the development of cultural competence?
- Do performance evaluations for managers and supervisors reward actions taken to reduce internal/friction/backlash related to diversity initiatives and the development of cultural competence?
- Do performance evaluations for officers reward meeting the special needs of specific groups: women, the elderly, minorities, juveniles?
- Do performance evaluations for officers reward sensitivity to diversity?
- Does the performance evaluation process allow the community opportunities for formal and informal input into the assessment?
- Do performance evaluations for officers reward them for initiating and maintaining community building and community-based problem-solving initiatives?
- Do performance evaluations for officers gauge success on whether their efforts attempted to improve quality of life in the community?

Source: Stewart, G. (2007). *Community policing explained: A guide for local governments.* Washington, DC: COPS.

to the individual performance level. Such alignment facilitates the linking of individual performance (look to Box 14.2) to organizational performance (GAO, 2006).

This is to demonstrate the importance of linking policy and individual performance reviews to the goals and objectives that guide a criminal justice agency into the future. This cyclic pattern of going from assessment to training to implementation to evaluation demonstrates a continual circle of development that uses past data to better face future challenges. This is the most effective means of utilizing real-world research to tailor-fit programs to the challenges within a jurisdiction. With this in mind, we once again point toward the work of Van Keulen (1988) who roughly 20 years ago noted that:

> Goals and objectives also play a critical role in evaluation by providing a standard against which to measure the program's success… having a statement of goals and objectives will enhance your program's credibility by showing that given careful thought has been given to what you are doing. (p. 1)

Van Keulen (1988) demonstrates the reasons why clarity in definition, point, and purpose behind a community corrections program is important. Thus, clearly articulated goals not only help crystallize the agency's philosophical orientation on the supervision process but also provide for more measurable constructs that lend themselves to effective evaluation. Clarity in the goals and objectives allows the agency to perform evaluative research to determine if its efforts are actually successful or if they are in need of improvement.

Such clarity then facilitates the ability of the agency to come "full circle" as the planning, implementation, evaluation, and refinement phases of agency operations unfold.

Agencies that are adept at implementing evaluative information and recommendations are sometimes referred to as learning organizations. **Learning organizations** have the inherent ability to adapt and change, improving performance through continual revision of goals, objectives, policies, and procedures. Throughout this process, learning organizations respond to the various pushes and pulls that are placed upon them by utilizing a continual process of data-driven, cyclical, and responsive decision-making that results in heightened adaptability of the organization. The ideal agency is a learning organization—one that can adjust to outside community needs and challenges as well as internal personnel and resource challenges. Lastly, in its ideal state, evaluation is an ongoing process that is embedded in the process of program planning, action setting, and later improvement. The Bureau of Justice Assistance, Center for Program Evaluation(2007) notes that evaluation findings can be used to revise policies, activities, goals, and objectives (see Figure 14-1) so that criminal justice agencies can provide the best possible services to the community to which they are accountable.

CURRENT EVENT
Police Agencies as Learning Organizations in the Global Community

As we have seen from our chapter readings, learning organizations are those that have the inherent ability to adapt and change, improving performance through continual revision of goals, objectives, policies, and procedures. Throughout this process, the agency will respond to pushes and pulls by utilizing a continual process of data-driven, cyclical, and responsive decision-making that *results in heightened* adaptability of the organization. Going further, it would appear that the idea of police agencies serving as learning organizations is one that has been considered a gold standard in operation by many police experts (Crank & Giacomazzi, 2009; Daniel, 2001; Filstad & Gottschalk, 2013). This is not, in all likelihood, a new or current innovation.

What is new, however, is that the idea is one that has come into vogue, with renewed interest, on an international level (Filstad & Gottschalk, 2013). This is particularly true in Norway where challenges to policing have called for the Norwegian police force to develop a learning organization that focuses on experience-based learning, the evaluation and identification of important learning arenas, knowledge sharing across boundaries and police districts, and the creation of a strong learning culture (Filstad & Gottschalk, 2013; Wathne, 2012). This approach is expected to assist police in Norway in learning from past responses and will prove useful in addressing issues related to minority populations in Norway. Problems with Pakistani and Somali communities in Norway have persisted in the country which has, historically speaking, been very homogeneous in demographic composition.

Indeed, Norway has been described as xenophobic, meaning that they are very suspicious and even hostile of

outsiders (Ladegaard, 2013). Issues related to immigration in general, and Islamic immigrant populations, in particular, have led to intense public debate in the past few years. Further, these issues are new to Norway, unlike many other countries throughout Europe and the rest of the world, because this country has typically consisted of persons from the Scandinavian area and/or areas of Europe that are close in proximity. Acts of racism and heated politics have become more prevalent in Norway (Ladegaard, 2013). Amidst these social conflicts, the Norwegian police must respond and, as we have seen in other areas of this text, they must contend with a number of issues that require culturally competent personnel and organizational response (Ladegaard, 2013). As a means of tracking the effectiveness of their service delivery and improving that service, policing in Norway has adopted a 'learning organization' approach that where personnel utilize data to improve these efforts (Wathne, 2012).

While we tout this as a current event – which it is – it is not exactly new in the United States or even other areas of the world. In fact, in the small nation of Wales, policing has also adopted a learning organization approach (Daniel, 2001) that extend back to the beginning of this millennium. In the United States, examples exist as far back as the 1990's, where police experts have noted that police departments, as learning organizations, should make a point to benefit from their own efforts as well as those of other agencies as a means of improving tactical and strategic operations (Geller, 1997). Nevertheless, the process of learning and refining operations is one that is ongoing and never ends, making it continually a 'current event' in policing as well as the rest of the criminal justice system, regardless of the area of the world in which it is implemented, by name or deed.

References: Crank, J. P. & Giacomazzi, A. (2009). A sheriffs office as a learning organization. *Police Quarterly, 12*(4), 351–369.

Daniel, C. (2001). The police service as a learning organization. *Continuing Professional Development Journal, 4*, 11–14.

Geller, W. A. (1997). Suppose We Were Really Serious About Police Departments Becoming "Learning Organizations"? Rockville, MD: *National Institute of Justice Journal, 234*, 2–8. Retrieved from: https://www.ncjrs.gov/pdffiles/jr000234.pdf

Ladegaard, I. (2013, January 28). Norway's problem with immigration. Science Nordic. Retrieved from: http://sciencenordic.com/norways-problem-immigration

Filstad, C. & Gottschalk, P. (2013). The police force: to be or not to be a learning organization? In A. Ortenblad (Ed.), Handbook of Research on the Learning Organization, pp. 176–195. Cheltenham, UK: Edward Elgar Publishing Ltd.

Wathne, C. T. (2012). The Norwegian Police Force: a learning organization?, *Policing: An International Journal of Police Strategies & Management, 35*(4), pp. 704–722.

EVALUATION RESEARCH AND CULTURAL COMPETENCE IN THE AGENCY

Research and evaluation is a critical dimension of criminal justice programs. Evaluations are needed for program monitoring and for decision making by program staff, criminal justice administrators, and policymakers. Evaluations provide accountability, identify strengths and weaknesses, and provide a basis for program revision. In addition, evaluation reports are useful learning tools for others who are interested in developing effective programs. Many treatment programs in the criminal justice system have operated without evaluations for many years, only to find out later that key outcome data are needed to justify program continuation.

Conducting an adequate evaluation requires one to formulate clearly the treatment model and reasonable program goals and specific objectives related to client needs. General goals must be translated into measurable outcomes. The evaluator generally works closely with program administrators to translate their evaluation guidelines into operational components. For example, general goals of helping program participants become drug and crime free can be operationalized into intermediate goals of changing behavior (e.g., reductions in rule infractions and fewer positive drug test results) while in a program. In essence, scientific principles for conducting research should be carefully adhered to in order to enhance the viability of findings.

There are three basic types of evaluation:

1. Implementation
2. Process
3. Outcome

An important note before we discuss the three main components of evaluation research is that whereas implementation and process evaluations can begin when the program is initiated, outcome evaluation should not begin until the program has been fully implemented. Outcome evaluations are generally more costly than other types of evaluation and are warranted for programs of longer duration that are aimed at modifying lifestyles (such as therapeutic communities), rather than drug education interventions that are less intensive and less likely to produce long-term effects.

Implementation Evaluation

Although programs often look promising in the proposal stage, many fail to materialize as planned in the security-oriented correctional environment. Other programs are rigidly implemented as planned and without adjustments for the realities of community corrections, often rendering them less effective. **Implementation evaluation** is aimed at identifying problems and accomplishments during the early phases of program development for feedback to agency staff. Such evaluations involve informal and formal interviews with administrators, staff, and community members to ascertain their degree of satisfaction with the program and their perceptions of problems.

Process Evaluation

Traditionally, **process evaluation** refers to assessment of the effects of the program on clients while they are in the program, making it possible to assess the institution's intermediary goals. Process evaluation involves analyzing records related to the following:

1. Type and amount of training provided.
2. Attendance and participation of staff in meetings.
3. Number of staff who complete the training.
4. Staff evaluations of instructor proficiency in training.

Outcome Evaluation

Outcome evaluations are more ambitious and expensive than implementation or process evaluations. **Outcome evaluation** involves quantitative research aimed at assessing the impact of the program on long-term treatment outcomes. Such evaluations are usually carefully designed studies that compare outcomes for a treatment group with outcomes for other less-intensive treatments or a no-treatment control group (i.e., a sample of offenders who meet the program admission criteria but who do not receive treatment), complex statistical analyses, and sophisticated report preparation.

Follow-up data (e.g., drug relapse, recidivism, employment status) are the heart of outcome evaluation. Follow-up data can be collected from criminal justice records and face-to-face interviews with individuals who participated in certain programs. Studies that use agency records are less expensive than locating participants and conducting follow-up interviews. Outcome evaluations can include cost-effectiveness and cost-benefit information that is important to policymakers. Because outcome research usually involves a relatively large investment of time and money, as well as the cooperation of a variety of people and agencies, it must be carefully planned. A research design may be very simple and easy to implement or it may be more complex. In the case of more complex studies, it is usually advisable to enlist the assistance of an experienced researcher.

Program Quality and Staffing Quality

Besides outcome and process measures, there are a number of other areas that agencies may wish to evaluate. These other areas may or may not require the input of the community and may integrate results from community satisfaction surveys. Some examples would be when agencies wish to assess the quality of their program, their staff, or their curricula. Each of these three components are very important but may go well beyond simple outcome evaluation measures. In some cases, such as with program curricula, there may be a connection to the general process measures used to evaluate the program. However, it is important when agencies evaluate curricula that they keep this separate and distinct from the blurring effects of staff that may modify the general process with their own therapeutic slant and/or means of implementing aspects of a job requirement. In other words, the individual preferences of different persons employed in the agency are not what you hope to observe in a curricular assessment but rather it is the uniform and written procedures that are of interest.

From the example with curricular assessment just noted, it is clear that evaluations can be quite complex and detailed, depending on the approach taken by the agency. The key to an effective and ethical evaluation is evaluative transparency. **Evaluative transparency** is when an agency's evaluative process allows for an outside person (whether an auditor, an evaluator, or the public-at-large) to have full view of the agency's operations, budgeting, policies, procedures, and outcomes. In transparent agencies there are no secrets and confidential information is only kept when ethical or legal requirements mandate that the information not be transparent, such as with a victim's personal identity. In such cases, the intent is a benevolent safeguarding of the individual's welfare, not the agency's own welfare.

If one is to evaluate the quality of a program, it stands to reason that the program must be transparent to the evaluator who is tasked with observing that program. Agencies that seek to meet high ethical standards must be transparent. This is a core requisite to ensuring the quality of the program that is implemented. Furthermore, programs of quality are accountable to the public and this is, in part, an element of transparency. Public accountability is a matter of good ethical bearing and this is consistent with the reason that ethical safeguards are put into place—to protect the public consumer. In the case of police and corrections agencies, the product that is "sold" to the public is community safety, and it is the obligation of the agency to be accountable and transparent to the public when providing services to its jurisdiction. Thus, the quality of the program should be appraised by its ability to deliver ethical, open, and honest services that hold community safety as paramount.

With regard to staffing quality, agencies should make a point to evaluate their standards as well as the support that they provide to their staff. Naturally, recruitment and hiring standards should be evaluated routinely, but it is also important that agencies examine their own support services for staff. Some examples might include the existence of an effective human resources division, sufficient budgeting for equipment to effectively do one's job, and the nature of the job design, particularly with regard to caseload. As one might guess, this is also related to the overall quality of the program as well.

Quite naturally, agencies should evaluate their hiring standards and should examine factors such as the number of complaints generated by the community regarding staff functioning in police, juvenile justice, or community corrections agencies. In prison systems or secure juvenile detention facilities, grievances and/or complaints by offenders can also be examined if it should turn out that there is some legitimacy to such complaints. Likewise, employee standards of conduct are important, as are incidents where employees do not meet expected standards that are expected by the agency. Moreover, staff should be consulted and evaluators should consider whether the line staff feel prepared and/or whether they consider their work environment to be on par with other agencies. All of this staff-related information provides a richer analysis of agency operations and also provides additional transparency to the day-to-day routines that occur.

Feedback Loops and Continual Improvement

In evaluating correctional agencies, it is important that the information obtained from the evaluation serve some useful purpose. The Bureau of Justice Assistance's (BJA) Center for Program Evaluation (2007) elaborates on the need for evaluations to be constructed in a manner that is useful to the stakeholders of the evaluation. **Stakeholders** in agency evaluations include the agency personnel, the community in which the agency is located, and even the offender population that is being supervised. According to the BJA Center for Program Evaluation, it is important for evaluators to be clear on what agency administrators wish to evaluate and it is also important that evaluators ensure that administrators understand that evaluative efforts are to remain objective and unbiased in nature.

Beyond the initial understanding between administrators and evaluators, it is always important that evaluators provide recommendations for agencies, based on the outcome of the evaluation (Bureau of Justice Assistance, Center for Program Evaluation, 2007). It is the use of these recommendations through which agencies can improve their overall services and enhance goal-setting strategies in the future. Indeed, evaluation information can be a powerful tool for a variety of stakeholders (Bureau of Justice Assistance, Center for Program Evaluation, 2007). Program managers can use the information to make changes in their programs that will enhance their effectiveness (Bureau of Justice Assistance, Center for Program Evaluation, 2007, in Using Evaluation Result). Decision-makers can ensure that they are funding effective programs. Other authorities can ensure that programs are developed as intended and have sufficient resources to implement activities and meet their goals and objectives (Bureau of Justice Assistance, Center for Program Evaluation, 2007).

Community Harm with Ineffective Programs, Separating Politics from Science in the Evaluative Process

As we near the close of this text, it is important to reflect on the potential consequences that might be incurred if agencies are allowed to operate ineffectively. The evaluation of criminal justice agencies is directly tied to the assessment component. Both process and outcome evaluations tend to examine data during the initial assessment against the data that is received when the evaluation is later conducted. Thus, the evaluation process is a feedback loop into the initial assessment process, demonstrating to agencies that their programs are (or are not) working. If they are found to be in need of improvement, evaluators can then determine if this is due to the initial assessment or if the deficiency is due to some process issue further within the program's service delivery. Checking the initial assessment and ensuring that this process is adequate follow a "garbage in—garbage out" philosophy.

It can be seen that this process creates a systemic loop whereby the agency is constantly assessing and evaluating itself. This is known as the **assessment–training–evaluation cycle**, which is the process whereby assessment data and evaluation data are compared, one with the other, to determine the effectiveness of programs and to find areas where improvement of agency services is required. Agencies that successfully implement the *assessment–evaluation cycle* tend to use public resources more effectively and also are not prone to placing the community at risk of future criminal activity. In other words, agencies using the *assessment–evaluation* cycle will operate at an optimal level, avoiding harm to the community and the mismanagement of resources. On the other hand, those agencies that do not successfully implement the *assessment–evaluation cycle* will be more likely to *both* waste agency resources and place the community at a level of risk that otherwise would be preventable.

Lastly, successful evaluation measures should (1) be linked to an agency's mission and goals, as indicated in Figure 14-1; (2) be clearly stated; (3) have quantifiable targets or other measurable values; (4) be reasonably free of significant bias or manipulation that would distort the accurate assessment of performance; (5) provide a reliable way to assess progress; (6) sufficiently cover a program's core activities; (7) have limited overlap with other measures; (8) have balance, or not emphasize one or two priorities at the expense of others; and (9) address agency-wide priorities (GAO, 2006).

Managers can use evaluation measures in a number of ways to improve programs and allocate resources more efficiently and effectively. Decision makers can use results from evaluative performance measurement to identify problems or weaknesses in programs, identify factors causing the problems, and modify services or processes to try to address problems (GAO, 2006). Conversely, evaluation can be used to identify and increase the use of program approaches that are working well and to consider alternative processes in areas where goals are not met. Separately, evaluative performance measures can also be used to identify priorities and allocate resources. Decision makers can compare performance measure results with program goals and subsequently determine where to target resources to improve performance (GAO, 2006). Furthermore, when considering cultural competence of service delivery, agencies can use performance measurement to assess progress toward meeting goals, both internal to the agency and external within the broader community (such as with police agencies, juvenile agencies, community corrections, or the courts) or among a population of offenders (such as with correctional prison systems). The intended effect of assessing such progress is a reduction in problems for the agency and better relations with the community. These practices that emerge are what we refer to as evidence-based practices.

EVIDENCE-BASED PRACTICES

Evidence-based practice is a significant trend throughout all human services that emphasize outcomes. Interventions within community corrections are considered effective when they reduce offender risk and subsequent recidivism and therefore make a positive long-term contribution to public safety. In this section of the chapter, students are presented with a model or framework based on a set of principles for effective offender interventions within state, local, or private correctional systems. Specifically, **evidence-based practice (EBP)** implies that (1) one outcome is desired over others; (2) it is measurable; and (3) it is defined according to practical realities (i.e., public safety) rather than immeasurable moral or value-oriented standards (Colorado Division of Criminal Justice, 2007). Thus, EBP is more appropriate for scientific exploration within any criminal justice agency. We now follow with the presentation of eight different EBPs, adapted from the National Institute of Justice (2005); these principles are detailed as follows:

EBP #1: Assess the Needs of Organizational Participants

This stage is similar to the assessment stage of our assessment–training–evaluation cycle. At this point, agencies simply attempt to determine the level of cultural competence that they currently possess. Students should again refer to Figure 14-1 for an example instrument that might be used to assess an agency's cultural competence.

EBP #2: Enhance Motivation of Participants

Humans respond better when motivated—rather than persuaded—to change their behavior. An essential principle of effective motivation might be through the use of performance reviews that include aspects of cultural competence, collaborative partnership, and community relations. Students should again refer to Box 14.2 for examples.

EBP #3: Target Operational Changes

Staff training and professionalism become an essential component of developing a culture of personal change: well-trained staff can—and must—role model and promote pro-social attitudes and behaviors even while maintaining a safe and secure environment (Colorado Division of Criminal Justice, 2007).

EBP #4: Provide Skill Training for Staff and Monitor Their Delivery of Services

EBP emphasizes culturally competent strategies and it is delivered by well-trained staff. Supervisors must coach staff to learn new techniques. In addition, staff must be continually and consistently committed to further improving their sense of cultural competence.

EBP #5: Increase Positive Reinforcement

Researchers have found that optimal staff influence and organizational change result when the ratio of reinforcements is four positive to every negative reinforcement. Thus, agencies should use rewards and incentives to encourage sound multicultural service delivery and should avoid punishments as much as possible, unless such is clearly warranted and simply unavoidable. The key is to use rewards so as to increase cohesion within the agency rather than dissension.

EBP #6: Engage Ongoing Support

Support for culturally competent practices has to be ongoing in nature. This should be done both through a top-down and sustained set of messages that support multiculturalism as well as support from throughout the ranks of personnel. Using continued reinforcements (i.e., giving duty assignments to those who demonstrate competence), incentives through individual performance reviews, and using these perspectives in making decisions for later promotion, agencies can optimize the likelihood that these types of initiatives have longevity and widespread impact on personnel.

EBP #7: Measure Relevant Processes/Practices

An accurate and detailed documentation of case information and staff performance, along with a formal and valid mechanism for measuring outcomes, is the foundation of EBP. Quality control and program fidelity play a central and ongoing role in maximizing service delivery (Colorado Division of Criminal Justice, 2007).

EBP #8: Provide Measurement Feedback

Providing feedback builds accountability and maintains integrity, ultimately improving outcomes. Offenders need feedback on their behavioral changes, and program staff need feedback on program integrity. It is important to reward positive behavior— of inmates succeeding in programs, and of staff delivering effective programming. Measurements that identify effective practices then need to be linked to resources, and resource decisions should be based on objective measurement (Colorado Division of Criminal Justice, 2007). Years of research have gone into the development of these EBPs. When applied appropriately, these practices have the best potential to reduce recidivism. These principles should guide criminal justice program development, implementation, and evaluation.

Individual Case-Level Implementation of EBP

At this level of implementation, the logical implication is that one must assess (EBP #1) prior to triage or targeting intervention (EBP #3), and that it is beneficial to begin building offender motivation (EBP #2) prior to engaging these offenders in skill-building activities (# 4). Similarly, positively reinforcing new skills (EBP #5) has more relevancy after the skills have been introduced and trained (EBP #4) and at least partially in advance of the offender's realignment with pro-social groups and friends (EBP #6). The seventh (measure relevant practices) and eighth (provide feedback) principles need to follow the activities described throughout all the proceeding principles. Assessing staff adoption of culturally competent practices is possible anywhere along the continuum. These last two principles can and should be applicable after any of the earlier principles, but they also can be considered cumulative.

Agency-Level Implementation of EBPs

The principles, when applied at the agency level, assist with more closely aligning staff behavior and agency operations with EBP. Initial assessment followed by motivational enhancement will help staff prepare for the significant changes ahead. Agency priorities must be clarified and new protocols established and trained. Increasing positive rewards for staff who demonstrate new skills and proficiency is straightforward and an accepted standard in many organizations. The sixth principle regarding providing ongoing support in natural communities can be related to teamwork within the agency as well as with external agency stakeholders. The seventh and eighth principles are primarily about developing quality assurance systems, both to provide outcome data within the agency and to provide data to assist with marketing the agency to external stakeholders (National Institute of Justice, 2005).

System-Level Implementation of EBPs

The application of the Framework Principles at the system level is not much different from the agency level in terms of sequence and recommended order though it is both the most critical and challenging level. Funding, for most systems, comes from state and local agencies that have oversight responsibilities. Demonstrating the value of EBP and effective interventions are crucial at this level, as is adherence to a coherent strategy for EBP. Another distinction in applying the principles at the system level is the need for greater abstraction and policy integration. The principles for EBP must be understood and supported by policymakers so that appropriate policy development coincides effectively with implementation (National Institute of Justice, 2005).

Research Evaluation for Effectiveness of EBPs

In this chapter, eight separate principles have been identified that are related to reduced recidivism outcomes in the research literature. Though we know that these are EBPs, at this point, we do not know how well supported each is by the evidence. Thus, students should understand that this research does not support each of these principles with equal volume and quality, and even if it did, each principle would

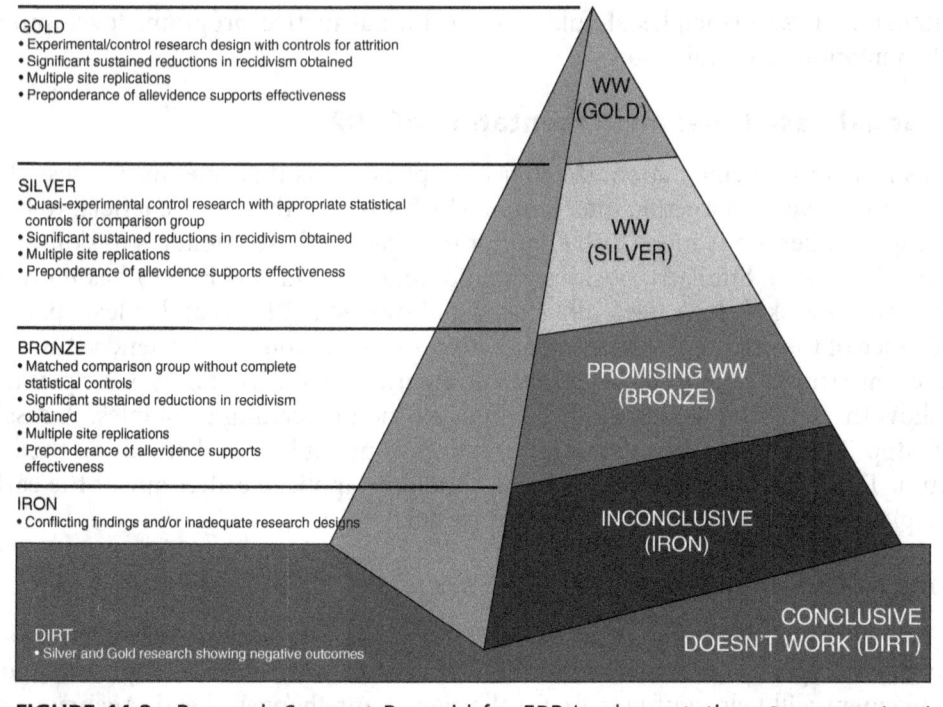

FIGURE 14-2 Research Support Pyramid for EBP Implementation. *Source:* National Institute of Justice. (2005). *Implementing evidence based practice in corrections.* Washington, DC: United States Department of Justice.

not necessarily have similar effects on outcomes. Too often programs or practices are promoted as having research support without any regard for either the quality or the research methods that were employed. Consequently, a research support pyramid (see Figure 14-2) has been included that shows how research support for each principle ranks.

The highest quality research support depicted in this schema (gold level) reflects interventions and practices that have been evaluated with experimental/control design and with multiple site replications that concluded significant sustained reductions in recidivism were associated with the intervention. The criteria for the next levels of support progressively decrease in terms of research rigor requirements (silver and bronze); however, all the top three levels require that a preponderance of all evidence supports effectiveness. The next rung lower in support (iron) is reserved for programs that have inconclusive support regarding their efficacy. Finally, the lowest level designation (dirt) is reserved for those programs that have research (utilizing methods and criteria associated with gold and silver levels) but the findings were negative and the programs were determined ineffective (National Institute of Justice, 2005).

CONCLUSION

Throughout this text, we have defined, discussed, and applied the notion of cultural competence in each segment of the criminal justice system. Whether an agency's role is policing, judicial processing, juvenile oriented, or correctional in nature, we have demonstrated that there is a bona fide need to consider diversity issues important and relevant to successfully providing effective services and meeting societal expectations of justice and ethical bearing. However, simply noting these needs is not sufficient, we must be able to specifically and concretely assess how well an agency addresses its ability to respond to a diverse multicultural society. Thus, the assessment of an agency's cultural competence was presented in this chapter as a first step in developing and maintaining the ability to address effective service delivery to a diverse population.

Once an agency is appropriately assessed, it must be determined whether services are sufficient or in need of further improvement. Thus, we have also presented information related to the implementation of cultural competence as an agency-wide supported ideal, in terms of both its initial introduction to agency staff and maintaining practices that are found to be sufficient. The key is to ensure that some type of baseline is generated so that agency administrators understand how well or how poorly their agency responds to diversity concerns, both within the organization itself and with regard to the public with which it deals (for police and courthouse operations) or with the offender population who is processed through the agency (as is the case for juvenile justice agencies, prison systems, and community corrections).

Whether an administrator wishes to implement new approaches or simply maintain current levels of culturally competent response, the need for training becomes quite clear. As we have noted in Chapter 5, the ability to infuse cultural competence into agency operations is related to the sense of proficiency that staff have in intercultural communication; communication of ideas, internally addressing staff needs and concerns, and an understanding of citizen priorities being key means of exhibiting cultural competence. We have provided numerous and specific suggestions regarding the development of effective training approaches for criminal justice agencies to cultivate cultural competence among staff and administrators. In fact, we have provided both classroom and hands-on-oriented training suggestions designed to empower staff ultimately to develop good judgment, discretion, and understanding, which can be applied to a multitude of settings. We do not simply provide ideas that are lecture-based in nature, but explain how effective training should be designed to mimic real-world circumstances and should challenge staff through doing, not just sitting and listening.

We have also demonstrated how goal setting within the agency should be interlaced with cultural competence as a key consideration. Agency objectives and activities should reflect the importance of goals related to cultural competence. Just as important is the fact that if agencies are serious about truly implementing these standards, they will also link individual performance evaluations, rewards, and incentives for staff to the goal of achieving or maintaining high levels of cultural competence. Having goals and objectives from top administration provides a strong top-down thematic message of support for cultural competence within the organization; tying this to individual performance reviews and reward systems provides a strong bottom-up incentive to take this thematic seriously and to, through inherent individual motivation, support the effort when conducting day-to-day activities in the agency and with the public-at-large.

Furthermore, we have shown that evaluation of cultural competence is very important in today's multicultural society. It is through the evaluative process that we are able to identify program strengths and weaknesses in providing culturally competent services. With evaluative data, we can determine whether our assessment and later training are effective in steering the agency toward goals and objectives of cultural competence. Thus, assessment can be seen as a measure of what goes into a program and evaluation can be seen as a measure of what comes out of the program. The two work hand-in-hand with one another. Because of this, students should be familiar with the assessment–training–evaluation cycle, since this is the primary means by which agencies measure their proficiency in delivering culturally competent services and since this is what ultimately determines whether an agency is meeting its goals and objectives.

When we find favorable outcomes through evaluation, those practices and processes that lead to this success are officially adopted as EBPS. The "evidence" being the evaluative data that we receive that shows that the practice is effective in achieving our goals of cultural competence in service delivery and community response. On the other hand, when agencies receive unfavorable evaluations, an examination of the policies and activities of that agency may be in order or, in some cases, a reassessment of the goals and objectives may be required to ensure that they are understood by staff and obtainable by the agency.

Chapter 14 Learning Check

1. The _____
_____ is founded on the idea that many of our greatest learning moments occur when we fail to achieve something, particularly when that failure either has consequences or leaves a long-term impression upon us.
   a. Failure Reduction Process
   b. Total Quality Improvement System (TQIS)
   c. Falling Fast Concept
   d. Failing Forward Concept
   e. None of the above

2. _____
_____ refers to assessment of the effects of the program on clients while they are in the program, making it possible to assess the institution's intermediary goals.
   a. Implementation evaluation
   b. Process evaluation
   c. Outcome evaluation
   d. Evidence-practice evaluation
   e. All of the above

3. The process of connecting cultural competency with evidence-based practices entails the following objectives:
   a. Cultural competence activities need to be imbedded within all stages of development, implementation, and evaluation of evidence-based practices
   b. Implementation should ensure that agency practices are tracked in a manner that yields a rubric or other evaluation scheme that can produce clear outcomes
   c. Attention should be paid to the effectiveness of evidence-based practices across cultural groups with data tracking maintained throughout
   d. Cross-culturally relevant strategies should be identified and defined in measurable terms, whenever possible
   e. All of the above

4. Culturally competent objectives are services or functions carried out by a program (i.e., what the program does) that are effective in responding to diverse populations.
   a. True
   b. False

5. Evidence-based practice (EBP) implies which of the following, if any?
   a. One outcome is desired over others
   b. The practice is measurable
   c. The practice is defined according to practical realities
   d. All of the above
   e. None of the above

6. Official in-service training on cultural competence topics should usually be conducted by personnel within the agency, and external instructors should be used to augment such training when and where desired by agency administrators.
   a. True
   b. False

7. Learning organizations have the inherent ability to adapt and change, improving performance through continual revision of goals, objectives, policies, and procedures.
   a. True
   b. False

8. _____
_____ is a governing principle of cultural competence that is reflected in the goals, objectives, and/or activities of the agency. It is a decision on an issue not resolved on the basis of facts and logic only.
   a. Goals of cultural competence
   b. Culturally competent policy
   c. Culturally competent activities
   d. Culturally competent objectives
   e. None of the above

9. Whenever possible, personnel from the local community should provide or at least assist in the training. This provides an added personal link between the agency and members of the community.
   a. True
   b. False
10. The _____
    _____ approach trains staff to

utilize their own sense of professional discretion, ethical bearing, and sound judgment to address scenarios where there is no absolutely clear response.
   a. Solution-Focused Learning Approach
   b. Discretion-Development Learning Approach
   c. Problem-Based Learning Approach
   d. Problem-Resolution Learning Approach
   e. None of the above

Essay Discussion Questions

1. Provide a discussion on why and how a community mediation agreement might be necessary and what it might address when considering the need for culturally competent agency responses.
2. Provide an overview of how the assessment–training–evaluation cycle is implemented within criminal justice agencies. Provide your own example of how you would implement this process into an agency.
3. Identify outcome evaluation and evidence-based practices. Explain how outcome evaluations are related to the development of evidence-based practices within an agency.

References

Bureau of Justice Assistance, Center for Program Evaluation. (2007). *Reporting and using evaluation results.* Washington, DC: Author. Retrieved from: http://www.ojp.usdoj.gov/BJA/evaluation/ sitemap.htm.

Colorado Division of Criminal Justice. (2007). *Evidence based correctional practices.* Denver, CO: Office of Research and Statistics.

Dana, R. H., Behn, J. D., & Gonwa, T. (1992). A checklist for the examination of cultural competence in social service agencies. *Research of Social Work Practice, 2*, 220–233.

Government Accountability Office. (2006). *Guidance and standards are needed for measuring the effectiveness of agencies' facility protection efforts.* Washington, DC: United States Government Accountability Office.

Friel, C. M. (2008). Advanced research design. Retrieved from: www.shsu.edu/~icc_cmf.

Johnson, C. (2006). Know the new neighbors: With Asian influx, Quincy leaders work on cultural competency. *Boston Globe.* Retrieved from: http://www.boston.com/news/local/articles/2006/04/20/know_the_new_neighbors.

National Crime Prevention Council. (1995). *Cultural diversity: An integral part of community oriented policing.* Arlington, VA: National Crime Prevention Council.

National Institute of Justice. (1992). *Evaluating drug control and system improvement projects: Guidelines for projects supported by the bureau of justice assistance.* Washington, DC: United States Department of Justice.

National Institute of Justice. (2005). *Implementing evidence based practice in corrections.* Washington, DC: United States Department of Justice.

New York State Office of Mental Health. (2008). *NYS OMH fact sheet: Cultural competence, evidenced based practices and planning.* Albany, NY: Author. Retrieved from: http://www.omh.state.ny.us/ omhweb/ebp/culturalcompetence.htm.

Robbins, S. P. (2005). *Organizational behavior* (11th ed.). Upper Saddle River, NJ: Prentice Hall.

Shusta, M., Levine, D. R., Wong, H. Z., Olson, A .T., & Harris, P. R. (2011). *Multicultural law enforcement: Strategies for peacekeeping in a diverse society* (5th ed.). Upper Saddle River, NJ: Prentice Hall.

United States Department of Justice Community Relations Service. (2005). *Mediation agreement between the Milwaukee Police Department and the Milwaukee Commission on Police Community Relations.* Chicago, IL: Midwest Regional Office for U. S. Department of Justice Community Relations Service.

Van Keulen, C. (1988). *Colorado alternative sentencing programs: Program guidelines.* Washington, DC: National Institute of Corrections. Retrieved from: http://www. nicic.org/pubs/pre/007064.pdf.

Future Multicultural Trends in Criminal Justice

LEARNING OBJECTIVES

After reading this chapter, students should be able to do the following:

1. Identify and discuss current trends within the criminal justice system that will impact minority relationships.
2. Understand various alternative criminal justice practices that are gaining in popularity and how these techniques may reduce minority disparities.
3. Discuss challenges for minority offenders related to recent trends.
4. Discuss how globalization and cultural changes impact the current criminal justice system.

KEY TERMS

Globalization

Community justice

Community policing

Environmental Crime Prevention

Addiction

Decriminalization

Legalization

Legalized

Loss of control

Drug courts

Evidence-based practices (EBPs)

Restorative justice

INTRODUCTION

The preceding chapters have provided an overview of what is known of the various minority and cultural groups and how the criminal justice system impacts their lives. The purpose of these chapters has been to show a broad historical context for how the present-day system evolved, present what is known about how minorities have been and continue to be affected by this system, and provide likelihoods of how the system will further evolve and impact minorities. In this context, race, culture, gender, and class intersect with the criminal justice system and in turn alter each other. Culture is changed related to how laws are written and how enforcement of the law occurs. For example, African American communities have been tremendously impacted by the War on Drugs and the subsequent high incarceration rates of young African American men. In part, the criminal justice system is responsible for removing male role models from African American communities, which disrupts family structures both emotionally and economically.

The criminal justice system also changes related to its involvement with minorities and how the public views these interactions. One example is that of the Rodney King assault. Because of the publicity gathered by this event, a nationwide dialog began that focused attention on police brutality and racial profiling. This media attention greatly influenced the laws and policies initiated by agencies and continues to affect how police interact with minorities. Given this, the criminal justice system should be understood as a dynamic entity that constantly changes related to its interaction with various cultural influences. This chapter is a summation of what has been presented in the previous chapters and, as such, will not include Current Events and International Focus features. This chapter will instead focus on, what we believe to be, likely future practices and trends in the criminal justice system of the United States, given the continued impact that both domestic and international cultural influences have upon society. With the focus being on the future practices and trends that are likely, given the impact of culture on the system.

Continued Globalization

As we noted at the beginning of this text, globalization will continue to be an important feature of the evolving criminalization system. As defined in previous chapters, **globalization** is defined as the instantaneous exchange between world cultures of ideas, capital, and goods that has occurred related to advances in telecommunications and travel over the last few decades. The creation of the internet and wireless devices has dramatically transformed our present age to lead some to conclude that "the world is flat." Thomas Friedman originally coined this term to refer to global economies; however, there is an increased awareness that globalization is also impacting all areas of the criminal justice system. As Friedman explains, advances in communications, travel, commerce, and technology have broken down barriers between nations and between individuals. Globalization has had a leveling effect, making the world more accessible to all. These advances have allowed small groups of criminals to achieve operational statuses that could only previously be achieved by nations or companies. Globalization has brought about the development of many newer/more sophisticated forms of crime, including human trafficking, cybercrime, homegrown terrorism, illegal immigration, etc. Moreover, globalization has changed the face of crime and how it is curtailed. In response to the changing of the criminal element, law enforcement has been forced to change as well. It is understood that enforcement in an age of globalization must rely on world partners in order to combat global crime.

The legal and judicial system is also being required to change in order to keep up with the current advances. One area of particular concern is how best to intercept communications between crime rings in order to prevent crimes from actually occurring. Because laws are often built around older technologies and require court orders, law enforcement is often slow to respond to these global threats. Laws that protect privacy frequently delay the response of enforcement agents. There will continue to be an ongoing debate about individual privacy rights and the need for advanced surveillance abilities.

An Emphasis on Cultural Competence Will Continue to Be Important

Chapter 5 of this text addressed cultural competence and the increasing representation of minority offenders in the criminal justice system. It is clear that the United States is becoming more racially and culturally diverse. Indeed, the need for multilingual skills and understanding of differing religious beliefs, lifestyle orientations, and other matters of diversity will become mandatory for future employees in the area of community corrections. The continued diversity among the offender population, along with other challenges (such as mental health needs), means that caseloads for officers are likely to become much more complicated in the future. Naturally, this can add to the already stressful conditions under which supervision officers work and will mean that agencies will need to find the means to mitigate these challenges and their associated stress.

There Will Be a Continued Reliance on Community Involvement and Community Justice

The community must be involved in the process. This means that the average citizen must both know of the offender and any programs where they can be involved. This is important and it requires that the agency provide aggressive advertisement and community awareness campaigns. Community supervision agents should visit not just the offender-client's home, but also other homes in the neighborhood to increase the informal social controls and human supervision that are in place.

During the past decade, community supervision has seen partnerships emerge between police agencies, faith-based organizations, civic associations, social service agencies, and a wide range of other specialized organizations. In this emerging collaborative schema, community supervision agencies are considered as the leader in addressing crime as a community-based social problem. Thus, community supervision agencies must often spearhead any conjoint community action when supervising special needs offenders. This is best achieved through the implementation of a community justice orientation. According to Clear and Cole (2002), **Community Justice** should be thought of as simultaneously being a philosophy of justice, a strategy of justice, and a combination of justice programs. When creating a community justice orientation within a given community, Clear and Cole (2002) note that there are three essential components: community policing, environmental crime prevention, and restorative justice.

Community Policing employs methods of creating partnerships between the police and the community. This means that programs such as neighborhood watch, citizens patrol, and so forth are utilized to create a working relationship between citizens and the police. Furthermore, community policing is intended to make the police the friends of the community and will often be decentralized in nature so that individual officers can mill about the community to build more personal and individualized relationships within the community. This form of policing is likewise effective when dealing with diverse communities. Indeed, the community policing model has been found to be particularly effective in fighting problems of gang infestation within racial and/or ethic-based communities. This is particularly true because often the gang members will victimize weaker members of their own racial group (such as with Chinese gangs or Latino gangs and protection or extortion rackets), making it difficult for officers to detect such crime. Officers who are fluent in the primary language of such a community will have more informal exposure to community members and is often in a better position to detect such subversive victimization.

Condon (2003) further notes how police will need to not only coordinate with the community citizen on a more effective level, but that it will be in the mutual best interests for police and community supervision officers to also routinely collaborate. For community supervision officers, rising caseloads place an ever-growing burden on individual officers and any supervisory assistance they can get makes their job, and the stress of that job, much easier to handle. Moreover, this makes the supervision process much more effective in detecting offender noncompliance. For police, the advantage is in the intensive background tracking that probation departments are able to provide, as well as the ability to search the homes, persons, and lives of those who are most likely to be repeat problems while they patrol their neighborhood beats. This eliminates much of the pain associated with policing, particular in communities that have disproportionate offender population. Thus, community policing officers and community supervision officers work hand-in-hand quite naturally and with little extra effort needed to substantially improve the quality of oversight of minority offenders.

Environmental Crime Prevention component of a community justice orientation will determine why certain areas of a jurisdiction are more crime prone than others. This is important in the prevention of crime and it is specifically important when attempting to supervise special needs offenders. Areas rampant with drugs are important to locate to deter drug offenders from recidivism, areas of the town where prostitution is known to occur should be monitored and supervised by community supervision and police officers to deter female offenders from engaging in the business of illicit sex services, and areas known to have gang problems should be saturated to diminish gang influence in that community and to improve the odds of prior gang member on community supervision who are trying to get out of their previous lifestyle.

POLICE WILL NEED INCREASED KNOWLEDGE ABOUT IMMIGRANT POPULATIONS AND YOUNGER POPULATIONS

As seen in Chapter 7, immigrant populations have continued to grow in various areas of the nation. This demographic development has required police agencies to consider various new programs and approaches to policing in their community. One of the key needs for these agencies is knowledge and training for officers. In many cases, agencies are reaching to the minority communities for a solution to these problems. Indeed, the use of citizen volunteers from these communities can provide the additional expertise needed in the agency and can also improve agency relations with the community. Furthermore, both community-wide and agency-wide training can be provided by these volunteers who work in tandem with police trainers, thereby further integrating training on immigrant minority issues and, at the same time, bridging gaps between the community and the agency.

We have also noted in Chapter 12 that among the juvenile population, there is an increased proportion who are (and will continue to be) of a racial or ethnic minority group. This is particularly true with the Latino American population. It is interesting to point out that while the Latino American population is the fastest growing minority within the borders of the United States, it also shares additional characteristics of other immigrant populations. However, as Latino American youth are born and raised in the United States, we have seen that fewer and fewer are learning or retaining their use of the Spanish language. Rather, they often speak English as their first language or speak English, only. Thus, over time, some of the language challenges for law enforcement will be ameliorated but, at the same time, we will see an increase in the younger population, particularly among the Latino American population, which has the highest birth rate in the nation.

There Will be a Movement away from Prisons toward Community Supervision

As previously identified in Chapter 11, perhaps the greatest obstacle facing the current practice of corrections is the sheer numbers of offenders being placed behind bars and the subsequent costs involved in housing these offenders. In the past three decades, the prison population has exploded largely related to stricter sentencing laws, the increased enforcement efforts that are part of the U.S. drug policy, and high recidivism rates. The United States maintains the lead as the world's top incarcerator. This is evidenced by noting that although the United States only constitutes 5 percent of the world's population, it maintains 25 percent of the world's incarcerated population. It is noteworthy that the groups most affected by this dramatic increase are African American and Hispanic, which are incarcerated at rates in excess of 4 times that of whites.

Coinciding with the increased number of prisoners is the associated societal costs of housing those prisoners. The visible costs of incarceration include the costs of prosecuting and housing offenders. This economic cost alone is staggering, noting that the Federal government spends approximately $68 billion annually on corrections combined with each state (which is approximately 7 percent of each state budget) and local government's apportionment. It is noteworthy that hidden costs, such as the financial and social effects of incarceration on the families and the inmate, are arguably far greater (in economic terms) than the visible costs.

Given the recent financial downturns associated with the recession of 2007, a strain has been created wherein Federal, state, and local governments are hard-pressed to finance the current incarceration trends. Arguably, prior to this downturn, there existed few economic reasons to change this course. To understand this, one only need to understand that the prison system, as an industry, employed over 600,000 persons nationally and provided substantial livelihoods to the communities that housed these facilities. However, this trend of building new facilities and incarcerating as a first option seems to have plateaued.

This can be evidenced by a recent Department of Labor report that indicates that the growth in the employment sector of correctional employees is only expected to grow by 5 percent per year until 2020. This rate of growth is below the rate of growth of other industries (average of 14 percent), noting that it is projected that prisons will be less relied on as a form of correction than alternative community options. In contrast, the Department of Labor anticipates a dramatic increase in the number of probation officers and caseworkers within the same period. One would naturally conclude that this implies that Federal, state, and local governments will increasingly rely on community-based supervision solutions to replace the more costly expense of incarceration.

This movement toward community supervision is a reasonable approach considering the types of offenses that are currently garnering prison sentences. It is estimated that fewer than 8 percent of Federal offenders, 52 percent of state offenders, and 28 percent of local offenders are behind bars related to violent offenses. Further, the rate of violent crime over the last 30 years has remained fairly constant, noting that the bulk of the rise in the rate of incarceration has been to accommodate non-violent drug offenders. The key rational for imprisonment over other forms of correction is that the offender is physically removed from the community in order to prevent further harm to the public. However, the truth behind the current incarceration trend is that the majority of offenders: (1) pose only slight risks to the community related to violence or physical harm to others, (2) will return to the community in a relatively short timeframe, (3) upon return will likely not have received treatment for the addictive disorder that precipitated the offense, and (4) will not have obtained appropriate skills and resources to successfully navigate the return to the community. Arguably, the non-violent offender is made worse off by the practice of incarceration, and as a result, becomes a further burden to society upon release.

Disable/Elderly Offender Populations Will Continue to Increase and Be Shifted to Community Supervision

The entire population is graying in the United States and in other industrialized countries. In addition, the prison population in the United States is graying at a faster rate than is the general society beyond prison walls. This issue has been given considerable attention in recent years, with Texas, California, Florida, New York, and Louisiana all experiencing a rise in per capita elderly inmates that are incarcerated. The states just mentioned either have the largest prison population or have the highest rates of incarceration in the United States. In all cases, the costs associated with the elderly inmate are exponentially higher than those associated with younger inmates. This leads to other issues for administrators, such as the possibility of early release of inmates who are expected to die soon and the implementation of human caregiver programs such as Hospice, as well as accountability to the public. It is this accountability that places prison administrators in a dilemma, since public safety is the primary concern for all custodial programs. The sobering reality is that, like it or not, society will, one way or another, pay the expenses of keeping elderly inmates.

It is with this point in mind that state-level correctional systems will need to increase their use of community supervision programs for elderly offenders, including those who are chronically ill. This may seem to be an oversimplified recommendation, but it is one that has not truly been implemented by many states. Most states do have programs designed for the early release of elderly inmates, but these programs are not used extensively. The recommendation here is that community supervision be automatically implemented when an inmate reaches the age of 60, unless the offender is a bona fide pedophile or child molester. In the case of pedophiles, the typical risk assessment methods should remain intact, since these offenders have such poor prognoses for reform. However, all other elderly inmates should be automatically placed on community supervision, since this would reduce costs of upkeep significantly.

Sentencing May Become More Indeterminate in Nature

In January 2005, the U.S. Supreme Court held in *United States v. Booker* that Federal judges no longer are required to follow the sentencing guidelines that had been in effect since 1987. The High Court held that Federal judges now must only consider these guidelines with certain other sentencing criteria when deciding a defendant's punishment. Because of this ruling, and because of the trend toward community supervision, alternative sanctions, and restorative justice, it is speculated that sentencing will become more indeterminate in nature.

Whether this is for the better or for the worse is not completely clear, but it has historically been the case that the criminal justice system operates on a spectrum with punitive philosophies being at one end while reformative philosophies are on the other. The previous 10–15 years have been reflective of a crime control model of criminal justice that has had an emphasis on mandatory minimums for sentencing as well as purely determinate sentencing schemes. Historically speaking, the timing may begin to swing toward less-restrictive prison sentencing, which may lead to more use of community corrections.

Although crime has decreased in the past few years, the populations within prisons and the resulting costs associated with this massive imprisonment continue to grow. It may well be that although the increased imprisonment rates may be speculated to be the cause for lower crime rates, other factors are at play. Furthermore, even if this is the main reason for lower crime rates, the public may not keep that in mind and instead can become lulled into comfort. Amidst this may the incorporation of alternative sanctions. And this might not be a detrimental shift to public safety if programs like house arrest and GPS tracking are utilized effectively (see Chapter 1).

Therefore, in the long term it is likely that we will see more and more special needs offenders within our community. Because these offenders are not necessarily more violent than other offenders, and because of the continued use of community sanctions, it is the belief of this author that special needs offenders will become an increasing area of focus as community supervision continues to develop.

Further, Paparozzi (2003) notes that both international and national research have been effective at determining those correctional programs that reduce offender recidivism from those that do not. In fact, the results from most of this research would extend a great degree of optimism toward the effectiveness of community supervision. However, the public perception of community supervision still remains negative due to misunderstanding and due to the failure of many agencies to not only provide clear evaluative data on their programs, but their failure to publicize this data, especially in the media. Paparozzi (2003) states that "the absence of clear and convincing program evaluation data establishes the foundation for ideologically driven, as opposed to the more preferred evidence-based policies, programs, and practices" (p. 47).

This is a very good point because criminal justice policy is often driven by ideology and by media portrayals of the justice system. Paparozzi (2003) contends that when given a more research-based approach of analysis that is more or less objective in nature, it will be found that a treatment-based approach is more likely to reduce crime the most on a long-term basis. This is of course, the contention of this text as well (as was indicated in Chapter 1). This support of rehabilitation (indeed, even forced treatment has some effect) will ultimately show that with rehabilitation-based offender supervision programs, there is a resultant decrease in recidivism rates within the same local area.

At the time of writing this piece, over 60 percent of all offenders who are in the custody of correctional systems around the nation are on probation or parole (Clear & Cole, 2002). Furthermore, over 60 percent of these offenders receive some form of specialized treatment for some factor that led to their criminal offending. Thus, it is clear that there will be an increased need for programs relevant to special needs offenders. How community supervision agencies meet this need will affect public opinion toward these programs, which in turn will affect the ability to gain community involvement and support. Thus, administrators within community supervision departments will become the lead advocates in demonstrating the usefulness and importance of community supervision with special needs offenders since it will be these personnel who will be tasked with supervising such offenders. Ensuring that the media correctly portrays such offenders and that public perceptions of safety are kept intact will be the job and concern of these administrators. This reflects the fact that special needs offenders must be understood to have unique and specialized challenges that require attention from us all since they are, in effect, part of the community in need. Moreover, it is the lack of attention to these needs that results in aberrant behavior—aberrant behavior that becomes criminal and disrupts our communities. Related to the publics' need to understand the specialized concerns of offenders in order to facilitate community healing, supervision agency administrators must play the role of community healer through the fostering of collaborations between the offender and all other members of the community at large.

Early Prevention of Criminal Behavior/Addictions Will Continue to Be Promoted

To reduce the likelihood of incarceration, special attention should be paid to those persons at risk for developing addictive diseases and/or engaging in delinquent behavior. Of all of the risks associated with incarceration, attention should be paid to the risk factors regarding the onset of drug use involvement on the part of adolescents (See Figure 15-1). This is related to the fact that **addiction** is considered a "disease of adolescents" and that if the use of addictive substances can be delayed past the young adulthood phase (25 years of age or younger), then the chances of developing addictions can likely be averted. As a consequence of avoiding addictions, criminal involvement is likewise deterred. This does not mean, however, that a strict focus on this developmental period can completely mitigate problems because many of the personality traits and behavioral symptoms become present at very young ages (as early as four years of age). What this approach does mean is that behavioral signs

Risk Factors	Domain	Protective Factors
Early Aggressive Behavior	Individual	Self-Control
Poor Social Skills	Individual	Positive Relationships
Lack of Parental Supervision	Family	Parental Monitoring and Support
Substance Abuse	Peer	Academic Competence
Drug Availability	School	Anti-Drug Use Policies
Poverty	Community	Strong Neighborhood Attachment

FIGURE 15-1 Examples of Risk and Protective Factors. *Source:* National Institute of Drug Abuse. (2008). *Drugs, brains, and behaviors: The science of addiction.* Retrieved from: http://www.drugabuse.gov/publications/science-addiction/drug-abuse-addiction.

and symptoms must be acknowledged for children who are at risk and those children should be provided special attention through educational, social, and community supports until they are established as young adults. School prevention measures are designed to address the drug involvement risk factors, enhance the protective factors, target children who have additional risk factors above what the average pupil encounters, and intervene with youth who have already begun drug use. These approaches have been proven to reduce drug use among school-aged children, thus also reducing their risk for further delinquency and criminal involvement. All of these points were noted in Chapters 12 and 13, but we present them here to show how this will continue to be a trend in the future. As we have seen, minority youth can benefit, in particular, from programs that address risk and protective factors.

Drug Enforcement Strategy Will Be Adjusted to Represent Demand-Side Strategies

As stated previously in Chapter 11, the United States' approach to substance abuse is the most significant factor for the current incarceration trend. Currently, the Federal government spends approximately two-thirds of its $24 billion drug enforcement budget on enforcement-related activities. Given this, one would naturally expect that arrests, prosecutions, and incarcerations would roughly imitate the focus of spending. In order for this trend to change, an alternate view of how to best impact the demand for drugs needs to be applied. Traditional enforcement strategies primarily focus on reducing the supply of drugs to the end consumer, whereas demand-side philosophies work to reduce the end consumers' demand for the drug. Two conjoint prominent viewpoints of demand-side drug demand reduction strategies involve the **decriminalization** of drugs and enhanced treatment options. Decriminalization refers to removing the criminal sanctions related to the possession of certain quantities of substances. This means that a person is allowed to possess up to a certain quantity of a drug before criminal sanctions are applied. Persons caught with a misdemeanor amount of drugs would be evaluated for a substance dependency issue, fined, and/or remanded to treatment. A perhaps even more liberal view of removing penalties for drug use would be the complete removal of any penalty for mere use of substances. This effectively is known as **legalization**. Legalization prescribes rules as to who can use substances and how they might be used as well as regulates how the drugs are manufactured and distributed. Examples of **legalized** drugs include alcohol, tobacco, and prescription narcotics.

The advantage to the decriminalization and/or legalization of drugs is the cost savings related to a reduction of criminal justice involvement with non-violent drug offenders (See Table 15-1). It is estimated that if drugs were legalized there would be a $41.3 billion costs saving per year to both Federal and state governments. Additionally, if drugs were regulated and taxed like other products, it is estimated that $46.7 billion would be collected through taxation ($8.7 billion from marijuana and $38 billion from all other drugs). It is understood in this model that the cost savings and taxes collected through decriminalization/legalization would be used to support treatment and prevention efforts, which are largely seen to be more effective at preventing the development of addictive illnesses (thus a switch to demand-side tactics).

TABLE 15-1 Federal Drug Control Spending by Function (Budget Authority in Millions)

Function	FY 2012 Final	FY 2013 Annualized Continuing Resolution	FY 2014 Request
Treatment	7,848.3	8,082.4	9,261.6
Percentage	32.0	32.9	36.5
Prevention	1,339.2	1,289.5	1,408.7
Percentage	5.5	5.3	5.5
Domestic Law Enforcement	9,439.5	9,348.8	9,562.9
Percentage	38.5	38.1	37.7
Interdiction	4,036.5	3,869.7	3,705.0
Percentage	16.5	15.8	14.6
International	1,833.7	1,946.0	1,455.0
Percentage	7.5	7.9	5.7
Total	**$24,497.2**	**$24,536.4**	**$25,393.2**

Source: National Drug Control Budget: FY 2014 Funding Highlights, Executive Office of the President, Office of National Drug Control Policy, April 2013, Table 1, p. 12.

Decriminalization and legalization are deeply divisive ideas with strong supporters on both sides of the issue. Proponents of decriminalization/legalization efforts point to Portugal's liberal approach to drug use through decriminalization. Twelve years after this experiment began (2001), Portugal claims to have reduced drug use by half, encouraged more problem users to engage in treatment, and ultimately saved the government millions of dollars. Naysayers to decriminalization/legalization efforts often note that the societal consequences are unknown and therefore cost savings may never actually be realized. The main societal concerns involve increased crime, exposure of youth to substances, an increase in mental disorders related to drug use, increased health burdens related to use, and increased number of accidental deaths related to drug use.

Treatment Strategy Will Become of Greater Importance as Enforcement Strategy Changes

It is estimated that for every dollar spent on substance abuse treatment there is up to $18.2 in societal costs that are saved. Treatment remains the most effective way to reduce crime and incarceration through ameliorating the most prominent underlying factor—addictions. Treatment strategies emphasize that addiction is not a crime but is rather a brain disorder that has been caused related to prolonged exposure to mood-altering substances. The symptoms of the disease of addiction are marked by a **loss of control** in which the addicted person no longer makes rational decisions about his/her general wellbeing. This loss of control explains why persons addicted to substances are capable of participating in activities that are irrational and often times illegal, all with the main purpose of obtaining more of the substance of dependence.

Drug courts have increasingly become a preferred model of treatment for substance abusing offenders. According to the National Association for Drug Court

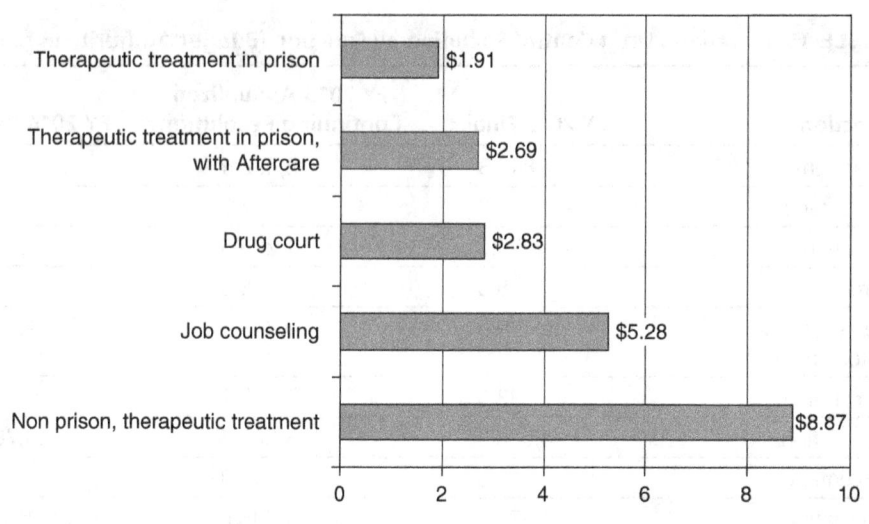

FIGURE 15-2 Treatment Alternatives Potential Cost Savings. *Source:* Aos, S., Phipps, P., Barnoski, R., & Lieb, R. (2001). The comparative costs and benefits of programs to reduce crime. Retrieved from: http://www.wsipp.wa.gov/rptfiles/costbenefit.pdf.

Professionals, drug courts are the most effective justice treatment option for non-violent drug offenders (see Figure 15-2).

Drug courts are defined as:

> A specially designed court calendar or docket, the purposes of which are to achieve a reduction in recidivism and substance abuse among nonviolent substance abusing offenders and to increase the offender's likelihood of successful habilitation through early, continuous, and intense judicially supervised treatment, mandatory periodic drug testing, community supervision, and use of appropriate sanctions and other rehabilitation services.

Although the drug court system proved to be an effective alternative to incarceration, there has been criticism that this approach has not been as effective for ethnic minorities. First, it is frequently remarked that ethnic minorities do not have equal representation in drug court programing. Drug court is seen as a lesser penalty and therefore critics would claim that minorities frequently receive harsher punishments

TABLE 15-2	**Minority Representation in Drug Courts Compared with Other Criminal Justice Programs**			
	African American	**% Difference in Drug Courts**	**Hispanic and Latino or Latina**	**% Difference in Drug Courts**
Drug Courts	21%		10%	
Arrestees	28%	−7%	Not Reported	
Probationers and Paroles	28%	−7%	13%	−3%
Jail Inmates	39%	−18%	16%	−6%
Prison Inmates	44%	−23%	20%	−10%

Source: Marlow, D. (2011). Achieving racial and ethnic fairness in drug courts. *Court Review, 49,* 40–47. (Adapted from: Huddleston, C. W., & Marlowe, D. B. (2011). *Painting the current picture: A national report on drug courts and other problem-solving court programs in the United States.* Washington, DC: National Drug Court Institute—Table 6.)

and that this fact is borne out in disparate drug court representation. This line of reasoning follows the basic trend for minorities who are placed on community supervision, noting that minorities are much more likely to receive prison or jail sentences vs. community supervision. Underrepresentation of minorities in drug courts relates to how persons are selected to participate in programming. To have equal representation between ethnic groups, one would expect parity between percentage of persons arrested and on probation and parole as is enrolled in drug court (Marlow, 2013). According to Huddleston and Marlow (2011) (above), African Americans are arrested and placed on probation and parole significantly more than they are remanded to participate in drug court (difference of 7 percent). Hispanic Americans similarly are afforded less access to drug treatment programing (difference of 3 percent). This may point to inequalities that, in part, are created by structural racism that is part of the judicial system. In any event, drug courts should begin to carefully consider the ethnic and racial makeup of participants to ensure that groups have equal access to programming. A second concern regarding drug courts includes the criticism that drug court programming may not actually meet the needs of minority clients. Substance abuse treatment programming has its early beginnings from the Alcoholics Anonymous (AA) movement, which began in the early part of the 20th century and was modeled after the Oxford Group. The Oxford Group was a program that attempted to recreate the principles of the early Christian Church. These principles included many of the ideologies that are maintained in AA that emphasize the "spiritual" components of addictive behaviors. As can be seen from the progression of the AA movement, AA principles (12 steps) were very useful for helping many persons recover. It is noteworthy though that these principles were likely easily integrated by those who sought recovery during this time period related to the fact that those seeking help were largely white males from Protestant backgrounds. One might conclude that the reasons why this approach was successful for this group of people were because it reinforced values and behaviors that were already part of the culture, it created a sense of familiarity related to the shared values, and it provided the necessary supports that are indicated when someone is attempting to recover from an addictive illness. Juxtaposed to the AA movement is a modern era of substance abuse treatment that is available to a more diverse group of persons from varied ethnic, racial, and religious groups. Despite the influx of more diverse backgrounds seeking treatment, the substance abuse treatment community has been slow at adopting many of the modern **evidence-based practices (EBPs)** that have been shown to be effective with these subpopulations. This slow integration of EBPs (those practices that have empirical research to support the claim of their effectiveness) is likely due to historical background of the substance abuse treatment field that has grown out of a paraprofessional group that found personal recovery through AA principles. As such, many of these same principles are reinforced despite the fact that there exists no empirical support that they are effective when working with diverse groups. A final criticism of drug courts is that they are not as effective for minorities as they are for non-minority groups. As noted previously, one reason for drug courts being less effective for minorities is that the treatment considerations frequently do not address minority's individual needs. Furthermore, minorities often experience more barriers to receiving treatment and recovering than do non-minorities. For example, non-minorities often do not have to struggle with transportation issues as do minorities. Other barriers may include the communities where minorities live (which are more likely to have both a criminal and drug presence), access to childcare, being able to develop healthy non-using supports, and concerns related to general poverty.

MENTAL HEALTH COURTS As stated in Chapter 10, one of the precipitants of the modern correctional influx is related to the deinstitutionalization process that began in the United States beginning in the early 1950s. A summarizing statement may conclude that, "prisons may now be the largest provider of mental health services in the United States" (Fellner, 2006, p 391). In general, minorities are less likely than non-minorities to receive quality mental healthcare within the community. Given this fact, they are more likely to have exacerbated mental health systems (e.g., untreated psychotic disorders) that lead to criminal charges. In part, untreated mental illness is responsible for the disparate treatment of minorities in the criminal justice system.

One possible community solution to incarceration of mentally ill minority offenders is through the use of mental health courts. Similar to their drug court counterpart, mental health courts are designed to create alternatives to incarceration, provide more appropriate long-term treatment for offenders, alleviate the burden on the criminal justice system, and reduce recidivism. Again, this is achieved in a similar fashion to the drug courts through the use of interdisciplinary teams from both treatment and judicial realms that work together to design programming that will best meet the needs of the offender.

There Will Continue to Be a Strong Emphasis on Reentry

As stated in Chapter 10, the practice of incarceration has "a tremendously negative effect on those incarcerated." Being incarcerated affects the offender's well-being, potentially places the community that he returns to at risk by a heightened exposure to communicable diseases, and unduly burdens families to which they will return. Unfortunately, despite the many strains that incarceration places on the offender and his/her support systems, few programs are in place to mitigate multiple stressors that offenders will experience when they return to their communities.

Once released, most offenders will return to the same communities where the same criminal risk factors are present. To reduce recidivism, effective reentry strategies must be implemented that target an offender's critical risk categories. Although there is no "one best fit" for reentry initiatives, there are general categories of focus that are known to reduce an offender's risk of recidivism. It is hoped that by reducing these risk factors recidivism can be reduced, thus significantly impacting the correctional system.

SUBSTANCE ABUSE Perhaps no greater reentry risk dominates the literature than that of substance abuse. Substance abuse is the most common health risk amongst the prison population, which has both public health and public safety implications. The most prevalent crime-linked drug, alcohol abuse, has being implicated in the commission of 80 percent of all crimes (Belenko, 1998). More than half of all state prisoners admit to being under the influence of alcohol or drugs at the time they committed their crime and nearly one in five prisoners admitted to performing a crime in order to get money to buy drugs (Mumola, 1999).

Despite the fact that there is a high prevalence of substance abuse illness within the prison system, there is virtually no treatment that exists within prisons. It has been estimated that fewer than 10 percent of prisoners that need substance abuse treatment ever receive it while incarcerated. Once released, there is little in the way of transitional substance abuse care and community follow-up. It has been estimated that as many as two-thirds of all substance abusers will relapse within three months of release (Wexler, Lipton, & Johnson, 1988).

COMMUNICABLE DISEASES   The second most prevalent health concern for returning offenders is that of communicable diseases. It has been estimated that nearly 25 percent of all those living with HIV/AIDS, nearly 33 percent of all those with Hep C, and nearly 33 percent of all those diagnosed with tuberculosis were released from prison within the last year. Communities where disproportionate numbers of offenders return often have heightened STD rates precipitated by both the offender's illness and transmissions to unsuspecting others with whom he/she may come into contact. Prevention of illness should begin with proper screening for STDs both while incarcerated and post release.

MENTAL ILLNESS   The third most prevalent health concern for returning prisoners is mental illness. It has been estimated that more than 25 to 65 percent of all inmates have at least one Axis I mental health diagnosis that requires treatment (Wilper et al. 2009). It is thought that this disparity is related to persons with mental illness being arrested at disproportionate rates for non-violent crimes (e.g., vagrancy).

Despite the fact that prisons as a whole have made considerable progress in the treatment of mental illness while incarcerated, most prisons offer little in linkages to community-based programs. In a polling of prison mental health providers, many admitted to giving reentering offenders referral information to mental health providers, but almost none actually secured the appointment for the offender (Beck & Maruschak, 2001). The result is that few offenders actually enter into community-based mental health treatments post release.

Although mental health concerns alone do not increase the risk of recidivism, a mental illness paired with an addictive disorder amplifies the recidivism risk (Case Western, 2012). With this in mind, proper mental health screening and intervention remain critical components for any substance abuse treatment programs.

EMPLOYMENT CHALLENGES   Just as there is a clear relationship between crime and substance abuse, there is an equally clear relationship between crime and work. Those who reenter communities with the ability to gain legitimate work with a higher income have the best odds of not re-offending. Unfortunately, there are multiple barriers to reentering offenders obtaining legal employment. First, offenders, on average, have low levels of education and employable skills prior to being arrested. This status continues because of an overall lack of emphasis on prison-based vocational training and education programs. Moreover, even when these programs are in place, there is often a lack of transitional support to aid a person in finding employment post release. A second problem for returning offenders related to employment is the sheer length of time that they have been out of the workforce. This interrupts the offender's developmental acquisition of work skills. In today's technologically driven culture, this places the returning offender at a significant disadvantage for obtaining employment. Finally, barriers associated with institutional practices restrict offenders from gaining employment. Some career fields discriminate against (either through legal statute or policy) the hiring of those with past felonious histories. Even if not expressly barred through rule, offenders certainly are barred based on stigma that is attached to being an offender. As a result, many offenders reengage in illegal activities because they are effectively hindered from obtaining legal employment.

HOUSING CHALLENGES   Once a person is released to the community, finding affordable/stable housing becomes an issue. This is because often the offender lacks the resources to place a deposit on a housing unit. Affordable public housing is restricted for felony offenders, which further limits options. With a severely restricted range of choices, the offender frequently chooses to live with family, who are often dysfunctional, or other associates, many of whom are criminally involved. Those who cannot find housing end up homeless, where they are at heightened risk for relapse and recidivism. In some states, it is estimated that more than 50 percent of those in homeless shelters were at one time incarcerated (Burt et al., 1999).

FAMILY CHALLENGES Social connectedness with family often becomes difficult while someone is incarcerated. Visits, phone calls, and letters (the primary means of connectedness) often are ineffective in maintaining a sufficient relationship for a number of reasons. First, the average prisoner lives in excess of 100 miles from home (note: This is especially true of Louisiana prisons that house state prisoners away from home communities due to public safety concerns). Once a person is allowed to visit, they are subjected to searches and other security measures that are unpleasant, which further dissuade family members from making the trip (Hairston, 2002). Visiting hours, although set, frequently change due to prison uncertainties (e.g., improper offender counts, unanticipated security concerns), leaving family members either waiting for hours on end to see their loved ones or else altogether turned around and not allowed to visit. It is not uncommon for a loved one to travel in excess of two hours from their homes only to be denied a visit. Calling on the phone is also problematic. Many facilities charge the inmate for phone calls through the selling of calling cards. These calls are exorbitantly priced, costing sometimes more than a $1 per minute. Given that the vast majority of offenders were impoverished before they entered prison, maintaining regular communication with family in the form of phone calls is not a possibility.

Once released, families may not be welcoming to their offender relative. Families may be unwilling to allow the offender back into the home for a number of health, financial, and legal reasons. One common reason for families not wanting the family member to live with them is fear that the offender will relapse or will become mentally unstable. A second reason is related to the fact that families perceive the offender to be a financial drain. Through years of incarceration, families have elected to send money to the offender as well as pay for many of his/her outside responsibilities (e.g., children). Often, this has caused resentment to build for the family. Finally, many returning offenders come from minority communities where public housing is common. Federal law bans offenders from living in Section 8 housing, thus jeopardizing the family's entitlement if the offender does move in.

A Continued Development of Varied Supervision/ Community Techniques

Electronic technology is one promising community supervision technique that is still in the developmental phases in the use of electronic technology as part of offender supervision plans. There are many forms of electronic monitoring techniques: (1) kiosk monitoring, (2) secure remote alcohol detection, (3) Global Positioning System devices (GPS), (4) closed circuit TV facial recognition system, and (5) radio frequency identification chips (RFIDs). These systems are used to assure that offenders are within appropriate areas and observe the requirements of probation or parole (e.g., not using alcohol). To date, these devices have not been proven, in and of themselves, to reduce criminal activity, but have been shown to have enhanced the quality of treatment and supervision. These qualities include participants in substance abuse treatment having a more favorable opinion of staff and being more likely to complete treatment. Furthermore, there is some evidence that these technologies make offenders more aware of getting caught committing a re-offense and therefore deter the contemplation of participation in criminal activity.

Restorative Justice seeks to make the victim, the community, and the offender whole by restoring each to the state that existed prior to the crime. While restorative justice has been discussed extensively throughout this text, there still remains one other key point that must be stated in this concluding chapter. Restorative justice is a global phenomenon that has been implemented to one extent or another in every continent in the world (Zvekic, 1996). Indeed, it is the prediction of this text that the United States will find itself being evermore synchronous with the rest of the global family and that this type of offender processing will become used with increasing regularity since this type of justice is ideally suited to tailoring sentences to both the needs of the victim and the unique issues of minority offenders.

CONCLUSION

Today's criminal justice system is in a process of rapid change that is occurring as a result of globalization, economic downtown-turn, and the rapid expansion of technologies. From a multicultural perspective, "the world has become flat" and diverse groups are interacting in ways that were previously unattainable. This has caused the nature of crime to change as well as the way in which crime is guarded against. The future development of the criminal justice system can be summarized by stating that future approaches will need to advance "smart on crime" strategies that find ways to best make use of tightening resources in order to protect the public more effectively. All groups will likely benefit from these enlightened trends in criminal justice, but none are likely to be more impacted than minorities. Historically, it has been observed that those with the least power in society always receive lesser treatments in the eyes of the law. Hopefully, the technologically advanced society will work diligently to ensure all people have equal protections and opportunities under the law.

Chapter 15 Learning Check

1. _____
   refers to the instantaneous exchange between world cultures of ideas, capital, and goods that has occurred related to advances in telecommunications and travel over the last few decades.
   a. Drug courts
   b. Globalization
   c. Restorative justice
   d. Evidence-based practices

2. The War on Drugs is responsible for the United States incarcerating more persons per capital than any country in the world.
   a. True
   b. False

3. EBP stands for:
   a. Enriched Blank Plans
   b. Every Bold Person
   c. Evidence-Based Practice
   d. Evident Because of Pretense

4. _____ is the percentage of the world's population that the United States incarcerates.
   a. 5%
   b. 10%
   c. 15%
   d. 25%

5. In general, minorities have more recidivism risk factors than do non-minorities.
   a. True
   b. False

Essay Discussion Questions

1. How does technology and innovation influence our modern culture? Give an example of how globalization has impacted the criminal justice system.

2. What are the factors that are most related to minorities being incarcerated at a greater rate than non-minorities? Do you believe this is a result of structural racism?

References

Belenko, S. (1998). *Behind Bars: Substance abuse and America's prison population.* New York: National Center on Addiction and Substance Abuse at Columbia University.

Beck, A. J., & Maruschak, L. M. (2001). *Mental health treatment in state prisons, 2000.* Washington, DC: US Department of Justice, Office of Justice Programs, Bureau of Justice Statistics.

Burt, M. R., Laudan Y., Aron, T. D., Valente, J., Lee, E., & Iwen, B. (1999). *Homelessness: Programs and the people they serve: Findings of the National Survey of Homeless Assistance Providers and Clients.* Washington DC: The Urban Institute.

Case Western Reserve University. (2012, January 19). Mental illness protects some inmates from returning to jail. *Medical News Today.* Retrieved from: http://www.medicalnewstoday.com/releases/240445.php.

Clear, T. R., & Cole, G. F. (2002). *American corrections* (6th ed.). Belmont, CA: Wadsworth/Thomson Learning.

Condon, C. D. (2003). Falling crime rates, rising caseload numbers: Using police-probation partnerships. *Corrections Today, 65*(1), 44–49.

Fellner, J. (2006). Corrections quandary: Mental illness and prison rules. *Harvard Civil Rights-Civil Liberties Law Review, 41,* 391.

Hairston, C. F. (2002). Prisoners and families: Parenting issues during incarceration. Paper prepared for the *From prison to home: The effect of incarceration and reentry on children, families, and communities,* national policy conference convened by the U.S. Department of Justice and the Urban Institute. Washington, DC: U.S. Department of Justice and the Urban Institute January 30–31.

Marlow, D. (2013). Achieving racial and ethnic fairness in drug courts. *American Judges Association Court Review, 49.* Retrieved From: http://aja.ncsc.dni.us/publications/courtrv/cr49-1/CR49-1Marlowe.pdf.

Mumola, C. J. (1999). Substance abuse and treatment: State and federal prisoners, 1997. *Bureau of Justice Statistics, Special Report.* Washington, DC: U.S. Department of Justice.

Paparozzi, M. (2003). Probation, parole and public safety: The need for principled practices versus faddism and circular policy development. *Corrections Today, 65*(5), 46–51.

Shusta, R. M., Levine, D. R., Wong, H. Z., & Harris, P. R. (2004). *Multicultural law enforcement: Strategies for peacekeeping in a diverse society* (3rd ed.). Upper Saddle Rive, NJ: Prentice Hall.

Wexler, H. K., Lipton, D. S., & Johnson, B. D. (1988). *A criminal justice system strategy for treating cocaine-heroin abusing offenders in custody.* Issues and practices paper in criminal justice (USGPO No. 1988-202-045:8-0082). Washington, DC: National Institute of Justice.

Wilper, A. P., Woolhandler, S., Boyd, J. W., Lasser, K. E., McCormick, D., Bor, D. H., & Himmelstein, D. U. (2009). The health and health care of US prisoners: Results of a nationwide survey. *American Journal of Public Health, 99*(4), 666–672.

Zvekic, U. (1996). Probation in an International Perspective. *Overcrowded Times, 7*(2), 5–8.

INDEX

A

Abuse
  abandonment, 67
  emotional abuse, 67
  exploitation, 67
  neglect, 67
  physical abuse, 66
  self-neglect, 67
  sexual abuse, 66
Acculturation, 29–30, 40–41
  adjusting, 112
  associated issues, 44
  categories of, 112
  choosing, 112
  definition, 29
  degree of, 112–13
  frame-of-reference, 36
  importance of, 326
  level of, 122
  preserving, 112
  surviving, 112
Activities of daily living, 67
ADA. See Americans with Disabilities Act (1990)
ADC. See Arab Anti-Discrimination Committee
Addams, Jane, 81
Addictions, 256–258
  addictive illnesses, conundrum of, 257
  drug policy, 258
  link between crime and substance abuse, 257
  recidivism, 257
  substance abusers, 258
  substance addiction-crime connection, 257–258
  substance use illness, 257
ADEA. See Age Discrimination in Employment Act (1967)
ADLs. See Activities of daily living
Adolescent Family Life (AFL) program, 314
Affirmative action, 285–287
African Americans, 20–23, 132–134
  biased and discriminatory laws, 132
  categories of, 21
  confidence in local police, 138
  crime, impact of, 136–137
  criminal justice, impact of, 136–137
  family cohesion, 23
  forms of abuses, 133
  historical victimization, 136
  income disparity, 21
  integration into mainstream society, 132
  intergenerational trauma, 22–23
  Jim Crow laws, 22
  law enforcement and, 137–139
  marginalization of, 135
  mass victimization, 20
  modern day community, 134–137
  as plantation owners, 20
  policing and, 139
  racial discrimination, 138
  racial profiling and, 139
  slavery, 133–134
  state of race relations, 138
  structural racism, 134–135
  violence, impact of, 136–137
  working conditions, 133
Afrocentric traits, 199
Age-based policy, 72

Age discrimination, 50, 61
  cultural adultism, 50
  elderly discrimination, 50
Age Discrimination in Employment Act (1967), 50, 61
Agency tokenism, 110
Age-related illnesses, 49
Alcoholics Anonymous (AA) movement, 399
Alcoholism, 51, 63, 87, 92
Alice Stebbin Wells, 76
Alzheimer's Disease, 57
  See also Dementia
American Correctional Association, 85, 300
American exceptionalism, 33
  politically reinforced, 33
  tenets of, 33
Americans with Disabilities Act (1990), 51–52, 61–62, 64, 81
Amnesty International, 283
Anti-Drug Abuse Act, 275, 280
Anti-Gay crime, 102–103
Anti-social personality disorder, 54
Appellate Court, 229
Arab Americans, 155–156
  discrimination against, 156
  discriminatory enforcement practices, 157
  hate crimes against, 156
  patrol jurisdictions, 155
  stereotyping of, 156
  violence and hatred, 157
Arab Anti-Discrimination Committee, 156
Arthritis, 48–49
Aryan Brotherhood, 291, 293–294
Arizona v. United States (2012), 171–172
Asian alone population, 12
Asian Americans, 12, 151–154
  crime victimization, 152–153
  criminal activity, 153–154
  cultural differences, 151
  domestic violence, 153
  generational status, 152
  house robbery, 154
  lack of cultural awareness, 151
  media-catching incidents, 151
  patriarchal values, 153
  rapport establishment, difficulties, 152
  sexual assaults, 154
  street gangs, 153
  utilitarian crimes, 153
ASPD. See Anti-social personality disorder
As pure justice, 236
Assessment-evaluation cycle, 380
Assimilation, 29–32, 40–41
  associated issues, 44
  cultural, 29
  degree of, 112–113
  frame-of-reference, 36
  personal attributes, and, 30–32
  policies of, 30
  principle of, 33
  for system-blame-oriented individuals, 31
Asylums, 252–253
  beggar lunatics, 252
  behavioral illnesses, 252
  drunkenness, 252

penitentiary system, 252
schizophrenia, 252

B

Baby boom, 48, 77
Back and spine problems, 49
Bacon's Rebellion (1660),254
  See also Slavery
Bail discriminations, 227
Bail, racial disparity in, 224–225
Bail setting, 224–226, 242
  cash bond (cash only), 226
  citation release (cite out), 226
  conditions of release, 226
  immigration bond, 226
  judicial discretion, 226
  process, 225
  property bond, 226
  released on recognizance, 226
  for religious offenses, 227–228
  surety bond, 226
  victim protective orders, 226
Barrio Azteca, 294
Beggar lunatics, 252
Behavioral illnesses, 256
Bem sex role inventory, 94
BGF. See Black Guerrilla Family
BIA. See Bureau of Indian Affairs
Bilateral exchange of money, goods, 9
Bi-lingual police officers, 119–120
Bipolar disorder, 42
Black Guerrilla Family, 291
Black Muslims Movement, 294
Black traits, 199
Blended families, 307
Bloods, 292, 294
Bloody code era, 251
Blue laws, 245
Bond setting process, 225
BOP. See Federal Bureau of Prisons
Broken homes, 307–308
Bureau of Indian Affairs, 149
Burnout, 63

C

California Appeals Court, 263
California Department of Correction (CDCR), 263
Canada
  diversity and, 218
  gender equality in, 218
Canadian Bar Association, 218
Caring law enforcement, 65–66
Cash Bond (cash only), 226
Category schemas, 117
Causal schemas, 118
Centers for Disease Control, 11, 48–49, 86, 151, 314, 319–321, 323
Chain gangs, 282, 284
Change of venue, 231
Charge reduction, 229–231
Child Saver Movement, 81
Chronic illnesses, 48
Church of Jesus Christ Christian, 267
Citation release (cite out), 226
Citizen review panels, 3, 170, 172
Citizen's advisory committee, 172
CIT. See Crisis intervention teams
Citizen's rights, violation of, 140
Civil Rights Act, 51, 91
  Title VII, 176–177, 179, 198

Civil Rights movement, 84, 136, 216, 222, 294, 319
Civil Rights of Institutionalized Persons Act, 294
Civil War, 37
CJCC. See Church of Jesus Christ Christian
Clark and Doll experiments, 198
Clink, 248
CLO. See Community liaison officer
Cognitive deficits, 68
Colorblindness, 197–198
  claim in court, 197
Colorism
  adjudication, 37
  arrests, 37
  bias, 37
  impact on criminal justice, 37
  sentencing, 37
  skin color, 37
Columbus, Christopher, 18
Commission for Racial Equality, 189
Communicable diseases, 72, 258, 400–401
Community involvement
  continued reliance on, 390–391
  trust-building and, 163–165
Community justice, 206, 390–391
Community leaders, 172, 180–181, 367
Community liaison officer, 174
Community mediation agreement, 369
Community policing, 3, 103, 126, 163–165, 170–175, 390–391
  community oriented, 163
  definition, 163
  diversity, 174–175
  emergence of, 175
  in minority community, 170
  Neighborhood Watch Programs, 174
  orientation of peace keeping, 165
  strategies, 165
  types of, 173
Community-relations issues, 12
Community relations in Puerto Rico, 145
Comprehensive Drug Abuse Prevention Act, 275
Comprehensive Immigration Reform Act, 10
Conditions of release, 226
Contextual discrimination, 236–237, 239
Convention on the Elimination of All Forms of Racial Discrimination, 15
Convict lease system, 280, 282, 284
Convict transportation, 250
Cooper v. Pate, 266
COPS. See Community Oriented Policing Services
Correctional system, 3, 16, 55, 245–246, 252, 259–260, 301, 354, 381, 393, 394
Correctional workers, 288–289
  bilingual workers, 289
  diversity training programs, 289
  gender composition, 288
  racial composition, 288
Corrections, 78, 101, 199, 260, 284–285, 289, 291–293, 296–298, 350
  fags, 298
  homosexuality, 298
  institutional racism and, 280–281
  jailhouse turnouts, 298

Index

Corrections (*continued*)
  male prison hierarchies, 298
  organizational changes, 299
  Prison Rape Elimination Act, 298–299
  punks, 298
  sexual orientation and, 297–299
  sexual victimization, 298
  turning out, 298
  wolves, 298
Court of appeals, 201, 234
Courts and religious offenses, 227–228
Court System of America, 200–201
  appellate courts, 201
  civil, 200
  Commissions, 201
  criminal, 200
  diversity and, 209
  drug courts, 208
  elder courts, 208
  family courts, 207–208
  judges selection, 201–202
  juvenile courts, 207
  mental health courts, 208–209
  minority held seats in, 203
  minority judges in special courts, 210
  representation by race/ethnicity, 210
  special courts, 200–201, 207–209
  Supreme Court, 201
  trial courts, 201
  tribal courts, 203–205
Creator or Great Spirit, 149
Crib job, 69
Crime reduction initiatives, 186
Crime victim's movement, 84
Criminal justice disparities, 37–38
Criminal justice immigration
    controversies, 10–11
Criminal justice multicultural (*See*
    Multicultural criminal justice)
Criminal justice practitioners, 7
Criminal proceedings, 40–41
Criminal subculture, 328
Crips, 292
Crisis intervention teams, 56
Cross-cultural communication
    misunderstandings in Hong
    Kong, 121
Cross-linguistic interrogation, 125
Cross-linguistic interviews, 124, 125
Cross-racial identification, 122
Cross-racial inmate, 299–301
  education, 301–302
  staff training, 382
Cross-racial recognition, 123
Cruz v. Beto, 266
CSA. *See* Comprehensive Drug Abuse
    Prevention Act
Cuban Americans, 146–147
Cultural adultism, 50
Cultural blindness, 110
Cultural competence, 27–28, 108–111,
    119, 127, 186–187, 209–211,
    289, 300, 363, 366–381, 384–
    386, 389–390
  acculturation, degree of, 112–113
  activities, 374
  aspects of, 381
  assessing agency, 363–366
  assimilation, degree of, 112–113
  community mediation agreement, 369
  continuum, 109–115
  cultural blindness, 110
  cultural destructiveness, 110
  cultural incapacity, 110
  cultural pre-competence, 110
  cultural sensitivity, 370
  cultural value orientation, 113–115
  culturally proficient, 111

definition, 108
diverse minority groups, 111–115
employee performance evaluation, 375
English competence, 113
evaluation of, 363, 385
evaluation research, 377–381
  continual improvement, 379–380
  feedback loops, 379–380
  implementation evaluation, 377–378
  outcome evaluation, 378
  process evaluation, 378
  program quality, 378–379
  staffing quality, 378–379
  with evidence-based practice, 366–368
  failing forward concept, 373
  gender and cross-cultural training in
      United Nations, 372
  generational status in the us, 111–112
  goals of, 374, 385
  ill-structured problem, 371, 373
  implementation of, 366–371, 385
  individual staff recognition, 374–376
  in-service training, 368
  judicial professionals and, 209–211
  as a key consideration, 385
  minority public defenders, 211
  multiple levels of achievement, 110
  objectives, 367, 374–375
  policy, 374
  pre-service training, 368
  problem-based learning approach, 371
  problem-solving, 373
  for public defenders, 211
  religious beliefs, 113–115
  self-assessment tool, 364–366
  of service delivery, 380
  states of, 110–111
  training for, 369
  training guidelines, 369–370
  training in large and small agencies,
      368–371
  training situations, 374
Cultural destructiveness, 110
Cultural diversity
  definition, 5–6
  political viewpoints, 5
  religious beliefs, 5
  United Nations' concern, 5
Cultural incapacity, 110
Culturally competent activities, 374
Culturally competent objectives, 374
Culturally competent policy, 374
Culturally pre-competence, 110
Culturally proficient, 111, 122
Culturally specific training, 187
Cutter v. Wilkinson, 267

D

Death penalty, 15, 199–200, 215, 223,
    237, 239–242, 245, 251
  Caucasian victims, 242
  offender vs. victim, 239–242
  prosecutorial death discretion
      outcome, 241
  prosecutor role, 240
  racial disparities, 241
Debt bondage, 249
Debtor's gaols, 249–250
Decriminalization, 396–397
Deinstitutionalization, 259, 400
Deliberate indifference, 299
Delinquency, 207, 305–309, 312, 317,
    327–330, 335–336, 338, 340–343,
    348, 351, 353, 355, 356, 396
  female, 312
  likelihood of, 305
  prevalence of, 308
  risk factors, 305

Delusions, 56
Dementia, 48, 57–58, 68
  diagnostic criteria, 58
  problems with, 58
Demographics challenges, 166
Dependency, 51, 69, 207, 252, 396
Depression, 57, 88
Diabetes, 48, 214
Diagnostic and Statistical Manual IV–
    Text Revision (DSM-IV–TR), 53
Diagnostic packages, 35
Differential stops, 139
Direct discrimination, 237–238
Disabilities Common to the Criminal
    Justice System, 52–53
Disability
  defined, 51
  discrimination, 50–52
Disabled as Criminal Justice Employees,
    62–64
Disabled as victims of crimes, 64–65
Discrimination, 34, 37, 236–237
  contextual, 237
  dark skin, 37
  direct, 237
  indirect, 237
  individual, 34, 237
  institutional, 34, 236
  interaction effect, 237
  pure justice, 236
  racial, 37
  types of, 236
  See also Colorism
Dismissal, 230
Disparate recidivism rates, 44
Disparities, 34–35
  detention, 41
  education levels, 42
  healthcare, 42
  juvenile cases, 41–42
  of incarceration, 42
  for minorities, 42
  psychiatric conditions, 42
  sentencing, 41–42
  totality of arrest records, 39
Disproportionate minority contact, 334,
    337–340, 354, 356
Diversity
  definitions, 2
  and gender equality, 218
  investigative approach, 3
Diversity training, 182, 184–189, 363–364
  demonstrated elements, 184
  goal of, 184
  immigrant-specific, 187–189
  in police agencies, 184–189
    challenges to diversity in England,
        188–189
    immigrant specific, 187–189
    rebrand the training, 187–188
  role of, 182
  role-reversal experiences, 189
Dix, Dorthia, 253, 259
DMC. *See* Disproportionate minority
    contact
Dominant culture, unfair treatment by, 5
Dominant group, 29, 34, 49, 246
Dow Jones, 14
Down's syndrome, 54
Drug abuse, 20, 56, 87, 275, 305
Drug courts, 201, 208, 397–400
  minority representation, 398
Drug criminalization, 274–276
Drug Enforcement Administration
    (DEA), 64
Drug Enforcement Agency (DEA), 275
Drug offenses, non-violent, 279
Drug policy, 258

Drug trafficking, 276, 293, 341, 346
Dual employment rates, 260–261
Due process, 215, 222–223, 242

E

EBPs. *See* Evidence-based practices
Elder Courts, 208
Elder financial and property crimes,
    69–70
  health insurance fraud, 69
  home equity conversion mortgages, 69
  house-flipping, 69
  investment schemes, 69
  reverse mortgages, 69
  telemarketing fraud, 69
Elderly as criminal justice employees,
    61–62
Elderly as victims of crimes, 66–69
  elder abuse, 66–67
  elderscide, 66
Elderly inmates, 3, 72, 393
Elderly offenders, 70
  inverse age-crime relationship, 70
Elderly in prison, 71
Elderly volunteers, 61–62
Elderscide, 66
Elder suicide, 70
Emancipation Proclamation, 134
English prison system, 71
Environmental crime prevention, 391
Equal employment opportunity, 76,
    179, 287
Equal Protection Clause, 233, 290
Escalera v. Terhune, 263
Establishment Clause, 267
Ethnic group
  assumptions, 32
  disparities, 37
Ethnicity, 28–29
  racial features, 28
  social categorization, 28
Ethnic succession, 260–261
Evaluative transparency, 379
Event schemas, 118
Evidence-based practices, 363, 367–368,
    381–384, 399
  agency-level implementation, 383
  individual case-level implementation,
      383
  measurement feedback, 382–383
  needs of organizational participants,
      381
  ongoing support, 382
  operational changes, 382
  participants motivation, 381
  positive reinforcement, 382
  relevant processes measure, 382
  research evaluation for effectiveness,
      383–384
  research support pyramid, 384
  services delivery monitoring, 382
  skill training, 382
  system-level implementation, 383
Evil other, 36
Ex parte Crow Dog, 204
Explicit stereotyping and attitudes, 197
Externalizing behaviors, 318, 329
External locus of control, 30–32
Externally oriented diversity, 165, 187

F

Fags, 298
Failing forward concept, 373–374
Family courts, 207–208
Farsi, 155
Federal Bureau of Investigation (FBI),
    64, 176
  diversity, 176

diversity by race/ethnicity, 183
minority specific programs, 178
advertising campaign, 179
Asian American/Pacific Islander
  program, 178
Black Affairs program, 178
Federal Women's program, 178
female officers, 181
Hispanic Employment program, 178
Federal Bureau of Prisons, 16, 291
Federal cost of incarcerating criminal
  aliens, 16
Federal drug control, 397
Federalism, 200
Federal law, 171
Federal preemption, 171
Federal prisons, 16, 279, 285, 287
Feedback loops, 379–380
Female offenders
  demographics of, 85–86
  drug abuse, 87
  mental health issues, 87–88
  as mothers in prison, 90
  negative effect on children, 91
  physical and/or sexual abuse, 86
  as mothers, 89
  separation between mother and
    child, 89
  sex industry activity, 86
  sexually transmitted diseases, 86–87
  as single mother, 88–91
Fetal alcohol syndrome, 54, 91
Feudalism, 248
Feudal system, 249
Forced labor, 247
Formal charges, filing of, 228
Formalist model, 196
Four standards of mental healthcare,
  58–59
Fourteenth Amendment, 222, 233,
  284, 290
Freedom
  American myth, 247
  importance of, 246
  of religion, 113, 266
Free Exercise Clause, 267–268
French prisons, 43
Fulton County jail, 225
Fulwood v. Clemmer, 266

G

Gangs
  affiliations, prison, 263
  corrections and, 350
  folks, 345
  G.R.E.A.T. initiative in Central
    America, 349
  Hmong Nation Society, 346
  juvenile females and, 348–350
    Latinas, 348
    sexual and physical abuse in the
      home, 348
  Latin Kings, 345
  Mexican Mafia, 346
  minority youth, 343–345
  racial affiliation and, 345–346
  reasons for joining, 343–345
  Vice Lords, 345
  youth compositions of, 341–343
Garbage in—garbage out philosophy,
  380
Gates v. Collier Prison Reform Case, 284
  See also Trusty system
Gay and lesbian employees, 91–96
  alcoholism, 91
  anti-gay crime, 102–103
  Bem sex role inventory, 94
  bisexual-identified victims, 99

discrimination in the professional
    setting, 96
gender identity of victims and
    survivors, 100
hate crimes against, 96–98
heterosexual, 99
HIV/AIDS, 98
hooking up, 101
institutional- and community-based
    components, 92
international focus, 95
legal marriage of same-sex partners, 94
lifestyle, 91–93
organizational culture of tolerance,
    94–96
in paramilitary agencies, 93–94
pedophilia, 98
primary and secondary victimization,
    98–99
professionalism in agencies, 93
protective pairing, 101
sexual harassment, 97–98
sexual orientation, 94, 99
stress-relate health problems, 92
undermining of religious institutions,
    98
victim characteristics, 99–100
victimization form, 98–103
vilification, 97–98
violent actions, 96–97
Gender as a minority status, 311–315
  female delinquency, 312
  gender-specific interventions, 312
  sexually transmitted disease, 313
  teenage mothers, 312–315
  unwanted pregnancies, 312–315
  victim-turned-offender hypothesis, 312
Gender equality, 218
  diversity and, 218
General Accounting Office, 241
Genocide, 19
Georgia (American Penal Colony), 251
Gerontocracy, 49
Gideon v. Wainwright, 223
Glass ceiling, 82–83
Global community, police agencies
    as learning organizations in,
    376–377
Globalization, 7–13, 324, 389
Granny Patrol, 61
Guadalupe Hidalgo, treaty of, 17
Gubernatorial appointment, 201
Gubernatorial processes, 202

H

Hallucinations, 55
Health insurance fraud, 69
Hearing impairment visual
    Impairment, 60
Heart problems, 49
Hispanic Outreach program, 190
Historical trauma, 17–18
  African Americans and, 20–23
  Native Americans and, 18–20
Historical victimization, 136
Holy days, 268
Hong Kong, cross-cultural
    communication
    misunderstandings in, 121
Homegrown challenges, 17–18
Hooliganism, 255
Hospitals, 252–253
  bedlam, 252
  early formation, 252
Houston Processing Center, 260
Human rights violations, North Korea
    in, 283
Hyper-masculine ideals, 104

I

IAT. *See* Implicit Association Test
ICE. *See* Immigration and Customs
    Enforcement
Ill-structured problem, 371
Immigrants, 259–264
  adjustment status, 8
  African Americans, 262–264
  Asian, 8, 11–13
  Asian Americans, 262
  backgrounds, 259
  black and white, 36
  challenges, 165–174
    cultural and racial diversity, 165
    fear of police, 168
    lack of awareness, 170
    language barriers, 167
    model police response, 172–174
    reluctance to report crime,
      167–168
    traditional honor system, 167
    trust-building efforts, 168
  Chinese, 31
  detainment on arrival, 259–260
  ethnic succession, 260
  Hispanic Americans, 261
  influx, 32
  Italian, 13
  Latino, 13
  Mariel boatlift, 260
  mass exodus, 9
  Mexican, 8–10
  Middle Eastern Muslims, 261–262
  native cultures, 30
  permanent residents, 8
  post-arrival arrest/imprisonment,
    260–261
  Russian-Jewish, 33
  temporary, 8
  unauthorized, 10
  younger population, approaches to
    policing, 391–403
    addiction, early prevention, 395–396
    communicable diseases, 401
    community supervision, 392–393
    correctional programs, 394
    criminal behavior, early
      prevention, 395–396
    decriminalization of drugs, 396
    drug courts, 397–398
    drug enforcement strategy,
      396–397
    electronic monitoring techniques,
      402
    employment challenges, 401
    family challenges, 402
    financial downturns, 392
    GPS tracking, 394
    house arrest, 394
    housing challenges, 401–402
    less-restrictive prison sentencing,
      394
    mental health courts, 400
    mental illness, 401
    minority representation in drug
      courts, 398
    prison population, 392
    recidivism-reducing strategies,
      400–402
    reentry strategies, 400–402
    research-based approach, 394
    risk and protective factors, 395
    sentencing criteria, 393–394
    substance abuse, 400
    supervision/community
      techniques, 402–403
    treatment strategy, 397–400
  Vietnamese, 31

Immigration
  Arizona v. United States (2012),
    171–172
  aspects of illegal, 172
  controversies and criminal justice,
    10–11
Immigration and Customs
    Enforcement, 10, 16, 169, 171
Immigration and Nationality Act,
    Section 287(g), 168–169
Immigration Bond, 226
Immigration lawyers, 14
Impairment, 49
Impartial judge, 196
Impartial justice, 193, 219
Implementation evaluation, 377–378
Implicit Association Test, 197
Implicit bias, 197–198
Imprisonment, minority treatment,
    281–285
  chain gangs, 284
  convict lease system, 282
  LSP Angola, 284–285
  old school corrections, 284–285
  pig laws, 281
  prison reform, 284–285
  race-based slavery, 281
  trusty system, 284–285
Incarceration
  industrial prison complex, 280
  institutional racism, 276
  mass incarceration, 280
  minorities and, 276–280
  native Americans experience, 276
  shift in, 273
  societal issues, 277
  women and, 279–280
Indentured servants, 36, 245, 253–254
Indentured servitude, 36, 251, 253, 281
Indian Reorganization Act, 205
Indigent defender system, 223–224
  low wages, 224
  minority defendants, 224
  prison delivers/plea deal, 224
Indirect discrimination, 237
Individual discrimination, 34, 237
Individualism vs. collectivism, 116
Industrial prison complex, 280
Initial screenings, 230
Inmate population in Japan, 71
Institutional discrimination, 34,
    236–237, 316
Institutional racism, 134, 137, 238, 276,
    280, 287, 325, 353
  corrections and, 280
Institutions of confinement, 247–248,
    259, 268
Integration
  benefits of, 29
  social, 29–30
Interaction, 164, 237, 369, 389
Intercultural communication, 115–127
  associated problems, 122
  bilingual and bicultural staff, 119
  citizen relations and agency
    operations, 126–127
  crime-fighting information, 120, 122
  cross-racial issues, 122–124
  cultural competence and, 127
  cultural variation, 116
  definition, 108
  effective, 125, 126
  important point, 123
  international focus, 121
  interrogation, 124–126
  interviewing, 124–126
  language interpretation, 122
  and linguistic competence, 119

Intercultural communication (*continued*)
  misunderstandings, 121
  multi-linguistic issues, 109, 124–126
  schemas, impact of, 117–118
  sign-language interpretation, 122
  studies and prospective research, 116–117
  top-down model, 127
Intergenerational trauma, 17
  See also Historical trauma
Internal control, 32
Internalizing behaviors, 317–318
Internal locus of control, 30–31
Internally oriented diversity, 165, 187
Internal responsibility, 32
International Court of Justice, 14
International Covenant on Civil and Political Rights, 14
International slave labor camps, 255–256
Interrogation
  cross-linguistic, 125
  misidentified Asian Indians for, 115
  multi-linguistic issues, 124–126
  perpetrator, 124
Interventions
  culturally competent, 4
  gender-specific, 4
Interview
  common probes, 124
  cross-linguistic, 124
  cross-racial factor, 123
  cultural competence, 210
  discomfort in, 123
  facial expressions, 126
  micro-expressions, 126
  multi-linguistic issues, 124–126
  nonverbal cues, 126
  quasi-fluent, 125
  social context, 124
  verbal behavior, 125
Intra-racial, 134, 136, 157–159, 237–238, 237–238
Iranians, 154–155
IRA. *See* Indian Reorganization Act
Islamic immigrant populations, 376

J
Jailhouse turnouts, 298
Jails, 42, 57, 101, 104, 248–253, 259, 268, 279, 285
  bridewell, 250
  debtor's gaols, 249–250
  houses of correction, 250
  poorhouses, 250
  serfdom, 249
  transportation, 250
  workhouses, 250
Japan, inmate population in, 71
Jewish population, 5
Jim Crow laws, 22, 37, 280
  See also African Americans
Joint or second parent adoption, 207–208
Judicial Appointments Commission, 218
Jury nullification, 233, 235
Jury selection, 231–233
  change of venue, 232
  Los Angeles Riots (1992), 232
  OJ Simpson trial, 232
  preemptory challenges, 232–233
  racism and, 234
  voir dire, 232–233
Just Detention International, 101
Juvenile
  age-appropriate language, use of, 310
  blended families, 307
  broken homes, 307
  caseworkers, 113

census in residential placement, 352–353
criminal subculture, 328
culturally relevant interventions, 330
detention and incarceration, disparity, 352–353
disproportionate minority contact, 337–340
  key points of processing, 339
  urbanicity, 339
drug-crime cycle drug-crime cycle, 356
education, 308–309
family, 306–308
Federal Advisory Committee, 342
female in custody, 350–352
  drug experience, 351
  residential treatment program, 351
  substance-related problems, 352
gangs
  composition in, 341–343
  and corrections, 350
  female gang members, 349–350
  involvement, 343–345
gender as a minority status, 311–315
  female delinquency, 312
  gender-specific interventions, 312
  sexually transmitted disease, 313
  teenage mothers, 312–315
  unwanted pregnancies, 312–315
  victim-turned-offender hypothesis, 312
health and wellness, 305–311
learning disabilities, 309
macro-effects, 329
micro-effects, 329
as minority, 305
minority confinement, 353–356
  cultural insensitivity, 354
  culturally and linguistically services, 354
  discretionary authority misuse, 354
  lack of alternatives, 354
  racial stereotyping, 354
minority issues, 325–326
nuclear family composition, 308
offending by age and gender, 334–337
  drug crimes, 335
  drug-related offenses, 335
  gang membership, 337
peer groups, 325–326
population, approaches to policing, 391–403
poverty, 326–328
prevention and intervention efforts, 356–357
protective factors, 305
racial discrimination, 315–319
  ability to adaptively cope, 316
  ability to socialize, 316
  externalizing behaviors, 318
  institutional discrimination, 316
  internalizing behaviors, 317–318
  legal and/or non-legal, 316
  macro-system, 317
  micro-system, 317
  social inequality, 315–316
risk factors, 305
sexual activity and, 310–311
sexual minority, 320–325
  attempted suicide and, 322–325
  carrying a gun to school, 320–321
  heterosexual, 320
  identity, sexual, 320
  physical fights at school, 321
  sexual assault and, 321–322
social class, 326–328
social contexts associated, 340–350
social factors, 305

social-environmental approach, 341
socialization, 306, 325–326
subculture, 325–326
suicide, 324
underclass, 326–328
violence in schools, 309–310
violent crime and gambling, 341
Juvenile courts, 207
Juvenile Justice and Delinquency Prevention Act (1974), 338
Juvenile probation officers, 82, 113, 310

K
Klinefelter's syndrome, 54

L
Latino Americans, 140–147
  Cuban Americans, 146–147
  immigration, 141–142
  Mexican Americans, 140–143
  Puerto Ricans, 143–144
Law enforcement, 13–17, 38–39
  arrests and, 38–39
  caring, 65–66
  communication cannels, 13
  community inclusion, 13
  consideration of race, 15
  culturally competent, 12
  death penalty, 15
  federal cost of incarcerating criminal aliens, 16
  foreign courts citations, 14
  global community's impact on, 14–15
  implications for criminal justice, 16–17
  international court, 15
  international factors, 14
  minority representation, 17
  racial diversity, 16
  trust building, 13
Law Enforcement Recruitment Toolkit, 174
Learning disabilities, 51, 309, 356
Learning organizations, 376–377
Legalization, 10, 395–396
Legislative appointment, 201
Lesbian, Gay, Bisexual, and Transgender Program, 185
Linguistic competence, 119
Locus of control, 30–32
  external, 30–32
  internal, 30–31
  responsibility, 31–32
Los Angeles riots (1992), 232
Loss of control, 397
LSP Angola, 284

M
Macro-level victimizations, 137
Macro-system effects, 317
Madhouse. *See* Asylums
Major Crime Act (1885), 204
Masculinity vs. femininity, 116
Mass incarceration, 268, 273, 278–279
Melting pot, 9, 33–34
Memphis Model, 56
Mental healthcare, four standards of, 58–59
Mental health courts, 208–209, 400
Mental illness, 34, 42, 53, 55, 57, 63, 88, 258–259, 401
  antipsychotic medications, 259
  deinstitutionalization era, 259
  deinstitutionalization process, 259
Mental impairment, 53–58
  Alzheimer's disease, 57
  anti-social personality disorder, 54
  dementia, 57–58

mental retardation, 54–55
mentally-ill offenders, 57–58
mood disorders, 57
multi-axial system, 53
psychosis and psychotic disorders, 55–57
Mentally retarded offenders, 14
Mental retardation, 54–55
  capital punishment and, 55
  causes for, 54
  Down's syndrome, 54
  Klinefelter's syndrome, 54
  mild, 54
  moderate, 54
  prevalence, 54
  profound, 54–55
  ranges of, 54
  severe, 54–55
Merit selection, 201–202
Mexican Americans, 140–143
  Immigration Concerns, 143
  Puerto Ricans, 143–144
Mexican-American war, 17–18
Mexican issues, 8
Mexican Mafia, 290–293, 346
Mexikanemi, 293
Micro-system effects, 317
Middle Eastern Americans, 154–157
  Arab Americans, 155–156
  courteous communication, 156
  family loyalty, 156
  Iranians, 154–155
  personal honor, 156
  socioeconomics differences, 155
  stereotyping of, 156
  Turks, 154–155
  victimization of, 156–157
Migration, 324
Minorities, recruitment and hiring in policing, 174–183
  commitment to hiring, 175–176
  community involvement, 180–181
  demographic compositions, 177
  legal considerations, 176–179
  minority retention, 182–183
  planning & techniques, 179–180
  young and old hiring, 181–182
Minority
  Caucasian American group, 7
  definition, 2, 4–5
  employment and retention of, 203
  historical trauma, 17–18
  homegrown challenges, 17–18
  interface of, 44
  investigative approach, 3
  minority status, 5
  model minority, 4
  negative stereotypes of, 31
  persons with disabilities, 3
  sentencing, 238–239
Minority defendants, 222–223
  Gideon v. Wainwright, 223
  Scottsboro case, 222–223
Minority held seats in court system, 203
Minority judiciary, 211–217
  Constance Baker Motley, 216
  Eric Hampton Holder, 216–217
  Florence Ellinwood Allen, 213
  Frank Howell Seay, 213
  Herbert Young Choy, 215
  Johnnie L. Cochran, Jr., 217
  Lance Ito, 215
  Michael Burrage, 213
  Reynaldo Guerra Garza, 215
  Sandra Day O'Conner, 214–215
  Sonia Sotomayor, 213–214
  Thurgood Marshall, 212–213
  William Henry Hastie, Jr., 212

Minority offenders and police, 158–159
  police response, 158
  social threat of racial minority, 159
  tense police-community relations, 158
  use-of-force in policing, 158
  victim-based selection bias, 159
Minority victims of crime, 157–158
  ethnic orientation, 157
  household and personal crimes, 157
  police response, 158
Minority Youth Transition Program, 355
Modern Prison Facilities, 285–287
Mood Disorders, suicide prevention, 57
Multicultural criminal justice, current
     events in, 10–11, 40–41, 65–66,
     90, 119–120
Multicultural hiring, best practice in, 179
Multiculturalism, 2–4, 7–13, 29–30, 44,
     139, 165, 174, 186, 192, 218, 300,
     315, 334, 339, 382
  Asian immigrants, 11–13
  definition, 7
  examination of, 4
  immigration, 8
  investigative approach, 3
  notion of, 2
Muslim prison
  inmates, 43
  population, 43

N

NAFTA. *See* North American Free
    Trade Alliance
National Association of Women Judges,
    81
National Coalition of Anti Violence
    Programs, 97
National Campaign to Prevent Teen
    and Unplanned Pregnancy
    (2010), 314
National Crime Prevention Council,
    164–165
National Crime Victimization Survey,
    134, 157
National Gang Crime Research Center,
    350
National Night Out, 164, 173
National Organization for Women Legal
    Defense and Education Fund, 81
National Security Entry-Exit
    Registration System, 261
Native Americans, 18–20, 147–151
  alcohol and drug abuse, 20
  brutalization process, 20
  categories of, 19
  child molestation, 150
  crime and criminal behavior, 20
  criminal victimization, 20
  declinations of criminal cases, 150
  definition of, 147
  domestic violence, 20
  genocide, 19
  intergenerational trauma, 20–21
  jurisdictions, 149
  physical assaults, 150
  sexual assaults, 150
  spirituality, 148–149
  traditional culture, 149
  unique legal status, 149–151
  values, 148–149
  victimization, 149
Naturalization Act, 37
Nazi concentration camps, 283
Nazi Low Riders, 293–294
NCAVP. *See* National Coalition of Anti
    Violence Programs
NCVS. *See* National Crime
    Victimization Survey

Neglect, 65–66
  active neglect, 67–68
  conditions, 68
  passive neglect, 67–68
  types, 67–68
Neighborhood watch, 3, 103, 164, 173,
    390
Ñeta, 292
New Debtors Prisons, 265
New York State Office of Mental Health,
    367
NGCRC. *See* National Gang Crime
    Research Center
NLR. *See* Nazi Low Riders
Nonpartisan election, 201–202
Non-violent drug offenses, 279
North American Free Trade Alliance
  economic impact, 9, 16
  implementation of, 9
  second phase, 9
North Korean prison camps, 283
Norwegian police force, 376
NYSOMH. *See* New York State Office of
    Mental Health

O

Offenders, female, 90
Office on Violence Against Women, 84
OJ Simpson trial, 232
Old school corrections, 284–285
One-drop rule, 37, 280
One-eighth rule, 37
Onomichi Prison, 71
Organizational culture, 83, 91, 168, 182,
    184, 288, 299, 301, 368
  in police agencies, 182
  within prison systems, 301
  role of supervisory staff, 299
  of tolerance, 94–96
  trustworthy, 182
  vision plan, 299
Osteoporosis, 48
Outcome evaluation, 378
Outing, 323
Over-identification, 187
OVW. *See* Office on Violence Against
    Women

P

Partisan election, 201–202
Peacemaking circles. *See* Sentencing
    circles
Peasants, 246, 248
Pelican Bay state prison, racial based
    classification system in, 263
Perpetrator, 98, 101, 123–124, 134, 153,
    159, 172, 238
Personality disorder
  borderline, 87
  multiple, 87
Person-blame, 31
Person-centeredness, 31
Person schemas, 117
Persons with disabilities, 3
Phrenology, 28–29
Physical disabilities, 59–60
  assistive aids, 59
  causes of, 59
  hearing impairment, 60
  range of, 59
  visual Impairment, 60
Pig laws, 281–282, 301
Pigmentocracy, 37
  See also Colorism
Plea bargaining, 229–230, 239, 242
Police abuses in Puerto Rico, 145
Police agencies
  in England, 188–189

as learning organizations in global
    community, 376–377
Police-community relations, 173, 181,
    192
Police hiring, best practices in, 180
Policing, 13, 159, 163–164, 182–183,
    188, 390
  diversity benefits, 174–175
  racial profiling in, 140
Poor laws (1388), 249
Post-traumatic stress disorder, 63, 87
Powell v. Alabama, 222–223
Power distance, 116
Preemptive challenges, 232–233
Pregnancy, teenage, 314–315
Prejudice, 34
Pre-service training, 368
President's Teen Pregnancy Prevention
    Initiative, 314
Price Waterhouse v. Hopkins (1989), 198
Prima facie, 233
Prison, 251–252, 295–298
  camps in North Korea, 283
  elderly in, 71
  emergence of, 281
  female offenders as mothers in, 90
  French, 43
  gang affiliations, 263
  imprisonment, 251
  inmates, Muslim, 43
  modern conception, 251
  pillory, 251
  population of Muslims in, 43
  prisonization and, 295–298
  race and, 289–290
  racial based classification
    system, 263
  religion and, 294
  slavery, 251
  staff and inmate dynamics, 295–296
  stocks, 251
  subcultures, 104
  symbiotic prison relationship, 295
  women in corrections, 296–297
Prison gangs, 290–294
  Aryan Brotherhood (AB), 291
  Barrio Azteca, 294
  Black Guerrilla Family (BGF), 291
  Bloods, 292
  Crips, 292
  Mexican Mafia, 291
  Mexikanemi, 293
  Nazi Low Riders (NLR), 293–294
  Ñeta, 292
  Texas Mexican Mafia, 293
  Texas Syndicate, 293
  United Blood Nation (UBN), 294
Prison reform, 253, 284–285
Private sector, racial profiling in, 140
Problem-based learning approach, 371
Problem solving courts, 209
Process evaluation, 378
Prohibition Era. *See* War on drugs
Property bond, 226
Prosecutorial death discretion outcome,
    241
Prosecutorial discretion, 228–231
  charge reduction, 230–231
  dismissal, 230
  filing of formal charges, 228
  initial screenings, 230
  plea bargaining, 231
  race of the victim effect, 230
Protective factors, 305, 307, 329,
    395–396
Protective orders, 225–226
Protestant ethic, 31
Protestant faith, 254

Psychosis and psychotic disorders
  cause, 56
  delusions, 55–56
  hallucinations, 55
  thought disorder, 55–56
PTSD. *See* Post-traumatic stress disorder
Puerto Rico Police Department, 145
Puerto Ricans, 143–144
  community relations, 145
  education level, 144
  homeownership, 144
  marital status, 144
  marriage and children, 144
  police abuses, 145
Punk, 80, 296, 298
Punk Prayer incident, 255–256
Pure justice, 236
Push factors, 142
Pussy riot, 255–256

R

Race
  Alaska Native, 6
  American Indian, 6
  Asian, 6
  black (African), 6
  categories of, 6, 29
  cultural and behavioral traits, 29
  definitions, 6
  sociological categorizations, 28
  of victim effect, 200, 230, 239
  white, 6
Racial allegiances, 4
Racial based classification system in
    prison, 263
Racial bias, 36–7
Racial discrimination, 15, 138, 233–234,
    315–319, 329, 340, 356
  ability to adaptively cope, 316
  ability to socialize, 316
  externalizing behaviors, 318
  institutional discrimination, 316
  internalizing behaviors, 317–318
  legal and/or non-legal types of, 316
  macro-system, 317
  micro-system, 317
  social inequality, 315–316
Racial disparity in bail, 224–225
Racial diversity, 6
Racial inequality, theory on, 316
Racial motivations, 4
Racial profiling, 7, 39–40, 139, 156–157,
    173, 260, 369, 389
  driving while black, 39
  image of police officers, 40
  key impetus for immigrant
    detainment, 260
  minorities and, 39–40
  in policing, 140
  in private sector, 140
  settlement phase, 39
  supportive evidence, 39
  training to prevent, 156
  UN definition, 139
Racial recognition, 123
Racial Segregation Case Law, 289–290
Racism, institutional, 36–37
Racism, claims of, 225
Ranking diversity committee, 203
Realist model, 196
Rebrand the training, 187–188
Reentry services, lack of, 44
Released on Recognizance, 226
Religion, 40–41
Religious beliefs, 113–115, 266–268
  appearance, 267
  Asian Indians, hate crimes against, 115
  Christianity, denomination of, 114

Religious beliefs (*continued*)
  church presence in African American culture, 114
  constitutional rights of inmates, 266
  dress, 267
  forced transformation, 114
  holy days, 268
  indigenous, 114
  karma and reincarnation, concepts of, 114
  non-traditional religions, 267–268
  religious diets, 268
  religious observance, 266
  right to practice faith, 266
  right to religion in prison, 266
  Satanist, 267–268
  Wicca, 267
Religious diets, 268
Religious Freedom Restoration Act, 294
Religious Land Use and Institutionalized Persons Act (2000), 266–267, 294
Religious offenses, courts and, 227–228
Restorative justice, 390, 394, 403
RFRA. *See* Religious Freedom Restoration Act
Rheumatism, 49, 53
Risk factors, 305–307, 317, 329, 339–340, 355, 395–396, 400
RLUIPA. *See* Religious Land Use and Institutionalized Persons Act (2000)
Rodney King police brutality trials, 231–232
  See also Jury selection
Role-reversal experiences, 189
Role schemas, 117
ROR. *See* Released on Recognizance
Rugged individualism, 31

S
SAMHSA. *See* Substance Abuse and Mental Health Services Administration
Schemas
  category, 117
  causal, 118
  cognitive structures, 117
  event, 118
  intercultural communication, 117–118
  interpretations of criminal behaviors, 118
  natural by-product, 118
  person, 117
  role, 117
  self, 117
Schizophrenia, 42
School violence, 309–310
SDT. *See* Social dominance theory
Secure Fence Act, 9
Seizing one's freedoms, concept of, 249
Self-construals, 116
Self-fulfilling prophesy, 40
Self schemas, 117
Sentencing circles, 205–206
  goals, 206
  implementation, 205–206
  learned lessons, 207
  multi-step procedure, 205

Sentencing, disparity in, 235–236
Separation of church, 5
Sexually transmitted diseases, 86–87, 310, 313, 401
  AIDS, 87
  genital warts, 87
  gonorrhea, 87
  hepatitis, 87
  herpes, 87
  syphilis, 87
  treatable, 87
Sexual minority youth, 305, 309–325, 330, 356
  attempted suicide and, 322–325
  heterosexual, 320
  identify themselves as a sexual minority, 320
  physical fights at school, 321
  sexual assault and, 321–322
  who carry a Gun to School, 320–321
Sexual orientation program, 185–186
SGA. *See* Substantial gainful activities
Shi'ah sect, 155
'Shop-and frisk' scandal. *See* policing, racial profiling in
Slave Codes, 136
Slavery, 6, 17–18, 36, 114, 132–134, 136, 245, 249, 251, 253–256, 280–285
  Catholic slave owners, 254
  chattel slavery, 254
  black race concept, 254
  disenfranchisements of, 254
  end of, 134
  ethnocentric culture, 254
  forms of abuses, 133
  indentured servants, 253–254
  indentured servitude, 253
  modern minorities, 256
  protestant slave owners, 254
  race-based, 254–255
  roots of, 253
  standard of living, 133
  working conditions, 133
Smarter Sentencing Bill, 279
Social dominance, 34–35
Social exchange theory, 68
Social factors, 305
Social inequality, 315–316
Socialization process, 306, 325
Social justice approach, 319
Social security administration, 52
Social security disability insurance, 52
Social status, importance of, 246
Spanish–American war, 17
Spanish Speaking Ride Along Program, 119, 190
Special courts, 201, 207–209
  drug courts, 208
  elder courts, 208
  family courts, 207–208
  juvenile courts, 207
  mental health courts, 208–209
SSA. *See* Social Security Administration
SSDI. *See* Social Security Disability Insurance
SSI. *See* Supplemental Security Income
Stakeholders, 165, 379–380
State law, 171

State prisons, 16, 211, 253, 285, 287
STDs. *See* Sexually transmitted diseases
Stereotyping behavior, 35–36
Stigma, 34
Stigmatization, 34
Stimulant drugs, 257
Strain theory, 238
Strive Act, 10
Structural racism, 134–135
  academic components, 135
  byproduct of, 134
  impact of, 134, 136–137
  practical components, 135
Substance Abuse and Mental Health Services Administration, 20
Substance abuse disorders, 253
Substantial gainful activities, 52
Subtle, 39, 49, 101, 237
Suicidal behaviors, 324
Suicide prevention, 57
Suicide, teenage, 324
Supplemental security income, 52
Supreme Court, 3, 14–15, 58, 61, 80–81, 95, 101, 143, 171, 198, 201–204, 212–213, 223, 227, 229, 233–234, 240, 265–267, 299, 393
Surety bond, 226
Symbiotic prison relationship, 295

T
Teenage mothers, 312–315
Teenage pregnancy, 314–315
Teenage suicide, 324
Telemarketing fraud, 69
Texas Mexican Mafia. *See* Mexikanemi
Texas syndicate, 290, 293
Theriault v. Carlson, 266
Tillery, Clovis, 286–287
Tolokonnikova, Nadezhda, 225–226
Top-down model, 127
Traumatic stress, 62–64
  burnout, 63
  car fatalities, 63
  critical-incident occupations, 64
  failed resuscitation attempts, 63
  morbidity risk, 63
  posttraumatic stress disorder, 63
Treaty of Guadalupe Hidalgo, 17
Trial by jury of one's peers, 248–249
Trial courts, 201
Tribal courts, 203–205
Tribal Law and Order Act (2010), 151
Troubled female youth, 311
Truancy officers, 113
Trust-building, community involvement and, 163–165
Trusty system, 284–285
Turks, 154–155
Turner v. Safley, 266, 268
Turning out, 298
Tyronne jurors, 199

U
UBN. *See* United Blood Nation
Uncertainty avoidance, 116
Undereducated, 264–265
United Blood Nation, 294
United Nations, 5, 15

United States Department of Justice (USDOJ), 84, 145, 149
Universal Theory of suicide, 70
Unwanted pregnancies, 312–315
Urbanicity, 339, 357
U.S. Bureau of the Census, 6

V
VAWA. *See* Violence Against Women Act
Vera Institute, 13
Victim-based selection bias, 159
Victims of Crime Act (VOCA), 84
Vilification, 97–98
Violence against women, 83–85
  Crime Victim's Movement, 84
  domestic abuse, 83
  domestic violence, 84–85
  Office on Violence Against Women (OVW), 84
  sexual assault, 83
  shelter movement, 84
  Victims of Crime Act, 84
  Violence Against Women Act, 84
Violence Against Women Act, 84
Violation of citizen's rights, 140
Virginia Racial Act, 37
Voir dire, 232–233
Volunteerism in policing, 189–192
  bilingual assistance, 190
  cultural liaisons, 190–191
  ethnic-specific responses, 191–192
  Hispanic outreach program, 190
  Spanish speaking ride along program, 190
  volunteers, 190–191

W
War on Drugs, 16, 91, 258, 264, 274–276, 278, 280, 302, 388
WASP. *See* White Anglo-Saxon Protestant
White Anglo-Saxon Protestant, 34
Wolf, 298, 348, 350, 355
Women in criminal justice, 76–83
  child saver movement, 81
  in corrections, 78–80
  in different types of police agencies, 78
  discrimination against women, 81
  female supervisors, 78–79
  glass ceiling, 82–83
  higher-level supervisors, 80
  International Association of Women Police, 76
  in judicial system, 80–81
  in juvenile justice system, 81–82
  in law enforcement, 76–78
  in male prisons, 79
  service-oriented approach, 79
  sexual harassment, 79
  as supervisors, 83
  on traffic-control, 78
World Health Organisation (WHO), 324
World Trade Center tragedy, 7, 9, 112, 154, 261

Y
Youth culture, 320, 323, 325, 327, 334